Atheism in France, 1650–1729

VOLUME I: THE ORTHODOX SOURCES OF DISBELIEF

Alan Charles Kors

PRINCETON UNIVERSITY PRESS
PRINCETON, NEW JERSEY

Published by Princeton University Press, 41 William Street,
Princeton, New Jersey 08540
In the United Kingdom: Princeton University Press, Oxford

Library of Congress Cataloging-in-Publication Data

Kors, Alan Charles.
Atheism in France, 1650–1729 / Alan Charles Kors.
p. cm.
Includes bibliographical references.
Contents: v. 1. The orthodox sources of disbelief
ISBN 0-691-05575-0 (v. 1)
1. Atheism—France—History—17th century. 2. Atheism—
France —History—18th century. 3. France—Intellectual
life—17th century. 4. France—Intellectual life—
18th century. I. Title.
BL2765.F8K67 1990 211'.8'094409032—dc20 89-28743

Publication of this book was made possible by a grant from the Publications Program of
the National Endowment for the Humanities, an independent Federal agency

This book has been composed in Linotron Sabon

Princeton University Press books are printed on acid-free paper,
and meet the guidelines for permanence and durability of the Committee on Production
Guidelines for Book Longevity of the Council on Library Resources

Printed in the United States of America by Princeton University Press,
Princeton, New Jersey
1 3 5 7 9 10 8 6 4 2

Atheism in France, 1650–1729

To the memory of my beloved mother

Belle Kors (1909–1978)

CONTENTS

PREFACE

THIS STUDY is the first of two volumes that, taken together, will seek to explain the emergence of atheism from the intellectual communities of early-modern France. Each study, however, is intended to stand alone, focused on issues of independent historical importance. This work is a study of the significance of "atheism" to the orthodox learned world of the late seventeenth and early eighteenth centuries. It is at once an analysis of the problem of atheism in early-modern French thought and, from that perspective, a portrait of a learned culture that would change the conceptual possibilities of France and, in many ways, the West. The second volume will explore the actual atheism that arose in the early eighteenth century, and its specific relationships to the crises of both orthodox and heterodox learned worlds.

The chronological boundaries of this study are less arbitrary than might appear from its curious dates, extending from the death of Descartes at one end to the death and posthumously discovered atheistic manuscript of the abbé Meslier at the other. It seeks to understand how, in the time between, the seemingly boundless theistic confidence of a culture, its ostensible sense of the utter unthinkability of atheism, was unraveled by its own hands, that is, by its own teachings, debates, tensions, and rivalries. It was a learned culture that claimed, again and again, that the existence of God was so evident and manifest that only a depraved and insincere libertine could even seek to disbelieve in it. Only depravity seeking assurance of impunity, it taught, could doubt that there was an independent and intelligent Supreme Being above and yet concerned with the world. It offered a great diversity of grounds, reasons, and formal demonstrations for belief in the existence of God, certain that these compelled belief. It also generated its own antithesis to that theistic conviction, and, temporarily, at least, it destroyed its own assurance in the *évidence*, both logical and empirical, of that belief. To understand the atheism and materialistic naturalism that arose from the early-modern learned world of France, one must understand the culture and crisis from which such conceptions emerged.

This book is *not* about the theoretical logic or implications of ideas (what minds somehow "ought" to have concluded from thoughts they had). It is *not* yet another analysis of the history of early-modern texts that later centuries declared "canonical" (and somehow a priori "influential" because of modern liking for them). It is *not* an attempt to establish a metadialogue between the seventeenth century and the past, or, for that matter, between the seventeenth century and the present. In fact, there is provocative and enlightening intellectual history done from all of these perspectives, but none of them is my choice for this work. Rather, this book is a study of the actual intellectual behavior, in context, of the French-speaking learned world of the late seventeenth and early eighteenth centuries. In the early decades of the eighteenth century, there emerged from the thought of that profoundly theistic community an unambiguously and explicitly atheistic current of speculation and judgment. I seek to understand how it was possible for that particular community to generate that particular current of thought.

Quantitatively, of course, atheism was a narrowly circumscribed current of thought. For every atheistic manuscript or treatise, there were thousands of theological, devotional, liturgical, and catechistical publications. Indeed, for every work about atheism, there were thousands and thousands of works on other burning issues in theology and ecclesiology: heresy, Jansenism, mysticism, quietism, grace, the Eucharist, deism, physical premotion, pantheism, Richerism, Gallicanism, ultramontanism, monasticism, propagation of the faith—and so on, and so on. Yet qualitatively, the debate over atheism was different from all of these, since virtually all religious works and all theological and ecclesiological debates would be rendered moot (and almost every substantive position taken within them would be nullified) if the atheists were right. As a subject of historical interest, the emergence of atheism should more than hold its own with the topics of current historical concern.

It is, however, a subject that touches by its nature a large number of deep and passionate concerns. Let me emphasize, then, indeed, let me promise, that it is only as a historian that I address any of these. It is not my intent, in any manner whatsoever, to do more here than disclose aspects of the actual human past. My concerns are neither philosophical, nor theological, nor antitheological in this work. I write as a historian.

Even in this regard, however, I am only too painfully aware of how many areas of scholarly specialization in intellectual, religious, and institutional history this book intersects, and, thus, of the countless monographs and studies that should inform it. One common meaning of *infinite* in the seventeenth century was simply "indefinite," the state of being, in practice, boundless, of having no limits that could be reached. In that sense, the literature I cross here—the history of belief and disbelief; the reception of the classics; the history of philosophy and philosophical theology; the evolution of learning; the effect of travel and discovery; the rivalries of monastic and other religious orders, to name but a few—is "infinite." There are surely, thus, countless works, secondary and primary, whose absence from my notes will be striking to diverse specialists. This is true both for general and particular issues, and doubly so for individual schools of thought, institutions, authors, and texts. Any offense given by this, either to the living or to the dead, is unintentional. I have worked on this study, with two years away for yet more important things, since 1975. For a frightening number of years, as I followed the readings of my learned community from one citation to another, the bibliography of works read grew arithmetically while the bibliography of works to be read grew exponentially. What prodigious readers and name-droppers the authors of early-modern France could be! How little I had known when filling out the "feasibility" portions of those grant proposals of what was still my youth!

I wanted to read everything, but when there were choices to be made, I always chose to read primary sources with my own mind's eyes rather than profit from the labors of others. (I hope that *you*, however, will not abandon me in similar pursuit!) The benefit of such a choice is that I believe myself to know what that learned world actually read and what it did not, what is representative and what is not, what is original and what is commonplace. Secondary works that influenced my choice of objects of study or that influenced, by my agreement or disagreement, my sense of people, places, issues, and ideas are listed in the bibliography that concludes volume II of this work. I trust that critics will let me know, in print, by letter, or in person, what I have missed that would have shed brighter or different light on the problems I have explored.

There surely are countless ways to analyze and explicate the emergence of atheism in early-modern France. I do not seek to argue with historians, however, on issues of theories of analysis and explication. From the premise that intellectual history, like all forms of history, is human curiosity critically examining the empirical record of the past, I have tried to know the French learned world of the late seventeenth and early eighteenth centuries as deeply and as broadly as I could, so that I could understand its inheritance, its education, its debates, its tensions, its procedures, its dilemmas, and its options. I have taken, so to speak, the courses its members both followed and gave, read the works it wrote or kept alive, overheard its arguments, studied its approbations and censures, examined the manuscripts it could not or would not dare to publish, opened its mail, and, in short, tried as much as I could to live questioningly among its minds for an extended period of time. One person's familiarity, of course, may well be another's superficial and misleading acquaintance, and immersion, alas, is not the same as enlightenment. My hope, however, is, at the least, that a learned community which altered the world will become at once more alive and more accurately analyzed for my readers than if I had not undertaken this endeavor, and, at the most, that the emergence of atheism from that community will come to make far more sense than before. I beg the reader to judge me in terms of those at once modest and ambitious hopes.

. . .

The learned community of early-modern France is at once remarkably familiar and remarkably foreign, since we of the modern learned world both are its offspring and have traveled to physical and mental worlds it could not have foreseen. It too had its innovators and its traditionalists, often unable to see how much in fact they shared; its university professors, like ours, kept one eye on eternal questions and the other on reputations and careers, and usually managed, as we do, to secure a peer review by colleagues sympathetic to their fundamental intellectual orientations and goals; it even worried, as we do, that the latest theories out of Paris were vitiating the integrity of the intellectual world. It was, in a European sense at least, a community that defined itself internationally, although, given Latin, its lingua franca, it had far less need of translators than we. It created, more often than not, the criteria of scholarship in the humanities and, indeed, of scholarly debate, on which we still fundamentally rely, gradually substituting critical method for tradition and intuition, although our variations on the trees often obscure the forest we share with them. To read its journals of scientific, philosophical, literary, and classical studies is to see the origins of those in which scholars still pursue or praise each other in terms that many of its scholars well would have understood. While most of the Western world has let its medieval and early-modern titles and professional pretensions go the way of sumptuary laws, the educated, especially the doctors of philosophy, divinity, law, and medicine whom universities then and now have sent forth into the world, still call themselves *docte*, that is, "learned," and somehow succeed even in these egalitarian times to get contemporaries to call them by august terms. Once a year, *our* doctors of philosophy even sport *its* bonnets and robes. On the other hand, our forebears in basic and esoteric *scientia* functioned in a world that their progeny would transform both physically and mentally in revolutionary ways. We certainly can see ourselves in the mirror of their curiosity, their methods, and their vanities, but the backdrop is different, indeed.

Like most learned communities in the history of the West since its time, and like many that preceded it, that of early-modern France wanted to know a great deal about the world in which it found itself. It was itself the heir, however, of two great traditions of knowledge, the classical and the Judeo-Christian, and it tried ceaselessly to come to terms with the tensions and paradoxes of that division in both its science and its wisdom. A Christian learned world, it in theory could have turned its back on pre-

Christian and non-Christian gentile thought, but it recognized too much of itself in those minds, and it knew in myriad ways that thought could not be indifferent to the history of thought. It would have found manifestly self-contradictory a modern world of thought that often treats as marginal or epiphenomenal (in academic texts, for learned audiences and for scholarly review, no less) the human effort to know and understand. Long before our arrival into the institutions in which it also transacted its mental affairs (universities, academies, publishing, and journals), the learned world of early-modern France grappled with the fundamental question of whether the universe in which humanity found itself was eternal or created, random or designed, explicable or inexplicable by natural knowledge alone, amoral or just, teleological or purposeless. In brief, it grappled with the problem of atheism. My undertaking is a study of the dynamics and consequences of that engagement. It is, thus, a study of early-modern France, of the learned community, and of the emergence of atheism. It is also a recognition from one learned world of the enduring significance of the mental life of another.

. . .

The reader should know a few things at the outset about my practices in this text. First, past words and thoughts are the data of intellectual history, and data must be shared. I believe it essential in such history to hear tone and nuance, to become familiar with the sound, so to speak, of one's subjects' voices. The numerous quotations in this book are the "charts and tables" of my particular craft; they are there to persuade you of a certain historical view of things. Second, and related, it is not enough in this study to discern what might strike one anachronistically as the "significant" texts of a culture. Since I am arguing a case often based on claims about influence and the "climate" of opinion, it is essential, not a luxury, that I demonstrate the breadth and representative character of certain phenomena. Third, a mere glance at certain intellectual phenomena is unworthy of your attention. Having identified specific tendencies as broad and general, I shall often take a longer, fuller, and more analytic look at individual instances of these.

There is an overarching argument to this book: the generation of disbelief by orthodox culture itself. What makes an argument valuable in history, however, is not its elegance or complexity, but its relationship to the data to which it is inductively bound. In sharing the data from which I believe my argument derived, I hope also to help you draw a richer portrait of that absorbing learned world. My pattern thus, in most chapters, will be to offer a characterization or account of a phenomenon essential to my argument; to establish such a phenomenon as broad, general, and possessing an interested audience; to examine it in specific embodiments that give you a fuller understanding of its nature; and to link it to the next claim of my thesis.

The footnotes, in addition to serving the usual function, are also a part of the effort at portraiture, and in that spirit, even the reader prepared to take me on faith is invited to use them extensively: early-modern title pages are a singular window onto their mental world. All early-modern titles are given in their early-modern spelling (and capitalization), in which there is great charm. Titles superfluously long, however, which early-modern titles can be, have been shortened, with the hiatuses noted.

. . .

In general, seventeenth- and eighteenth-century authors did *not* emphasize text by italicization or underlining, which often served merely to indicate direct quotation in their works. I, on the other hand, want to ensure that certain aspects of a quotation do not pass by without your having noticed them with particular attention. *All emphases, unless otherwise indicated, are therefore my own.*

All foreign-language quotations are given here in English, since surely one of the functions of an American historian of France is to make a foreign culture accessible to compatriots. All translations, unless otherwise indicated, are my own. Where I believe the French or Latin to be ambiguous, however, or where I think the reader plausibly might find a different meaning, I have provided the original, without modernizing the spelling. The footnotes should allow the reader in all cases to consult the original language on his or her own. I know Europeans who take American historians to task for their presentation of French-language data, including quotations, in English. At the same time, however, these persons often justifiably criticize seemingly well-educated Americans for their ignorance of the cultures and histories of the world's diverse peoples. Surely, the two criticisms cannot be made simultaneously in good faith, and the individual American cannot be asked to learn ten languages. American historians of foreign cultures should not be blind to the needs of their own.

Problematic attributions of authorship abound in early-modern France. Since my arguments all turn on the generality of phenomena, specific attributions are rarely critical, and I have accepted the standard attributions of the Bibliothèque Nationale or other major libraries. Where there are variations in the spelling of names, I have sought to utilize those most commonly employed. In my next study, focused on heterodox thought itself, where issues of attribution relate substantively to my argument, all such problems will be both specified and addressed.

In almost all instances, I have consulted early-modern editions of ancient, medieval, and early-modern texts, both for the sensual and intellectual pleasure of holding in my hands what early-modern readers themselves held, and to be certain that it was their versions of texts that would inform my work. The exceptions generally are only later critical editions of their works or standard editions based on their own early-modern texts. It is not always easy, however, to do European history from these shores, for the need and the ability to consult abroad do not always coincide, and the reader will note a few editions of works later than those held by early-modern hands. These are minor exceptions to my rule, however, and I do not think any of them critical. Wherever possible and unproblematic, especially in the case of ancient and medieval texts, I have tried to provide you with accessible alternatives for your own consultation. Where I think the specialist might want more information or data than I have provided in the main body of my text, I have added such to the footnotes. Enough self-justification, however!

. . .

Research for this book benefited at critical junctures from the aid of others. I am deeply grateful to the American Council of Learned Societies (1975–1976) and the Shelby Cullom Davis Center for Historical Studies at Princeton University (1986–1987) for their support. At the roulette tables of funding, fortune often smiles more favorably upon those setting out on some adventure than on those near the end of one. I am doubly indebted, therefore, to the Davis Center for its willingness to assist in the completion of this study. The generosity of Shelby Cullom Davis, Jr. and the capacious wisdom and dedication of Lawrence Stone as director of the Davis Center have contributed in exemplary fashion to academic research and dialogue. The Davis Center was a genuine oasis of collegiality, of intellectual diversity and tolerance, and of ongoing academic stimulation. I am indebted to Alfred J. Rieber, who, when Chair of the Department of History at the University of Pennsylvania, did so much to gain for me the time to bring this project to completion. I also am indebted to Vartan Gregorian, who, when Dean of Arts and Sciences and then Provost of the University of Pennsylvania, which he served full well, was so supportive of my work.

I should like to thank my dear friend Joe Maline for his technical assistance, and to acknowledge my indebtedness to Pyramid Technology Corporation for the use of their computer in preparation of the manuscript.

Many people offered me readings and criticisms of my work, in whole or in part, from which I have benefited. In particular, I am pleased to acknowledge my gratitude to my colleagues at Pennsylvania, Gary Hatfield, Bruce Kuklick, Edward Peters, and Marc Trachtenberg, and to Father Michael J. Buckley, S.J., Roger Emerson, Werner Gundersheimer, Michael Hobart, Dale Van Kley, and Zachary Schiffman. Each offered sage counsel from which I hope that I have profited.

I also thank (in order of appearance) Marvin L. Sachs, Julius Mackie, John Glick, and William Powlis.

This manuscript also has benefited from the wise and sensitive copyediting of Lauren Lepow.

Above all, I am indebted to my beloved family, Erika, Samantha, and Brian, whose love, support, and patience are boundless, and who give me infinitely more than I possibly should try to acknowledge in this place.

Atheism in France, 1650–1729

INTELLECTUAL HISTORY AND THE HISTORY OF ATHEISM

THE EMERGENCE OF ATHEISM from the French learned world of the late seventeenth and early eighteenth centuries is a dramatic moment of human culture, and it is tempting to seek to explain it by means of long-term phenomena. My own penchant, however, is for understanding human affairs in terms of the actual specific contexts in which they occur. Immersion in the data and details of contextual phenomena creates, of course, a vested interest in the significance of the particular. It also allows, however, a sense of a unique time and place in which, quite wonderfully, the "short-term" assumes phases and dynamics of its own and becomes, as befits any moment of human history, inordinately complex. As one studies the learned world of early-modern France from this vantage, longer-term phenomena become interesting only by virtue of their embodiment in more immediate dynamics of this singular period of French history.

To one familiar with the intricacies of the short-term, the broadest categories of the long-term, such as "secularization" or "desacralization," may begin to sound, at worst, vague beyond utility, or, at best, like complex abstractions whose particular sources are not yet understood. Nonetheless, for those who think more boldly, I should hope that if this work has been done well, it will link in some way with their broadest concerns, confirming, perhaps, someone's general views in the particular, or, at the least, making someone's agencies more clear as they acted in one time and place. Nonetheless, it is upon the French early-modern learned world, its ways of thinking and acting, and what emerged from these, that I shall lavish what time I have here.

There is a sense, however, in which this work certainly does reflect, and, indeed, arose from, a concern with the modestly longer-term. If the sequence of research determined the sequence of narrative, I should begin here with the late eighteenth century, with the atheism of d'Holbach, Naigeon, and Diderot, and work back to the clandestine atheistic manuscripts of the early eighteenth century, and, from there, to the debates and dilemmas of the generation that began (since I must stop somewhere) in the year of Descartes's death. That is, in fact, how I have studied the phenomenon of French disbelief. Tracing the sources of late Enlightenment atheism to, among other things, the atheistic manuscripts of the early eighteenth century, I sought, in turn, the roots of the disbelief and philosophical motifs of the first "modern" atheists in France. That inquiry led not to a prior history of free thought, most of which culminated in deeply theistic deisms or in antiphilosophical skepticisms, but to the orthodox culture of the late seventeenth and early eighteenth centuries in France. It was, above all, within the deeply Christian learned culture of those years that there occurred inquiries and debates that generated the components of atheistic thought. It was, to say the least, not what I had expected; it indeed was what I found. I begin, then, with this volume, to retrace my steps in reverse. The thrill (and often tedium) of the detective's trail was in the research; to you I now offer the first part of the dossier thus compiled. Before one can understand the heterodoxy of early-modern atheism, one first must understand the orthodox sources of disbelief. That is the goal of this volume.

. . .

This book is not an argument with other historians. Although I shall begin with what a few historians have had to say, and shall use one or two to make a point now and then, I am, in matters academic, far more tempted by the eremitic than the mutually referential, that is, the historiographical, and, indeed, regret the combative tone I have taken at other times with historians with whom I have disagreed. There are truly countless valuable ways to try to know something about human life before our own appearance in this world, and we should all be fools to close our minds' ears to each other's honest accounts of long study and familiarity with parts of it.

The general kind of history I do—with its often misleading modifier, *intellectual*—goes in and out of favor and through various metamorphoses with startling rapidity. It is, in the final analysis, curiosity applied to the history of human conceptual behavior. Whatever the weight diverse schools of *thought* give to that behavior as cause or effect, it seems one of the things that most sets us apart from all other species, and, indeed, that gives us a history which is more than a "biology" (although, of course, the whole concept of "biology" arises from conceptual behavior and itself has an intellectual history). The point seems obvious, but it may be one of those forests ignored in favor of particular trees.

. . .

In 1729, a rural priest named Jean Meslier died, leaving behind him, to the scandal of those who knew of it, a "Testament" of explicit and combative atheism. Although, as we shall see, the great teachers and learned figures of his culture taught that the existence of God was a truth so luminous that only a depraved or ignorant "fool" could disbelieve it, Meslier was not persuaded by their claims. Significantly, he did not believe himself in any way obliged, in order to disagree with them, to abandon the habits of "reason," "evidence," or "demonstration" that those teachers also sought to inculcate. To the contrary, one knows from the content of his manuscript, and even from his marginalia to the great Fénelon's published "demonstrations" of the existence of God, that he was committed to rational and evidential grounds for his disbelief.[1] This work will seek to explain how it became conceptually possible for someone like Meslier to disbelieve the most essential proposition of his culture's view of the world, that "God exists." It is not in any way focused on Meslier himself, to whom I shall return at great length in my next volume, but, at times, it will use him as a foil. Our central question here is this: from what phenomena and sources in their learned culture did the authors of the atheistic manuscripts of the early eighteenth century derive their grounds for rejecting the claim that the existence of God was indubitable? The alternative views of the world that followed such a rejection, and the (often equally surprising) identification of the sources and debates from which those were derived, will constitute our next "dossier."

. . .

Meslier's rejection of belief in God raises two questions (among others): one, about Meslier, and his life; the other, about the intellectual sources of his disbelief. Most historians, I suspect, would find the former the more "empirical" of the questions, and the latter the more "speculative." For myself, I would reverse those descriptions. The more *speculative* question, it seems to me, is why Meslier was so disaffected from the culture that engendered him. Who has a satisfactory theory of such motivation? The usual attempts at explanation focus on phenomena that, if "causes" of alienation, should have produced tens of thousands of Mesliers, where, in fact, there were few indeed. The more "empirical" question, I should think, is that of what sources, conceptions, and intellectual contexts and dynamics made possible the actual *content* of his beliefs.

Accounts of the social, political, or economic roots of Meslier's disaffection *might* tell us why he detached himself from the mental world of his Church, but they simply cannot explicate the particular substance of his disaffection. Why did he not become a Huguenot, a Lutheran, a sorcerer, a deist, a libertine, a skeptic, a Socinian, or, for that matter, *if merely being preserved as a notion sufficed to make some particular heterodoxy a real option*, a Manichaean? The tendency of Meslier's mind to think in particular, specific ways is simply unexplained by any amount of

[1] Meslier's "Testament" and his notes on Fénelon can be found in the invaluable critical edition by Jean Deprun, Roland Desné and Albert Soboul, eds., *Oeuvres complètes de Jean Meslier*, 3 vols. (Paris, 1970–1972).

social, political, or economic analysis. In fact, the culture in which he participated made it possible for Meslier to achieve a restructuring of his view of reality that involved the most radical break then imaginable from his Church: he became an atheist. That was his specific form of belief and disbelief. How was such an option available to Meslier? With what ideas could someone think atheistically by then? With what replies and objections could someone reject what the culture had taken to be unshakable proofs of the existence of God? Why was atheism a real option for the authors of France as the eighteenth century dawned? In the face of claims of universal consent, of Aristotelian or Scholastic a posteriori proofs of God, of Cartesian or Malebranchist a priori proofs of God, how was it now possible, conceptually, to declare and believe the world to be without compelling proof of God, without plan, without providence, without immaterial prime mover, without necessary perfect being? What mental events now made atheism an actual alternative for a mind of the late seventeenth or early eighteenth centuries? In short, can one account in those terms for the atheism that emerged from the learned world in France, leaving to others the psychohistory, social history, or metahistory of why atheists chose or were impelled to think in such ways?

This distinction between explaining motivation and explaining the specific content of human conceptions is too easily overlooked. Explanations of why, in noncognitive terms, someone revolts against or simply rejects the fundamental beliefs or values of his or her culture may shed light on rebellion or alienation or creativity, whatever the case may be, but they cannot possibly specify why this or that *particular* content and form are the *particular* conceptual expression of such rebellion, alienation, or creative act, or even why such content and form are available to such a person at such a time. Consider, by analogy, the problem of accounting for specific notions of the just society. A rise in prices or taxes, a sense of traditional expectations altered, or any number of phenomena might well explain the impulse to revolt, but without attention to the history of cognition and conceptualization, the history of how issues were defined and debated and transformed, one will never know why revolt has spoken in a myriad of specific conceptions. As the Benedictine educator Porcheron wrote in 1690, the mind can be compared to "a naked guest who comes to live in a furnished palace."[2] Let us explore some of that furniture together.

. . .

Two major and provocative historical works, one old, one new, have discussed the problem of "atheism" in *sixteenth-century* France, which is

[2] David-Placide Porcheron, O.S.B., *Maximes pour l'éducation d'un jeune seigneur* . . . (Paris, 1690).

not without interest for a study that wishes to analyze the sources of disbelief in the France of the second half of the seventeenth century. Lucien Febvre and François Berriot both sought to make sense of the use of the term *atheist* in sixteenth-century theology, moral commentary, and polemic, and to infer plausible conclusions about the persons and groups so described.[3] Febvre saw clearly how imprecisely and polemically the term was used in the sixteenth century, but he perhaps assumed too hastily that this settled the cognitive matter, and that any "speculative" atheism was literally unthinkable in a society so permeated by the structures, symbols, and experiences of religious life and understanding. One may think about "unthinkability" differently, as we shall see.

Berriot understood full well the connection drawn by the early-modern orthodox mind between rejection of traditional values and denial of the God assumed to be the author of those values, but he supposed, perhaps arbitrarily, that some of the alienated and marginal figures denounced by clerical observers indeed may have rejected that God in some cognitive sense and may have been correctly identified as "atheists" in terms that link them to later phenomena. Let us look at Febvre and Berriot in the thickets of sixteenth-century polemic.

. . .

For Lucien Febvre, it was evident enough that the sixteenth century hurled about the charge of atheism with great abandon, even when it specified that those accused in some sense had evidenced a disbelief in God. "To say that atheism is the act of denying the deity," he noted, "is not to say anything very precise." The accusation of atheism, he concluded, could mean many things, none of which was what one would mean by the term today. Calvin, Luther, Zwingli, and Erasmus, among other reformers or critics of sixteenth-century creed or practice, all were termed atheists by diverse adversaries. Indeed, for Febvre, the charge was generally just a rhetorical device to express the strongest disapproval, or simply "a kind of obscenity meant to cause a shudder in an audience of the faithful." Saint Paul, in his Epistle to the Ephesians, had termed the pagans who knew neither Christ nor the Jewish covenant "without God in the world," and in that sense, *atheist* continued to be an epithet applied to anyone who "did not think about [religious] things exactly the way everyone else did." The Church had built bridges between Christian theology and Aristotelian philosophy, Febvre also argued, but felt forever

[3] Lucien Febvre, *The Problem of Unbelief in the Sixteenth Century: The Religion of Rabelais*, trans. B. Gottlieb (Cambridge, Mass., 1982). The English translation is preferable to the French editions, being more precise in its citations and translations from the Latin than the original and revised French editions of Paris, 1942, and Paris, 1947; François Berriot, *Athéismes et athéistes au XVIe siècle en France*, 2 vols. (Lille, [1977]).

threatened by what it took to be the heterodox Aristotelianism of Averroes. Those whom it perceived to be followers of the suspect commentator, such as Pomponazzi, also could be identified as atheistic.[4] As a description of almost all the particular accusations he examines, Febvre's account seems just right.

Being Lucien Febvre, however, and interested in a deeper history of the French mentality, he went much further. A central part of Febvre's agenda in this work was not merely the contextual analysis of actual accusations, but the larger argument that atheism was, in some fundamental sense, "unthinkable" before the philosophical revolution of the seventeenth century. Atheism required philosophical "free flights" of thought, Febvre argued, and the sixteenth century could only speculate in Latin, "a language made to express the intellectual processes of a civilization that had been dead for a thousand years." Radical new modes of speculation might reach "the threshold of philosophical consciousness," but not until the Cartesian revolution in philosophical language could a fundamental departure from past ways of thought emerge.[5] In addition to lacking a language, atheism, for Febvre, also lacked a medium. The sixteenth century, he argued, was "a century that wanted to believe," a culture saturated with a religiosity that presupposed an unchallenged belief in the existence of God.[6] What, then, were all the theological references to actual incredulity within the flock, to complaints against providence, to refusal to believe? For Febvre, they were, at most, references to occasional "personal impulses and moods." Such impulses and moods, deprived of any systematic or linguistic foundation for coherent disbelief, evidenced merely an ephemeral "unbelief of despair, expressed in the shout of a poor man covered with bruises. . . . or perhaps the unbelief that was a revolt against the triumph of injustice."[7] Febvre did not deny the possibility that faced with tragic experience, or aching to offend the smug, individuals in the sixteenth century might rage at the heavens, but this, if it occurred, was "disbelief" without historical significance:

> To deny, to deny effectively, no matter what the denial is directed against, is not simply to say, out of caprice, whim, or a vain wish to attract attention, "I deny." To deny is to say deliberately and calmly, "For such and such reasons, which are valid for every man and every normally constituted intellect, it appears impossible to me, truly impossible, to accept such and such a system." . . . [Such reasons] could not be fragmentary reasons or special reasons. They had to form a veritable cluster of coherent reasons lending each other

[4] Febvre, *Unbelief*, 131–46. (The seventeenth century did not share the doubts of some scholars and theologians today concerning the authorship of Ephesians.)

[5] Ibid., 206, 364–69.

[6] Ibid., "Conclusion."

[7] Ibid., 459–60.

support. . . . If this cluster could not be formed . . . the denial was without significance. It was inconsequential. It hardly deserves to be discussed.[8]

As strong as Febvre's case might be for the nature of so many sixteenth-century accusations of atheism against prominent heretics, philosophers, and men of letters, his case for the "unthinkability" of atheism seems, in several ways, problematic. First, it is by no means evident that his enumeration of accusations is adequate, or that far more precise charges were not made. Second, the argument about Latin is interesting, but certainly arbitrary in and of itself, and seemingly belied by both prior and later Latin works expressing fundamental challenges to the beliefs of the dominant culture. The most notorious "atheistic" manuscript of the seventeenth century, for example, was the Latin *Theophrastus redivivus*, which revealed far more familiarity with the "dead" than with the living, and with Latinity than with the vernacular.[9] Third, his thesis begs the question of the relationship between, on the one hand, "impulse and mood" and, on the other, formal thought in matters of denial and disbelief. New and positive metaphysical and conceptual systems certainly require some pattern of thought similar to that described by Febvre's rather strict criteria for historical significance, but it is by no means clear that disbelief and denial, to achieve significant causal agency or to merit historical attention, need occur in such ways. Finally, with Rabelais and the poets as his quarry, Febvre looked more at literary culture than at theological and philosophical culture, and it is possible that the view would not be the same from other vantages.

François Berriot found Febvre arbitrary in almost all regards and concluded that Christian apologists of the sixteenth and early seventeenth centuries had identified and described contemporaneous incredulity with enough detail that one might find in their works the atheists' "catechism" that the century would not permit the atheists themselves to write. Where for Febvre anathematizations of atheism were above all a window into the minds of the anathematizers, for Berriot they were a window into the minds of the anathematized. The sixteenth century, in his view, was an age of deep political, economic, social, and religious crises, producing alienated and marginal elements in whom the impulse to reject dominant beliefs resulted in a genuine and even codifiable atheism. At the dawn of capitalism, he would have it, the sixteenth century reacted to the anguish of the world by providing France with its "first atheists."[10] Heterodoxy and skepticism "seem indeed to culminate, toward the year 1550, in diverse forms of deism and even atheism, in the lettered public at least."

[8] Ibid., 352.

[9] Guido Canziani and Gianni Paganini, eds., *Théophrastus Redivivus, edizione prima e critica*, 2 vols. (Florence, 1981–1982). See infra, pt. 2, chap. 7.

[10] Berriot, *Athéismes*.

Since such men obviously could not publish, "we are thus reduced to knowing such opinions from the testimony of those who combat them . . . which allows us to determine quite well what were the theories of the first 'atheists.' "[11]

The *marginaux* whose anguished lives, for Berriot, contributed to the first appearance of atheism, tend to disappear from view, however, once he turns to the atheists of the "catechism," who would seem to be simply heterodox men of letters. There is a strange chasm between the socially alienated figures of the first half of Berriot's work and the alleged authors of the atheists' catechism. Further, this atheistic "catechism" turns out often enough to be precisely what Febvre himself had in mind as evidence for his own thesis that almost any heterodoxy could earn the label of atheism. Berriot offers evidence of unspecified doubts about creation and providence; heterodox or rationalist critiques of orthodox Christian beliefs, or aspects of Christian beliefs; Judaizing monotheism; pantheism; and the justification of the pursuit of pleasure.[12] The issue, however, is not whether the sixteenth century witnessed heterodox thought, magical naturalism, Averroistic revivals or continuities, Satanism, and new superstitions, the heart of Berriot's cognitive evidence, but, given his title ("Atheisms and Atheists in Sixteenth-Century France"), whether or not it produced an atheism in any way distinguishable from these. There is nothing in Berriot's two volumes to suggest that it did.[13]

Above all, from Berriot's own evidence, the portrait of the atheist is behavioral and normative, not conceptual and cognitive: he is described as being without religion, as living without God, as attached to the sensual things of this world, as voluptuous, carnal, and, the seemingly most common source of the charge, as given to frequent taking of the Lord's name in vain. Protestant apologists might well have termed "atheists" those Catholic soldiers who supposedly called out, while slaughtering Calvinists, "Where is your God now?" but historians should perhaps avoid reading too much disbelief into such insult added to ultimate injury.[14] The question of whether the sixteenth-century homosexual ever expressed doubts about the providential ordering of nature and society is both important and profound, but it is not answered by Berriot's recognition that "the accusation of atheism goes hand in hand with that of

[11] Ibid., II, 593.

[12] Ibid., 591–818.

[13] Berriot, for example, ends vol. I with a long analysis of the heterodox *De tribus impostoribus*, after having conceded (I, 546–76) that "the famous pamphlet is indeed the work of a deist and not an atheist." He also conceded (I, 575) that "the 'libertines' of the end of the sixteenth and the beginning of the seventeenth century, with just a few exceptions [whom he does not specify], often will limit themselves to repeating the arguments of Julian [the Apostate] and above all of Celsus." That is to say, they limited themselves to arguments not for atheism, but against Christianity.

[14] Ibid., I, 128–39.

homosexuality [in the sixteenth century]."[15] Indeed, that recognition would seem to support Febvre's thesis, or, more precisely, the simple equation of "atheism" and moral "ungodliness" in early-modern usage. Inferring belief from behavior (on the assumption that no one who believed in God, for example, could employ an oath that violated God's commandment), early-modern sermonizers could well confound blasphemous curses and "denial of God."[16] The historian (from mere acquaintance with colleagues, let alone the past) should not be so precipitous. For example, Berriot's sharpest example of a "negateur de Dieu" in his discussion of blasphemy and sacrilege is that of a man who merely refused to attend vespers and masses, and who was described by accusers who did attend Catholic services as living solely for pleasure.[17] It is undeniable, to cite another case, that apologists often could not believe rural bestiality compatible with belief in God, but this is *not* the stuff of "catechisms" of disbelief.[18] In his own conclusion, Berriot recognizes that the atheist is portrayed, above all else, as a libertine, as someone seeking a rationale for pursuing the pleasures of the earth.[19] This is surely a window into the minds of the accusers and, perhaps, taking account of polemical exaggerations, onto the worldly behavior of the accused; it is certainly not evident that it is a window into the minds of the accused.

Berriot, in brief, has begged the issue of what one should infer from accusations of atheism; Febvre has begged the issue of thinkable disbelief in orthodox Latin Christendom. I shall address both issues directly in the course of this work.

. . .

A culture that, in general, chose to conflate behavioral and conceptual "atheism," the "denial" of God being the perceived sin, whatever its precise manifestation, has confused countless scholars. At times, it could confuse itself. In the spring of 1728, the priest Guillaume, curé of Fresnes, was placed in the Bastille as "an atheist." The abbé Couet, *grand vicaire* and canon of Notre Dame, examined Guillaume's papers for the police and found in his writings "several false principles contrary to sound theology," above all touching on what virtually all theologians took to be the thorny issue of the nature of God's ideas of the creatures. As Couet noted, however, "one could not accuse someone of impiety who has lost his way in matters so abstract, *unless one found other proofs of his cor-*

[15] Ibid., 389.

[16] In all of Berriot's discussion of "blasphemers and deniers of God" (I, 128–39), there is not a single example of anything more "atheistic" than the taking of God's name in vain.

[17] Ibid., I, 136.

[18] Ibid., 171.

[19] Ibid., II, 819–45.

rupted sentiments." In fact, Couet concluded, what makes Guillaume's writings so suspect is "the manifest debauchery and libertinism of his morals . . . and [his] jokes on [the subject of] religion." Guillaume was sentenced to ten months in the Bastille, after which he was sent into monastic seclusion.[20] In short, perhaps a lover, or a drunken joke at some superior's expense, and a notebook of abstract and earnest theology, were all that were involved in such a case.

Further, a culture that often did not distinguish between denying the "true" God and denying that there was a Supreme Being at all could produce similar confusions. In August 1729, for example, a police memoir warned of the "self-proclaimed wits" of the Parisian cafés who spoke against "religion." "If order is not restored," the inspector urged, "the number of atheists *or* deists will grow, and many people will make a religion of their own design for themselves, as in England."[21] This may be no more than a response to irreverence toward the Catholic church. In that same month, the police noted the case of the bookseller Morléon, who was selling, "to many people, abbés and others . . . several works filled with impieties and maxims contrary to the existence of God." Now there, at last, is a phrase that sounds specific enough, "maxims contrary to the existence of God." It is the phrase that in the yet looser language of the sixteenth century made Berriot quite certain of the reality of actual atheists. However, when police agent Haymier was asked to examine Morléon's case, he reported on the content of the texts in these terms: "The manuscripts that [Morléon] is selling . . . treat of the history of earliest times, of the first man, of the history of Egypt, of the patriarchs from the calling of Abraham to the exodus of the Israelites. He has others that discuss the life of Jesus Christ, his origin, and the errors introduced after his death." Morléon was released after one month, having promised never again to sell works "filled with impiety."[22]

. . .

If one accepts the culture's equation of any heterodox views with "atheism," the result, while scholarly, can sound more than paradoxical. Don Cameron Allen's study of "faith and skepticism," *Doubt's Boundless Sea*, focused on such figures as Pomponazzi, Cardan, Vanini, Montaigne, Charron, Bodin, Blount, Oldham, and Rochester.[23] While the chapter ti-

[20] François Ravaisson, ed., *Archives de la Bastille: Documents inédits*. 19 vols. (Paris, 1866–1902), XIV, 197–201.

[21] Ibid., 221–22.

[22] Ibid.

[23] Don Cameron Allen, *Doubt's Boundless Sea: Skepticism and Faith in the Renaissance* (Baltimore, 1964).

tles spoke of "Three Italian Atheists," "Three French Atheists," and "The Atheist Redeemed," Allen's preface made plain the limits of these terms:

> For the Renaissance, in general, an atheist was one who could not accept any religious principle shared by all Christian creeds. A Jew, a Mohammedan, a deist was an atheist, and the definition could be narrower: to many Protestants, the Pope was the chief of Roman Catholic atheists; to many a Roman Catholic, Canterbury was head of the Anglican atheists. None of the men in my present study called himself an atheist, none denied the existence of God. With very few exceptions, this statement holds true for all the atheists indicted by the orthodox opposition.[24]

Let us leave the historians, however, who can speak for themselves, and turn to France in the early-modern age.[25]

[24] Ibid., vi.

[25] For other approaches to and conceptions of the problem, see also *Actes du colloque international de Sommières*, ed. André Stegmann: *Aspects du libertinisme au XVIe siècle* (Paris, 1974); Antoine Adam, *Le mouvement philosophique dans la première moitié du XVIIIe siècle* (Paris, 1967) and *Théophile de Viau et la libre pensée française en 1620* 2d ed. (Geneva, 1965); Henri Busson, *La pensée religieuse française de Charron à Pascal* (Paris, 1933) and *La religion des classiques (1660–1685)* (Paris, 1948) and *Les sources et le développement du rationalisme dans la littérature française de la renaissance*, rev. ed. (Paris, 1957); Cornelio Fabro, *God in Exile: Modern Atheism. A Study of the Internal Dynamic of Modern Atheism, from Its Roots in the Cartesian 'Cogito' to the Present Day*, trans. Arthur Gibson (New York, 1968) [translated from his *Introduzione all'ateismo moderno* (1964)]; Tullio Gregory, *Theophrastus Redivivus: Erudizione e ateismo nel Seicento* (Naples, 1979); Tullio Gregory, G. Paganini, et al., *Ricerche su letteratura libertina e letteratura clandestina nel Seicento* . . . (Florence, 1981); Hermann Ley, *Geschichte der Aufklärung und des Atheismus*, 5 vols. to date (Berlin, 1966–); Fritz Mauthner, *Der Atheismus und seine Geschichte im Abendlande* (Stuttgart and Berlin, 1921); René Pintard, *Le libertinage érudit dans la première moitié du XVIIe siècle*, 2 vols. (Paris, 1943); J. S. Spink, *French Free-Thought from Gassendi to Voltaire* (London, 1960); and D. P. Walker, *The Ancient Theology: Studies in Christian Platonism from the Fifteenth to the Eighteenth Century* (Ithaca, 1972), 132–63. [After this book was completed, a new work by Michael J. Buckley, S.J., *At the Origins of Modern Atheism* (New Haven, 1987), was sent to me for review. Father Buckley already has illuminated some of the most difficult questions in the long-term history of philosophical theology (see his capacious and acute *Motion and Motion's God: Thematic Variations in Aristotle, Cicero, Newton and Hegel* [Princeton, 1971]). His new work is a rich and provocative study of three centuries of religious (or, more precisely, areligious) development, and what he sees as the "self-alienation" of religion. As history of ideas, its approach and findings in many ways make an interesting two-sided coin with my own study of the behavior of an intellectual community. As readers will infer from my discussion of the Cartesian and Malebranchist theological impulse, however, infra, pt. 3, chap. 10, I am not sure that one *historically* should distinguish quite so categorically as he perhaps does between "philosophy" and "religious experience." The interested reader will find my review of Father Buckley's work in *Eighteenth-Century Studies* XXII, no. 4 (Summer 1989), 614–17.]

PART ONE

Atheists without Atheism; Atheism without Atheists

Chapter One

ATHEISTS WITHOUT ATHEISM

To JUDGE by a commonplace theme of the learned literature of the age, "the atheist" was almost everywhere in early-modern France but, strictly speaking, did not exist. This was a paradox appropriate to a culture that was at times obsessed by the image of the atheist and that simultaneously claimed to dismiss his would-be conclusions as unthinkable.

The atheist could be both ubiquitous and without true atheism, since *being an atheist*, book after book agreed, was a function solely of the will, while *thinking as an atheist* obviously referred in some essential way to a function of the mind. The atheist, it was claimed, could *will* himself into being but could not truly *think* atheistically. In that sense, the atheist was presented as a distorted mirror image of the idealized believer. The ideal of Christian intellectual life was faith in search of understanding. The Christian, in his own self-portrait, believing by the will in revelation (with many a different view of the relationship between grace and volition), sought to understand, and discovered in the content of belief, to the delight of the mind, a satisfying, true knowledge of what otherwise made no or little sense. The atheist, in Christian portrait, disbelieving in God only by his will, sought intellectual justification for that disbelief but could go no further than ignorance and self-contradiction. The existence of God, the great majority of teachers proclaimed, was so manifest and inescapable a truth that no people ever had not recognized it, no sane philosopher ever had denied it, no sincere seeker after truth ever had disbelieved it. It was the "fool," the "*homo stultus*," "*l'insensé*," of the Fourteenth Psalm who had said "in his heart" that "there is no God." The culture taught that he had to be a fool, for no one of sense could say that; and he had to say it in his heart, for no one could think it in his mind. As the Jesuit Rapin put it, early in the eighteenth century, "Of all natural truths, the most deeply engraved in the heart of man is the existence of God. . . . All times, all nations and all schools agree on it." Thus, "there is nothing more monstrous in nature than atheism:

> It is a disorder of the mind conceived in libertinism. . . . [The atheist] will be a little mind, puffed up by the success of a sonnet or a madrigal . . . a debauched person who never has had a head free enough nor a mind clear enough to judge sanely of anything. . . . [Atheism is found only among those]

whose minds are the most disordered and whose hearts are the most corrupted.[1]

However, there was a second paradox in the manner in which the learned of the culture generally addressed an atheism that, they argued, could not truly be conceived: they explicated and analyzed it in erudite depth and detail, and they demanded that all systems of philosophical theology overcome it. Why should there be so many accounts and refutations of unthinkable ways of thought? Why should there be so many demonstrations of what was evident? Why were there so many cries of intellectual, not only moral, alarm? What, one well might ask, was on their minds?

. . .

It is often difficult, we have seen, to know precisely what early-modern theologians meant by the terms *atheist* and *atheism*. Among the many reasons for this was the seeming equivocation, inherited perhaps from the ancient world itself, in the meaning of godlessness. As Drachmann has argued for the Greeks, *atheistic* generally meant "ungodly," in the sense of living as if there were no gods or divine laws.[2] As the early Christians learned when they themselves were accused of atheism, it also meant denying the specific "true" gods of specific places. Saint Justin Martyr's *First Apology* addressed both meanings. He responded to the charge of atheism against the Christians by replying, "We do proclaim ourselves atheists as regards those whom you call gods, but not with respect to the Most True God." Addressing the cause of what he took to be the source of actual disbelief, he wrote: "Before God no man has an excuse if he does evil, for all men have been created with the power to reason and to reflect. If anyone does not believe that God takes an interest in these things [virtue and vice], *he will by some artifice imply either that God does not exist*, . . . or that He is [as unmoved] as a stone [by human choice]."[3]

[1] René Rapin, S.J., *Oeuvres de P[ère]. Rapin*, 3 vols. (The Hague, 1725), I, 422.

[2] A. B. Drachmann, *Atheism in Pagan Antiquity*, trans. I. Anderson (Copenhagen, 1922), 1–13.

[3] St. Justin Martyr, *Writings of Saint Justin Martyr*, ed. and trans. Thomas B. Falls (Washington, 1948), c.6 and c.28. The charge of atheism against the Christians was commonly known through many patristic works, especially that of Lactantius. When Henricus Sivers addressed this issue in a thesis presented under the direction of the eminent German philosopher and theologian Christian Kortholt, in *De Atheismo, veteribus Christianis, ob Templorum inprimis adversationem, objecto, in que eosdem a nostris retorto, Excercitatio* (Kiel, 1689), 1–38, he concluded that the pagan charge of atheism against the early Christians was based on the fact that the latter had no temples, sacrifices, or images devoted to the gods of the country; he noted and cited the many Fathers who, struck by the "iniquity" of the accusation, were obliged to respond to it.

For almost all early-modern theologians there was, from a Christian perspective, no equivocation here. It was clear to them that those who lived immoral lives would seek to persuade themselves, in desperation, that there was no need to believe in a God who would judge and punish them. To live as if there were no God was to place oneself in peril if there were a God. The "ungodly" atheist, then—that is to say, the immoral man—sought to deflect his terror by denying the specific God who judged and punished mankind and by closing his mind to the abundance of arguments that proved His existence. Indeed, this was also the view taken by Saint Justin Martyr. The atheist could be discerned by his morals, by his opposition to the providential and judgmental Christian God, or by his denial of any Supreme Being. Indeed, in a Catholic context, if one believed Protestants merely to be seeking to avoid the justice of God by denying the Roman church's possession of the keys to the kingdom of heaven, a judgment more of the sixteenth than of the seventeenth century, then one plausibly could call them atheists too. These were all aspects of the same phenomenon. Further, any argument deemed to give comfort to the morally ungodly might be characterized, as a result, as "atheistic."[4] Such perspectives allowed moderate polemicists to identify any position that they took to be perverse, willful blindness to religious truth as "atheism," and to identify this with an immoral life. Less temperate polemicists could look at the effect of arguments without regard for the element of perverse intent, since an argument that plausibly *could* be used by the perverse achieved the same effect. Almost all polemicists inferred atheism from immoral behavior. Superb at making distinctions, the early-modern commentator could distinguish theoretically among a great variety of possible forms of atheistic expression, only to conflate them all in the end under the rubric of libertine immorality. This sequence of distinction and conflation has confused historians, who, given what followed, understandably have looked for the origins of philosophical atheism, but it appears to have made sense to most early-modern minds. Sometimes the latter formulated the issue in the more formal (and, to us, familiar) terms of a distinction between "practical" and "speculative" atheism, but they generally did so only to make the argument that the second was merely an incoherent product of the first.[5]

[4] For example, Mathurin Veyssière de La Croze, in his *Entretiens sur divers sujets d'histoire, de littérature, de religion, et de critique* (Cologne, 1733), 384, acknowledged that people termed atheists were "accused, rightly or wrongly, of having called into question [*d'avoir revoqué en doute*] the existence of God and the immortality of the soul, *or of having maliciously furnished others with reasons for doubting these*."

[5] On the development of this distinction in early-modern European formal philosophy, see the interesting article by David Berman, "The Theoretical/Practical Distinction as Ap-

There were, to be sure, countless variations on the theme of atheism, but the identification of atheism with willed stupidity in support of a depraved life was one of the commonplaces, albeit occasionally challenged, of early-modern theology. Its premise was that atheism (and often the behavior that produced it) was *contra natura*. As Gautier had noted, long before Febvre and Berriot, "In the sixteenth century, two *savants* and two theologians could not dispute without accusing each other reciprocally of sodomy and atheism."[6] The reason for this phenomenon was not simply polemical, nor in any way necessarily based on any philosophical or skeptical disbelief on the part of the "*marginaux*"; above all, it followed from an assumption about the congruence of behavior and belief. If living as if God would not punish according to His law implied disbelief of doctrines essential to demonstrating divine justice (foremost among which, obviously, was the very existence of God), then why not simply infer the one from the other? The suspect thinker was surely depraved, and the depraved libertine was surely a suspect thinker. The etiology of atheism, it was assumed, was in the depraved will, but the symptoms could be in doubts and objections.

There were many scriptural sources for such a view of disbelief and ungodliness. Before assuming that scandalized theologians correctly recorded the correlations of their culture, then, we should recognize the extent to which the equation of "immoral" behavior and "denial of God" was merely a repetition of biblical commonplaces encountered frequently in their clerical education. First and foremost, there was the "fool" of the Fourteenth (and Fifty-third) Psalm "[who] hath said in his heart, 'There is no God.' " This denial was linked to mankind's iniquity: "They are corrupt, they have done abominable works. . . . they are all together become filthy. . . . Have all the workers of iniquity no knowledge?" The Seventy-third Psalm taught of "the ungodly," who were characterized by pride, violence, oppression, wealth, gluttony, and corruption. The Seventy-fourth Psalm decried the "enemies" of God, the "foolish people" who "have blasphemed Thy name" and forgotten the covenant. The Seventy-eighth Psalm explained God's anger against the Israelites for disobedience of His law as punishment of their disbelief: "because they believed not in God; and trusted not in His salvation." The Ninety-fourth Psalm spoke of those who slew the widow, the stranger, and the fatherless, but who believed that "the Lord shall not see." In addition to being wicked, such disbelievers in providential justice were "brutish" and "fools." There were "the wicked" of Job 21:14–15, who asked, "What profit should we have, if we pray unto Him?" and who "say unto God,

plied to the Existence of God from Locke to Kant," in *Trivium* XII (1977), 92–108, which draws examples primarily from British thought.

[6] Théophile Gautier, *Les grotesques* (Paris, 1853), 71.

Depart from us." In the New Testament, Jude 4–19 spoke of "ungodly men, turning the grace of our God into lasciviousness, and denying the only Lord God, and our Lord Jesus Christ." These ungodly men could be recognized in three ways: they "believed not"; they committed "ungodly deeds," including perversions, fornication, and "filthy" dreams; and they complained of and mocked the divine while walking "after their own ungodly lusts." In short, the ungodly were those "who separate themselves, sensual, having not the Spirit." To many a theologian, Jude could well have been describing the *libertins érudits*, or perhaps even providing a category in which any description of libertinism had to occur. In Ephesians 3:12, Paul described the gentiles who had known neither Christ nor the Jewish covenant as "without God in this world," a source for seeing denial or even ignorance of the "true" God as atheism. Finally, much weight was placed on Saint Paul's judgment, in Romans 1:19–20, that unbelievers were "without excuse," since the "invisible things" of God were so very "manifest" and "clearly seen" in the visible world. In the verses that followed (Romans 1:21–32), such unbelief was linked to unclean lusts and homosexuality, and, in a breathtaking sequence, to a vast array of sins, all exacerbated by the voluntary nature of both crimes and disbelief:

> unrighteousness, fornication, wickedness, covetousness, maliciousness; full of envy, murder, debate, deceit, malignity; whisperers, backbiters, haters of God, despiteful, proud, boasters, inventors of evil things, disobedient to parents, without understanding, covenant breakers, without natural affection, implacable, unmerciful: Who knowing the judgment of God, that they which commit such things are worthy of death, not only do the same, but have pleasure in them that do them.[7]

Saint Paul, however, did not undertake to articulate, dissect, and disprove at great length that which was so inane and depraved as to be "without excuse." The internal dissonance of early-modern attitudes toward "atheism" derived precisely from seeing it as both "without excuse," and, for whatever reasons, as in need of extensive commentary and refutation. To introduce this dissonance, let us look briefly at four commentaries, drawn from a period of almost one hundred years and from both Catholic and Huguenot worlds of thought.

. . .

In 1641, André d'Abillon, priest and doctor of theology, wrote a "defense" of God against the atheists, *La Divinité défendue contre les athées*.

[7] Rather than translate from diverse seventeenth-century French Bibles into English, I simply have used the King James version whenever appropriate.

The existence of God, he observed, was both manifest in all of nature and taught by all schools of philosophy. Those who denied this truth were reckless atheists whose "impiety and ignorance" arose solely from the fear, given "the dissoluteness [*débordement*] of their morals," that God justly would punish them. Knowledge of God's being in no way depended upon faith or religious experience, since there were a "host" of arguments and demonstrations that established it with the uttermost evidence and certainty. It might well be that there were no atheists "in nature," but even then, it would be worthwhile to shed light on the adored truth of God's existence. If there were such atheists, they were a handful of rash figures who said "either by their mouths or, from fear of human justice, by their hearts, that there is no God in the world." He offered a small and unforbidding list of those who might be characterized as such: among the ancients, Lucian, Diagoras, Theodorus, and Protagoras; among the moderns, Vanini, "and several others." Given the "libertines" of this current century, however, he urged the importance of showing that one could only be an atheist by an act of willful ignorance.[8]

However, having established a clear agenda—namely, to deprive would-be fearless libertines of any grounds for hoping that they might avoid divine justice—d'Abillon, like almost all of his contemporaries who wrote on the subject, proceeded to weaken the central assumption of his work, the inanity of any atheistic conclusions, by taking these conclusions quite seriously. Eloquence against the atheists was not enough, he urged; one needed "all the rigor of the most scholastic theology" to be sure that "the force of my syllogisms forces the atheists, with enough power, to confess their temerity and ignorance."[9] To do that, one had to reason one's way through the difficulties of a term, "God," that was "full of equivocation and analogy," a difficult task, and to establish His existence demonstratively against "the principal objections of the atheists," objections that should be stated "with all possible force."[10] Where most medieval summae and commentaries had done this rather concisely, d'Abillon would go on for more than 250 pages, proving God from subtle Scotist arguments, from the Thomist "five ways," from miracles, from demonology, from prophecy, from conscience, and from the consequences of abandoning such belief, both for society and for the sciences. Along the way, he proposed "atheistic" objections to each of his proofs, some quite easily dismissed (e.g., that the sun was the first cause of all things), and some the object of a bit more concern (e.g., that conscience and human law did not require supernatural explanation).[11] Having proved God against particular objections, he defended his conclusion for yet another

[8] André d'Abillon, *La divinité défendue contre les athées* (Paris, 1641), 1–44.

[9] Ibid., 1–11, 38–44.

[10] Ibid., "Avis au lecteur," and 15–28, 315–16.

[11] Ibid., 45–314.

85 pages against what he presented as the strongest "propositions" of the atheists. His readers may have found these weak, and many could have identified them as commonplace objections long offered to students of divinity to sharpen their minds upon, but they were not quite what one might expect from debauched fools: (1) that "if a sovereign providence governed this world, there would not be such obvious disorders"; (2) that since "all that we see in the world is . . . composed of matter," and since "everything that falls under our senses is a simple . . . or mixed body," we could have no knowledge of a God who "doesn't fall under our senses"; (3) that "nature . . . suffices to produce all the operations that we admire in the world," and we need not multiply beings unnecessarily to explain phenomena; (4) that the existence of evil is incompatible with the existence of God, since "if there were a God . . . there would be an infinite goodness . . . [that] would destroy entirely the contrary which is opposed to it"; and (5) that "mysteries," insisted upon by God, would involve God in impossibilities.[12] Such atheistic propositions, d'Abillon concluded, were so "frivolous" that to risk an eternity of pain on their behalf, when one lost nothing by believing in God, could only be the triumph of malice over reason. All atheists had gone from vice to depravity to blindness to denial of God, and they must never be allowed to tempt any believer onto the same path. For this reason, "there is no punishment violent enough for so dark a crime."[13] For the two doctors of the Sorbonne who approved the publication of his work, d'Abillon's "solid doctrine and powerful reasons" were "capable of confounding atheism," which was ringing endorsement, but curious for a culture that saw such atheism as "frivolous" from beginning to end.[14]

Similarly, the Huguenot David Derodon's *L'athéisme convaincu* (1659) defined the atheists as "those whom debauchery, bad company, or little knowledge of good letters have so corrupted that they dare to deny publicly the Being who gave them their being."[15] Against such debauched ignorant men, Derodon offered nine proofs of God, including, among others, the necessity of a creator (from the noneternity of the world), the order of the universe, universal consent, conscience and the awareness of one's sins, and the need for a prime mover.[16] He warned "those who dispute against the atheists," however, that they "always should use this first proof [from the noneternity of the world], as being the principal one that demonstratively proves a Divinity. . . . For as to the other proofs, . . . they do not entirely close the atheists' mouth, not be-

[12] Ibid., 317–402.
[13] Ibid., 396–402.
[14] Ibid., "Approbation."
[15] David Derodon, *L'athéisme convaincu. Traité demonstrant par raisons naturelles qu'il y a un Dieu* (Orange, 1659), 4.
[16] Ibid., 3–147.

cause they have solid replies to overturn them, but because they have enough evasions to elude them."[17] Might one not think the evasion of eight of nine proofs a solid accomplishment for those who were atheists by debauchery, bad friends, and ignorance?

In the Jesuit Jean Dez's posthumously published *La foy des chrétiens . . . justifiée* (1714), belief in God was presented as a principle accepted by "all times, all peoples, and all men," such that "atheists, *if there be any*," would have to argue that nature "had belied her reputation [for wisdom] on this point alone by deceiving all mankind." The "few atheists whom people have believed to see in all centuries" were abominable enemies of goodness and probity.[18] Nonetheless, he portrayed them in terms often assigned by the very learned to the great multitude of the less learned, as those "who want to believe only what they see," and he attempted to refute them by reference to metaphysical demonstrations from contingency, necessary being, degrees of perfection, natural order, first cause, and prime mover, and to proofs from universal consent, the desire for beatitude, and the willingness to suffer martyrdom for the good.[19]

In Mathurin Veyssière de La Croze's "Dissertation sur l'athéisme et sur les athées modernes" (1733), the former Benedictine and now Huguenot author explained that atheism would not be such a terrible crime if it were, in fact, "only an error of the understanding." Given the incomparable clarity of the proofs of the Divinity, however, it was obvious that it was impossible for it to be such an error. "Atheism," he wrote, "cannot be born elsewhere than in a very disordered and very corrupted heart" and is always sired by "the unruliness of the will." It was not "natural to men," but produced by pride, self-love, and libertinism. Far from being a "system," it was voluntary doubt, taking the form of "difficulties" posed to the proofs we have of God. Such being the case, he warned, there could be no more "extravagant" or dangerous opinion than what he described as the widely articulated view that "great minds are more subject to atheism than others," and the learned should stop accusing each other falsely of this utmost crime.[20]

In short, then, atheism was a willful refusal to believe, and it was with-

[17] Ibid., 134.

[18] Jean Dez, S.J., *La foy des chrétiens . . . justifiée contre les déistes, les juifs, les sociniens et les autres hérétiques . . . où l'on montre qu'elle est toujours conforme à la raison*, ed. P. de Laubrussel, 4 vols. (Paris, 1714), III, 12, 41, 45–47. Dez had been *recteur* of the Jesuit seminary of Strasbourg from 1682 to 1691, and *recteur* of the University of Strasbourg from 1704 to 1708 and from 1711 until his death in 1712, and had been *gouverneur* of the Jesuits in "Champagne, Gallo-Belgique et Paris."

[19] The reference to "*les athées, qui ne veulent croire que ce qu'ils voyent*" is found in ibid., III, 36; the refutation of atheism is found in III, 14–55.

[20] Veyssière de La Croze, "Dissertation sur l'athéisme et sur les athées modernes," in *Entretiens*, 250–457. See, in particular, 250–84.

out serious intellectual foundation. Nonetheless, it should be combated by metaphysical and complex proofs that repelled its objections to belief. As synonymous with insincerity in religious belief, it was a common term of polemical abuse and could be seen as both widespread, and, if one saw the age as increasingly libertine, burgeoning. As synonymous with any authentic inability to be persuaded of the existence of God, it was seen as so rare that it could be opposed by an appeal to universal consent. Whether or not "real atheists" existed was open to doubt, but the malicious and ignorant fool (at times an ancient philosopher of no small repute) who sought to protect himself from knowledge of God's justice was real, and the lies he told himself were both inane and the stuff of intense theological scrutiny and discussion. Within these conceptions and conventions, on the whole, early-modern France confronted the "atheists" and attempted to note, or at times simply to imagine, or even, in the case of those allegedly circumspect (and thus silent) atheists of the heart, to assign their arguments. In theory and practice, atheism, as ungodliness, referred to behavior far more than to belief throughout most of the early-modern period, but this behavior was deemed to give rise to objections, doubts, and ways of thinking that in some sense "removed" God from the world. Thus, if we interrogate the authors of the early-modern learned world on whether or not there were atheists before the turn of the eighteenth century, their answers are inherently equivocal, and we must proceed with extreme caution with regard to the congruence of our notions and theirs. If we ask them what people called atheists believed, they may tell us only what they expected people seeking to hide from divine justice to believe. With these initial caveats, let us proceed, nevertheless, to ask them such things.

. . .

Let us begin with what they wanted to believe. The monk and theologian Yves de Paris wrote a popular system of natural theology that by 1640 was in its fourth edition. Arraying a wide variety of proofs of God's existence, the Capuchin spoke for most of his culture when he noted that, given the evidence of these demonstrations, a person could only deny God "by madness, by ambition, and by effort of persuading himself of this in order to secure the annulment of all his crimes."[21] The priest and educator Claude Fleury, writing a generation later, with equal popularity, sketched the spectrum of sins against the faith, from idolatry and superstition

[21] Yves de Paris, O.F.M., Capuchin, *La théologie naturelle. Tome premier: Divisé en deux parties. La première traictant de l'existence de Dieu . . .*, 4th ed., rev. and corr. (Paris, 1640). The quotation is from 83–84.

through Judaism and heresy to the most egregious of all such sins, "impiety" and "irreligion," the latter being defined as "the indifference of libertines *who live as if there were neither God nor religion*."[22] The nuances were different, but the essential diagnosis was the same: the source of atheism lay in the criminal immorality of those who *lived* "without God." In a work that saw three editions by 1706 and was reprinted in the 1720s and 1750s, the Oratorian Bernard Lamy, mathematician, Cartesian philosopher, and theologian, described such unbelievers in those same common terms: "For given the manner in which they live, having no chance of hoping for reward on the part of God, *they must hope that there were nothing to fear*, which they cannot do except by persuading themselves that everything that is said about religion is without solidity."[23]

These characterizations were not new to the seventeenth century. In the sixteenth century, in France, the widespread accusations of atheism that caught the attention of Febvre, Allen, and Berriot might be looser (the seventeenth century increasingly could not quite bring itself to see sectarian differences as justifying the charge), but the linkage to immorality was generally the same. In 1578, Guy le Fevre de la Boderie, the translator of Ficino's exposition of Christian doctrine, decried his "unfortunate century, with its corruption of laws, customs, good morals, and the chaos and confusion of sects which gush forth and multiply rapidly from day to day" as one that "nourishes, like the serpent in its breast, Atheism, which secretly creeps into the hearts and minds of several voluptuous and depraved men."[24] Catholic, Calvinist, and heterodox freethinkers could agree on such a portrait. Gentillet's discourses against the "atheist" Machiavelli described the ancient and modern atheists as those who have freed themselves from the fear of God's punishment of their crimes, denying "a God who sees what they do and who must punish them for these."[25] The Swiss Calvinist reformer Pierre Viret similarly expressed his fear of those who "*do not want to be subjects either of God or of any creature*, but [who want] to do everything that pleases them."[26] Geoffroy Vallée, an antireligious advocate of reason as an "antidote" to fear and

[22] Claude Fleury, *Catéchisme historique. Contenant en abrégé l'histoire sainte et la doctrine chrétienne*, 2 vols. (Paris, 1683), II, 248.

[23] Bernard Lamy, Oratory, *Entretiens sur les sciences* . . . [first published in Grenoble and Lyon, 1684]. Critical ed. by François Girbal and Pierre Clair [from the 3d ed., rev. and aug. (Lyon, 1706)] (Paris, 1966), 69.

[24] Guy Le Fevre de La Boderie, "Epistre" [unpaginated, xi pp.], in Marcelo Ficino, *De la religion chrestienne* . . . , trans. G. Le Fevre de La Boderie (Paris, 1578).

[25] Innocent Gentillet, *Discours sur les moyens de bien gouverner . . . contre Nicolas Machiavel Florentin* (n.p., 1576), 172–75.

[26] Pierre Viret, *Deux dialogues: L'alcumie du purgatoire; L'homme naturel* [first published, respectively, in 1544 and 1561], ed. Jacques Courvoisier, (Lausanne, 1971), 32.

dogma, who was denounced by his contemporaries as an atheist for his notorious condemnation of existing creeds and churches, in fact held views similar to those of the orthodox on the subject of atheism. Although "it is true that *man can never be an atheist* and is created thus by God," he wrote, there are those who, having abandoned themselves to voluptuousness, attempt unsuccessfully to suppress all thought of the divine and to live "without God." Such an atheist, "or [rather]," Vallée concluded, "the one who calls himself such, because *it is not possible for man to be without God*," lives always in torment.[27]

Toward the end of the sixteenth century, two works in particular undertook a systematic analysis of atheism and its causes: Pierre Charron's *Les trois véritez* (1595) and Laurent Pollot's *Dialogues contre la pluralité des religions et l'athéisme* (1595). Charron allowed much of what he loathed in the world to be a contributor to atheism, from pride to "interminable" theological dispute, and he made it clear, at least between the lines, that the issue was more one of God's providence than of His existence. In truth, he averred, there was a "universal consent" to the existence of God, since "nothing has been so unanimously and perpetually received and advocated by all men as the belief and apprehension of the Deity, of a first, sovereign, and omnipotent cause." Nonetheless, he acknowledged, there were "beasts" so deformed and monstrous that they sought to deny such a truth, above all, the truth of a Providence that watched over all things. For this atheism, there were five primary "causes" or "occasions," all of which, he believed, the Scriptures had explained. First and foremost, there was "*insipientia*," the "foolishness" of which the Psalmist wrote, which Charron identified with brutishness and madness. Second, there was "*impunitas*," the evil soul in search of exemption from punishment, described by the Ninth Psalm. Third, there was "*ignorantia consiliorum Dei*," described by the Second Psalm, an unwillingness to heed the counsel and affairs of God. For Charron, this was the act of questioning the ways in which the world was governed from above, of raising difficulties about the course of things that led one to believe "that there is not at all a God or a master governor, but that everything goes as it would." Fourth, there was "*impatientia*," the impatience described by Exodus 17 and Job 21, the state of having solicited God by prayer and vow, and, not receiving what one begged for, having decided that "there is no one who hears." Finally, as described by 2 Peter 3, there was belief in "*perpetuus ordo et tenor natura*," the failure to discern the author of the regularity of nature, concluding, pitiably, that

[27] Geoffroy Vallée, *La béatitude des chrestiens ou le fléo de la foy* (n.p., 1573?; Paris, 1867 [limited ed. 120 copies, by the "Académie des bibliophiles"]), 10–13.

things "have, of themselves, always gone thus."[28] In reverse order, then, Charron presents us with an atheism born of hasty judgment by impatient and selfish souls who ignore the counsel of God, seeking to avoid merited punishment in their brutishness and madness. The categories of such judgment, he believed, including a failure to see beyond the operations of nature, had been described by Scripture itself.

Pollot, in his dialogue on atheism, also argued for the absolute evidence of the existence of God, judging that atheists were freaks, monsters void of all judgment, men so depraved that "*they had gouged out their own eyes expressly in order not to see God in His works nor in His word.*"[29] There were three groups of atheists, he explained: enemies of Christianity "who do not know the true God"; those who "doubt or even feel or speak ill of God's providence"; and, finally, "those *who force themselves to erase all sentiment of divinity from their heart*, and blaspheming miserably, say that there is no God."[30] Having made these distinctions and identified the last group as the only subject of his dialogue, however, Pollot proceeded to redefine these real atheists by merging the three groups: "We call atheists those who deny the true God, or even all Divinity, together with religion: just as the word itself provides its meaning, which signifies without God." These monsters could be identified by fourteen "oppositions and objections," almost all of which were merely heterodox theistic views, many simply Protestant, but three of which did involve providence, creation, and the immortality of the soul.[31] After dealing with the intellectual substance of these "atheistic views," Pollot concluded with the visible manifestations of such atheism: faithlessness toward God and one's fellow men; deceit; lack of conscience; hatred of equity and virtue; love of all vice, debauchery, and wickedness; public and private tyranny and extortion; and, in the end, contempt for and profanation of religion and all that depends on it.[32] In short, atheism was a willful blindness, expressed in "oppositions and objections" to orthodox beliefs, and visible in an unjust, dissolute, ungodly life.

The seeming flowering of courtly and aristocratic "libertinism" in the early seventeenth century, and the survivals, revivals, and reassertions of diverse heterodox (including Protestant) criticisms of prevailing doctrines only reinforced the belief among the learned Catholic devout that "atheism" was ever more rampant in France. In 1623–1624, three works ap-

[28] Pierre Charron, *Toutes les oeuvres de Pierre Charron . . . Dernière edition*, 2 vols. (Paris, 1635), II, 1–8.

[29] Laurent Pollot, *Dialogues contre la pluralité des religions et l'athéisme* (La Rochelle, 1595), 97r.

[30] Ibid., 97v–98r.

[31] Ibid., 98r–99r.

[32] Ibid., 99r–172v.

peared that sought to link libertine life-styles, heterodox thought, and "atheism": the Jesuit François Garasse's *La doctrine curieuse des beaux esprits de ce temps* (1623); and two books by the savant Minim monk Marin Mersenne, his *Quaestiones celeberrimae in Genesim* (1623), and his *L'impiété des déistes, athées, et libertins de ce temps* (1624). They seem, most essentially, a response of clerics to a growing lay world of letters whose orthodoxy and morals, from ecclesiastical perspectives, seemed dubious at best. Garasse distinguished between "libertines," who were "apprentices" of atheism and "have no other god but their stomachs," and actual atheists, who feigned belief in God but who, in their secret, private language, denied Him among themselves.[33] At times, he linked such real atheism with what he termed a substitution of nature for God, but his actual target here was concupiscent behavior far more than ideas. Atheistic naturalism was not philosophical materialism, but carnal self-indulgence. Having "no divinity . . . but nature" meant "refusing nothing to our bodies or to our senses of what they desire." Further, such "atheists" might even believe in God privately, but this was not a significant excuse; to avoid atheism, one must also accept the Incarnation, the Eucharist, the resurrection of the dead, heaven, and hell.[34] Belief in "fate" or "destiny" was equally atheistic for Garasse, such that all who cast horoscopes or took them into account were deniers of God. To grant God but deny angels, demons, and demonic possession also constituted atheism. Pagan polytheism was "a branch of atheism." Sodomy was atheism.[35] The atheists, in short, were those who mocked, denied, or questioned, by word or by behavior, articles of belief deemed essential by Garasse, and they were motivated by "malice" and appetite.

Berriot might find the stuff of the "atheists' catechism" in Garasse's accounts, but the population of atheists was not quite what one might imagine. Trying to distinguish among degrees of disbelief, Garasse had identified as "perfect [complete] atheists" the Manichaeans, Luther, Vanini, and the poets of the libertine *Parnasse satyrique*.[36] In the course of the *Doctrine curieuse*, the following individuals and groups were classified as unambiguously atheistic: Cain, Nimrod, Esau, Judas, Diagoras, Democritus, Epicurus, Diogenes, Leucippus, Sardanapalus, Calvin and *all* his disciples, all astrologers, the Parisian satiric poets, Zwingli, Erasmus, Béza, all "sodomites," Pasquier, Machiavelli, Osiander, and Mo-

[33] François Garasse, S.J., *La doctrine curieuse des beaux esprits de ce temps, ou prétendus tels*, 2 vols. (Paris, 1623), I, 1–98.

[34] Ibid., II, 675–946.

[35] This recitation of "atheistic" beliefs and practices is found throughout the text, but see, in particular, ibid., I, 205–468.

[36] Ibid., 39–46.

hammed.[37] Not one of these, however, it should be noted well, actually could *think* atheistically, in Garasse's view. "The most hopeless ne'er-do-well imaginable," he wrote, "does not have enough resolve to persuade himself with force of this proposition 'That there is no God,' " which was why it could be said only by "the heart."[38]

Mersenne's *Quaestiones in Genesim* offered and replied to twenty-six "objections" of the "atheists," drawn essentially from the classics and from standard Scholastic *sed contra* "objections" to proofs of God that theology students long had been given as exercises. These referred primarily to difficulties concerning orthodox notions of creation, providence, and the problem of evil.[39] Mersenne claimed that there were fifty thousand atheists in Paris alone.[40] His actual atheists, however, sounded far from learned. For example, they were described as claiming that the Catholic church would not survive past 1661, the year in which all roman numerals would be used (MVCLXI, in some early seventeenth-century usage), after which atheists and deists would reign. In brief, Mersenne's "atheists" seemed far more superstitious than formally disputational.[41] In the end, as Lenoble noted in his study of Mersenne, the learned monk would direct "the ancient reproach of atheism . . . at whoever will demonstrate any liberty with regard to tradition. . . . For him, . . . belief and atheism are above all an acceptance or a denial of the established religion."[42] When Mersenne explained the causes of atheism, the first two were stupidity and the fear of divine punishment.[43]

In 1624, his analysis and refutation of "the impiety of the deists, atheists, and libertines of these times" made his perspective yet clearer. The occasion of his denunciation of impiety was his discovery of the notorious "Quatrains of the deist," referred to by Mersenne as "the Poem of the deist." Such overt rejection of Christianity, for Mersenne, was a station on that road to atheism initiated by Luther and Calvin. While primarily directed against the deists, Mersenne's treatise undertook to prove God against "the atheists," although, he confessed, it was astonishing to have to do so, given that everything in the universe bespoke the Divinity. Such being the case, he noted, "I believe that one would have to have a wondrously brutish soul to reach the point of thinking that there is no God."[44]

[37] Ibid., I and II.

[38] Ibid., I, 158–61.

[39] Marin Mersenne, Minim, *Quaestiones celeberrimae in Genesim . . . In hoc volumine athei, et deistae impugnatur, et expugnatur . . .* (Paris, 1623), cols. 235–462.

[40] Ibid., cols. 669–74.

[41] Ibid., "Praefatio."

[42] Robert Lenoble, *Mersenne ou la naissance du mécanisme* (Paris, 1943), 171–73.

[43] Mersenne, *Quaestiones*, cols. 225–26.

[44] Marin Mersenne, Minim, *L'impiété des déistes, athées, et libertins de ce temps, combatuë, et renversée de point en point par raisons tirées de la philosophie et de la théologie.*

Huguenot theologians, of course, bristled at any linking of the Reformation and atheism, but they fully shared the view that atheism was a set of objections to conventional belief motivated by a debased soul in search of impunity. Derodon argued that there were three sorts of atheists. First, there were "the refined," who under the guise of being philosophical skeptics raised objections to formal proofs of God's existence. He claimed to have known personally some four or five such men, all of whom, he warned, had perished horribly shortly after expressing their objections. These, however, only "feign doubt," he assured his readers, since their infection by spiritual poison was what truly was at work. Second, there were "the debauched," generally young men from wealthy and powerful families who, ignored and undisciplined as children, now lived immorally without God. These, he agreed, were a far larger group than the first. Third, there were "the ignorant," the largest group, who professed belief in God and thought they knew Him, but who in fact were not truly persuaded. If they actually believed that He existed, then how could they possibly offend Him by the frequent vices of their lives?[45] Louis Cappel, professor of theology at Saumur, attributed all atheism quite simply to the perversion of the will, to "effeminacy," and to the depraved search for material prosperity and pleasure.[46]

In 1660, the national synod of French Reformed churches, meeting at Loudun, denounced "the atheism, the impiety, the blasphemy, the injustice, the dissolution, and the luxury" of the age.[47] Samuel Cottiby, a former Huguenot now converted to Catholicism, wrote in reply that atheism could never be overcome without the Catholic practice of auricular confession, since until confronted with and discharged of his sins the sinner could only hope that there were no God.[48] The Huguenot Jean Daillé dismissed this as absurd, since it so dramatically underestimated the "entrenched sin" of atheism, which was above all else a product of an insolent will.[49]

The portrait of the atheist offered by Molière in *Dom Juan*, that of a debauched immoralist whose cleverness consisted primarily in his skill at self-serving deceit and seduction, and only secondarily in witty blas-

---

Ensemble la réfutation du Poème des Déistes, 2 vols. (Paris, 1624), passim. The final quotation is from I, 72–73.

45 Derodon, *L'athéisme*, 148–51.

46 Louis Cappel, *Le pivot de la foi et religion, ou Preuve de la divinité contre les athées et les profanes* (Saumur, 1643), "Préface." The *Pivot* was translated into English by Philip Marinel as *The Hinge of the Faith and Religion . . .* (London, 1660).

47 Jean Daillé, *Lettre escrite à Monsieur Le Coq . . . sur le changement de religion de M. Cottiby* (Charenton, 1660), "Préface," [ii–v].

48 "Lettre de M. Cottiby envoyée . . . aux Pasteurs et Anciens de l'Eglise Reformée de Pictiers," in ibid., [vi–xxii].

49 Ibid., 16–18.

phemy, was simply the dramatic representation of a commonplace. The valet Sganarelle's description of his master could have been drawn from almost all accounts of the unbeliever: "the greatest miscreant that the earth has ever known, a madman, a dog, a devil, a Turk, a heretic, who believes in neither heaven, nor saint, nor God, nor werewolf; who spends this life truly as a brutish animal; a pig of Epicurus; a true Sardanapalus, who closes his ears to all Christian remonstrances that can be made to him, and treats everything that we believe as nonsense."[50]

[50] This is the text of the quickly suppressed edition "noncartonnée" of 1682, available in Jean-Baptiste Molière, *Oeuvres complètes de Molière*, ed. Gustave Michaut (Paris, 1947), v, 24. Allowing Don Juan explicitly to deny "God" was deemed too strong, however, and in the authorized, altered edition, *Les oeuvres de Monsieur de Molière. Revuës, corrigées et augmentées*, 8 vols. (Paris, 1682 [and Paris, 1683]), VII, 134, the line was changed to "who believes in neither heaven, nor hell, nor werewolf." Many were offended that Molière had portrayed a debauched atheist onstage, and found his violent death at the end of the play too contrived, but the playwright had said nothing new. The original language was maintained in the Amsterdam edition of 1683: *Le festin de Pierre, comédie par J.G.P. de M., edition nouvelle, & toute differente de celle qui a paru jusqu'à present*, which was also reprinted in Brussels, 1694. The model of the particular provocation offered by Molière's Don Juan, who, when asked what he believed, answered with the truths of addition, was taken almost literally from an anecdote privately recorded by Tallement des Réaux sometime after 1657: "It is told of a German prince strongly given over to Mathematics, that asked at the point of death by his confessor if he did not believe, etc. 'We mathematicians,' he replied, 'believe that two and two make four, and four and four make eight,' " in *Les historiettes de Tallemant des Réaux*, ed. De Monmergué and P. Paris, 3d ed. (Paris, 1854–1860), I, 493. The context in the *Historiettes* related to the choice between Catholic and Protestant creeds rather than to atheism, however. Jean Louis Guez, sieur de Balzac, in his posthumously published *Socrate chrestien . . . et autres oeuvres . . .* (Arnhem, 1675), 127, also told the same tale, this time in the context of impiety and atheism, but identified its subject as "a French prince" and noted that since it was "a domestic secret, known to few persons," he would not identify the prince. The words by which the valet described his atheistic master appear to have originated in Pollot, *Dialogues*, 2r–2v: "Atheists, who believe neither in God, nor angel, nor devil, nor paradise, nor hell [*Athéistes, qui ne croyent, ny Dieu, ny Ange, ny diable, ny Paradis, ny enfer*]." Among those offended by the manner in which Molière brought an atheist to the stage, see the sieur de Rochemont's *Observations sur une comédie de Molière intitulée Le Festin de Pierre* (Paris, 1665), 1–27, which denounced Molière as "a writer of farces . . . who makes the majesty of God the plaything of a theatrical master and valet, of an atheist who laughs at it and of a valet more impious than his master." Don Juan, for de Rochemont, was "an atheist struck down in appearance . . . [but in reality] an atheist who in fact strikes down and overturns all the foundations of religion." In particular, he decried scenes showing "an atheist who reduces all faith to two plus two make four and four plus four make eight." See also Armand de Bourbon, prince de Conti, *Traité de la comédie et des spectacles, selon la tradition de l'église, tirée des conciles et des saints pères*, 2d ed. (Paris, 1669), 67–68: "Is there a more overt School of Atheism than the *Festin de Pierre*, where after having put into the mouth of an atheist who has much wit all of the most horrible impieties, the author confides the cause of God to a valet, who, to support it, is made to say all the impertinences in the world; and he [Molière] claims to justify his play at the end, a play so full of blasphemies, by means of a bomb that he makes the ridiculous agency of divine vengeance."

Molière's critic, de Rochemont, saw this portrait as only too accurate. He noted, "I know that one does not fall into atheism in one blow. One descends only by degrees into this abyss. One goes there only by a long sequence of vices and by a chain of evil behavior that leads from one to the other. . . . [It is] by these degrees that Molière has shown atheism upon the stage."[51]

For de Rochemont, Molière's play put on public display all four of the varieties of disbelief: (1) blasphemy; (2) overt worship joined to a covert denial of God "in the depth of the heart"; (3) belief in a God whom one did not fear, a God viewed as "either blind or impotent"; and (4) the seeming defense of religion "only in order to destroy it, by maliciously weakening its proofs or by skillfully debasing the dignity of its mysteries." Molière's atheist was a mocking libertine whose vice led to blasphemies that the playwright never should have allowed him to utter with wit.[52]

By the late seventeenth century, then, theologians and other commentators on the scandals of irreligion had a well-defined character in place: the wicked atheist without real conviction. On the surface, nothing had changed in the caricature. Atheistic disbelief might be attributed less and less to a variety of merely heterodox views or doubts, but atheism as the "denial" of God continued to be conceived of both as the widespread phenomenon of libertine life-styles and, intellectually, as an inanity so extreme that it could only be a function of the will. Spizelius's widely read *De Atheismi Radice* (1666) accepted Mersenne's figures for atheists in France, but made clear what the real target was by naming it the "libertine-atheistic doctrine."[53]

The atheist, then, the great majority of commentators would have had their readers believe, was a real threat in his behavior, but no threat at all in his ideas. The Oratorian priest and theologian Denis Amelote assured his readers that "there are no civilized nations that do not agree to the truth of a sovereign being"; he described atheism simply as "license that seeks impunity," but that cannot even convince itself, given the primordial consciousness of God in all mankind.[54] The erudite Protestant Frideric Spanheim saw the evidence for God as so universal that it took the willful lowering of oneself from human to subbestial status to doubt it, and required that the *insensé* be utterly "wicked" as well. The problem, for Spanheim, was not speculative atheists, but "these covert atheists who live as if there were no God," outraging Him by their immoral thoughts,

[51] De Rochemont, *Observations*, 10–25.

[52] Ibid., 27–34.

[53] Theophilus Spizelius, *De Atheismi Radice* (Augsburg, 1666), 19–24.

[54] Denis Amelote, Oratory, *Abbrégé de la théologie, ou des principales veritez de la religion* (Paris, 1675), 1–43.

conduct, and pursuit of pleasure.[55] As the theologian and canon François Diroys explained in his popular defense of Catholicism against "false religions and atheism," contestation of the truths of God, providence, and the distinction between good and evil could only come from those who "do not want to be persuaded of them," having "a vast disorder of the mind and will which makes them prefer the shadows . . . to the light."[56] Rochefort's *Dictionnaire* quoted with approval Théophile de Viau's defense of himself against the charge of atheism, that no creature could ignore the truth of God's existence imprinted by God Himself in every soul, and defined the atheists as those who "do everything to persuade their souls that they have no souls, and their vices that there is no God to punish them."[57] For the eminent Dominican and Thomist theologian Noel Alexandre, only those who were "abandoned to the desires of their hearts . . . immersing themselves in impurity . . . [and] dishonored in their own bodies" could disbelieve. Homosexuals, he charged, were terrified of knowing God and were typically atheists. Their partners in denying God were the wicked, fornicators, the greedy, the envious, murderers, cheats, the corrupt, and the vain. Atheists, in short, were not philosophers, but people "who study to invent new ways of doing evil."[58]

It is important to understand, before turning to the seeming paradox of early-modern presentations of serious atheistic views, how widespread this insistence was that there could be no sincere atheistic belief. As Paul-Philippe de Chaumont, retired bishop of Acqs, assured his readers, persuasion of the existence of God was an "instinct" in all men, a "light independent of their reason," which was why it could be universal even among the unlettered; it was also irrefutably demonstrable. Atheism, then, was merely a pose by a handful of "libertines," but even these showed their true colors when confronted by adversity, maintaining their "criminal profession of being atheists" only "until a violent illness" led them to acknowledge "the true sentiments that they have on the existence of God."[59] Laurent Bordelon, man of letters and commentator on the ancients, conceded that there was merely virtual but not perfect universal consent to the existence of God, but argued that the exceptions were ei-

[55] Frideric Spanheim, *L'athée convaincu en quatre sermons sur les paroles du Pseaume XIV. vers I. 'L'insensé a dit en son coeur, il n'y a point de Dieu'* . . . (Leiden, 1676), 85–91.

[56] François Diroys, *Preuves et préjugez de la religion chrestienne et catholique contre les fausses religions et l'athéisme* (Paris, 1683), 3–4.

[57] César de Rochefort, *Dictionnaire général et curieux* . . . (Lyon, 1685), 22.

[58] Noel Alexandre, O.P., *Abrégé de la foi et de la morale de l'Eglise* . . . , 2 vols. (Paris, 1686), II, 160–62.

[59] Paul Philippe de Chaumont, bishop of Acqs, *Réflexions sur le christianisme, enseigné dans l'Eglise Catholique. Tirées de diverses preuves que la RAISON fournit touchant la religion chrétienne, enseignée dans l'Eglise Catholique*, 2 vols. (Paris, 1692–1693), I, 13–19.

ther wholly barbarous peoples utterly devoid of natural light, or thinkers whose reason having been "corrupted by sensual pleasures or by self-conceit, another form of madness . . . *try* not to believe in God."[60] The atomist Samuel Sorbière, for all his philosophical heterodoxy, shared these views fully. There were atheists out of debauchery and ignorance, he wrote, but "in their adversities" they evidenced their *real* beliefs by always "having recourse to a Supreme Cause." As for atheists by thought, Sorbière admitted that "I cannot conceive [of them]."[61] For the Jesuit Jean Crasset, all disbelief—pagan, Jewish, heretical, and atheistic—was the product of pride, malice, unregulated passions, ambition, envy, avarice, and incontinence; put simply, "the sins of the body extinguish the light of reason and of faith." As for the atheist per se, Crasset offered the formula that "every atheist is a lewd person, and every lewd person must be an atheist," explaining that this was "a virtually necessary consequence, . . . because God avenges on the mind the shameful sins of the flesh."[62]

One of the most popular portraits of the atheist was La Bruyère's essay on "*esprits forts*" in his frequently reprinted *Caractères*. For La Bruyère, knowledge of God was given in human nature itself and could not be genuinely disbelieved. There were indeed rich and powerful men so lazy and so attached to the world that they were indifferent to God, and this indifference had been confused with actual denials of God, but this was an error: "they do not deny these things, nor grant them; they do not think on them." In the same way that people managed to convince themselves that commerce with a loose woman was not a sin, people in perfect health seeking pleasure allowed themselves to doubt, temporarily, the reality of God, but "when they become sick and dropsy occurs, they abandon their concubines and they believe in God." Were there actually people who could abandon belief given by nature at birth and by all subsequent experience and thought? Even if there were, La Bruyère concluded, "that would prove only the existence of monsters," but in fact, "atheism does not exist." There were depraved, immoral men who might wish that God did not exist, but "I would like to see a sober, moderate, chaste, equitable man utter the phrase that there is no God. He, at least, would speak without self-interest, *but this man cannot be found*."[63] As the erudite Benedictine Malebranchist François Lamy explained to his readers in 1694:

[60] Laurent Bordelon, *Les oeuvres de Monsieur Bordelon*, 3 vols. (Paris, 1689–1690), II, 400–405.

[61] Samuel Sorbière, *Sorbierana, ou bons mots, recontres agréables, pensées judicieuses, et observations curieuses de M. Sorbière*, ed. G. L. Colomyez (Paris, 1694), 2, "Athées."

[62] Jean Crasset, S.J., *La foy victorieuse de l'infidelité et du libertinage*, 2 vols. (Paris, 1693), I, 9–86.

[63] Jean de La Bruyère, *Les Caractères de Théophraste . . . avec Les caractères ou les*

> Who doubts that there is a God? We are no longer in the time of atheists. There are none, unless they are atheists of the heart: I mean men similar to those of whom the prophet speaks, who, impelled by the corruption of their heart, *wish* that there were no God, and even affect to appear to doubt His existence. But as for atheists of the mind, who deny this existence, or who doubt it in good faith, that is what I cannot believe that one could find.[64]

This was a view seemingly held across the spectrum of a generally fractious French intellectual life. For the eminent Jansenist Pierre Nicole, we were obliged to believe in God not by faith, which in fact followed such belief, but because God has manifested His existence, divinity, and power "in a manner so clear *that there is only the corruption of their heart that could make them [the atheists] fail to surrender to these lights*." "Faith," Nicole elaborated, pertained to submission to God, not belief in Him, since even demons *knew* that God existed, "being constrained by the evidence of the proofs."[65] The eminent Jesuit theologian Louis Bourdaloue agreed. The world was filled with "atheists . . . by their morals," but he was doubtful that there were any "atheists . . . by belief." Belief in the existence and providence of God were universal "general notions" that the libertine could only seek to "erase" from his mind gradually and by self-interest, not ever by a search for truth. The only men who "ever" had disbelieved in God were "those for whom it would be expedient that there in fact not be such [a God], and who would find their advantage in the system of this atheism."[66] The worldly and often irreverent Guy Patin, quoted in a 1709 edition of *Patiniana*, agreed:

> I never have been able to believe that there were true atheists. The idea of God is in all men. . . . Those who combat it speak at the bidding of their corrupted heart, but they do not follow the lights of their mind. They would wish that there were no God who punishes their immoralities: that is the goal of their sentiments. But they know despite themselves that this God exists.[67]

Similarly, Pierre-Jacques Brillon, continuator of La Bruyère's *Caractères*, conceded that, in theory, a "virtuous" atheist might be with excuse

---

moeurs de ce siècle, ed. Pierre-Jacques Brillon, new ed., aug., 2 vols. (Paris, 1700; Amsterdam, 1701), II, 84–90.

[64] François Lamy, O.S.B., *Vérité evidente de la religion chrétienne* . . . (Paris, 1694), "Préface," [iii–iv].

[65] Pierre Nicole, *Instructions théologiques et morales, sur le premier commandement du Decalogue* . . . , new ed., 2 vols. (Paris, 1723 [first published, 1708]), I, 23.

[66] Louis Bourdaloue, S.J., *Oeuvres de Bourdaloue*, 16 vols. (Paris, 1826 [first published Paris, 1703–1734]), III, 196–97; VII, 87–88; and see also I, 357–60.

[67] Guy Patin, *L'esprit de Guy Patin, tiré de ses conversations, de son cabinet, de ses lettres, & de ses autres ouvrages*, [ed. Laurent Bordelon or perhaps Antoine Lancelot] (Amsterdam, 1709), 171.

for such crime, but he insisted that such a man never could exist: "I never have been able to imagine to myself that there were true atheists." The "fool" of Scripture knew in his "mind" that he was wrong, but he spoke "in his heart . . . that is to say, the fool *hoped that there were no God*."[68] The deistic, freethinking *Espion Turc* held a similar view of atheists, describing them as "declared enemies of belief in a God; infamous and heedless, who do not dare to remain alone, out of the fear that coming to think on themselves, they would become wiser." Atheists, who dared to joke about God, were effeminate slaves to criminal passions and were interested primarily in eating and drinking their fill before they became dust.[69] The young Montesquieu, whose own *Lettres Persanes* owed much to the *Espion Turc*, wrote in his private notebooks that he could not believe that atheists of philosophical conviction could possibly exist, given the indubitable evidence of God's existence.[70] For the philosophical skeptic Saint-Hyacinthe, even those who sought to deny God in their discourses revealed their actual belief in Him by assigning the qualities of God to other forces or entities. "We have," he urged, "an ineffaceable sentiment of the Supreme Being, and professed atheists recognize Him despite themselves." Idolatry and indifference to God were what had been labeled atheism. It was possible, though highly doubtful, that there were men who did not believe in God in the sense of never thinking of Him properly or, indeed, never thinking of Him, but "if by *atheist* one means a man who formally denies a God without recognizing under some other name the attributes of this God, one can say that there are absolutely no atheists." However, although there could be no denial of God by the mind, there certainly was "a true atheism of denying God by behavior."[71] Jean Denyse, respected professor of philosophy at the University of Paris, agreed. Whatever "names" men may have used for God, he wrote in 1717, all minds have recognized the metaphysical attributes of the Supreme Being. Since no one seriously could deny the reality of a metaphysical necessary being, "it does not seem to me that there ever have been atheists in this sense." The point of disbelief, however, was not metaphysical, but a deep fear of the system of divine rewards and punishments, since "it is in this sense alone that [the existence of God] can have an essential relationship to morality and that it influences the entire con-

[68] Pierre-Jacques Brillon, *Suite des Caractères de Theophraste, et des Pensées de Mr. Pascal* (Amsterdam, 1708), 24–26.

[69] Paolo Marana, *L'espion dans les cours des princes chrêtiens . . .* [*L'espion Turc*], new ed., aug., 6 vols. (Cologne, 1710), II, 209–16.

[70] Charles-Louis de Secondat, baron de Montesquieu, *Oeuvres complètes*, ed. Daniel Oster (Paris, 1964), 955.

[71] Thémiseul de Saint-Hyacinthe, *Mémoires littéraires*, 2 vols. (The Hague, 1716), I, 13–23.

duct of life." Atheists would be delighted to acknowledge metaphysical truth, for example, if they could be allowed to deny eternal punishments by denying the soul's immortality. Atheists, however, did not really think about such matters as creation or whether substances could exist except by divine omnipotence. Rather, "When they refuse to recognize the existence of a God, it is of a God who affects their interests, and knowledge of whom must have an influence on the entire conduct of their life . . . [of a God] who punishes the wicked . . . for an eternity."[72]

In 1705, Michel Levasseur, priest and popularizer of more formal treatises on religion, in a work published with an unusually large number of approbations from doctors of the Sorbonne, reiterated the view that there had been and was a universal consent to the existence of God, explaining that most charges of atheism had been simply criticisms of idolatrous belief, and concluding that "there never have been true atheists."[73] In 1714, the influential "rationalist" Huguenot Jacques Bernard explained that all men were born with the ineradicable idea of the Divinity. Those "called atheists," for Bernard, were not exceptions to this universal consent, but simply "monsters" forced by their immoral lives "to fight against this idea with all their strength . . . because if there is a God, [they] have nothing for which to hope and everything to fear." Although dread led them to say repeatedly to themselves that God did not exist, their own reason and conscience assured them otherwise, and they knew, inside, that their attempted disbelief was impossible.[74] In 1727, the Huguenot *Bibliothèque Anglaise*, reporting on the Boyle lectures of 1721–1722, shared the view that Spinoza, though himself self-contradictory, was the only systematic atheist of the modern world; the lectures had attributed atheism to the love of singularity, an overreaction to religious fraud (for which Roman Catholicism was blamed), and, above all, to the libertine desire to gratify all vicious passions.[75] David-Augustin de Brueys, who converted from Calvinism to Catholicism, explained that there were no "real" atheists and never had been, which was why Scripture portrayed the fool as "saying" rather than "believing" that there was no God. "All" of those who passed for atheists merely had been critics of the absurdities of polytheistic fable. Even if there were those who out of vanity tried to convince

[72] Jean Denyse, *La vérité de la religion chrétienne démontrée par ordre géométrique*, 2d ed. (Paris, 1719 [first published Paris, 1717]), "Préface" [unpaginated, 66 pp.], [i–xvii].

[73] Michel Levasseur, *Entretiens sur la religion contre les athées, les déistes, et tous les autres ennemis de la foy catholique* (Blois and Paris, 1705), 1–12.

[74] Jacques Bernard, *De l'excellence de la religion*, 2 vols. (Amsterdam, 1714), vii–viii, 79–92.

[75] Armand de La Chapelle and Michel de La Roche, eds., *Bibliothèque Anglaise, ou Histoire littéraire de la Grande Bretagne*, 15 vols. [La Roche, vols. I–V; La Chapelle, vols. VI–XV] (Amsterdam, 1717–1728), XIV (1727), 499–519.

themselves that God did not exist, they could not succeed in persuading themselves. Whatever their blasphemies (blasphemies, he noted, that assumed a being to be blasphemed), they all acknowledged the reality of God at times of trouble, danger, pain, despair, or approach of death.[76]

Because such portraits of the atheist dominated learned publication and teaching, they of course also dominated the widely disseminated journals of the learned world. In *comptes rendus* of works that discussed the problem of atheism, the popular journals shared and embellished the traditional presentations of disbelievers. Atheists who were not struck by the marvels of nature in a manner sufficient to convince them of God's existence, the *Histoire des Ouvrages des Savans* explained in 1689, would not be impressed by *any* argument:

> One can be an atheist by the heart, but one cannot be one by the mind. They [atheists] perhaps imagine that they have replied to everything when they have extinguished the remorse of conscience. . . . But examine these heroes of atheism at their death; you will see the mask that falls from their faces, and very few of these braggarts carry this affected incredulity [*cette incrédulité étudiée*] up to the edge of the grave.[77]

Men truly immersed in incredulity, the same journal explained in 1696, will not be touched by argument, since they "do not surrender easily to arguments which culminate in imposing inconvenient laws on their thoughts and on their conduct."[78] Reviewing a Genevan Calvinist work on fundamental issues of Christian theology, the *Nouvelles de la République des Lettres* noted its view that while there were "several men who live as if they were [atheists] . . . those who lived like atheists and who boasted of being such, gave the lie to this [*se sont démentis*] at the hour of their death."[79] In 1702, the *Histoire des Ouvrages des Savans* favorably explained an author's view that the argument from universal consent was not weakened by a few dissenters: "If one listens to them, one will note that they attack the Divinity more by witticisms or by debauchery of mind than by reason. They hope that God is not, because He inconveniences and constrains their passions; thus, one can disdain their judgment."[80] Reviewing a work by Basnage two years later, the journal urged upon its readers his view that "death is almost the sole proof recognized

[76] David-Augustin de Brueys, *Traité du légitime usage de la raison, principalement sur les objets de la foy. Où l'on démontre que les hérétiques, les athées, et les libertins ne font point le légitime usage que les hommes sont obligés de faire de leur raison, sur les objets de la foy* (Paris, 1728 [first published in 1727]), "Préface" and 42–92.

[77] *Histoire des Ouvrages des Savans*, mars 1689, 81–82.

[78] Ibid., sept. 1696, 18.

[79] *Nouvelles de la République des Lettres*, nov. 1701, 487–88.

[80] *Histoire des Ouvrages des Savans*, avril 1702, 183.

by atheists. They are rarely converted by reason . . . but at the approach of death their conscience betrays them . . . and they show plainly that they fear a God that they have feigned not to believe in [*ils laissent voir qu'ils craignent un Dieu qu'ils font semblant de ne pas croire*]."[81] In June 1705, challenging Bayle's effort to separate issues of belief from issues of behavior, the *Journal de Trévoux* assured its readers, concerning atheists, that "there is not any one of them in whom brutal vices or pride did not precede atheism; there is not any one of them who did not have an interest in combating the existence of God."[82] Returning to this theme a month later, the Jesuit journal insisted that "it is only in his heart, the prophet King [David] says, that the fool says there is no God; his mind disavows this aberration [*égarement*] of his heart; he wishes that there were no God and cannot prevent himself from believing that there is one [*il voudroit qu'il n'y eut point de Dieu, & ne peut s'empêcher de croire qu'il y en a un*]."[83] Commenting extensively on the same topic in 1707, the *Nouvelles de la République des Lettres* explained that

> these proofs [of the existence of God] appear so clear and so certain, to us who are persuaded of this existence, that we cannot understand that men . . . reject them, unless the existence of a God inconveniences them and they have some secret interest in rejecting it; that is to say, to explain the thing otherwise, unless they are vicious and the persuasion of the existence of a God impedes them in their vices [*à moins qu'ils ne soient vicieux; & que la persuasion de l'existence d'un Dieu ne les gêne dans leurs vices*].[84]

In 1708, the *Histoire des Ouvrages des Savans* endorsed a model of the etiology of disbelief that put the matter quite succinctly: without "corruption of morals," knowledge never made an atheist. Rather, "Libertinism of behavior leads them to libertinism of speculation. They believe nothing, because in believing it would be necessary to renounce their passions and their favorite vices."[85] In 1706, reviewing Levasseur's *Entretiens sur la religion*, the *Journal de Trévoux* supported the priest's argument that the existence of God was so perfectly manifest from observation of the wonders of the creation, that "there never were genuine atheists, and if there are found peoples who do not know God . . . they are peoples so

[81] Ibid., août 1704, 349.

[82] *Journal de Trévoux*, juin 1705, 924.

[83] Ibid., juillet 1705, 1103–4.

[84] *Nouvelles de la République des Lettres*, mars 1707, 263–64. This was the third of an eight-part review of Bayle's *Réponse aux questions d'un provincial* by the current editor, Jacques Bernard, published throughout the course of 1707. In content and tone, it was quite similar to Bernard's long *compte rendu* of Bayle's *Continuation des Pensées diverses* in the January and March 1705 issues of the journal. See also his reviews of Bayle on these themes in the issues of November 1703 and January and February 1706.

[85] *Histoire des Ouvrages des Savans*, avril 1708, 161.

gross that they made no reflection at all, neither on the universe, nor on the arrangement of the creatures, nor on themselves."[86] Commenting favorably on a theological work by a professor of law, the *Journal de Trévoux* noted, in 1718, that the author understood that "in order to be [an atheist] in fact, it would be necessary to be deprived of the lights of reason," since "[a] man enlightened by reason could not fail to perceive a thousand proofs of this truth [of the existence of God]."[87] Six years later, the Jesuit publication reviewed an author whom it found "learned and concise" and explained that "he does not recognize any atheist, any atheistic people . . . any atheistic particular person." People may have tried to become atheists, but "to endeavor to become one, is not to be one; it is not to be one and to know it."[88]

In brief, then, for most voices of the learned world, since atheists were actual beings who could not maintain any actual true atheism, there were atheists without atheism. The Oratorian Pouget, in the Montpellier catechism for adults, which the archbishop of Paris authorized for use in his archdiocese as well, summarized it all in response to the question "Are we certain that there is a God?" He replied:

> It is a truth so clear that one must be an *insensé* to deny it or to put it in doubt. . . . These words, "The fool has said in his heart," are remarkable. They make us understand that when it comes to this excess of madness, saying that there is no God, the mind in one sense has less of a role in this extravagance than the heart. That is to say, that the ungodly person [*l'impie*] wishes that there were no God, in order to be able to smother all remorse and gratify his passions with more liberty. The depravity of his heart impels him later to say to himself that there is no God. But he tries in vain to numb himself to this truth; it is so strongly imprinted in the mind of man, that it is virtually impossible for it to be entirely effaced.[89]

Chevigny's popular educational guide for the aristocracy, *La science des personnes de la cour, de l'épée et de la robe*, a series of questions and answers, replied to the query "You are thus not persuaded that there are atheists?" with the common answer: "I believe that there can be [atheists] of the heart; but there certainly are not any [atheists] of the mind." Such atheism, Chevigny explained, could not be undone by education, since it was an "ignorance being more in the heart than in the mind." If men denied the existence of God, it was only "because they live in a manner

[86] *Journal de Trévoux*, oct. 1706, 1733.

[87] Ibid., sept. 1718, 396.

[88] Ibid., nov. 1724, 1926.

[89] François Aimé Pouget, Oratory, *Instructions générales en forme de Catéchisme* . . . [the "Catéchisme de Montpellier . . ."], new ed., rev. and aug. (Paris, 1707), 7–8.

that makes them wish that there were no God."[90] As the learned Jesuit Tournemine, primary editor of the *Journal de Trévoux*, wrote in his unauthorized preface to Fénélon's celebrated demonstrations of God's existence, "There never have been true atheists." Rage, despair, and fear of God's justice indeed have formed the bizarre obstinacy of "some would-be atheists," but "they could not prevent themselves from believing in the existence of God [even] during the times that they tried their hardest to prevent themselves from believing it." Concerning "the alleged atheists of paganism," a category he presented solely as the invention of Pierre Bayle, Tournemine agreed with a recent work by a fellow Jesuit, Michel Morgues's *Plan théologique du paganisme* (1712), that these were simply, in Tournemine's phrase, "the least impious of all the pagans," ardent monotheistic critics of polytheism. For Tournemine, Bayle's assertion of the reality of pagan atheism was not credible and was, at its strongest, the unsupported claim that there had been "only five or six [unnamed] Spinozists" who did not distinguish between the world and its cause. Even these, however, if they were real, would not be philosophers but, literally, madmen. Further, he noted, we have had, in the seventeenth century, experience with the conversion to Catholicism of many men who had been "impious," and "of these converted unbelievers, there is not even a single one up to now who has acknowledged having been persuaded for even one single moment that there were no God . . . however hard each tried."[91]

. . .

One can understand, thus, the deeper significance of seventeenth-century debates about "universal consent" and the existence or even the possibility of "virtuous atheists," debates we shall in due course explore. Even without these strains of early-modern French culture, however, a problem obvious to the very authors we have cited remained. If belief in God were universal and ineradicable, and if denial of God were volitional and not intellectual, then for whom and to what end were so many treatises on the existence of God written? Chevigny's and Tournemine's answers to *that* question, for example, suggest that perhaps the problem of atheism was not quite so unthreatening as the learned culture would have had its

[90] Le sieur de Chevigny, *La science des personnes de la cour, de l'epée et de la robe . . .*, new ed., aug., 2 vols. (Amsterdam, 1707), I, 69–70. According to the *Journal de Trévoux*, juin 1724, 1066–70, in a review of the second edition of a posthumous revised edition of Chevigny's work, augmented by additions by de Limiers (and first published in 1714), the original editions had enjoyed four printings.

[91] René-Joseph Tournemine, S.J., "Réflexions . . . sur l'athéisme . . . ," in François de Salignac de la Motte Fénélon, archbishop of Cambray, *Oeuvres philosophiques . . .* (Paris, 1718), 523–29. Tournemine's "Réflexions" first appeared in 1713.

audience believe. Chevigny posed the question explicitly and answered in two parts. First, they were written "to destroy the sophisms of the libertines, which could not fail to take the simple by surprise." Second, "if these treatises do not serve as an antidote for those who deny the existence of God because they live in a manner that makes them wish that there were no God, *they can serve as protection [préservatif] for the others*."[92] Tournemine explained that, obviously, since "it is certain that there are no true atheists, it is not for them that one writes on the existence of God." Why then? First, he replied, "*one wants to strengthen shaken minds [des esprits ébranlez]*." Second, "it is not an established error that one combats: *it is doubts that one forestalls [qu'on prévient], and that one dissipates*."[93]

The same *Histoire des Ouvrages des Savans* that found the existence of God so evident that no one could disbelieve it in good faith posed the same problem to itself: if that were the case, "it seems that in so refined a century as our own, there is no need to enlighten minds about it." It concluded, however, that one did not write for any atheists themselves: "On the contrary, it is in order to convince the learned [*les Savans*] and to appease their objections and their difficulties [*pour les desarmer de leurs objections & de leurs difficultez*] that it is necessary to assemble everything that study and reason can provide in the way of proofs and demonstrations."[94]

The same *Nouvelles de la République des Lettres*, under Jacques Bernard's direction, that found the notion of sincere atheists inconceivable, nonetheless granted that in addition to atheists by ignorance and atheists by sins of the heart, there probably were indeed "atheists of the mind [*Athées de l'esprit*]," indeed, "only too many, who succumbing under the weight, although light, of certain difficulties, come to put the existence of God among the number of things that are very dubious and of which one cannot be assured, and have positive and confirmed doubts on this subject [*qui succombant sous le poids, quoi que léger, de certaines difficultez, viennent à mettre l'existence de Dieu au nombre de ces choses fort douteuses, & dont on ne peut bien s'assurer, & ont des doutes positifs & confirmez sur ce sujet*]."[95]

What "*others*," and what "*savans*," if only simpletons or depraved immoralists could disbelieve? What "*shaken minds*," if the etiology of atheism were in the will alone? What "*doubts*," let alone what "*positive and confirmed doubts*," if belief in God were so ineradicable that it required a positive action of perversity to cast any shadow on it at all?

[92] Chevigny, *La science des personnes de la cour*, I, 69–70.

[93] Tournemine, "Réflexions," 529–32.

[94] *Histoire des Ouvrages des Savans*, sept. 1696, 16–17.

[95] *Nouvelles de la République des Lettres*, nov. 1701, 488–90.

Chapter Two

THINKING ABOUT THE UNTHINKABLE

LET US TURN, then, as we all on occasion should do, from consideration of depraved souls and perverse wills to contemplation of thinking minds and conceivable thoughts. As we have seen, the very literature that addressed atheism as a behavioral and volitional phenomenon often referred to its manifestation in formal "objections" and "doubts," sought to demonstrate the existence of God against its "arguments," and, even when dismissing "veritable atheism" as oxymoronic and mentally impossible, often explicated its cognitive nature. Early-modern theologians and savants, however equivocal their polemical uses of the terms *atheist* and *atheism*, were capable of defining these terms, when they deemed it appropriate, with a certain philosophical exactitude, or, at the least, of making distinctions that included reference to a specific disbelief in the existence of any Supreme Being whatsoever.

It long had been a theological commonplace to distinguish, as Saint Augustine had done, three modes of belief concerning God: "*credere Deum*," to believe *that God exists*; "*credere Deo*," to believe God, to believe His revelation in Scripture; and *credere in Deum*, to believe in God, that is, to rely on Him with the full conviction of faith and loving obedience.[1] Many early-modern minds well might want to dismiss the

[1] See the interesting article by Jean-Claude Schmitt, "Du Bon Usage du 'Credo,' " in *Faire croire: Modalités de la diffusion et de la réception des messages religieux du XIIe au XVe siècle*, ed. l'Ecole Française de Rome (Rome, 1981), 337–61. Schmitt argues that the distinctions date from the thirteenth century, despite the fact that "in the Middle Ages, theologians left no place for disbelief [*l'incroyance*]: they thought that only fools could deny the existence of God." The need for the distinctions, for Schmitt, was to differentiate the gentiles' simple belief *that* God exists from, first, the belief in what God revealed (even if it did not affect behavior), and, second, from the Christians' loving and obedient belief "in God." The real issues for the thirteenth century, for Schmitt, were those that concerned the quality of faith: *viva* or *mortua*; *formata* or *informis*; *non ficta* or *ficta*; *magna* or *modica*; and, above all, *explicita* or *implicita*. For two typical instances of the same distinctions among forms of *credere* in the seventeenth century, see Henri-Louis Chasteigner de la Rochepozay, bishop of Poitiers, *Celebriorum distinctionum tum philosophicarum tum theologicarum synopsis* (Poitier, 1612), 14 ("*Credere Deum, est credere Deum esse; Credere Deo, est credere verbus ejus . . . ; Credere in Deum, est adhaerere Deo per cognitionem et amorem*"); and Charles-Gaspard de La Feuille, O.P., *Théologie du coeur et de l'esprit*, 3 vols. 5th ed. (Chaumont, 1710), I, 52–53 (which distinguished among "*croire Dieu*," to be certain that there is a God; "*croire à Dieu*," to be certain that all He says is true; and "*croire en Dieu*," to be certain that God exists and that all He says is true, and to have full confidence and

first without the second and third forms of belief as worthless and, thus, in some significant sense for them, "atheistic." It was (and perhaps remains) a never-ending source of astonishment and dismay for pious believers that people who claimed to know *that* God exists could fail to put full faith in Him, let alone live in a manner that seemed to belie such knowledge.

Most early-modern thinkers well might want to argue, at least most of the time, that no one truly could not "*credere Deum.*" However, they certainly could posit the *category* of disbelief "that God exists," and define *atheism* as such. Indeed, we shall see, even those who declared "atheism" inconceivable still could give it a highly complex theoretical content. The meaning of *atheism* as *the belief that God did not exist* was essential, of course, even to their arguments that it could not be a "real" phenomenon. The Carthusian monk and savant Bonaventure (Noel) d'Argonne sought to maintain a distinction between the atheist's "thought," which might be real, and his "knowledge": "the libertines who say that there is no God perhaps say what they think; but they do not say what they know."[2]

Thus, the *Dictionnaire* of the Académie française, published in 1694, defined *atheist* as "one who does not recognize any God" ("*celui qui ne reconnoist point de Dieu*") and *atheism* as "an impiety which consists of not recognizing any Divinity" ("*impiété qui consiste à ne reconnoistre aucune Divinité*").[3] If one kept to this definition, accusations of atheism arising from disagreements over lesser matters would not be valid. The Jesuit Le Valois, for example, who declaimed against the implications of the Cartesian view of substance for the Eucharist, condemned, in 1680, those of his allies who "continually accuse [Descartes] of atheism . . . with more passion than reason." He urged his fellow anti-Cartesians to distinguish between "atheism" and mere "works in which there are five or six places that are too bold and dangerous in matters of religion."[4] La Mothe Le Vayer denounced the prevalence of superstitious impiety, but warned that "there is an extreme difference between denying absolutely any sort of divinity and having superstitious and erroneous opinions of it." He urged that "we reserve this great and outrageous term of abuse [atheism]" for those individuals "who did not recognize any Power on high . . . or

love of Him). The first four editions of La Feuille's work were published under the title *Instruction Chrétienne*, the first edition of which was in 1698.

[2] Noel Bonaventure d'Argonne, Carthusian, *L'éducation, maximes et réflexions* . . . (Rouen, 1691), 181.

[3] *Le Dictionnaire de l'Académie Françoise, dedié au roy*, 2 vols. (Paris, 1694), I, 62.

[4] Louis Le Valois [pseud.: Louis De La Ville], S.J., *Sentiments de M. Descartes touchant l'essence et les propriétés du corps, opposés à la doctrine de l'Eglise et conformes aux erreurs de Calvin sur le sujet de l'Eucharistie* (Paris, 1680), 89.

who admit no other god than the four elements."[5] The popular *Mémoires pour servir à l'histoire des hommes illustres dans la République des Lettres*, begun by the theologian Jean-Pierre Niceron in 1727, denounced accusations of atheism against Guillaume Postel "since there is not one of his writings in which he does not presuppose the Divinity," and against Jerôme Cardan, whom it described as "a superstitious man and not an '*esprit fort*,' . . . [despite] what is commonly said of him." Many have treated Cardan as an atheist, Niceron observed, but only because they have confounded "fanaticism" and "atheism."[6] The *Mémoires* strongly approved of Nieuwentyt's distinction between, on the one hand, the irreligious "who indeed believe that there is a God, but who deny [His] revelation" and, on the other, authentic atheists who denied "the existence of an omnipotent, omniscient, and wholly good Supreme Being."[7] Similarly, the deist Claude Gilbert, in his *Histoire de Caléjava*, after declaring the proofs of the existence of God to be so evident that it was doubtful that there ever had been genuine atheists, praised Clement of Alexandria (with perhaps a certain ironic self-interestedness) for having seen that ancient accusations of atheism were made falsely against those who rejected polytheism and "believed in the unity of God." Gilbert warned against confusing atheism with critiques of sectarian religion or with libertinism: "In society, people do not [adequately] distinguish atheism from irreligion, and irreligion from an abandonment to all sorts of vice."[8]

Even authors who polemically merged "libertinism" and "atheism," however, could distinguish the second as an explicit denial of the proposition "that there is a God." Veyssière de La Croze admitted that "speaking in a strict sense [*à la rigueur*], true atheism consists in one indivisible point, that is to say in the abnegation of the existence of God." This "manifest denial" constituted a "real atheism which unites that of the heart *and that of the mind*."[9] Buddeus's treatise on atheism, widely read in Latin in France and later translated into the vernacular, distinguished between two classes of atheism. The first, indeed, was "a malign and perverse disposition of the mind, by which, without paying attention to the activity of conscience, one smothers its inspirations and feelings of re-

[5] François La Mothe Le Vayer, *Oeuvres*, 15 vols. new ed., aug. [3d ed.] (Paris, 1684), XII, 217–24.

[6] Jean-Pierre Niceron et al., *Mémoires pour servir à l'histoire des hommes illustres dans la République des Lettres* . . . , 43 vols. (Paris, 1727–1745), VIII, 318 (re Postel); XIV, 243, 254–55, 265 (re Cardan).

[7] Ibid., XIII, 359–60.

[8] Claude Gilbert, *Histoire de Caléjava, ou de l'isle des hommes raisonnables, avec le parallèle de leur morale et du christianisme* ([Dijon], 1700), 83–86.

[9] Veyssière de La Croze, "Dissertation sur l'Athéisme . . . ," in *Entretiens*, 252, 266.

morse, and tries to persuade oneself thereby that there is no God." The second, however, he defined as one "in which one approves and stubbornly defends certain *opinions* from which it follows by a natural and necessary consequence, that cannot be avoided, that there is no God."[10] Michel de La Roche's *Bibliothèque Anglaise* translated Sir Richard Blackmore's definition for its readers: "By an atheist, I understand a man who openly declares that he does not believe in the existence of God."[11] The abbé de Gérard's *Philosophie des gens de cour* (1680) specifically distinguished "libertines," who argued against this or that perfection of God (the denial of providence and divine justice, for example) from atheists, who denied "that there is a God."[12] Jenkin Philipps's celebrated and, in France, widely utilized discourse on atheism, published in 1716, addressed "the characteristics by which atheists can be discerned." While he deplored the misuse of the term for purposes of religious calumny, he said that he understood the appeal of terming atheists those who denied the immortality of the soul, the Resurrection, and the Last Judgment, and who were atheists "by [logical] consequence, and indirectly [*per consequentiam, et indirectè*]." He urged, however, that one reserve the term only for those "who either are ignorant of the existence of the Supreme Will . . . or who believe and persuade themselves that God does not exist." Only those who maintain propositions "against the existence of God," he concluded, should be called "systematic atheists." All other unbelievers were merely blasphemers, heretics, or unorthodox thinkers.[13] Similarly, in 1717, the French edition of Samuel Clarke's sermons on God's existence—while it accepted the use of the term *atheists* for those who feigned disbelief in God or denied specific divine attributes, and while it acknowledged that much disbelief came from stupidity and moral debauchery—distinguished as a class of atheists those who actually rejected belief in the existence of God "from speculation and reasoning."[14]

The identification of atheism as a specific *intellectual* denial that God

[10] Johann Franz von Buddeus, *Traité de l'athéisme et de la superstition, par feu Mr. Jean-François Buddeus . . . Avec des remarques historiques et philosophiques*, trans. Louis Philon, ed. Jean-Chrétien Fischer (Amsterdam, 1740), 98–99. The treatise was first published in Latin as *Theses theologicae de atheismo et superstitione variis* . . . (Jena, 1717, rpt. 1718); 2d ed. (Jena, 1722); 3d ed. (Utrecht [Trajecti ad Rhenum], 1737).

[11] *Bibliothèque Anglaise*, I (1717), 357.

[12] Abbé Armand de Gérard, *La philosophie des gens de cour* (Paris, 1680), 123.

[13] J. Thomasio Philipps [Jenkin Thomas Philipps], *Dissertatio Historico-Philologica de Atheismo. sive Historia Atheismi in qua multi Scriptores Vetusti & Recentiores, Impietatis falsò postulati, liberantur à turpi 'Atheismi' stigmatei alii verò qui de supremo Numine sentire videntur minus rectè, corripiuntur meritò* (London, 1716), 23–26. Cf. Spizelius, *De Atheismi Radice*, 15–17.

[14] Samuel Clarke, *De l'existence et des attributs de Dieu* . . . , trans. [Pierre] Ricotier (Amsterdam, 1717), 1–13.

existed was distinguishable, of course, from the claim that such a denial actually or sincerely had occurred in the past or present, but it allowed authors to recognize abuses and imprecision in accusations of ultimate disbelief. This was particularly useful to authors so accused. Bayle, who did believe that there were "real" atheists, termed it "infamous" that he himself was accused of atheism for having made such a historical claim, and he reminded his readers that Descartes had been denounced for atheism despite works "in which the true God is found everywhere and was the foundation, the key, and the linchpin of the entire system," and that volumes had been written denouncing Lutherans and Calvinists in similar terms.[15] What theologians really wanted to denounce as atheism, Bayle urged elsewhere, were above all "libels violently attacking the disorders of the clergy."[16] He also noted the paradox that while denying any "real" atheism, theologians sought to enhance the importance of their treatises on the existence of God by exaggerating the number of "atheists," taking "for atheists a large quantity of people who merely proposed some objection with too much ardor, or who gave themselves license in spreading profane raillery."[17]

In 1663, the royal physician Charles Lussauld denounced the common accusation of "atheism" against physicians, identifying it with the view that medical doctors "deferred too much to Nature and did not have any religion." This was absurd, Lussauld wrote, since atheism was neither the claim that many things could be explained in terms of the operations of nature, nor (though wholly false when applied to physicians, he added) irreligion, but the denial of the existence of God, which no physician, indeed, no people or philosopher ever had maintained. If one acknowledged a God as the "Author of Nature," he explained, as all physicians did, one could not be an atheist. It was, he argued, the ancient physicians' contempt for pagan polytheism and polytheistic religion that had led to their reputation for impiety.[18] In 1666, the priest and theologian Louis Marais, with approbation, rejected with outrage the charges of atheism leveled against him for his attack on the doctrine of papal infallibility.[19] The deist Tyssot de Patot recalled that as a student, he had been de-

[15] Pierre Bayle, "Additions aux Pensées diverses" [first published in 1694], in *Pensées diverses écrites à un docteur de Sorbonne, à l'occasion de la comète qui parut au mois de décembre 1680*, new ed., corr., 4 vols. (Rotterdam, 1721), II, 317–18.

[16] Pierre Bayle, *Dictionnaire historique et critique*, 2 vols. (Rotterdam, 1697), art. "Pierre Aretin."

[17] Pierre Bayle, *Continuation des Pensées diverses* in *Pensées diverses*, III, 257–58.

[18] Charles Lussauld, *Apologie pour les médecins, contre ceux qui les accusent de déférer trop à la nature, & de n'avoir point de religion* (Paris, 1663). His target was Moïse Amyraut, *La morale chrétienne*, 6 vols. (Saumur, 1652–1660).

[19] Louis Marais, *Discours de la défense de la verité . . . prononcé . . . en présence de Mr. le recteur de toute l'université . . .* (Paris, 1666), 43–44.

nounced for atheism for having embraced Copernicanism after its condemnation by the Holy Office.[20] The sixteenth and early seventeenth centuries' use of *atheist* as a term of general abuse was increasingly out of fashion or, at the least, under attack in a learned world that was coming to pride itself on its precision.

In 1737, the apologist abbé François Ilharet de La Chambre, in his *Traité de la véritable religion*, addressed the question of whether or not there were or ever had been "true atheists." As prelude to an answer, he explained the theoretical distinctions theology should make with regard to disbelief. First, there were two possible kinds of atheism: "practical atheism," defined as "the nonbelief [*non-croyance*] in the existence of a Supreme Being, which has as its principle the goal of not feeling any remorse while abandoning oneself to all of one's passions"; and "speculative atheism," defined as the same disbelief if it occurred "without malice and the corruption of the heart playing any role in it." The latter could be distinguished further into "negative speculative atheism," defined as disbelief by virtue of "stupidity," inability to reason, or utter ignorance, on the one hand, and, on the other, "positive speculative atheism," defined as "the formal negation of the existence of a Supreme Being, supported by reasoning and reflection." This positive speculative atheism would be the "judgment that this point [the existence of God], far from being proven, is solidly defeated by clear and evident arguments." There certainly were "practical atheists," given wickedness. There certainly were "negative speculative" atheists, given people "stupid and incapable of any reasoning." "Thus," he concluded, "the precise issue of the question of the reality of atheism comes down to knowing if there are *positive speculative atheists of reason and of good faith* [italics his], that is to say, persons who deny the existence of a Supreme Being . . . because they judge that this point is not proven, and that the arguments that attack it are better than those that seem to establish it."[21]

As we have seen, there was, in the seventeenth and early eighteenth centuries, a common and widespread assertion that such a "positive speculative" atheism, let alone any atheism held in "good faith," was unimaginable. We also have seen some possible difficulties with the ascription of so self-assured a view to the members of the learned world. Was an actual atheism of good faith truly as "inconceivable" to them as they tried to convince their readers, or, perhaps, as they tried to convince themselves? Let us reflect for a moment on the ways in which the notion of the

[20] Simon Tyssot de Patot, *Voyages et avantures de Jaques* [*sic*] *Massé* (Bordeaux, 1710), 9–10.

[21] Abbé François Ilharet de La Chambre, *Traité de la véritable religion. Contre les athées, les déistes, le païens, les juifs, les mahometans & toutes les fausses religions*, 5 vols. (Paris, 1737), I, 5–8.

"speculative atheist" might be useful or even necessary to seventeenth-century minds. Sometimes it helps to ask simple questions. Why did they need the concept of such a being at all?

. . .

The "atheist" could serve any number of classificatory and, indeed, heuristic functions in early-modern texts. One needed a description of what those who lived "as if" there were no God would have to believe *if* they sought a justification of their lives. The "atheist" was above all such a character. He also was the ignorant or inattentive soul unaware of what in fact he "knew." The "atheist," however, could serve other roles. He was the formulator of the "objections" that theology or philosophy overcame. He was the tabula rasa on which nature might imprint evidence of the Divinity. He was the listener about to be persuaded by one's own compelling proofs of God's existence. He was the potential consistent reasoner who could be brought into being by the implications of one's rival's well-intentioned but foolish premises or logical fallacies. He was the short-sighted thinker who seemed to have no need for God in his explanations of the cosmos or earth. He was, simply by logical or merely etymological necessity, the antipode of the theist.

In addition, the "atheist" was a specter of which theologians, in particular, were keenly aware: he was what anyone would be who surrendered to doubts. Febvre surely was correct that naming doubt without consequence "atheism" is more than equivocal, but the argument begs certain historical questions, among them Febvre's own thesis about unthinkability.[22] Christianity, like the Greek, Roman, and Hebrew religious worlds that had preceded it, understood full well the "incredulity," even if ephemeral, of unanswered doubts about providence, the origin of evil, the meaning of suffering—in short, about the ultimate justice and coherence of the world. It was the disbeliever, real or feigned, possessed of such incredulity, who advanced the *sed contra* arguments to which virtually all theologians learned to reply. The "atheist," in that sense, could be found lurking, on occasion, in the world of ancient texts, in the questions of men and women known to the theologian, or indeed, perhaps, in a dark corner of the theologian's own mind. The "thought" of such an "atheist" was *not* impossible or even difficult for defenders of the faith to describe. Atheism, even if hypothetical, could be an inability to believe in a God who stood in any relationship to this world of such pain and suffering and injustice; a failure to be persuaded by formal proofs of His existence; a reaction against poor arguments; a natural philosophy that did not re-

[22] See supra, pt. 1, chap. 1.

quire God for any explanation of other beings and their behavior; an incapacity to rid oneself of fundamental doubts. To argue that such atheism was not tenable was not to believe it unimaginable. Indeed, atheism thus conceived was no more "unimaginable" for the early-modern French than it had been for two of their most celebrated authorities, Cicero and Aquinas.

Cicero's *De natura deorum*, read in Jesuit collèges in the second year of Latin, more for its rhetoric than for its ideas, was, among other things, an extended reflection on the problem of providence and evil as confronted by competing Epicurean, Stoic, and Academic (that is, skeptical) schools of ancient philosophy. The skeptical Cotta's attack on Balbus's Stoic views of providence, while seemingly intended to criticize a rational theology and to defend, as an alternative, one grounded simply in tradition and authority, specifically dismissed Balbus's views of providence as insufficient to establish the existence of the gods. From the folly of men, the prosperity of the wicked, the suffering of the good, and the triumphs of injustice, one would conclude, in Cotta's view, if not for the nonexistence of the gods, then at least the problematic nature of the question. Balbus recognized that Cotta's skeptical arguments might be "from conviction" or "from mere pretense," but he also saw that the issue was one of belief or disbelief in the proposition "that the gods exist."[23]

For Aquinas, the conceivability of atheism followed from logic and was confirmed by the Psalmist's reference to the fool, who for Aquinas, employed his mind as well as his heart. As he wrote in the *Summa Theologiae*, "The opposite of the proposition 'God exists' can be thought." Men ought to know that God is the object of their desire, but, in fact, "the awareness that God exists is not implanted in us in any clear or specific way." While Aquinas was wholly convinced that God's existence could be made certain by demonstration, he posited three bases for the philosophical rejection of such a conviction: (1) "since . . . faith is concerned with the unseen, its propositions cannot be demonstrated. . . . It is therefore impossible to demonstrate that God exists"; (2) "the central link of demonstration is a definition. But Damascene tells us that we cannot define what God is, but only what he is not. Hence we cannot demonstrate that God exists"; and (3) "if demonstration of God's existence were possible, this could only be by arguing from his effects. Now God [being

[23] Cicero, *De natura deorum*. The early-modern edition I have used is *Entretiens de Cicero sur la Nature des Dieux*, 3 vols. trans. abbé d'Olivet (Paris, 1721). For Balbus's speech about the "impiety" of such arguments, whatever their motivation, see II, 185–86. On the place of the *De natura deorum* in the curriculum for Greek and Latin in the Jesuit collèges in France as late as 1692, see François de Dainville, S.J., *L'éducation des jésuites (XVIe–XVIIIe siècles)*, ed. M.-M. Compère (Paris, 1978), 222–23. (Compère's volume is a welcome collection of Dainville's scattered articles.)

infinite] and his effects [being finite] are incommensurable. . . . Consequently, since effects incommensurate with their cause cannot make it evident, it does not seem possible to demonstrate that God exists." When he offered his five proofs of God's existence, Aquinas proposed two objections to be overcome, objections that led one to conclude that "it seems that there is no God." Anyone who held such objections and reached such a conclusion, was, in theory at least, an atheist. What would such an atheist object to belief that God exists? First, he would raise the problem of evil: "If God then existed, nobody would ever encounter evil. But evil is encountered in the world. God therefore does not exist." Second, he would raise the claim of the sufficiency of natural explanations: "If a few causes fully account for some effect, one does not seek more. Now it seems that everything we observe in this world can be fully accounted for by other causes, without assuming a God. Thus natural effects are explained by natural causes, and contrived effects by human reasoning and will. There is therefore no need to suppose that a God exists."[24]

The *Summa Contra Gentiles* added to this catalog of the atheist's formal arguments. An objector to claims for the demonstrability of God could argue that "if, as is shown in [Aristotle's] *Posterior Analytics*, the knowledge of the principles of demonstration takes its origin from sense, whatever transcends all sense and sensibles seems to be indemonstrable. That God exists appears to be a proposition of this sort and is therefore indemonstrable."[25] The medieval doctors of the Church and their heirs might disbelieve in the sincerity of "atheists," but, masterful dialecticians, they had little difficulty imagining what intellectual forms atheism as the denial of God's existence would take.

If Cicero and Aquinas could conceive that suffering and injustice, evil in general, and reliance upon natural explanation alone might lead to disbelief in God, so could an early-modern age that read them both assiduously. In an analysis of the origins of incredulity, the Jesuit Louis Bourdaloue, one of the most celebrated preachers of Louis XIV's reign, saw doubts concerning providence as the final, decisive phase in the formation of "atheists." "Reflections that they make on the events of the world," he explained, "make them doubt if there is a providence . . . [and] no longer knowing if there is a providence, they no longer know if there is a God."[26] In two of Bishop Bossuet's sermons "on providence," he also commented that doubts concerning providence were the major cause of doubts con-

[24] Thomas Aquinas, *Summa Theologica S. Thomae Aquinatis* . . . , ed. Jean Nicolai, O.P. (Paris, 1663 [in folio]), Ia. q.2, a.1–3.

[25] Thomas Aquinas, O.P., *Summa Contra Gentiles* I. c.12. I am using the translation of Anton C. Pegis, ed. and trans., St. Thomas Aquinas, *Summa Contra Gentiles, Book One: God* (Notre Dame and London, 1975).

[26] Bourdaloue, S.J., *Oeuvres*, III, 196–97.

cerning the very existence of God.[27] Such doubt and its consequence were in some real sense quite thinkable.

Early-modern graduates of universities, so many of them still theologians, had been praised, rewarded, and judged on the basis of their abilities to master arguments, to reason, to speculate. They were at home with the most abstract matters of conceptualization and analysis. They were deeply versed in the classics, in the canonical philosophers and doctors of the Church and, indeed, of the West in general. They played with ideas as masterfully as others played with cards. They were taught, formally and informally, to generate "objections" to all of their own most cherished beliefs, indeed, we shall see, to anticipate the strongest possible objections and to overcome these. In certain modes, they surely did find it "unthinkable" that anyone could fail to be persuaded of their most essential belief, the existence of God. In other modes, however, they rehearsed the arguments of atheism, entertained them, so to speak, and became familiar with them, all for purposes of triumphant refutation. They could explain what their antithesis believed, and some understood, often despite themselves, that one might hold such views "sincerely" and even involuntarily.

Nicole might well write that "only the corruption of their heart" could lead the atheists to deny the evidence of God's existence, but in a letter urging the efficacy of "extraordinary events" (such as demonic possessions) for convincing the unbeliever, published posthumously in 1718, he urged "that *there are all sorts of atheists, of good faith*, of bad faith, determined, vacillating, and tempted." "Speculative reasons," he argued, "have little influence on the minds of those men," while "with a miracle . . . you will win everything."[28] When Malebranche, in his *Conversations chrétiennes* (1677), provided his Christian with an interlocutor, he created someone sincerely unconvinced of the existence of God, someone who seemed quite far from willfully ignorant depravity:

> When I think of all the things that you told us yesterday, I cannot doubt the existence of a God who governs all that occurs in the world. But when I reflect that there are clever men [*gens habiles*] who do doubt it, and that Mr. ——— and several other very learned and very intelligent persons have assured me that they had need of faith to believe it, a certain apprehension remains with me that your proofs are not certain.[29]

[27] Jacques-Bénigne Bossuet, bishop of Meaux, *Oeuvres de Bossuet*, 4 vols. [Institut de France ed.] (Paris, 1849), I, 414–17; II, 715–24.

[28] Pierre Nicole, *Lettres de feu M. Nicole*, new ed., rev., corr., and aug., 2 vols. (Lille, 1718), I, 205–6.

[29] Nicolas Malebranche, Oratory, *Conversations chrétiennes* [1677], in *Oeuvres complètes de Malebranche*, gen. ed., André Robinet, 21 vols. (Paris, 1958–1970), IV, 57.

In brief, theologians could not have drawn a square circle, for that truly was unthinkable. They could draw the portrait of the atheist.

. . .

When the Catholic convert Cottiby had suggested that auricular confession would aid in the conversion of atheists, since it would allow them to confront the sins that led to their would-be disbelief, the Huguenot Daillé, we have seen, had replied that the argument was absurd, since the depraved person would not choose to go to confession. In response, Cottiby, who defined atheism as "this full-grown impiety [*impiété formée*] which denies the Divinity and which does not believe in providence," revealed that he either knew or indeed could imagine atheism under a different light:

> First, it is false that atheists never go to confession, or that they go only for worldly reasons; *for how many there are among them who not believing in God, make every effort possible to believe in Him*, and who only having fallen into this accursed belief [atheism] by a certain mental carelessness, seek every occasion to rescue themselves from it. . . . It would be easy to provide you with examples of these unfortunates, even some of the most obstinate [who "profess that there is no God"].[30]

Niceron described the theologian Jean-Baptiste Morin's *Quod sit Deus* (1635), an attempt to demonstrate God "by the geometric method," as having been written for "one of his friends, who had fallen into atheism."[31] More informally, the same Guy Patin who denied that there could be "true atheists" and who attributed all disbelief to "corruption of the heart," allowed himself the phrase "a lovely soul before God, if he believed in Him [*belle ame devant Dieu, s'il y croyait*]" with reference to several dead or dying notables.[32]

Such views were not new. Charron, in 1595, formally proclaimed that belief in God was universal, engraved on all minds and hearts, and "virtually impossible to dislodge." He acknowledged, however, "a monstrous but true thing," namely, that *there are several who doubt it*, several who aver it weakly or coldly, several who are not concerned with it, *and even several who contest it and argue for the contrary*." When he analyzed the species of unbelievers, he began with real atheists, those who "flatly deny the Deity [*tout à plat nient la Deïté*] and by their discourse want to persuade that there is no God at all." He characterized "this kind of atheism"

[30] Samuel Cottiby, *Réplique à la lettre de Monsieur Daillé* . . . (Poitiers, 1660), 51–53.

[31] Niceron et al., *Mémoires*, III, 96–97.

[32] Guy Patin, *Lettres de Gui Patin*, ed. J.-H. Reveillé-Parise, new ed., aug., 3 vols. (Paris, 1846), I, 233; III, 154 and 227.

as "primary, overt [*insigne*], full-grown [*formée*], and comprehensive [*universelle*]," to distinguish it from lesser and weaker forms of disbelief. Although he described the soul possessed of such atheism by the cliché " 'furious and maniacal' [*forcenée et maniacle*]," he also noted that it must be "an extremely strong and hardy soul," since it required "perhaps as much force and firmness [*roideur*] of soul to refute and resolutely divest oneself of the apprehension of and belief in God" as it did to hold "inviolably" to that belief. Most people, he argued, fell somewhere in between, an interesting acknowledgment of the doubts that he saw plaguing most believers at least on occasion, or, at the very least, of the imaginability of such sincere doubts.[33]

In his "Reflections on the Existence of God" (1704), the Huguenot Jacques Basnage argued that during good health, "there is no man more firm than the atheist," who, while easy to defeat in argument, is difficult to convince and convert. The atheists' fear of death, however, evidenced their actual belief in God, he insisted, and those who were "atheists of vice," disbelieving in God "by self-interest," given their sins, would return to belief in God from fear and passion at the approach of their end. There was, however, Basnage urged, a separate class of atheists, namely, "atheists of speculation who pride themselves on their purity of morals, their laying aside of passions, their grandeur of soul and strength of mind which raise them above the vulgar." These speculative atheists, he conceded, were "virtually invincible," but the theologian should not ignore them. They should not be confused, he insisted, with "atheists from vice . . . from desire," and they were usually not guilty of the worldly crimes with which they were charged. The task of the theologian was to address them with formal arguments: virtual universal consent; the incapacity of the creatures to be self-caused; the utter improbability that order and regularity in nature could be the product of chance; and the reality of spirit.[34]

The learned, devout, and widely respected Frideric Spanheim, when he reflected in general terms on the nature of atheism, found it easy to dismiss it as the extravagant and mad beliefs of "the corrupted man and the wicked man," and to attribute it to Caligula, Nero, and Claudius. There were many, he noted, who "live *as if there were no God* [italics his]," and the Psalmist had described them well. However, when he asked himself the explicit question—Have there ever been real atheists?—he answered that while it would seem impossible, "several men," nevertheless, "have been irresolute [*ont flotté*] on this subject [of God's existence], and have doubted that there was a God." Among these, he claimed, were Protago-

[33] Charron, *Oeuvres*, II, 4–6.

[34] Jacques Basnage, "Réflexions sur l'Existence de Dieu," in *Histoire du vieux et du nouveau testament . . . On y ajoûte deux Discours pour prouver l'existence d'un Dieu . . .* (Amsterdam, 1704), "Préface," Discours No. 1 [unpaginated; twelve double-columned pp.].

ras, Pliny, and (based on an "anecdote" Protestants enjoyed passing on), "Pope Clement . . . who while dying said that he soon would be enlightened on *three things that he had doubted all of his life, if there were a God*," if the soul were immortal, and if there were a heaven and hell. Further, there were those who now believed that they could explain all things without reference to a God. The Psalmist, he concluded, had not met the likes of these and had described those who simply had questioned the providence of God out of fear of being judged by Him. There was, however, unaddressed by Scripture, an explicit atheism, a belief that "in fact . . . *there is no God* [italics his], that there is no Sovereign Cause." This genuine disbelief "seems to have been unknown to David . . . having not yet appeared in his time."[35]

Samuel Clarke's translated treatise posited three kinds of atheists: those who did not believe that God exists; those who simply affected such a disbelief; and those who denied the proper attributes of the divine nature. The atheism of those who truly denied God, he urged, could stem from any one of three sources or causes: first, stupidity; second, moral debauchery; but third,

> Atheists of speculation and reasoning, who basing themselves on the principles of philosophy, maintain that the arguments against the existence and attributes of God, after the most considered and exact examination of which they are capable, appear to them stronger and more conclusive than those employed to establish these great truths.[36]

For Clarke, since the only atheists capable of reason were these "atheists of speculation," they alone were the proper object of the theologian's efforts of demonstration. He was able to articulate the essential elements of their thought for his readers: atheists argued that the moral disorders of the world were incompatible with the existence of a Supreme Being (which, for Clarke, proved that they wished for the world to be ruled by providence rather than chance); and they argued that belief in God had a political origin (which showed that they found it desirable for God to exist, since it served the interest of society). In short, he argued, his atheistic readers could be persuaded at the outset that they should want to be convinced that God existed. He described their belief (or disbelief) as based on a view of "man abandoned to himself . . . neither protected nor guided by a Supreme Being . . . in a state that is more miserable and sad than he would be in given the supposition of the existence of a God." Such "sincere" atheists, "whom interest and passion have not rendered unbelievers," but who were such from "reason and philosophy," should have

[35] Spanheim, *L'athée*, 3–49.

[36] Clarke, *De l'existence de Dieu*, 1–13.

nothing to do with scoffers and mockers, should be satisfied if the theologian proved God "possible and such that there is no demonstration to the contrary," and should want to find a "good demonstration" that would address every one of their objections and compel assent incontestably.[37]

If Catholic and Protestant theologians could imagine a sincere atheist with genuine doubts, significant objections, and a disbelief that might even be in search of reasons to believe, so could popular men of letters, despite, in some cases, their very own protestations to the contrary. The adventurer Charles d'Assoucy, himself accused of atheism for his lifestyle and irreligious wit, distinguished, after the "conversion" he claimed to experience during his imprisonment by the Roman Inquisition, between "false atheists" and "true atheists." The former came to atheism from their wickedness, out of fear of God's justice, and were more "enemies of God and His glory . . . than men unaware of His being and power." These, he claimed, were the men he knew only too well, and the company he had kept. The "true atheists," however, from whom he dissociated his libertine circles, were those who "lost knowledge of God for having wanted to know Him too well and for having searched for Him with too much curiosity." Such atheists certainly never blasphemed, "since they would be ashamed to attack what in their imagination could only be a chimera." Further, unlike the dissolute wits, such atheists would keep their disbelief discreetly "under lock and key" and never risk the respect of the world. Finally, unlike the libertines, such atheists would be "intrepid at the approach of death, since they regard it as the end of human sufferings."[38] La Mothe Le Vayer might write of universal consent to belief in God, but he acknowledged that there were so many different ideas of God that, without grace, "the mind becomes lost . . . because being unable to discern the true from the false, it falls into irreligion, or into an indifference that is not far removed from atheism."[39] Despite his earlier denial of the reality of atheism in an essay devoted to that precise topic, Saint-Hyacinthe, in a discussion of the universal equation of virtue and happiness, accepted a traveler's description of a Siam whose thinkers were in fact truly atheistic, and noted: "It is surprising that, recognizing no God, the belief that one can only be happy by means of virtue should be so strong" among them.[40] Saint-Evremond, noting that serious study revealed the same thoughts, uncertainties, beliefs, and disbeliefs in all centuries, observed that "the most devout person can never succeed in always

[37] Ibid.

[38] Charles Coypeau d'Assoucy, *Les pensées de Monsieur Dassoucy dans le S. Office de Rome* (Paris, 1675 [1676 according to "Privilège" and "Achevé d'imprimer"]), 46–50.

[39] La Mothe Le Vayer, *Oeuvres*, XI, 415.

[40] Saint-Hyacinthe, *Méms. litts.*, I, 44.

believing, nor the most impious person in never believing."[41] It was best, he concluded, to follow theology docilely and not as a science of demonstration. To make his point, he argued that the very modes of Christian intellectual life made thinkable what the society was determined to treat as unthinkable:

> We burn a man unfortunate enough [to disbelieve] for not believing in a God, and nevertheless we inquire publicly in the schools *if there is a God* [emphasis his]. In this way, you shake the conviction of weak minds, you cast suspicion into the defiant, you arm the furious, and you permit them to seek pernicious reasons by which they combat their own sentiments and the true impressions of Nature.[42]

As Jean Bernier noted in the 1690s, justifying his decision to begin his history of medicine with an inquiry into whether there was an actual medical science, "Theology even calls the existence of God into question before speaking of His attributes and the cult due to Him," so that it might overcome the primary objections to its entire enterprise, the incredulity of the atheists.[43]

• • •

Saint-Evremond distinguished between the learned who posed the question of God's existence and the weak, defiant, or furious people who were tempted by it into doubt or disbelief. One indication that atheism might be conceived quite differently from simply the triumph of fury, ignorance, and defiant will over temperance, knowledge, and reason, however, was the assertion by others that it was more an affair of the thoughtful and well-educated than of the simple and unlettered. D'Assoucy attributed the phenomenon of "genuine" atheism to the world of higher learning and belles lettres, to the exceptionally learned who, he wrote, knew much about this world and little about the next. Such atheists were "extremely subtle and shrewd minds [*des esprits extrêmement fins et déliés*]" who "not content with seeing and understanding the Divinity from the excellence of His works like the rest of mankind . . . want to have a knowledge of Him that surpasses our natural capacities." Seeking "to study, search for, and contemplate Him from too close," the atheist lost all vision of Him, "like those who lose their sight from the effects of contemplating

[41] Charles de Saint-Evremond, *Oeuvres mêlées de Mr. de Saint-Evremond, publiées sur les manuscrits de l'auteur*, new ed., rev., corr., and aug., 5 vols. (Amsterdam, 1706), I, 135–36.

[42] Ibid., 184–85.

[43] Jean Bernier, *Histoire cronologique de la médecine, et des médecins, où il est traité de l'origine, du progrès, et de tout ce qui apartient à cette science*, 2d ed. (Paris, 1695), 1.

the sun."[44] In 1679, the pious apologist the abbé de Gérard observed that while "ignorance almost always produces superstitious and credulous men," it was "learning [*la science*]" that "produces atheists and impious men."[45]

As Boureau-Deslandes explained in 1712, "It is ordinarily from the effects of studying religion that one finds oneself committed to believing nothing. *The uncertainty of great men is founded on the same principles that serve to convince the vulgar*." He recognized that this was not the would-be consensus of the learned world and added quickly that "I fear to have said too much on so delicate a matter."[46] Writing of the death of Lucilio Vanini, "burned for the crime of atheism," he noted that this "savant" had remained brave throughout his final ordeal, and he concluded, "Let them say after this that the spirit of incredulity is always a mark of debauchery."[47] The *Naudaeana* of 1703 quoted Gabriel Naudé as having noted the paradox that the Italy which he believed so full of "atheists who believe nothing" was also a great center of religious publication, from which he had concluded that "I think that these same writers do not believe any more than the others; *for it is a maxim that I hold as certain that the doubt which they have is one of the primary causes that obliges them to write [of God and immortality]*." In many ways, he insisted, it was precisely the writings of the learned, of authors trying to persuade themselves, that led to the doubts of others: "Instead of providing instruction, [these writings] are fit [more] to put everything into doubt."[48]

According to Jean d'Espagne, in a work published in English in 1648 and in French in 1674, the view that "knowledge produces atheism" was widespread. "The common people reproach the learned with atheism," he noted, a charge that was "only too true with respect to many." Although he insisted that such a crime must be imputed "to their ignorance, not their knowledge," and that "there never was an atheist who was not ignorant, nor a complete philosopher who did not acknowledge a God," he admitted that the "atheism" of the learned came from their being "so enclosed in the thoughts of a body of knowledge, or a particular faculty," from their excessive naturalism, and from their inability, in their specu-

[44] D'Assoucy, *Les pensées*, 33–41.

[45] Abbé Armand de Gérard, *Le véritable chrestien qui combat les abus du siècle, ou maximes et réflexions chrestiennes sur quelques points essentiels de la religion* (Paris, 1679), 3.

[46] A.-F. Boureau-Deslandes, *Réflexions sur les grands hommes qui sont mort en plaisantant* (Amsterdam, 1712), 124–25.

[47] Ibid., 142–44.

[48] Antoine Lancelot, ed., *Naudaeana et Patiniana, ou singularitez remarquables prises des conversations de Mess. Naudé et Patin*, 2d ed., rev., corr., and aug. (Amsterdam, 1703), 46–47.

lations "on the higher causes," to reach the First Cause.[49] Writing on modern philosophers, the Huguenot Isaac Jacquelot observed in 1697 that "everyone says that there is a God," but he insisted that this could be "a dangerous equivocation," since there were those who "nevertheless had no idea of the divinity beyond that of the matter of the universe." We might want to believe in universal consent to the existence of God, he noted, but alas, this was not the case: "It is in vain that we say that it is a principle against which no one ever should speak. It would be desirable if that were so, but it is not." In the preface to his diverse proofs of God's existence, he implicitly acknowledged that there could be sincere, learned dissenters: "Those who remain unpersuaded after the attentive reading of [my] book are invited to communicate to me their doubts and their difficulties."[50]

The famous Jesuit apologist Pierre Coton, in a dialogue written in about 1610 and published in 1683 by the later Jesuit Michel Boutauld, indeed declared atheism to be the product of "pride and sin." Nonetheless, he allowed his "libertine" to observe that many theologians "have recognized that it was the mark of a well-formed mind wisely to form difficulties concerning the existence of God, since they never exerted greater efforts nor produced more beautiful works than in responding to these." His own voice, the "theologian," replied that such efforts "were never done to convince atheists and persuade them that God exists, but to persuade all other men that atheists are madmen less reasonable than animals." When the libertine, however, feigned belief in God and requested to be instructed in those efforts so that he might be "incapable of ever doubting it ["the existence of God"]," the theologian replied that it were better not to so inquire. "The true way to forget and ignore what we know naturally ["that God exists"]," he warned, "is to want to know it philosophically and to examine it by indiscreet reflections." He offered the lesson of Protagoras, who in his youth was wise and believed in God, but who became an atheist when he sought to "know by reasoning." Atheists might well be "less reasonable than animals," but, for Coton, as the case of Protagoras showed, reason was not always their enemy:

> He learned to forget what he knew for forty years. The reasons that he found served him only to teach publicly and scandalously that there was no God. You are wise today . . . you know with certainty that God exists. Content yourself with this certainty that nature and faith have given you: for if you

[49] Jean d'Espagne, *Les Oeuvres de Jean Despagne* . . . , 2 vols. (The Hague, 1674), II, 20–24.

[50] Isaac Jacquelot, *Dissertations sur l'existence de Dieu, où l'on démontre cette vérité par l'histoire universelle, par la réfutation d'Epicure et de Spinosa* . . . (The Hague, 1697), "Préface." [There also is an edition of 3 vols. (Paris, 1744).]

want to know better by speculations and convictions . . . tomorrow you no longer will know it.[51]

Boutauld independently agreed with such sentiments. The learned find it "lovely," he wrote, to discuss all things, including divinity, in an "assembly of the curious." This seemed without suspicion, he noted, but he warned that "the most dangerous thinkers" often appear to be the least suspect, "the most chaste and the most modest." By their very "wisdom," however, they provided tools to the corruption of the heart. Those who began by proposing doubts for intellectual amusement often ended by asking "how they came to know that the world was made by a Creator." At all costs, he warned, "do not follow masters who seek to establish their school on the edge of a precipice" where it would only take "a puff of wind to push them to the bottom of an abyss."[52]

In 1706, there appeared a posthumous edition of the apologist Louis Ferrand's treatise on the existence of God, with "Remarks" and emendations by its anonymous editor, all with the approbation of the theologian and royal censor Bigres. The author of the prefatory remarks explained that there were two different choices made by those who wrote on the existence of God, either an emphasis on combating atheism, overcoming objections to God's existence and providence by means of human reasoning, or an emphasis on instructing those who already knew and loved God, relying on revelation, authority, and tradition. Ferrand, he observed, succeeded in both modes. He noted, however, that after familiarizing himself with the objections of the atheists, he now realized that he should "retouch" Ferrand's work. Had Ferrand known these arguments, he assured his readers, he also would have wanted "to multiply his proofs," "to relate a larger number of objections," and, of course, "to ruin these objections by reasonings of a proper scope, fortified by good authorities, according to his custom." We could not know how many people were familiar with atheistic objections and in need of answers to them. It was clear, he insisted, that we required a book much stronger than that which Ferrand had written. Not only did atheists "abuse their reason . . . build new systems . . . propose subtleties, and invent sophisms," but they searched antiquity and the history of philosophy for all the old objections,

[51] Pierre Coton, S.J., and Michel Boutauld, S.J., *Le théologien dans les conversations avec les sages et les grands du monde* (Paris, 1683), 16–18. Coton flourished as an apologist in the early years of the seventeenth century; this work was edited and updated by Boutauld from Coton's manuscripts. It enjoyed a 2d ed. (Paris, 1689 [two printings]); and a 3d ed. (Lyon, 1696).

[52] Michel Boutauld, S.J., *Les conseils de la sagesse, ou le recueil des maximes de Salomon les plus nécessaires à l'homme pour se conduire sagement. Avec des réflexions sur ces maximes* (Paris, 1677), 105–9. This is part of Boutauld's "Réflexion" on the verse from Ecclesiastes, "*In cogitationibus impii interrogatio erit.*"

looking for support from even the most celebrated philosophers, and offering "a pompous array of badly interpreted citations." To overcome these, one must clarify, as forcefully as possible, "the most important difficulties of the unbelievers," since "the good cause suffers when one allows one's adversaries to believe that one has dissimulated and that one fears their objections." Nothing could "better reassure the faithful," he concluded, "than knowledge of the errors against which one arms them." It is easiest "to avoid a trap," he advised, "when one anticipates it."[53] One might have hypothesized that nothing could better reassure the faithful than the common claim that atheism was so unimaginable that a mind required a positive self-blinding even to entertain it.

. . .

If it required proofs of the existence of God and the resolution of objections to overcome the speculative atheist, then the ability to conceive of an intelligent, sincere thinker as yet unconvinced by such proofs or unable to overcome specific objections to them was, in some sense, the ability to conceive quite clearly of such an atheist. Coton's apologetic work presented its readers with a thinker (eventually overcome) who granted the essential importance of belief in the existence of God, but who lamented "that it seems that one never will find, like the philosopher's stone [or] perpetual motion, the demonstration of the existence and the truth of God." Indeed, he claimed "that I have been searching for a long time for someone to disclose it [such a demonstration] to me, and who will be more fortunate than so many others whose treatises and writings have not satisfied enlightened philosophers very much." When the theologian of the dialogue expressed anger that anyone would even pose such an "imprudent and unreasonable question," and asked the unbeliever to clarify what he meant, the imagined atheist replied: "I desire . . . to hear some reason that proves and demonstratively convinces that there is a God."[54] In brief, it was not at all unthinkable to Coton that someone still might await such a demonstration.

Nor, as we have intimated, was it at all unthinkable to such theologians that someone might have doubts and objections which remained unsatisfied by putative proofs, above all concerning the incompatibility of evil with the existence of God. When the astute Jesuit missionary Matteo Ricci wrote a treatise of Christian theology for the philosophers of China in 1603, he noted that "the truth about the Lord of Heaven is already in the hearts of men," but he recognized that "human beings do not imme-

[53] Anonymous preface to Louis Ferrand, *De la connaissance de Dieu . . . Avec des Remarques de M**** (Paris, 1706), [i–viii, unpaginated].

[54] Coton and Boutauld, *Le théologien*, 12–13.

diately realize this and, furthermore, they are not prone to reflect about such a matter." He also spoke of "a foolish man who thinks that what his eyes cannot see does not exist." Against such tendencies, he asked his Chinese audience to reflect on a serious problem for the state: "If this Honored One did not exist, or if He exists but does not intervene in human affairs, would this not be to shut the gate of doing good and to open the road of doing evil?" Finally, he acknowledged the roots of actual atheism: "When some people see that lightning only strikes dead trees but not villains, they doubt that there exists a Lord above."[55]

This particular resistance to belief in God, real or imagined, did not depend, as Ricci's dates indicate, on any philosophical revolution of the later seventeenth century (indeed, the objection concerning lightning was an ancient Epicurean commonplace), but could be conceived of as virtually a universal tendency of the human mind. In the thirteenth century, Ramon Lull had begun his *Libre de meravelles* with reference to his hero Felix's religious doubt, a doubt that had been occasioned by the sad fate of his beloved and that had been overcome only by a holy hermit's proof to him by various arguments of the existence of God.[56] Pollot himself, in 1595, could formulate what it was that an atheist would object to belief in a God of providence: that it contradicts our experience of human liberty; that "things proceed and occur following the ordinary course of nature"; and that there is too much corruptibility in the world.[57] In that same year, Charron listed among the causes of atheism the unbeliever's "sense that there are several absurdities in the course and governance of this world, several difficulties." For Charron, the inability to resolve these leads the atheist to become "resolved that there is no God at all, nor governing master, but that everything proceeds as it would."[58] His contemporary Du Bartas (Guillaume de Saluste) wrote of "men without God" who use the suffering of the good to raise doubts about the existence of God.[59] The editor of the 1611 posthumous edition of Du Bartas's works noted that "since there are only too many Epicureans and atheists who howl against the doctrine of the providence of God, it also does occur sometimes to faithful and true Christians to be as if dazzled by the vain splendor of the profane and astonished by the almost continual affliction of the good." He declared this a "paradox that human reason never will

[55] Matteo Ricci, S.J., *The True Meaning of the Lord of Heaven (T'ien-chu shih-i)* [Beijing, 1603], trans. Douglas Lancashire and Peter Hu Kuo-Chen, S.J., ed. Edward J. Malatesta, S.J. (Taipei and Paris, 1985), 61.

[56] Ramon Lull, *Libre de meravelles*, I. c.1 (Barcelona, 1931), I, 32. [The *Libre de meravelles* was not published until 1750].

[57] Pollot, *Dialogues*, 104v–118v.

[58] Charron, *La Sagesse*, in *Oeuvres*, II, 7–8.

[59] Guillaume de Saluste, sieur Du Bartas, *Les Oeuvres de G. de Saluste . . . Dernière édition* . . . , rev., corr., and aug. (Paris, 1611), 312D–313A.

be able to understand" and conceded that it could be overcome only by faith and the acceptance of Christian doctrine.[60] Mersenne in 1623 attributed similar doubts to the atheist: "Since it would be better if there were no sins in this world, and nevertheless these reign, there is no God, for otherwise He would not allow them." If God existed, he continued, there could be no "monsters" and no depraved wills, and yet there were such things. If God existed, Mersenne's atheist proposed, "He is the creator of evil," which would be absurd.[61]

The Jesuit Théophile Raynaud, in his *Theologia naturalis*, reprinted in his posthumous *Opera omnia* of 1665, conceded that atheists, however inane, indeed existed. While he claimed that such atheists were atheists of the heart and of stupidity, never of thought (although they included Diagoras, Theodorus, and Protagoras), he assigned specific arguments to them. They claimed that no being such as God could be knowable to the human faculties. They claimed that the existence of an infinite being was disproven by the reality of things that He was not, and thus, that limited His being. First and foremost, however, they claimed that if God existed, there would be no evil, and the world could not go in the wicked, chaotic ways that it did.[62] Elsewhere, he argued that all denial or doubt concerning the compatibility of providence and evil resolved itself necessarily into atheism.[63] Spanheim, in 1676, wrote that he found atheism astonishing, perverse, absurd, and incomprehensible, but attributed it above all to the inability to understand how, if God existed, there could be so much evil and sin in the world, or how pain and suffering could fall upon the good and bad alike:

> It is that, my brothers, that has for all time provided the great pretext of atheists and libertines, and that has led a large number of men to doubt either of a God or of a providence. . . . And certainly, I admit that to consider things from this perspective, the flesh has the wherewithal to doubt [*la chair a dequoy doûter*].[64]

When the influential critic and editor Jean Le Clerc thought about the atheist's motivation, he attributed such ultimate disbelief to "pride" and "prejudice," and to presumption, negligence, and laziness. When he thought about the atheist's opinions and attitudes, however, he attributed atheism above all to efforts to judge God's actions by human values rather than simply to submit to providence: "One concludes that there is

[60] Ibid., 325A–325C.

[61] Mersenne, *Quaestiones*, cols. 281–312, 315–48, 403–12, 431–36.

[62] Théophile Raynaud, S.J., *Opera omnia* . . . , 19 vols. [in folio!] (Lyon, 1665), v, 292–98.

[63] Théophile Raynaud, S.J., *Erotemata de malis ac bonis libris* . . . (Lyon, 1653), 17–25.

[64] Spanheim, *L'athée*, 323–99.

no God from [the fact] that He does not govern the human race in the manner in which one judges that He should guide it."[65]

The Huguenot theologian Jean La Placette wrote that the great Christian theologians and philosophers, including the seventeenth-century "Cartesian" Catholics Arnauld, Malebranche, and Régis, had proven the existence of God so decisively that even "if these proofs do not convince the atheists," believers now may be assured that no atheistic objections could overturn such demonstrations. The great danger, he warned, however, was the fideistic claim that faith was opposed to reason, argued above all on the basis of the incompatibility of evil and sin with the existence of God. This concession was virtually the only thing, he remonstrated, that could open the gates to confident atheism. God being free, La Placette urged, He could do what would appear to us as "contradiction." Arguments that there was any actual incompatibility between the existence of God and the reality of evil, La Placette warned, would lead not to Manichaeanism, as he alleged Bayle had suggested, but rather would "give proselytes to atheism and to the philosophy of Epicurus [the denial of providence]." The problem of evil, he insisted, was the problem of atheism.[66]

As Brillon put it in his continuation of La Bruyère's portrait of the unbeliever: "Incapable of knowing these things [of providence], we want to fathom the judgments of God, we ask Him to be accountable to us for His conduct, *we make His wisdom responsible for our doubts*."[67] Reviewing Keill's *Introductio ad veram Astronomiam* in 1719, La Roche asserted that since astronomy led our gaze away from the moral chaos of this earthly world to the beauty and order of celestial things, it brought us with the most assurance to recognition of the existence, wisdom, goodness, and omnipotence of God. This was a vital function for La Roche, since "atheism is based principally on [consideration of] the corruption and disorder that reigns among men," and, in particular, on "the prosperity of the wicked," a phenomenon, he noted, that had led many of the most virtuous faithful into fundamental doubt.[68]

. . .

Doubts about the existence of God based on the problem of evil, suffering, and injustice, however, were far from the only conceivable model of

[65] Jean Le Clerc, *De l'incrédulité, où l'on examine les motifs & les raisons générales qui portent les INCREDULES à rejetter la religion chrétienne* (Amsterdam, 1696), 60–64.

[66] Jean La Placette, *Réponse à deux objections, qu'on oppose de la part de la raison à ce que la foi nous apprend sur l'origine du mal, & sur le mystère de la trinité* (Amsterdam, 1707), "Préface" [30 pp., unpaginated].

[67] Brillon, *Suite des Caractères*, 20–22.

[68] *Bibliothèque Anglaise* II (1718), 336–39.

the atheist's rejection of belief in God. At the simplest level, priests and theologians of the seventeenth and early eighteenth centuries had talked of God, at some point in their lives, with common, unlearned people, and they knew at first hand that what they took at times to be a truth so clear and luminous that all mankind came to it naturally nevertheless could be quite foreign to even the partially schooled. Thus, the celebrated Boudon, grand archdeacon of Evreux, wrote of his pastoral visits to Church schools, noting sadly that "we teach every day to children that there is a God, but they have no understanding of it . . . ; they say without intelligence, like animals, that there is a God. In truth, there is nothing that they know less." Children learned of God "by memory," he complained, but they had only the words, not the idea:

> We make visits and we question the children, sometimes quite advanced in age, some of them thirteen or fourteen years old: they answer perfectly all the questions that are found in the catechism. . . . But if you ask them about their thoughts and their sentiments with regard to God, . . . you will see that they do not have the least knowledge of Him. . . . They will tell you that the Holy Virgin is God . . . ; that God has not always been. . . . They do not understand in any manner what they are talking about; they are without comprehension.[69]

The problems with the truly well-educated, however, could be far greater. The learned world of early-modern France often understood that demonstration was an art as well as a science, and that the clever logician could even "prove," in theory, the unprovable. Gédéon Tallemant des Réaux recounted in his *Historiettes*, written in the mid-seventeenth century, an anecdote told about the Cardinal Du Perron:

> One day he gave a discourse, in front of Henry III, to prove that there was a God, and after having done it he offered to prove, by a completely contrary discourse, that there was not a God. That displeased the King. . . . Several persons persuaded the King, as apparently it was the truth, that the poor man had offered to give this discourse opposed to the other only in order to demonstrate his wit.[70]

On a more formal level, Charron, in 1595, wrote of those who, although "not resolved to the negation of the Deity . . . yet are not of the affirmative." "Such men," he opined, "having no God and not believing in any God, are truly atheists."[71] In a manuscript on his attempts to con-

[69] Henri-Marie Boudon, *Oeuvres complètes de Boudon, grand archidiacre d'Evreux* . . . , ed. J.-P. Migne, 3 vols. (Paris, 1856), I, 269–70. This was from Boudon's essay "Dieu Inconnu." Boudon died in 1702.

[70] Tallemant des Réaux, *Les historiettes*, II, 103–4. Tallement des Réaux died in 1690.

[71] Charron, *La Sagesse*, in *Oeuvres*, II, 6–7.

vert what he saw as three distinct groups in Asia, the "atheists," the "infidels," and the "pagans," the priest Jean d'Aubry, writing in the mid-seventeenth century, noted that "the Atheists laughed at what I said." This, he confessed, was unsettling: "I was plunged into a profound melancholy, seeing that our Religion . . . could not be usefully communicated."[72]

The culture, then, could offer a portrait of a sincere inability to be convinced by proofs of God's existence. This could be conceived to occur at the level of those ignorant of theology, as in the case of the Asian "atheists," or at the level of the learned. Spanheim wrote of those who "complain that the existence of a God cannot be mathematically verified [*ne peut estre verifiée mathématiquement*]," and urged them to recognize that neither could "His nonexistence." He blamed the reality of such atheists on the "criminal" exercises in the schools whereby students were encouraged to argue against God's being in order to show the weakness of such atheistic positions. What prince, he asked, would allow "a subject, in order to exercise his mind, to dispute his birth and his authority?" What if such an exercise, he cautioned, actually persuaded someone that the feigned arguments were stronger than the replies in defense of God's existence? To adopt the persona of the atheist for intellectual purposes, he noted, was to become worse than the devil, who at least never questioned God's being. "Who doesn't know," he asked, "that by touching pitch or dung, one is made filthy by it?"[73]

Such warnings, however, went wholly unheeded, perhaps because the culture indeed was in theory so committed to the notion, which it nonetheless belied again and again, that atheism involved only the will and never the mind. The Capuchin theologian Anaclet du Havre, in a work quite representative of almost all treatises of philosophical theology, felt absolutely obliged to share the strongest possible "reasonings of the atheists to prove that there is no God" with his order's students of theology, so that they could be in a position "to destroy these by opposed, solid, and convincing responses." What "arguments" might "the atheist" make? He offered two atheistic "propositions" and five atheistic "reasonings." The propositions, which he attributed to Aquinas's "objections" rather than to any modern thinkers, were first, that one could explain the universe without God, simply by reference to matter in motion, and second, that people believed in God "only because they are told from their earliest youth that there is one, and because princes have used this opinion." The atheistic "reasonings" were aimed at the problems of demon-

[72] Fragments of the manuscript were published by Niceron et al., *Mémoires*, XXII, 263–67.

[73] Spanheim, *L'athée*, 53–58.

stration of God's existence. First, there was no contradiction in "progression to the infinite [infinite regression of causes]," invalidating the proof of a necessary first cause. Second, we could have no clear idea of God, and, hence, no proof of a being whom we did not adequately conceive. Third, the idea of God was self-contradictory (e.g., among many putative "self-contradictions" cited, He was supposed to be both immobile and the cause of motion). Fourth, if God existed, there would be no evil in the world. Fifth, if there were a God, He would have infinite knowledge and thus would know the last number, but there can be no last number. Finally, if there were a God, He was either unable or unwilling to prevent crime, both of which possibilities negated the existence of a perfect being.[74] None of these "arguments" was new to Anaclet du Havre, but now almost all Capuchin students could conceive of them as well.

As Aquinas indeed had done, but in Latin and before printing, Anaclet du Havre also considered, but in the vernacular and with dramatic new means of dissemination, the "reasonings of several theologians to prove that one cannot demonstrate the existence of God." Anaclet du Havre explicated such arguments with great precision, again so that his students could "destroy them by opposed, solid, and convincing replies and reasons." First, God must be proven either by His cause or His effects, but as the first being He admits of no prior cause, and as a necessary, infinite cause, He cannot be demonstrated from contingent, finite effects. Second, God could not possibly be the object of sense experience, and thus, "the existence of God cannot be demonstrated by sensible effects, nor by natural reasons based on those same effects." Third, there are peoples who do not believe in God, so it is evident that it is not a necessary or innate idea. Fourth, since God's essence and existence would have to be identical, and the human mind could not possibly know the essence of an infinite being by natural lights, it could not possibly know the existence of God.[75]

If one believed that all such objections to proof of God's being fell of their own illogic virtually at first glance—an assumption implicit in the many assurances that only a madman or depraved fool could will himself to deny the evidence of God's existence—then indeed one need not fear them intellectually. Reviewing favorably an English theological work that treated atheism as "a monster against which all nature and reason itself rises up and revolts," the *Histoire des Ouvrages des Savans*, in 1696, noted that "the author nonetheless introduces the atheists, proposing their miserable objections. The most specious is taken from the disorder

[74] N. Anaclet du Havre, O.F.M., Capuchin, *Sujet de conférences sur la théologie positive . . . A l'usage des Capucins*, 3 vols. (Rouen, 1712), I, pt. 3, 59–61.

[75] Ibid., 61–62.

and the irregularity that they claim to notice in the works of God."[76] Commenting on the propriety of repeating objections to the existence of God, the *Nouvelles de la République des Lettres* reassured its readers in 1718 that "those who would let themselves be persuaded by the objections rather than by the replies would be persons who already had taken sides with atheism against religion."[77] At times, however, voices in the culture indeed worried that such objections could be stated too forcefully. In November 1705, the same journal, referring to Thomas Campanella's *Atheismus triumphatus* (Atheism vanquished), had noted that "it is claimed that Campanella, pretending to combat the atheists in this work, favored them, by lending them arguments of which they never would have thought and by replying to these very weakly."[78] In October 1706, the *Histoire des Ouvrages des Savans*, commenting on the same topic, observed similarly that Campanella's work "caused a great stir, but less because he refuted the atheists well in it, than because he gave them arguments that they never would have invented themselves."[79] Two decades later, Niceron's series of *Mémoires* circulated the same view.[80] In May 1718, *L'Europe Savante* reported that one Leiden theologian had accused another of atheism because of the strength of the latter's "objections" against proof of God and noted that many "satires" had appeared on this affair.[81]

Vanini had charged Aquinas's *Summa Contra Gentiles* with the same weakness, that is, "that there was not one objection of the atheists that was well resolved there."[82] A century later, David Durand accused Vanini of *intentionally* having done the same. For Durand, "the true key to his pernicious work" was "this method of attacking what one makes believe one is defending." In his view, Vanini "refuted" the atheists' arguments and objections weakly, so that he could, in fact, repeat their arguments positively for his audience. For Durand, such a deceit had obtained the required theological approbations for Vanini's *Amphitheatrum*, a work, he believed, that intentionally had given too much strength to formulations of atheistic objections and never had resolved essential atheistic "difficulties." Vanini, Durand concluded, feigned pride in his proofs of God, but in fact his work "casts shadows on the divine existence."[83] Para-

[76] *Histoire des Ouvrages des Savans*, oct. 1696, 85–86.

[77] *Nouvelles de la République des Lettres*, jan.–fév. 1718, 78–79.

[78] Ibid., nov. 1705, 512.

[79] *Histoire des Ouvrages des Savans*, oct. 1706, 450.

[80] Niceron et al., *Mémoires*, VII, 81.

[81] *L'Europe Savante* III, pt. 1 (mai 1718), 162–65.

[82] Lucilio Vanini, *Amphitheatrum aeternae providentiae divino-magicum* (Lyon, 1615), "Candido Lectore."

[83] David Durand, *La vie et les sentimens de Lucilio Vanini* (Rotterdam, 1717), 37–38, 67–69, 73–89, 102–20.

phrasing Durand's work, *L'Europe Savante* explained that Vanini merely "gives the appearance of combating ancient and modern atheists, and truly he gives them the victory [*la cause gagnée*] by the weakness and impertinence of his replies."[84]

Many thinkers attributed atheistic conclusions, regardless of intentions, to schools of philosophy to which they were opposed. As we later shall see, this became a common motif of both Scholastic-Cartesian polemic and histories of ancient philosophy, but it was not limited to this. Many thinkers, including Charron, Jean de Silhon, the Huguenot Jacques Bernard, and the Jesuit Théophile Raynaud thought that skeptical natural philosophy, either Pyrrhonian, or, for some, any variant of Academic skepticism, would culminate in atheism or its equivalent, a failure to recognize that one knew of the existence of God. De Volder, professor of philosophy at the University of Leiden, was convinced that there were almost no genuine atheists, but that there were indeed skeptical schools of philosophy that denied proofs of the existence of God and gave the appearance of atheism.[85]

To believe that there were strong reasons and appearances on both sides of the question of God's existence, Charron urged, was to be indifferent to this most essential question and, in the final analysis, atheistic. Likewise, for Charron, the Epicurean denial of God's providence was fundamentally atheistic: "For it is scarcely better, and perhaps worse, to believe in an impotent, nonchalant God, without concern for and providence over his works . . . than not to believe in Him at all." Thus, for Charron, such men "in a certain sense, can be called atheists."[86] Jean de Silhon argued in 1661 that the Academic principle that "there are no indubitable [propositions]" clearly entailed that "the existence of God, for example, is a truth of which one can doubt," and that the discovery of God's being could not be decided with certainty. This, he noted, would place all revelation in doubt, since it would be the alleged word of "an uncertain Being."[87] In 1718, Jacques Bernard, in the widely read *Nouvelles de la République des Lettres*, defended philosophical skeptics such as La Mothe Le Vayer from the charge of atheism, but he noted that "one sees in him many marks of Pyrrhonism, and *if this malady extends all the way to doubting if there is God, it is very close to atheism*."[88]

[84] *L'Europe Savante* IV, pt. 1 (juillet 1718), 77–114. See also *Journal de Trévoux*, mars 1711, 480–84.

[85] Burchardus de Volder, *Disputationes Philosophicae omnes contra Atheos* (Mittelburg, 1685). The *Disputationes* were a defense of Descartes's two proofs of God, offered as Plato's and St. Augustine's, as the only (and utterly triumphant) alternative to skeptical criticism of proof of God.

[86] Charron, *La Sagesse*, II, 6–7.

[87] Jean de Silhon, *De la certitude des connoissances humaines* (Paris, 1661), 1–5.

[88] *Nouvelles de la République des Lettres*, mars–avril 1718, 278–79.

In short, many early-modern French minds easily could imagine a person unpersuaded, from a variety of perspectives, of the existence of God. Not all proofs of God were compelling, and until the sincere searcher after truth found such a proof, he was, in some sense, an atheist. Raynaud's *Theologia naturalis* might attribute disbelief merely to the fool, but Raynaud, for example, agreed with Saint Thomas that Anselm's proof of God was not compelling, and that, indeed, no "a priori" proof of God was persuasive. He further argued, however, that "the atheist" could find escapes from Aquinas's own proofs from contingent being, from motion, and from the impossibility of an infinite regress of efficient causes, and he insisted that only the complex proof "from the subordination of causes" could eliminate the refuge of the atheist. He also argued that skeptical philosophy, eliminating the possibility of such a proof, would lead, if unrefuted, to atheistic conclusions.[89]

While Pierre Nicole thought proofs of God's existence from Scripture, miracles, and the gift of prophecy the most convincing, he acknowledged that the atheist would not concede the factual basis of these. For such atheists, the theologian should provide metaphysical and, above all, "more proportioned to the majority of minds," sensible proofs. The strongest "sensible proof," he argued, was the "natural instinct" to believe in God from the impression that the world makes on us. He acknowledged, however, that such reasoning, whatever its force, was not ideal: "If *it is not an invincible reason*, it is a sentiment and a vision that do not have less force than all the [formal] reasons." It was more natural to give in to it, he concluded, than to contradict it.[90] In many ways, this conceded a great deal to theoretical disbelief. The philosophical skeptic Saint-Evremond, however, would concede even more. Most believers, the fideistic man of letters concluded in 1684, believed by their "will . . . by desires," and thus achieved a belief in God "that the Understanding refuses them by its lights." Indeed, he added, "*I have known devout believers who in a certain opposition between the heart and the mind, truly loved God without really believing in Him.*"[91]

Equally problematic for a legion of theologians was what they took to be the tendency toward excessive "naturalism" in mankind. The Lockean "revolution" often is conceived to have broken radically with a less empirical tradition (although who was more committed than Aristotle, in theory at least, to the priority of the senses in the derivation of knowledge?). Hobbes's contemporaneous critics have convinced many historians that he proposed a materialized view of the objects of our knowledge

[89] Raynaud, S.J., *Opera omnia*, v, 205–17, 292–98.

[90] Pierre Nicole, *Essais de morale, contenus en divers traitez sur plusieurs devoirs importans*, 6th ed., rev. and corr., 4 vols. (The Hague, 1688), II, 22–23.

[91] Saint-Evremond, *Oeuvres*, IV, 317 [mispaginated as 417].

which departed dramatically from the spiritualized consciousness of his age. Seventeenth-century apologists, however, forever complained that their fellow creatures, educated and uneducated alike, were hopelessly tied to sense experience alone, were unable to conceive of anything that was not material, and were blind to the quotidian reality of spiritual causal agency. For many, this phenomenon, informally, in everyday life, and formally, in philosophy, also raised the specter of atheism. Some of these complaints, to be sure, were directed against a notion of Epicureanism known more from patristic and scholarly sources than from any daily contact, and some were directed merely against crude sensualism. Certainly, there were idiosyncratic criteria and polemical hyperbole involved in determinations of such excessive "naturalism." Nonetheless, the early-modern learned world clearly could conceive of minds blind to all but "what they could see." The person who thought he did not need God to explain his world, or that all explanations were limited by what could be experienced sensibly, also was a model for the would-be "atheist."[92]

Pollot, in 1595, had written of thinkers who attributed "this beautiful order and all of its coherence . . . to nature," expressing his contempt at their failure to see that such a "nature" would require the very attributes of divinity. He noted that Saint Augustine had denounced such blind philosophers in book 3 of *De Trinitate*, and he shared (and paraphrased) Augustine's view of them as men who "attributed to nature and to secondary causes what belongs to the First Cause, to such an extent did they ignore God." For Pollot, it was "an abominable sacrilege to attribute to the creature the title, office, and dignity that suits the Creator alone."[93] In 1625, Naudé had cited the Scholastic Vasquez to the effect that sorcery at least forced the irreligious to be "saved from atheism, by recognizing . . . that there are other substances than those that can be judged by touch and by sight."[94] Mersenne, in 1623, had included, among the atheist's views, the notion that since unnecessary causes should not be added to explanations, "whatever is referred to God and miracles can be referred to natural causes; therefore, there is no need to add God."[95]

This view of atheism persisted throughout the early-modern period. In 1674, the Jesuit Petiot wrote of "the atheists, who attribute all of these [natural] effects to a stupid nature." He did not, however, think that they

[92] Dez, S.J., *La foy des chrétiens*, III, 36, wrote of "the atheists, who only want to believe what they see [*qui ne veulent croire que ce qu'ils voyent*]."

[93] Pollot, *Dialogues*, 104v–118v.

[94] Gabriel Naudé, *Apologie pour les grands hommes soupçonnez de magie. Dernière édition* (Amsterdam, 1712) [first published in Paris, 1625], 378–79. The original title was *Apologie pour tous les grands personnages qui ont esté faussement soupçonnez de magie*.

[95] Mersenne, *Quaestiones*, cols. 379–90.

could sustain such views in the face of natural catastrophe, noting, concerning earthquakes for example, that "I do not believe that there are atheists so fanatical and so obstinate that they have not implored the mercy of God when seeing the earth give way beneath their feet."[96] In 1676, the freethinking d'Assoucy likewise denounced those atheists who "assign everything to destiny and fatality and deny God the glory of having made the world, in order to attribute it to chance." For d'Assoucy, it was evident that nature was arranged in harmonious and purposeful ways "of which blind nature, devoid of all intelligence, is not capable." If nature proceeded without God, d'Assoucy noted, "it would put our feet where we have our heads."[97] When Spanheim denounced what he took to be the unparalleled profusion of "covert or overt" modern atheists, he attributed it to three reasons, primary among which was that too much was "attributed . . . to secondary causes" (vanity and libertinism being the other two).[98]

For Brillon, writing in 1708, the highest degree of atheistic incredulity was that of the man who "attributes everything to the course of nature, and the course of nature . . . to chance and necessity." Although he was certain such unbelievers would invoke God at the approach of their death, they were, nonetheless, the "true atheists" among the impious.[99] For his contemporary, the Capuchin Anaclet du Havre, we have seen, the refutation of atheism began with the refutation of the claim that one can explain the universe without reference to God, solely in terms of matter in motion. He feared that the path to this claim was cleared by the insistence of certain theologians themselves that belief in God required faith, since "the existence of God cannot be demonstrated by sensible effects, nor by natural reasons based on those same effects."[100]

In 1716, the Cartesian abbé Charles Claude Genest, member of the Académie française and chaplain to the duchesse d'Orléans, published a well-received poetic exposition of his philosophy, including his "natural proofs of the existence of God." In it, he offered a portrait of the ancient and modern "Epicurean" atheists who believed that in explaining "what moves the universe," "Destiny, Nature, Chance, Mind, or God" were equally plausible and equally obscure.[101] For Blackmore, as reported in

[96] Estenne Petiot, S.J., *Demonstrations théologiques pour établir la foy chrestienne, et catholique. Contre les superstitions, et les erreurs de toutes les sectes infidelles* (Metz, 1674), 146, 159.

[97] D'Assoucy, *Les pensées*, 62–93.

[98] Spanheim, *L'athée*, 232–74.

[99] Brillon, *Suite des Caractères*, 22–24.

[100] Anaclet du Havre, O.F.M., Capuchin, *Théologie positive*, I, pt. 3, 59–61.

[101] Abbé Charles Claude Genest, *Principes de philosophie, ou Preuves naturelles de l'existence de Dieu et de l'immortalité de l'ame* (Paris, 1716), 30.

the *Bibliothèque Anglaise*, the Greeks gave rise to atheism, since it was only with the advent of their philosophical systems that men who had found God indispensable to account for the cosmos now "attribute to other causes the formation and the conservation of the universe."[102] Montesquieu, in his notebooks, averred that he found it incredible that anyone could attribute the "laws of nature" to "a blind power," but offered the portrait of a disbeliever who, he claimed, did reason exactly in such a way to him:

> No man ever has been mad enough to say that chance produced the world; everyone has known perfectly well that a leaf could not make itself except by natural causes or natural laws, and, by extension, [that this is true of] all the productions of nature. The most that one could say of this . . . is that . . . one has discovered the [natural] cause of the formation of several things . . . and that it was the same for all the rest; that if we did not discover it [the natural cause], it was because we did not see enough things to allow us to discover the majority of the effects and operations of nature. It was like a problem of geometry in which one did not know all the conditions.[103]

Although Montesquieu believed that such an unbeliever would be undone by the simple question "Who established these laws of nature?" he had no difficulty imagining what might be going on in the mind of such an atheist. For Montesquieu, "the least reflection suffices for man to cure himself of atheism," but that reflection had to conclude in the recognition that "there is an intelligent being who produces this order that we see in the world." The Epicurean attribution of order to chance "is insupportable, since it attacks the existence of a being whose name is written everywhere," but it was a position in need of refutation.[104]

That sense—that the signature of God was everywhere in the world, externally manifest to the senses and internally manifest to the mind or soul—both supported and explained for many what was proclaimed so widely as universal consent to the existence of God. Who could deny the existence of what all men believed, since such conviction could only come from the fact that all things taught it? The atheist, however, was obviously such a being, and to imagine him, one would have to imagine alternative explanations for putative universal consent. This was why the reaction to what was perceived as "Machiavellianism" was so strong. It was one thing to point out that religious truth was useful to the state, that is to say, to argue that belief in the existence of God, derived from experience and reflection, was also essential to the preservation of civil order.

[102] *Bibliothèque Anglaise* I (1717), 355–62.
[103] Montesquieu, *Oeuvres complètes*, 417.
[104] Ibid., 417 and 955.

It was quite a different thing, however, to suggest that belief in God arose from its indispensability to civil rulers. The early-modern age, despite its insistence that universal consent could only come from the natural self-evidence or evidence of God's existence, could posit and explicate a very different explanation.

Charron, for example, in 1595, urged that theologians *not* argue for the existence of God from the "utility" of that conviction to society, since this would play directly into the hands of "the atheists." The suggestion of "utility," he warned, implied that it was not a matter of "truth," but "a tall tale [*une bourde*], an artificial invention of great utility to the powerful." For atheists, he noted, "wise princes believe nothing of it in their souls, but utilize it to prevail over . . . their subjects."[105] The Capuchin Yves de Paris indeed argued for the "utility" of belief in God and stressed that "all the ancient lawgivers made this belief primary, as the most necessary for their laws," but he insisted that it did not proceed from "the invention of princes." Having stated that only madness or malice could account for atheism, he nonetheless offered a long refutation of the view that belief in God arose from the need for a society to secure respect of its laws, and he declared it appalling that so many "libertines" of his age had been "seduced" by such an account of its origin. Since belief in God co-existed with uncivilized states and humbled rather than exalted the princes, he concluded, universal consent to it could only show how natural it was so to believe and how ubiquitous in nature the cause and evidence for such belief must be.[106] For the deist Marana, in his popular *Espion Turc*, one of the sad impulses toward atheism was the misplaced desire not to be "duped" by "a stratagem invented" by the powerful, arising from a belief that theism was "merely an artifice of politics."[107] For Anaclet du Havre, a fundamental atheistic proposition was the assertion that people believed in God "only because they are told from their earliest youth that there is one, and because princes have utilized this opinion."[108]

Further, there were those who were perfectly aware of the equally ancient claim that belief in the gods, and thus God, arose from the fear and helplessness of mankind before the forces of nature. Genest's proof of the existence of God identified the atheistic enemy as seeking to explain the origin of the idea of God in this manner. In his poetry (which, knowing my limits, I shall render in prose), Genest offered a portrait of the arguments of such a man. The atheist believed that:

[105] Charron, *La Sagesse*, in *Oeuvres*, II, 9–10.

[106] Yves de Paris, O.F.M., Capuchin, *La théologie naturelle*, 45–101.

[107] Marana, *L'espion Turc*, II, 209–16.

[108] Anaclet du Havre, O.F.M., Capuchin, *Théologie positive*, I, pt. 3, 59.

> Mortal men . . . gripped by fear, exposed to pains, weak, and miserable, placed on their altars either fearsome gods or helpful deities, phantoms that error adored as avengers or as helpmates. Poor mortals, holding on, in suffering, to a life that is both so brief and so uncertain. . . . in pains and in miseries. Complaining of the misfortunes of their condition, they knew how to fabricate, at their will, images the contrary of these; [and] at the bidding of their wishes and their passion, to hear, amplify, and combine [such] chimeras, and to forge for themselves a Being in whom a limitless power and infinite goodness were united.[109]

One might say many things of such a passage: that it drew on commonplaces of classical incredulity; that it satisfied Genest's need to establish with force and elegance a point of view worthy of his refutation; that it showed the ability to imagine and embellish a position antithetical to his own. What one would *not* be tempted to say, however, no matter the extent to which Genest stressed the inconceivability of atheistic conclusions, was that it indicated a mind to whom such disbelief was truly unthinkable.

• • •

Perhaps they protested too much, these learned minds of the seventeenth and early eighteenth centuries, about an atheism that only could be embraced by willfully imbecilic criminals in pitiably desperate and hopeless search for impunity. The erudite Petiot shifted his tone dramatically when he thought of such men in 1674, in ways that suggested more danger than a handful of incapable dissenters from universal consent would seem to represent: "We must pile up stones to crush them; we must take up torches and firebrands to burn them; we must aim cannons to overcome them; it is necessary that God be glorified and that the atheists be exterminated."[110] A generation later, Jacques Bernard expressed a similar "sovereign horror" at the thought of such "monsters" who would "do everything to efface from their heart the persuasion of the existence of God." Bernard added that he could almost feel a certain "pity" for them, but not quite, because they were such freaks of nature:

> Their misery frightens me . . . these perpetual uncertainties . . . these shadows . . . this frightful night. . . . I want neither to have any commerce with them, nor to interrogate them on their state. I would be afraid that they would disclose thoughts to me that would throw me into a fear from which I would not be able to return.[111]

[109] Genest, *Principes*, 25–26.
[110] Petiot, S.J., *Demonstrations*, 303.
[111] Bernard, *De l'excellence de la religion*, 97–98.

The philosophical Catholic canon Simon Foucher understood well that to be educated in a culture that asked one always to consider the antithesis of all of one's views was to risk having honest doubts become disbelief. "We are so accustomed in the world to judge," he noted, urging a healthy skeptical philosophy as an alternative to this dilemma, "that we don't fail to support the negative of a proposition as soon as we cease supporting its affirmative."[112] If that were the case, however, then the ability to entertain doubts about the existence of God could be dramatic indeed. As we have seen, such doubts could be entertained, even if only for heuristic purposes. In his informal notebooks, Bossuet observed that "there is an atheism hidden in every heart, which breaks out into every action. We count God for nothing: we believe that when we have recourse to God, it is because things are desperate and there is nothing more to be done."[113] This was a practical atheism of which he spoke, one should imagine, but these *every*s were not what one would expect from the foremost spokesman of a Catholic culture that claimed to find "atheism" so aberrant and restricted a phenomenon.

The "problem" of atheism, whatever its particular manifestations in the conceptual and rhetorical categories of early-modern France, was a problem that touched on more timeless aspects of the human experience—and certainly on the Greek and thus Western propensity to fear that the world was without purpose or meaning, and that all might be chaos in the end. Perhaps, despite protestations to the contrary, it was only too real a problem, even if only at rare times, for the very souls obliged to reassure the faithful against those doubts and objections that the ancient Greeks, the medieval Scholastics, and the ongoing community of Christian theologians always could summon to mind. Perhaps one does not always need to seek sources of atheism somehow exogenous to Christendom. To insist not only upon order and purpose, but also upon the manifest evidence of these, was to create a potential susceptibility to disbelief, however limited, that belied the confident claim that incredulity was so very exorbitant. Who, in one sense of *believe*, could have believed more deeply than the Jansenist mother superior Angélique de Saint-Jean, whose perseverance and pious resolve impressed so many during her lead-

[112] Simon Foucher, *Dissertation sur la Recherche de la vérité, contenant l'Apologie des académiciens. Où l'on fait voir que leur manière de philosopher est la plus utile pour la religion, et la plus conforme au bon sens* . . . (Paris, 1687), 21. Foucher has been studied in lucid and penetrating fashion by Richard A. Watson, *The Downfall of Cartesianism 1673–1712* . . . (The Hague, 1966), which focuses on Foucher's epistemological critiques of Cartesian and Malebranchist notions of "idea" and on their philosophical implications for the whole ontological scheme of the seventeenth century. The title may be inflated (whose is not, these days?), but the book is a rare joy.

[113] Bossuet, "Pensées détachées," in *Oeuvres*, IV, 780.

ership of the nuns at Port-Royal-des-Champs in its most trying days? There were, however, other senses of *believe*, as Angélique de Saint-Jean herself was well aware, and these indeed could entail an element of fundamental doubt deep within the soul of the believer. She described

> a kind of doubt about all the things of faith and providence, at which I pause so little from fear of reasoning or of giving more entry to temptation, that it seems to me that my mind rejects it with a certain perspective that itself could be considered contrary to the faith, because it encloses a kind of doubt. It is as if I were saying that when there could be something uncertain in what seemed to me to be the truth, and that everything that I believe . . . could be doubtful, I should have no better choice to make than that of always following prudence. I frighten myself by writing that . . . [for] is not something missing from the certainty of the faith when one is capable of these [doubting] thoughts? I have not dared to speak to anyone of these thoughts, since they seem so dangerous to me that I should fear to give them the least exposure to those to whom I would have to speak my pain.[114]

Reviewing and paraphrasing a work by Basnage in 1704, the *Histoire des Ouvrages des Savans* offered a portrait of "the atheist" quite different from its usual characterizations. "The atheist," it told its readers, "boasts that his attachment to his opinions is disinterested; no passion engages him to it." This should give the faithful hope, the review explained, that such atheists might indeed be "cured" by presentation of the truth. These atheists "do not dive into debauchery and do not abandon themselves to the *voluptés* of the world." Rather, "they ordinarily seek seclusion [*la retraite*], and little concerned for applause, they make their most sensible pleasure consist of meditation and contentment of mind." Unlike fanatics, they respect the laws of humanity. However, "Even if atheists are adorned with several appearances of virtue," they suffer from specific vices of the heart: "They put themselves above the vulgar, above popular errors. They look with disdain upon those who are enchained to religion, as slaves who do not perceive that it [religion] is a yoke imposed on the people by artifice and by political design."[115] The reviewer paused to make certain the readers knew what sort of atheists Basnage had in mind here, and how they compared to the commonplace depraved atheists. In so doing, he said perhaps more than he meant to say:

> Mr. Basnage speaks there only of speculative and rational atheists [*Athées de speculation et de raisonnement*]; for there are atheists from vice [*Athées vi-*

[114] This "fragment" from the remarkable Angélique de Saint-Jean Arnauld d'Andilly (1624–1684) was published by Léon Cognet in *La Table Ronde*, déc. 1954, 52. My attention was called to it by Lucien Goldmann, *Le Dieu caché. Etude sur la vision tragique dans les 'Pensées' de Pascal & dans le théâtre de Racine* (Paris, 1975), 328.

[115] *Histoire des Ouvrages des Savans*, août 1704, 349–51.

> *cieux*], who deny the existence of a God only because they do not want there to be one. But if these [latter] atheists are the most detestable, they are not the most dangerous. It is easier to lead them back from it [atheism], because they hold to it *only* from vice, and age or disgust suffices to make them return from it. But the others are more undocile. They pride themselves that if they believe nothing, *it is from reflection*, and as a consequence they make it a point of honor never to surrender themselves [to us].[116]

The Benedictine savant François Lamy wrote in 1710 of "men who contend against [*qui combatent*] the existence of God" by pointing to contradictions among "the perfections that we attribute to Him," including the seeming contradiction between God's equity and the actual conduct of the governance of the world. He saw the incredulity of such men neither as solely volitional, nor as inconceivable. Indeed, he urged them to hold intellectually to the definition of God as "the infinitely perfect being," a being he believed established by Descartes's proofs, and "to accustom themselves to dissipate, by this means, all the clouds of doubts that are raised in their minds, and to break against this rock all the little insurrections [*soulèvemens*] of their heart." He knew the utility of this personally, he admitted: "I confess to you that this is the method that I use for myself for those doubts that I sometimes feel." Although he was in most of his works a consistently confident Christian rationalist, he acknowledged here that he indeed could feel "agitated against the justice of God, against His goodness, against His providence," and that at such times, he simply "appealed against [such doubts] to His infinite perfection . . . sure that nothing unjust . . . cruel . . . or hard could pertain to the infinitely perfect being."[117] If these "doubts" were those that led to the contestation of "the *existence* of God," then atheism was far from unimaginable to him.

The emergence of atheism in France would not be an affair of a merely nominal Christian culture, but, rather, in very large part, an affair precisely of the Christian mind or soul. "Theism" entails the concept, if not the categories, of "atheism." It is a believing culture that generates its own antithesis, disbelief in the principles of its own belief. Early-modern theists, Catholic, Protestant, and heterodox, sought to reassure themselves that no one could give doubts about God's being coherent argument or positive content. They themselves, however, were the source or conduit of such argument and the discoverers or creators of such atheistic teaching. Such an argument may sound paradoxical, but, we shall see, it restores both the potential and the reality of atheism to the culture of which

[116] Ibid., 351–52.

[117] François Lamy, O.S.B., *L'incrédule amené à la religion par la raison, en quelques entretiens où l'on traite de l'aliance de la raison avec la foy* (Paris, 1710), 116–18.

they were themselves a living part. We know, in one sense, the end of the story: the emergence of an atheistic strain of thought in early-modern France. Let us examine more closely what made such atheism possible, and, in one sense, even theologically "necessary." After that, let us examine what appears to have effected that potential into actual being as a philosophical and attitudinal position embraced by some and offered to all.

Chapter Three

ATHEISM WITHOUT ATHEISTS

PEOPLE do not learn from "a" society, of course, but from the mediating institutions, relationships, places, and events that actually link individual lives to larger groups, structures, and histories, and that separate, often dramatically, beings of the same historical era. The same phenomena, however, if not always the same lessons learned from them, can permeate whole strata of a diverse world. The educated public of the French seventeenth century, whose own thought in so many ways would transform fundamentally the mental and material culture of its heirs, was indeed diverse, but, on the whole, it shared a certain manner of formal education that provided a great many of its ways of being and thinking. We cannot understand it without knowing, among other things, some essential elements of the education through which it passed and the expectations and habits created there. In particular, the necessity of "atheism" *in some form* followed from that education.

Early-modern thinkers who denied that there could be any genuine "speculative" atheists knew that there nonetheless had to be an "atheism" in the form of atheistic argumentation, whether or not there were any minds who actually held to or proselytized for such a point of view. It did not require an atheistic mind to conceive of an atheistic objection to claims of theistic proof. If atheism in that sense did not exist, the members of the learned world would have had to invent it. Simply put, there was, in the very imperatives of the manner of thought into which almost all of them were educated, the obligation to create the antithesis of their own belief.

. . .

Before a university student moved to the higher faculties, such as that of theology, he studied at the faculty of arts, and there, after two years of Latin, Greek, rhetoric, and grammar, he spent at least two years in the study of philosophy, an exercise devoted primarily to the mastering of Aristotelian thought. This was the rule at all of the *collèges de plein exercise*. At the heart of this, in the first year of reading philosophy, lay what the culture saw as the "method" or "system," Aristotle's *Organon*. Most directors of education still believed, deeply, that the culture truly possessed in Aristotle's logic and modes of inquiry rules for the use of mind that allowed what could be known by our natural faculties to become the property of human understanding. The Jesuit *Ratio Studiorum* instructed each professor of philosophy that "in matters of any importance, let him not depart from Aristotle [unless Aristotle conflicts in any particular instance with the conclusions of Christian teaching]."[1] The texts and logic of Aristotle held central place in philosophical training in the collèges and universities, and the immediate goal of the study of that logic was the ability to participate in disputations.[2]

In Aristotle's dialectic and discussions of methods, in *The Categories*, *On Interpretation*, the *Prior Analytics*, the *Posterior Analytics*, and the *Topica*, the student discovered how those born or chosen to contemplate and know could achieve coherence and science—certain, systematic knowledge—on behalf of that great majority of Christian mankind whose conditions or circumstances did not allow them to escape from the rule of sweat and toil. We would be wrong to think of "seventeenth-century texts" as necessarily *written* in the seventeenth century; they were, of course, whatever works were *read* in that time. (The Bible, to make the point clearer, was not merely a text of the first centuries.) Aristotle was in that sense, however much challenged and however differently the age's students read him from students before or after, the most seventeenth-century philosopher of all. On certain topics of logic and method, however, he seemed amenable to only one interpretation. In the *Topica*, for example, through whose difficult lessons virtually all educated minds of early-modern France had passed, students were instructed, as their peers had been for centuries, on the requirement to interpose objection and antithetical argument between proposition and conviction.

"In dealing with any thesis," Aristotle informed them, "we must examine the argument both for and against, and having discovered it, we must immediately seek the solution; for the result will be that we shall have trained ourselves at the same time both for question and for answer." What, however, if there were no one who actually advanced or held views antithetical to our own? Aristotle had an answer to that from which a solemn intellectual obligation followed:

> *If we have no one else with whom to argue, we must do so with ourselves.* Also, one must choose arguments relating to the same thesis and compare them; for this procedure supplies an abundance of material for carrying the position by storm and is very helpful in refutation, when one has plenty of arguments both for and against; for the result is that one is put on one's

[1] *Ratio Atque Institutio Studiorum Societatis Jesu* (1599). I have used the translation by A. R. Ball, "The Ratio Studiorum," in *St. Ignatius and the Ratio Studiorum* ed. Edward A. Fitzpatrick (New York and London, 1933), 119–254. The quotation is from 168.

[2] Ibid., 171–74.

> guard against contrary arguments. Also, to take and to have taken in at a glance the results of each of two hypotheses is no mean instrument for the cultivation of knowledge and philosophical wisdom; for then it only remains to make a correct choice of one of them. For such a process one must possess a certain natural ability, and real natural ability consists in being able correctly to choose the true and avoid the false. Men of natural ability can do this; for they judge correctly what is best by a correct feeling of love [attraction] or hatred [revulsion] for what is set before them.[3]

In order to reach an appropriate level of understanding, Aristotle instructed them, it was essential to learn by practice how to form, to challenge, and to defend propositions relevant to an issue. "These are the sources of ability in discussion," he concluded, "and the purpose of exercise is the acquisition of ability, particularly in connection with propositions and objections; for, to put the matter simply, the man who can make propositions and objections is the skilled dialectician [logician]." He advised against disputing with an unskilled interlocutor, since one needed to learn to argue with the best. Argument had two fundamental modes: "to make a proposition," which trained one in synthesis; and "to make an objection," which taught one the essential skill of analysis. "To make an objection," Aristotle taught, "is to turn one thing into many; for the objector distinguishes or demolishes, conceding one proposition and refusing to concede another."[4]

The forms and exercises of late-medieval and early-modern university education, both as investigations and as controversies for the sake of controversy, reflected and strongly reinforced this Aristotelian injunction. Aquinas had made the issue one of common sense: "Men who look for the truth without considering their doubts first are like people who do not look where they are going."[5] In addition to teaching by public readings from and appropriate commentary on the received texts (the "lectures," literally, "readings," whose meaning has undergone such evolution), medieval universities institutionalized education by disputation. On any

[3] Aristotle, *Organon: Topica* VIII.xiv.163b1–19. The translation is by E. S. Forster, in Aristotle, *Organon*, ed. and trans. H. P. Cooke, H. Tredennick, and E. S. Forster, 2 vols. (Cambridge, Mass., 1933 and 1960), II. The seventeenth-century edition consulted is Guillaume Du Val, ed., *Aristotelis Opera Omnia, graece et latine, doctissimorum virorum interpretatione et notis emendatissima . . . Guillelmus Du Vallius . . .*, 3d ed., 4 vols. [in folio] (Paris, 1654). [The 1st ed. of the Du Val Aristotle, in Greek and Latin, was Paris, 1619; the 2d ed. was Paris, 1629.] Some seventeenth-century French scholars and students came to use the (Latin only) edition of the *Aristotelis Opera quae extant omnia . . .*, ed. Sylvestro Mauro, 6 vols. (Rome, 1668).

[4] Ibid. 163b19–164b20.

[5] Aquinas, *Expositiones in duodecim libros Metaphysices Aristotelis* [*Commentary on the Metaphysics*] I.III, lect. 1., in *Opera Omnia*, ed. Jean Nicolai, O.P., 23 vols. (Paris, 1660), IV.

question, at the *disputatio*, the master or doctor would choose some particular thesis or proposition as the topic at hand. Master and students raised the strongest objections to such a thesis that they could summon, and the disputant then upheld the thesis by appropriate response and argument. The master or doctor had the right to reach the final conclusion, and to return to the subject at length in his own next class. There, he generally repeated the thesis; restated, strengthened, and added to the arguments that could be opposed to it; and, finally, defended his own conclusion by, among other things, formally refuting the objections he had raised. So many theological and philosophical titles that emerged from the universities reflected their source in disputations: *Quaestiones disputatae*, *Quaestiones quodlibetales*, *Sophismata*, *Impossibilia*, and *Insolubilia*. Even in formal synthetic summae, the *quaestio* was the unit of inquiry. It proceeded from statements of the question or thesis to be examined (*Quaeritur utrum . . . videtur quod sic . . .* or *quod non . . .*) to the strong objections that could be opposed to such a thesis (*Sed contra . . .*) to the strongest reply to such objections (*Dicendum . . .* or *Intelligendum . . .* or *Solutio, responsio . . .*) to one's final conclusions for or against (*Ad rationes dicendum . . .* or *Ad rationes in oppositum dicendum . . .*). Abelard's model of the *sic et non*, the for and against on all disputed issues, linked to the formal requirements of Aristotelian method, had become the means by which the universities sought to make certain both that rigor would prevail among the educated and that the learned never would be caught off guard by argument against their rightful views.[6]

This still was the case well into the seventeenth century. To advance from *baccalauréat* to *licence*, the would-be theologian at the Faculty of Theology at Paris passed through three disputations (the "*petite ordinaire*," the "*grande ordinaire*," and the "*Sorbonnique*"), in which one's ranking as a deft disputant determined the order of one's place in the presentation of candidates for the doctorate.[7] Historians might well want

[6] See the classic and lively discussions of the institutionalization of the Scholastic method in Fernand van Steenberghen, *Histoire de la philosophie: Période chrétienne* (Paris and Louvain, 1964), 77–82; Etienne Gilson, *History of Christian Philosophy in the Middle Ages* (New York, 1955), 246–50; and F. C. Copleston, *A History of Medieval Philosophy* (London, 1972), 150–59. The structure of argument by *quaestio* in Aquinas receives particularly cogent analysis by Thomas Gilby, O.P., in his introduction to vol. 1, pt. 1 of the Blackfriars edition of the *Summa Theologiae*.

[7] Charles Jourdain, *Histoire de l'Université de Paris au XVIIe et au XVIIIe siècle*, 2d ed., 2 vols. (Paris, 1888), I, 46–49. See also François Lebrun et al., *De Gutenberg aux Lumières*, vol. IV of the *Histoire générale de l'enseignement et de l'éducation en France* (Paris, 1981); M.-M Compère and D. Julia, *Les collèges français: 16e–18e siècles* (Paris, 1984); J. Lelièvre, *L'éducation en France du XVIe au XVIIe siècle* (Brussels, 1975); G. Snyders, *La pédagogie en France aux XVIIe et XVIIIe siècles* (Paris, 1972); F. de Dainville, S.J., *L'éducation des jésuites (XVIe–XVIIIe siècles)* (Paris, 1978); W. Frijhoff and D. Julia, *Ecole et société dans la France de l'Ancien Régime* (Paris, 1975); J. de Viguerie, *Une oeuvre d'éducation sous*

to caricature the years of philosophical (and theological) study in the seventeenth century as the minutiae of logical hairsplitting and forced distinctions, but that should leave them hard-pressed to imagine how such a philosophical education produced the mental dexterity of the likes of Bacon, Locke, Hobbes, Newton, Descartes, Gassendi, Bayle, Arnauld, and Malebranche, who all passed through it. In their direct encounters with the universities and with the texts of the great medieval philosophers, theologians, and subsequent commentators, seventeenth-century students were taught explicitly and by example that the first obligation of the educated mind in its proper natural role was the logical analysis of any thesis whatsoever into its strengths and its weaknesses, and, in brief, the articulation and confrontation of all possibly cogent objections to their own arguments. Minds nurtured on *quaestiones* presented in such form, and on *sophismata*, *insolubilia*, and countless formal *disputationes* of all kinds were minds predisposed to the entertaining of beliefs wholly opposed to their own. The Jesuit Denis Petau, who objected strongly to this Scholastic system in the seventeenth century and invited students to concentrate on a positive theology derived deferentially from Scripture and patristic sources, conceded that "this [his own] course of positive theology is less well attended, if indeed it is not sometimes utterly ignored, compared to the other [Scholastic] course in which a quarrelsome and contentious theology has the knack of attracting minds." Even he, however, insisted that such dialectic was a wondrously efficacious means of defeating the enemies of the faith and was an appropriate response to

l'Ancien Régime: Les Pères de la Doctrine chrétienne en France et en Italie, 1592–1792 (Paris, 1985); R. Chartier et al., *L'éducation en France du XVIe au XVIIIe siècle* (Paris, 1976); S. Guénée, *Bibliographie de l'histoire des universités françaises des origines à la révolution*, vol. II (Paris, 1978). The Scholastic method persisted well into the eighteenth century at the French universities, which annoys Bernard Plongeron, *La vie quotidienne du clergé français au XVIIIe siècle* (Paris, 1974), 195–97, who terms the obligatory two years of philosophy (of the eight years of university study required for the doctorate in theology) an encounter with "this bastardized scholasticism." It is the contention of C. B. Schmitt, "The Rediscovery of Skepticism," in *The Skeptical Tradition*, ed. Myles Burneat (Berkeley, 1983), 241, that "the medieval tradition of criticism and logical analysis (*sophismata, insolubilia*, etc.), of course, had something in common with ancient skepticism, but was an independent development, not genetically tied to the literary remains of the [Academically skeptical] ancients. . . . [T]hey functioned as two different historical strands." The reader also might want to examine an interesting article on the twelfth-century origins of the "disputatio," A. G. Landgraf, "Zur Technik und Ueberliferung der Disputation," in *Collecteana Franciscana* XX (1950), 173–88. See also abbé T. J. Pichon, *Des études théologiques . . .* (Avignon, 1767); P. Lallemand, *Histoire de l'éducation dans l'ancien Oratoire de France* (Paris, 1887); M. Targe, *Professeurs et régents de collège dans l'ancien Université de Paris* (Paris, 1902); G. Rigault, *Histoire générale de l'Institut des Frères des Ecoles Chrétiennes*, 8 vols. (Paris, 1947–1953); and L. W. Brockliss, *French Higher Education in the Seventeenth and Eighteenth Centuries: A Cultural History* (Oxford, 1987).

Saint Paul's call for reasonable assent.[8] In brief, historians should be careful not to confuse the methods by which the learned chose to deal with heresy or to teach children and the uneducated (as in the catechisms *pro pueris et indoctis* called for by the Council of Trent) with the methods by which they trained their own minds.

The intriguing figure of the *protervus* of the late-medieval university was in many ways the model for what the critical (and safely Christian) mind should do for itself. The *protervus* (literally, the bold or impudent person), as Gilson described him, was not the "devil's advocate," since the devil's advocate merely assumed the arguments that might be assigned to the devil himself. Rather, the *protervus* was "an obstinate dialectician who never gives up so long as he has one argument left with which to oppose any conclusion in philosophy or theology." His role was essential, since "against a conclusively proved thesis, no objection should remain possible. What can still be opposed by the *protervus* remains a mere probability."[9] It was a goal of Scholastic education that this boldness and impudence be internalized, and no small amount of dissatisfaction with the "endless quibbling" of Scholastic method was in fact a reaction against this remarkably self-critical function of mind. The irony, of course, was that the Scholastics themselves attributed "boldness" and "rashness" primarily to their opponents.

Although Thomas Aquinas did not enjoy quite the extraordinary prestige in Catholic secondary schools and universities that he would have from the nineteenth century on, he was the most deeply respected doctor of the Church in the seventeenth century, and there was indeed a Thomistic revival that proceeded throughout the early-modern age.[10] Jean

[8] J.-C. Vital Chatellain, *Le Père Denis Petau d'Orléans, Jésuite: Sa vie et ses oeuvres* (Paris, 1884), 154–308. The quotation is from a letter of 1631 from Petau to Mutius Vitelleschi, S.J., general of the Society. On his harsh words for the excesses of Scholastic method, along with his recognition of its essential utility to defending truth from error, see Denis Petau, S.J., "Praefatio" to *Theologicorum Dogmatum*, vol. I: *De Deo Uno, Deique proprietatibus agitur* (Paris, 1644).

[9] Gilson, *Christian Philosophy*, 500.

[10] Popular historians often write as if Scholasticism were no longer an influence on anyone's mind by the seventeenth century, appearing to agree with Edward John Kearns, *Ideas in Seventeenth-Century France* (New York, 1979), 10–11, that "all historians recognize that by 1650 or at the latest 1670 it was clear that scholasticism was intellectually dead." They might want to look at Jean Nicolai, O.P., et al., eds., *Sancti Thomae Aquinatis, . . . Opera omnia . . .*, 23 vols. (Paris, 1660 [the Societatem bibliopolarum ed.]), which also appeared that same year in a 20-vol. Paris edition. This did not include the *Summa Theologiae* (*ST*), published separately as Jean Nicolai, O.P., ed. *Summa Theologica S. Thomae Aquinatis . . .*, 1 vol. [in folio] (Paris 1663). In addition to his edition of the *ST* (with more than ten thousand marginal glosses), the Dominican scholar Nicolai, professor at the Faculty of Theology at the University of Paris, separately published Aquinas's work on the four books of the *Sentences*, *Sancti Tomae Aquinatis . . . Commentaria in quatuor libros Sententiarum Petri Lombardi . . .*, 4 tomes in 2 fol. vols. (Paris, 1659). There were also the ongoing

d'Espagne complained that "if Saint Paul returned to the world, he would be barely capable of being received as a doctor of theology, for lack of having studied Thomas Aquinas."[11] The Jesuits' *Ratio Studiorum*, the essential text at their vital collèges, instructed professors that (with the exception of Thomas's views of the conception of Mary and the solemnity of vows) "all members of our Order shall follow the teaching of St. Thomas in scholastic theology and consider him as their special teacher;

---

reprintings of the Louvain/Douai edition of the *ST*, first published in Douai, 1614, and reprinted in Paris, 1617; Paris, 1639; and Paris, 1662. There was also the Marandé abridged translation of the *ST* into French, as *La clef, ou Abbrégé de la Somme de S. Thomas . . .*, 2 tomes in 1 vol., published in Paris, 1649, and reprinted in a 10-vol. edition in Paris, 1668–1669. In Lyon, a new commentary by Philippe de la Très Sainte Trinité, the *Disputationes theologicae . . . in primam partem divi Thomae . . .*, 4 tomes in 2 vols. [in folio] (Lyon, 1653), was reprinted in 4 vols. [in folio] in 1664. Between 1649 and 1670, then, there was a remarkable outpouring of critical editions of St. Thomas, commentaries upon his work, and published encyclopedic or synoptic courses on his philosophy and theology. Among the most notable and successful of the latter were the multivolumed works of Jean-Baptiste Gonet, O.P., *Clypeus theologiae thomisticae contra novos ejus impugnatores* (Bordeaux, 1659–1669); Pierre Labat, O.P., *Theologia scholastica secundum illibatam S. Thomae doctrinam . . .* (Toulouse, 1658–1661); Jerome De Medicis, *Formalis explicatio Summae theologicae divi Thomae Aquinatis . . .* (Paris, 1657); Antoine Regnault, *Doctrinae Divi Thomae Aquinatis . . .* (Toulouse, 1670); and, in the vernacular, the abbé N. de Hauteville's 10-vol. *La theologie de saint Thomas . . .* (Paris, 1670) [De Hauteville was a doctor of theology from the University of Paris]. Seventeenth-century French scholars and publishers also produced major editions of the works of Albertus Magnus, *Beati Alberti Magni, . . . Opera quae hactenus haberi potuerunt . . .*, 21 vols. [in folio], ed. Pierre Jammy (Lyon, 1651) [preceded by an *Index Operum B. Alberti Magni . . .* (Paris, 1646)]; of Saint Bonaventure, *Sancti Bonaventurae, . . . Opera . . .*, 8 vols. [in folio] (Lyon, 1668) [followed by the . . . *Tabula, seu Index generalis in Opera omnia S. Bonaventurae* (Lyon, 1681)]; extensive volumes of contemporary Franciscan commentary on St. Bonaventure: Bartholomaeus de Barberiis, O.F.M., *Cursus theologicus ad mentem seraphici doctorus S. Bonaventurae . . .*, 2 tomes in 1 vol. [in folio] (Lyon, 1687) and . . . *Cursus philosophicus ad mentem sancti Bonaventurae . . .*, 3 vols. (Lyon, 1677) and . . . *Glossa, seu Summa ex omnibus S. Bonaventurae expositionibus in Sacram Scripturam . . .*, 4 vols. [in folio] (Lyon, 1681–1685); of Duns Scotus, *R.P.F. Joannis Duns Scoti, . . . Opera omnia quae hucusque reperiri potuerunt . . .*, ed. Luke Wadding, O.F.M., 12 tomes in 13 vols. [in folio], (Lyon, 1639) [with extensive commentary, scholia, and notes by seven leading Scotist commentators]; the major commentary on and defense of Scotus published by Barthelemy Durand, O.F.M., the *Clypeus scoticae theologiae . . .*, 4 vols. (Marseille, 1685–1686), and republished in 1700 and 1709; two rich new commentaries by the seventeenth-century commentator Claude Frassen, O.F.M., the *Philosophia academica, quam ex selectissimis Aristotelis et Doctoris subtilis Scoti rationibus ac sententiis . . .*, of which see the 2d ed. 4 tomes in 1 vol. (Paris, 1668) and the 3d ed. 4 tomes in 2 vols. (Toulouse, 1686), and the *Scotus academicus, seu Universa Doctoris subtilis Theologica dogmata, quae ad nitidam et solidam Academiae parisiensis docendi methodum concinnavit . . .*, 4 vols. (Paris, 1672–1677) and 3d ed. (Paris, 1683); the Scotist Peter of Tarentasia (Pope Innocent V), *Innocenti Quinti . . . qui antea Petrus de Tarantasia dicebatur, In IV libros sententiarum commentaria . . .*, 2 vols. [in folio] (Toulouse, 1649–1652); and William of Auvergne, *Guilielmi Alverni, . . . Opera omnia . . .*, 2 vols. [in folio] (Paris, 1674). Some cadaver!

[11] Jean d'Espagne, *Erreurs populaires*, in *Oeuvres*, II, 37.

they shall center all their efforts in him so that their pupils may esteem him as highly as possible."[12] Students of his summae were taught by his example to be bold and rash indeed in formulating objections to their own most essential propositions of belief. Even the Jesuits who opposed (or believed they opposed) Thomas's Dominican followers on issues of grace embraced him on fundamental structures and modes of philosophical theology. In Aquinas, they found a method that they believed had stood the test of time. A question is posed (or a thesis advanced), followed by objections deemed not at all malicious in intent but, above all, logical or factual in character. Against these objections, further objections are posed, generally on behalf of the argument to be supported in the end. Then Aquinas commits himself, often on the basis of authorities logically analyzed, and, to leave no doubts, he replies to objections, modifying or nuancing, if necessary, his own earlier objections to those objections. It was scarcely a model for hiding from antithetical views.

Thus, when Niceron, in the early eighteenth century, paraphrased the reply of the fifteenth-century philosopher Bartolomeo Platina to the accusation that he (Platina) and others had "put the immortality of the soul and the existence of God into dispute," he was sharing a view that embodied the very ethos of the traditional learned world: "that all philosophers and theologians placed the most certain truths into dispute in order to assure themselves of their certainty."[13] Pierre Bayle was in no manner innovative when he declared it a primary responsibility of demonstration "to foresee all the objections of the adversary and to deprive him, as much as possible, of all defensive and offensive arms."[14] If an author did not "anticipate objections [*aller audevant des objections*]," Bayle warned, he would be subject to legitimate attacks by his critics.[15] This was the general rule of the educated. When Malebranche's unfortunate and persecuted defender among the Jesuits, Yves-Marie André, wrote to his hero in anguish, caught between his obligation to teach the philosophy favored by the order in which he had taken his vows and his commitment to a Malebranchist philosophy that the Jesuits had condemned, Malebranche reminded him of the latitude of intellectual life:

> I believe nonetheless that you could present as clearly as possible the views of the *corps* [the Jesuits] with their best proofs [arguments] and [you could present] the other [Malebranchist] views *in the form of objections*, warning your disciples [students] to yield only to what is evident, without [your] af-

[12] *Ratio Studiorum*, 160.

[13] Niceron et al., *Mémoires*, VIII, 222–23.

[14] Pierre Bayle, *Réponse aux questions d'un provincial*, in *Oeuvres diverses* . . . [henceforth, *OD*], 4 vols. (The Hague, 1727[–1731]), III, pt. 2, 526.

[15] Bayle, *OD*, III, pt. 2, 631.

firming anything too positively. To expose them to the opinions of others, although false, is not to deceive them; to the contrary, it is to incite them to use their mind in order to recognize the most true [opinions].[16]

It was understood, thus, that in a demonstration of the existence of God one would share the atheist's objections or if necessary create them, since such a confrontation was entailed by the very ethic and methodology of the educated. It was precisely this that a pious critic of Scholasticism, such as Adam Tribbechou, held against the tradition: the Aristotelian doctors put everything into doubt with their "*Dubitationum et Disputationum*," "even the existence of God."[17] For most members of the learned world, however, this was a virtue. The priest Claude Fleury's very popular *Catéchisme historique* (1683), published with an approbation by Bossuet himself, argued that if anyone who had studied formally were an atheist, he would have to be someone who *only* read the "objections," ignoring "the proofs." Further, Fleury insisted, those who in the name of "faith" denounced serious analysis of such matters offered "merely vain pretexts by which to excuse ignorance and laziness." "The true religion," he assured his readers, "does not fear being known; it teaches nothing that cannot support itself under the brightest light of day."[18] The Capuchin theologian Grégoire de Lyons, whose *Nouveau catéchisme théologique* enjoyed four editions by 1698, explained that while positive theology, deriving all of its truths from God's revealed Word, was taught and accepted without argument, Scholastic theology was "necessary in the Church . . . to confirm the faithful in the belief of the truths of our religion." It "put in order all the questions which are treated, *or which can be framed* on the different matters of which one speaks in theology."[19] Jean Le Clerc was a philosophical and theological adversary of Pierre Bayle's, but he warned the latter's critics not to cast suspicion on Bayle for the force of his "objections" and reminded them of the appropriateness of Bayle's activity:

One must take the difficulties that he proposes for those objections that it is permitted to make in an auditorium of Theology and of Philosophy, where

16 Malebranche to Y.-M. André, S.J., in Malebranche, *Oeuvres complètes*, XIX, 797.

17 Adam Tribbechou, *De Doctoribus Scholasticis, et corrupta per eos divinarum humanarumque rerum scientia*, 2d ed. (Jena, 1719), 129–38.

18 Fleury, *Catéchisme historique*, I, 3–6. Shortly after this (I, 16–19), he explained that "the method and style of scholastic theology" was "wholly appropriate" to anyone who studied logic, philosophy, or theology but would not be understood by "a merchant or an *homme d'affaires* who has not been to a collège"; the latter, he warned, "will form only a confused idea from a discourse that regards God and religion."

19 Grégoire de Lyons, O.F.M., Capuchin, *Le nouveau catéchisme théologique, qui donne brièvement et d'une manière particulière les définitions, & l'explication des principales dificultés dont on traite en théologie*, new [4th] ed. (Lyon, 1698), 1–5.

the more [strongly] one advances a difficulty, the more [the difficulty] honors those who can resolve it [*où plus on pousse une difficulté, plus elle fait honneur à ceux qui la peuvent résoudre*]. It is a justice that he [Bayle] has the right to demand from his readers, and that cannot be refused him.[20]

In 1690, Charles Gobinet, priest, theologian, doctor of theology from the Sorbonne, and principal of the collège du Plessis-Sorbonne, wrote an "Instruction" on "the manner of studying well." He acknowledged that "simple [religious] belief suffices [for] simple and ignorant persons," but he insisted that "it is not the same for the learned." "It is not enough for a student to know and to believe that there is a God who created heaven and earth," Gobinet wrote; "He must know all these truths more distinctly in order to understand them well and in order to explain them to others who are in need." When he examined theology as a science, he listed among its primary tasks that of "responding to the difficulties that can be proposed against it." He traced the development of theology from Saint Augustine to Saint Thomas, seeing Aquinas as the author of "what is most solid in the theology that is taught today in the Schools." Such a theology, he observed, was essential to the Church, not only because it could "combat [errors] when they are advanced," but because it could "anticipate errors." Positive theology examined the revealed Word of God, but Scholastic theology alone could reach those who did not accept that Word, and who needed to be led "by reasoning and the precepts of dialectic." This Scholasticism, he averred, had added "order and method" to theology, and criticism of its "superfluous questions" ignored the issue of its rightness and truth. It needed its exercises in logic not to dispute the Word of God, but to provide the Christian world with rules of reasoning that made it able to demonstrate its truth.[21]

Thus, as the Jesuit de Fénis explained in the context of Catholic-Protestant debate, training in Scholastic disputation left its beneficiary strongly armed against error. The "ignorant people" might be overwhelmed by objections, but "I challenge you to propose these objections in our schools of theology, and you will see that the students who sit on our benches will silence all your doctors."[22] If that confidence was the fruit of training in the dialectic of objections and replies, then who had a right to complain of it? Most Huguenots, products of the same education in what they all took to be Aristotelian dialectic, would have agreed with

[20] Jean Le Clerc, *Parrhasiana, ou Pensées diverses sur des matières de critique* . . . , 2 vols. (Amsterdam, 1699–1701), I, 301–3.

[21] Charles Gobinet, *Instruction sur la manière de bien étudier* (Paris, 1690), 153–59, 236–47.

[22] J.-L. de Fénis, S.J., *Traité de la présence réelle du corps de Jesus-Christ dans l'eucharistie* (Paris, 1683), 56–57.

the general attitude toward anticipation of "objections" to even the most fundamental propositions of belief. As Isaac Papin noted, before his conversion to Catholicism, in a work otherwise quite critical of the place given to logical exercise and *scientia* in Christian education, society did need *some* thinkers, at least, who spent their time in the "exercise" of their intelligence, so that "the more simple and less instructed" could be reassured about the existence of God and of rewards and punishments. The certitude of such necessary thinkers would gain its solidity from "the examination of all the difficulties that can be formed against the truths of religion and of all the responses to these difficulties."[23] Writing to a Catholic correspondent about the work of another Huguenot theologian, Isaac Jacquelot's demonstration of the existence of God, Pierre Bayle criticized it specifically because "he does not propose the objections with all the strength that the libertines could put in them."[24]

. . .

Twelve years before, Bayle had praised a demonstration of the existence of God and of the truth of Christianity precisely *for* the strength with which it had objected to its own propositions, noting, in its favor, that it pursued unbelievers unto their "final fortifications" and never "weakened" the real force of their "objections."[25] This book, despite its having been written by a Huguenot theologian, Jacques Abbadie, was, in fact, of all works examining objections to theistic and Christian belief, the best received in early-modern Catholic France. Its praise from Catholic theologians was remarkable for the time and makes it of great utility to the historian, since it obviously was a work that simply read "right" to most early-modern French minds and embodied the ways in which the skillful, persuasive apologist was supposed to think. First published in 1684, Abbadie's *Traité de la vérité de la religion chrétienne* enjoyed seven editions in French (most with several printings) by 1729. Reviewing the second edition of 1688, the Huguenot *Histoire des Ouvrages des Savans* noted with astonishment and pride that "this work has had so much applause in the world and has been so well received even by the Catholics, despite their distrust of everything that comes from the hands of those whom they call heretics, that nothing could be more useful than to make a new edition of it."[26] The Catholic *Mémoires pour servir à l'histoire des hommes illustres dans la République des Lettres* termed it "one of the best works

[23] Isaac Papin, *La vanité des sciences ou réfléxions d'un philosophe chrétien sur le véritable bonheur* (Amsterdam, 1688), 94–95, 125–27.

[24] Bayle to the abbé Du Bos, December 1696, in *OD*, IV, 725–26.

[25] *Nouvelles de la République des Lettres*, nov. 1684, 399–410.

[26] *Histoire des Ouvrages des Savans*, jan. 1688, 38–39.

that has been written on this subject."[27] In his letters, published in 1697, Bussy-Rabutin spoke of it many times, calling it "the only book to be read to the world," "a divine book . . . [that] compels my reason not to doubt," "the most divine of all books"; he noted that some people were certain that Jesus Christ would never let Abbadie die a Protestant, and that "it seems that the Holy Spirit dictated his thoughts and his proofs."[28] The Catholic author of the preface to Louis Ferrand's apologetic works noted that "Abbadie . . . the Protestant . . . succeeded better than all the others in this sort of combat [of defending God against His enemies]."[29] The Capuchin theologian and educator Anaclet du Havre recommended to his students only two non-Catholic writers on the existence of God: Cicero and "the Protestant Abbadie."[30] Jean Denyse, professor of philosophy at the collège de Montaigu at the University of Paris, commented, in the preface to his own major apologetic work, that while everyone said that nothing could be added to Abbadie, he, Denyse, did things a little bit differently, he was briefer than Abbadie, and it was not true that *everyone* in France had read the Huguenot. He conceded, however, that Abbadie already had used the most convincing demonstrations available in natural theology.[31] Denyse's colleague, Guillaume Dagoumer, in his course on metaphysics at the University of Paris, cited Abbadie favorably to his students as a source of philosophical demonstration of the existence of God.[32] In 1725, a bookseller was arrested for distributing suspicious books, including one by a Protestant author, but was released upon report by Catholic examiners that none of the books was dangerous. The priest Levillier, a Parisian curé, informed the police that the Protestant work, Abbadie's *Traité*, was "in everyone's hands," and that "it establishes so well the existence and truth of religion in general, that whatever he says favorable to his [Protestant] camp cannot cause any prejudice in the mind of its readers."[33]

Here, then, is a work reprinted throughout the early-modern period, extraordinarily popular among Catholics and Protestants alike, and deeply admired for its intellectual manner. Here, also, given the learned culture it expressed, is a work in which one met the atheism of the "ob-

[27] Niceron et al., *Mémoires*, XXXIII, 381ff.

[28] Roger de Rabutin, comte de Bussy, *Les lettres de Messire Roger de Rabutin comte de Bussy*, 4 vols. (Paris, 1697), II, 206, 209–10, 214–15.

[29] In the unpaginated "Préface" to Ferrand, *De la connaissance de Dieu*, [i–ii].

[30] Anaclet du Havre, O.F.M., Capuchin, *Théologie positive*, I, pt. 3, 48–49.

[31] Denyse, *La vérité de la religion*, "Préface," [xxxvi–lxvi].

[32] Guillaume Dagoumer, *Philosophia ad usum scholae accommodata*. 4 vols. (Paris, 1702–1703), III (*Metaphysica*), 215–16. Dagoumer's *Philosophia* also was published in 4 vols. in Lyon, 1702–1703. It enjoyed a 3d ed., 6 vols. (Lyon, 1757), which also was published in Dresden and Leipzig.

[33] *Archives de la Bastille*, XIII, 513–16.

jector" in full force. As Abbadie himself informed his readers, one of his primary goals was "to consider separately the most prominent [*apparentes*] objections of the atheists," even though, as he also informed them, there were only atheists "by their heart," "there could not be any who were [atheists] by their mind," and there was a belief in the existence of God that was universal to mankind, whatever changes in society and education had occurred or might occur.[34]

What, then, was this intellectual atheism without intellectual atheists? How, for example, would it deal with universal consent? First, the hypothetical atheist would deny the implication that universal consent proved the truth of the existence of God: "One will say, perhaps, that [belief in the existence of God] is due to the policy of some prince who believed that this opinion would be a restraint to retain his subjects in the obedience due to him." Second, he would claim that such belief was a prejudice rather than a logical inference, since God did not come under the senses: "To reject as a speculation what one does not see and touch forms one of the prejudices of the atheists, who do not believe that there is a God because they do not see Him."[35]

For Abbadie, however, universal consent was less a proof in itself than a consequence of the force of all proofs of God. What would the atheist object to these proofs? Foremost, for Abbadie, there was the proof from the design, the marvels, and the purposes of nature. To this, Abbadie's atheist would pose two "difficulties." First, he would charge the theist with examining only the evidence that supported the proof, ignoring, for example, rain wasted on uninhabited deserts, flies and other noxious insects, parasites, and pests, and he would ask why "the lack of order and wisdom that we find in several other parts of the Universe" does not lead to "a wholly contrary conclusion?" Second, he would claim that we had inadequate knowledge to conclude that something could not be attributed to the operations of natural forces and therefore required attribution to God: "that we do not know the admirable manner in which the production of natural things occurs, and that if these mysteries of Nature were well understood, we perhaps would find nothing in them that constrained us to recognize a First Cause."[36]

Next, there was the proof from the very existence of matter and of motion, neither of which could be self-caused, and from the fact that matter moved specifically in ways that allowed for the existence of this ordered world and of life within it. The atheist would object to this by means of three arguments. First, he would argue that the eternal being of

[34] Jacques Abbadie, *Traité de la vérité de la religion chrétienne*, 2 vols. (Rotterdam, 1684), I, "Préface," 5, 11–14, 131–47.

[35] Ibid., 14–21.

[36] Ibid., 28–32.

matter posed no problem, since "every being is determined to exist by the very fact that it is a being." Second, he would argue that "it is essential to [of the essence of] matter to be in motion of itself [*de se mouvoir*]." Third, he would argue that the particular products of eternal matter essentially in motion were the effects of "chance [*le hazard*]." Even thought itself would be explained by the atheist in terms of matter in motion, for he would attribute wisdom and intelligence to a particular arrangement of matter from which they "emerge [*sortent*]," one of the outcomes of matter in motion "diversified in an infinity of varieties."[37]

Next, there was the proof of God from the need for a first cause, given the impossibility of infinite regress. Here, even "if the atheist is obliged to say that he derives his birth from his father, and the latter from another," he will argue to the theist that "he who recognizes the existence of God must also think in a similar manner, that God existed a thousand centuries before the creation of the world, and a million centuries before these thousand, all the way to infinity." To the argument that since natural history taught us that men have not always inhabited the world, and must have God as their first cause, the atheist would "say with some that man was formed from the clay of Egypt heated by the rays of the sun, or with several others that he emerged from the sea," in short, that "secondary," natural causes sufficed to account for our presence.[38]

Finally, there was a more ad hominem appeal to human experience as a proof of God, a consideration of our human nature, the adaptation of our minds and bodies to our needs, our ineffable desires for the good and sacred, all evidence of a design beyond the capacity of mere nature, of a design that made us "the chef d'oeuvre of the visible creatures." Abbadie's atheist would be unmoved by this, replying "that he [man] is only a point beside these immense spaces that surround him and that he is the center of infirmities and maladies . . . that he is the plaything of storms and tempests, the prey of animals stronger than he; that his life is in the hands of an insect and grubworm."[39]

In addition to objecting to universal consent and particular proofs, Abbadie's atheist would propose an independent set of "principal difficulties" to the theist. First, he would argue that God cannot be seen and thus cannot be known, from which it follows that "it is impossible to understand what this Supreme Being is," a being conceived so differently by different minds that it is a case of "different turns of imagination." Next, the atheist would argue that a real idea of God would either be innate or acquired by the senses, but that in fact it could be neither, since it de-

[37] Ibid., 33–38, 48–51, 66–70.
[38] Ibid., 74–76, 91–92.
[39] Ibid., 105–10.

pended upon education and was acknowledged by theists themselves to refer to a being "above" the sensible world. The atheist would claim, further, that in addition to being incomprehensible, "the idea of this Supreme Being contains a thousand contradictions [such as omnipresence and transcendence, infinity and particularity] and destroys itself as a consequence." Finally, the atheist would claim that everything which the theist attempts to assign to God could be assigned simply to "the Universe itself."[40]

These "principal difficulties," however, did not exhaust the atheist's arsenal, and there were a set of "several small objections" that also required response. We have heard some of them before, but it is the sheer cumulative energy of Abbadie's hypothetical atheist in this theologically beloved best-seller that is, among other things, so striking, so let us not pause. The atheist argued that if a God who answered prayer existed, He would be involved necessarily in contradictions; that if a God who was the sovereign good existed, there could be no evil, which, nonetheless, there was; that if a God who was omniscient existed, He would know the last number, which contradicted the ability to add to any number. Finally, among these "small objections," the atheist would deny all claims of evident providence, unpersuaded by the theist's citation of the "economy" of man's moral nature: "The atheists, on the contrary, try to establish their sentiment by means of the disorder of thoughts and passions and by means of the crimes that God permits men to commit." For the atheist, God would lack either the will or the desire to prevent evil, but either lack would contradict His putative perfection.[41]

. . .

Most of these arguments, above all the general and "principal" ones, and the objection from evil, were offered a generation later by the atheistic manuscripts that have so captured the attention of historians of atheistic thought. The temptation has been to consider many of them daring and original formulations capable of startling the orthodox mind. In fact, the classicist or medievalist will see at once, some of these arguments originated in Greek thought, and some in the commonplace "objections" of the Scholastic summae. Others, we shall see, arose in prior surveys—classical, patristic, and early-modern—of "atheistic" thought. Others, Abbadie himself informed his readers, arose from the implications of some contemporary philosophy. Their widest and most influential circulation in the early-modern period, then, was certainly *not* in the later clandestine

[40] Ibid., 117–24.
[41] Ibid., 124–31.

manuscripts, but precisely in immensely popular and well-received works by theologians such as Abbadie.

. . .

Abbadie himself, and virtually all of his readers, were certain that his "replies" to these objections and difficulties were decisive and compelling. The critical element in our longer tale, then, will not be the generation of atheistic theses, which abounded, but the development of the possibility of seeing these as stronger than the replies to them. First, however, it is important fully to understand how ubiquitous these atheistic theses indeed were in the theistic learned world. Cicero's Stoic Balbus might have believed that "the habit of arguing against the gods is a wicked and evil practice, whether done in sincerity or feigned [*sive ex animo id fit sive simulate*],"[42] but learned Christendom found this custom essential and useful to its quest for understanding and solidity. Such objections, of course, had to receive replies. Bossuet rebuked Richard Simon for simply explicating Socinian views, noting that "under this pretext one would be obliged only to treat all the arguments of the atheists . . . without making any response."[43] Further, it would raise eyebrows, we have seen, if the replies to the objections were perceived as not sufficiently compelling. Mathieu Marais recalled in his diary that the abbé Houtteville would be "forever reproached for having assembled, at the end of his book, twelve very strong objections against religion to which he does not oppose adequately strong replies," and Marais termed it "very dangerous to give to the public these objections heaped up in one and the same place, even if one did reply well." "Did he believe," Marais asked, "that he could do better than Abbadie?"[44] More than a century after his death, Vanini was still being denounced as someone who had written "a book designed to refute [atheistic] sentiments, but in which while he feigns combating them with all his strength, he gives them a victory in some manner by the weakness of his replies."[45] Nonetheless, an author was expected not only *not* to hide such objections from his readers, but indeed to forewarn them clearly about them. As was noted in 1706 by the editor who, with ecclesiastical approval, *strengthened* the atheistic objections in Louis Ferrand's defense of belief in God, "The good cause suffers when one allows one's adversaries to fancy [*se figurer*] that one dissimulates or that one fears

[42] Cicero, *La Nature des Dieux* [Olivet ed. of 1721], II, 186.

[43] Bossuet, *Oeuvres*, I, 518.

[44] Mathieu Marais, *Journal et mémoires de Mathieu Marais, avocat au parlement de Paris, sur la régence et le règne de Louis* XV . . . , ed. De Lescure, 4 vols. (Paris, 1863–1868), II, 244.

[45] Niceron et al., *Mémoires*, XXVI, 374–75.

their objections; . . . nothing is more capable of reassuring the faithful than knowledge of the errors against which one arms them." The alternative, he noted, was the awful danger of being caught unawares; by contrast, "it is easy to avoid a trap when one foresees it."[46]

This view, and its relationship in the minds of those who held it to the whole question of atheism, was clearly expressed in Sforza Cardinal Pallavicino's defense of the Scholastic adherence to Aristotelian method. In his popular history of the Council of Trent, Paolo Sarpi had remarked that many had hoped for a condemnation of "the subtlety of the scholastics, *who put everything into dispute* and ordinarily were attached to questions of philosophy." He himself described "the Scholastics" as "positing the philosophy of Aristotle as the foundation of Christian doctrine . . . ; and turning everything into a problem, *going so far as to dispute if there is a God*."[47] Pallavicino defended the Council against Sarpi. He was particularly outraged by Sarpi's charge that, in Pallavicino's paraphrase, "the scholastics . . . called everything into question [*ont . . . revoqué tout en doûte*], even to the point of questioning if there is a God and discussing the pros and the cons [*jusqu'à mettre en question s'il y a un Dieu, et discuter le pour et le contre*]." The cardinal replied, on the whole, for a post-Tridentine Church that reaffirmed its deep affinity with the ways of thinking that it associated with Aristotle, Albertus Magnus, Thomas Aquinas, Duns Scotus, and the centuries of Scholastic education of which it was itself the heir. "In truth," he responded, "it is the duty of the theologian to destroy objections that are drawn from philosophy to devise arguments against religion." There could be nothing to fear from such a role, since "against truth there are no demonstrations that can stand." Sarpi, Pallavicino assured his readers, misunderstood the function of Scholastic exercise: "They do not [really] put the existence of God into doubt, as Sarpi stupidly accuses them of doing; if they put it into doubt, it is in discussion, since it is necessary to put into doubt all propositions which are not evident by themselves and from the relationship of the terms that express them." For Pallavicino, our intelligence was "narrow and lazy," and if it accepted a conclusion on the basis of what it took to be indubitable propositions, it was likely to reject the conclusion and not merely the propositions if someone succeeded in making the latter dubious. The logical exercises of the Scholastics prevented this:

> Thus, it is very usefully that the scholastics, and, at their head, Saint Thomas, discuss all sorts of questions with so much care, *and above all, that which is the foundation of all religion, if there is a God*; which, although it appears

[46] Ferrand, *De la connaissance de Dieu*, "Préface," [vii].

[47] Fra Paolo Sarpi, *Histoire du Concile de Trente*, trans. A. N. Amelot de Houssaye, 3d ed. (Amsterdam, 1704), 172.

> superfluous from the perspective of the topic, which in itself is very certain, nevertheless because of the weight of our imagination, which with difficulty disengages itself from matter, and because of the dissipation of our passions, which do not want there to be an observer of those monstrous acts from which they do not want to abstain, is perhaps as necessary as it seems derisory to Sarpi; and may it please God that it is not necessary particularly for him.[48]

The great early-modern discussions of atheism, then, not only gave voice to and disseminated the objections of "the atheist," but, in so doing, honored the most venerated traditions of the learned world. It was in no way surprising for Charron to advise his readers: "Let us now hear the atheists speak; and let us see their objections, which are . . . propositions of the errors, absurdities, contradictions, and ill consequences that they want to derive and infer from the establishment of the Deity." Seeking these objections, Charron went no farther than arguments commonly assigned to the ancients. It was Sextus Empiricus who urged, in Charron's *Trois véritez*, that there could be no immaterial Supreme Being who would be "alive," life depending on senses and physical faculties, and that there could be no infinite being capable of acting in one place and then another, infinity and movement being incompatible. It was Euripides and Pliny who argued in Charron that there could be no omnipotent being, since nothing could make fire cold, snow black, or two tens equal to anything but twenty. It was Epicurus who voiced the view in Charron that there could be no supremely good, wise, and great being, given the uselessness, harmfulness, and vileness of so much of the universe.[49]

In 1641, André d'Abillon's *Divinité défendue contre les athées* noted that demonstrations of God's existence carried the utmost evidence and certainty, and that there were a great "host" of them, of which he would propose nine "that seem to me to have the most weight." Nonetheless, its author, a priest and doctor of theology, understood his obligation to give full voice to the adversary: "I will never flatter my own side, giving [rather] all the strength possible to the imaginary arguments of the atheists. I will omit no arrow that they could let fly against the source of light [*Je n'ometray aucun trait qu'ils puissent décocher contre le soleil*], so that they do not believe that they have been [badly] armed in order for us to fight them."[50]

[48] Sforza Cardinal Pallavicino, *Histoire du Concile de Trente* . . . , ed. abbé Migne, 3 vols. (Montrouge, 1844–1845), II, 196–201. Pallavicino's history was published in Rome, 1656–1657, but the learned world in France would have read the edition published as *Vera Concilii Tridentini historia contra falsem Petre Suavis Polani [Paolo Sarpi] narrationem scripta*, 3 pts. (Antwerp, 1673).

[49] Charron, *Trois véritez*, in *Oeuvres*, II, 41–46.

[50] D'Abillon, *La divinité défendue*, 38–44.

To d'Abillon's first proof, from the possibility of a necessary being to the actual necessity of such a being, the "atheist" objected that it was logically impossible to move from the possible to the actual; that the notion of a "self-caused being" was self-contradictory, since such an entity would have had to exist before it existed; and, finally, that the argument presupposed what it sought to prove, a necessary being. To d'Abillon's second proof, from universal consent, the atheist replied (long before Bayle) both that such a criterion would have established polytheism in the ancient world and that it arbitrarily presupposed the impossibility of universal error. To d'Abillon's third proof, from the contingency of the creatures to the necessity of their First Cause, the atheist argued that natural causes account for natural effects, and that the putative contingent "mass" ["*gros*," meaning here, "whole"] of all beings was "imaginary," since each particular being was always caused by a preceding particular being, and, thus, "infinite regress in causes and principles is not impossible."[51]

D'Abillon offered no formal atheistic objections to his fourth and fifth proofs, which he believed were compelling from ordinary human experience, namely, "from the beautiful order and admirable rapport in so great a diversity of creatures," and "from miracles." Nonetheless, he shared the atheist's perspective on such proofs: the atheist would have to attribute order, with Democritus and Epicurus, to "a fortuitous meeting of atoms," and he would have to deny the testimony of all witnesses to miracles, declaring the alleged events to be "fables" and "inventions." Against his sixth proof, equally drawn from "experience," but, in this instance, "of the existence of spirits, demons, magicians, witches, and the demonically possessed," the atheist denied the reality of spirits, asserting that "all things are corporeal, and of the same nature as those which fall under our senses." Against his seventh proof, based on the reality of "prophecy," the atheist again denied the factual basis of the evidence, seeing all prophecies as tales designed to fool the simple and the innocent.[52]

D'Abillon's final proofs, his eighth and ninth, were more ad hominem. The eighth argued that conscience and morals proved the existence of God, and the ninth averred that all certainty in all sciences depended upon the existence of God, since nothing could be better known than that. To the eighth, the atheist objected that the social consequences of disbelief were not a proof, that mankind was protected by human laws and punishments, and that conscience was a human phenomenon not dependent on belief in or the existence of God. To the ninth, the atheist did not reply.[53]

[51] Ibid., 51–59, 68–84, 95–113.

[52] Ibid., 134–40, 206–11, 221–44, 278–86.

[53] Ibid., 290–305.

D'Abillon's atheist was not finished, however. Having replied to most of d'Abillon's proofs, the disbeliever was now free to advance five of his own general arguments against belief in God. D'Abillon accepted his responsibility to advance these boldly: "I shall give them all the force and all the coloration that they could borrow from the cunning and the temerity of a sophist." He began with what he offered as "the first and strongest opposition that the atheists formulate," an objection so powerful that it "seems at first glance to be without reply": "If there were a God in the universe, there would be a providence; now, *if a sovereign providence governed this world, there would not be such manifest disorders in it*." Long before a Meslier formulated an atheism grounded in, among other things, the claim that the suffering of the poor and innocent was incompatible with the existence of a God, d'Abillon's hypothetical atheist made the same claim in a widely circulated work published with imprimatur to general approval. If there were a God, the wicked

> would not be prosperous in abundance, at the highest enjoyment of glory, while at the same time virtuous persons sigh in the midst of contempt, in poverty and in sufferings. . . . An innocent laborer and a poor artisan, whose lives are without stain, would not be constrained to earn their livelihood by the sweat of their brow, while a vicious prince bathes in an ocean of delights. In a word, if there were some divinity in the world, it would dispense its favors more liberally on virtuous persons, and would hurl thunderbolts on criminal heads, and would dispense happiness and misfortune, punishment and rewards with more justice.

In brief, the atheist would object "that all things in this world succeed as if there were no divinity. . . . Thus, . . . there is not a general providence that governs all the world."[54]

Second, d'Abillon's atheist would formulate an objection that had the most influence on "the simple people," in d'Abillon's view, since it was based on an appeal to sense experience. Failing to distinguish between God's works, which are sensible, and God Himself, who is known "mediately" as cause "in the effects that He produces," the theoretical objector to theism, before Hobbes and long before the Enlightenment materialists, would argue that we could not have any knowledge of God, since "Everything that we see in the world . . . is made and composed of matter: everything which falls under our senses is either a simple body . . . or a mixed body. . . . but we do not see spirits; God and angels do not fall under our senses."[55]

[54] Ibid., 315–16 ["*Je leur donneray toute la force, et toute la couleur, qu'elle peuvent emprunter des ruses, et de la témérité d'un sophiste*"], 317–47.

[55] Ibid., 348–60.

Third, in an objection that d'Abillon specifically identified as "borrowed" from Aquinas's objections, the atheist would urge the principle of parsimony, the sufficiency of natural causes to account for natural effects, deriding theism as the unnecessary multiplication of causes. Long before Diderot, d'Abillon's atheist averred:

> Only a bad philosopher would multiply beings without necessity. It is useless to utilize several things where the use of a lesser number would suffice. And given that all the effects that we see in nature, however high and difficult, can be attributed to natural and sensible causes, what need is there of saying that there is a spiritual, sovereign, and necessary Being, except to augment the number of beings, without being constrained to this by any necessity.

The atheist would argue, in effect, that "all the productions which fall under our experience can be referred sufficiently to two principles: . . . to the artifice . . . of reason; or . . . to nature." "Let nature act," the atheist would conclude, "since it suffices to produce all the operations that we admire in the world."[56]

While the fifth objection related solely to Christianity and its mysteries, and was directed simply against the particular Christian idea of God, the fourth was general, and, again, "borrowed" from Aquinas (and, d'Abillon noted, Augustine). It argued that there was an incompatibility between the evil that we knew to be real in the world and a God defined as infinitely good: "If there is a God . . . there is an infinite goodness; now, if there is a goodness without limits, it follows that there is not any evil in the world, because an infinite opposite [the infinite goodness of God] will entirely destroy the contrary that is opposed to it."[57]

In Derodon's *L'athéisme convaincu*, first published in 1659 and reprinted in 1665 in *La lumière de la raison*, God was only proven conclusively, in the author's view, by the argument that the world and all its phenomena could not be "from all eternity," and that since nothing could produce itself, the world must have been created by a transcendent, eternal being, which is what we mean by God. Derodon allowed the atheist nine objections to this proof and claimed that he had heard these with his own ears. Although he denounced the sources of these objections as "atheists," he did specify that he included in that category "certain very dangerous minds who profess to be [philosophical] skeptics and pretend to doubt all things, so that they can be able thus to discourse doubtfully of the Divinity."[58]

Since one of the central issues in Derodon's proof was a particularly

[56] Ibid., 361–75.
[57] Ibid., 375–79.
[58] Derodon, *L'athéisme*, 3–22, 148–49.

thorny Scholastic question—the categories to which the argument from the impossibility of infinite regress did or did not apply—Derodon's "atheist" was given some subtle arguments to advance. The first urged "that successive things could have been from all eternity collectively, and not distributively." While all particular entities necessarily had a beginning, the atheist argued, "taken together" as the "collectivity" of all entities, sequences, and generations, there was no contradiction in their being "from all eternity." Derodon, in fact, conceded that the objection might be true of "possible" beings but denied that it could apply to "actual" beings. Second, the atheist objected that if there could be no *past* eternity because of the impossibility of an infinite sequence of real beings, then there could be no *future* eternity, which the theist, and particularly the Christian, nonetheless believed possible, indeed certain. Third, the atheist would deny that he had to accept a "formal infinity" of beings to accept the eternity of the world, arguing that his hypothesis of the eternity of the world entailed merely an indefinite infinity, a collectivity of men and days that "cannot be numbered."[59]

If the theist argued that much in the world that we observed bore the marks of relative newness, the atheist could continue to maintain objections based on the eternity of the world. He could argue, fourth, "that the world has not been from all eternity in the state that it is in at present." He could argue, fifth, "that there has been from all eternity a matter without form." Indeed, the ancient atomists believed this, Derodon noted, convinced that "it was this matter, to wit, the atoms, which with time, by a fortuitous concourse, composed the world in the state it presently has." He could argue, sixth and seventh, that even if men have not always existed, they could have been the product of purely natural causes, and composed of "eternal" elements, and "it would not follow that they had been produced by some superior and divine cause." Indeed, the atheist could speculate, eighth, that it was just as likely that the world was "produced from the matter of an other world which previously had been, and that this other world had been produced from the matter of another world which was before it, and so on, consecutively," in some endless cycle. Finally, the atheist would argue that whatever is theoretically possible cannot be appealed to as a logical self-contradiction, and that Christians would have to limit the omnipotence of their God to deny Him the power of creating an eternal world; if such a world were possible, however, then the whole proof from the impossibility of an eternal world collapses:

> Christians admit that God could have created the world from all eternity, although they believe that he created it only in the course of time. Now it is

[59] Ibid., 23[mispaginated as "32"]–24, 52–54, 59–62. His discussion of a "possible" world without sequence and this "real" world occurs on 32–39.

a wholly true axiom that *posito possibili nihil sequitur absurdi*, that is to say, that if one actually posits a possible thing, no absurdity follows from it. And given thus that the world could have been from all eternity, there is no ill consequence or contradiction in positing that it actually is from all eternity.[60]

Bear in mind the constant here: these are the theologians explaining such views to an ever-larger audience!

• • •

In the fifth volume of his published *Cursus philosophicus* (1671), a course on peripatetic (Aristotelian) metaphysics, Jean Vincent, priest, member of the Congregation of Christian Doctrine, and professor of philosophy at the University of Toulouse, demonstrated the existence of God by standard Thomistic arguments and then made certain that his students were familiar with all of the major objections to these. Some of the most eminent Catholic theologians and philosophers, he noted, denied the principle on which Saint Thomas's proofs seemed to stand, that "whatever is moved is moved by something else," claiming that Christians certainly would not admit that this was true of spirits. Some denied the principle that what was true of the parts (the impossibility of their eternity) was necessarily true of the whole. Some denied that contingency entailed dependence. Some denied that the higher was necessarily the cause of the lower. Some denied that a perfect being could be inferred from the imperfections of the world. Some turned Aristotle against Thomas, arguing that since the Stagirite's notion of certainty depended upon knowledge of effects from their causes, there could be no certainty in our knowledge of a God admittedly known only from His effects. Some turned Thomas against himself (it was Aquinas, however, who had posed the same objection), arguing that if, as Thomas reasoned, it were true both that God's essence and existence were identical and that we could not know God's essence, then it followed that we could not know God's existence. Vincent conceded that some medieval doctors had concluded that God could not be proven, but referred his students to Thomas's condemnation of these. Whoever denied these "Aristotelian" proofs, Vincent himself concluded, did not necessarily err in faith, but certainly erred in physics and metaphysics.[61]

François Feu, priest, curé of Saint Gervais, and doctor of theology from

[60] Ibid., 93–94, 104–5, 109–10, 114–19, 119–20, 123–25. The concluding quotation is from 123–25.

[61] Jean Vincent, Doctrinaire, *Cursus philosophicus, in quo totius scholae quaestiones fere omnes, aequâ perspicuitate, ac doctrinâ, in utramque partem propugnantur*, 5 vols. (Toulouse, 1658–1671), v (*Complectens Metaphysicam*), 599–619.

the Sorbonne, in a textbook written for doctoral candidates in theology, his *Theologici Tractatus* (1692–1695), received great praise from his superiors, specifically from Claude Gallio, "moderator" of the Faculty of Theology at Paris, for his efforts "against atheists and idolators."[62] As part of that effort, he sought to arm his students against all of the atheists' arguments (despite his proclamation that atheism was always of the "will," an "*errore practico*," and never of the "intellect," an "*errore speculativo*"). Against the argument from universal consent, Feu's atheist cited the notorious atheists of antiquity (Protagoras, Diagoras, Theodorus, and others) and Scripture's own references to those who did not know God. Feu's atheist shared Vincent's atheist's objection that if God's essence and existence were inseparable, the unknowability of the former entailed the unknowability of the latter. He also shared the objection that if, as Aristotelians (such as Vincent and Feu) believed, all knowledge originated in the senses, it would not be possible to know God either intuitively or by abstraction. Further, even if the atheist granted that God could be known, in theory, from certain effects, he would deny that a God could be inferred from the world we in fact observe. A cause must be proportionate to effects from which it is inferred, the atheist would object, but by the theist's own admission, God and the creatures are infinitely disproportionate. All ideas derived from experience of this world are contingent, he would argue, and how can anything necessary be inferred from the contingent? All sensible knowledge is merely "probable," so how could certain knowledge of an indubitable being be derived? Indeed, the atheist would object, all patristic and Scholastic proofs of the existence of God *presuppose* that the world could not be eternal, begging the question that could leave their proofs without foundation, and *presuppose* that causes are all parts of some collective whole, begging the question of infinite regress. How could the mind possibly find, in "a collection of confused and contingent" beings, evidence of a perfect and necessary God? Attempts to circumvent these problems, such as Augustine's and Anselm's proofs *from* the perfection of God, the atheist would insist, contradict the received Aristotelian theory of knowledge, dependent upon sense experience, and rely on discredited notions of universals.[63]

At the opposite pole of the philosophical spectrum of French Catholicism, the Cartesian Benedictine monk and philosopher François Lamy felt equally obliged, in 1710, to confront not only the actual but also the possible mind of the atheist. "If by atheism," he observed, "one understands only the sentiment of those who could not believe in the existence of

[62] François Feu, *Theologici Tractatus ex Sacris Codicibus, et Sanctorum Patrum Monumentis Excerpti*, 2 vols. (Paris, 1692–1695), I, "Approbations."

[63] Ibid., I, 6–21.

God," then one simple demonstration would suffice to lead them to proper belief: that thought itself requires an immaterial and omnipotent cause. This solution of what he took to be the only real problem of contemporary "atheism," a need for one persuasive proof, was not adequate to the responsibility of the apologist, however, who must deal with all of the atheist's *possible* "objections" and "difficulties" of any weight. Lamy could conceive of four: (1) that there was no reason to posit an unproduced First Being; (2) that "there are only material beings, and matter is necessary and eternal"; (3) that nature itself could be the first cause necessary to physics; and (4) that the educated Chinese, an enlightened group, believed matter to be eternal. He sounded an ominous note by asserting that while Cartesian philosophy in fact could reply efficaciously to these atheistic objections, the Aristotelians would be helpless in the face of them.[64]

The Capuchin Anaclet du Havre, a philosophical eclectic who recommended both Lamy's and Abbadie's work to his students, along with Thomistic, Augustinian, Malebranchist, and fideist texts, published his "conferences" on theology in 1712. The very questions with which he approached the issue of God's existence revealed his commitment to the forms inherited from the *quaestio* and *disputatio*. First, he asked, "*Are we certain that there is a God*? Are there several atheists who have dared to deny His existence, or at least have doubted it? What are the reasons by which one can convince them of the necessary existence of a God? Can one demonstrate it to them by natural reasons?" Second, he explored the thinking of the atheist: "Can one be invincibly ignorant that there is a God?" For Anaclet du Havre, there indeed were atheists such as he had defined, but the answer to the question of invincibility was no. Five proofs, he taught, conclusively demonstrated God's being: the design of the universe; the need for a first cause; the need for a first mover; the need for a cause of thought; and universal consent.[65]

To the latter argument, the Capuchin's model of the atheist objected that belief in God was acquired through education and originated in the policies of princes seeking means of exacting obedience from their subjects. More generally, the atheist argued that one could explain the universe without God, by means of a vast extended matter arranged by motion.[66]

Turning to specific formal demonstrations, his atheist raised the standard objections. He denied that "a progression to infinity" entailed any contradiction; denied that we had any precise idea of God; claimed that

[64] F. Lamy, O.S.B., *L'incrédule*, 78–88.

[65] Anaclet du Havre, O.F.M., Capuchin, *Théologie positive*, I, pt. 3, 48–49; II, pt. 1, 1–7.

[66] Ibid., II, pt. 1, 5; I, pt. 3, 59.

the concept of God was inherently self-contradictory, His putative attributes being mutually exclusive; claimed that the existence of evil disproved the existence of any supreme goodness; raised the problem of "omniscience" and the "last number"; and claimed with Epicurus that given sin and crime, God either could not or would not prevent them, in which case there was either no omnipotence or no sovereign goodness. Anaclet du Havre also raised fideistic objections, attributed to Christian theologians themselves, to the whole notion that God's existence was amenable to demonstration. There was the familiar theoretical problem of the inseparability of God's existence and unknowable essence. More specifically, God could not be known as the effect of any prior cause, since nothing was deemed to precede Him, nor as the cause of observable effects, since there was no proportion between the finite and the infinite one sought to infer. Further, that which transcended the senses could not be known from the senses. If God could not be known from the senses, he could be known only from an innate idea of Him, but there existed peoples who knew of no God, and thus, the idea was not innate.[67]

Even Voltaire, when he turned to metaphysics, retained this method from his Jesuit education. His *Traité de métaphysique* (1734) devoted a chapter to the question of "if there is a God," concluding that the "difficulties" that the atheist could oppose to the theist's system were vastly outweighed by the "absurdities" that the theist could disclose in atheism. Nonetheless, it sought to make the atheist's "objections" clear: the world had to be eternal, since nothing could come from nothing; the idea of creation by a perfect being was self-contradictory, since either creation was necessary (and thus from all eternity and not a creation at all) or it was freely chosen (and thus an immutable being had changed His will); the more we knew, the more we explained in nature by reference to natural laws, not God; and, finally, the destructiveness, suffering, and mutual slaughter of the creatures were incompatible with the existence of a supremely good being. Further, the atheist would claim that even if he accepted that the contingency of the world entailed a necessary being, "the material world" could be that being.[68] From Aquinas to Voltaire, the tradition had been passed on.

Indeed, Aquinas's "objections" to his own demonstrations, themselves derived primarily from patristic accounts of and inferences from Greek philosophy, provided the essential portrait of the hypothetical atheist. It was a portrait offered in the thirteenth century to that small handful of theologians who might encounter the non-Christian world and who stood in need of philosophical rigor to deal with those not graced from

[67] Ibid., I, pt. 3, 60–70.

[68] Voltaire, *Traité de métaphysique* [1734], chap. 2.

birth with possession of the Word of God, and thus in need of natural arguments. Aristotle had taught Aquinas that to succeed in natural argument, one had to anticipate, in their full strength, the objections to one's beliefs. The thirteenth century, confronting the texts and beliefs of a post-classical non-Christian world, wished its theologians to have adequate philosophical armament in dealing with, for example, Islamic doctors not committed to the Trinity or to other essential beliefs of Christianity. In fact, although the "proofs" of God came first in logical sequence, they were not perceived as under real challenge anywhere. The objections of the atheist were almost incidental to the heart of Aquinas's concerns. It was a portrait offered in the seventeenth century, however, to a relatively vast learned world being buffeted by new discoveries, new schools of thought, new debates, and new convergences of intellectual phenomena. In this new age of printed texts, growing literacy, avid readership, and the ongoing influx of nonclerics into the universities, the arguments of the theoretical atheists were explicated to all who passed through higher education, to all who read works of formal theology and philosophy, and to all who read the vulgarizations and popularizations of these.

Recall Aquinas's formulations of the atheist's objections in the *Summa Theologiae*: the incompatibility of evil and the existence of God; and the parsimony of explaining all phenomena by reference to nature alone. How well, indeed, these anticipated the atheistic perspectives that were to come! These formulations in orthodox literature persisted, but Aquinas's context did not: at a structural level, the institutions and the dynamics of the learned world had been profoundly changed, and at an intellectual level, the "problem" of evil and the meaning of naturalism were being transformed in the consciousness of the seventeenth century. In response to his general thesis that God could be proven by natural reason, Aquinas had formulated objections that related to the philosophical epistemology of natural theology: that God was unseen, while man was dependent upon the senses; that God could not be adequately defined, while demonstration depended upon clear definition; that an infinite God could not be inferred from finite effects, since "God and his effects are incommensurable." Again, how correct the anticipation of the forms that atheistic criticism of theistic proof would take! These persisted also in the "objections" of the seventeenth century, but, again, in a different context, and with new debates to intersect. In the *Summa Contra Gentiles*, Aquinas addressed at greater length "the opinion of those who say that the existence of God cannot be demonstrated." These were fideists, not atheists, but their arguments became part of the formal Christian portrait of the atheist. In addition to the objections of the *Summa Theologiae*, the *Summa Contra Gentiles* raised the difficulty of knowing God's existence if it were identical with His unknowable essence; and that of how a being that "transcends all sense and sensibles" could be anything but "indemonstrable."[69] These might be casual objections in the thirteenth century, but in the seventeenth century, we shall see, they took on new meaning.

The obligation to propose objections to its own most sacred beliefs was a salient characteristic of that philosophical and theological tribe descended from the Greeks, from the men deemed Fathers of the Church, and from the medieval doctors. From the first centuries of the Church's intellectual life to the seventeenth century, of course, there were always other Christian voices, many of them, insistent that the commitment to Greek philosophy, and to logic in particular, conflicted with the piety, humility, inspiration, and simple faith that they believed to have been prescribed by Christ and the inspired apostles. Even a rationalist such as Descartes could object to the process, decrying a philosophical (as opposed to a geometrical) tradition "in which each believing that all of his propositions are problematic, few give themselves over to the search for truth; and many even . . . study nothing else but how to fight arrogantly against the most obvious truths."[70] Yet the Church at Trent had reaffirmed its commitment to Scholastic logic and proof, insisting that its defenders be prepared to do rigorous battle with enemies real or possible, and its institutions of learning, expanding rapidly, set loose a dynamic of mental dialectic into the Western world. Jean Denyse, priest and professor, saw only two ways of proving conclusions, including the truths of religion, a task he took to be the obligation of Christian professors in Christian universities: the geometrical method, which he preferred; and the method of "the Schools." The main difference between the two, he thought, was that proponents of the first reasoned from principles taken as axioms or propositions of faith, while proponents of the second believed that they must reason from propositions that were based on "*proofs*" derived from first principles of thought. The latter was a good and rigorous method, he conceded, but it left one too long in uncertainty while awaiting conclusive proofs of the propositions with which one would reason about the faith, and it deliberately produced students who were contentious toward any proposition put to them. It invited the student to be "rather like the adversary than like the disciple" and trained him "to try to support, at whatever cost necessary, the opposite of what one wants to prove to him," and always "[to resist] ceding . . . and being vanquished."[71]

[69] Aquinas, *Summa Contra Gentiles* l.I. c.XII. [vol. XIII of the Nicolai, O.P. ed.].

[70] René Descartes, [Dedication] "To Messieurs the deans and doctors of the Sacred Faculty of Theology of Paris," in *Meditationes de Prima Philosophia in qua Dei existentia et animae immortalitas demonstratur* (Paris, 1641). For the text in an excellent modern edition, see Descartes, *Oeuvres philosophiques*, ed. F. Alquié, 3 vols. (Paris, 1963–1973), II, 387.

[71] Denyse, *La vérité de la religion*, "Préface," [xxviii–xxxvi].

The dominant model of education, then, recognized the theological and philosophical necessity of atheism, and it offered first to its chosen students, then to a vast reading public, a catalog of all of the basic categories, objections, and difficulties of antitheistic thought. Scholastic minds had accepted a breathtaking invitation: "If we have no one else with whom to argue, we must do so with ourselves." One did not have to search for atheistic views in the seventeenth century; they were published with permission and approval.

The atheist of the objections, then, was a heuristic device, a hypothetical mind whose need to be convinced by argument of theistic proofs allowed the establishment beyond even hypothetical doubt of one's natural belief in God. This atheist could be derived from a great diversity of sources and could stand in for oneself and one's students awaiting compelling proof. On questions of providence and, perhaps, other issues as well, he even could be the doubts one encountered alive in one's own mind. He shared one's principles of dialectic and science, and he was generally cooperative or, at least, silent after one replied to him with insistence. He was, as the analysis of his will by Christian authors almost always showed, the worst miscreant among men. He was also, as their inquiries and apologias almost always showed, an indispensable and even intimate intellectual companion. In the course of the seventeenth and early eighteenth centuries, to the astonishment of most, he would come to life and seek converts of his own. From one perspective, the voices of the Christian learned world, seeing his nature primarily in terms of a perverted will, denied his right to share the world with them. From another perspective, we next shall see, they invited him to enter.

Chapter Four

BEFORE BELIEF: PHILOSOPHY AND PREAMBLE

THE OBLIGATION to prove God against the objections of the "atheists" was understood by the learned culture in a diversity of ways, most of which made no explicit claims about the role of demonstration in religious belief. Proof against "atheistic" objections could be an exercise in the science and art of demonstration; a warning to the immoral that nothing could support their enterprise to secure impunity; a self-reassurance, consistent with received philosophies, that there was no conflict between natural light and supernatural faith on this most essential element of Christian theistic belief. Indeed, if these had been the only reasons for such an obligation, the drama of early-modern French theology might have been far different from what in fact it turned out to be. Some, indeed, emphatically understood such a duty only in one or more of those terms. Others, however, as we shall see, framed the issue of overcoming theoretical atheism as if demonstration were a prerequisite, in some way, of educated belief. By making natural "*évidence*" of God's existence in any way *essential* to theistic belief in the minds of many, prominent theological and philosophical voices raised the issue of demonstration and proof to a prominence that made its perceived outcomes far more influential than any mere exercise, warning, or reassurance would be. From some, the message was quite explicit: if we do not persuade you demonstratively, do not believe! It was a message issued, we shall see in subsequent chapters, at the very time when the factions within a divided Christian intellectual world were explaining to one and all why each other's proofs should never persuade![1]

The necessity of proof is not an issue that ever would come to light, however, if one examined only what the Church taught its uninitiated and its children. Let us sample the catechisms from twenty-one diverse early-modern dioceses in the northern half of France (including that from Montpellier, which was authorized for use in Paris).[2] Instructed formally

[1] What the proper role and consequences of natural proof or disproof in fundamental issues of theology *should be* is not, of course, a historical question and does not in any way concern us here. My purpose is simply to analyze what the theological community in the learned world of early-modern France thought about and taught concerning such a matter, so that we later may understand how these conceptions and formulations helped to shape contemporaneous expectations, debates, choices, and behaviors.

[2] The call number of the catechism in the *Imprimés* of the Bibliothèque Nationale is in-

by the Council of Trent of the need for better religious instruction (and informally by the polemics of a Christendom now divided into competing claims of rightful succession to the original Church), French Catholicism sought in the seventeenth century not only to improve the education of its own clergy and teachers, but to catechize the less educated faithful in a proper understanding of the creed. In these catechisms, a rich source for understanding the Church's view of appropriate popular thought, language, and religious teaching, there is generally not a hint of "objections" to be overcome, "difficulties" to be resolved, or "arguments with oneself" to the end of firmer and somehow more rigorous conviction of the existence of God.

The catechisms could be quite open to problems of understanding the divine attributes, perhaps in response to questions students actually raised (e.g., if God *could not* commit sin, how could one say He was omnipotent?).[3] It clearly never occurred to bishops, theologians, and pedagogues, however, that the broad task of popular Christian education was the production of philosophers and dialecticians. The catechisms contained the essential truths of positive theology, and the *fruits* but not the *mode* of Scholastic theology. Their goal, from the obvious perspective of their authors, was not in this instance to form the natural faculties, but

---

dicated in parentheses after each listing here. Angers: *Catéchisme à l'usage du diocèse d'Angers*, 13th ed. (Angers, 1738) (D.88814); Autun: *Catéchisme ou abrégé de la foy et des véritez chrestiennes* (Moulins, 1703) (D.14307); Beauvais: *Catéchisme de la doctrine chrestienne* (Beauvais, 1681) (D.14347); Besançon: *Catéchisme nouveau . . . pour . . . faciliter à aprendre les vérités du christianisme* (Besançon, 1698) (D.14348); Boulogne: *Catéchisme du diocèse de Boulogne* (Boulogne, 1726) (D.28161); Bourges: *Catéchismes ou abrégés de la doctrine chrétienne* (Bourges, 1690) (D. 14370); Cambrai: *Catéchisme ou sommaire de la doctrine chrétienne* (Cambrai, 1692) (D. 28179); Chartres: *Catéchisme du diocèse de Chartres* (Chartres, 1699); Clermont: *Catéchisme de la foy et des moeurs chrétiennes* (Clermont, 1674) (D.28222); Meaux: *Catéchisme du diocèse de Meaux . . .* (Paris, 1701) (D.28529); Metz: *Catéchisme du diocèse de Metz* (Metz, 1701) (D.14397); Montpellier (authorized also for use in Paris): *Catéchismes du diocèse de Montpellier* (Paris, 1703) (D.28559); Orléans: *Catéchisme du diocèse d'Orléans* (Orléans, 1709) (D.28690); Paris: *Catéchisme ou abrégé de la foy et des véritez chrestiennes* (Paris, 1709) (D.14416); Quimper: *Catéchisme françois-breton dressé en faveur des enfans* (Quimper, 1717) (D.28817); Reims: *Catéchisme ou doctrine chrétienne* (Paris, 1692) (D.28824); Rouen: *Catéchisme ou abrégé de la doctrine chrétienne* (Rouen, 1720) (D.28873); Soissons: *Catéchisme ou doctrine chrétienne* (Soisson, 1711) (D.28978); Strasbourg: *Catechismus, oder kurzer Begrif der christlichen Lehr* (Strasbourg, n.d. [1700]) (D.29311); Toul: *Catéchisme du diocèse de Toul* (Toul, 1703) (D.14481); Troyes: *Catéchisme du diocèse de Troyes . . . avec un règlement pour la manière de faire le catéchisme et un abrégé de l'histoire sainte* (Troyes, 1705) (D.14484).

[3] *Reims*, 75–89 (which explained that sin was always an effect of impotence). *Clermont*, 21–25, asked, "How does God, who is infinitely wise, allow harmful things and monsters in nature?" (answering that "harmful things serve several good designs of Providence extremely well; they are fit among other things to lead us to repentance and to detach us from the present life"; as for monsters, "they give a certain brilliance [*éclat*] to the perfect works of nature, as shadows in a painting give luster to the colors").

to fill the mind and heart with religious truth. They offered not topics for disputation, but those specific conclusions that Christians must believe and act upon to be members of God's Church. Among other things, they explained what the Church meant by the "God" in whom it taught the necessity of belief: an eternal, infinite spirit, creator and providential governor of all things in the universe, omnipotent, omniscient, ubiquitous, immutable, blessed, and supremely good, who knew and judged all the secrets of the human heart. A few added to this general listing of attributes the more Augustinian, or Cartesian, or Malebranchist-sounding formula, "an infinitely perfect being," or "an infinitely perfect spirit."[4] Only two catechisms acknowledged, indeed stressed, that the definitions of God they offered were problematic "in this life" and could only with the most manifest imperfection represent God to us: the catechism of Soissons and, Meslier scholars take note, the singular catechism of Reims.[5]

In addressing the obligation to believe in God, ten of the twenty-one catechisms simply presupposed His existence, nine beginning with the question, "What is God?" and one with the question of why we are to believe in only *one* God.[6] Of the remaining eleven, nine posed a first question about the obvious fact of the students' finding themselves alive in this world, eight asking, "Who put you in this world?" and one asking if the world always had been, and all nine immediately concluding without explanation that "God" was the source of life and world.[7] One began simply with the question of the duty to believe, "Are we obligated to believe that there is a God?"[8] *Only one*, that of Reims, posed the question in terms that suggested a *choice* between intellectual belief and disbelief, "Is there a God?"[9]

Only three of the twenty-one catechisms, those of Toul, Montpellier, and, again, Reims, asked, "How do we know that there is a God?" and presented means and reasons by which one came to have knowledge of such a truth. The Toul catechism, in its instructions to the catechizer on

[4] The phrase "infinitely perfect" occurs only in *Autun*, 1; *Chartres*, 1; *Montpellier*, 3; *Quimper*, 14–15; and *Troyes*, 23.

[5] *Soissons*, 35 ("*On ne saurait bien dire en cette vie ce que c'est que Dieu . . . parce que Dieu est infiniment au-dessus de ce que nous pouvons penser et concevoir, étant sur la Terre*"); *Reims*, IIème Leçon ("*Demande: Qu'est-ce que Dieu? Réponse: "C'est là une demande à laquelle nous ne pouvons répondre que fort imparfaitement pendant que nous sommes en cette vie. . . . Dieu est infiniment au-dessus de tout ce que nous pouvons penser et concevoir de plus grand et de plus élevé pendant que nous sommes en ce monde*").

[6] *Autun*; *Boulogne*; *Bourges*; *Chartres*; *Clermont*; *Montpellier*; *Paris*; *Soissons*; *Strasbourg*; *Troyes* (which begins its section on God with, "Why do you say that there cannot be several Gods?").

[7] *Angers*; *Beauvais*; *Besançon*; *Cambrai*; *Meaux*; *Metz*; *Orléans*; *Quimper* ("Has the world always been?"); *Rouen*.

[8] *Toul*, 9.

[9] *Reims*, 75 ("Question: Is there a God? [*Y-a-t-il un Dieu*?] Answer: Yes, there is a God, and one would have to have neither senses nor reason in order not to know this truth").

"the order and method of the catechism," noted that the proper meaning of religious belief should be explained: "To believe is to be assured of a thing because it has been told us. . . . What is it thus to believe that there is a God? It is to be assured that there is a God because it has been told us. Who told us? God Himself." In the body of the Toul catechism, then, the question of "why" we believe in God was answered first by the explanation that God taught us in Scripture of His own existence, and, thus, that given its source, this information could not be doubted. The Toul catechism also answered its "How do we know?" question, however, by the explanation that "all creatures" teach the same truth by virtue of the order and beauty of the creation. Faith *and* reason, then, the Toul catechism stressed, which it identified as "two infallible sources," provided us with the same certain knowledge of God's being. The Montpellier catechism offered three interrelated and wholly natural sources of its knowledge that God existed: the order of nature; the impossibility of the self-construction of the world; and the impossibility that blind chance could have arranged the creatures as we observe them. The Reims catechism also linked its claim of knowledge of God's existence to solely natural reasons: the order and beauty of nature; and the fact of universal consent, supported by a natural sentiment of God in every heart and mind, and by human behavior in times of adversity.[10] These three, however, were clearly exceptions to the prevailing mode of basic instruction. *Eighteen* of the twenty-one catechisms *did not address at all* the issue of *how* we acquired such knowledge of God's existence. God's reality simply was assumed, and His attributes were stated and, in diverse ways, explained. It was the propagation of the first article of the creed that mattered here, not its philosophical justification, let alone the suggestion that legitimate knowledge of it in any way depended upon natural sources or philosophical demonstration.[11]

The catechisms commanded assent, students were taught, because they spoke what God's own infallible Word and Church had taught as the creed. The educated Catholic had no problem whatsoever with the central assumption in this, namely, that what God indeed revealed commanded unequivocal assent. The logical sequence of belief, however, posed a problem of its own. Believing the articles of faith because one believed that there was a God who had revealed them made perfect sense. In almost all of the catechisms, however, belief *that* God existed was

[10] *Toul*, 9 (the second question asked about God); *Montpellier*, 3–4 (the fifth question asked about God); *Reims*, 75–89 (the second question asked about God: "Why do you say that one would have to have neither senses nor reason," etc. For each of the reasons given, there is a subsequent "How do we know by . . ." question).

[11] We know so little about how these catechisms were actually received and internalized by their auditors. Recall, supra, the observations of Boudon, in *Oeuvres complètes*, I, 269–70.

merged with belief of God and affective belief in God, such that the existence of God was presented as one of those articles of the faith itself. For most of the learned, trained in the analysis and classification of arguments and demonstrations, it was self-evidently circular to believe in the existence of God because of the creed and in the creed because it came from God. *As a mode of faith*, there was no problem with such a phenomenon; *as a natural argument*, it clearly involved a *pétition de principe*, that is, it presupposed the very object it set out to prove.

Given the learned community's supreme confidence in the demonstrability of God, however, this was an utterly unnecessary paralogism for them, and, thus, one that they need not defend in the abstract, let alone to unbelievers. What was divine was to be believed, but as Aquinas had noted about the logical priority of persuasion when he addressed "the gentiles," "We must set down in the beginning that whereby His existence is demonstrated, as the necessary foundation of the whole work. For, if we do not demonstrate that God exists, all consideration of divine things is necessarily suppressed."[12] In short, for the learned, there was an essential distinction to be drawn, though ever so uneasily delineated, between, on the one hand, the "articles of the faith," revealed by God in Scripture, tradition, and the teaching of the Church, and, on the other, those "preambles" without which "all consideration of divine things is necessarily suppressed." Such categories arose not from self-examination of the phenomenon of personal belief, but from consideration of the logical sequence of an argument designed to lead even the theoretical unbeliever from atheism to full acceptance of the Christian creed.

. . .

It is a thorny phrase, "preamble" of the faith. Medieval and early-modern texts used diverse Latin terms to say it: *praembula fidei, praeamblum ad articulos fidei, aliquid praecedens articulos fidei*, all of which might be

[12] Aquinas, *Summa Contra Gentiles* l.i. c.9. par.5. (in Pegis translation). Bernardino M. Bonansea, in *God and Atheism: A Philosophical Approach to the Problem of God* (Washington, D.C., 1979), 172–73, notes well, I think, that among the medieval Scholastics, demonstration of the existence of God, as a "praeambula fidei," always occurred "within a theological framework and in the service of the data of revelation . . . within an atmosphere of serenity rather than of anguish." Aquinas, for Bonansea, "wants to prove the existence of God . . . by truly demonstrative arguments. Yet it is a God whom he has already found." See also the interesting discussion of "praeambula fidei" by S. Harent in A. Vacant, et al., *Dictionnaire de théologie catholique*, vi, 171–237 (art. "Foi," sec. 6, "Préparation rationelle de la Foi"). On the problems of assessing the place of demonstration in Aquinas's thought, see the exceptionally encyclopedic and thoughtful work of Fernand van Steenberghen, *Le problème de l'existence de Dieu dans les écrits de S. Thomas d'Aquin* (Louvain-la-Neuve, 1980).

understood with differences of nuance that in different contexts could loom large or small. If the focus of discussion were on the kind of belief in God that served a salvific function or that honored God, there was, at least until quite late in the seventeenth century, no disagreement among Catholic theologians: the belief of a person who could not articulate grounds beyond faith and obedience for a belief in God's being was in no manner inferior to that of a dialectician who could prove God by a variety of natural proofs. Other things being unequal, such as purity of intention, it could be deemed superior to that of a learned philosopher.

Indeed, there had been and in the seventeenth century still were those who questioned not only the validity, but even the whole theological and moral status of efforts to demonstrate the existence of God, "fideists" of diverse stripes, who, wishing to stress either the incapacity of fallen human reason or the virtue of faith (or, indeed, both) argued that belief in God was a matter of faith alone. Almost every Scholastic theologian who addressed the question of God's existence felt formally obliged to deal with the opinion of those for whom God's existence could not be demonstrated by natural means and could be believed by faith alone, "*de opinione dicentium quod Deum esse demonstrari non potest, sed sola fide tenetur*," as the commonplace formulation put it. In that context, the Church—for a variety of reasons, not least among which were its refusal to concede the terrain of natural knowledge to its real or possible enemies and its supreme confidence in the rational and evidential demonstrability of this most fundamental preamble or foundation of its belief—formally condemned (but never fully suppressed) such fideism. Aquinas believed that "what led some persons to hold this view was the weakness of the arguments which had been brought forth by others to prove that God exists," a problem that he thought resolved by demonstrative proofs.[13]

Saint Thomas's respected seventeenth-century editor and commentator, the Dominican Jean Nicolai, *premier régent* of the *grand couvent des Jacobins*, believing himself the beneficiary of such demonstrative proofs, explained that the existence of God was *manifest*, and that faith pertained only to that which was inevident.[14] It was the almost universal understanding of the eighth session of the Fifth Lateran Council (1513) that it was now an article of faith that knowledge of the existence of God, while it could be legitimately and even wonderfully derived from faith alone, did not *depend* on faith alone.[15] The widely admired Minim monk and teacher Emmanuel Maignan, theologian, mathematician, and philoso-

[13] Aquinas, *Summa Contra Gentiles* l.I. c.12.

[14] Jean Nicolai, O.P., ed., *Summa Theologica S. Thomae Aquinatis* q.2, art. 2, Nicolai's note "P."

[15] Charles-Joseph Hefele, ed., *Histoire des Conciles d'après les documents inédits*, trans. J. Cardinal Hergenroether, tome VIII (Paris, 1917), pt. 1, 420–22.

pher, in his *Philosophia Sacra*, termed any opposition to this view, at best, an absolute "theological error," but, most probably, an actual heresy, "entirely and expressly against the faith."[16] There were potentially embarrassing departures from such assurance to be found among admired medieval theologians, but well before the seventeenth century, the issue was "officially" settled. Indeed, in France, the Faculty of Theology of the University of Paris explicitly had condemned any fideistic claims that God could not be proven by natural reason.[17] In 1701, the Jesuit *Journal de Trévoux* noted that important theologians opposed what they took to be the "Thomist" view that "the existence of God *cannot* pertain to Faith," but insisted that this was a misreading of Saint Thomas, a "*malentendu*."[18]

From the thirteenth to sixteenth centuries, the Church's primary adversaries may have attacked specific "articles" of the creed, but *not* the foundational belief in the existence of God; the only challenge to "universal consent" was the "fool" of Scripture or perhaps a few pagans beyond the intellectual pale. In such a context, theologians and councils could consider the topic of God's demonstrability in purely abstract terms. They appear to have given more weight to the *theoretical* issue of the priority of *praembulae* in the sequence of belief than perhaps has suited their heirs in the more contestatory world of the nineteenth and twentieth centuries. Although the First Vatican Council reaffirmed, in the nineteenth century, the traditional understanding of the dictum of 1513, a growing number of theologians since then seem to have found the doctrine of the philosophical demonstrability of God's existence either irrelevant to their primary religious concerns or, indeed, an outright bother.[19]

[16] Emmanuel Maignan, Minim, *Philosophia Sacra, sive entis tum supernaturalis, tum increati, ubi de iis quae Theologia habet seu quoad Substantiam, seu quoad modum Physica, vel similia Physicis; tum circa Deum secundum se, eiusque ut Unius ac Trini perfectiones; . . . agitur Physice, et vi luminis naturalis; quandasam adhibitis etiam, ubi opus est, Sacris Fidei luminibus* (Paris [and Toulouse], 1661), [in folio], 85–86. There would be a 2d ed. of the *Philosophia Sacra* (Lyon, 1672).

[17] *Chartularium Universitatis Parisiensis*, ed. Henri Denifle, O.P., tome II (Paris, 1891), pièce 1124, 576ff.

[18] *Journal de Trévoux*, mai–juin 1701, 35–36.

[19] Vatican I (see G. Schneeman and T. Granderath, eds., *Acta et decreta sacrorum conciliorum recentiorum*, 7 vols. [Freiburg, 1892], VII, cols. 250 and 255) would be quite explicit: "The . . . Church . . . holds and teaches that by the natural light of reason, God . . . can be shown with certainty by means of created things." Indeed, it even pronounced anathema against anyone who "says that the unique and true God, our Creator and Lord, cannot be known with certainty by means of created entities." As a result, no Catholic theologian or historian of theology, in theory, should be able to say, with the Lutheran Paul Tillich, *Systematic Theology*, vol. I (Chicago, 1951), 237, that "the question of the existence of God can be neither asked nor answered. . . . It is as atheistic to affirm the existence of God as it is to deny it." (Cf., however, Arnobius of Sicca, *Contra Gentes* l.1, c. 32, where the patristic

Such a tendency perhaps has led some modern commentators on medieval thought to minimize the place of proof in Scholastic and above all Thomistic views of the sequence of belief. Nonetheless, Aquinas undeniably argued that God could be proven by natural lights, and he undeniably saw the existence of God as a "preamble" to the faith. The Church, in some fashion, accepted both views. To what extent the notion of "preamble" he used was intended to mean "prerequisite" or "foundation" of belief, and to what extent such terms radically differ, is a problem for medievalists to decide. The Church did not permit doubt that an individual believer ignorant of formal proofs of the "preamble" could believe sufficiently by faith and be saved. Few catechisms, we have seen, felt obliged either to make the distinction or to share the proofs.

Nonetheless, in the seventeenth century, we just have seen, Saint Thomas's leading Dominican editor drew a categorical distinction between the evident truths of philosophy and the revealed articles of the faith, and saw Aquinas as placing belief in the bare existence of God in the first category alone. Why not? Surely, for him and most contemporaneous theologians, the exhilaration of their enterprise began with the investigation of the revealed attributes and will of God, with the Trinity, and with the relationship of God to man. Let the philosophers or philosophically minded have the pleasure of reminding mankind, with Rom. 1:19–21, that it was "without excuse" if it did not see the evidence for God even without benefit of revelation or particular grace.

Although Aquinas was discussing merely *knowledge of* (as opposed to experience of or belief in) the faith, the phrase met most often in his texts to describe natural proofs of God was simply "*praeambula fidei*," and it was in that form that the early-modern reader in France generally encountered it. The context of that encounter is critical. The seventeenth century in France was marked by a growing and striking tendency of the learned world to distinguish its knowledge and its ways of knowing from

---

apologist declares that "it matters very little and makes no difference, whether you deny that He exists or assert and admit that He does, since both an assertion of such a thing and the denial of an unbelieving opponent are equally blameworthy" [Arnobius of Sicca, *The Case Against the Pagans*, trans. George E. McCracken, 2 vols. (Westminster, Md., 1949), I, 81–82]). Nonetheless, the growing historical separation between the would-be claims of academic philosophy and the would-be claims of religious experience clearly has led to an impatience on the part of many religious sensibilities with demands that they "satisfy" the "requirements" of natural, philosophical "proof" of the elements of belief. Gilson, in *L'Athéisme difficile* (Paris, 1979), 11, surely was not alone among twentieth-century Catholic intellectuals in his view: "I often have been requested, at times summoned, sometimes defied to give proofs of the existence of God. I never have been able to be impassioned about the question. I feel so certain that a reality that transcends the world and myself corresponds to the word God that the prospect of seeking proofs for that of which I am so certain seems to me devoid of interest."

those of the "vulgar," demanding "*évidence*," either logical or empirical (or both), for natural and even, increasingly, supernatural belief, a tendency reinforced by both prevailing Aristotelian notions of *scientia* and Cartesian criteria of rational assent.[20] The Church taught its educated minds that belief in the mere existence of God was a "preamble" to the faith, demonstrable by philosophy, not an "article" of the faith itself. Belief in a God who revealed was logically prior and in that sense prefatory to belief in the content of revelation. The Church further taught that such demonstrations were compelling and that it was, somewhat paradoxically to modern ears, a matter of faith that belief in God's being was entailed by natural lights. If that were the case, such demonstrability must be evident in the actual world. All of this elevated the issue of philosophical proofs to a remarkable and dynamic place in the intellectual life of the culture, one that, ironically, would contribute mightily to the possibility of atheistic belief. Let us examine, then, what the culture found in the works of its most revered doctor about the issue of preamble, and how it interpreted the issue. The stakes and some of the intensities of the enterprise of philosophical theology in the seventeenth century indeed should become much clearer.

• • •

Aquinas had distinguished explicitly between "preamble" and "article" of the faith. In his *Quaestiones de Veritate*, he explained it this way: "That God exists is not an article of faith but a preamble to an article of faith, unless we understand something else along with God's existence, for example, that He has a unity of essence with a trinity of persons and other similar things."[21] In short, there was some sort of categorical distinction between the status of knowledge (though by no means necessarily belief) that God existed, which did not require faith, and the status of knowledge that God existed in a manner made known only by revelation by God Himself, which did require faith. For Aquinas, as he explained in his commentary on Boethius, the truths dependent on grace neither replaced nor destroyed "the light of knowledge," but built on and "per-

[20] By *scientia*, virtually all Aristotelians in the seventeenth century still meant only knowledge that was logically certain and indubitable, but, we shall see in later chapters, since Aristotle had ascribed this attribute only to knowledge "from causes," it raised problems of proof of God; the Cartesians' "clear and distinct ideas" entailed certainty and indubitability also, but, we shall see, since Descartes had assigned God the role of guaranteeing the validity of such a criterion by His incapacity to deceive, it also raised problems of proving God *before* establishing the certainty of a means of proof.

[21] Aquinas, *Quaestiones disputatae . . . de Veritate* q. 10, art. 12 [vol. XII of the Nicolai, O.P. ed.]. I have used the translation in Bonansea, *God and Atheism*, 172.

fected" it. Sacred doctrine and a philosophy "founded on the natural light of reason" were dramatically asymmetrical, the first going far beyond the second, but they were consistent and related. He formulated the nature of that relationship straightforwardly: philosophy "contains . . . certain resemblances to what belongs to faith, *and certain preambles to faith.*" Since truth could not contradict truth, philosophy was useful to theology in diverse ways. It could refute philosophical arguments against the articles of faith, for example, and it could clarify faith by means of "resemblances" to natural truths. Foremost among its uses, however, was the proof of the "preambles":

> First, we can use it [philosophy] to demonstrate the preambles of the faith, *which are necessary to the science of faith* as being those things that are proven of God by natural arguments, *for example, that God exists*, that God is one, or similar propositions concerning God or created beings *that faith presupposes as having been proven in philosophy.*[22]

Aquinas did not say that philosophical demonstration of the existence of God was necessary to any act of faith, but simply to the *scientia* of sacred things, that is, to the science of theology. He did not claim in any way that such theology was necessary to salvific belief and faith. If one wished a *scientia* of things divine, however, philosophical demonstration of the existence of God was a presupposition of such a science. Thus, in the *Summa Theologiae*, Saint Thomas explained both the essential relationship of preambles to a theologically scientific faith *and* the unessential nature of the preambles to any other valid sort of faith:

> The truths about God which St. Paul says we can know by our natural powers of reasoning—that God exists, for example—are not numbered among the articles of faith, *but are presupposed to them. For faith presupposes natural knowledge* just as grace does nature and all perfections that which they perfect. However, there is nothing to stop a man accepting on faith some truth which he personally cannot demonstrate, even if that truth in itself is such that demonstration could make it evident.[23]

By the seventeenth century, even a philosophical skeptic and seeming fideist could accept what he took to be Aquinas's distinctions. "So that we can recognize by the forces of Nature alone that there is a God," La Mothe Le Vayer wrote, "Saint Thomas resolved very well [*a fort bien determiné*] that our belief on this matter is not an article of the Faith." An article of faith, the skeptic explained, "concerns only things that are not

[22] Aquinas, *Expositio in Librum Boetii de Trinitate* q. 2, art. 3 [vol. xx of the Nicolai, O.P. ed.]. I have used (but modified) the translation by Anton C. Pegis, offered in his general introduction to the *Summa Contra Gentiles*.

[23] Aquinas, *ST* 1a, q.2, art. 2.

evident and never manifest truths, which are, like this one [the existence of God], plain [*notoires*] to everyone."[24]

To those with great confidence in philosophy, of course, it was a distinction that suggested nothing problematic whatsoever. Indeed, the theological community in France encouraged such a confidence in philosophy. At the pinnacle of that community, in terms of the hierarchy of its institutions of learning, was the eminent inner sanctum of intellectual accomplishment at the Faculty of Theology at Paris, the Société de Sorbonne. As the Oratorian priest Denis Amelote reminded his readers in a biography of the late spiritual leader of the Oratory, Charles de Condren:

> It is one of the laws of the celebrated faculty of the Sorbonne that those who aspire to the honor of its Société must publicly teach a course of philosophy in the University of Paris. This study produces many excellent effects, for *it obliges its doctors to make themselves masters in the human sciences in order to be able to become masters in the divine wisdom* [*elle oblige ses Docteurs de se rendre Maistres dans les sciences humaines, afin de le pouvoir devenir dans la Sagesse divine*]; . . . it provides them a rich harvest of all the arts and all the bodies of knowledge which can originate [*naistre*] in the field of human reason, of which philosophy is more an ample treasury than a particular science.[25]

In an extremely well-received text on education, Charles Rollin, who served a term as *recteur* of the University of Paris and later was professor of eloquence at the collège royale, made claims that expressed quite well much of the learned world's confidence about the role of philosophy in the acquisition of knowledge about God: "One of the great effects and the most essential fruit of philosophy is to raise man to knowledge of the grandeur of God, of His power, of His wisdom, of His goodness; to make him attentive to His providence; to teach him to ascend all the way to Him by the consideration of the marvels of nature."[26]

[24] La Mothe le Vayer, *Oeuvres*, XI, 408–9.

[25] Denis Amelote, Oratory, *La vie du Père Charles de Condren, second supérieur général de la Congrégation de l'Oratoire de Jésus*, 2d ed., rev. and aug. (Paris, 1657), 153–54. The 1st ed. of Amelote's *Vie de Condren* was in 1643.

[26] Charles Rollin, *De la manière d'enseigner et d'étudier les belles lettres par rapport à l'esprit et au coeur*, 2d ed., rev. and corr., 4 vols. (Paris, 1728), IV, 409. Reviewing the last two volumes of this edition, the *Journal de Trévoux* (juillet 1728, 1161) noted, "as a happy augury" for volumes III and IV, that the first two volumes had sold out quickly and that the second edition had come merely two years after the first. Reviewing the first edition of 1726 with great enthusiasm, the *Journal de Trévoux* devoted thirty pages to its *compte rendu* (août 1726, 1400–1430) and termed it "a fruit of his [Rollin's] gratitude [*reconnaissance*] toward the University of Paris," noting that it was based "not on his particular views, but on what is practiced in the University of Paris . . . [on] what he has seen the *Maîtres* practice."

In a text published with the approbation of three leading doctors of theology from the Sorbonne, the theologian and royal professor of philosophy Louis Ellies Dupin observed in 1703 that good philosophy formed a "natural theology" of great utility to the faith. Obviously, from the perspective of dealing with unbelief, it "served and still serves to prove the existence and unity of a God against the atheists."[27] The believer, of course, did not require such proofs but should understand their benefits: "Although . . . it suffices for salvation to believe with simplicity the articles of the Faith that the Church teaches, one cannot doubt nevertheless that it is very useful . . . not to ignore the foundations and proofs of their belief, and to be prepared to give reasons for these, and to respond to the difficulties that can be opposed to them."[28] This "utility" became apparent, for Dupin, from consideration of the sequence of belief. "The certitude of the truths of religion," he explained, depended upon the fact of a divine revelation that made it eminently reasonable to submit our reason to such truths. What made such submission reasonable, however, was the certainty that "God cannot deceive men by revealing falsities as truths," which we knew not by faith (which would be circular), but by "natural reason." Knowledge by natural light that there was a God who was "supremely perfect, and consequently supremely wise and supremely good, convinces us in an evident manner of His veracity." Such *knowledge* of the existence of God, by the same logic, could not be from revelation but, rather, was "known by the lights of nature, and provable by reason." This was also the case for knowledge of "His attributes and the majority of the principles of morality," which allowed one to reason from His existence as a supremely good being to the necessity of His veracity. The necessity of these natural truths in the sequence of reasonable belief in Christian doctrine, then, made it "permissible, useful, *and even necessary to join Reason to Faith in order to establish them*."[29]

Thus, the English Catholic Henry Holden's examination of faith, *De Fide*, published in Paris with the approbation of a leading theologian of the Sorbonne, began with the observation that "it is evident that in the question which I undertake to discuss [faith], *diverse things are to be supposed as demonstrated elsewhere*," first among which was "that there is a God."[30] Discussing *De Fide* two generations later in his *Bibliothèque des auteurs ecclésiastiques*, Dupin paraphrased that simple introduction as follows:

[27] Louis Ellies Dupin, *Traité de la doctrine chrétienne et orthodoxe* . . . (Paris, 1703), 606–8.

[28] Ibid., "Avertissement."

[29] Ibid., 3–10, 552–56.

[30] Henry Holden, *An Analysis of the Divine Faith*, trans. W. G. (Paris, 1658), 1–2.

With regard to the existence of God, he [Holden] believes it *a preamble necessary to the Faith, rather than an Article of Faith*, because it is impossible to believe any Article on the basis of the authority of God who revealed it, unless one presupposes the existence of God: *and he does not believe that one can give one's consent to this proposition, "God exists," because God revealed it.*[31]

Aquinas surely had not said *that*, but there was the argument stated plainly enough, that the faith itself, and assent to its foundation, required an anterior demonstration of God's existence. If that were the case, then the proofs of the preambles were a serious business indeed.

To the counterargument that a proper Christian *philosophy* should *begin* with unquestioning belief in the existence of God, France's leading Aristotelian philosopher of the latter half of the seventeenth century, Pierre Barbay, replied that it should not. Barbay, whose courses in Aristotelian philosophy at the University of Paris helped to shape the thinking of a generation, acknowledged that some wanted the proposition "God exists [*Deus est*]" to be a "first principle of Metaphysics" that must be adhered to "indisputably [*sine controversia*]." He explicitly and vigorously rejected this claim, however, arguing that such a proposition was clearly disputable, even if only a fool could dispute it. The *only* indisputable first principle, he argued, was that "it is impossible for something to be and not to be at the same time," from which one was obliged to demonstrate other truths.[32] For Barbay, such proofs were easily derived a posteriori by "natural reason" from the series of essentially dependent causes that constituted the contingency of the observed world and from the order of the heavens. Only then could philosophy address the issues of divine attributes (such as His veracity, upon which knowledge of the truth of revelation logically depended).[33]

The Minim monk Emmanuel Maignan, who taught philosophy and theology at the University of Toulouse, explained to his students that while philosophy dealt with natural things and theology with supernatural things, theology could rely upon natural lights to create a "sacred philosophy," the object of which would be to demonstrate the existence of God, to understand God's works in nature, and to establish the foundations of religion. The fruit of this, his *Philosophia Sacra* (1661), was published with an unusually large number of approbations from the superiors

[31] Louis Ellies Dupin, *Bibliothèque des auteurs ecclésiastiques du dix-septième siècle*, 7 vols. (Paris, 1708), II, 166.

[32] Pierre Barbay, *Commentarius in Aristotelis Metaphysicam*, 2d ed., rev. (Paris, 1676), 24–29. The 1st ed. of Barbay's *In Aristotelis Metaphysicam* was 1674. His *In universam Aristotelis philosophiam introductio* was in a 5th ed. by 1707.

[33] Pierre Barbay, *In Aristotelis Metaphysicam*, 361–72.

of his Minim order, from Minim professors of theology at Toulouse, from a *professeur-régent* of theology at Toulouse, and from several Carmelite theologians. For Maignan, while theologians legitimately could presuppose the existence of God as the "first principle of the faith [*primum fidei principium*]," they obviously could *not* prove it to the unbeliever from revelation, and needed to appeal to universal consent and demonstration from natural philosophy to establish that principle when challenged. The Christian, for Maignan, was irrevocably committed to the view that any gentile's disbelief in God's existence was "inexcusable" not because it violated "Scripture," which the gentile could not know, or "probability," or "hypothesis," but precisely because it violated indubitable philosophical knowledge, that is to say, natural "*scientia*."[34]

The theologian Jean-Claude Sommier, protonotary apostolic and soon to be a cardinal, in a work dedicated to Pope Clement XI and published with approbations from Oratorian and Jesuit theologians, from professors at the collège royale and the collège d'Epinal, and with the imprimatur of the count-bishop of Toul, wrote in 1708 that reason was absolutely "necessary" to the faith. Without rational foundations, he insisted, even faith would fall, since faith was obeyed voluntarily, which meant "on the basis of a full hearing of the evidence [*avec connoissance de cause*]": "One never could believe sincerely what one did not see and perceive, if one were not truly persuaded [by reason] that one must believe it. . . . *Without true reason, and without evident knowledge, there cannot be true religion*." It was above all because of this that "it would be a heresy to say that one cannot know the existence of God without faith."[35] As François Feu, doctor of theology from the Sorbonne, reminded his readers, proof of the existence of God was essential not only because the faith must be armed "against various temptations" offered by the miscreant atheists, but because it was the obvious *precondition* of all theology.[36] The preface of John Ray's work on the existence of God, translated into French in 1714, put the matter quite simply. Theology, like all sciences, properly could assume rather than prove the existence of its object of inquiry, but that created an essential need for a natural philosophical proof of God's being:

> Since the principle foundation of religion is the belief in and fear of God, and since one could not love Him nor serve Him without knowing Him, and

[34] Maignan, Minim, *Philosophia Sacra*, 57–104. The discussion of the "*primum fidei principium*" is found on 59–60.

[35] Jean-Claude Sommier, *Histoire dogmatique de la religion; ou La religion prouvée par l'authorité divine et humaine, et par les lumières de la raison*, 3 vols. (Paris, 1708–1711), I, i–ii.

[36] Feu, *Theologici Tractatus*, I, 2.

> without being fully persuaded of His existence, it is absolutely necessary to establish firmly this first principle.[37]

Those concerned with fideistic claims felt obliged to make this point quite strongly. When Descartes imagined the atheist faced only by a philosophical skeptic, he found the consequences unacceptable. In the dedication of his *Meditations*, Descartes urged that proof of God and proof of the immortal soul were "the principal [questions] that should be demonstrated rather by the arguments of philosophy than of theology." While it was "sufficient" for those of us "who are faithful to believe by faith [*par la foi*] that there is a God," he advised, "certainly it does not seem possible ever to persuade the unfaithful of any religion, nor scarcely of any moral virtue, *if in the first place one does not prove these two things [the existence of God and the immortality of the soul] by natural reason [si premièrement on ne leur prouve ces deux choses par raison naturelle]*."[38]

In 1661, Jean de Silhon, in his effort to warn the faithful of the incompatibility of skeptical philosophy and faith despite fideistic claims to the contrary, insisted that "three constant and indubitable truths" lay at the foundation of Christianity, and that if they were rendered dubious by natural philosophy, the faith itself could not stand: first, "that there is some Sovereign Being to whom all nature is subject, and who . . . can be neither deceived Himself in His knowledge nor want to deceive others"; second, that His signs to our senses cannot be imaginary or illusory (as the skeptics would claim); and third, that His signs could only be from Him. Before one could accept the faith one had to accept the existence of the God who revealed the faith, and before one could know the existence of that God, the certainty of knowledge had to be secured against skeptical philosophy. Only "*évidence*," a certainty beyond opinion and probability, made possible that "science" on which the truths essential to the establishment of the faith depended.[39]

In 1675, faced with the skeptical Academic philosophy of Canon Simon Foucher, the Benedictine monk and philosopher Dom Robert Desgabets declared himself wholly unimpressed by "the Academics [skeptical philosophers] who make a profession of piety [and] say that Faith suffices for us." While he did not question Foucher's piety or sincerity, he observed that "one is right to say to them [the fideists] that it is not an in-

[37] John Ray, *L'existence et la sagesse de Dieu, manifestées dans les oeuvres de la création*, trans. G. Broedelet (Utrecht, 1714), "Préface."

[38] Descartes, "A Messieurs les doyens et docteurs de la Sacrée Faculté de Théologie de Paris," in *Oeuvres philosophiques* (Alquié), II, 383.

[39] De Silhon, *De la certitude*, 6–7, 60–68, 546–54.

considerable evil [*mal*] to reverse as much as they do the natural order *which requires that one be convinced by reason of the immortality of the soul and of the existence of God before one proposes our mysteries to the unbelievers [l'ordre naturel qui veut que l'on soit convaincu par raison . . . de l'existence de Dieu auparavant qu'on propose de sa part aux infidelles nos mystères*].”[40] In 1696, his fellow Benedictine, the philosopher Dom François Lamy, seeking to refute Spinoza rather than the skeptics, put the matter bluntly indeed. Metaphysics was a matter of paramount importance, Lamy wrote, for on the basis of its conclusions “one will be persuaded that there is a God, or that there is not; that He is free and intelligent, or that He is not; that He has a providence full of light and wisdom, or that He has not; that He is just, veracious, omnipotent, [and] the true cause of everything that has being, or that He is not.” Obviously, Lamy noted, “all our ethics and our religion must vary extremely according to the diversity of these alternatives.” That being the case, “*nothing is more important to man than the knowledge of a science [“metaphysics”] which alone can give him the means of sorting out the best parts of all that.*” In short, he advised: “*Religion and the certitude of the faith themselves depend in some fashion on metaphysics*, in that it is necessary for it [metaphysical philosophy] to prove for them at least that there is a God; that this God is not a deceiver; and that His testimony is infallible.”[41]

Was this a marginal work? To the contrary, it was published with the approbation of Fénélon himself, and with further approbations from the powerful Hideux, theologian, doctor of the Sorbonne, and *curé des Saints Innocents*, and from Coulau, the influential director of the Bibliothèque Mazarine.[42] Ten years later, in his *Premiers élémens des sciences*, Lamy reiterated these same themes: reason first must establish the existence of God before faith in His Word can occur; to believe by faith that God exists would be to accept the word of a being whom you did not yet know to exist, which would be absurd.[43]

No less a theologian and philosopher than Malebranche himself com-

[40] Dom Robert Desgabets, O.S.B., *Critique de la Critique de la Recherche de la vérité, où l'on découvre le chemin qui conduit aux connaissances solides. Pour servir de réponse à la Lettre d'un académicien* (Paris, 1675), 7–11. In his discussion of skepticism and God (ibid., 57–71), Desgabets warned that without a principle of certainty, “we would not be assured that there is a real world, a Religion, a God, etc. [*nous ne serions pas assurés qu'il y a un vray monde, une Religion, un Dieu, etc.*].”

[41] Dom François Lamy, O.S.B., *Le nouvel athéisme renversé, ou réfutation du sistême de Spinosa. Tirée pour la plupart de la conaissance de la nature de l'homme* (Paris, 1696), 5–8.

[42] Ibid. The approbations *follow* the “Avertissement.”

[43] Dom François Lamy, O.S.B., *Les premiers élémens des sciences, ou Entrée aux connoissances solides, en divers entretiens, proportionnés à la portée des commerçans, et suivis d'un essay de logique* (Paris, 1706), 68–94.

pleted the equation of "preamble" with a concept of an essential obligation to prove God by reason prior to real faith. In his *Conversations chrétiennes*, first published in 1676, one of his interlocutors, Aristarque, declares himself "convinced [of the existence of God] by faith; but I confess that I am not fully convinced of it by reason." Malebranche's Théodore replied:

> If you say things as you think them, you are convinced of it neither by reason nor by faith. For do you not see that the certitude of the faith comes from the authority of a God who speaks, and who cannot be a deceiver. *If, therefore, you are not convinced by reason that there is a God, how will you be convinced that He has spoken?* Can you know that He has spoken, without knowing [first] that He is?[44]

If that were the case, then demonstration of God was, to say the least, no simple logical exercise, and to whatever extent one accepted Malebranche's view, to that extent one's belief in God depended in one's own mind precisely upon philosophical demonstration. For Malebranche, this posed no problem, since "everything proves God."[45] Nonetheless, it clearly raised the stakes of philosophy or philosophical theology dramatically.

. . .

In Malebranche's congregation, the Oratory, such views were as common as they were among the erudite Benedictines, and in 1700, they caused a minor scandal. The affair in one sense could be seen as a preservation of the rights of faith against the claims of the need to prove God by natural lights, since, viewed from the Sorbonne, that was its official outcome. Its most dramatic element, however, that sheds the most light on the nature of the growing tendency to conflate "preamble" and "requirement for faith," was the remarkable extent to which such a pious and spiritual Congregation confidently could go (with a bishop's support, we shall see) not simply in emphasizing the role of natural lights in the sequence of belief, but, indeed, in insisting on its indispensable place there.

In the summer of 1700, the Oratorian fathers in Vendôme upheld a doctoral thesis in theology that had been dedicated to the bishop of Blois, who himself was present at the defense. The thesis contained a proposition that the Vendôme Oratory accepted, but that the doctoral candidate had to defend against vigorous opposition from a theology student from

[44] Malebranche, Oratory, *Conversations chrétiennes* in *Oeuvres complètes*, IV, 14. The *Conversations chrétiennes* enjoyed seven editions.

[45] Malebranche, *De la recherche de la vérité*, in ibid., II, 19, 103–4 (where he urges that in fact, nothing has more proofs than God's existence).

Paris who had attended the session: "The existence of God does not pertain to faith, *nor can it pertain to faith*. So Saint Thomas judged. [*Existentia Dei ad fidem nec attinet, nec attinere potest. Ita sentit S. Thomas*]." Defending this proposition orally, the candidate, to the approval of his Oratorian professors, committed himself formally to three other propositions that seemed to be entailed by it: (1) "The existence of God is not revealed, nor can it be revealed by God"; (2) "No one can elicit an act of faith about the existence of God"; and (3) "The Church does not require a positive act of faith about the existence of God." The protesting visitor, scandalized by the thesis, was a licentiate from the Faculty of Theology at Paris, de Becquereau, scheduled to seek his own doctorate from the Sorbonne in the coming winter. It was his spirited criticism of the thesis, and questioning by the bishop of Blois, that led the Oratorian theologian to add the three additional propositions concerning faith and belief in God. De Becquereau became vehement in his denunciation of the propositions, and he formally appealed to the bishop to intervene. The bishop of Blois held several conferences with the Parisian student, but he refused to give him satisfaction, at which point de Becquereau stated his intention to get the propositions denounced by theologians at the Sorbonne.[46] According to one contemporary account, the affair caused "much stir in the city [of Vendôme]."[47]

When de Becquereau returned to Paris later that year, he presented the four propositions to a large number of theologians at the Faculty of Theology and found about forty—many (if not most) of them Jansenist supporters often sympathetic to the Oratory—willing to draft and sign a censure of them. The censure, which relied most heavily on Saint Augustine's views of faith and reason, argued that "nothing prevents the existence of God from being known by the same man through reason as well as faith" and pointed out that "there are many other things which [both] reason and faith also teach." There was nothing wrong in believing in God by means of reason, or, for that matter, by means of human authority, "on the assumption that faith would suffice if reason had not been explored." It conceded that "faith presupposes revelation" and that "revelation presupposes the existence of an entity who reveals," but insisted that both of those presuppositions could be believed by faith alone. Since "not all men are capable of understanding the reasons that prove the existence of God," since even those who are so capable "can be persuaded . . . much more easily and clearly . . . through faith," and since without faith many men from the time of the Fall had become "doubtful of His existence,"

[46] Bibliothèque Nationale, MSS.: Fonds français, 19312, 1r–2r.

[47] *Nouvelles de la République des Lettres*, avril 1701, 476–77 (a letter from a correspondent in France, among the "Extraits des Diverses Lettres").

the indispensability of faith was evident. One could accept Saint Augustine's own proofs of God and, of course, simultaneously engage in "an act of faith" on the same matter, but one could not deny that a purely rational belief in God was "without [salvific] merit [*meritoria non est*]." Sound doctrine, it insisted, "damns those who might not believe that God exists through faith unless they were to ascertain it by reason." All Saint Thomas meant when he argued that the existence of God was not among "the articles of faith" (the defense of Thomas being brief, indeed, in this Augustinian censure) was that God's being was not inevident to us and did not depend upon faith alone for our knowledge of it.[48] In their summation, the drafters of the censure did not defend (or address) Saint Thomas, but simply termed the Oratory's propositions "false, scandalous, erroneous, impious, and contrary to the word of God."[49] Five Dominican theologians at the Sorbonne, including the formidable Noel Alexandre, separately, in a supporting set of signatures, also termed the propositions "false, erroneous, rash, offensive [*malêsonantes*], . . . scandalous, and contrary to the word of God." They cited Hebrews 11:6 ("But without faith it is impossible to please Him: for he that cometh to God must believe that He is") as the specific "word of God" the thesis contravened. Sensitive to the use in the censured thesis of their order's Angelic Doctor, however, they specifically added among their terms of censure that the propositions were "injurious to Saint Thomas."[50]

While the outcome at the Sorbonne was clear enough, many details surrounding the censure reveal the ambiguities inherent in this effort to define the proper place of demonstration in the sequence of belief. First, de Becquereau had worried about achieving the censure if the names, affiliations, and stations of the persons censured were known, and he presented the propositions to the Sorbonne theologians "*in abstracto*." Interested observers in Paris were not told the identities of those who had supported the censured propositions until *after* the censure. Second, the archbishop of Paris was so angered by de Becquereau's behavior that he "forbade him from performing any function in his diocese, even saying the mass." Third, even after being informed of all of the Parisian details, the bishop of Blois declared himself "greatly shocked by this censure."[51] Clearly, then, not every theologian or ecclesiastic found the Oratory's thesis on the indispensability of rational proof of God manifestly contrary to the faith.

Equally (if not more) striking, however, is the list of signatories to the censure, for it reveals how critical was the *context* of the denunciation of

[48] Bibliothèque Nationale, MSS.: Fonds français, 19312, 2v–9v.

[49] Ibid., 9v–10r.

[50] Ibid., 10v–10r.

[51] Ibid., 1r–2r; *Nouvelles de la République des Lettres*, avril 1701, 476–77.

such views, in this case an explicit appeal to Jansenizing and to Dominican theologians to judge as a matter of pure theory the use of Saint Thomas to support the proposition that natural proof of God's existence was an essential *precondition* of faith. I have cited Malebranche's rhetorical question, urged on behalf of the view that faith in God's existence, absent rational conviction to that effect, was illogical: "If . . . you are not convinced by reason that there is a God, how will you be convinced that He has spoken?" Among the signatories to the censure, however, was Malebranche's editor and frequent approbator, Blampignon. I have cited the Benedictine François Lamy's thesis that "religion and the certitude of the faith" *depended* on metaphysical proof of God, but among the signatories to the censure was Hideux, who gave warm approbation to the very work in which Lamy made such an argument. Eight years after the censure, Sommier—soon to be made a cardinal—repeated and, in effect, extended the most extreme implications of Lamy's and Malebranche's argument, making sincere religious belief entirely dependent upon prior rational and natural conviction of the existence of God; he received the approbation of Pissonat, another signatory to the censure. Much depended, then, upon the *context* of the question. If the issue were explicitly the status of faith, then these figures could censure such an elevation of philosophical demonstration. If the issue were philosophical skepticism or actual disbelief, however, the same censurers could find nothing unsound, threatening, or exceptional in the claim of reason's indispensability to faith, or, more precisely, in the argument that faith required anterior philosophical demonstration of God's existence.[52] Augustinians, they could be moved, depending on that context, both by their sense of the

[52] See approbations in the works listed in nn. 38–41. The study of approbations is exceptionally helpful in the analysis of the patterns and alliances of the theological community. A full examination of the early-modern approbation would allow us to identify the theological and religious sympathies (and learn much about the strategies) of large numbers of doctors of theology throughout France. This is especially important given the intensity of divisions among Catholic schools of thought (each with eminent defenders). Even in times requiring the greatest prudence, authors knew where to turn for needed approbations, and there were not only distinct groups of Thomist, Molinist, and Jansenist censors and superiors who could be counted on to grant permissions to works that competing schools found both essentially dangerous to the faith and often libelous of other theologians, but there were similar camps of Aristotelian, Cartesian, Malebranchist, and fideistic censors. Usually, censors simply noted that a work "contained nothing contrary to the faith," a criterion that allowed a great deal of *philosophical* latitude. Occasionally, as in the first editions of Pascal's *Pensées*, they used their approbations for their own polemical purposes, offering an extended defense of an author's work. Thémiseul de Saint-Hyacinthe, in his parody of the world of learning and letters, the mordant *Le chef d'oeuvre d'un inconnu* (The Hague, 1714), "Approbations," mocked the institution of the approbation; his imaginary censors said such things as, "We have found nothing in this that is not wholly in conformity with our [own] sentiments, and, as a consquence, nothing that is not wholly orthodox."

need for faith since the Fall *and* by their sense of the divine illumination of the rational mind. The censure of 1701, a defense of the rights of faith, had little audience. The works of Malebranche, François Lamy, and Jean-Claude Sommier, which could appeal to all who believed in a light within, had, by comparison, a very large one.

. . .

The Jesuit journal of the arts and sciences, the *Journal de Trévoux*, almost always criticized and evaluated works in metaphysical theology and philosophy from a perspective it deemed grounded in Aquinas and the main traditions of revered Scholastic doctors consistent with Saint Thomas's broad philosophical theology. In general, it did not admire the frequently Jansenist, Cartesian, or Malebranchist theologians of either the Oratory or the Benedictines, to say the least, and it clearly saw itself as a sober voice of orthodoxy in a divided French Catholic church. In 1727, it reviewed a translation into French of the major statement of ancient skeptical philosophy, *Les Hipotiposes . . . de Sextus Empiricus*. The context, thus, was a consideration of the claim that natural human reason and the natural senses could not attain or provide a means to attain certainty. If such a claim were true, the Jesuit journal asked, "how save the idea of God from this general wreckage of ideas?" The reviewer was not thinking about the religious priority of faith over philosophy, a perspective that might have informed a review of an excessively naturalist or rationalist work, but about the implications of skepticism for a sequence of belief that should culminate in acceptance of the Christian creed. His argument, to the journal's large and diverse audience, showed again how critical the issue of rational proof of the "preamble" of the faith could be made to appear. His use of the pronoun *I* placed the Christian, and not the unbeliever, into the sequence that must begin with *philosophical* certainty:

> How will I believe that there is a God if I must distrust my *reason* which tells me it, the wonders of nature which announce it to me, geometrical truths which are even more suited to my intelligence, and more sensibly evident? [If] I have no *Criterium*, no discernment, no rule of truth or certainty, what will assure me thus of the existence of this God? . . . for it is to these blasphemies that one comes by reasoning consequentially [from philosophical skepticism].[53]

Important theological and philosophical voices, then, with great confidence in the support offered to theology by philosophy, could claim that conviction by natural lights of the existence of God was a prerequisite of

[53] *Journal de Trévoux*, jan. 1727, 53–54.

reasonable and perhaps of all faith, if not on the part of the unlearned, then at least on the part of those who taught them. They made such claims in works published with often high approbation and explicit ecclesiastical support. To many, such a claim, in the right context, obviously did not seem problematic. Atheism, the culture taught, was unthinkable and inexcusable precisely because it was so eminently demonstrable that there was a God. Only a miscreant seeking to blind himself to truth could be an atheist. Fideism and even behavioral evidence of disbelief threatened such confidence, so the culture, confronting these, argued often from its sense of the *évidence* of the preamble or foundation of its creed. It generally denounced fideism as disturbing to sincere Christians, contrary to divine teaching, and irrational. Fideism, considered as an abandonment of reason, was no comfort to the faithful: one could not demonstrate the inexcusability and stultified nature of disbelief if it required grace and faith to believe in God. Fideism, considered as a critique of the rationality of belief in God, was incorrect: God, the Church itself taught as doctrine, was demonstrable. Fideism, considered as a philosophical position, was illogical: before one believed in revelation, one needed to be certain of the existence of the God who truly revealed, a certainty available from philosophy. Disbelief was a moral and not a philosophical phenomenon. Indeed, it was so evident to the natural faculties that God existed, the main voices of theological and intellectual culture insisted, that there existed a virtual universal consent among all peoples and sages to such a belief. Such views formed powerful barriers against the notion that there could be any such thing as reasonable disbelief, critical barriers at a time when major voices could declare demonstration and proper belief inseparable. What, in the life of the learned world, could challenge such confident convictions?

PART TWO

Other Peoples and Other Minds: Thinking about Universal Consent

Chapter Five

OTHER PEOPLES

MEETINGS OF CULTURES are always extraordinary affairs. It was both profoundly stimulating and profoundly disconcerting for Europeans to confront the other peoples of the globe and to try to comprehend their ways of being and thinking. (It surely was at least that for those other peoples to confront the Europeans!) Few early-modern French, of course, actually set eyes on distantly foreign climes or nations. As the reading public grew, however, publishers became aware of (and to some extent created) its insatiable curiosity concerning the earth's diversities. The flora, fauna, human mores, and religious practices and beliefs of other lands were objects of boundless fascination. Missionaries and secular travelers were, among many other things, the variously reliable eyes and ears of a learned world avid to know with whom and with what it shared its abode. European authors and readers attempted to learn a great deal about their earth, and, with often far less success, to integrate all of this new information into their traditional received notions of things. In the long term, such encounters, for the learned world, expanded its "data base" exponentially, created whole new sciences, and gave rise to theoretical problems that culminated in distinctly novel ways of thinking anthropologically, sociologically, historically, and, in the broadest sense, geographically. In the short term, such encounters added a large amount of specific knowledge to the European storehouse, engendered new degrees of relativism in some quarters, educed in diverse minds increased or decreased self-confidence in the superiority of Christian, European culture, and, for our purposes here, occasioned something of a major crisis in the proof of God from universal consent.

The Parisian medical doctor and traveler Charles Patin, writing merely on the basis of travels to other *European* lands, noted, in his *Relations . . . de voyage* (1674), that "nothing is less similar to a man than a man. . . . They are different things, one people and another people, one nation and another nation." What one people delighted in, another people detested; "everywhere, one finds new customs, new religions, new manners of dressing, eating, living, and even dying." "The diversity of opinions and sentiments . . . among men," Patin observed, was enormously provocative: "It impels the mind to the search for truth and keeps it from indolence by giving it a second breath."[1] The force of the argument from universal consent lay precisely in the view that any common human beliefs within such startling diversity were proof of the obvious and, thus, compelling evidence indeed. Increased familiarity with accounts of that diversity, however, exposed readers to a striking line of testimony, rightly or wrongly offered, that there was no such universal consent to the existence of God. A majority of travelers found what they took to be belief in God almost everywhere, but that was not news. A significant number believed that they had encountered atheistic peoples, and some virtuous ones at that, and this was news indeed.

As we have seen, authors of all kinds offered the argument from universal consent to the existence of God both as a dramatic fact about the world and as grounds for belief in what was unanimously agreed to by all mankind. It served to reassure the faithful about the foundational article of their beliefs, and to humiliate the would-be atheist by showing how piteously alone and singularly ignorant such a figure would be. While a few writers found it a sufficient proof of God's existence, it generally was recognized to be an argument of a special kind. For most, it was a "moral" proof, persuasive without being logically demonstrative.

The learned world of the seventeenth century commonly distinguished between "demonstrative" and "moral" proofs. Demonstrative proofs satisfied the full measure of the criteria of necessary, entailed conclusions. Moral proofs satisfied any sincere and reasonable person's search for truth, although the dogged disputant could show that such proofs did not close the issue from a formally logical point of view, often using some cleverly feigned hypothesis to avoid conceding a conclusion. That two things each equal to a third were equal to each other could be shown demonstratively. That Julius Caesar actually had lived could not be "demonstrated" as such, but only an arbitrary hypothesis (concerning some deliberate fraud by almost all of the ancients, for example) could keep the issue open. The "*évidence*" of a moral proof compelled sincere belief, but it did not compel necessary logical certainty. It was deemed "moral" in the sense of the Latin "*mos*," referring to the will, inclination, character, and morals of the person to whom it was directed, a sense present in the French "*morale*" as well, referring to the whole range of human mental and ethical phenomena. In that sense, it took a rather perverse soul and mind to withhold assent from its conclusions, precisely the status assigned to the atheist. It could be put quite simply: one had to be insane, imbecilic, or depraved to disbelieve what the world had taught everyone else.

[1] Charles Patin, *Relations historiques et curieuses de voyages en Allemagne, Angleterre, Hollande, Bohème, Suisse, etc.* (Lyon, 1674), 49–53.

For almost all early-modern theologians and philosophers, then, the argument from "universal consent" on behalf of God's existence, while not a demonstrative proof, was as strong a moral proof as one could imagine, and one, thus, that ought to persuade all reasonable minds. If every nation that ever had lived and recorded its sense of the world had reached the conclusion that there was some God, who could doubt that it was an evident and inescapable truth? We have seen the effort to portray atheism as so impossible a conclusion that only an act of the will overriding all reason and evidence could sustain it. The argument from universal consent loomed large in such an effort. The atheist, real or imagined, sought to defend a conclusion so bizarre and extravagant that no peoples ever had reached it from their knowledge of self and world. He might just as well argue that there was no sun or no moon.

From the Christian perspective, the weakness of mankind's reason and the power of its passions often had led to scandalous misconceptions of God, and while some theologians sought to find "anticipations" of Christianity in natural theological knowledge, most distinguished categorically between a proper Christian notion of the Divinity and diverse idolatrous and anthropomorphic conceptions of God. It was not only that the gentile nations did not know the revealed truth of the Trinity, but that whole (if not most) peoples had failed to understand essential aspects of God's providence, spirituality, immutability, independence, and creative agency. Some saw such misunderstandings as "atheistic" by implication, since false beliefs about divine attributes either misrepresented the real God or posited a self-contradiction in the divine being (e.g., for Christians, a God without providence or independence was no true God at all). Almost everyone, however, saw such errors as having arisen from a failure of non-Christian theists to understand what followed from the infinity and perfection of the God that mind in fact had discerned. Nonetheless, even peoples foolish or dissolute enough to project general or, worse, human imperfections upon their gods did recognize a Supreme Being in some form, and this was considered powerful testimony to the ineluctable truth of His existence. Minucius Felix, a Latin Father of the Church, had noted with pleasure how even the most common people among the pagans acknowledged the God of the heavens, and he insisted that this arose from "the natural language of the common crowd" that did not require a "profession of faith made by a Christian" but was the portion of "even those who acknowledge Jupiter to be supreme."[2] His heirs claimed to

[2] Minucius Felix, *Octavius* cap. 18, #11. I have used the translation of R. Arbesmann, Minucius Felix, *Octavius*, in *The Fathers of the Church: A New Translation*, vol. x (New York, 1950). There were at least fifteen editions of the *Octavius* published in France from 1600 to 1712, of which five were published after 1652.

believe this to be true not only of the Greeks and Romans, but of all peoples whatsoever.

The source most widely cited by early-modern theologians and philosophers for the factual basis and the "moral" validity of the argument from universal consent was Cicero's *Tusculanae disputationes*. Having observed that men had known the gods from "the suggestions of nature [*natura admonente*]" even before they had acquired a "grasp of a reasoned system of causation," Cicero cited and defended his own culture's conclusion from this, a conclusion that also would be received as a commonplace of philosophical and pastoral theology within the Christian world:

> Furthermore, . . . this seems to be advanced as the surest basis for our belief in the existence of the gods, that there is no [people] so uncivilized, no one in the world, we are told, so barbarous that his mind has no inkling of a belief in [the] gods[.] [It is] true that many have wrong notions about the gods, for this usually is a result of a corrupt nature; nevertheless all men think that a divine power and divine nature exist, and that it is not the result of human conference or convention. . . . regulation or statute. . . . *[I]n every inquiry the unanimity of the [peoples] of the world must be regarded as a law of nature.*[3]

As Du Plessis d'Argentré put it in his *Elementa Theologica* (1702), in a general discussion of *évidence*, doubt was absurd in the presence of "general evidence," where all men who paid even minimal intellectual attention consented easily to the same belief. Truths generally obvious to all should be taken as "primary principles," since only fools would resist what all "sincere men" acknowledged to be certain. Arguments against what was universally recognized, for this doctor of the Sorbonne, invariably were made for the sake of argument alone, without sincere persuasion. It was more than foolishness to doubt what "all and diverse times and nations of mankind see as evident truth." This criterion did not hold for *negative* beliefs, for things might occur that people thought impossible, but held fully for *positive* beliefs.[4] The atheist, thus, would place himself against the common experience and thought of all mankind. As Alexander Ross's frequently reprinted survey of the world's religions, his *Pansebia*, put it, in a French edition of 1666, "How could atheists avoid

[3] Cicero, *Tusculanae disputationes* I.xiii. I have used the translation by J. E. King, ed. and trans., *Tusculan Disputations* (Loeb Classical Library, 1927), 20–30, changing his punctuation and substituting "peoples" for "races." The early-modern French reader would have consulted *Les Tusculanes de Cicéro*, trans. P. Du Ryer (Paris, 1655 [first published, Paris 1643]), or any number of Latin editions.

[4] Abbé Charles Du Plessis d'Argentré, *Elementa Theologica, in quibus de autoritate ac pondere cujuslibet argumenti theologici diligenter et accuratè disputatur* (Paris, 1702), 301–7. Du Plessis d'Argentré was a doctor of theology from the Sorbonne and a member of the Société de Sorbonne; his benefice was as abbé de la Sainte Croix.

shame and ignominy when they read this book, in which they will see that there is no people, however abominable it has been, that has renounced a Divinity?"[5] For Ross, "all the peoples know, even from the harmony and established order [of the world], from the marvelous operations of nature, and the beauty of the world, that there is a God."[6] We have seen how widespread in France the use of this argument had become.[7] As the *Journal de Trévoux* put it in 1724, favorably paraphrasing a fellow Jesuit, "*We have scarcely any stronger proofs against the atheists* than to show them this knowledge [of God's existence], so appropriate to human nature that it exists in all times, in all nations, in all minds." Despite all the varieties of human religions, there was, concerning the existence of God, "unanimity of belief on this fundamental preliminary [article] [*l'unanimité de créance sur ce préliminaire fondamental*]."[8] Thinkers might disagree on whether this demonstrated the *innateness* of the idea of the Deity, imprinted on the soul and mind by God Himself, or simply the obviousness of God's existence from the merest regard of the evidence of nature, but as the claims of almost all theologians insisted, no people was so benighted as to disbelieve in a divine being. The problem was that despite the commonplace status of the premise that all peoples believed in God, it was not, after all, a principle of reasoning that this was so, but a claim about the actual behavior of the world. The data on which such a claim was based, however, became increasingly problematic.

. . .

Concerning almost all topics that regard early-modern atheism, there is disproportionate attention paid to the role of Pierre Bayle. Ironically, this has elevated a thinker whose influence in many ways derived from his erudite study of the thought and texts of others to the position of a particularly innovative philosopher. Perhaps because those who have studied Bayle have studied him so brilliantly, there is a tendency to attribute phenomena general to the culture to Bayle and to his putative singularity. This has been done both with regard to the seventeenth century's obsession with the "problem" of providence and with regard to the unraveling of the argument from universal consent. Indeed, to hear some historians tell the tale, the argument from universal consent was scarcely challenged, in theory or in detail, except for Pierre Bayle's late seventeenth-century

[5] Alexander Ross, *Les religions du monde, ou Démonstration de toutes les religions et hérésies de l'Asie, Afrique, Amérique, et de l'Europe, depuis le commencement du monde jusqu'à présent*, trans. Thomas La Grue (Amsterdam, 1666), "Préface."

[6] Ibid., 370.

[7] See supra, pt. 1, chap. 1.

[8] *Journal de Trévoux*, sept. 1724, 1571–2.

assault upon it from the Huguenot *Refuge*. Frank Manuel offered this view:

> He [Bayle] denied the common Christian tradition that nations of atheists could not exist and flouted the orthodox proposition that an idea of God or divinity was in all men . . . Bayle combed the travel literature for accounts of atheist savages, in order to demolish the argument . . . that the general consensus of nations was a witness to the existence of a divinity. . . . And he followed his evidence on the existence of atheist savage nations with the astounding report that these primitives who were without religion, far from being bestial and vicious, were benign and mild toward one another.[9]

I, too, shall flirt with overemphasis on Bayle, but, we shall see, it was in fact difficult to *avoid* finding evidence against universal consent in seventeenth-century literature. Far from astonishing his audience, Bayle was reporting on materials commonplace by the time he wrote, materials that long had influenced the learned world. Generations before Bayle wrote, Gassendi had placed the existence of God among those "things that are nevertheless not so universally admitted that certain peoples—as recent accounts of the New World attest—and even a host of philosophers—as emerges from ancient history—persuaded of the opposite, are not prepared, if I take them not to be sane and whole in their minds, to argue that it is rather I who am ill and deprived of judgment."[10]

Bayle indeed had done something with more force than had most of his learned contemporaries, although not more forcefully than ancient skeptics with whom they were quite familiar: he had criticized the argument from universal consent on *theoretical* grounds. That is to say, he had urged that *even if its factual basis were correct*, it did not prove anything. Most thinkers would have agreed if the issue were formal demonstration, but Bayle, in his *Pensées diverses sur la comète*, his *Additions aux Pensées diverses*, his *Continuation des Pensées diverses*, and his *Réponses aux questions d'un provincial* was attacking its status as even a moral proof. He did not find it compelling at all.

If one reduces the argument to a convenient syllogism, proof from universal consent ran as follows:

Major premise:	what is universally believed by all peoples is true.
Minor premise:	all peoples past and present have believed that God exists.
Conclusion:	that "God exists" is true.

[9] Frank E. Manuel, *The Eighteenth Century Confronts the Gods* (New York, 1967 [first published Cambridge, Mass., 1959]), 34.

[10] Pierre Gassendi, *Ad Librum Domini Edoardi Herberti, Angli, De Vertitate, EPISTOLA*, ed. and trans. Bernard Rochot, in *Actes du Congrès du Tricentenaire de Pierre Gassendi* (n.p., n.d.), 251–87. The quotation is from 278.

Bayle attacked the major premise (which for most others was indeed *not* a principle of reason but merely a morally persuasive assumption) in arguments that gained a certain notoriety. He claimed that it presupposed that nature's general impressions on us were an infallible mark of truth; that it would have established the truth of polytheism throughout most of human history, against the Jews and against the first Christians; that it reinforced each people's particular prejudices; and, perhaps his essential purpose, that it perniciously would authorize countless superstitions, such as astrology, divination, and fear of comets as ill omens. Against the minor premise, Bayle argued primarily that it would be impossible for us to know if all peoples past, present, and future acknowledged any truth, and, indeed, he raised examples or claims of particular instances of atheism.[11]

Where for Bayle the theoretical criticisms were the most telling, he in fact was directing them against an argument that people found *persuasive* even if not logically demonstrative, *if its facts were correct*. In some sense, Bayle missed the spirit with which his age approached the question of *moral* proof. A reviewer in the *Nouvelles de la République des Lettres*, writing in 1705, paraphrased Bayle's arguments quite cogently, but he persisted in his beliefs that "one must never reject an opinion, above all when it is generally received, on the pretext that it is subject to difficulties, or that one can make objections against it." The proof was simply too good to be abandoned on hypothetical grounds: "The argument in question having been received as good by all that there have been of great minds in all the centuries is a prejudice in its favor, and it would be necessary for the difficulties that one opposes to it to be of the greatest force in order to be able to shake one's persuasion of it." As for our limited knowledge of "all peoples," this was merely a "perhaps" that Bayle had introduced, a purely hypothetical "perhaps" of no consequence. As for claims of atheistic peoples, these surely were either "romances by honest men" that passed for genuine travel literature or the reports of "travelers without lights, without judgment, of no reputation, and perhaps without good faith." Most importantly, however, for the reviewer, Bayle had simply confused the requirements of metaphysical and moral arguments; a few exceptions would not shake the latter:

> The force of the argument in question does not depend at all on a metaphysical universality. If Cicero or someone else has proposed it as such, we are not obliged to defend their view. Assail them as much as you wish, the blows

[11] Pierre Bayle, *Pensées diverses*. This "new edition" of Rotterdam, 1721, contained the *Pensées diverses*, the *Additions aux Pensées diverses*, and the *Continuation des pensées diverses*); it was republished, with the *Réponse aux questions d'un provincial* in vol. III of the *OD*.

> will not fall on us. It is sufficient that most nations, those, above all, that are enlightened, and that are in agreement on virtually nothing else beside this, unanimously consent to acknowledge a Divinity, to persuade me that this belief is based on a solid and unshakable foundation.[12]

This review is particularly interesting and concedes more than its author may have known. On the one hand, of course, it simply drew the common distinction between a metaphysical proof, a category in which it did not place the argument from universal consent, and a persuasive moral proof that it felt remained unimperiled by Bayle's criticisms. On the other hand, however, it abandoned the claim of "all nations" in favor of one of "most nations, those, above all, that are enlightened," and sought to discredit sources of evidence to the contrary. In these modifications, it accurately reflected the real drama of the argument from universal consent in the seventeenth century, which centered far less upon any issue of the validity of the criterion than upon the essential issue of whether or not the minor premise, that all peoples believed in God, could be sustained. That, after all, was what made atheism seem so unthinkable. The issue for us, of course, is not what the facts of the world actually might or might not have been concerning religious belief in diverse nations, but what contemporaneous travelers and commentators taught about this to the early-modern French learned world. The Huguenot reviewer of Bayle wanted his readers to see those who reported on atheistic peoples as either writers of fiction or as manifestly impeachable witnesses. It was not difficult, however, for contemporaries to reach far different conclusions.

. . .

The seventeenth century read or knew of a vast literature, much of it emanating from the French encounter with the natives of the New World, that, simply put, raised the profoundest doubt about universal consent to the existence of God. It was difficult indeed to attribute all grounds for such doubt to "romances by honest men" or to "travelers without lights, without judgment, of no reputation, and perhaps without good faith." From Jean de Léry's *Voyage* of 1578 until the dawn of the Enlightenment, a host of pious and respected authors noted that "despite Cicero's belief" (or "despite St. Augustine's," who had repeated it), they had found whole peoples and nations without any notion whatsoever of God. Many authors wrote to the contrary, but negative evidence, that is, evidence of the "exceptions," logically counted all the more in an argument from the universality of a phenomenon.

[12] *Nouvelles de la République des Lettres*, fév. 1705, 123–37.

Léry was a French Calvinist, an eventual refugee and Genevan pastor, who had lived among the Indians of Brazil for a year. His *Voyage* was first published in La Rochelle in 1578 but was reprinted in 1580, 1585, 1595, 1599, 1600, 1611, 1642, and 1677. Writing of the Carib Indians, the Huguenot explorer observed that "with regard to what is termed religion among other peoples, it can be said openly that not only do these poor savages have none at all, but that, also, if there is a nation which is without God and which lives without God in the world, it is truly they [*s'il y a nation qui soit et vive sans Dieu au monde, ce sont vraiment eux*]."[13] For Léry, in fact, "this sentence of Cicero" was not vitiated by the Caribs, since he believed that we should recognize their "fear of thunder" (or any of their "superstitions") as a vestigial recognition of God's existence. Nonetheless, when he concluded his discussion of the beliefs of the American Indians, he acknowledged that "having considered them thus empty and deprived of all sound sentiment of God," he could have found his faith in God "shaken," were it not "supported by other things."[14] Further, he contrasted the Indians of Brazil to both the ancient pagans and the Indians of Peru, the Caribs being not only ignorant of the one true God, but devoid even of polytheism: "They neither acknowledge nor adore any celestial or terrestrial gods." Finally, he declared them to share with "the most demonically possessed atheists" the desire to make others believe "that there is not any God."[15]

Others proclaimed the Indians of Florida, the Caribbean, and South America as without any such "vestiges" at all. René Laudonnière, in 1586, declared the Indians of Florida to have "no knowledge of God or any religion."[16] The Capuchin missionary Claude d'Abbeville assured his readers in 1614 that the "Topinamba Indians" of the Maranón basin had "neither faith nor any shadow of religion."[17] The explorer Jean Mocquet described "all the peoples of Brazil" as being "without faith and without law, and without any certain belief in any Divinity, true or false, not even worshiping idols or other things."[18]

[13] Jean de Léry, *Histoire d'un voyage fait en la terre du Brésil* . . . [La Rochelle, 1578], ed. Michel Contat (Lausanne, 1972), 25–26.

[14] Ibid., 187–207. His discussion of the effect upon his faith of seeing these people "without God" occurs on 206–7.

[15] Ibid., 187–91.

[16] René Laudonnière, *L'Histoire notable de la Floride* . . . [1586]; see the critical edition, René Laudonnière, *Three Voyages*, ed. and trans. Charles E. Bennet (Gainesville, Fl., 1975), 11–13.

[17] Claude d'Abbeville, O.F.M., Capuchin, *Histoire de la mission des pères capucins en l'Isle de Maragnan et terre circonvoisines* (Paris, 1614), 328.

[18] Jean Mocquet, *Voyages en Afrique, Asie, Indes Orientales & Occidentales* . . . (Paris, 1617), 133. (The 1st ed. of Mocquet's *Voyages* was Paris, 1616; it was also published in Rouen, 1645, and Rouen, 1665.)

By the mid- to late seventeenth century, such views of the "Carib Indians" were expressed quite frequently. Charles de Rochefort's popular *Histoire naturelle et morale des Iles Antilles de l'Amérique*, published in 1658 and again in a revised edition of 1681, reminded his readers of Cicero's view, and of the arguments that "nature itself imprinted knowledge of the Divinity in the mind of every man" and that every nation had "a natural sentiment of God," even when "wrapped in the shadows of Paganism." If Cicero had known the Caribs, however, de Rochefort concluded, he would have been more circumspect. Even when we explain God and the creation to them, he informed his readers, "they do not recognize the Lord of nature in this admirable work of the universe." Indeed, he insisted, "those . . . who have conversed among the island-dwelling Caribs [*les Caraïbes Insulaires*] are obliged to admit that they have just about smothered all knowledge that nature gave them of the Divinity by the violence of their brutal passions. . . . They do not even have any name in order to express [the idea of] Divinity, let alone in order to serve Him." Further, even after "listening with great patience to every discourse" we made to them about God, they responded "as if by mockery" rather than with agreement, more impressed by how well we spoke than by what we said. Nor were they alone in their disbelief. Travel literature had made Cicero's dictum seem quite problematic:

> But it seems that it is today quite difficult [*malaisé*] to confirm the famous words of this incomparable Orator. For the poor savages of the ancient people of the Andes in Peru and of the two provinces of Chirhuanes or Cheriganes, of most of the regions of New France, of New Mexico, of New Holland, of Brazil, of the New Low Countries, of Tierra del Fuego, of the Arouäges, of the habitations of the Cayenne River, of the Iles des Larrons and of several other [islands], from what chroniclers report, do not have any spirit of religion and adore no sovereign power.[19]

In short, "these barbarians [the Caribs] . . . have not been able at all to discern or recognize the honor that God has done them by revealing Himself to them in so many beautiful creatures . . . [and] they have remained without hope and without God in the world."[20]

In a work published in 1664, Antoine Biet, priest and curé of Sainte Geneviève de Senlis, wrote from French Guyana, where he was father superior of the missionaries, about Indian disbelief in God. He too explicitly stated that Cicero's rule of universal consent, the assertion that "there have not been any nations so barbarous" not to know or invent God or

[19] Charles de Rochefort, *Histoire naturelle et morale des Iles Antilles de l'Amérique* (Rotterdam, 1658), 413–14. (In ibid., final ed., rev. and aug. [Rotterdam, 1681], this discussion is on 468–69.)

[20] Ibid., 423. (In ed. of 1681, 478.)

gods, did *not* apply to the new French colony. The issue was not the truth or falsity, the coherence or superstition of the Indians' view of God, but the fact that "not recognizing any Divinity, they do not have any words to name Him," which, he noted, made it difficult to discuss religion with them. Biet knew full well that his observations went against the assumptions of his culture:

> It is a wholly astonishing thing that these peoples among whom we live have not been restrained until the present by any divine or human laws, *living in a perfect ignorance of any divinity, either true or false . . . [without] the least tincture, that is to say, even some small bit of knowledge of some divinity.*[21]

Later in the 1660s, the Dominican missionary Jean-Baptiste Du Tertre, writing from the Antilles, disagreed with the view that the Caribs had no sense of any God.[22] Nonetheless, he claimed that he had met black slaves in the Antilles who were genuine atheists. While some blacks, he wrote, were Christians and some Muslims, "I have found a large quantity of them who had no religion and who were neither idolators nor Muslims; who adored no Divinity, and never had made any reflection that there was a God."[23] Almost two generations later, the Dominican Jean-Baptiste Labat, in a work first published in 1722 and reprinted in 1724, undertook explicitly to update Du Tertre's study, which he termed "admirable for the time in which he wrote it." He disagreed with Du Tertre about the black slaves, almost all of whom he found not atheistic but idolatrous.[24] On the Carib Indians, however, he denied his predecessor's attribution of some religious sense to them. "What I know very well," he wrote, "is that they have no religion nor any fixed cult; they seem to know no other beings but material ones; they do not even have in their language any term to express God or a spirit."[25] In January 1717, Jacques Bernard's *Nouvelles de la République des Lettres* informed its readers of a French Catholic royal engineer's trip to the western coast of South America. According to the widely read learned journal, he had sought to inform himself of the religious beliefs of the Indians and had learned from the missionaries and others "that they had none." Indeed, he had been assured by "a Jesuit . . . that they were true atheists, that they adored nothing at

[21] Antoine Biet, *Voyages de France Equinoxiale en l'Isle de Cayenne, entrepris par les françois en l'année M.DC.LII.* (Paris, 1664), 359–62.

[22] Jean-Baptiste Du Tertre, O.P., *Histoire générale des Antilles habitées par les françois*, 4 vols. (Paris, 1667–1671), II, 364.

[23] Ibid., 502.

[24] Jean-Baptiste Labat, O.P., *Nouveau voyage aux Isles de l'Amérique*, 2 vols. (The Hague, 1724), II, 46. This work was first published in Paris, 1722.

[25] Ibid., II, 123.

all, and that they mocked everything that one tried to tell them on this subject."[26]

Far from being a discredited theme, then, the view that whole Indian nations might be considered exceptions to "universal consent" was maintained by travelers and missionaries who might well be taken as the best informed observers by elements of the reading public. In 1710, Jacques Bernard published a letter from a correspondent who had settled in the Carolinas, and whom he described as "a savant who is very well known to me," criticizing Bernard for having argued that the Indians of Carolina adored a God and Creator. "That would make them quite learned and quite religious," Bernard's critic wrote, but, in fact, "it is not known at the present if they even know that there is a God. One does not see much probability of it."[27]

Travel, missionary, and settler literature from New France was much more abundant and also could offer grounds for rejecting the argument from universal consent. While Jacques Cartier had declared the Indians of Canada to have "no belief in God [*aucune créance de Dieu*]," his own account of their views contradicted this, and he even assigned a term in their vocabulary for the Deity.[28] Reports from other early explorers, however, were more problematic. In his first works on New France, Samuel de Champlain had portrayed the Indians as idolatrous and, from the Christian perspective, confused, as when "they say that God is not very good." Nonetheless, the Indians he wrote of in 1603 "believe there is a God," and those discussed in 1613, while they had "no religion," likewise believed in His existence.[29] In his description of his travels from 1615 to 1618, however, published in 1619, Champlain now claimed to have met "settled tribes with a taste for tillage of the soil, but without faith or law, living without God and without religion like brute beasts."[30] He described a village whose "poor creatures" lived and died "without any knowledge of God."[31] He described the Hurons in starkly atheistic terms: "They recognize no divinity, they adore and believe in no God nor in

[26] *Nouvelles de la République des Lettres*, jan.–fév. 1717, 109. The work reported on was Amédée-François Frezier, *Relation du voyage de la mer de sud aux côtes de Chili, du Pérou, et du Brézil, fait pendant les années 1712, 1713, & 1714*, 2 vols. (Amsterdam, 1717).

[27] *Nouvelles de la République des Lettres*, avril 1710, 468.

[28] Jacques Cartier, *Bref récit, et succincte narration, de la navigation faicte es Ysles de Canada* . . . [Paris, 1545], in *Trois voyages au Canada* ["Collection Voyages et Découvertes"], ed. Bertrand Guégan (Paris, n.d.), 40–41, 60.

[29] Samuel de Champlain, *The Works of Samuel de Champlain* [in French and English], gen. ed. H. P. Biggar, trans. H. H. Langton and W. F. Ganong, 6 vols. (Toronto, 1922–1936), I, 111–12, 115; II, 46–47. The translation is theirs.

[30] Ibid., III, 15–16.

[31] Ibid., 51–52.

anything whatsoever."[32] A 1632 edition of his travels shared his view of an Indian tribe encountered along the Atlantic coast: "They do not differ from our Souriquois and Canadian Indians, who worship neither sun nor moon nor anything, and pray no more than beasts."[33] Marc Lescarbot's *Histoire de la Nouvelle France* (1609, and in a third edition by 1617), describing the "Souriquois, and other neighboring tribes," assured its readers "that they are devoid of all knowledge of God."[34] He, too, knew that he was contradicting Cicero, and he conceded that many Indian tribes were merely idolatrous, but, nonetheless, he was certain of the atheism of whole Indian nations:

> But even though Cicero has said, speaking of the nature of the gods, that there is no people so savage, so brutal, nor so barbarous that it is not imbued with some opinion of them [the gods], yet it is so that in these last centuries nations have been found that do not have any sense of them at all.[35]

Large numbers of Jesuit missionaries in North America seemed to hesitate in their characterizations of Canadian Indian beliefs. At some level, they seemed to sense how difficult it was to portray the worldview of an alien people; at another, they seemed to pull back from the brink of declaring whole peoples atheistic in contradiction of their tradition. Paul Le Jeune, in a narrative published in 1632, wrote of the Iroquois that they "think only about how to live and take revenge upon their enemies. They are not tied to the worship of any particular Divinity."[36] He did not declare them atheistic, however. Charles L'Allemant was convinced that the Iroquois worshiped the sun and acknowledged a creator but did not give Him any homage.[37] Paul Raqueneau, discussing the Hurons, wrote rather ambiguously that, "to tell the truth, none of the peoples of these lands has received from its ancestors any knowledge of a God. . . . Nonetheless, although they are barbarians, there has remained in their hearts a secret idea of the Divinity and of a First Principle, author of all things, whom they call on without knowing Him." However, he added, "they do not know who He is; they have neither fear . . . [nor] love . . . [nor] respect . . . [nor] worship."[38] Jacques Bordier quoted for his readers from the

[32] Ibid., 143, and IV, 319–20.

[33] Ibid., III, 407.

[34] Marc Lescarbot, *Histoire de la Nouvelle France . . .*, 3d ed. (Paris, 1617), 92.

[35] Ibid., 709–11.

[36] Paul Le Jeune, S.J., *Briève relation du voyage de la Nouvelle France . . .* (Paris, 1632), 28.

[37] Charles L'Allemant, S.J., *Lettre du père Charles L'Allemant superieur de la Mission de Canada, de la Compagnie de Jésus . . ., oú sont contenus les moeurs et façons de vivre des sauvages habitans de ce païs là . . .* (Paris, 1627), 7.

[38] Paul Raqueneau, S.J., *Relation de ce qui s'est passé dans le pays des Hurons, pays de la Nouvelle France . . .*, in *Relation de . . . 1647 & 1648* (Paris, 1649), pt. 2, 117–20.

journal of his fellow Jesuit, Allouez, who had studied the religion of the Ottawa Indians. According to Allouez, the Indians " 'do not recognize any purely spiritual Divinity,' " but they were difficult to categorize religiously. He concluded, concerning the Ottawas, that they were " 'not very far removed from recognizing the Creator of the world,' " which seemed to leave them somewhere in between belief and disbelief.[39]

Many formulas tried to capture that same sense of slender connection to Christian theological terms. For Pierre Biard, the Indians had "a certain tenuous notion [*tenuem quandam habent cognitionem*]" of God.[40] For the author of the *Relatio Rerum Gestarum in Novo-Francia Missione Annis 1613 & 1614*, they should be understood as "having scarcely any conception of Divinity [*vix ulla Numinis cogitatione*]."[41] For Joseph Jouvency, writing almost a hundred years later, the Indians had no system of or concern for religion, and the object of their honor "has no defined character." Nonetheless, he concluded, "they sense . . . as if by twilight that there exists some deity."[42] For François Du Creux, in his *Historiae Canadensis* (1664), it had to be, as Saint Augustine had written, that "there do not exist any peoples so fierce and so barbaric that God does not speak to their hearts," but he confessed that Indian creation legends seemed "quite odd and quite dubious" to the Indians themselves, and that "the Indians cannot conceive of anything incorporeal."[43] When the Jesuits first arrived in Canada, Du Creux insisted, they encountered among the Indians "a darkness so thick that . . . there was barely any trace left of knowledge of the great and good God." At most, he conceded, "there still remains, in the farthest corners of their hearts, some faint conception of the Divinity."[44]

The development of the Jesuit Paul Le Jeune's thinking on this matter is particularly striking, for it shows both the possibilities of interpretation increasingly open to the learned culture and the perils faced by the argument from universal consent. In 1632, we have seen above, he was perplexed by Indian beliefs but saw no atheism in them. In 1633, he noted

[39] Jacques Bordier, S.J., *Relation de ce qui s'est passé de plus remarquable aux missions des pères de la Compagnie de Jésus en la Nouvelle France, les années 1666 & 1667* (Paris, 1668), 55–57, 103–4.

[40] Pierre Biard, S.J., *Missio Canadensis. Epistola ex Portu-regali in Acadia* . . . (Dillingen, n.d.), 15–16. Biard's *Epistola* was translated into French as the *Relation de la Nouvelle France* . . . (cited infra n. 75).

[41] *Relatio Rerum Gestarum in Novo-Francia Missione Annis 1613 & 1614*, in *Annuae Litterae Societatis Iesu, Anni MDCXIIX* (Lyon, 1618), 564.

[42] Joseph Jouvency, S.J., *De Regione et Moribus Canadensium, seu Barbarorum Novae Franciae* (Rome, 1710), 347.

[43] François Du Creux, S.J., *Historiae Canadensis seu Novae Franciae libri decem* (Paris, 1664), 77–78, 87.

[44] Ibid., 1–2.

the widespread descriptions of the Algonquins as atheistic, declared that when he had read such things back in France, he had been "astonished," and reassured his readers that such a characterization was "a great mistake," even if understandable: "I admit that the Indians have no . . . prayer . . . or worship . . . and that their knowledge is more like a darkness, but one cannot deny that they recognize some being superior to man. . . . I do not know their inner thoughts, but . . . it can be seen that they acknowledge some Divinity."[45]

By 1634, he was lamenting the fact that the Indians thought only "of the present life" and had no God to whom they prayed or made promises, which still could be dismissed as relating merely to religion and not to the issue of any natural recognition of a God.[46] By 1635, however, his commitment to universal consent was under severe strain. Concerning the Hurons, whom he knew best, he still maintained that "it is so obvious, so evident that a Divinity who made heaven and earth exists that our Hurons cannot remain completely ignorant of Him." "Although their mind's vision is so very obscured by the darkness of a lengthy ignorance and by their vices and their sins," he observed, "they still perceive something of Him, although they misunderstand Him grossly." He was increasingly despairing, however, over his inability to converse with the Hurons about God. He complained that "if you ask them who made the sky . . . their only reply is that they do not know anything about that," and that "when we preach one God, Creator . . . to them," their only reply is "that this is fine for our land but not for theirs, that every land has its own ways."[47] Further, he recently had met the Indians of Cap Bréton, and, for the first time, based now on increased experience, he was not certain that the "universal" knowledge was theirs:

> *What they lack is knowledge of God*. . . . It is wondrous that we have as yet been unable to discover any trace of this knowledge [of God] in what we know about their language. Perhaps we shall discover more, . . . for it is incredible that nature's light should be completely extinguished in them, or that they never converse among themselves about what they cannot be completely ignorant of. For all of that, however, we have not noticed, up to the present, any more religion among these piteous savages than among the animals.[48]

Note well that it was a freethinking deist, the baron de La Hontan, who worked with more diligence than anyone "to rescue" the North American

[45] Paul Le Jeune, S.J., *Relation de ce qui s'est passé en la Nouvelle France en l'année 1633* (Paris, 1634), 75–79.

[46] Paul Le Jeune, S.J., *Relation de . . . 1634* (Paris, 1635), 82.

[47] Paul Le Jeune, S.J., *Relation de . . . 1635* (Paris, 1636), 166–69.

[48] Ibid., 210–13.

Indians from charges of atheism, and to portray them as those virtuous natural religionists whom the Rousseauist elements of the later Enlightenment would so admire. While learned Christian culture puzzled over the appropriate categories for understanding Indian beliefs and disbeliefs, it was La Hontan who assigned to the North Americans a deistic profession of faith, based upon an empirical, wholly natural inference of a purposeful creation, immortality of the soul, and natural knowledge of good and evil.[49] Why should the culture have taken the heterodox thinker as a more reliable guide to matters theological than orthodox missionaries and travelers?

. . .

Indeed, the missionary status of so many chroniclers of global patterns of belief and the prestige of so many writers of travel literature surely made it impossible for many to dismiss claims of atheistic peoples and schools of thought in the world as merely "romances" or reports "without good faith." The Jesuit missionary Alexandre de Rhodes, writing in midcentury from Tonkin, characterized the Confucianism he met there as "appropriate to forming good morals," but noted that Confucius "makes no mention [in his works] of God, the sovereign principle of everything." Confucius, he assured his readers, "makes the first principle corporeal, without knowledge, without reason, without soul, incapable, and unworthy of cult and adoration," all of which, he noted, "manifestly leads to atheism." De Rhodes also promulgated what we soon shall see was a common view of Buddhist "atheism," informing his audience that there was a public idolatrous Buddhism for the amusement and distraction of the common people, and an atheistic doctrine passed on by Buddha to "the most ingenious and the most cunning of his disciples [*les plus ingenieux et les plus malins de ses disciples*]" and kept alive to this day.[50] Three years after de Rhodes's work was translated from the Latin of its first edition into French, Charles Chaulmer's *Tableau d'Afrique* portrayed the tribes west of the Niger river as living "without recognizing any Divinity." He described the "Kaffirs" in unambiguously atheistic terms: "They know neither any God nor any religion whatsoever [*Ils ne connoissent ny*

[49] Louis-Armand, baron de La Hontan, *Nouveaux voyages de Mr. le Baron de la Hontan dans l'Amérique Septentrionale*, 2 vols. (The Hague, 1703). Although the title page says "1703," this edition was reviewed in the *Histoire des Ouvrages des Savans*, août 1702, 342–50.

[50] Alexandre de Rhodes, S.J., *Histoire du royaume de Tunquin, et des grands progrez que la prédication de l'Evangile y a faits en la conversion des infidelles. Depuis l'année* 1627 *jusques à l'année* 1646, trans. Henry Albi, S.J., [from the Latin] (Lyon, 1651), 61–66.

Dieu ny Religion quelconque]."[51] Chaulmer was not just any traveler but offered to his audience the title of royal *historiographe de France.* It was the Jesuit missionary Ferdinand Verbiest who in 1684 asserted that the eastern Tartars of China, unlike the western Tartars, were a people "the majority of whom have no religion and do not believe in any God [*dont la plûpart n'ont aucune Religion et ne croyent point de Dieu*]."[52]

In general, the authors of the most popular commentaries on foreign lands and beliefs were figures of genuine prestige. Sir Paul Rycaut's account of the Ottoman Empire, for example, was quickly translated from English into French in 1670, in which form (and others) it enjoyed multiple editions. Rycaut had been King Charles II's ambassador from Great Britain to the Ottoman court. While Ottoman religion occupied only a minor part of his attention, it was a subject on which Rycaut had disturbing things to say. Discussing the varieties of "sects" among the Turks, he noted that "it will not be inappropriate to make it known . . . to what an extent atheism has introduced itself into that country." The "sect" of atheists, however, as described by Rycaut, was not composed of some mere handful of the most ignorant men of Constantinople, but of a significant number of the most educated:

> Those, thus, who profess atheism, refer to each other among themselves as "Muserins," that is to say, "we possess the true secret," and this secret is nothing other than to deny the Divinity absolutely, to maintain affirmatively that it is nature, or the internal principle of each individual entity, that directs the ordinary course of all the things that we see and that we admire; . . . and that man germinates, grows, and withers like grasses and like flowers. *It is a surprising thing to see the large number of persons who are of this opinion in Constantinople, the majority of them being "cadis" and learned in the writings of the Arabs.*[53]

The atheistic "Muserins" even had a notable martyr, according to Rycaut, one Mahomet Effendi, "prosperous and well versed in the knowledge of Oriental sciences," who he claimed was executed "during my stay in Constantinople, for having insolently proffered several blasphemies against the existence of God." Effendi's best-known argument, he noted,

[51] Charles, sieur de Chaulmer, *Le tableau d'Afrique* (Paris, 1654), 199–201, 279–81.

[52] Ferdinand Verbiest, S.J., *Lettre du P. Ferdinand Verbiest de la Compagnie de Jésus, écrite de la cour de Pékin sur un voyage que l'empereur de la Chine a fait l'an 1683 dans la Tartarie* (Paris, 1684). The *Lettre* is quite brief. It was reprinted in Paris in 1685 and 1688 (bound with other works) and also in Pierre Bayle, ed., *Retour des pièces choisies* (Emmerich, 1687), 72–96. The quotation in the Bayle edition is found on 76–77. Verbiest's account of eastern Tartar "atheism" was also shared by the *Nouvelles de la République des Lettres*, fév. 1685, 199–203.

[53] Paul Rycaut, *Histoire de l'état présent de l'Empire Ottoman . . .*, trans. M. Briot [from the English] (Paris, 1670), 237–40.

went like this: " 'Either there is no God . . . or He is neither so able nor so wise as our doctors want to persuade us; for if that were so [that God existed], He would not have let me live so long, I who am the greatest opponent of His existence who ever has been in the world, and who speaks of it [God's existence] with the greatest disdain.' " Further, Effendi (in Rycaut's portrait) showed a striking constancy of character for an atheist. Offered the chance to save his life by disavowing his doctrine, "he preferred to die in his impiety than to retract it, saying that the love that he had for the truth obliged him to suffer martyrdom, although he was certain that he had no recompense for which to hope."[54]

Rycaut was wholly aware that such things were not supposed to be, which in many ways only added force to his narrative. "I admit that until now," he wrote, "I was unable to believe that there was genuine atheism in the world, persuaded, as I am, that the existence of God can be demonstrated by natural light and by reason." Events in Constantinople, however, had changed his mind: "[Effendi's] invincible obstinacy made me understand that there are men who have extinguished these bright lights of nature and of reason in their hearts, in a horrifying manner." Nor, again, was this an affair of the ignorant and marginal: "The poison of this [atheistic] doctrine is so subtle that it has penetrated even into the chambers of the seraglio, into the apartments of the women and eunuchs, and infected the pashas and all their court."[55]

Reviewing a 1709 French reedition of Rycaut's work, the *Nouvelles de la République des Lettres* explained that "atheism has made great progress among [the Turks]," faithfully paraphrased the views of the "Muserrim" and their martyr Effendi, and explicated the absolute naturalism that purportedly underlay their denial of God. In a rare departure from his normal procedure, the editor, Jacques Bernard, inserted himself explicitly in his *compte rendu* to argue with the Turkish atheists, insisting that their concept of a Nature capable of design by its own principles led to absurdities and could not be an entity distinct from God Himself; that Effendi mistakenly seemed to think that his insults could in any way harm God; and that "the resolution he took to be the Martyr of Atheism . . . only proves that there is no mental oddity [*point de travers d'esprit*] of which man could not be capable."[56] Readers might find that well said, but they scarcely could have found all this supportive of the factual premise of the argument from universal consent.

For readers who did not purchase or read travel literature directly, the learned journals, we just have seen, made certain that its "discoveries"

[54] Ibid.
[55] Ibid.
[56] *Nouvelles de la République des Lettres*, nov. 1709, 493–96.

were widely shared. Indeed, if one missed an argument against universal consent in original works (as I myself have learned), one was sure to discover it in the journals. In 1702, for example, journals gave broad coverage to publication of the Jesuit Charles Le Gobien's *Relation des Isles Marianes* (1701). Readers of both the *Histoire des Ouvrages des Savans* and the *Nouvelles de la République des Lettres* in 1702 confronted the missionary's pronouncement that "the inhabitants of the Mariana Islands have no idea [of religion] and do not acknowledge any Divinity."[57] Two years later, readers of the *Histoire des Ouvrages des Savans* encountered the same distinction that the Jesuit de Rhodes had made (for Tonkin) between popular Buddhist idolatry and educated Buddhist atheism, only now it was being applied to Formosa. Readers discovered that a learned study of that island nation had concluded from familiarity with its inhabitants that "the religion of the Formosans is not uniform: idolatry is the religion of the people, and atheism is that of those men who rise a bit above the vulgar."[58]

Engelbert Kaempfer's study of Japan, translated into French in 1729, did not analyze Buddhism similarly in its discussion of the major religions of the island empire, which he characterized as Buddhist, Shinto, Confucian, and Christian. Discussing the Japanese variant of Confucianism, however, the Protestant philosopher, natural historian, and world traveler informed his readers that *its* adherents were atheistic: "They believe the world eternal and suppose that men and animals have been produced by . . . the sky and the five sublunar elements. *Since they acknowledge no Gods*, they have neither temples, nor . . . cult."[59]

Again, such assertions of actual atheism were by no means the prevailing French discussions of religion in any of these lands, but again, they were not made by suspect witnesses, and the issue was one where evidence against "universal" belief counted logically more than evidence for such a phenomenon. In the space of some thirteen years, three discussions of the religion of the Siamese provided readers with a sequence that well could have seemed one of growing understanding. In 1678, Jean-Baptiste Tavernier's *Six voyages* reported on his conversations with Siamese bonzes and perhaps left his readers somewhat confused: "If one asks

[57] *Histoire des Ouvrages des Savans*, mars 1702, 114; *Nouvelles de la République des Lettres*, mars 1702, 322–23.

[58] *Histoire des Ouvrages des Savans*, nov. 1704, 519.

[59] Engelbert Kaempfer, *Histoire naturelle, civile, et ecclésiastique de l'Empire du Japon*, trans. P. Des Maizeaux, 2 vols. (The Hague, 1729), I, 215–17. This was a translation from the English edition, which had been translated from the German by J.-G. Scheuchezer. The entire discussion of Japanese religion, primarily focused on Buddhism and Shinto, is found in I, 175–217. The "Vie de l'Auteur" that would have impressed readers with Kaempfer's credentials is found in I, v–xii.

them where their God is, they answer that He has disappeared and that they do not know where He is."[60] Ten years later, Nicolas Gervaise's *Histoire naturelle et politique du royaume de Siam* conceded that the Siamese believed in neither a "First Principle" nor an "Author of all things." "According to them," he further acknowledged, "the world has no Creator or Master; it is the work of chance; and all of the parts that compose it were assembled on their own; it has always been or rather one could not indicate any instant when it has not been." Nonetheless, he insisted, these were heathen misunderstandings of God, in whom the Siamese in fact believed. They had a principle of Divinity, even if they did not link it to the formation of the world.[61] In 1691, however, the *Du royaume de Siam* appeared, by Simon de La Loubère, who had lived there for two years as Louis XIV's *envoyé extraordinaire.* La Loubère explicitly addressed the issue of whether the Siamese merely had a misunderstanding about God's nature, and concluded that "they have no sort of theology, and one perhaps could exculpate them of the accusation of a cult of false divinities by means of a yet more culpable impiety, which is *to know no Divinity, neither true nor false.*"[62] In a separate discussion of Siamese beliefs, he reported that, in particular, "men of letters . . . today have no sentiment of religion and believe neither in the existence of any God nor in the immortality of the soul." They "acknowledge no intelligent [Supreme] Being, . . . [but] only a blind fatality." Claiming to have presented "the entire teachings of the Siamese," he described these as a "doctrine in which I find *no idea of Divinity.*" The ancient pagans, he noted, indeed had possessed confused views of things divine but nonetheless had believed in Divinity, even an Epicurus who denied the providence of the gods. "But the Siamese," he insisted, "have no similar idea. . . . [and] I believe that one can be certain that [they] have no idea of any God." With learned citations that indeed must have seemed more serious discussion than that of any of his predecessors, the French king's representative in Siam sought to refute every claim of any Siamese theism, insisting that Siam had "lost . . . the idea of Divinity" totally and without any ambiguity. Travelers had confused a cult of respect to deceased ancestors with religious worship and falsely inferred some remnant of belief in God; study of Siamese sources and discussions with them disabused one of such a view. In brief,

[60] Jean-Baptiste Tavernier, baron Aubonne, *Les six voyages . . . en Turquie, en Perse et aux Indes pendant l'espace de quarante ans . . .* (Paris, 1678), II, 516.

[61] Nicolas Gervaise, *Histoire naturelle et politique du royaume de Siam* (Paris, 1688), 158–59.

[62] Simon de La Loubère, *Du royaume de Siam, par Monsr. De La Loubère, envoyé extraordinaire du Roy auprès du Roy de Siam en 1687 & 1688*, 2 vols. (Amsterdam, 1691), I, 188.

"they should be called atheists rather than idolators."[63] It required no Pierre Bayle to cast doubt on the argument from universal consent.

. . .

Given the weight placed by the culture on the volitional rather than intellectual etiology of atheism, the theme of "virtuous" atheists in this missionary and travel literature was a striking one, and quite subversive of the view of disbelief that learned France sought to hold. Again, one should not exaggerate Bayle's role in challenging the educated world's assumption that atheism was the worst and most depraved mode of human life. Indeed, Bayle made the largely theoretical argument that a hypothetical community of "virtuous atheists" could exist. In fact, Bayle's argument, made in the context of his claim that atheism was no worse than idolatry (and perhaps, from a Christian perspective, a good deal better) was simply a lively (but certainly riveting) variation on Plutarch's celebrated thesis that superstition was even more dreadful than atheism.[64] More significantly, missionary and travel literature that offered portraits of virtuous atheists preceded, surrounded, and in essential ways obviated the need for Bayle's argument. The empirical claim that there lived atheists who were not morally debased obviously was far more compelling than the theoretical claim that such men could exist. Most importantly, of course, such a theme threatened the very foundation of the assurance that atheism need not be related to matters of mind, since it could only be the effect of the darkest depravity.

The portrait of the "virtuous" atheist, in fact, was not an uncommon motif, and its widespread dissemination provided the possibility for a quite different view of disbelief from the quasi-official account. Léry described his "savages" as being "without God," but, also, without "mistrust . . . avarice . . . envy and ambition," and despite their constant nakedness, without lewdness, shame, or infidelity.[65] They were cruel to their enemies, the Huguenot Léry acknowledged, but he asked his readers rhetorically if they were more cruel than the usurers of Europe or the butchers of the Saint Bartholomew's Day massacre in France.[66] The Catholic priest and missionary Antoine Biet may have seen the Indians of Guyana as being in "a complete ignorance of any Divinity, either true or false," but he also praised their respect for their elders (though not their respect

[63] Ibid., 359–68, 380–435.

[64] See supra, n. 11; see Plutarch, "On Superstition," in the *Moralia*. On the place of the *Moralia* in early-modern learned culture and on the editions consulted by that culture, see infra, chap. 6.

[65] Léry, *Histoire*, 96–98, 108–9.

[66] Ibid., 164–85.

for their wives) and thought rather well of their mental state: "They are not lacking in wit [*esprit*]; the only shortcoming [*défaut*] is that it is not cultivated. They reason quite well [*ils raisonnent fort bien*] and do nothing that they have not thought about closely, undertaking no matter of importance without having taken good counsel among themselves."[67] They were indeed licentious in sexuality and marriage, but this stemmed in part from an admirable general trait: "They refuse nothing one to another." For Biet, despite their atheism and ignorance of divine laws, they inviolably kept their traditions; they avoided all inequalities (indeed, which surprised him, "they have no king"); they maintained ordered assemblies, ordered travel, and ordered warfare; they learned numerous things "only by means of natural light," such as how to be punctual by attention to the celestial bodies; and they were clever enough to distinguish among the French, Spanish, English, and Flemish by sight alone.[68]

The Dominican missionary Jean-Baptiste Du Tertre had written of atheistic black slaves encountered in the Antilles, men who in his account had never even thought that there might be a God. He and his culture had been taught by almost all authorities that such atheists would have to be the most depraved and selfish of men, but Du Tertre's description of them suggested otherwise:

> The love that they have one for another is extremely tender, and those on the same land have connections among themselves that are so close and so intimate that they assist each other in all their illnesses, take an interest in the treatment that each other receives, and cannot see companions mistreated without feeling their pains [*sans compatir à leurs peines*].[69]

This was not Rousseau describing indigenous North American "deists" from his quarters in France, but a Dominican priest, a century earlier, describing naturally compassionate "atheistic" African slaves whom he claimed to have encountered at first hand. Surely, for those familiar with such literature, this was more telling than any purely theoretical argument!

Similarly, Charles de Rochefort, for all of his insistence on the Caribs as exceptions to Cicero's rule, also insisted on their natural simplicity and described them as "sweet and good-natured [*doux et bénin*]." They were "modest," "decent," and although without laws, they detested theft of any kind and were wonderfully respectful toward their elders. (Europeans seemed impressed by attitudes toward elders everywhere they traveled.) If readers were shocked to learn of their atheism, how much more

[67] Biet, *Voyages*, 352–56.
[68] Ibid., 361–94. The quotation ("*Ils ne se refusent rien les uns aux autres*") is on 388.
[69] Du Tertre, O.P., *Histoire*, II, 499–500.

shocked must they have been to learn that these "barbarians," who lived "without acknowledging God," felt morally superior to the Europeans? "Ordinarily, they reproach us for our greed," de Rochefort wrote, and they are amazed by our love of gold. By contrast, "They live in great harmony and love one another very much [*Ils vivent en grande union et s'entr'aiment beaucoup les uns les autres*]."[70]

The priest and missionary Chrestien Le Clerq, who lived among the Indians of the Gaspé Peninsula, was not certain if these "sun-worshipers" should be seen as idolators or as atheists, since, as he equivocated, they "never truly have known any Divinity." Nonetheless, he noted in 1691, "the savages are charitable beyond anything imaginable in Europe."[71] Marc Lescarbot, on the other hand, was certain that he indeed had met atheistic peoples. Writing early in the seventeenth century, he so described the Armouchiquois Indians but also praised their moral qualities. They were far more virtuous, he insisted, than idol-worshiping tribes. Indeed, they already could be counted a "fortunate people" and would be "a thousand times more fortunate" than the idolatrous tribes he had met if only they had "knowledge of God."[72] Throughout his text, Lescarbot frequently assigned the adjective *noble* to tribes he had found atheistic. After describing most tribes of New France as "without God," he still assured his readers that "they have merit, fidelity, liberality, and humanity, and theirs is a hospitality so natural and praiseworthy that they receive every man with it who is not their enemy." Further, "they speak with much good judgment and reason."[73]

Similarly, the Jesuit Le Jeune described the Indians of Cap Bréton, who had surprised him by their "lack . . . [of] knowledge of God," as modest, intelligent, serious, agreeable, exceptionally clever, honest, and decent.[74] The Jesuit Pierre Biard was not at all certain that the Indians of New France actually believed in God, but he was struck by their chasteness, their lack of avarice, and their honest pride. They were, he noted, "always busy with and occupied by either the material things of life or their own mores and customs," and yet, he added, "I am not sure that, in truth, they don't have a reason to prefer their own sort of happiness to ours (which they do), at least if we are talking of temporal happiness." They were "so very generous and unmalicious . . . [with] a cheerful disposition, and a

[70] De Rochefort, *Histoire*, 455–68.

[71] Chrestien Le Clerq, *Nouvelle relation de la Gaspésie, qui contient les moeurs et la religion des sauvages gaspésiens Porte-Croix* . . . (Paris, 1691), 165–66 (his hesitation about how to classify their beliefs) and 230 (his view of their charity). Le Clerq's work enjoyed a 2d ed. (Lyon, 1692) and a 3d ed. (Paris, 1758).

[72] Lescarbot, *Histoire*, 551–54.

[73] Ibid., 8.

[74] Le Jeune, S.J., *Relation de . . . 1635*, 210–13.

good capacity for judging and evaluating material and ordinary things, reasoning deductively with great skill, and always seasoning their reasons with some lovely comparison."[75] Such missionaries indeed saw themselves on a Christianizing and colonizing endeavor, but they also were simply educated and lively observers, clearly fascinated by all that was new and different around them. With the confidence of those who could cross oceans and northern forests in early-modern times, they were not afraid of what they encountered there, and could report honestly to their contemporaries on what they believed they had witnessed.

Bayle may get historical credit for the assertion that it would be easier to convert atheists than idolators to the truth, since the former were a tabula rasa while the latter were benighted by false ideas (a view obviously perilous to the commonplace characterization of the source of an atheism), but he was not saying anything new. Listen to Lescarbot almost a century before. Commenting on how strange it was to find atheistic tribes surrounded by idolatrous tribes, he noted:

> And nevertheless, everything considered, since the condition of the former and the latter is deplorable, I should prefer to deal with [the tribe] that worships nothing rather than the one that adores creatures . . . for such as it is, it at least does not blaspheme and does not assign God's glory to another . . . but the latter [the idolatrous tribe] is yet more brutish in adoring something dead. . . . And further, the one that is not imbued with any wrong opinion [of God] is much more susceptible of true adoration than the other: being similar to a blank canvas. . . . That is why our nations of New France [whom Lescarbot had found to be atheistic] will surrender themselves more easily to receiving the Christian doctrine [than idolators] once the province is seriously settled.[76]

Travelers to Asia often wrote in similar terms. Confucius may have been without any notion of God for the Jesuit de Rhodes, but his books nonetheless provided "instructions appropriate to forming good morals."[77] Kaempfer's Japanese Confucians were also portrayed as godless, yet he praised their practice of virtue, the purity of their consciences, the goodness and honesty of their lives. They were so virtuous, he noted, that other Japanese suspected them of being Christians![78] Rycaut's Ottoman sect of naturalistic atheists were "frank and generous toward each other, and prompt to do each other services, even to excess." Indeed, his popular chronicle presented the "atheists" in terms that obviously belied the common view of such souls: "Those who declare for this sect love each other

[75] Pierre Biard, S.J., *Relation de la Nouvelle France, de ses terres, naturel du païs, et de ses habitans* (Lyon, 1616), 36–39, 62, 92–98.

[76] Lescarbot, *Histoire*, 709–11.

[77] De Rhodes, S.J., *Histoire*, 61–65.

[78] Kaempfer, *Histoire*, I, 215–17.

and protect each other exceedingly; they are kind and hospitable."[79] La Loubère's Siamese atheists, utterly without even the idea of God, were praised by the author for their goodness, their excellent morals, their conjugal fidelity and family closeness, their respect for their elders, the rarity of murder among them, and the integrity of their word. He found them overly prone to thievery, avarice, vengefulness, and false flattery, but insisted that they were more moderate in such things than the Europeans.[80]

On the one hand, then, formal discussions of atheism generally portrayed it as the manifestation in would-be disbelief of viciousness, egregious immorality, and imbecilic self-indulgence and blindness; on the other hand, however, widely read explorers, pious missionaries, and prestigious travelers often told a remarkably different tale. If one believed their tale, however, the culture's entire analysis of atheism, which had made it synonymous with perversely willful madness, stood in doubt. Atheism became more than "thinkable" by the eighteenth century, and it is not enough to look for the sources of that phenomenon in some alleged underground culture of the prior century, especially when broad currents of orthodox culture were creating virtually all of its preconditions.

. . .

The question of the actuality of atheism and atheistic virtue received its most extended airing in the intense, acrimonious, scandalous (and, thus, for early-modern readers, spellbinding) debate among French Catholic missionaries, religious orders, orthodox commentators, and theologians on the issue of Chinese beliefs and practices. The complex "Chinese rites" controversy was not primarily about "Chinese atheism." It was precisely the case, however, that issues arising in one context of the learned world could in another context occasion profound discussions about disbelief and, as a consequence, alter the ways in which the culture thought about disbelief in God.

In the case of the rites controversy, the essential and initial contestation was certainly not over the nature of proof from universal consent, but over the Jesuits' tactical integration of Chinese terms and rituals into the process of Christianization. What accommodations to make to ancestor worship, for example, was a more central question than whether or not Confucius could conceive of a Supreme Being. The controversy, however, provided a welcome occasion for Catholic orders and movements aggrieved by the seemingly irresistible ascent of the Jesuits to assail their powerful rivals on matters of utmost concern. Fearful or resentful of the growing authority of the Jesuits in the collèges, the universities, the con-

[79] Rycaut, *Histoire*, 237–39.
[80] La Loubère, *Royaume de Siam*, 223–33.

fessionals of the privileged, and the foreign and colonial missions, and seeking to weaken what they believed was a special relationship to the papacy, enemies of the Society found in the Chinese controversy an issue wherein the Jesuits could be made to appear not only willing to compromise essential aspects of the faith, but, indeed, to compromise them with "atheism." For the reading public, it became dramatic theater, indeed.

Dominicans, Franciscans, and, in France, Jansenists, Gallicans, and all of their diverse sympathizers, joined forces to assail Jesuit practices in China. The controversy, beneath all the flights of rhetoric, continued to be about how to undertake conversions in China and about whose view of such an enterprise, the Jesuit or the Dominican and Franciscan, was to be upheld or condemned. In the course of a century of claims and counterclaims, however, a contest that reached its apex of bitterness and publicity as a cause célèbre at the dawn of the eighteenth century, the charged issue of atheism came to occupy a larger and larger part of the discussion. Discussion of that issue raised profound questions for the culture's understanding of the interrelated themes of universal consent and the moral status of the atheist. The rites issue, therefore, provides us with our first (but by no means our last) example of how ecclesiastical rivalries, and competition for the sympathy of the growing reading public, unintentionally could bring subversive views of atheism and its "thinkability" to the avid attention of educated minds.

Having made "the atheist" one of their most terrible figures and symbols, and, as such, a most efficacious polemical foil, theologians tended to take him along on most of their skirmishes. Perhaps they did not fully understand who their audience had become. Here was a battle royal that captivated the public, and "the atheist" was indeed in the middle of the fray. If anyone who read in learned literature had remained ignorant of the peril into which the argument from universal consent had been placed by accounts of the New World, Africa, Japan, Siam, and the Ottoman Empire, the Chinese rites controversy made it almost impossible to remain in such bliss.

. . .

The earliest Jesuit missionaries in China were struck by many things: the division in Chinese religious life between a popular, "idolatrous" religion, with its seeming veneration of statues of Buddha, and a "religion of the lettered," focused on ethics and civil virtue; the high moral intelligence of Confucius and Mencius, authors of the books on which the doctrine of the lettered was based; the Chinese chronology, and the problems of integrating it with the history revealed in Scripture; the stable civilization of China, and its solid civic, cultural, and scholarly accomplishments. They were not meeting "savages" or "barbarians" at the Chinese emperor's court, the missionaries knew from the start, but cultivated minds. Sorting out what such people believed about God and nature was a problem that demanded great attention and analysis. It was an understanding that might satisfy many a curious question, and it was an understanding essential to the strategy of the entire missionary enterprise.

Initially, the most interesting debate about "Chinese atheism" had been between successive leaders of the Jesuit mission there. The singular Matteo Ricci had been quite impressed by the ethical standards and moral philosophy of Confucianism, convinced that it reflected some original Chinese understanding of God's revelation to mankind, even if only His natural revelation, and that this Confucian natural theology could serve as a *foundation* for the Christianization of China. Focusing on conversion of the emperor's court as the most efficacious means of leading the Chinese to Christianity, Ricci concentrated on the Confucian elite. Exploring issues of theology and philosophy with them, Ricci became convinced that the Chinese characters *Tien* and *Xam-ti*, understood as "Heaven" and/or "Lord of Heaven," signified the "God" of Christian natural theology. The uneducated Chinese were idolators and eventually would have to be led away from false gods to recognition of the true God; the educated Chinese, with a few exceptions, were natural theists and needed to be led merely from natural to revealed religion. Conversions and catechisms could proceed from that premise.[81]

Ricci's successor, Niccolo Longobardo, was not convinced of this, although his doubts initially obsessed only the missionaries of China themselves and a papacy forced to adjudicate the issues that his analysis (or, more precisely, the analyses that he relied upon) had raised. For Longobardo, the division in Chinese religious life was between those who had fallen into idolatry and those who had descended into atheism. Longobardo, whose work would be given broad circulation much later, at the height of the controversy, advanced the thesis that the Confucian Chinese had no concept of spiritual substance, and that the "Heaven" they revered was the material sky and its supposed creative, material forces. For Longobardo, the Chinese Confucians, thus, had no proper notion of God, and their materialistic naturalism was nothing less than the "atheism of the lettered."[82]

Eventually, and with many a twist, turn, nuance, and exception, most

[81] Matteo Ricci, S.J., *De Christiana Expeditione apud Sinas suscepta ab Societate Jesu . . .* (Augsburg, 1615); Nicolas Trigault, S.J., ed., *Histoire de l'expédition chrestienne au royaume de la Chine entreprise par les PP. de la Compagnie de Jésus, tirée des commentaires de Riccius*, trans. F. de Riguebourg-Trigault (Lyon, 1616). See also supra, pt. 1, chap. 2, n. 55.

[82] N. Longobardo, S.J., *Traité sur quelques points de la religion des Chinois*, trans. abbé de Cicé, new ed. (Paris, 1701). The *Traité* was originally published in France as *Nouveau advis du grande royaume de la Chine*, trans. Jean de Bordes, S.J. (Paris, 1602).

Jesuits agreed with Ricci's analysis and proceeded on the assumption (and, for missionaries, the tactically convenient view) that Confucian and Christian elements, terms, and ceremonies could be mixed, temporarily at least, without any harm to the true faith. Eventually, and with equal twists and turns, the most vocal (if not most) Dominican and Franciscan missionaries—and, in time, most domestic French Catholic opponents of the Jesuits—came to agree with Longobardo's conclusions. For them, the Jesuits were doing nothing less than compromising with the *least* tolerable of all states of mind and soul—atheism—and any admixture of Christian and Confucian elements, terms, and ceremonies threatened the very foundation of the creed. There, then, were the essential questions set loose in the learned world: first, were Confucian and Christian beliefs and practices at all compatible and to what extent? And second, intimately related to the first, were the most educated Chinese theists or atheists?

Throughout the seventeenth century, the issues simmered, decided this way or that in turn, and gathering force from the intensity of ecclesiastical rivalries. In the end, both Rome and the Sorbonne decided for the anti-Jesuit view. The whole debate easily *could have been* simply about whether or not Confucians believed in the "true" God, not about their theism or atheism. In the heat of polemic, however, positions lost their nuances, and a concert of voices insisted that what most educated French took to be the most learned minds of the most civilized nation outside of Europe were "atheists" pure and simple. France did not need Pierre Bayle, then, to present to it the issue of whether a nation of atheists could endure, and, indeed, could endure in civic virtue; its own Church would come to insist that this was not a theoretical possibility, but a historical fact. If one accepted the widely circulated view of the excellence of Confucian ethics *and* the official determination by both Rome and the Faculty of Theology at Paris that Confucianism was atheistic, this conclusion followed ineluctably. Let us see to what views the reading public was exposed.

• • •

To begin, even Ricci himself, and fellow Jesuits sympathetic to most of his views, saw evidence for something that they wished to label as atheism among *some* of the most educated Chinese. In 1616, for example, Nicolas Trigault's translation, compilation, and exposition of Ricci's accounts of the Jesuits in China had described Confucianism as worshiping "one sole God" and as honoring Confucius merely as a prince of philosophers. Nonetheless, Trigault noted that without supernatural grace, if some of the Chinese indeed had been led by natural lights to abandon idolatry, "there are a few of them who from a much greater descent fell into atheism."[83] Divided into too many sects, he warned, the Chinese were becoming increasingly irreligious, and some had embraced "the very grave errors of atheism."[84] The very order most committed to a positive view of Chinese theism, thus, still asserted that a current of atheism could flourish among the well-educated and civic-minded mandarins. This analysis was repeated in 1696 by the Jesuit most in the public eye as an apologist for his order's Chinese mission.[85]

In 1687, a group of Jesuit missionaries undertook to settle the issues of Chinese teachings once and for all, and to defend their practice of intermixing Confucian and Christian terms and rituals by celebrating the antiquity, reasonableness, and theism of the former. In Philippe Couplet's long preliminary discourse to the *Confucius Sinarum Philosophus sive Scientia Sinensis*, he insisted that Ricci and Trigault had been confused by some *superstitious* elements of a *late* Confucianism infected by a Buddhism that he described as "the most terrible of evils." For Couplet, however, as for Ricci, the preserved teachings of Confucius evidenced only the purest theism. Confucius had expressed a true notion of God, and the words *Tien* and *Xam-ti* indeed expressed the Divinity.[86] Even for Couplet, however, there indeed were strains of non-Confucian "Chinese atheism." Emphasizing the Jesuit contrast between respectable Confucianism and intolerable Buddhism, for example, he repeated the increasingly commonplace description of the latter as divided between an "idolatrous" popular religion and an explicitly "atheistic" lettered doctrine.[87] Nonetheless, for Couplet, Europeans must grant China its due. Whatever Buddhist degeneration had occurred, it was evident from Confucian tradition and *scientia* that China, this "singular and propitious" land, had taught the true God two thousand years before the Incarnation of Christ. Confucians worshiped, in their "Lord of Heaven," the "Supreme Emperor" whom Christians knew as "God." Their virtue was no mere "external appearance," as some Franciscan and Dominican missionaries had claimed, but a sincere internal virtue, manifested in "seriousness, modesty, continence, abstinence, [and] decorum."[88] Since atheism could *not* be virtuous, Couplet pointed out, the Confucians could not be atheists. It was clear to him that "just as frequent and serious crimes and dissolution of morals finally leads down the road to the greatest of all crimes, athe-

[83] Trigault, S.J., *Histoire*, 165–68.

[84] Ibid., 188.

[85] Louis Le Comte, S.J., *Nouveaux mémoires sur l'état présent de la Chine*, 3 vols. [first published, (Paris, 1696], 3d ed., (Paris 1697), 145–48.

[86] Philippe Couplet, "Proëmialis Declaratio," in Prospero Intorcetta, S.J., Christianus Herdtrich, S.J., François Rougemont, S.J., and Philippe Couplet, S.J., *Confucius Sinarum Philosophus sive Scientia Sinensis Latine Exposita* (Paris, 1687), ix–cxxiv. See especially xxxviii–lxix and lxxxii–cvi.

[87] Ibid., xxvii–xxxiv, xxxviii–lxix.

[88] Ibid., xxxiv–xxxviii, lxix–lxxxviii.

ism, so all virtue, concern with how one lives one's life, [and] pious administration of the people are clear indications of true religion."[89] In part, he was warning that to call the virtuous Confucians atheists would be to concede that disbelief in God could arise from reasons other than moral depravity.

That, however, was precisely what the anti-Jesuits insisted upon doing, giving their readers the problem of how to reconcile such conclusions about Confucius's atheism with admiring accounts of the virtue of the Chinese sage. In the latter vein, for example, Canon Simon Foucher insisted that Confucian and Christian morality were in virtually perfect conformity, such that, indeed, Confucius might well be considered "a kind of Prophet, who foretold the coming of the Messiah."[90] One way of accepting both accounts, of course, was to concede the possibility of virtuous atheism. Basing his account on various Franciscan and Dominican commentaries, for example, Simon de La Loubère's popular work in effect reached such a disturbing conclusion: "Several accounts of China assure us that their men of letters, who are the most important citizens in this country . . . today have no sentiment of religion and do not believe in the existence of any God."[91] For La Loubère, the Chinese Confucians, whose morality he admired profoundly, did not revere a genuine God, but merely "the material principle of the entire world, or of its most beautiful part, which is the Sky"; they recognized no spiritual principle, no providence, and no omnipotence. Confucius himself may have been theologically ambiguous, but his deepest philosophical discussions of God "had no other intention than to describe [Him] as impossible, since he found Him nowhere."[92] In modern China, it was precisely the most educated part of the population, "men of letters, that is to say those who have passed their tests in [Confucian] literature and who alone participate in the government," who "had become completely impious," and who recognized only "a blind fatality," "without," in fact, "having changed anything in the language of their predecessors."[93]

The formidable Antoine Arnauld entered these debates in the 1690s, siding almost wholly with the opponents of the Jesuits. The essential object of Arnauld's polemics in this was not, of course, the nature of Chinese thought, but, as reflected above all for Arnauld in the bitter Jansenist-Jesuit debates, what he took to be the fatally compromised Jesuit positions in moral theology. The notion that the Jesuits had gone so far as to

[89] Ibid., lxxxii.

[90] Simon Foucher, *Lettre sur la morale de Confucius, philosophe de la Chine* (Amsterdam and Paris, 1688), passim. It is on 43–44 that Foucher suggests that Confucius might have been "*une espèce de Prophète, qui a prédit la venuë du Messie.*"

[91] La Loubère, *Royaume de Siam*, 370.

[92] Ibid., 396–99.

[93] Ibid., 404–5.

tolerate Chinese atheism to enhance their reputation for efficacious proselytization was too tempting a characterization not to be used against them. Thus, in *La morale pratique des Jésuites*, published in 1691 (and in a second edition of 1717), Arnauld retold the whole story. Ricci, he noted, was certain that the Chinese characters for material sky meant the true God. Longobardo, in his account, knew this to be wrong from the start but remained silent during Ricci's lifetime. Since then, a large number of missionaries had shown unmistakably that the Chinese philosophers and sages were indeed wholly materialistic; these Dominicans and Franciscans "*prove by utterly convincing testimony the atheism of the sect of the lettered [Confucianism].*"[94] He declared that he wished the Jesuits in China could be as honest and humble as the Franciscan missionaries in Canada, who had written, he noted, that " 'These nations, which profess no religion, appear incapable of the most common reasoning that leads other men to the true or false knowledge of a Divinity.' " The Jesuits knew this about China, but tried to hide this fact from the world.[95] Among the Dominicans, spokesmen for the missions insisted upon Chinese atheism,[96] and their formidable professor of theology at the Sorbonne, Noel Alexandre, undertook a major defense of such a thesis.[97]

[94] Antoine Arnauld, *Oeuvres*, XXXIV, 303–7 [*La morale pratique des Jésuites*, VI, chap. 3]. See also the publication of separate parts of *La morale pratique* as Arnauld, *Histoire des différens que les missionnaires Jésuites d'une part, & ceux des Ordres de S. Dominique & de S. François de l'autre, ont touchant les cultes ques les Chinois rendent à leur maître Confucius* . . . ([Cologne?], 1692); *Suite de l'histoire des différens entre les Jésuites de la Chine d'une part & des missionnaires des Ordres de St. Dominique et de St. François de l'autre* . . . ([Cologne?], 1693). Concerning China, Arnauld appears to have found most scandalous what he took to be the Jesuit China mission's indifference to Christological teaching, specifically, the redemptive power of the Crucifixion and Resurrection, in their communications with the Chinese, believing them to be "ashamed" of preaching Christ rather than natural theology to the gentiles.

[95] Arnauld, *Oeuvres*, XXXIV, 697–98 [*La morale pratique*, VII, chap. 11].

[96] The constant stream of Dominican and Franciscan denunciations of Jesuit practices and accounts came from the superiors in the missions of those orders. There were frequent claims, widely accepted, that in the "rank and file" of these missions, Jesuit "accommodations" were imitated. We shall not attempt to sort out such issues here, since our concern is not with the underlying institutional reality in China, but with the views that these contestations succeeded in placing before the reading public in France. For a good sense of the criticisms of the Jesuits, see, for example, the anonymous *Lettre de Mrs. des missions étrangères au Pape, sur les idolâtries & superstitions Chinoises* (n.p., n.d. [ca. 1699]); *Lettre 1. 2. & 3. d'un docteur de l'Order de St. Dominique sur les cérémonies de la Chine* . . . (Cologne, n.d. [ca. 1699]); *Conformité des cérémonies Chinoises avec l'idolatrie Grecque et Romaine. Pour servir de confirmation à l'apologie des Dominicains missionaires de la Chine* . . . (Cologne, n.d. [ca. 1699]). As the titles indicate well, the issue of atheism was not the primary focus of the debate but was raised as part of the far more general issue of "conformity," that is to say, of the "compatibility" of Confucian and Christian doctrines and practices.

[97] Noel Alexandre, O.P., *Apologie des Dominicains missionaires de la Chine* . . . (Cologne, 1699). Alexandre defended the censure of the Jesuit view of China in his *Lettre d'une*

Again, it is essential to see the *convergence* of competing claims—Confucian virtue and Confucian atheism—in a debate that had caught the fancy of that burgeoning reading public "before whom," as one reviewer of Arnauld commented, "the trial is continuing."[98] The Jesuit *Confucius Sinarum Philosophus* was immensely influential. In addition to insisting that Confucius had possessed a true idea of God, it attributed to him "a morality that might be said to proceed from the school of Jesus Christ" and stressed the sincere Confucian commitment to duty, reason, sound governance, charity, concern for the sovereign good, obedience, respect, filial devotion, repentance, dignity, and civility.[99] The next year, La Brune's *La morale de Confucius* (1688) agreed, amazed that "destitute of the lights of divine revelation," Confucius had formulated a morality "so well developed . . . [and] with so much force." Confucius's teachings "had as their goal nothing other than to dissipate the shadows of the mind, to banish vices, to reestablish that integrity which he was certain had been a gift of Heaven . . . to obey, fear, and serve [God], to love his neighbor as himself, to conquer [his passions] and submit them to reason."[100] The public, however, would have to reconcile this to Arnauld's notion that Confucius never in any way had known any being apart from those of the material world.[101] If it missed Arnauld, there was the sympathetic review of his work in the *Histoire des Ouvrages des Savans* in 1692, which reminded readers that Ricci had thought the *Xam-ti* of the educated Chinese to be "God," but that we now knew otherwise:

> There are three sects among the Chinese; that of the lettered is the dominant religion. Father Ricci . . . learned the language of the country and read their philosopher Confucius with attention. . . . He sought in the principles of this philosopher some conformity with the Christian religion and found that by the *Xam-ti* of which so many lettered spoke, meaning literally "the King on high," Confucius had understood the true God. *The truth nevertheless is that Confucius recognized no spiritual being distinct from matter, and that he*

personne de piété sur un écrit des Jésuits contre la censure de quelques propositions . . . (Cologne, 1701). Cologne was both a major center and a major false imprint for the publication of Dominican and Jansenist anti-Jesuit literature intended for French audiences.

98 *Histoire des Ouvrages des Savans*, oct. 1692, 94–99.

99 Intorcetta, S.J., and Couplet, S.J., et al., *Confucius*, cxvii–cxxiv (and see also xxxviii–lxix).

100 J. de La Brune, *La morale de Confucius, philosophe de la Chine* (Amsterdam, [1688]), "Avertissement" ("*destituée des lumières de la révélation divine*"), and 2–8, 20–21 ("*Confucius dans toute sa doctrine n'avait pour but que de dissiper les ténèbres de l'esprit, bannir les vices, rétablir cette integrité qu'il assurait avoir été un présent du Ciel . . . [et faire apprendre aux hommes] à obéir au ciel, à le craindre, à le servir, à aimer son prochain comme soi-même, à se vaincre, à soumettre ses passions à la raison*"), and, in the same vein, 39, 62, 73–77, 93–94.

101 Arnauld, *Histoire des différens*, passim.

attributed the construction of the world to the fortuitous movement of formless matter.[102]

In 1699, Noel Alexandre explicated the Dominican perspective just before the whole issue would be submitted to the review of the Sorbonne and of Rome. For Alexandre, there were two dominant religions in China, Buddhism and Confucianism, each subdivided into further sects. The former was idolatrous in its popular mode, but among educated adherents it reflected the "atheism" that Buddha had taught just before his death. Confucianism was nothing but "a refined atheism" and naturalism in which "the lettered or savants of China speak of nature as of a Divinity" and revere "merely the material sky." While, like the Buddhists, the educated Confucians gave the people a popular religion of superstition and idolatry, "they are atheists according to their arcane doctrine. They say in their heart, 'There is no God.' They refer everything to nature."[103] Confucius himself was manifestly "an atheist and a damned man." His followers then and today "are almost all atheists . . . [and] are convinced that the world was made by and is governed by chance." "All [Confucian] principles," he concluded, "are the principles of atheism."[104] In 1701, he assured his readers that the early Jesuits had understood the atheism of China, that current Jesuit admiration of Confucianism was a decision "to prefer in this the view of several atheistic doctors to that of Catholic doctors," and that, in fact, all of the Chinese were either "idolators or atheists."[105] Reviewing Alexandre in 1699, the *Histoire des Ouvrages des Savans* reversed his view of "popular" and "secret" doctrine, perhaps confused about how a doctrine could be both "arcane" and "apparent," but shared with its significant audience the heart of his thesis: "The lettered recognize no other Divinity but Nature . . . such that it [their 'sect'] is a disguised and subtle atheism. . . . [T]hey recognize only material substances. . . . They are idolators according to their secret doctrine and atheists according to their apparent and popular doctrine."[106]

Reviewing three Dominican works on the subject in 1700, the same journal noted that the debate was now as much a struggle for public opinion as for ecclesiastical approval:

> As the dispute heats up on this matter, the publications multiply. The fear or hope of the judgment that is awaited from Rome excites equally the Jesuits

[102] *Histoire des Ouvrages des Savans*, oct. 1692, 94–99.

[103] Alexandre, O.P., *Apologie des Dominicains missionaires*, 7–16.

[104] Ibid., 40 ("*un Athée et un damné*"), 73–87 ("*Or tous ces principes sont les principes de l'Athéisme*").

[105] Alexandre, O.P., *Lettre d'une personne de piété*, 56–67, 86. The quotation to the effect that the Jesuits seem to "*préferer en cela le sentiment de quelques Docteurs Athées [the 'sectateurs de Confucius'] à celui des Docteurs Catholiques*" is on 67.

[106] *Histoire des Ouvrages des Savans*, août 1699, 344–56.

and their adversaries to convince the world of the justice of their cause. It is not known if it is the difficulty or the embarrassing nature of the question which delays the decision, or if political considerations affect these extensions and delays. But in the final analysis the trial proceeds just as instructively before the Public as before the Tribunal which must pronounce on it. . . . Let us see what the Dominicans answer [to a Jesuit critic].[107]

This review also touched on one of the great ironies of the Chinese rites controversy, one that reveals the issue of "atheism" to have been far more a polemical device for those who raised it than the heart and soul of the debate. The Jesuits had permitted their newly converted Chinese disciples to continue in ceremonies of homage to Confucius and their ancestors. On this issue it was their adversaries who insisted that, in some sense, these disciples (whom in other contexts they portrayed as atheists) worshiped Confucius and ancestors idolatrously, as gods. The Jesuits, however, on *this* issue, argued, the reviewer noted, that "sacrifices, libations, and other ceremonies made with such solemnity on their tombs" were *not* "an idolatrous and superstitious cult" with which there could be no compromise; rather, "to show that these are merely civil honors, it is [claimed] that the sect of the lettered, of whom the Emperor is the head, profess atheism [before conversion to Christianity]." "As a result," he paraphrased the Jesuit view, "if one enters into their minds and their intentions, one will agree that they cannot offer divine and religious honors to them," an argument, he noted, that "does not appear compelling to the Dominicans."[108] Richard Simon wondered how the *Jesuits* could save the argument from universal consent and account for the evidence of Chinese "idolatry," given their claims of "the complete atheism that these [Jesuit] fathers attribute to the sect of the lettered, and on which they principally base themselves in order to maintain that their religion [the homage to Confucius and ancestors] is merely civil."[109]

In short, wherever one turned, one found the claim that learned atheism was the belief (or disbelief) of a mandarin group so often described as the embodiment of civic virtue. All this indeed confused the public, but, inadvertently, it also could only further disseminate the grounds for thinking that there might be peoples, indeed exceptionally "civilized" peoples, who sincerely and disinterestedly reached the conclusion that the universe was neither created, designed, governed, nor in any way in rela-

[107] Ibid., juin 1700, 266–67.

[108] Ibid., 267–68.

[109] Richard Simon, *Bibliothèque critique, ou Recueil de diverses pièces critiques, dont la plûpart ne sont point imprimées, ou ne se trouvent que très-difficilement* . . . , ed. de Sainjore, 4 vols. (Paris, 1708–1710), II, 62–63.

tionship with a being that transcended the natural world. What a breathtaking consideration that must have been for some minds!

From 1696 until 1700, the well-connected Jesuit Louis Le Comte, confessor to the duchesse de Bourgogne, sought to settle all of these matters but, ironically, provided the very case by which the Jesuit position was condemned both in Paris and in Rome. In his *Nouveaux mémoires sur l'état présent de la Chine*, dedicated to the king, and frequently reissued, he attempted both to secure the Jesuit view of Confucius and to appease his order's adversaries. For Le Comte, borrowing from earlier Jesuit accounts, the Chinese philosopher was an admirable sage and a brilliant moralist whose writings were a design for good and ethical government. He possessed and advocated disdain for the things of this world, and manifested in his life and writings the virtues of gravity, kindness, abstinence, sobriety, humility, and modesty. His ethical maxims were excellent, and while it was surprising that the Chinese had never made a god of him, in fact they had not. Everything about him "would give grounds for judging that he was not a pure philosopher formed by reason, but a man inspired by God for the reformation of this new world."[110] Nonetheless, Le Comte sought to make sense of his opponents' views, or, perhaps more accurately, to give his reader a way of accepting the Jesuits' view of Confucianism without having to dismiss as absurd all other accounts and views. In doing so, however—in a work that attracted a remarkable amount of attention, enjoying a third edition within one year of its publication in 1696 and a fourth by 1701—he would give scant comfort to supporters of the argument from universal consent or the argument that all atheists were immoralists.

First, however, he did insist that the Jesuits were essentially correct about the theology of Confucius and Mencius themselves, and that their texts demonstrated that the Chinese "always conserved knowledge of God" for more than two thousand years (after Noah), until their religion had become "infected" by the superstitions and impieties of a far more recent Buddhism. There were still so many vestiges of true religion in Confucianism, he urged, and these were proper foundations for a Christian education in China, but, alas, European observers frequently only saw the "idolatry" and the "atheism" of the Buddhist legacy. It was idolatrous and atheistic at the same time, he wrote, sharing the common view, because Buddha had established *both* doctrines:

[110] Louis Le Comte, S.J., *Nouveaux mémoires*, I, 326–53. See also I, 211–12, where Le Comte observes that "it must be admitted that the Chinese nation has had great qualities: much *douceur* and politeness in worldly practices; common sense and order in their affairs; zeal for the public good; just ideas on government; a mediocre intellect, in truth, in the speculative sciences, but right and sure in moral philosophy, which they have always conserved in strict conformity with reason."

> He died at the age of sixty-nine, and to crown his impiety, after having established idolatry during his life, he tried to inspire atheism at his death. At that point, he declared to his disciples that he had spoken in all his discourses in enigmas, and that it was self-deception to look beyond nothingness for the first principle of things [*on s'abusoit, si l'on cherchoit hors du néant le premier principe des choses*]. "It is from this nothingness," he said, "that everything emerged; it is into this nothingness that everything must fall again. There is the abyss in which all our hopes end." . . . [S]ince impiety finds more partisans than virtue, he founded among the bonzes a particular sect of atheists, based upon these last words of their master. The others, who found it difficult to disabuse themselves of their prejudices, held to the earlier [idolatrous] errors.[111]

Le Comte's adversaries, however, whatever their view of Buddhist bonzes, had wished to declare Confucian mandarins atheists; the Jesuits could concede a bit of that charge (after all, they had admitted in the past that there were *some*), and they did stand in need of at least a few converts whose homage to Confucius could not conceivably be considered at all "idolatrous." For an instant, in Le Comte's text, the two views proved useful to each other. Le Comte believed, perhaps, that he could make a partial peace by reviving Ricci's and Trigault's arguments that there were *three*, not *two* primary Chinese "sects": Confucians; Buddhists; and, third, "the sect of the savants," arising among the mandarins, which falsely tried to present itself as genuine Confucianism, but which in fact was atheism in disguise. Le Comte made the case for this view without ambiguity:

> They speak of the Divinity as if it were nothing but nature. . . . It is no longer this sovereign Emperor of the Heavens, just, omnipotent, the first of the spiritual entities and the arbiter of all creatures. One sees in their work only a refined atheism and an estrangement from every religious cult. . . . [T]hey give to nature virtually all the qualities that we recognize in God.[112]

The emperor and all genuine Confucians, Le Comte insisted, truly and sincerely believe in God. This atheistic "sect of savants," however, "honor God by word and by their lips," but in their hearts, "they give to these words an impious meaning that destroys the Divinity and smothers all religious sentiment." At first imbued with true notions of God, thus, the Chinese have descended into "superstition, magic, paganism, and finally into atheism, moving thus by degrees from precipice to precipice, and have become from this enemies of the reason that they had followed so constantly, and the very horror of the nature to whom they give at

[111] Ibid., II, 110–26.
[112] Ibid., 145–47.

present such great honors."[113] Thus, in a book that sold out as rapidly as it was printed and that attracted the most intense scrutiny, a leading Jesuit merely had declared the most educated of the Buddhist monks and the most educated of the Confucian mandarins, two of the most powerful groups in a flourishing empire, to be skeptical or naturalistic atheists.

None of these "concessions" to his ecclesiastical opponents was sufficient, however. Indeed, almost all that Le Comte's adversaries noticed in his work was, for them, the utterly unacceptable view that pure Confucianism was anything but atheism, or that the Chinese had ever in their texts given witness to an original natural knowledge of the Divinity at the time of the chosen Jews. The Dominicans submitted Le Comte's book to Rome and the University of Paris for condemnation. He defended himself in a work that argued for the admirable ethics and theism of Confucian thought and insisted that *Tien* meant *not* "the material sky," but God Himself.[114] In a second defense, after he knew that the Dominicans had extracted several propositions from his *Etat Présent* and submitted them to Rome for papal condemnation, he pleaded with his critics for two things above all. First, he asked them to recognize that he never had claimed that God had given the Chinese knowledge of Christian truth through Confucius, such as the Fall of Adam and redemption through Christ, but merely that they had "implicit" true knowledge of God, evidence that God had not abandoned all nations but the Jews to darkness in the centuries before Christ. Second, he insisted that "the majority of Chinese savants" still believed in God and were in no way atheistic. If any reader had failed to see the implications of this debate for the argument from universal consent, Le Comte now made sure that they understood these full well:

> Would it not to the contrary be far more dangerous [for religion] to condemn what one reproves here in my book [*L'état présent*], by saying that the ancient Chinese, like those of the present, were atheists? *For would not the Libertines draw great advantage from the confession that would be made to them, that in so vast, so ancient, so enlightened, so solidly established, and so flourishing an Empire, [measured] either by the multitude of its inhabitants or by the invention of almost all the arts, the Divinity never had been acknowledged? What would become thus of the arguments that the holy fathers, in proving the existence of God, drew from the consent of all peoples, in whom they claimed that nature had so deeply imprinted the idea of Him,*

[113] Ibid., 147–153.

[114] Louis Le Comte, S.J., *Lettre . . . sur les cérémonies de la Chine* (Paris, 1700), passim. See, especially, 33–40, 60–75, and 106–10 (where he seeks to demonstrate that *Tien* does *not* mean "*le Ciel matériel*." One of his central arguments here (especially 110ff.) is that it is Buddhist idolatry, not Confucianism, that has created religious problems in China.

> *that nothing could erase it.* And, above all, why would they have gone to all the trouble of assembling with so much care all the testimonies that they could find in the books of the gentile philosophers to establish this truth, if they had not believed that it was extremely important to use it in that way . . . ?[115]

This plea, recall, was from a Jesuit who himself had limited atheism merely to educated Buddhist monks able "to disabuse themselves of their prejudices" and to the mandarin "sect of the savants"!

Neither the Sorbonne nor Rome heeded Le Comte's warning, however. With a clash of titans holding the reading public rapt (between 1660 and 1714 there would be more than 130 books published on the rites controversies in France alone, far more if one included imprints from Amsterdam and Cologne widely read in France), and with the fate of the argument from universal consent explicitly emphasized by the author whose works had become the lightning rod for the whole affair, the Faculty of Theology in Paris, as the eighteenth century dawned, censured Le Comte's works.[116] Louis XIV removed him from his post as confessor to the duchesse de Bourgogne, and Jansenists such as Dupin who themselves had been victims of theological censures orchestrated by the Jesuits now rejoiced in turn.[117]

While the question was pending at Rome, the doctors of theology at the University of Paris determined that, in fact, the critics of the Jesuits were essentially correct. The ancient Chinese had not preserved in Confucianism any knowledge of the God foundational to Christian belief. Confucius himself had not had such knowledge. To the specific question of whether Confucian terms could be used as appropriate Chinese translations of "God," 132 doctors of theology replied that they could not: since "the [two] words . . . signify the *material* sky or a certain force of

[115] Louis Le Comte, S.J., *Eclaircissement sur la dénonciation faite à N.S.P. le Pape, des Nouveaux mémoires de la Chine* . . . (n.p. 1700), 1–15. It is on 13–15 that he argues, "*Ne seroit-il pas au contraire bien plus dangereux de condamner ce qu'on reprend d'icy dans mon Livre, en disant que les anciens Chinois, comme ceux d'à présent, étoient Athées. Car les Libertins ne tireroient-ils pas avantage de l'aveu qu'on leur feroit, que dans un Empire si vaste, si ancien, si éclairé, établi si solidement, et si florissant, soit par le multitude de ses Habitans, soit par l'invention de presque tous les Arts, on n'auroit jamais reconnu de Divinité? Que deviendroient donc les raisonnemens que les saints Pères, en prouvant l'existence de Dieu, ont tiré du consentement de tous les Peuples, ausquels ils prétendent que la nature en a imprimé si profondément l'idée, que rien ne la peut effacer.*"

[116] For a bibliography of more than 130 books on the controversy, as noted by a contemporary, see Louis Ellies Dupin, *Histoire ecclésiastique du dix-septième siècle*, 4 vols. (Paris, 1727), IV, 722–33. The correct text of the censure, which occurred in October 1700, can be found in ibid., IV, 168–79, and in Dupin, *Défense de la Censure de la Faculté de Théologie de Paris, du 18 octobre 1700* . . . (Paris, 1701), xxiii–xxxvi.

[117] Dupin, *Défense de la Censure*.

this sky, missionaries may not utilize them to mean God, since they do not give their auditors the opportunity to think that God is anything other than the sky or its power." Further, concerning "the philosophy and doctrine of the lettered Chinese," the Sorbonne concluded that it was not only "extremely opposed to the Christian religion," but that, at the least, we knew enough to understand "that it leads to atheism," recognizing nothing beyond the material world.[118] In a defense of the censure, published with the approbation of four of its major authors, the theologian Dupin, still royal professor of philosophy at the collège de France, wrote that in China, "idolatry and atheism divide between them all minds," the common people being "sunken into idolatry" and "the savants or lettered infected with atheism."[119] The works of Confucius himself "contain two capital errors: atheism and sorcery. . . . God is not spoken of in his commentaries." Confucius and his followers throughout the ages attributed nothing whatsoever to a Divinity but referred all, even the formation of the world, to "subtle matter." Indeed, Dupin insisted, in all of the ancient or current beliefs or laws of the Confucians, "one meets *no vestige there*" of recognition of God; rather, one sees "impiety and atheism clearly established." What people have taken to mean "God" in Confucius's thought never, in fact, meant "God," but merely "the visible and material sky."[120] "The quality of 'a man inspired by God,' " which Le Comte had dared to assign to Confucius, "is attributed [in his book] to an atheistic philosopher."[121] Far removed from the Jesuit portrait of them, the ancient Chinese in fact lived "without religion and without God."[122] In brief,

> Confucius, whose religion and virtue the author of the *Mémoires* [Le Comte] so praises that he calls him "a saint" and "a man inspired by God for the reformation of this new world," was at bottom a notorious atheist [*étoit au fond un insigne Athée*] . . . and so strongly inspired atheism in his followers [*sectateurs*] . . . that for two thousand years there has not been even one who has not been an atheist like him.[123]

The *Histoire des Ouvrages des Savans*, reviewing Dupin's defense of the censure, summarized this issue quite succinctly for its readers: "The lettered, who are the dominant sect, openly profess atheism, and the rest

[118] Dupin, *Histoire ecclésiastique*, IV, 168–79 (and, his own explication of the contestation and censure, in ibid., IV, 99–168, much of it seemingly drawn, without acknowledgment, from Arnauld, *La morale pratique des Jésuites*, VI, chap. 3).

[119] Dupin, *Défense de la Censure*, 49–50, 64.

[120] Ibid., 73–82. See also 88–135 for an extended discussion of this.

[121] Ibid., 374.

[122] Ibid., 151.

[123] Ibid., 135.

of the people always have been idolatrous."[124] Longobardo's *Traité* to the same effect was translated from Latin into French and published now by the enemies of the late Jesuit's order.[125]

The Jesuits mounted a major campaign to prevent a similar finding by Rome. They argued that the issue was not theological but historical, since the debate was over *what* in fact the Chinese believed, an issue which had to precede the theological issue of doctrinal compatibility.[126] The *Journal de Trévoux* continued to insist, censure or no censure, that it simply was not true that the Chinese worshiped "the material sky"; Confucians truly worshiped "the living God, the Sovereign Master of the Universe . . . the God of the Heavens."[127] Le Comte himself went to Rome to try to justify his works and was received by the pope and by leading theologians who would decide the issue.[128] In 1702, as the *Histoire des Ouvrages des Savans* correctly described it, the Jesuits "produced a document that they make a great deal out of, presenting it as of great weight in such a contestation," namely, an affidavit from the emperor of China himself upholding the Jesuit positions.[129] An apostolic emissary and papally designated bishop for China, however, Marin Labbé, replied forcefully and bitterly, in a public letter to Rome, insisting that the emperor, whom he described alternately as both "atheistic" and "superstitious," was utterly indifferent to all religions and would have signed anything put to him. Why, the bishop asked, didn't the Jesuits ask him if *Tien* or *Xam-ti* in any way indicated a spiritual or eternal or intelligent or infinite being, or, in fact, a being in any manner independent of the material world?[130] The *Nouvelles de la République des Lettres* called Labbé's work "the most appropriate for satisfying the readers . . . of all the texts that have been published on the great affair [of] the Jesuits . . . touching the religion of the Chinese."[131] The *Histoire des Ouvrages des Savans* explained Labbé's

[124] *Histoire des Ouvrages des Savans*, jan. 1702, 3–12. The quotation is from 4 of the review.

[125] See supra, n. 82.

[126] See, for example, the anonymous Jesuit *Journal Historique des Assemblées tenuës en Sorbonne, pour condamner les Mémoires de la Chine* (n.p., 1701), which argued vehemently against the right of the doctors of the Sorbonne to decide a historical issue without appropriate knowledge.

[127] *Journal de Trévoux*, mars 1702, 136–38.

[128] Dom Jean Mabillon, O.S.B., *Correspondance inédite de Mabillon et de Montfaucon avec l'Italie, contenant un grand nombre de faits sur l'histoire religieuse et littéraire du 17ᵉ siècle . . .*, ed. M. Valéry, 3 vols. (Paris, 1846), III, 109.

[129] *Histoire des Ouvrages des Savans*, juin 1702, 274–76.

[130] Marin Labbé, bishop of Tiliopolis, *Lettre de M. Marin Labbé nommé par le Saint Siège evêque de Tiliopolis & coadjuteur au vicariat apostolique de la Cochinchine, au Pape, sur le CERTIFICAT de l'Empereur de la Chine . . .* (Antwerp, 1702).

[131] *Nouvelles de la République des Lettres*, juillet 1702, 22–23.

views of the emperor to its readers: "He is truly an atheist by his principles . . . he does not believe in any God."[132]

At last, Rome answered. The Holy Office and the Congregation for the Propagation of the Faith agreed with the Sorbonne; in France, Jansenizing bishops celebrated the comeuppance of their rivals, delighted that, in censure of the Jesuits, the educated elite of the great Chinese Empire had been pronounced atheists by Rome.[133] What was the importance of the argument from universal consent compared to a defeat for the enemies of Jansen and (they believed) Saint Augustine? Contrary to the views of Manuel,[134] who needed Bayle? who had "to comb" the literature? who would be "astonished" to learn of the coexistence of civilization and atheism? Here is how the *Histoire des Ouvrages des Savans* described it all in May 1701, reviewing four Jansenist and Dominican celebrations and defenses of the Sorbonne's decision: "The censure of the propositions extracted from the books of Father Le Comte has caused such a stir, that there is almost nothing new to be taught to the public on that matter [*a fait tant de bruit, qu'on ne peut presque rien apprendre au public là-dessus*]." Reporting on the views of the bishop of Conon, Maigrot, the journal shared his opinion that the matter was open and shut: "It is evident from the books of Confucius that he was a genuine atheist. He recognized no other principle than matter devoid of knowledge and of liberty." It endorsed such a view: "That is so true that the lettered who follow the sentiments of Confucius make an open profession of atheism [*font profession ouverte d'athéïsme*]."[135]

Nor did the issue quickly fade away. Polemics kept it before the reading public for decades. In 1710, an anonymous defense of the Jesuits conceded that *Tien* and *Xam-ti* were "equivocal" names for God but argued that this was true of most languages, and that the best way to combat the contemporary "Chinese atheists" was to show them that despite their own materialism, their ancestors had possessed terms for the Divinity.[136] Now, even Jesuit apologists were conceding the atheism of modern China.

132 *Histoire des Ouvrages des Savans*, juin 1702, 277.

133 See, for example, Artus de Lionne, bishop of Rosalie, *Observationes in quaesita Sinarum imperatori a Patribus Societatis Jesu proposita, et illius ad ea responsionem circa coeli, avorum, et Confucii cultum* . . . (n.p., n.d. [1704]), which gloated over these events. De Lionne believed himself injured by the Jesuits in these debates in 1700, from which arose his brief (26 pp.) *Lettre de Mgr. l'évêque de Rosalie aux RR. PP. Jésuites* (n.p., n.d. [1706]) and an anonymous defense of de Lionne's positions, the *Lettre à Mr. de Lionne sur le libelle des Jésuites contre Mr. l'Evêque de Rosalie son fils* [36 pp.] (Rome, 1701).

134 See supra, n. 9.

135 *Histoire des Ouvrages des Savans*, mai 1701, 203–11.

136 *Epistola . . . in quâ explicatur Mens et Doctrina Patrum Societatis Jesu, circa Controversiam Sinensem* [24 pp.] (n.p., 1710).

In 1729, a small anonymous brochure, embodying or sympathetic to Jesuit perspectives, sought to qualify that, however, declaring that "if the Chinese are atheists, it is of a singular species," since they certainly seemed to make a Divinity of the heavens.[137] Reviewing this work, the *Nouvelliste du Parnasse* spoke not from some heterodox position, but from the "official" orthodoxy of his culture: "Allow me to point out to you how little use of logic is made by the author. From the moment that he admits that the lettered recognize no other Divinity than a power spread throughout the Universe, and above all in the material sky . . . , why make [the issue of] if they are atheists a problem? Was there ever a more decided atheism?"[138]

Bayle, in 1703, wrote to a friend that to deal with philosophical objections to his theoretical critique of "the argument for the divine existence drawn from the consent of all the nations," he was now "obliged to read what Locke said against innate ideas in his *Essay on [Human] Understanding.*"[139] French Catholics who had read either their popular travel and missionary literature or any of the voluminous literature on the Chinese would have had no such need. The Huguenot Jacques Bernard still defended the argument in 1705, conceding that there obviously were peoples who did not believe in God, but claiming that theirs was "a negative atheism" that derived solely from their ignorance.[140] It was hard to make such an argument about the learned Chinese. The Huguenot Elie Benoist undertook a similar defense in 1712, but he now had to argue that "in moral proofs one does not count votes, one weighs them." In weighing testimonies of modern atheisms, he noted, we can both grant their truth and discount their significance, since Cicero's observation counts for more, recording as it did the views of mankind during a period much closer to the creation, before centuries of subsequent degeneration of the peoples of the world.[141] Again, however, the now official French Catholic view was that even the ancient Chinese themselves never had acknowledged God. In 1724, the Jesuit Joseph François Lafitau's *Moeurs des sau-*

[137] *Idée générale du gouvernement et de la morale des Chinois* [38 pp.] (n.p., 1729).

[138] P.-F.-G. Desfontaines and François Granet, eds., *Le Nouvelliste du Parnasse, ou Réflexions sur les ouvrages nouveaux*, 2d ed., 2 vols. (Paris, 1734 [first published, Paris, 1731–1732]), I, 405–7.

[139] Pierre Bayle, *Lettres de Mr. Bayle, publiées sur les originaux*, ed. Pierre Des Maizeaux, 3 vols. (Amsterdam, 1729), III, 945.

[140] See Bernard's editorial interjection in a review of an English book that utilized the argument from universal consent, in *Nouvelles de la République des Lettres*, mai 1705, 523–25.

[141] Elie Benoist, *Mélange de remarques critiques, historiques, philosophiques, théologiques sur les deux dissertations de M. Toland, . . . avec une Dissertation . . . où on examine l'argument tiré du consentement de tous les peoples, pour prouver l'existence de Dieu . . .* (Delft, 1712), "Préface, contentant une Dissertation . . . ," [separately paginated, 3–100].

vages Amériquaines expressed his "extreme distress" at all of the accounts in "most of the travel narrations" that depicted the Indians as "without any knowledge of a Divinity." These were, he pleaded with his readers, "errors made even by missionaries and honest men who . . . wrote too hastily," and, above all, "*who did not foresee the disastrous conclusions that could be drawn from the expression of a judgment that is so pernicious to religion.*" In fact, Lafitau cited Bayle *in favor of* universal consent on the grounds where it most mattered, issues of fact, since Bayle, he thought, understood that American Indian beliefs presupposed a Divinity. Yet, he acknowledged, the characterizations of peoples as atheistic continued, despite the awful danger. "What argument," the Jesuit asked his vast audience, "do we not provide to the atheists in this manner?" He answered his own question in terms the atheists indeed would come to use:

> One of the strongest proofs against them . . . is the unanimous consent of all peoples in acknowledging a Supreme Being. . . . This argument would give way, however, if it were true that there is a multitude of diverse nations . . . that . . . have no idea of any God. . . . From that, the atheist would seem to reason correctly by concluding that if there is almost an entire world of peoples that have no religion, that found among other peoples is the work of human discretion and is a contrivance of legislators who created it to control the people by fear, the mother of superstition.[142]

He sought to reestablish this proof, however, not against the arguments of any atheists, but against a whole seventeenth-century tradition of his fellow learned Christians.

[142] Joseph François Lafitau, S.J., *Les Moeurs des sauvages Amériquains comparées aux moeurs des premiers temps*, 2 vols. [the quarto ed.] (Paris, 1724), I, 5–6.

Chapter Six

THE ANCIENTS

THE ARGUMENT from universal consent did not disappear from the literature in the wake of missionary and travel accounts that alleged the "atheism" of many peoples. Within the learned culture of early-modern France, however, there now were widely discussed grounds for rejecting the factual basis of that argument. Was unbelief in God in fact so unnatural and so exceptional that it had to be attributed to a depravity of will beyond that which all the heirs of Adam shared? As Lafitau and Le Comte had recognized and warned against, there now were orthodox voices suggesting that whole peoples did not share the essential foundation (or had not reached the essential conclusion) of European theism. The common formulation, "all peoples and all sages," was challenged directly in its first claim, "all peoples." It also was challenged, we now shall see, in its claim about seekers after wisdom. For those convinced by such accounts, analyses, and debates that neither all peoples nor all sages believed in God, the argument from universal consent, with all of its implications and reassurances, was effectively obsolete.

Those who generated or responded to such claims and suggestions, of course, were not necessarily concerned primarily (or, indeed, at all) with theoretical sequences of theistic belief, let alone with the categories into which historians might choose someday to place them. On the whole, they were concerned with describing what they saw or read; with a particular people, philosopher, or school of thought; with problems of conversion or with the issue of the congruence of foreign beliefs and Christian notions. Intentions and consequences, however, can lead separate lives.

. . .

For the theologically minded who explicitly discussed universal consent, there were two fundamental options, each with an obvious appeal and an implicit danger. A narrow definition of atheism would secure the *consensus gentium*, the universal consent of mankind to common theistic notions, but at the risk of sacrificing all rigor in defining a minimally Judeo-Christian concept of Divinity. Could a people not believe in the providence, intelligence, spirituality, or absolute independence of the object of its reverence, for example, and still be accounted to believe in any sense in God? A broad definition of atheism would secure a proper understanding, from Christian perspective, of what attributes were essential to the Divinity, but at the risk of making atheism seem widespread and, thus, quite thinkable indeed. Did all those peoples whose views and language did not reflect belief in such attributes dissent from theism itself? Despite warnings, many authors chose to write from a broad definition of atheism, most of them seeing nothing in common between the Christian belief in God and diverse heathenish views of the world, and most so secure in their theism that it probably never occurred to them that their critiques of explicit or implicit philosophical views as "atheistic" could suggest anything more than the superiority of Christian culture.

In human affairs, however, it is so often convergence that counts: these discussions occurred at a time when the reading public and its means of dissemination of thought had grown dramatically; when more and more minds were committed to a logically and empirically secure theology; when disturbingly different foreign or ancient mentalities were being explored with unprecedented scrutiny; and when the culture as a whole was undergoing a profound series of debates, engaging that broader reading public, about the proper grounds for belief and understanding. In that convergence, the argument from universal consent was a strong barrier against doubt or disbelief that might be occasioned by the expansion and alteration of knowledge and the struggles among competing philosophical systems. It was a barrier with many a breach. Perhaps there always had been savants aware of those breaches; in the circumstances of the seventeenth century, however, such awareness became common and notorious knowledge. Anomalies are powerful agencies for focusing the mind. The more some denied exceptions to a theistic *consensus gentium* while others insisted upon them, the more the seeming contradictions would invite consideration and debate.

• • •

Moral proof from a unanimous consent of all mankind to the existence of God certainly did not lose its appeal. The influential Jesuit savant and editor René-Joseph Tournemine, for example, was one of countless authors who continued to hold to a narrow definition of atheism and to endorse wholeheartedly the argument from a *consensus gentium*. As he wrote in 1702, he believed that in even the most absurd ancient fables about corporeal, imperfect gods, we saw "this ineffaceable idea of the Divinity that the Creator has engraved in our hearts." Even those who claimed that natural fear might have created the ancient gods, he insisted, must acknowledge that "[fear] never could have created them if men had not had previously some idea of the Divinity."[1] The Jesuit Lafitau was certain that even "the bacchanalia . . . and the mysteries of Isis and Osiris," indeed, even "all the darkness of idolatry and the horrors of magic . . . presuppose a religion sacred in its original state, before it became corrupted." The worst abuses of "the pagan peoples [*la gentilité*] . . . [were in fundamental] conformity . . . with the true religion." If atheists attack the *consensus gentium*, he was convinced, they "claim authority for their disbelief in vain."[2] The Jesuit scholar Pierre Lescalopier, editor of a Latin edition of Cicero's *De natura deorum*, defended the proof of God by universal consent from Cotta's attack on it in the dialogue. All peoples, he argued, believed in God or the gods, and the voice of all peoples is the very voice and certainty of nature herself. An individual might be mistaken, but not the human species.[3] The *Nouvelles de la République des Lettres*, in 1689, noted a Catholic author who declared the proof from universal consent to be in fact demonstrative, and not merely "moral."[4] Almost thirty years later, in that same journal, Jacques Bernard claimed that critics of the proof had confused irreligion and atheism, and he insisted (in a clause, however, whose rhetoric perhaps indicated how powerful the case *against* universal consent had become) that "those who doubt this fact [that atheism is widespread in the world] are not entirely blameworthy [*ceux qui doutent de ce fait ne sont pas tout-à-fait blâmables*]."[5] The deist Gilbert, in the *Histoire de Caléjava*, also asserted that all peoples and thinkers denounced as atheists simply had held incorrect ideas about divine attributes, doubting His unity, for example, or simply had established no exterior cult.[6] Richard Simon similarly insisted that we should not confound "confused" ideas of God with atheism, particularly since it was the view of Saint Augustine himself "that knowledge of God is so natural to us that it cannot be absolutely effaced."[7]

From the mid-seventeenth century to the early decades of the eighteenth, formal apologetic treatises continued to offer the proof from universal consent as a strong (indeed, often as their first or second) argument on behalf of God's existence, as if the travel and missionary literature never had been written. *The question, however, is whether in the presence of that literature, such continued use of the argument did not raise more*

[1] *Journal de Trévoux*, nov.–déc. 1702, 108–9 (in a series of articles by Tournemine on ancient fables).

[2] Lafitau, S.J., *Les Moeurs*, I, 108–54, 452–55.

[3] Cicero, *De natura deorum*, ed. Pierre Lescalopier, S.J. (Paris, 1668), l.1, 87. ["*Possunt errare singuli, labi possunt nonnunquam viri sapientes, sibi, suoque arbitrio permissi; at totat hominis naturam tanta erroris contagio facilè invadere non potest.*"]

[4] *Nouvelles de la République des Lettres*, jan. 1689, 5–9.

[5] Ibid., jan.–fév. 1717, 109–10.

[6] Gilbert, *Histoire de Caléjava*, 83–86.

[7] Simon, *Bibliothèque critique*, II, 62–63.

doubts in at least a few minds than it resolved. Nonetheless, insistence on its factual and persuasive validity remained a central part of theological literature. In 1641, d'Abillon had proposed it as his second proof, acknowledging, with most, that it was "a moral proof," but pronouncing it appropriate to "every truly sensible man [*tout homme bien sensé*]." Long before Bayle made the case historians persist in finding original, however, d'Abillon himself offered what he took to be three obvious "objections" to his own use of the proof, two theoretical, and one factual. The theoretical arguments were that it embodied a criterion that would have established the plurality of the gods (which he rejected for equating what was clear in an idea of divinity with what was "confused" in such an idea); and that human knowledge was too fallible to provide a *criterium* from its own resources (which he rejected on the grounds that "a universal ignorance is morally impossible"). The factual objection was that several pagan philosophers had rejected the Divinity. D'Abillon conceded that last claim, but he argued that they comprised only "five or six" out of "a thousand" philosophers, that they all were vile and immoral, and that they often were justly put to death by their own societies. It was safe to conclude, he reassured his audience, that "one hundred thousand of the wisest and most learned men since the birth of the world, in all centuries, in all ages, and in all academies, have firmly believed this truth [that God exists]." Unless it was an evident truth, he asked, "how could it be that all the sects of philosophers and theologians, who glory in stubbornly contradicting each other, nevertheless have fallen into agreement over this proposition?"[8]

In 1674, the Jesuit Petiot made it his first demonstration, certain that being the belief "of all the peoples and of all the sages," it could not possibly be false.[9] Pierre-Daniel Huet's enormously popular *Demonstratio Evangelica*, which saw four editions between 1675 and 1694, and an eighth edition by 1733, gave the argument from universal consent a preponderant weight in its proof of God's existence. A growing *philosophical* skeptic, the future bishop found the argument ideal, since it obviated the need for dogmatic philosophical systems to be brought to bear on matters of religious belief.[10] Reviewing his work, the *Journal des Sçavans* described his demonstration of God to be "founded of the constant experience and the unanimous consent of all men," on beliefs that "always have been accepted by the universal consent of all nations and of all centuries."[11] In 1683, François Diroys, doctor of theology from the Sor-

[8] D'Abillon, *La divinité défendue*, 60–84.

[9] Petiot, S.J., *Démonstrations*, 11–14.

[10] Pierre-Daniel Huet (later, bishop of Avranches), *Demonstratio Evangelica* (Paris, 1679); 3d ed. (Paris, 1690); 5th ed. (Leipzig, 1703).

[11] *Journal des Sçavans*, 9 juin 1679, 5–6.

bonne, offered it as his first proof, insisting that it was compelling precisely because it was most true of "Peoples among whom reason has been cultivated a bit [*les Peuples où l'on a un peu cultivé la raison*]." The fact of "the ignorance of certain Peoples [that God exists] and the contradiction of several atheists" did not vitiate it, given the general universality of belief in God's existence. Very few people ever denied it, and most of those were skeptics who would deny the *certainty* of anything.[12]

As we see, however, even proponents of the argument often found that they had to deal with exceptions to their rule. Louis Ferrand's posthumously published apologetical work, *De la connaissance de Dieu*, made it the third argument for God's existence, assuring its readers that the "handful" of exceptions only proved the rule and that all of these could be explained by criminal self-interest.[13] By this time, however, Ferrand's editor in 1706 felt obliged to concede that many saw more than a "handful" of ancient atheists, but he argued that these did not comprise "a sufficient exception" to weaken the proof. First, it was difficult to establish the true beliefs of ancient philosophers (an argument, we should note, that could cut both ways). Second, if one eliminated from the category of atheists both ancient critics of a false polytheism and ancient materialists whose denial of all spiritual being merely indicated that they "badly conceived of His nature," then there remained "few persons" indeed who "embraced atheism."[14]

For the Protestant Elie Benoist, we have seen in part, the argument from universal consent had been abused by apologists who made it too categorical, but it stood as a moral proof if one weighed the *quality* of opinions, even if some "obscurities and shadows" continued to cloud it. In "moral proofs," he averred, "one does not count votes, one weighs them," and where most proponents of the proof insisted on citing "the multitude," in fact, "the multitude, in this, loses all of its authority, and often a very small number of persons carries the issue over millions of witnesses incapable of saying anything useful to the question."[15] In short, he urged that it was the universal consent of minds worth taking seriously that established the indubitableness of their common belief. If that were the case, then the history and analysis of philosophies loomed large in the equation. As the young Montesquieu saw all too clearly, however, it was not uncommon for savants to find atheism among those otherwise reputed wise:

> I have seen a manuscript by Father Castel [the celebrated Jesuit natural philosopher], which is a critical examination of the system of M. Newton. . . .

[12] Diroys, *Preuves et préjugez*, 6–11.

[13] Ferrand, *De la connaissance de Dieu*, 109–18.

[14] Ibid., 118–33.

[15] Benoist, "Dissertation," in *Mélange*, 3–25.

> Father Castel, like every Jesuit, does not fail to attack M. Newton on the orthodoxy of his principles, which he says lead to atheism. . . . I don't know how it happens that it is impossible to frame a system of the World without first being accused of atheism: Descartes, Newton, Gassendi, Malebranche. By that one accomplishes nothing else but to prove atheism and give it strength, in making people believe that atheism is so natural that all systems, however different they may be, always lead to it [*En quoi on ne fait autre chose que prouver l'athéisme et lui donner des forces, en faisant croire que l'athéisme est si naturel que tous les systèmes, quelques differents qu'ils soient, y tendent toujours*].[16]

In 1738, the journal *Mercure et Minerve* noted that for the longest time (that is to say, the very period on which we focus), it was the tendency to identify precisely the most innovative and intelligent new thought as atheistic, a danger, indeed, for the faith:

> As soon as a philosopher of a superior order arises, who strays from the beaten path and who, generously freeing himself from received prejudice, proposes clear and distinct ideas in place of the words formerly in use, just so soon do people not fail to exclaim against atheism [*aussi-tôt on ne manque pas de crier à l'Athéisme*]. . . . That is how people treated the greatest philosophers of paganism . . . and I do not know from what motive there are found today savants who are pleased to perpetuate these calumnies. . . . *Would it be a gain for religion if one could convict all of the great philosophers of atheism?* Completely to the contrary, it would follow from this that it suffices to meditate and to have ideas superior to those of the vulgar in order to feel the weakness of religion and to disabuse oneself of it.[17]

For some, then, the orthodox themselves had eviscerated the argument from universal consent. Indeed, such was the case, and in early-modern encounters with the classics and patristics (both increasingly, one should note, translated into the vernacular), with classical scholarship, and with the newly emerging science of the history of philosophy, the gutting of theistic consensus went on apace. In the presence of accounts of atheistic peoples, defenders of the argument asked their readers "to weigh" the voices. Confucius and Buddha already had been "weighed" by many on the side of the atheists. What of the sages of Greece and Rome?

. . .

If all one read were certain specific histories of philosophy, the issue of ancient atheism would not have seemed a problem at all; many accounts

[16] Montesquieu, "Spicilége," in *Oeuvres complètes* [*L'Intégrale*], 413.

[17] *Suite* of the *Mercure et Minerve*, avril–juillet 1738, in *Amusemens littéraires, moraux & politiques*, ed. rev. and aug. (Berlin, 1739), 193–94.

of prior thought saw virtually no dissent whatsoever among the ancients from universal consent to belief in God. Vossius's well-received *De Theologia gentili*, in a third edition by 1675, saw most ancient sages not only as theistic but as essentially monotheistic, a condition maintained, he believed, until the follies of superstition led to the excesses of pagan polytheism and idolatry. For Vossius, the pagan philosophers understood that God was free, perfect, and incorporeal, even if they often could not see the full implications of that conception. "Almost all of them, by the light of nature," had reached an essential conception of the Divinity, however imperfect compared to Christian understanding. He acknowledged that there were those who doubted if the pagan philosophers "even can be said to have any sense of God," but cited against them Saint Paul's words to the Epicureans and Stoics in Acts 17, which he saw as charging them with *incorrect* views of the Divinity, not in any way with atheism. For Vossius, the original lights of the pagans degenerated in two ways, neither of which should be confused with speculative disbelief. Above all, there was the growth of superstition, which he identified with the improper worship of the Divine, culminating in the gross errors of idolatry. Further, there was "impiety," by which he explicitly meant "ignoring" God in one's moral life, an "atheism" (which Vossius termed "a word often loosely used") that was not a philosophical denial of God, but an indifference to worship and an expression of hope that there would be no divine justice. "Atheism," for Vossius, arose not in mind, but in any one of four volitional or affective states: "madness"; loss of either hope in God or fear of Him; forgetfulness that He cared about our lives; or the cynical worship of Him for earthly rewards. In the first state, "madness," the "atheist" might well "convince himself, for a time at least, that there is no God," and this was the "impiety" of the "fool" described by the Psalmist, but illness or misfortune would reawaken the underlying awareness of Divinity in such a man.[18] In brief, for Vossius the traditional and commonplace view of atheism stood unthreatened by familiarity with the ancients.

Four works quite popular in the vernacular in France, Gilles de Launay's *Introduction à la philosophie* (2d edition, 1675), Louis Thomassin's *La méthode d'étudier . . . chrétiennement . . . la philosophie* (1685), Laurent Bordelon's *Théatre philosophique* (1692), and Michel Morgues's *Plan théologique du paganisme* (1712), also did not take attributions of ancient atheism seriously at all. De Launay, *historiographe du roy* and professor of philosophy, found the charges of atheism that some directed against the Epicureans, for example, to be nothing but libels by Stoics

[18] Gerardus Joannes Vossius, *De Theologia gentili et physiologia christiana, sive De origine ac progressu idololatriae, ad veterum gesta ac rerum naturam reductae, deque naturae mirandis, quibus homo adducitur ad Deum* . . . , 3d ed., aug. (Frankfurt, 1675), I, 8–17.

envious of Epicurus's reputation. Indeed, de Launay only identified *one* atheist explicitly, "Theodorus, named the Atheist for having maintained that there were no Gods," and described him as having arisen from a school of "debauchery."[19] Thomassin, an Oratorian priest and educator, had as his explicit goal "to show everywhere the rapport and alliance of Philosophy in general, and, in particular, of the Logic, Physics, and Ethics of the ancient philosophers, with Religion."[20] Not only did all the later schools of Greek philosophy recognize an intelligent first cause, but so did the Greek poets, the pre-Socratics, and, indeed, the Indian, Phoenician, Egyptian, and "barbarian and African" philosophers.[21] For Thomassin, the myth of disbelief or materialism among the pre-Socratics arose solely from their having ended their inquiries at secondary causes. Nonetheless, he insisted, the thought of Anaxagoras, who recognized the role of a Divine Mind in forming the world we observe, was surely derived from his predecessors, and thus showed "the likelihood that the first Ionic philosophers, presupposing what was incontestable and up until then uncontested, the first efficient cause of all things, spoke merely of secondary causes." Indeed, he assured his readers, "these [pre-Socratic] philosophers had lofty notions of the Divinity."[22] Once past the pre-Socratics, Thomassin had clear sailing: Pythagoras, Plato, and Aristotle clearly recognized "the supreme Intelligence of God"; the skeptics only "feigned doubt" the better to make truth intelligible; the Stoics, while holding absurd views on the corporeality of God, sometimes saw Him as "a pure Intelligence," and their errors were pardonable.[23] Only the Epicureans were suspect, not because they denied the gods, which they did not, but because they denied divine providence, and Cicero was correct that to deny providence is *by implication* to deny God.[24]

Bordelon also had difficulty with Epicurus (above all because his atoms were, in Bordelon's explication, "uncreated, immortal, eternal, incorruptible, and self-moving"), but Gassendi had shown how Epicurus could be made compatible with Christian theism.[25] As for other supposed atheists, such classifications were based on misunderstandings. Empedocles, for example, merely believed that we could not comprehend the na-

[19] Gilles de Launay, *Introduction à la philosophie*, 2d ed., corr. and aug. (Paris, 1675), 83–84, 109–16.

[20] Louis Thomassin, Oratory, *La méthode d'étudier et d'enseigner chrétiennement et solidement la philosophie par rapport à la religion chrestienne et aux Ecritures* (Paris, 1685), 1.

[21] Ibid., 1–157.

[22] Ibid., 157–65.

[23] Ibid., 165–215.

[24] Ibid., 227–38

[25] Laurent Bordelon, *Théatre philosophique sur lequel on represente . . . les philosophes anciens et modernes . . .* (Paris, 1692), 36, 51–56.

ture of God.[26] Diagoras had merely posed the honest *question*, asked by a multitude of decent men who never stand accused of atheism, if there were gods. In Bordelon's portrait, Diagoras himself recognized "that there are no real atheists," but only those who wished there were no gods. He invented a fragment for Diagoras, allowing him to ask, "Can one have reason and eyes and doubt that there is a Divinity?"[27] Bion had been accused of atheism merely for having questioned the notion that God would punish children for the sins of their fathers.[28] Democritus may have made atoms and void the physical principles of all things, and may have posited a corporeal God, but he believed nonetheless that "God is the soul of the world."[29]

The Jesuit Morgues went the furthest of them all in seeking to dismiss any notion of Greek atheism. The learned philosophers of paganism not only recognized the "unity" of God, but never confused "belief in a Supreme God" with the "host of 'Gods in name [only]' " found in popular pagan religions.[30] All of the Ionic school believed that Divine Intelligence brought order out of chaos. The Eleatic school saw God as "the Whole [*le Tout*]," for which some condemned them for an atheistic equation of God and nature, but which in fact was the very opposite of atheism, reflecting their pious belief that God was unique, unchanging, self-created, immortal, ungenerated, infinite, and immobile. The Italic school rendered a formal cult to God, and in the case of Pythagoras recognized one God as father, intelligence, soul, and motor of the world. Many sages who appeared polytheistic (Socrates, Plato, and Cicero, for example) in fact were monotheistic in their beliefs but feigned polytheism to avoid difficulties with the superstitious multitudes.[31]

For Morgues, it was precisely the bolder monotheistic sages, those who explicitly attacked the absurdities of polytheism, who ironically had come to be known as "atheists": they "did not reject the Supreme God, but merely the subaltern Divinities." Assuring his readers that he long had "attentively considered the prodigious aberrations of the pagans on the issue of [the nature of] the Divinity," he informed them that "there never yet has crossed my eyes any truly declared atheist." All those so described had simply opposed popular superstition because they believed in the

[26] Ibid., 142.

[27] Ibid., 153–58.

[28] Ibid., 230–31.

[29] Ibid., 247–48.

[30] Michel Morgues, S.J., *Plan théologique du Pythagorisme, et des autres sectes sçavantes de la Grèce, pour servir d'éclaircissement aux ouvrages polémiques des Pères contre les payens* [title page of vol. II changes title to *Plan théologique du paganisme* . . .] 2 vols. (Toulouse, 1712), I, 15.

[31] Ibid., I, 15–36.

unity of God: "Their atheism attacked only polytheism." He asked his readers to trust him that while it was conceivable that perhaps *one* of the thirty tyrants of Athens had been an atheist, there were none among the philosophers: "Neither in Greece, nor in Italy, nor among the savants, nor among the people did any complete atheism appear, or any real Atheist who absolutely denied all Divinity." He knew all too well, he allowed, about "the six famous atheists of paganism" (Protagoras, Prodicus, Diagoras, Theodorus, Euhemerus, and Critias). Perhaps Critias, if we assumed that there was no hyperbole in the accounts given of his views, might be the one exception, but, in fact, if one examined them all closely, and weighed all of the charges of atheism against them, "one will find that their atheism attacked only inferior Divinities, either political or poetic, without reaching either to the First God," or even to "genies who were invisible gods."[32]

Published outside of France, but well-known within it, the Huguenot Benjamin Binet's *Idée générale de la théologie payenne* (1699) had made much the same argument, insisting that ancient thinkers who had been deemed impious merely had mocked the plurality of gods, and that the pagan philosophers had possessed "the natural idea of God," which, though useless for salvation, had sufficed to make them aware not only of the existence of God but of many of His essential properties. The ancient sages "knew God as well as a corrupted creature can know Him without the aid of grace."[33] Such views were common. They were seemingly contradicted, however, as we shall see, by much of classical and patristic literature itself, and by scholarly commentary. Morgues's extended title was revealing: "to serve as clarification of the polemical works of the Fathers [of the Church] against the pagans." As Morgues knew, there were other views of pagan atheism than his own, they came with excellent credentials, and they were better known than the *Plan théologique*. There was, indeed, a great deal being published and read in the seventeenth century on the subject of ancient "atheism."

. . .

The educated early-modern world knew the ancient thinkers in many ways and believed itself to be on intimate terms with the complexities and meanings of their views. On the whole, it knew the most celebrated of them directly, through early-modern editions of their texts. It knew, through fragments quoted and commentary offered in the texts it did pos-

[32] Ibid., 91–110.

[33] Benjamin Binet, *Idée générale de la théologie payenne . . . ou Traitté historique des dieux du paganisme* (Amsterdam, 1699), 30–85.

sess, a large cast of thinkers whose works had not been preserved intact. While lacking the convenience of Diels's nineteenth-century collection of such "fragments" for the pre-Socratics, it already had found and explicitly analyzed most of these in a great variety of ancient accounts of and quotations from their lost works.[34] The ancients themselves, of course, had offered compilations and explications of prior classical philosophy, and these studies of the *placita* (teachings, or opinions) of the philosophers were convenient and widely read sources of views with which all savants were expected to be familiar. If for any reason one shunned profane literature, although few did, there were similar fragments, accounts, explications, and implicit collections of *placita* in patristic literature. The Fathers of the Church had been diversely concerned with the pagan philosophers, and early-modern students of the patristics (benefiting from a large number of new and critical editions of such apologetic and doctrinal works) could not avoid their frequent discussions of ancient philosophies. Finally, the seventeenth and early eighteenth centuries saw a great flowering of both highly learned and more popular studies of the history of philosophy, some of them even explicitly focused on the issue of atheism, but most of them touching on that issue at least indirectly.

• • •

The ancients, in fact, whether rightly or wrongly understood from *our* learned culture's point of view, long had been the sources of so many of the "atheistic" objections framed (and responded to) in medieval and

[34] The following sources for pre-Socratic "fragments" were widely available in seventeenth-century France (with an asterisk for those available in French translation also): Aëtius* [see infra, under pseudo-Plutarch]; Aristotle*; Arnobius; Athenagoras* [French translations from the sixteenth century only]; Athenaeus* (the *Deipnosophistae*); St. Augustine*; Censorinus (the *De Die Natali*); Chalcidius; Cicero*; Clement of Alexandria*; Diodorus of Sicily* [French translations from the sixteenth and early eighteenth centuries]; Diogenes Laertius*; Epictetus*; Epiphanius; Euripides (the *Bacchae*); Eusebius; Galen; Hermeias (the *Irrisus Gentilium Philosophorum*); Hermes Trismegistus*; Hesychius of Miletus; Hippolytus; Josephus Flavius*; Irenaeus; Lactantius*; Lucretius*; Origen [+ French translation of the *Contra Celsum* in 1700]; Philo Judaeus*; Philostratus (Flavius)*; Plato*; Pliny the Elder*; Plutarch*; [pseudo-]Plutarch* (the *De Placitis Philosophorum*, included in early-modern editions of the *Moralia* and now generally attributed to Aëtius); Proclus; Seneca*; Sextus Empiricus [+ French translation, 1725]; Tertullian*; Theodoretus*; Theophrastus; Xenophon*; and Zacharias Scholasticus. Less available sources, but works that could be consulted in diverse libraries, were late sixteenth- or very early seventeenth-century editions of Hippocrates of Côs; Iambilichus (+ a Greek-Latin publication of the *De Vita Pythagorae* and the *Protrepticae orationes ad philosophiam* [Amsterdam, 1707]); Joannes Diaconus; Plotinus; Scipio Aquilianus (*De Placitis philosophorum, qui ante Aristotelis tempora floruerunt*); Simplicius (in countless sixteenth-century Venetian editions, but virtually unpublished in early-modern France itself); and Themistus.

early-modern philosophical theology, often without specific attribution. By the seventeenth century, more and more minds were confronting the originals of these formulations at first hand. They came, in general, in two forms. First, there were the arguments of the "atheists" of tradition, explicitly seen as such. Second, there were arguments that neither the author nor the source of the "fragment" necessarily identified as atheistic, but that raised problems of interpretation which led some or many to see atheism explicitly or implicitly there. Many arguments that had been read as innocuous for centuries came to be seen, in the particular contexts of other early-modern philosophical debates, as far more dangerous than first had been understood. There was an intriguing interplay between classical and early-modern thought, the former often engendering classifications of the latter and the latter often engendering reclassifications of the former. Now, let us see what "atheism" the "moderns" encountered among the ancients, and where they might encounter it.

Who were the atheists of tradition? While some early-modern thinkers, we have seen, insisted that all such "atheists" merely had been misunderstood, there was a general consensus about the reality of certain atheists in the ancient world, exceptions to the rule. Protagoras of Abdera, Prodicus, Theodorus of Cyrene, Diagoras of Melos, and Critias, for example, were almost universally identified as such, and Euhemerus frequently. Why? In the case of Protagoras, two fragments earned him this reputation. In the first, he was cited—by Sextus Empiricus, Plato, and Diogenes Laertius, among others—as arguing that "man is the measure of all things, of the things that are, that they are, and of the things that are not, that they are not."[35] In the second, and more dramatic, he was quoted by Eusebius and Laertius (among others) as denying the *evidence* of Divinity: "About the gods, *I am not able to know whether they exist or do not exist*, nor what they are like in form; for the factors preventing knowledge are many: the obscurity of the subject and the shortness of human life."[36] Here, then, most believed, was a man "without God." Prodicus also was so identified for having articulated a theory about the origin of the gods,

[35] Sources widely available in early-modern France: Sextus Empiricus, *Adversus mathematicos* VII.60; Diogenes Laertius, *De Vita . . . Philosophorum* IX.51; Plato, *Theaetatus* 151E–152A. See infra, for discussion of early-modern editions of Sextus and Laertius. (Translation used: Kathleen Freeman, ed. and trans., *Ancilla to the Pre-Socratic Philosophers: A Complete Translation of the Fragments in Diels,* Fragmente der Vorsokratiker [Oxford, 1948], 125).

[36] Sources widely available in early-modern France: Diogenes Laertius, *De Vita . . . Philosophorum* IX.51; Eusebius, *De Praeparatio Evangelica* XIV.3.7 (Freeman, *Ancilla*, 126). Eusebius's *De Praeparatio Evangelica* had been translated into Latin by George of Trebizond and first printed as early as 1470. His works were published in Paris, 1581; Paris, 1628; and Cologne, 1688. Individually, both the *Praeparatio* and the *Demonstratio* were widely available in Greek or Latin, but there were no early-modern editions in French.

namely, that things useful to mankind (the sun and moon, rivers, wine, etc.) came to be regarded as divine simply by virtue of their utility, a view also developed by Euhemerus, Theodorus, and Diagoras. Such an opinion was in theory compatible with criticism of "polytheistic superstition," although it did not in fact speak of any "corruption" of an original idea of God; while Euhemerus sometimes got the benefit of the doubt, however, Prodicus, Theodorus, and Diagoras generally did not, perhaps because of the large role their views played in Cicero's *De natura deorum* and in Sextus Empiricus, or simply because of the difference of their treatment by later commentators. Theodorus, of course, was doomed in reputation by the label attached to his very name throughout the ages, "Theodorus the Atheist."[37] In the frequently republished patristic work of Minucius Felix, the *Octavius*, the pagan interlocutor Caecilius spoke of the "atheism" of Theodorus, Diagoras, and Protagoras, who, "by asserting there were no gods, cut at the root of all the fear and reverence by which mankind is governed."[38] The Athenian Critias, known (among other places) in Sextus Empiricus, (pseudo-)Plutarch, and Xenophon, also was seen as atheistic for his view of the origins of belief in the gods. As recorded fragments of his satiric play *Sisyphus* expressed his view, mankind, in a state of nature ruled by force and brutishness, devised laws of retribution to secure justice but worried about crimes that might be committed in secret. To deal with that concern, "some wise and clever man" invented gods that would be feared:

> Hence he introduced the Divine, saying that there is a God flourishing with immortal life, hearing and seeing with his mind, and thinking of everything and caring about those things, and having divine nature, who will hear everything said among mortals and will be able to see all that is done. . . . In saying these words, he introduced the pleasantest of teachings, covering up the truth with a false theory. . . . With such fears did he surround mankind, through which he well established the deity with his argument . . . and quenched lawlessness among men. . . . Thus, I think, for the first time did someone persuade mortals to believe in a race of deities.[39]

In general, the pre-Socratic philosophers, as paraphrased or cited by later thinkers, posed grave problems of interpretation, above all because

[37] On the "school" of Prodicus, Euhemerus, Theodorus and Diagoras, see Cicero, *De natura deorum* I.37.118; II.5, 13, 23, 59; Sextus Empiricus, *Adv. math.* IX.18.51–52. On the role of the *De natura deorum*, see infra.

[38] Minucius Felix, *Octavius* VIII.

[39] Sources widely available in early-modern France: Sextus Empiricus, *Adv. math.* I.52; Xenophon, *Memorabilia* I.iv.18 (Freeman, *Ancilla*, 157–58). See also, infra, nn. 89–94. Xenophon's *Opera* were widely available in Greek, Greek and Latin, Latin, and French editions throughout the early-modern period. The *Memorabilia Socratis* was published separately, in French, in Paris, 1650, and Amsterdam, 1699.

so many of them were seen as having understood the "first principle" of things to be material, and, usually, to be a specific element. While early-modern debates indeed influenced such perceptions (if one wished to denounce Hobbes as "atheistic" for his corporealism or Spinoza for his monism and denial of providence, how could one not reach the same conclusion about so much of pre-Socratic thought?), the problems had been posed long before. In particular, much of a patristic literature deemed wise by virtue of the sanctity of its authors drew disturbing conclusions about widespread atheism in the ancient world.

Irenaeus saw most of the pre-Socratics as "atheists" in their materialist explanations of the origin of the world, including Homer, Thales, Anaximander, Empedocles, and even Anaxagoras.[40] Theophilus believed that Empedocles "taught atheism."[41] Clement of Alexandria saw Thales, Anaximenes, Diogenes of Apollonia, Parmenides, Heraclitus, Empedocles, and all the atomists as such.[42] For Lactantius, in the *Divinae Institutiones*, the issue of whether the world was formed and governed by providence or by chance was the issue of a theistic or atheistic view of the world, and he condemned as atheistic Democritus and Epicurus on such grounds. He added to that same category "Protagoras, who called the gods into doubt, and, afterwards, Diagoras, who later excluded them, and some others who did not think that the gods existed." Despite this, however, he found these exceptions so minimal that he held to the argument from universal consent; his readers, from his own accounting, however, could reach their own conclusion about that.[43]

Indeed, in the *De Ira Dei*, Lactantius again identified Protagoras, Diagoras ("who said that there was no god whatsoever, and for this opinion he was named an atheist"), and Theodorus as atheists, and, equating the Epicurean denial of providence with implicit atheism, himself provided substantial (and also anecdotal) grounds for seeing Leucippus, Democritus, and, above all, Epicurus as atheistic:

> But if He cares for nothing [and] provides for nothing, He has lost all Divinity. He who takes away all force, [and,] therefore, all substance from God,

[40] Irenaeus, *Adversus haereses* II.xiv.1–6. There were Latin editions of Irenaeus's work in Paris, 1639; Paris, 1675; and Paris, 1710. It is not clear whom Irenaeus confused with Anaxagoras.

[41] Theophilus, *Adversus Autol.* III.2.

[42] Clement of Alexandria, *Protrepticus* 64.2–3; *Stromateis* I.xi.52.4. See infra, n. 49.

[43] Lactantius, *Divinae Institutiones* I.2; III.17; III.28. There were many editions of Lactantius in the seventeenth century, the most commonly utilized after midcentury being the *Lucii Coelii Lactantii Firmiani Opera quae extant* . . . (Lyon, 1660). The *Divinae Institutiones* was translated into French in 1710, but libraries also held French translations from the sixteenth century, when five vernacular editions were printed. I have used the English translation in Lactantius, *The Divine Institutes: Books I–VIII*, trans. Sister Mary Francis McDonald (Washington, D.C., 1964).

> *what else does he say except that there is no God at all*? Marcus Tullius [Cicero], in fact, relates that it was said by Posidonius that Epicurus believed this, that there were no gods, but that the things which he spoke about the gods he had said for the sake of driving away ill will, so in his words he left the gods, but in very fact he removed them, to whom he assigned no motion [and] no function.[44]

Athenagoras, in his "plea" for the Christians against accusations of atheism, the *Legatio*, had undertaken what in many ways was a sustained examination and redefinition of the term *atheism* (as used by the pagans) to exonerate the Christians of the charge. His criteria for what made the Christians antithetical to atheists—above all else their distinction of God from matter, and their insistence that the first principle was eternal, one, infinite, and omnipotent—led him to characterize much of pagan theology as implicitly atheistic, recognizing merely composite, unstable, changeable, material beings. Also, he noted, it was the pagans who had given examples of explicitly and unambiguously atheistic men: Diagoras was a genuine atheist, Athenagoras wrote, for "he bluntly declared that there is no God at all."[45] Arnobius of Sicca's *Adversus Gentes* was direct in its insistence on strains of pagan atheism, *especially* among the philosophers:

> For we hear that some who give themselves to the study of philosophy deny that there is any divine force; and that others daily inquire whether it exists; that others construct the whole sum of things by chance accidents and random collisions and fashion it by the propulsions of different-shaped things.[46]

Was Arnobius an "obscure" early-modern source? In fact, the *Adversus Gentes* was published seven times in the seventeenth century, including editions of 1651 and 1666. For Arnobius, there was no doubt at all about the reality of atheistic schools of thought in the pagan world: "So, too, some deny categorically that gods exist; others say they doubt

[44] Lactantius, *De Ira Dei* IV, IX–XIII. The final quotation is from c. IV. I have used the English translation in Lactantius, *The Minor Works*, trans. Sister Mary Francis McDonald (Washington, D.C., 1965).

[45] Athenagoras, *Legatio* 4.1–30.6. The quotation concerning Diagoras is found in 4.1. Athenagoras was available in many early-modern editions in Greek and Latin. The *Legatio*, more commonly then termed the *Apologia*, was available in libraries in French translation in two late sixteenth-century editions of 1574 and 1577. I have used the English translation in Athenagoras, *Legatio and De Resurrectione*, ed. and trans. William R. Schoedel (Oxford, 1972).

[46] Arnobius of Sicca, *Adversus Gentes* I.31–32. The Bibliothèque Nationale (*Imprimés*: C.1618) has a copy of the edition of 1651 with manuscript notes by Bishop Pierre-Daniel Huet. I have used the English translation in Arnobius of Sicca, *The Case against the Pagans*, trans. George E. McCracken (Westminster, Md., 1949).

whether they exist anywhere."[47] Further, yet another source of Bayle's views (although with Plutarch, we shall see, as one, who needs to count?), Arnobius found such atheism to be *less* blameworthy than "blasphemous" pagan idolatry:

> A man who doubts the existence of the gods or who completely denies their existence, although the boldness of his ideas may give him the appearance of following monstrous views, nevertheless without reviling the faith of anyone, merely does not agree to things that are obscure. . . . But you who assert that you are the champions and protagonists of their [the gods'] immortality, have you passed by [or] overlooked any single one of them and left him unabused by your maledictions? And is there any kind of insult so damnable in the belief of all that you have hesitated to use it on them?[48]

Clement of Alexandria's *Stromateis* was widely available in Latin (and in the original Greek) throughout the seventeenth century in France and was translated into the vernacular in Parisian editions of 1696 and 1701.[49] Clement admired so much of Greek philosophy as a gift from God, but he termed Epicurus "the initiator of men into atheism" and, we have seen, described much of pre-Socratic thought as utter disbelief in God: "Certain [philosophers] revere the elements: Diogenes the air, Thales water, Hippasos fire, and, finally, some make atoms the principle of everything; they cloak themselves in the term *philosopher*, but they are only atheistic abortions."[50] At times, Clement used the term *atheist* equivocally, for he applied it to explicit disbelief, to certain forms of erroneous belief (denial of providence, for example), to those who used God as "accomplices to man's own evil," and to those who infused the Divinity with the worst passions of men.[51] He was precise enough, however, to make evident that he saw actual denial of the existence of Divinity in the world of Greek philosophy, distinct from denial of God's providence and justice: "Those . . . who have not seen the liberty of the human soul . . . are irritated by what is done by unpunished injustice, *and disbelieve in the existence of God.* Similar to them in belief are those who . . . despairing

[47] Ibid. II.56–57.

[48] Ibid. V.30.

[49] Clement of Alexandria was available to the early-modern reader in Greek and Latin in his *Opera . . . quae exstant* . . . (Lyon, 1616; Paris, 1629; and [two printings], Paris, 1641); and in the vernacular in *Les Oeuvres de S. Clément d'Alexandrie* (Paris, 1696; and Paris, 1701).

[50] Clement of Alexandria, *Stromateis* I.ii.1.11 (re Epicurus); I.xi.54.2 (re the "atheistic" philosophers). In ibid. I.xi.51.1, Clement reminded his readers that "the Stoics . . . say quite basely that God is corporeal."

[51] Ibid. VII.iii.15 and iv.23.1–3.

at their sufferings, *say that there is no God*, or that if He does exist, He is not in charge of everything."[52]

Saint Augustine's *De Civitate Dei*, always widely read, but particularly so in France after Jansenism focused so much attention on his works, offered a review of Greek philosophy that saw the "Ionian" (Milesian) tradition more as hopelessly confused about God than as in any way atheistic. By insisting on its materialism and denial of divine intelligence, however, he gave adequate grounds to readers with a less capacious concept of theism to assign them to an atheistic camp, which, we shall see, many did. His individual characterizations of the Ionians were commonplace by his time and still commonplace in the seventeenth century, but the authority of Augustine among Fathers and doctors of the Church was for many sui generis and compelling.[53] Concerning Thales, he wrote, "His main theory was that the primary stuff of all things is water, and that from this principle originated the elements, the cosmos, and everything which the world produced. As far as he was concerned, nothing of all this universe . . . was directed by divine intelligence." He described Thales' disciple, Anaximander, as believing the universe to be material principles producing "uncounted worlds" in "endless succession of dissolution and becoming," and averred that, "like Thales, he found no place for any divine direction in the processes of nature." Anaximenes neither "denied nor ignored the gods" like his predecessor, but "taught that they were creatures of the air and not its creators." Not until Anaxagoras, Diogenes of Apollonia, and Archelaus, for Saint Augustine, did the Ionians recognize "the divine mind" and "the agency of the divine reason" in the production of things *from* coeternal material principles.[54] When he compared the pre-Socratics to his much-admired Plato, the materialism of the former was made clear:

[52] Ibid. vii.iii.15

[53] There were two remarkable editions of Augustine's works in the seventeenth century in France, the *Opera* edited by the theologians of Louvain, the *S. Aurelii Augustini, . . . Opera . . . per theologos Lovanienses . . . ac emendata . . .*, 10 tomes in 6 [fol.] vols., ed. Th. Gozalum and J. Molanum (Paris, 1613–1614) (reprinted in 11 tomes in 7 vols., Paris, 1635–1637; and in Paris, 1636–1651); and the both celebrated and (for its Jansenizing commentary) harassed *Opera* edited by the Maurist Benedictines, the *Sancti Aurelii Augustini, . . . Operum . . . post Lovaniensium theologorum recensionen castigatus . . . Opera ex studio monachorum Ordinis S. Benedicit et Congregatione S. Mauri . . .*, 11 tomes in 15 [fol.] vols., ed. T. Blampin, O.S.B. et al. (Paris, 1679–1700) (new ed., 12 tomes in 9 vols., Antwerp, 1700–1703). The *De Civitate Dei* was widely translated into French, including the 1-vol. folio ed. of *De la Cité de Dieu*, trans. le sieur de Ceriziers (Paris, 1655); *De la Cité de Dieu*, trans. Louis Giry, 2 vols. (Paris, 1665–1667); and, enjoying three printings, *La Cité de Dieu de Saint Augustin*, trans. Pierre Lombert, 2 vols. (Paris, 1675; Paris, 1693; and Paris, 1701). I have utilized the English translation in St. Augustine, *The City of God*, trans. D. B. Zema, S.J., D. J. Honan, S.J., and G.-G. Walsh, S.J., 3 vols. (New York, 1950–1954).

[54] St. Augustine, *De Civitate Dei*, l.viii, c.2 (his discussion of the Ionian school).

So, too, those philosophers, the materialists who believe that the ultimate principles of nature are corporeal, should yield to those great ["Platonists"] who had knowledge of so great a God. Such were Thales, who found the cause and principle of things in water, Anaximenes in air, the Stoics in fire, Epicurus in atoms. . . . And so of the rest, whose names it is needless to mention, who maintained that bodies, simple or compound, animate or inanimate, but nevertheless material, were the root of all reality.[55]

Similarly, in the *Contra Academicos*, Saint Augustine did not accuse the Academy of atheism but did describe a materialism that others could use to support such a charge. He portrayed Zeno as believing "that there is nothing beyond the present world of the senses and nothing transpires in it except through corporeal agency." This appealed to the ancients, Augustine insisted, because "people will most readily, however harmfully, believe because of their familiarity with material things, that everything is corporeal." This "pernicious doctrine of materialism" endured in the Academy, for Augustine, until refuted successfully by Carneades.[56]

. . .

If one thought that perhaps the early Fathers were being in any way unfair to the ancients, there were always the ancients themselves to testify about those thinkers known only in fragments, witnesses whom the early-modern world also revered and read with great fervor. Aristotle's *Metaphysics* presented the thought of the pre-Socratic sages as limited to a thoroughgoing corporeal materialism, explaining that "many of the earlier philosophers regard body as being or primary being and regard all else as modifiers of a body, so that the principles of bodies are the principles of things."[57] This view of them was offered precisely to distinguish them from his own view, which (he was sure) they had not anticipated, "that there is a primary being, eternal and unmovable and separate from sensible things . . . without parts and indivisible."[58] As we shall see, that Aristotelian distinction would inform a large number of early-modern attempts to separate Greek "atheism" from Greek "theism." Where Aristotle did not raise the issue of "atheism" explicitly, however, Plato indeed had done so in the widely cited book 10 of the *Laws*, which sought to address not only those who portray the gods as corporeal, corruptible,

[55] Ibid. l.VIII, c.5.

[56] St. Augustine, *Contra Academicos* l.III, 38. I have used the English translation of St. Augustine, *Against the Academics*, trans. John J. O'Meara (Westminster, Md., 1950).

[57] Aristotle, *Metaphysica* I, passim; III.5 (1002a), where one finds the quotation. I have used the English translation of Aristotle, *Metaphysics*, trans. Richard Hope (Ann Arbor, 1963).

[58] Ibid. XII.7 (1073a).

or without providence, but those who "deny the existence of the gods." When the Cretan interlocutor asked if it were not easy to convince atheists from "the evidence of the earth, the sun, the stars, and all the universe, and the beautiful ordering of the seasons, . . . and . . . the further fact that all Greeks and Barbarians believe in the existence of the gods," the Athenian interlocutor replied that it was not so simple as that:

> It is rather the novel views of our modern [natural philosophers] that we must hold responsible as the true cause of [this] mischief [of atheism]. For the result of the arguments of such people is this, that when you and I try to prove the existence of the gods by pointing to these very objects—sun, moon, stars and earth—as instances of deity and divinity, people who have been converted by these scientists will assert that these things are simply earth and stone, incapable of paying any heed to human affairs, and that these beliefs of ours are speciously [derived] with arguments to [try to] make them plausible.[59]

This, of course, still could be seen by early-modern minds as relevant merely to a debate over polytheism. The heart of Plato's analysis of atheism in the *Laws*, however, as it would be for so many in the seventeenth century, was the issue of whether or not the agency of chance or of design should be inferred from the world. For the "atheist," in Plato's description, "the greatest and most beautiful things are the work of nature and of chance, and the lesser things [those made by man] that of art." Contemporaneous unbelievers, Plato claimed, were convinced that the elements exist by nature and by chance, and that all things have been "brought into existence" solely "by means of these, which are all inanimate." For many, then, "it is by chance that these elements move, by the interplay of their respective forces, and accordingly as they meet together and combine fittingly . . . in this way and by these means they have brought into being the whole Heaven and all that is in the Heaven, and all animals, too, and plants, . . . and all this, as they assert, *not owing to reason, nor to any god or art, but owing, as we have said, to nature and chance*."[60]

If pressed to account for the widespread belief in gods, the atheists, the Athenian explained, have a ready answer: "The first statement . . . which these people make about the gods is that they exist by art and not by nature—by certain legal conventions which differ from place to place,

[59] Plato, *Noumia* x, passim (the quotation is from 886A). The *Laws* was included in the Dacier translation of *Les Oeuvres de Platon* . . . , 2 vols. (Paris, 1699); 2d ed. (Paris, 1701). I have used the translation in Plato, *Laws*, ed. and trans. R. G. Bury, 2 vols. (Cambridge, Mass., 1926).

[60] Ibid. (888D–889D).

according as each tribe agreed when forming their laws."[61] One cannot deny the existence of such atheists, since "if the assertions mentioned had not been sown . . . well-nigh over the whole world of men, there would have been no need of counter-arguments to defend the existence of the gods; *but as it is, they are necessary*."[62] Finally, while belief in the gods was necessary to the virtue of the state, there were (Bayle students, again take note) individual atheists who could be wholly virtuous. Although such virtuous atheists were to be punished because of the danger they posed to society, Plato acknowledged that there were "those who, *though they utterly disbelieve in the existence of the gods, possess by nature a just character, [and] both hate evil, and, because of their dislike of injustice, are incapable of being induced to commit unjust actions, and flee from unjust men and love the just*."[63]

. . .

Again, it is essential to remind oneself that the texts in which such views appeared were not exotic or esoteric texts for the early-modern learned world, but works of great immediacy, broad dissemination, and easy accessibility, both materially and mentally. It is difficult to exaggerate the "presence" in early-modern minds of classical and patristic thought. Historians who lose sight of that may believe themselves obliged to hunt high and low for possible sources of early-modern views of atheism and may attribute to Bayle's "Remarks" in the *Dictionnaire* what was omnipresent in his culture. As in the case of travel and missionary literature, so also in that of the ancients, contradictions of the quasi-official apologetic views were indeed ubiquitous. With that in mind, let us examine both the compendia of philosophical views most popular and widely cited in the early-modern world and the fruits of early-modern commentary, in order that we may yet deepen our appreciation of the role of traditional and "orthodox" culture in generating the possibility and categories of atheistic thought.

. . .

Two of the most authoritative and influential guides to ancient thought for the seventeenth century were Diogenes Laertius's *De Vita et Moribus Philosophorum* and Plutarch's *Moralia*, which then included (pseudo-Plutarch's) *De Placitis Philosophorum*. The *De Vita* was widely available

[61] Ibid. (889E).
[62] Ibid. (891B).
[63] Ibid. (908B–908C).

in Greek, in Latin translation, and in three vernacular editions, the last of these in 1668. The *De Placitis*, now generally attributed to Aëtius, was widely available in all reprintings of the 16th-century Stephanus edition of the *Moralia*, and in all reprintings of Bishop Jacques Amyot's translation into the French. These were, as much as any books, standard reference works of the early-modern world. Recommending them to students in the sixteenth century, Juan Luis Vives, although concerned primarily with the views of nature in them, expressed what remained a popular view, especially among those not particularly enamored of prior philosophy: "Plutarch . . . [in] his four books *de Placitis Philosophorum* as well as Diogenes Laertius in his *de Vita . . . Philosophorum* will serve to show the intelligent student how many kinds of absurd opinions well-known philosophers have held. . . . Students will see that they, too, were men, and often held mistaken opinions on matters which are most self-evident."[64] As R. D. Hicks has reminded us, the influence and dissemination of Laertius's *Lives* were of primary cultural significance in early-modern thought, and such influential savants as Casaubon, Henri Estienne (Stephanus), Ménage, and Gassendi "became his interpreters"; he noted that "before long, histories of philosophy began to be written, and pioneers like Stanley and Brücker did little more than rearrange and amplify the contents of his work."[65] His latter observation is an exaggeration (and we shall meet earlier "pioneers" than he acknowledges), but it was indeed an enormously influential work. As was *De Placitis Philosophorum*! Bayle's father owned Amyot's translation of the *Moralia*, and Bayle obviously read the *De Placitis* carefully, for it is everywhere in his citations and views.[66] Indeed, it was one of the most widely cited of all sources in almost all works of seventeenth-century classical scholarship. What did these two works have to say that pertained to universal consent?

First, Laertius presented so much of pre-Socratic thought as wholly materialist, although he did not ascribe atheism explicitly to the first poets, sages, or philosophers of antiquity. He wrote of the magi and "their views concerning the being and origin of the gods, whom they hold to be fire, earth and water."[67] The Egyptians "say *that matter was the first principle*;

[64] Juan Luis Vives, *On Education: A Translation of the De Tradendis Disciplinis*, trans. Foster Watson (Cambridge, 1913). The *De Disciplinis* was first published in 1531 and enjoyed an edition in Leiden, 1636.

[65] R. D. Hicks's "Introduction" to Diogenes Laertius, *Lives of Eminent Philosophers*, ed. and trans. R. D. Hicks, 2 vols. (Loeb Classical Library 1925), ix–xi.

[66] Elisabeth Labrousse, *Pierre Bayle*, 2 vols. (The Hague, 1963–1964), I, 55; see also Ruth Elizabeth Cowdrick, *The Early Reading of Pierre Bayle . . .* (Scottsdale, Pa., 1939). In the *Dictionnaire*, Bayle almost invariably cites Plutarch in "the Amiot edition."

[67] Diogenes Laertius, *De la vie des philosophes. Traduction nouvelle*, trans. Gilles Boileau, 2 vols. (Paris, 1668), I.6. (Throughout, I have utilized the translation of R. D. Hicks, ed. and trans., *Lives*.)

next the four elements were derived from matter, and thus living things of every species were produced."[68] Anaxagoras, for Laertius, "was the first who set mind above matter," and all of the Ionians before him had defined the first principle to be material.[69] Among the Cyreniacs there was Theodorus, "a man who utterly rejected the current belief in the gods."[70] Stilpo and Bion were presented as doubters about divinity, willing to express themselves candidly only in private. When asked about the gods, "[Stilpo] is said to have replied: 'Don't put such a question in the street, simpleton, but when we are alone!' It is said that Bion, when he was asked the same question whether there are gods, replied: 'Will you not scatter the crowd from me?' "[71] Indeed, Bion was portrayed as a philosopher who was convinced of atheism, temporarily at least, *by argument*: "Next he went over to Theodorean views, after he had heard the lectures of Theodorus the Atheist, who used every kind of sophistical argument." Laertius's Bion could be used to show that the atheist could not sustain his disbelief at the approach of death, but that side of the story was problematic, while the reality of his atheism was (in Laertius's portrait) indubitable:

> In his familiar talk he would often vehemently assail belief in the gods, a taste which he had derived from Theodorus. Afterwards, when he fell ill . . . , he was persuaded to wear an amulet and to repent of his offenses against religion. . . . [In] these lines I have taken him to task: "We hear that Bion . . . denied that the gods really exist. Had he persisted in holding his opinion, it would have been right to say, 'He thinks as he pleases: wrongly, to be sure, but still he does think so.' But in fact, when he fell ill . . . and feared death, he who denied the existence of the gods . . . cheerfully allowed an old woman to put a charm round his neck . . . as if the gods existed just when Bion chose to recognize them."[72]

Laertius's Plato, Aristotle, and the Stoics recognized both the existence and the spirituality of the Divinity. The believer in universal consent could get from book 5 to book 7 unscathed. The philosophies of Empedocles, Heraclitus, and Parmenides, however, were presented without a single mention of God or the gods, and, in the last instance, as expressly explaining order by reference to corporeal elements alone: "He held that there were two elements, fire and earth, and that the former discharged the function of a craftsman, the latter of his material."[73] Melissus was

[68] Ibid. I.10.
[69] Ibid. I–II, passim. The discussion of Anaxagoras's views occurs in II.6–9.
[70] Ibid. II.97.
[71] Ibid. II.117.
[72] Ibid. IV.54–57.
[73] Ibid. VIII–IX, passim. The quotation concerning Parmenides is found in IX.21–22.

portrayed as believing "that the universe was unlimited, unchangeable and immovable, and was one, uniform and full of matter." Concerning the gods, Melissus was, at some level, without belief: "He said that we ought not to make any statements about the gods, for it was impossible to have knowledge of them."[74] This view and others equally incredulous were attributed to Protagoras as well:

> In another work he began thus: "As to the gods, I have no means of knowing either that they exist or that they do not exist. For many are the obstacles that impede knowledge, both the obscurity of the question, and the shortness of human life." For this introduction to his book the Athenians expelled him; and they burnt his works in the market place, after sending round a herald to collect them from all who had copies in their possession.[75]

As for the skeptics, in Laertius's portrait, such a suspension of belief was explicit or implicit in almost all of their views, especially among those called "Ephetics" (who suspended judgment on every question) and "Aporetics" (who remained always in perplexity over every question). They all derived, for Laertius, from Pyrrho, whose "most noble philosophy" he described as "taking the form of agnosticism and suspension of judgment. . . . And so, universally, he held that there is nothing really existent, but custom and convention govern human action; for no single thing is in itself any more this than that."[76]

In the Amyot edition of the *De Placitis Philosophorum*,[77] all philosophy prior to that of Anaxagoras was presented as seeing the "principles"

[74] Ibid. IX.24.

[75] Ibid. IX.51–52.

[76] Ibid. IX.61–108.

[77] [Pseudo-]Plutarch, *De Placitis Philosophorum*, in Plutarch, *Les Oeuvres morales et philosophiques de Plutarque*, ed. and trans. Jacques Amyot, bishop of Auxerre, new ed., rev., corr., and aug., 2 [fol.] vols. (Paris, 1618), II, 439vE–460vF. The sixteenth century first knew Plutarch in the Aldine Greek editions and the Greek-Latin Xylander editions. In 1572, the remarkable scholar, editor and publisher Henri Estienne (Stephanus) produced his Greek-Latin critical edition in 13 vols., which was translated into French, with revisions, by Bishop Jacques Amyot (Paris, 1559–1572), who had consulted many of the Paris manuscripts and offered some critical emendations. The Amyot edition was published again in a new, revised edition of 1618 and was widely available throughout the seventeenth century. The *De Placitis Philosophorum* was placed in 439E–460F of the *Moralia* in the Stephanus and Amyot editions and is now omitted from editions of Plutarch, generally being attributed to Aëtius in a guess perhaps as good as any other. Amyot understood that the compendium was problematic; in a marginal note to ibid., 439v, he noted: "This entire opuscule of the opinions of the philosophers is miserably corrupted and defective in the original Greek, and can be restored only by conjecture . . . [until] by some lucky encounter we find a complete ancient copy . . . and for that [reason] I do not guarantee the present translation." It was such a convenient compendium, however, and the prestige of Plutarch so high, that work after work relied on it for certain views of ancient philosophy.

of nature, defined as the agents that engendered all of the natural elements, as purely material. Anaxagoras should be praised as the first who "added the worker to matter." Before him (and, in the case of some, after him), corporeal entities were seen as uncreated, immortal, eternal, incorruptible, and the source of all beings.[78] Recall that Aquinas's summae had taught generation after generation of Christian students that the antithesis to theism was a naturalism which believed all things explicable in terms of material principles and elements alone. When those same students read *De Placitis*, however, they learned that for large numbers of Greek sages, "the world came to be formed . . . in this manner: indivisible atoms having a fortuitous, unplanned, and undeliberated motion, and moving lightly and continuously, several bodies came to collide together [*les Atomes indivisibles aiants un mouvement fortuit et non consulté ny de propos delibéré, et se movant très légèrement et continuellement, plusieurs corps sont venus à se rencontrer ensemble*]."[79]

Further, in *De Placitis*, while most philosophers assigned the status of Divinity to diverse material principles, several "held resolutely that there were not any Gods [*ont tenu resoluëment qu'il n'estoit point de Dieux*]," including Diagoras, Theodorus, Euhemerus, and, although he tried "to conceal" his views, Euripides, who was clearly "an atheist," attributing all belief in gods to political need and a strategy for restraint of criminals.[80] Lending support to either the view that the Stoics and the atomists retained *some* understanding of God or that, correctly and rigorously understood, their views were atheistic, *De Placitis* observed that for the Stoics "the world is God" and that for the atomists, "all the gods were formed from man."[81]

The rest of Plutarch's *Moralia*, increasingly absorbed in the vernacular throughout the seventeenth century, also offered (among many other things) a textbook of ancient views toward atheism. First, of course, and unmistakably the primary locus of Bayle's arguments that idolatry was worse than superstition, there was Plutarch's essay "On Superstition," introduced by Amyot with the caution that "this treatise is dangerous to read and contains a false doctrine, for it is certain that superstition is less evil and much closer to true religion than impiety and atheism . . . the sin of sins."[82]

[78] Ibid., 440B–440G.

[79] Ibid., 441F–441H.

[80] Ibid., 442H–443B. This was a frequently quoted section on the reality and nature of Greek atheism.

[81] Ibid., 443G.

[82] *De Superstitione*, a lengthy essay, is found in vol. I of the Amyot edition of the *Moralia*, 119vE–124rB [in Stephanus and modern editions, 164E–171F]. My citations from Plutarch

"On Superstition" not only made atheism appear widespread but characterized it as merely "a false judgment about [the existence of] God [*un faulx jugement de Dieu*]," while, in contrast, "superstition" was treated as relating to the emotions, "a passion produced by a false judgment." Better to hear no music at all, Plutarch urged, than to go mad from it! Atheists, while tragically ignorant of an important truth, merely "do not recognize the gods at all . . . disregard them . . . and [reach a state of] indifference"; the superstitious "think that they exist and are evil," reaching a state of "equal agitation and fear toward the things that could help them," and suffering terribly. The atheist can accept his fate without complaint, since he always has denied that justice, providence, and order govern the world; the superstitious person, feeling punished by the gods in any misfortune, lives in "fears and frights, suspicions and trepidations." When ill, the atheist looks to his diet or excesses; the superstitious man, by contrast, feels helpless and passive. Where the latter is inconsolable, "it is possible in the case of a man unconvinced of the existence of gods, when he is in grief and great distress . . . to wipe away a tear" and do something constructive.[83] In an argument that Bayle would make central to his own thesis, Plutarch argued that superstition insulted Divinity far more than did atheism: "For me, I should prefer men to say about me that I never was born at all, and that Plutarch does not exist, than to say that Plutarch is an inconsistent, fickle, ill-tempered, vindictive person."[84]

Again, note that in describing ancient "atheism," Plutarch made it a product of thought, while describing superstition as a product of bondage to passion: "The atheist believes there are no gods; the superstitious man . . . believes in them . . . for he is afraid not to believe . . . and he would call the condition of the atheist happy because it is a state of freedom." Atheists, Plutarch insisted, became such not out of "dissatisfaction" with man's lot, but, rather, out of the "absurd behavior and emotions of superstition." Many, then, "say that it would be better if there were no gods at all than gods . . . [who are] so tyrannical, petty, and easily angered."[85] For Plutarch, this view made sense. It would be far better for a people to have "no gods," he concluded, than to have gods to whom they offer human sacrifice. It would have been far better for the Carthaginians to have had the atheists "Critias or Diagoras frame their laws at the outset, and thus not believe in any divine power or god, rather than offer such [blood] sacrifices as they offered to Cronos." Indeed, Plutarch urged, it is precisely the effort to escape from the worst abuses of superstition that

himself are from the Amyot edition, with the Stephanus locations in brackets. Amyot's caution is found on 119vE.

[83] Ibid., 119vE–122vG [164E–168E].

[84] Ibid., 122vG–123rA [169E–170D].

[85] Ibid., 123rD–123vF [170F–171B].

has caused "some persons, in trying to escape [these], to rush into a raw and hardened atheism."[86]

Further, in his essay *De Communibus Notitiis Adversus Stoicos*, Plutarch, arguing against what he took to be the Stoic notion of corporeal and thus destructible Divinity, portrayed "the atheists" in a manner that made it more than difficult for early-modern readers to see them as merely rejecting such false idolatrous ideas:

> There has not been a single man who, conceiving of god, did not conceive him to be indestructible and everlasting. Indeed, those unfortunates who have been called atheists, a Theodorus, a Diagoras, and a Hippon, did not dare to say that God is corruptible, but denied that there was incorruptible substance.[87]

. . .

On the whole, in discussing these works, I have omitted discussions of Epicurus and Lucretius, to show how widespread the identifications of "atheism" among the ancients could be, even without them. I shall turn my attention, in my next volume, to their place in seventeenth-century thought, but, we soon shall see, many early-modern historians of philosophy characterized their obvious naturalism, and their denial of spirit, design, creation, and providence, as "atheistic." It should be clear by now, however, that from the sources widely utilized in early-modern France, the "exceptions" to universal consent among the ancients could only with great difficulty be limited to them. Others, the most reputable sources announced, disbelieved in God, *or offered arguments that they believed unanswerable against the existence of any Divinity.* Among those who did the latter, explicated at length in an ancient source widely noted in early-modern France, were the formally skeptical Greek philosophers, the followers of Pyrrho, or, simply, "the Pyrrhonians." Let us turn, then, to the much-read and much-discussed Sextus Empiricus, and his *Hypotyposes* or *Outlines of Pyrrhonism.*[88]

[86] Ibid., 123vF–124rB [171B–171F].

[87] Ibid., II, 582E [1075A].

[88] As early-modern scholars now know well, interest in Sextus Empiricus was high from the first publication of extant Greek and Latin translation manuscripts in the sixteenth century. It was above all the Stephanus edition of the *Hypotyposes* in Latin (Paris, 1562), that stimulated so much attention to Sextus and Greek skepticism, followed by a Latin edition of the *Adversus Mathematicos* in Paris, 1569. Despite the availability of Sextus in Latin, there was a Greek *Sexti Empirici Opera quae extant* . . . in Paris (and Geneva), 1621, under the guidance of P. and J. Chouet. (The Stephanus Latin and Chouet Greek would be combined in the *Sexti Empirici Opera, graece et latine* . . . [Leipzig, 1718].) The *Hypotyposes* was translated anonymously into French as *Les Hipotiposes, ou Institutions pirroniennes*

In one sense, of course, the central philosophical position of the *Hypotyposes*, that no certainty was possible at all, entailed, if true, that no philosophical certainty was possible concerning the existence of God. In presenting the views of the Pyrrhonian school, however, Sextus Empiricus not only advanced such a view by general criticism of all criteria of truth and compelling demonstration, but offered specific criticisms of any claims of knowledge of Divinity. For seventeenth-century readers and authors who believed that such criticism favored or reflected atheism (the Pyrrhonians themselves, as presented by Sextus Empiricus, claimed to believe in the gods despite the absence of demonstration), the *Hypotyposes* could only further weaken the argument from a consent appearing less and less universal.

The dramatic third book of the *Hypotyposes* was precisely focused on the issue of knowledge of God. First, Sextus Empiricus explained, the dogmatic philosophers themselves did not agree about the nature of God, and "how shall we be able to reach a conception of God when we have no agreement about His substance or His form or His place of abode?" They tell us, then, he noted, simply to regard whatever being we conceive to be "imperishable and blessed" as that God, "but this is foolish," since, first, not knowing the substance of God, we cannot learn of or conceive of His properties, and, second, the term *blessed* is utterly equivocal. Is there not, however, some universal belief in Him? The Pyrrhonians replied:

> In order to form a concept of God it is necessary . . . to suspend judgment as to His existence or nonexistence, for the existence of God is not evident a priori. For if we were impressed spontaneously by God [with knowledge of Him], the dogmatic philosophers would be in agreement concerning His essence, nature, and place, when in fact their endless disagreement has made Him seem nonevident to us, and in need of demonstration.[89]

How could an uncertain God be *demonstrated*, however, the Pyrrhonians asked? If He could be demonstrated by self-evident things, He would be self-evident, which we know He is not, but everything "nonevident" from which we would seek to demonstrate Him would itself need proof

---

de Sextus Empiricus, en trois livres, traduites du grec, avec des notes (n.p., 1725; reprint, London [?], 1735). For the *Hypotyposes*, the page numbers in brackets are from the French edition of 1725. For the modern reader, see Sextus Empiricus, *Outlines of Pyrrhonism*, trans. R. G. Bury (Cambridge, Mass., 1933); *Against the Logicians* trans. R. G. Bury (Cambridge, Mass., 1935); and *Against the Physicists. Against the Ethicists*, trans. R. G. Bury (Cambridge, Mass., 1936), which together form the Loeb Classical Library's Greek and English edition of *Sextus Empiricus* in three volumes. For a most provocative and enlightening study, see Richard H. Popkin, *The History of Scepticism from Erasmus to Descartes*, rev. ed. (Assen, 1964).

[89] Sextus Empiricus, *Hyptotyposes* III, passim. [*Hipotiposes* (Paris, 1725), 271–76.]

from something "nonevident" and "prior," ad infinitum. Further, given the obvious reality of evil in the world, which no dogmatist (they thought) denies, the existence of God cannot be known. Either He is providential, or He is not. If He is providential, however, "there would have been nothing evil and no evil in the world, yet all things, they say, are full of evil." If God is not providential, however, then He is weaker than the cause that prevents His power of providence, and is no God (since "it contradicts our idea of God that He should be weaker than anything"); further, if He is not providential, then no work or production in the world is His, "and no one could name the source of the perception of God's existence." Given evil, the reality of which everyone concedes, God would be either "weak or malign," both of which would contradict His being. From this, Sextus concluded, it is demonstrated "that it cannot be known if there is a God [*Voilà donc encore les raisons qui prouvent que l'on ne peut pas conaitre s'il y a un Dieu*]."[90] Further, the Pyrrhonians noted, both the reality of genuine atheism in Greece and differences of definitions of God from place to place and school to school leave one in endless irresolvable controversies (and, we should note, far from universal consent): "For while most affirm that gods exist, some deny their existence, like the school of Diagoras of Melos, and Theodorus, and Critias the Athenian."[91] The term *school*, one should note, suggested also that these were not isolated unbelievers.

Unlike the *Hypotyposes*, Sextus Empiricus's *Adversus Dogmaticos* was untranslated into French, but it was widely read in Latin translation, and it too raised profound questions about universal consent. In a chapter on the gods, Sextus Empiricus strongly presented the arguments for and against the existence of any Divinity. Finding nothing to choose between them ("*those who maintain the non-existence of Gods do not fall short of the former with respect to their equipollence [equal weight]*"), he called for a "skeptical suspension of judgment" on the question. In arguing against universal consent, however, Sextus Empiricus provided both a large cast of characters and thumbnail sketches of their grounds for disbelief. There were "a host" of atheists, he claimed. They included Euhemerus (for whom "those counted as Gods were certain men of power"); Prodicus (for whom "what [in nature] benefits life is [termed] God"); Diagoras of Melos (who, "at first . . . [was] God-fearing . . . but when he had been wronged [with impunity] . . . changed round and asserted that God does not exist"); Critias (who believed that "the ancient lawgivers invented God as a kind of overseer of the right and wrong actions of men"); Theodorus the Atheist (who "demolished the theological beliefs

[90] Ibid.

[91] Ibid. III.218–19. [*Hipotiposes* (Paris, 1725), 399–401.]

of the Greeks by a variety of arguments"); Protagoras (who was " 'unable to say . . . whether they exist' "); Epicurus (who, "according to some . . . in his popular exposition allows the existence of God but in expounding the real nature of things he does not allow it"); and the skeptics themselves (who find "equipollence of the opposed arguments" and conclude that "the Gods are existent 'no more' than non-existent").[92]

. . .

When the *Hypotyposes* was published in a French-language edition in 1725, its anonymous translator insisted that he saw no theological application of its arguments but merely presented to his readers Sextus's "great knowledge of the opinions of the ancient philosophers" and his "very subtle arguments." Although occasionally wrong, Sextus Empiricus was "a great philosopher" himself, so there was no need to justify the translation: "It is enough that the reading of this work pleased me, and that I believed that it also could please several persons who would prefer more to read this author in French than in Greek or Latin." He was "simply exposing the doctrine of the skeptics." Further, "so many great men have been Pyrrhonians," among both the ancients and the moderns, including many eminent theologians. As for Sextus Empiricus on God, the reader was asked to recognize that the Greek did not "want to prove absolutely that there is no God," but merely to show that from the definitions of God given by the philosophers, "there is not [any God]." This, for the translator, was "another thing altogether."[93]

Following Sextus's discussion of Divinity, the translator added his own "Reflections . . . on the preceding chapter." The reader should not become indignant "against Sextus, and perhaps against me," he explained, since the Christian believer was unthreatened by Sextus's views. First, all of Sextus's objections and difficulties, he insisted, "are confined, virtually, *to those that have been proposed an infinite number of times with regard to physical evil, or to the evils to which animals and men are exposed, or to moral evil.*" The Christian, however, has answers to these (which he did not specify); indeed, he added, every system of theology has different answers to these with which it is "satisfied [*content*]." Second, Cicero's *De natura deorum* was "more dangerous" than the *Hypotyposes*, but it was universally admired, and indeed, its myriad translators had not been reproached for their work. Thus, he informed or reminded his readers with lengthy direct quotation, the celebrated translator of Cicero's dia-

[92] Sextus Empiricus, *Adversus Dogmaticos* III.i.13–48. I have utilized the translation by R. G. Bury cited supra, n. 88, for whom it is *Against the Physicists* I.13–48.

[93] Sextus Empiricus, *Les Hipotiposes* (Paris, 1725), "Préface" [unpaginated, xxii pp.].

logue on the gods, the abbé d'Olivet, had explained that only the God of the philosophers, not the Christian God, was assailed by any of its arguments. Finally, how could one condemn a Sextus "who had no knowledge of Christianity when he attacked the dogmatic philosophers [by arguing] against the existence of God"? His arguments may have been "crushing against *them*," but the Christian had a revelation that proved God, and this remained unaffected.[94]

Readers of the more popular journals who had missed this edition had it called to their attention in January 1727 by a long, informative review in the Jesuit *Journal de Trévoux*. The reviewer noted "with indignation" that although no one should fear that "doubting everything" ever would be "contagious," it was "dangerous" that the work of Sextus Empiricus had been "brought onstage" so often for so long, "sometimes in Greek, sometimes in Latin, and now in French." He distinguished between a scholar who explicated views fatal to religion in order to refute them, and someone who, as in this case, merely allowed such dangerous ancient arguments to stand alone. He quoted with outrage the translator's admission that he would leave the refutation to someone else who now could be well-informed about the skepticism in need of refutation, since, the translator had said, he himself was "not strong enough" for the task, as if it were difficult to overcome such objections. All skeptics, the *Journal* informed its readers, "*want one to doubt . . . if there is a Providence, [and] if there is a God*," among other indubitable truths. Such skeptics claimed that their doubt was a pure humility, a confession "that they knew nothing," but one should *not* be fooled into thinking that they said this "in good faith." Far from being a humble doubter, the Jesuit journal insisted, "Sextus denies the existence of God and of a Providence." With that said, of course, and Sextus identified with a whole school of philosophy, how would it be possible to sustain the argument for universal consent?[95]

The translator, in fact, had insisted (sincerely or insincerely) that Christian theism was sheltered from all of Sextus's criticisms. His Jesuit reviewer disagreed, however, insisting that if one granted even the Pyrrhonian theoretical criticism of a *criterium* of truth (that the criterion's truth itself would depend on a prior criterion, ad infinitum), *not even faith could "save the idea of God,"* since belief in that God would require a prior God to assure one "of the existence of this God." The *Journal* also shared (with indignation but with lengthy quotation as well) the translator's reply that each sect and system had a particular reply to Sextus that satisfied it. In case any reader had failed to see the most dangerous impli-

[94] Ibid., 277–84.

[95] *Journal de Trévoux*, jan. 1727, 36–62.

cation of that argument, the reviewer noted that "thus belief in God will be in each the effect of his sect, of his system, of his manner of thinking, and perhaps of the caprice [*bizarrerie*] of his mind." As for the translator's view that only the God of the philosophers, not the Christian God, was the object of Pyrrhonian criticism, the *Journal* insisted that if Sextus's arguments in fact did not deny the existence of the real God, then "all idolators are atheists," and "all the [Greek] philosophers" are atheists, which would *not* be reassuring. In fact, however, the Jesuit journal concluded, Sextus was not attacking pagan religion, but precisely "the true idea of God and of His Providence," which was why, indeed, "his book is dangerous for us." The reviewer wanted no ambiguity about that at all: "I even observe that Sextus scarcely combats anything except sound ideas, and those that we ourselves have of the Divinity [*Je remarque même que Sextus ne combat guères que les idées saines, & celles que nous avons de la Divinité nous mêmes*]." The "Academy" directly attacked the very foundations of theistic belief.[96]

First, then, there was Sextus Empiricus, widely available, as the *Journal* had noted, in Greek and Latin. The most erudite would read these. Then, there was a translation into French, by an anonymous savant who at least feigned the belief that Sextus's arguments could not threaten a Christian's theism but merely showed the absurdities one would reach from pagan philosophical premises. Those willing to read a difficult work of philosophy in the vernacular could read that. For those who merely wanted to keep up with the latest titles and news, however, or had missed the aspects of Sextus's views most dangerous to theistic consensus, there was a long, sincere *compte rendu* in the leading French Catholic journal of review and opinion, which called the translation to the attention of all of its readers, made the most atheistic implications of all of its arguments manifest to them, and placed the school of Pyrrhonian Academic skepticism squarely in the camp of a group, the speculative atheists, that was not supposed to exist. The ancients who posed a threat to belief in universal consent to the existence of God were an early-modern presence in a complex multitude of ways.

. . .

If the *Journal de Trévoux* was appalled by the ancient skeptics, which indeed it was, it could be generally enthusiastic about the Stoics, reflecting, in this, the general attitudes of the larger Catholic culture, and indeed, of much patristic literature itself. Reviewing, in June 1722, a translation into French by the abbé Le Masson of Cicero's *De natura deorum*,

[96] Ibid.

the *Journal* focused on the proof of "the existence of the Gods by the structure and harmony of the world" offered by the Stoic interlocutor Balbus, and, in particular, on Balbus's citation of Aristotle on this subject, which the *Journal* termed "this reflection so just and so sound from one of the greatest philosophers of antiquity upon the existence of the Divinity." Nonetheless, it noted that Cicero had presented arguments both for and against the existence of Divinity without combating all of the latter with equal force, and it therefore cautioned the reading public that "it would be appropriate for all translators never to undertake a version of profane authors without having taken care to refute the pernicious errors found there that they are exposing to the public." From that concern, it praised Le Masson's scholarly notes, claiming that they "make one feel the impiety and blindness of *the other philosophers who have attacked the truth of a first and sovereign being*," which was exceptionally important given "several extremely dangerous [errors] in this *Treatise on the Nature of the Gods*" that Cicero had left uncriticized. Le Masson's notes (unlike those of the anonymous translator of Sextus Empiricus) "made up for Cicero's fault."[97]

The *Journal de Trévoux*'s ambivalence toward Cicero's philosophical theology was in many ways representative of that of the broader Catholic culture, which tended to find him exquisite as a model of Latin grammar and rhetoric, Stoic and in many ways admirable in his moral philosophy, but disturbingly Academic, that is to say, skeptical, in his broader metaphysical outlook. It was a curious ambivalence, however, for it did not threaten his special place, and, indeed, that of the *De natura deorum* in particular, in the curriculum of the Jesuits.[98] In the collèges, however, it was read only in Latin and always with guidance. Seven months before its review of Le Masson's edition, the *Journal* had reviewed the translation of *De natura deorum* by the eminent abbé d'Olivet, member of the Académie française, and had reflected at greater length on the character of this widely read and frequently translated dialogue. It saw Cicero's work as essentially a confrontation between Epicurean and Stoic views, and it characterized that debate as follows: "Cicero limited himself to the two principal [theologies], of which the first, that is to say, that of the Epicureans [represented by Velleius], *admitted the Gods in appearance*

[97] Ibid., juin 1722, 984–89.

[98] According to Joseph de Jouvancy, S.J., *Christianis litterarum magistris de ratione discendi et docendi* (Paris, 1692), c.II, art. II, #5, the "Second Class" in the Jesuit collèges pursued the study of Greek and Latin through Isocrates, Lucian, Theophrastus, Homer, and a great deal of Cicero, including the *De natura deorum.* Students returned to Cicero in the fourth through sixth classes as well. The Jesuit *Ratio Studiorum*, 208–12, 216–20, 228–29, 233–34, wanted "[Latin] style . . . to be learned from Cicero only" and assigned his works a major place in the curriculum.

only, and in name rather than in fact; and of which the second, that is to say, that of the Stoics [represented by Balbus], recognized them sincerely."[99]

Nonetheless, the reviewer, aware of Cicero's skeptical side, as embodied in the interlocutor Cotta, was deeply worried about that philosophical strain in Cicero's dialogue. He observed that Cotta, after criticizing the flaws of both theologies, should have established the truth, "but he could not do it without leaving his character of the Academic philosopher, and the indifference of his sect which professes to espouse no opinion." Because of this,

> however lovely this work may be, there are people who doubt if it is appropriate to place it indifferently between everyone's hands by translating it. What gives rise to [this] doubt is that from the manner in which this work is treated, *it appears to lead gradually [insensiblement] to Atheism*, . . . for Cicero . . . abandons his reader to a doubt and an uncertainty always dangerous in the matter of religion.[100]

D'Olivet, however, the reviewer noted, resolved that problem with his notes and with an appended essay on the theology of the pagan philosophers, an essay that not only succeeded in clarifying what Cicero had left unclear, but constituted "a particular pleasure for those who want to pursue their curiosity" and "to understand" the developments of pagan philosophy. It was an essay "written with as much discernment as clarity and civility." D'Olivet is "a good critic" and "takes sides extremely well when different teachings must be discussed." In short, once again, we have a much-studied classic, its translation, and attention called to it (this time positively) in a journal that had been established precisely so that French readers might have a dependable Catholic perspective on the world of thought and letters—a journal that declared d'Olivet sufficient guard against any theological dangers.[101] Let us see what the reader would have found in all this.

To begin, let us note that there was a vast audience for *De natura deorum* in early-modern France, beyond its place in the curriculum. It was reprinted and given new editions and translations throughout the period. It surely was far more widely known than most of the seventeenth-cen-

[99] *Journal de Trévoux*, nov. 1721, 2015–41. The characterization of the dialogue occurs on 2016–19.

[100] Ibid., 2019–20. Typical of so much of the culture, with its concern for reputation and belles-lettres, it should be noted, the reviewer did not devote the largest part of his lengthy *compte rendu* to such theological and philosophical issues, however, but to a defense of the Jesuit Lescalopier's earlier edition of Cicero, some of the scholarship of which d'Olivet had found wanting, and in compliments to d'Olivet's qualities as a translator from the Latin.

[101] Ibid., passim.

tury texts from which historians tend to derive their notions of the intellectual furniture of the age. It was read for its form, its heuristic value in grammar and logic, and its historical value as light shed on the curiosities of ancient philosophy. It also, of course, was a text of philosophical theology, and that, its most salient characteristic, could not be wholly ignored. While most of *De natura deorum* turned on issues of providence—of whether or not the gods are concerned with the world and with mankind—the issue of atheism, of whether or not *any* Divinity exists, formed a significant aspect of the dialogue, and, of course, a qualitatively essential one for Christian readers in the context of debate over universal consent. At the outset, the reader learned that "most thinkers have affirmed that the gods exist, and this is the most probable view, and the one to which we are led by nature's guidance; but Protagoras declared himself uncertain, and Diagoras of Melos and Theodorus of Cyrene held that there are no gods at all."[102]

Velleius's exposition of Epicurean theology in book 1, however, while it denied providence and criticized the conceptions of Divinity in all other philosophical systems as both mutually- and self-contradictory, provided one of the strongest statements of the argument from universal consent. For Velleius, since nothing could be inferred about Divinity from the operations of nature, it was precisely (if not solely) on the basis of that consent that Epicurus could establish the existence of the gods:

> For he alone perceived, first, that the gods exist, because nature herself has imprinted a concept of them on the minds of all mankind. For what nation or what tribe of men is there but possesses untaught [*sine doctrina*] some preconception of the gods. . . . For the belief in the gods has not been established by authority, custom, or law, but rests on the unanimous and abiding consensus of mankind; their existence is therefore a necessary inference . . . ; a belief which all men by nature share [*de quo autem omnium natura consentit*] must necessarily be true; therefore it must be admitted that the gods exist. And . . . this truth is almost universally accepted not only among the philosophers but also among the unlearned.[103]

It was, thus, precisely this proof that Cotta the skeptical philosopher sought to undermine, although he first admitted that "many disturbing reflections occur to my mind, which sometimes make me think that there are no gods at all [*Multa enim occurrunt quae conturbent, ut interdum nulli esse videantur*]," which d'Olivet translated as "*J'ai peine à me défendre de certaines pensées, qui de temps en temps me troublent, et me*

[102] Cicero, *La Nature des Dieux* [Olivet ed. of 1721], I, 5–7 [standard citation: I.i].
[103] Ibid., I, 60–62 [I.xvi–xvii].

rendent presque incrédule à cet égard ['sur l'existence des Dieux']."[104] Cotta's real quarry, however, was the argument from the alleged *consensus gentium*, and his critique of it was yet another clear source of the culture's (and of Bayle's) views. Cotta declared the proof both "inconclusive and untrue." It was inconclusive because there is no way to know what foreign races believe, since most of the world is unknown to us, which d'Olivet rendered straightforwardly as "*Car d'où savez-vous ce que pensent toutes les nations?*"—an argument that in the seventeenth century, of course, now intersected a whole tradition of travel and missionary literature. It was untrue because we know there to be atheists, since Diagoras and Theodorus "openly deny the divine existence." Further, once Protagoras of Abdera found himself banished and his books burned for his having claimed not to know if the gods did or did not exist, the world confronted "an example that I can well believe has discouraged many people [ever] since from professing atheism, since the mere expression of doubt did not succeed in escaping punishment [d'Olivet: '*Sa punition . . . empêcha que beaucoup d'autres ne fissent profession ouverte d'athéisme, quand ils virent que sur le simple doute on ne lui avait pas fait grace*']."[105]

As if to take several last swings at the alleged *consensus gentium*, Cotta assailed the "self-contradiction" of the Epicurean gods without providence, which for the Academic "actually abolishes the gods, although professedly retaining them"; added Critias, Prodicus, and Euhemerus to his list of "atheists"; and declared that "Epicurus did not believe in the gods; . . . and [that] everything that he said about them was only to protect himself from the indignation of the public [d'Olivet: '*Epicure ne croyait point de Dieux; et . . . tout ce qu'il en disait, n'était que pour se dérober à l'indignation du Public.*']," an argument he reiterated in book 3.[106] Indeed, much of Cotta's later critique of Balbus's Stoic proofs of the gods was an argument that the Stoic gods were necessarily corporeal, composed, mutable, and destructible, and, thus, merely material entities and no real gods at all.[107]

Recall, now, that the *Journal de Trévoux* considered any translation of the work into the vernacular, which, of course, dramatically increased its audience, to be "dangerous" if done without adequate reply to such arguments. It declared itself reassured, however, by d'Olivet's notes and by his essay on pagan theology. Indeed, the edition came with reassuring credentials: it was translated by an eminent member of the royal Acadé-

[104] Ibid., I, 76–80 [I.xxii].

[105] Ibid., I, 81–84 [I.xxiii].

[106] Ibid., I, 84–160 [I.xxiii–xliv]. The expanded list of atheists and the view of Epicurus's belief as wholly feigned is found on I, 149–60. See also III, 4–5 [III.i].

[107] Ibid., III, 27–85 [III, viii–xxv].

mie française, with glosses on the Latin by Bouhier, *président à mortier* of the parlement de Dijon; it was dedicated to the king; finally, it was published with an approbation that termed it "very useful and very agreeable as much for persons who seek faithful and elegant translations as for savants who are attached to the study either of ancient philosophy or of criticism."[108] The orthodoxy of d'Olivet's commentaries may have seemed beyond reproach, but there is an irony there, for, in fact, they offered anything but support to defenders of the argument from universal consent.

The notes, which accompanied the French text and preceded the essay, accepted all of the identifications of the traditional atheists. Protagoras was "a famous sophist" who was punished for "making the existence of the Gods problematic"; Diagoras was "thrown into atheism . . . by seeing that the Gods tolerated the prosperity of a man he knew to be guilty," for which "the Athenians put a price on his head"; Theodorus "wrote against the existence of the Gods," for which "he was at last condemned to take poison."[109] Cotta the skeptic, who so strongly assailed the *consensus gentium* was "a fine mind [*un bel esprit*, so perhaps merely 'a wit'] who in his quality of Academic philosopher takes the task of embarrassing the other interlocutors and toying with every opinion, without allowing his own to be known."[110] Stoic theology rejected Plato's spirituality and "only allowed bodies."[111] When the Stoics referred to God they meant "nothing except the fire of the ether," and when they referred to His intelligence, they meant "nothing other than the laws of mechanics."[112] Balbus, thus, "denies the existence of the real God" and believes in nothing but the existence of the physical universe, so it is correct "to place him in the ranks of the atheists."[113] Although Cotta first claimed that Epicurus believed in God, he would later contradict himself, so "perhaps he wanted to spare Velleius here and not first offend him by holding Epicurus's atheism against him."[114] Some Greeks indeed saw God as "merely an invention of the political leaders," including not only Critias, but Euripides as well, and Prodicus indeed saw the introduction of the idea of the divine arising from a ploy of rulers to get people to care for useful animals by declaring them to be gods.[115] In the notes to the Latin text, Bouhier termed Euhemerus "this famous atheist."[116]

108 Ibid., title page; "Epître au Roi"; notes to Latin text; "Approbation" after "Préface."

109 Ibid., I, 5, n. 2 (Protagoras); I, 5–6, n. 2 (Diagoras); I, 6, n. 4 (Theodorus).

110 Ibid., 22–23, n. 8.

111 Ibid., 31, n. 1.

112 Ibid., II, 38–39, n. 9.

113 Ibid., 45, n. 3.

114 Ibid., I, 113, n. 2.

115 Ibid., 150, n. 1 and 151–52, n. 2

116 Ibid., 219, Rem. 73.

In his lengthy appended essay, d'Olivet sought to rescue the pre-Socratics from the common charge of atheism, but he conceded that we could never know them well: we had only truncated fragments to go by; we saw them only through the eyes of commentators and Scholastic philosophers; and the terms that they used no longer had the same meaning. While it was true that none before Anaxagoras posited a divine intelligence "absolutely distinct and separated from matter," why not grant that they saw Divinity infused in matter, "unless one takes a secret pleasure in augmenting the number of materialists?" Nonetheless, he immediately conceded that while some of the ancients (all of whom, he noted, believed in the eternity of matter whatever their theologies) believed that matter had achieved order only under the guidance of a divine intelligence, many others saw "a natural and spontaneous motion by which . . . matter finally attained an arrangement which little by little became what we see."[117]

Once past the earliest pre-Socratics, however, d'Olivet shifted his philosophical analysis and took a most capacious view of atheism. Indeed, he explicitly identified most Greek philosophers (with the exception of Plato, some of his disciples, and Pythagoras) as belonging to that camp. Xenophon merely defined the material "whole of the universe" as "God"; Parmenides also believed that "God and the Universe were one and the same thing"; Democritus's gods were "nothing else but atoms," and despite defenses of him by Bayle and Malebranche, he was "a pagan suspected of atheism by the pagans themselves." Concerning Aristotle, d'Olivet reminded his readers that "several [pious theologians] declare him an atheist in all regards," and averred that almost anyone can find justification for any view of him, given "the impenetrable obscurity" of his writings.[118]

Dramatically, d'Olivet explained at great length that not only was the Epicurean philosophy represented in the *De natura deorum* "atheistic," but that the Stoic philosophy itself was also wholly "implicated in this accusation of atheism." For d'Olivet, Strato and Epicurus both were fallen into "the most gross atheism," the former meaning by *God* merely "the mechanical laws of weight and movement," and the latter using the term merely to avoid opprobrium, being a strict materialist who recognized no superior intelligence whatsoever. The reader, he urged, should not be fooled by their prudent use of the term *Gods* but should judge each "by the logical consequences of his principles and by how the totality of his hypothesis obliges him to think." By that criterion, Zeno and all subsequent Stoics were pure materialists and "must be placed among the

[117] Ibid., III, 235–53.
[118] Ibid., 268–92.

number of those who recognized only the existence of bodies." It may have amused and protected them to call material principles "God," but we should not be deceived and should "give to them the title that they deserve, I mean, the title of Atheists."[119]

. . .

What underlay d'Olivet's whole approach here was a tradition of Christian attitudes toward the pagans as venerable as any tradition of defense of the argument from universal consent. The problem in the early-modern world was that the two traditions were so frequently placed together before a vast reading public already assailed, we soon shall see, by fundamental theological debate about knowledge of Divinity. The perspective of d'Olivet's essay is easily explained. There was order in the world. If one attributed that order to an intelligence beyond mere matter, one believed in God, however confused one's notion of that intelligence might be. Anaxagoras, thus, may have believed in the eternity of matter, but he saw the need for an intelligence apart from material principles to guide the formation of the ordered world from matter, and, thus, however dimly, he believed in Divinity. If one believed that matter itself, blindly and without design, could achieve the world that we observed, one was an atheist. If many had held the latter view, a naturalism deemed patently absurd by most Christian theologians, then it was an edifying lesson, indeed, on how unaided human reason could lead us into the abyss.[120] It was this corrective edification that d'Olivet had provided, thereby reassuring the *Journal de Trévoux* that he had met his Christian obligations as a translator. All this was fine for distinguishing "enlightened" Christian philosophical theology from the "darkness" of the pagans, but by making that distinction so often one between belief in God and atheism, it seriously undermined the argument from universal consent. If all one meant by universal consent was that no whole people ever had failed to recognize something as a Divinity, that argument was being undermined by travel and missionary literature. If the use of the term *gods* by philosophical schools analyzed to be "atheistic" was taken somehow as an indication that the "idea of God" remained ineffaceable, that argument was being undermined by references to schools that used the term only in order to avoid opprobrium in their societies.

For d'Olivet, thus, in a work commended by the *Journal de Trévoux*, the Greeks had descended precisely into that atheistic abyss. Almost all Greek philosophers, for d'Olivet, attributed order to the necessary oper-

[119] Ibid., 297–309.
[120] See, above all, ibid., 309--30.

ations of inanimate matter without intelligence or design. Since this was true of both Epicureans and Stoics, he believed, then Cotta's attacks against those two schools were not directed against the "real" God, real not even in the strict sense of the revealed Trinity, but simply in the sense of a free, intelligent being apart from matter. Thus, Cotta's skeptical assaults had no bearing, he could urge, upon "God such as we define Him," the very analysis that led the translator of Sextus Empiricus to believe that he safely could make the same argument.[121] From the perspective of "universal consent," however, this "defense" of Cicero's text cast almost all Greek philosophers into dissent from this evanescent "consensus," precisely when the "weighing" of opinions was being urged.

D'Olivet was explicit here. The issue of "whether the ancient philosophers must be placed in the ranks of the atheists" could not possibly be decided by whether they used a term, either *God* or *the gods*, upon which their societies insisted. The issue was whether or not they posited any intelligent cause of the world we observed. Some philosophers, he insisted, such as Anaximenes, Epicurus, and Strato, conceived of nothing beyond "matter alone, deprived of awareness [*sentiment*] and reason" as the cause of everything, "and the atheism of these philosophers is visibly the most gross of all, since the first cause that they recognized is only an inanimate matter." Others disagreed with them, seeing "too beautiful an order" in the world not to assign intelligence to its cause, such as most of the Stoics, "but conceiving of nothing that was not material, they believed that intelligence was part of matter," a step away from the crudest atheism, but atheism nonetheless. Only Anaxagoras and Plato as major Greek philosophers "understood that intelligence could not be material" and took a step toward any minimal idea of an actual God. Thus, in limiting his criticism to Epicurean and Stoic views, Cicero's Cotta attacked merely "the chimera that the philosophers put in the place of the real God."[122]

If anyone missed the implications of all this for the issue of whether atheism were sincerely thinkable, d'Olivet again addressed the issue explicitly in his conclusion. He anticipated that his critics would raise the *consensus gentium*, advising him that "instead of bringing the errors of the ancient philosophers to light, would it not be better to take advantage of what is obscure in the remains of their doctrine to try to make them appear orthodox, and *by that to have one more proof against the atheists*?" He found such an objection insufficient to restrain an honest and accurate reading of the Greeks. First, he noted, the proof from universal consent itself was "equivocal." Second, he asked, why would anyone unpersuaded by the testimony of Moses and Christ be moved by Pythagoras

[121] Ibid., 309–23.

[122] Ibid., 233–330, passim, and especially 309–23.

or Aristotle, a question that essentially ignored the point of *universal* consent. Finally, he insisted, the atheism of the ancients still could be attributed to qualities of depravity: "their pride, . . . the confidence that they had in their own lights . . . [and] reason." Against such arrogance, he argued, a work like Cicero's, that showed "the futility of human reason" unless enlightened by faith, surely was a remedy, for it reminded us that Moses taught truths far beyond "everything that was imagined on this subject [of Divinity] by the philosophers of Greece."[123] It was indeed a pious conclusion, but it was offered to a culture otherwise instructed that the existence of God was precisely an essential natural and rational "preamble" to the very acceptance of that scriptural faith!

. . .

While two sets of translations and reviews from the 1720s have allowed us to deal conveniently with such themes in early-modern accounts of Sextus Empiricus and Cicero, the chronology should not mislead us here. Throughout the seventeenth century, these classical sources, and, we have seen, many others, offered the same views to a growing body of readers. These were commonplaces for the early-modern learned world, not radical new perspectives, and whatever the continued use of the argument from universal consent, there now were countless evidential grounds for rejecting it. This meant, of course, that for some, atheism no longer needed to be seen as the last refuge of the willfully blind and irrational.

In 1670, Abraham Roger's very popular account of his travels was translated into French. Roger had noted that "navigation" confirmed universal consent.[124] His French editor, however, well before Bayle would address the same theme in theory, felt obliged, in a lengthy footnote, to dispute such a view on factual grounds. Referring the reader to a few Dutch travel accounts analogous to the literature we have described for France, Roger's editor noted that while the claim of universal consent had been stated and reiterated by so many, "navigation has made exactly the opposite known to those of our time, at least according to what they have been able to observe." Further, he added, if one read the four most obvious sources about ancient thought, specifically, Cicero's *De natura deorum*, Diogenes Laertius's *Vita*, Plutarch's *De Placitis Philosophorum* and Sextus Empiricus's *Hypotyposes*, one learned that there was widespread disbelief in God among the ancients. It was obvious, he concluded, that atheists were common then, and, in foreign lands, now; all one could

[123] Ibid., 325–30.

[124] Abraham Roger, *La Porte ouverte, pour parvenir à la connoissance du PAGANISME caché . . .*, trans. Thomas La Grue (Amsterdam, 1670), 139–49.

hope is that among us, who profess Christianity, there could not be "persons who are of a similar opinion."[125] At the very least, the erosion of belief in universal consent made it more likely that there would be such.

Twenty years later, John Locke himself referred to the same literature, not to weaken the evidence of belief in God, but to demonstrate, for his own epistemological purposes, that the idea of God could not possibly be innate. He referred to that literature not as something in need of lengthy identification, but, indeed, as something that would be familiar to all:

> *Besides the atheists taken notice of amongst the ancients, and left branded upon the records of history, hath not navigation discovered, in these latter ages, whole nations amongst whom there was to be found no notion of a God*, no religion? There are instances of nations where nature has been left to itself without the help of letters and discipline, and the improvements of arts and sciences. But there are others to be found [China? Siam?] who have enjoyed these in a very great measure, who yet, for want of a due application of their thoughts this way, want [lack] the idea and knowledge of God.[126]

Locke's work was translated into French at the dawn of the eighteenth century and was favorably reviewed by the *Journal de Trévoux*. Reviewing Coste's translation in 1700, the *Histoire des Ouvrages des Savans* reiterated, as a casual matter of fact, Locke's argument: "If there is any innate idea, it is that of the existence of God. Nonetheless, there are atheists who deny it, and travelers have met peoples who have no notion of the Divinity."[127] If that were the case, then indeed, from the very teaching of the learned and orthodox culture, this essential preamble to the faith was not guaranteed by any consensus from which only a madman could dissent, and it stood in urgent need of demonstration. Certain works in the emerging inquiry into the history of philosophy would not only disseminate these views far and wide but, by explicating ancient thinkers at great length, inadvertently would offer virtual courses on the substance of "atheistic" perspectives on the world.

[125] Ibid., editor's note, 139–40.

[126] John Locke, *An Essay Concerning Human Understanding* [1689] (London, 1690), I.iv.

[127] *Journal de Trévoux*, jan.–fév. 1701, 116–31, and *Histoire des Ouvrages des Savans*, juillet 1700, 294–95.

Chapter Seven

THE HISTORY OF PHILOSOPHY

FROM THE PATRISTICS to the early-moderns, thus, Christian apologists, chroniclers, commentators, and, eventually, editors made available to seventeenth-century readers the "atheism," "materialism," and "naturalism" of the ancients, often explicating at great length why benighted, non-Christian ways of thinking led to antitheistic conclusions. Although Christian education and received culture insured that almost all found folly or, at best, puzzling curiosities in such schools or instances of disbelief, it should not surprise us, given the individual variations of human thought, if some minds at some times actually found wisdom in the heterodox inheritance of the past.

The *private* effects of encountering such thought in different ages and contexts, whether (with Lucretius or Sextus Empiricus) in their originals or (with the pre-Socratics and the atheists of tradition) in accounts of their works, cannot be known. While it surely would have been difficult to construct a worldview from the lot of them, it is not impossible that some readers secretly, either ephemerally or, indeed, for the duration of their lives, were shaken loose from theistic certainties by them. Speculation on such matters, however, seems of little historical utility. The *Theophrastus Redivivus*, a manuscript from sometime in the seventeenth century, allows us to see one such private response (which I shall discuss presently), and, if nothing else, should make us wary of *categorical* pronouncements upon what was or was not individually "thinkable" before certain general developments reframed problems for larger numbers of the educated. We know nothing particular about its author or the circumstances of its composition. We simply do *not* know if other minds, earlier or contemporaneous, were affected similarly by late-Renaissance transmissions of the classical legacy itself. On the whole, the world of Western, Christian culture, believing that its theologians and philosophers had replied to each and every possible objection to belief in God and spiritual substance, and that theistic Platonists, neo-Platonists, Aristotelians, and Stoics were more serious ancient philosophers than pre-Socratics, Pyrrhonians, and atomists, did not seem terribly alarmed by such "atheistic" views. It generally categorized them simply as so confused and self-contradictory as to be readily dismissed from serious consideration. Indeed, their presence was often useful, to show the darkness into which unaided human reason could lead us, and to provide the "objections" to which the Christian theologians and philosophers confidently could reply.

From the thirteenth through the sixteenth centuries, the recovery and, eventually, publication of ancient texts had proceeded apace, usually in Greek or in Latin translation, and Christian minds had to confront new or newly understood pagan minds and schools of thought. These confrontations often occasioned dramatic debates within Christendom, with each generation's "pious" believers declaring scandalous that each generation's "curious" believers could find profane pagan philosophy to be of positive interest, edification, or even essential utility to Christianity. This was true of the encounter with Aristotle and his Arabic commentators in the thirteenth century;[1] it was true of the encounter with Sextus Empiricus in the sixteenth century.[2] Those who loved philosophy sought to assimilate what could be assimilated, use what was useful, refute what needed refutation, or refer to wiser minds or to faith that which seemed contrary to the creed but difficult to resolve. Those who found philosophy a distraction from true spiritual life, or a sin of pride, or a yet more ominous temptation of the faithful, either ignored such works, or, often, painted them as darkest incredulity precisely to warn the beneficiaries of revelation away from unhallowed works from unhallowed times.

From the longest-term perspectives, it is undeniable that for all the benefits and delights that ancient philosophy brought to Christian mental life, there were *potential* dangers in almost all natural philosophies that eventually surfaced to confirm someone's worst prior fears. The Fathers and doctors of the Church inherited ancient philosophical concepts, and their heirs inherited the patristic and Scholastic legacy. The Church, after all, believed that it required a philosophical language with which to explicate its doctrines and views, and it produced a ceaseless stream of philosophers who linked themselves to ancient schools. Aristotelian naturalism and Pyrrhonic skepticism, for example, if of magnificent utility for some in allowing the Thomistic syntheses in the first case and the humbling of arrogant human reason in the second, might well be blamed by others for planting the seeds of exclusive natural explanation or of total doubt in the gardens of Christian thought. To the extent that Western Christendom expressed its experience, religious and otherwise, in lan-

[1] See, for example, Roland Hissette, *Enquête sur les 219 articles condamnés à Paris le 7 mars 1277* (Louvain and Paris, 1977); Fernand van Steenberghen, *Aristotle in the West: The Origins of Latin Aristotelianism*, trans. Leonard Johnston, 2d ed. (Louvain, 1970) [a much fuller work than the French 1st ed., *Aristote en Occident: Les origines de l'aristotélisme Parisien* (Louvain, 1946)] and *Thomas Aquinas and Radical Aristotelianism* (Washington, D.C., 1980).

[2] See, for example, Popkin, *History of Scepticism*.

guage and concepts derived from the Greeks and Romans, both symbioses and conflicts were inevitable. Christian theology and ancient philosophy were in a pas de deux of infinite complexity.

The centuries of the Renaissance led to dramatically increased awareness among the erudite and curious of the radical heterodoxy and "impiety" (from Christian perspective) of ancient views noted in the preceding chapter. By the sixteenth and very early seventeenth centuries, before the brief but powerful restoration of Aristotelian philosophical order in France and before the dramatic and widespread reform of Catholic education there, a singular group of Italian philosophers alarmed and perplexed the French Catholic world, often citing the most heterodox ancient views for reasons at best unclear to their contemporaries. Cardan, Vanini, Pomponazzi, Bruno, and Campanella, among others, offered startling admixtures of naturalism, spiritualism, magic, mysticism, empiricism, intuition, astrology, dialectical pyrotechnics, fideism, and rationalism to their readers. They used whatever was at hand and borrowed heavily from a wide variety of Greeks. They were authors who quickly seemed anachronistic in France, irrelevant to new debates, and their influence on the seventeenth century seems minimal indeed, except insofar as the often violent suppression of their views reinforced philosophical orthodoxy.

It is true that they often did refer readers to what for Christian thinkers were the most disturbing strains of ancient thought. Such references, however, were not obscure. Further, they claimed to refute these, and there is simply too much spiritualism and magic in the Italian thinkers for them to be taken seriously as naturalists and materialists in terms remotely relevant to the late seventeenth or early eighteenth centuries. Their severest clerical critics, however, found them at once so heterodox, disconcerting, and unsuccessful at refutation that they often were deemed to be advancing the very views they ostensibly assailed. On the assumption that like produces like—an assumption more suited to genetics, perhaps, than to history—some have seen late-Renaissance magical naturalists as important players in the history of atheism,[3] but neither the likeness nor the influence is there. It is more plausible that their roles in that history were simple ones: to alert a few readers (who had many other sources) to just how naturalist and materialist certain strains of ancient thought could appear; and, however misinterpreted, to serve occasionally, themselves, as exceptions to universal consent in later histories of philosophy.

Nonetheless, there is the case of the intriguing *Theophrastus Redivivus*, a manuscript compilation of ancient "atheism" that occasionally cited a

[3] See, for example, Gregory et al., *Ricerche*, 3–47.

Cardan, a Vanini, and a Pomponazzi (among so many other primarily ancient authors, compilers, and commentators) as sources of its views of the materialistic or atheistic strain of Greek thought. It is too easy to exaggerate the significance both of this single manuscript, whose actual provenance is unknown, and of the late-Renaissance authors it cites primarily as conveyers of the Greeks. Those who have sought to demystify its place in the intellectual history of radical free thought have the evidence on their side.[4]

• • •

As we have seen, accounts of ancient "atheism," "materialism," "naturalism," and "political" explanations of the origins of belief in the gods abounded in literature widely available in the early-modern world. To say the least, one did not have to search very hard for them. At some point in the seventeenth century, some anonymous reader, perhaps French, perhaps not, composed a lengthy Latin compilation and explication of such views, clearly believing that these ancients were correct in rejecting God or gods, providence, creation, spirit, immortality, and religion. It was a bold and heady compendium of everything that could be found in the ancient sources that seemed antithetical to contemporaneous seventeenth-century beliefs, but none of it was new. It is, of course, not without human significance that someone was thus affected and persuaded by arguments found or believed to be found in the ancients. Nonetheless, as Jerôme Vercruysse has argued persuasively, "the philosophical milieus of the eighteenth century seem to ignore the *Theophrastus Redivivus* almost totally."[5] The same could be said of the seventeenth century too. Indeed, there is no reason whatsoever to see it as typical of even minor currents of seventeenth-century response to the ancients, let alone as influential on a Europe in which it was in effect unread.

Had it been widely read, it would have added very little to what already was generally at hand. Although some students of the work have seen it as original for not concluding merely in Pyrrhonism, or have described it as undertaking some new "anthropology" of religious life,[6] such formal skepticism, as we have seen, was merely one element of the recovered "impious" inheritance, and its explication of religion in terms of political

[4] Jerôme Vercruysse, "Le *Theophrastus Redivivus* au 18e siècle: mythe et réalité," in Gregory et al., *Ricerche*, 297–303. See also supra, Introduction.

[5] Vercruysse, "Le *Theophrastus Redivivus*."

[6] See, for example, the provocative interpretations of G. Canziani and G. Paganini, eds., *Theophrastus Redivivus*, xv–xxxv; and Lorenzo Bianchi, "Sapiente e Popolo nel Theophrastus Redivivus," *Studi Storici* xxiv, nos. 1–2 (1983), 137–64.

need appears to have been merely a summary of a whole ancient tradition concerning the origin of ancient gods. Its distinction between natural knowledge and religious myth, which some also have seen as innovative,[7] seems far less an anticipation of the new than merely a repetition of the generalities of the Epicurean tradition as transmitted by Lucretius. Although its most serious recent commentator, the brilliant Tullio Gregory, agreed with those who saw it as a continuity or bridge between Italian Renaissance traditions and the philosophical and even "scientific" agendas of the "moderns,"[8] it certainly appears to have had very little in common, conceptually or linguistically, with the "moderns" of the seventeenth century. Indeed, the author/compiler of the *Theophrastus Redivivus* seems quite singular in his almost exclusive reliance upon the ancients, in his general unfamiliarity with seventeenth-century commentary on these, and in the seriousness with which he takes Cardan, Pomponazzi, and Vanini. Whatever one's view of this compilation or text, however, it is difficult if not impossible to establish any serious line of argument for its conceptual *influence*, and it seems far more interesting as effect than as cause. As I earlier indicated concerning the Febvre thesis, the *Theophrastus Redivivus* is a document useful to refute the categorical notion that the ability to think "atheistically" depended on a revolution in philosophy that eschewed Latinity for the vernacular, or, indeed, on any specific philosophical revolution. It is also useful in showing how the classical knowledge widely disseminated in traditional and orthodox learned culture contained enough potential "atheism" to make the argument from universal consent seem wildly erroneous.

What occurs in the *Theophrastus Redivivus*? It is divided into six Latin *tractati*: on the gods; on the eternity of the world; on religion; on the mortality of the soul; on disdain for and fearlessness in the face of death; and on living according to nature. Its sources, for virtually all of its arguments, were standard accounts of ancient philosophy, above all as found in or as noted by Diogenes Laertius, Lucretius, Sextus Empiricus, Cicero, Diodorus of Sicily, Lactantius, Plato, and Seneca, and, occasionally, as presented in Cardan, Pomponazzi, and Vanini.

Its treatise on the gods was essentially a mere catalog of the names and assertions of the traditional atheists, which, emphasizing the notion that belief in the gods and religion arose from political utility, also cited as unbelievers almost any ancients who had written at all of such a purpose, including Plato and Aristotle. It generally ignored Christian responses to

[7] Canziani and Paganini, eds., *Theophrastus*, xv–xvii.

[8] Gregory, *Theophrastus*. The reader should note with appropriate caution that I find myself in disagreement here with some particularly astute and erudite scholars about the nature of the *Theophrastus Redivivus*.

such a theme. If one had read Sextus Empiricus and Lucretius, one learned nothing new about such ancient attitudes. The compiler presented them with obvious enthusiasm, but he even nominally denied agreement with such incredulity. Whatever case one might make for the boldness of its views of the phenomenon of religion in the later treatises, it was a work that did very little indeed with the formal issue of atheism.[9]

The second treatise, drawing both on the ancients' belief in the eternity of the world and on sixteenth-century attempts to evaluate that virtual unanimity, dismissed the notion of creation with arguments wholly familiar to any reader of Diogenes Laertius, Sextus Empiricus, Plutarch, and Lucretius, drawing a bit on Averroes and Ocellus Lucanas. The "debate" was not between the ancients and the Christian tradition, but between almost all the Greeks, on the one hand, and the Plato of the *Timaeus* (no longer an atheist by "Tractatus Secundus"), on the other.[10] The third treatise, accepting as its axiom what it saw as one strain of ancient thought, that "there are no gods such as those the laws put forth, and the world is eternal," examined the purely "political art" of religion, again following the arguments of the traditional atheists and of Lucretius.[11] The fourth treatise concluded for the inexplicability and incomprehensibility of "spiritual soul" from the "contradictions" and "disagreements" of the ancients.[12] The fifth treatise, drawing above all on Lucretius, Cicero, and Epicurus, sought to dispel any belief in an afterlife and, thus, any fear of death.[13] The sixth treatise—with the gods, religion, and the afterlife dismissed—asked the reader to live happily and according to nature, which it defined in terms of the Golden Rule, and more in keeping with a natural equality that had been destroyed by laws, arts, and sciences. Since the *Theophrastus Redivivus* revealed a certain familiarity with sixteenth- and early seventeenth-century travel literature that described the Indians of North and South America as living primitively without property or religion, the likely source for such views lay there.[14] Many authors explicated, albeit without approval, these same views. There were no significant epistemological claims about belief or disbelief in God in the *Theophrastus Redivivus*. Drawing upon Epicurean and Aristotelian sensationalism, the new Theophrastus asked us to learn *only* from the experience of the senses, but this certainly was not a new theoretical idea for a culture drenched with peripatetic empirical epistemology. Above all, we see from this manuscript that, to say the least, the

[9] Canziani and Paganini, eds., *Theophrastus*, 1–163.

[10] Ibid., 175–337.

[11] Ibid., 342–558.

[12] Ibid., 559–716.

[13] Ibid., 717–82.

[14] Ibid., 758–926.

ancient sources of disbelief were a real presence in early-modern learned culture and constituted a tradition that for some readers clearly vitiated the argument from universal consent.

· · ·

Far more important for the dynamic life of seventeenth-century French educated culture than this manuscript without progeny, however, was an emerging genre, the history of "atheistic" philosophy, that attracted a broad and, to judge by the different levels of complexity and erudition at which it was written, diverse audience. As the popularity of classical thought, travel literature, and exotica such as the *Thousand and One Nights* indicate, the reading public of the seventeenth and early eighteenth centuries loved to leave, in thought, the world around them, and to travel far in geographical space and historical time to explore the varieties of human experience. Education increased curiosity (as in some epochs it actually does), and the numbers of the educated were growing dramatically in the wake of Tridentine educational reforms, the efforts of Jesuits and Christian Brothers, increased support in education for the bright but modest in means, and the perceived or at least rewarded social and administrative utility of having more critically trained sons of the privileged. In an age when travel was difficult and few were attuned to the visual arts as sources of knowledge, books, for educated minds, were often the only windows on the world beyond their immediate boundaries. It is difficult to recapture now the early-modern thirst for books, the avidity with which the learned sought, read, and discussed printed texts. The history of atheistic philosophy, however serious its intent in purely analytic, interpretative, or theological terms, appealed greatly to readers eager to look through such windows at such an exotic sight, and it was a genre of growing importance.

· · ·

Once deciphered and pursued, the sometimes cryptic footnotes and marginalia of early-modern French discussions of prior philosophy lead one to a mutually referential set of treatises, histories, and theses, usually written in Latin, and part of the general Western symposium that a common language made possible. These works were cited, reviewed, discussed, and occasionally translated in France, where, as everywhere in the West, students of history (including the history of "error") very clearly felt themselves part of a community of inquiry far broader than that which merely vernacular linguistic boundaries allowed. Most learned journals published in French not only offered reviews and explications (and thus advertisements) of such works, but, indeed, they had specific sections for philosophical, theological, and literary news from abroad, focused above all else on new erudite publications. The learned world whose journals spoke of "the savants" and "the republic of letters" was cosmopolitan in its counsel and debates. One genre to which the Germans and English contributed with particular éclat was the history of "atheism," ancient, and, in some claims, modern. From London, Augsburg, Halle, Jena, Bremen, Kiel, Wittenberg, Hildesheim, Leipzig, and Lubeck, German and English savants added their diverse voices to the French consideration of atheism and, thus, of universal consent. There was a wide array of orthodox and pious learned voices before, contemporaneous with, and after Bayle to offer increasingly commonplace views of the history of philosophy. Bayle, of course, knew this full well, citing his predecessors and peers with great accuracy and frequency. Before looking at Bayle separately, then, let us examine the international erudite community of which he was a part.

• • •

Two works from the 1660s were typical of the genre: the second edition of Anton Reiser's *De Origine, Progressu et Incremento Antitheismi, seu Atheismi* and Theophilus Spizelius's *De Atheismi Radice.*[15] While Reiser began with schema for distinguishing among "atheisms" ("direct and indirect," "formal and virtual," "theoretical and practical," "inchoate and fully formed," "subtle and gross," "[based on] ignorance" and "[based on] denial," etc.), his two primary objects were, first, the scriptural revelation about atheism (it started with Cain and was the thought of all those who disbelieved in divine judgment) and, second, the relationship of ancient disbelief and modern thought.[16] On the second subject, Reiser saw three things as the essence of the "antitheism" whose "origin, progress, and increase" he wished to address: the denial of providence, the explanation of all phenomena by natural causes alone, and the thesis that belief in Divinity arose from political considerations. For Reiser, the reckless charges of "atheism" amid the hyperbolic polemics of Reformation debates had distorted our whole understanding of the problem, and, if taken seriously, would lead one to believe that all Catholics, Calvinists, Lutherans, Muslims, and Jews were atheists, which none, in fact, could be. The real "antitheists," past and present, however, could be identified by their

[15] Anton Reiser, *De Origine, Progressu et Incremento Antitheismi, seu Atheismi epistolaris dissertatio* . . . , 2d ed. (Augsburg, 1669); Spizelius, *De Atheismi Radice.*

[16] See Reiser, *De Origine*, 12–25, for his discussion of classificatory schemes. His discussion of Cain (26–28) inaugurates a lengthy general discussion of Scripture on atheism (26–226).

denial of providence, their naturalism, and their "political" explanation of theism. They arose from Epicurus's wholehearted attack on divine providence, Aristotle's denial of sublunar providence, Pyrrhonian skepticism, atomistic and Stoic naturalism, and the entire Greek and Lucretian tradition of explaining religion politically. As we shall see, a whole strain of early-modern consideration of the history of philosophy and atheism would stay within precisely that framework. While he acknowledged that there was obviously bitter debate among scholars about whether Aristotle were "atheistic" or "orthodox," Reiser found the denial of earthly providence a veiled but thoroughgoing naturalism at best. For Reiser, identification of the heirs of such thought among the moderns allowed a proper—as opposed to loose and irresponsible—identification of genuine atheists, among whom he placed (the list was far more extensive) Machiavelli and all the "*politiques*" of the French religious wars; the "naturalists" Aretino (Aretin), Politiano (Politien), Cremonius, and Barbaro; Descartes (by naturalist and "skeptical" implication, he believed, if not by intent); and Vanini and Campanella.[17] Indeed, these were charges that in almost every case Bayle himself felt obliged to address in articles in the *Dictionnaire*, precisely because they already were before the learned world.

Spizelius's *De Atheismi Radice*, while refraining from some of the accusations his colleague in Augsburg had offered, had high praise for the first edition of Reiser's *De Origine*.[18] For Spizelius, while atheism could not triumph over natural light without Satanic assistance, such aid obviously had occurred, and atheism was indeed manifest and growing in the world. Spizelius argued explicitly that patristic literature offered the clearest guide to current debates about atheism. The Fathers, he urged, had identified two evident atheisms around them: the "political atheism" of the likes of Critias; and the materialistic atheism of Epicurean and other naturalisms that dispensed with God in explanation of the world. This, for Spizelius, was the proper model for specifying disbelief. First, there was the atheism of those ancients and moderns "who reduce all religion to political art." This "political atheism," the view that belief in God arose from the needs of statecraft, was the atheism making the greatest progress in these times. Machiavelli and his heirs, such as (of all people!) Grotius, were "monstrous" and "impious" embodiments of it. Second, there was the atheism of those who "make everything the effect of Nature," to which category he assigned most peripatetics, insisting that Scholastic theologians were hard-pressed to equate Aristotle's material prime mover with any theological notion of God, and adding, from

[17] Ibid., 28–32, 226–342. The discussion of debates over Aristotle is found on 322–28.
[18] Spizelius, *De Atheismi Radice*, 1–3.

among more recent "naturalists," both Campanella and Vanini. There was, he conceded, based on our knowledge of China, an "atheism" of absolute ignorance of God, of the supernatural, and of providence, but such atheists could be persuaded by argument of the proposition "God exists," as missionary efforts in China had shown. There was also, he insisted, the far graver problem of "perverse" atheists, who required a miracle for their conversion.[19] Against the thesis that Bacon, Descartes, Galileo, Gassendi, and Hobbes should be added to the list comprising naturalist Aristotelians, Campanella, and Vanini, he agreed with the argument of the German scholar Philipp Jacob Spener that these corpuscular philosophers had assigned only magnitude, figure, and acquired movement to bodies, not self-existence, self-subsistence, spontaneous motion, or coherence, and, thus, that they properly and intentionally offered support to belief in the incorporeal and the Divinity.[20] In short, in works that explicitly sought to counter "loose" charges of atheism, likely to be dismissed, the respected Reiser and Spizelius had given seemingly rigorous (if diverse) grounds for rejecting the notion of universal consent.

Derived ultimately from the same patristic and classical sources, these works, in fact, bore striking resemblance precisely to a text such as Campanella's *Atheismus Triumphatus* (Atheism vanquished) (1631). Campanella had cited the same schools of thought (including Machiavelli, the peripatetics, and the atomists) as atheistic, but he had had the misfortune to quote from them at great length while failing to satisfy his severest critics about the quality of his refutation. To their view, he should have titled his book *Atheismus Triumphans*, although it seems, indeed, an obviously sincere attempt to identify and resolve the same naturalistic and political themes.[21] What all this tells us, however, is that potentially atheistic readings of main classical traditions were everywhere and were being disseminated by a diversity of means. It should not surprise us, then, to discover them in the most diverse early-modern historians of thought.

While it is striking to see the frequency with which the anti-Aristotelianism of some extended to the accusation of ultimate disbelief against Aristotle or his disciples, it should not be too surprising. From (at least) the thirteenth century on, the problem of "radical" (generally meaning Averroistic) Aristotelianism had haunted Christian philosophy, although far more of it had to do with Averroes' doctrine of the univocity of soul

[19] Ibid., 3–107. The discussion of the patristics as ideal guides occurs on 17–35.

[20] Ibid., 125–33. Several other seventeenth-century classical scholars also cite the work of Philipp Jacob Spener, *Confessio Naturae Contra Atheistas*, but I have been unable to locate it among the many works of Spener, despite much effort. Has anyone seen it?

[21] Thomasso Campanella, *Atheismus Triumphatus seu Reductio ad Religionem per Scientiarum Veritates* (Rome, 1631 [also published Paris, 1636]). See, in particular, 1–38, 53–71, 155–82

than with any essential problems in Averroes on divine existence. There never had been a period when there were not a goodly number of Christian minds certain that the embrace of Aristotle by Christian thought was an illicit affair, and the issue of his "naturalism" generally was central to such a view. Nonetheless, close to four hundred years after the censure of primarily peripatetic naturalism in Paris in 1277, critics still could place Aristotelians, not to mention Aristotle himself, at times, in the camp of the "atheists," as dramatic a blow against universal consent as could be struck for most seventeenth-century minds. When done by savants *without* commitments to Cartesian thought, as in the case of Reiser and Spizelius, the argument might appear less "tactical" than when coming from those involved in the great Cartesian-Aristotelian struggle of seventeenth-century philosophy, but in any context in which it occurred, its effect was subversive. Once one had designated "the atheist" as the epitome of unspeakable thought, what better charge to make against one's adversary? When done with discrimination and in the language of "speculative" atheism, however, especially directed against the Stagirite himself, what worse service to the cause of universal consent?

Thus, from London, Jenkin Thomas Philipps, in his *Dissertatio Historico-Philologica de Atheismo* (1716) argued that Aristotelian philosophy (which he termed "Aristotelian stupidity") *led* ineluctably to absolute naturalism, a genuine atheism from which, he insisted, Descartes had rescued contemporary philosophy.[22] Philipps was part of a long-standing tradition of similar analysis that often went beyond his charge against Aristotelian implications. In France, the Capuchin Valérien Magni (the preceptor, in so many ways, of his order), in an essay entitled *De atheismus Aristotelis*, published in a collection of his treatises in 1652, offered broad grounds for seeing the ancient (and perhaps some less ancient) peripatetics as explicitly atheistic.[23] In 1653, Jean de Launoy, respected professor of philosophy in Paris, reminded a fascinated audience (that discussed his work for two generations) of all the grounds on which Parisian theologians and philosophers had identified Aristotle as atheistic in the past, and of the fact that this had occurred both well before and well after 1277.[24] Samuel Parker, in his *Disputationes de Deo et providentia divina* (1678) also made the case for the real atheism of both Aristotle and his

[22] Philipps, *De Atheismo*, 6–22.

[23] Valerianus Magnus, O.F.M., Cap., *[De] atheismus Aristotelis*, in *Principia et specimen philosophiae axiomata; . . . atheismus Aristotelis; soliloquia animae cum Deo* (Cologne, 1652).

[24] Jean de Launoy, *De varia Aristotelis in Academia Parisiensi Fortuna* (Paris, 1653) [there is an ed. (n.p., n.d.) also, that may have preceded this]; 2d ed. (The Hague, 1656); 3d ed. (Paris, 1662); 4th ed. (Wittenberg, 1720). There were many printings of the Paris editions.

ancient disciples.[25] We have heard from Reiser and Spizelius. In 1725, the respected German savant Jacob Friedrich Reimmann, trying to sort out "false" from "deserved" attributions of atheism, argued that it was clear that Aristotle himself was no atheist, but that some of the later Greek peripatetics certainly appeared to have been such.[26] The debates among historians of prior thought became interesting indeed.

• • •

Thomas Stanley's popular *History of Philosophy*, widely noted in France and eventually available in Latin translation, found Aristotle not only sagely theistic, but cognizant of God as "immovable, one, eternal and indivisible, void of all quantity . . . most perfect . . . [and with] infinite power."[27] Further, he believed that the Ionic philosophers all had acknowledged God (however confused their notions of Him might be); he argued, elegantly, that their "first principles" were intended by them to refer to physics alone. His Thales believed in God and providence; his Anaximander failed to ascribe eternity to his gods but manifestly recognized divinity as an attribute; his Anaxagoras believed in an "infinite self-moving Mind"; his Archelaus, though he denied the creation, properly saw Mind as the first principle.[28] His Stoics, though they equated God and "the whole World and heaven," also had many proper notions of Divinity.[29] His Epicureans unquestionably believed in the gods, whatever their denial of providence.[30]

For Stanley, however, there was indeed a history of Greek atheism. It began with the Cyrenaics, and his frequent (though not constant) use of the singular *God* in describing what they negated made it impossible for his portraits to seem compatible with the view that such philosophers

[25] Samuel Parker, *Disputationes de Deo et providentia divina* . . . (London, 1678), disp. 1, sec. 24.

[26] Jacob Friedrich Reimmann, *Historia Universalis Atheismi et Atheorum falso & merito suspectorum* . . . (Hildesheim, 1725), 133–270, where he also assigns "merited" status to accusations of atheism against Zeno, Galen, Lucretius, Varro, all the Greek skeptics, Pliny the Elder, and a host of lesser figures, and notes that *many* more of the ancients *may* have been such.

[27] Thomas Stanley, *The History of Philosophy: Containing the Lives, Opinions, Actions and Discourses of the Philosophers of every Sect*, 3d ed. (London, 1701), 227–69. [The 1st ed. was 3 vols. (London, 1655–1662); 2d ed. (London, 1687).] The work was well received in the English editions, and widely cited, which justified a Latin translation as the *Historia Philosophiae vitas, opiniones, resque gesta et dicta philosophorum sectae cujusvis complexa*, trans. G. Olearius (Leipzig, 1711). My citations are all from the 3d ed. (London, 1701).

[28] Ibid., 6, 60–73.

[29] Ibid., 333–35.

[30] Ibid., 533–63.

were enemies merely of polytheism. Theodorus "held there was no God"; Bion was an absolute disciple of "Theodorus the Atheist . . . to whose opinions he addicted himself." More ambiguously, his Protagoras claimed not to know if "the gods" existed.[31] Finally, although he accepted the skeptical Pyrrhonians' claim to believe in "God" despite the absence of proof, he emphasized the latter side of their thought, explicating at length their argument that "it is necessary we suspend [judgment] whether he [God] is or he is not," since God for them was neither self-evident nor demonstrable.[32]

For some scholars, modern accusations of atheism focused attention more clearly on the ancients. Examining the philosophical system of Spinoza's *Ethica*, the eminent Johann Franz von Buddeus sought to specify what made it an atheistic text for him. In his *Dissertatio Philosophica de Spinozismo ante Spinozam*, he expressed his dissatisfaction with what he took to be the usual criticism and refutation of Spinoza, namely, that he merely had confused nature and God and absurdly assigned the powers of the latter to the former. For Buddeus, rather, the heart of Spinoza's "atheism" lay above all in three interrelated propositions: that only one substance can exist; that a substance cannot produce another substance; and that substance acts always from necessity. If only one substance could exist, he explained, then if that substance is not God (and note that Buddeus does not equate monism per se with atheism), the system is atheistic. Since that which is impotent to create another substance could not be God, and since that which acts from necessity could not be God, Spinozism, for Buddeus, was pure and genuine atheism. Having thus clarified the charge, Buddeus believed himself able to discover prior atheists from their adherence to similar propositions. The list he offered was long, indeed, since he concluded from this analysis that virtually all Greek philosophy, with the exception of the Platonic school, adhered to these atheistic theses. Most cases were open and shut for Buddeus: all the Eleatics and all the atomists were atheists. Discussing individuals, he also specified (in order of appearance in his treatise) Strato, Epicurus, Xenophanes, Parmenides, Theodorus, Leucippus, Democritus, Anaxagoras, and Alexander the Epicurean as unequivocal atheists. The Stoic school was strongly suspect and very close to atheism. Aristotle himself could not be wholly absolved of the charge. Acknowledging that it was not an accusation that ever should be made lightly, Buddeus nonetheless claimed that after the ancients, David of Dinant, Almaric, Abelard, and Cesalpino were atheists.[33]

[31] Ibid., 132–53.

[32] Ibid., 470–532.

[33] Johann Franz von Buddeus, *Dissertatio Philosophica de Spinozismo ante Spinozam* (Halle, 1701) [32 pp.].

Some of his particular judgments would change, but the essential analyses of his later, celebrated *Theses theologicae de atheismo & superstitione variis* (1716) were in place. Think on the implications of Buddeus's dissertation, however. A reader perplexed by the abstract metaphysics of Spinoza's *Ethica* might well turn to a work that sought to define its thesis and its lineage. He would discover, in Buddeus, first, that the *Ethica* should be read as atheism, and, second, that it was derived consistently from eminent schools of Greek philosophy!

There were, of course, savants who rushed to refute such notions of almost universal ancient atheism. Johann Christian Wolff (of Hamburg) indeed charged that Buddeus's analysis greatly strengthened the appeal of atheism not only by identifying so many "great philosophers" as such, but by including among them thinkers for whose minds and rigor the early Fathers of the Church themselves had declared their admiration.[34] The latter charge, we shall see, clearly got under Buddeus's skin, and he would make frequent references to it in his later work.

Johannes Henricus Foppius, from Bremen, replied in defense of Buddeus's thesis, which he saw as part of a broader school of proper analysis of the ancients that correctly had identified their essential atheism. For Foppius, we must indeed be prudent in charging anyone with atheism, and he deplored the "rashness" of Mersenne and others who had made "irresponsible" accusations. Nonetheless, he argued, if believers, whatever their disagreements, affirm God as in some way the intelligent, free cause of a world from which He is distinct and whose imperfections He does not share, then surely the "direct," unequivocal atheists must be those who "explicitly remove God from the world, or who make God to be another brute being." Those who equate God with the brute world are deniers of Divinity in just the same way as are those who simply state that God does not exist, since a being neither free, distinct from matter, nor independently eternal cannot conceivably be God. While the Eleatic and Ionic schools, for Foppius, initially believed in God, both degenerated into an absolute atheism from which few later Greek schools were exempt. Against the notion that modern scholars were "creating" too many atheists, Foppius replied that the gentile philosophers themselves had let us know how very widespread atheism was among them by their own charges against Euhemerus, Protagoras, Prodicus, Diagoras, Critias, Hippon, and Dionysius of Syracuse.[35]

Jacob Hase, also from Bremen, defended Wolff in his *De Gentilium Philosophis Atheismi Falso Suspectis* (1716), but his defense sheds inter-

[34] Johann Christian Wolffius, *Dissertatio de Atheismi falso suspectis* (Hamburg, n.d.).

[35] Johannes Foppius, *Exercitatio I. De Atheismo Philosophorum Gentilium Celebriorum* (Bremen, [1714]) [16 pp.].

esting light on the balance of forces in contemporaneous classical studies. Citing English, French, German, and Dutch scholarship, Hase claimed that it was clearly the dominant tendency now to label as atheists ancient thinkers who had wanted to assert the existence of God, however confused their notions of Divinity. Against this tendency, he urged that the ancients "anticipated" rather than denied our idea of the Supreme Being. They knew that God was the "most perfect being," which was the essence of philosophical belief in Him, and the reason they deemed Him corporeal was that corporeality was part of their idea of perfection. They could not fairly be accused of atheistic naturalism, because they assigned intelligence to even their corporeal God. Thus understood, *all* of the ancient philosophers recognized God.[36] It was a dissertation useful in one sense to universal consent, but in another sense, it communicated explicitly that most scholars in fact found widespread atheism among the Greeks.

Philipps's *De Atheismo*, published that same year, also declared itself sensitive to what it presented as a sad history of loose and reckless charges of atheism, although its conviction of Aristotle as an atheist would have struck many as reckless indeed. Philipps deplored the misuse of the term *atheist* for religious calumny and explicitly rejected Spizelius's charges against Grotius and others who (in Philipps's view) had simply deplored the misuse of religion in political life. He had equal contempt for Reiser's view of Cain as an atheist, insisting that immoral rebellion against God presupposes belief in the existence of God. Some chroniclers and commentators, he complained, created so many false categories of atheism that "all men" could be placed in at least one class of them. He ridiculed the writers of the early seventeenth century who found atheism everywhere, confounding it with heresy, indifference, superstition, deism, libertinism, and so on. The term *atheist*, he insisted, should be reserved for those "who either ignore the existence of the Supreme Divinity . . . or who believe and persuade themselves that God does not exist."[37] Such men, however, abounded in his own history.

For Philipps, there were only two categories of atheism that made sense: disbelief in God that followed "by [logical] consequence" from one's philosophy, such as from denial of providence and divine judgment; and "systematic" disbelief, the atheism of those who support explicit propositions "against the existence of God." Since God could not be conceived of except as spirit, however, he argued that "whoever denies the truth of incorporeal substance necessarily becomes an atheist," which settled the fate of many of the Greeks.[38] On the basis of these categories, he

[36] Jacobus Hasaeus [Jacob Hase], *Dissertatio Philosophica, de Gentilium Philosophis Atheismi Falso Suspectis* . . . (Bremen, 1716) [38 pp.].

[37] Philipps, *De Atheismo*, 24–29, 97, 114–15.

[38] Ibid., 24–26.

placed Epicurus, Lucretius, Thales, Anaximander, Anaximenes, Empedocles, Diagoras, Protagoras, Theodorus, and Strato in the atheistic camp (though some merely "indirectly," from the logical consequences of their materialism).[39] Further, while he attempted to save many medieval, Renaissance, and seventeenth-century thinkers from the charge of atheism, he did so in most erudite fashion, referring the reader to large numbers of contemporaneous or recent works, many of them otherwise quite obscure, in which those charges were made. Finally, Bruno, Campanella, Hobbes, and Spinoza were truly atheists (though not, he argued, Vanini, Pomponazzi, or Cardan), and there had been, in recent times, genuine denials of the existence of God, including those of the "Polish nobleman" Casimir Brzesky, who argued, he claimed, that " 'God is not the creator of man, but man is the creator of God . . . *ex nihilo*,' " Mahomet Effendi (to whom both he and we were introduced by Rycaut), and several others.[40]

Other English voices also received consideration in France on the subject of atheism. Thomas Wise's *Confutation of Atheism* (1706)—the introduction to which attracted attention, one should note, by criticizing Bayle's accusation that the Cambridge Platonists had found too much atheism everywhere—included an illustration of four "Theists," Aristotle, Plato, Socrates, and Pythagoras, standing under laurels of victory, and four "Atheists," Anaximander, Strato, Democritus, and Epicurus, standing under the wilted laurels of defeat.[41] For Wise, who nonetheless insisted that the number of atheists was sufficiently small not to discredit universal consent,[42] atheistic atomism, founded by Leucippus, Democritus, and (he somehow added) Protagoras, and later developed by Epicurus, was "a Philosophical Form of Atheology, a Gygantic Attempt to dethrone the Deity." Greek atomism, for Wise, established "Principles, [from] which it must needs follow, that there could be neither a corporeal nor incorporeal Deity."[43] Strato's animation of matter with "a self-active power," he also concluded, was necessarily atheistic, and, properly analyzed, many schools of Greek thought, based on the material causation of

[39] Ibid., 30–74.

[40] Ibid., 75–147. His concluding chapter is a lengthy bibliography of works the reader should consult to be informed of the debates and conclusions of authors concerned with the history of atheism, and it includes many savants who had painted the history of atheism with a broad brush indeed.

[41] Thomas Wise, *A Confutation of the Reason and Philosophy of Atheism* . . . (London, 1706). The portrait is located immediately before the title page; the "Introduction" was 143 pp., paginated separately. Wise was a Fellow of Exeter College, Oxford, and chaplain to the duke of Ormond. The *Confutation* was dedicated to the archbishop of Canterbury.

[42] Ibid., 441–99.

[43] Ibid., 1–51.

all things without the role of divine mind, were indistinguishable from such atheism.[44]

In 1717, the *Bibliothèque Anglaise*, published precisely to keep a French-language audience aware of English publications, reported extensively on Richard Blackmore's *Essays Upon Several Subjects*, which included a lengthy disquisition of the reality of atheism. According to the *Bibliothèque*, Blackmore was quite precise in his definition of the atheist: he was either "a man who openly declares that he does not believe in the existence of God," or he was someone who, without openly declaring his atheism, assigned *all* causality in the universe to other causes. The reviewer shared the list of genuine atheists that Blackmore derived from antiquity by his criteria: Aristippus, Aristotle, Bion, Democritus, Diagoras, Dicearchus, Epicurus (against Bayle, the reviewer noted, who argued that Epicurus was *not* an atheist), Leucippus, Lucian, Lucretius, Pliny the Elder, Protagoras, Pyrrho and *all* the skeptical Pyrrhonians, Strato, and Theodorus. Applied to the moderns, the *Bibliothèque* explained, Blackmore's criterion exculpated Cardan but led him to identify as genuine atheists Bergardo, Cesalpino, Hobbes, Mahomet Effendi, Matthias Knutzen, Spinoza, and Vanini.[45] One can perhaps understand better now the warnings of other savants such as Morgues about the implications of such attributions for universal consent.[46]

. . .

Even scholars who took those warnings seriously, however, could reach conclusions far from reassuring to believers in the *consensus gentium*. In 1725, Jacob Friedrich Reimmann's *Historia Universalis Atheismi et Atheorum falso & merito suspectorum* sought to make sense of the diverse assessments of the extent of atheism in the ancient and modern world. As with almost all of these authors, he explicitly referred his readers to an international literature in which the issue of "real atheism" had been and was being debated. Addressing the charges group by group, he argued that most accusations of atheism directed against diverse ancient peoples and thinkers before the flowering of Greek philosophy were problematic and question-begging, that others were dubious, but that,

[44] Ibid., 51–74.

[45] *Bibliothèque Anglaise* I, 355–62. Earlier (I, 39–41) the *Bibliothèque Anglaise* had alerted its readers to Blackmore's "plan to publish a Discourse in which he will go back to the origin of atheism and will present for inspection all the atheists from century to century up to our days [*il remontera jusqu'à l'origine de l'Athéisme, et fera passer en révue tous les Athées de siècle en siècle jusqu'à nos jours*]."

[46] See supra, pt. 2, chap. 6.

indeed, there were a few "probable" atheists and a few "real" ones.[47] Turning to the Greeks, he exonerated all of the thinkers of the early "Italian" school of Greek philosophy and similarly absolved most of the Ionics of the charge, but he saw Hippon and Archelaus as quite possibly atheists and Diogenes of Apollonia as quite certainly one.[48] Plato was clearly a theist for Reimmann; there were, however, strains of manifest atheism among his disciples. Similarly, an Aristotle who believed in God nonetheless gave rise to later Greek peripatetics who were difficult to find innocent of the charge. The (early) Academics were exculpated by Saint Augustine himself, which closed the case for Reimmann, but it was clear to him that Clitomachus was an atheist. He found most Cyrenaics acceptable but made exceptions in the cases of Bion and Euhemerus. The Stoics were innocent, with the exceptions of Zeno and Arisochius.[49] Although Epicureanism was synonymous with atheism for many, and the case of the Eleatics was particularly "difficult," Reimmann noted, there were too many pious defenders of both groups and too many problems of interpretation of the atomists to conclude generally for their atheism.[50] All the (Pyrrhonian) skeptics, however, were obviously atheistic, as were Galen, Philip of Macedonia, and Dionysius of Syracuse.[51] Among the Romans, Lucretius and Ovid were unmistakably theoretical atheists (which, in the case of Lucretius, would seem to cast doubt back on the exoneration of Epicurus), as were Varro, Pliny, and Caligula.[52] In brief, his clarifications left readers very far from any view of universal consent. When he turned to more recent thought, however, Reimmann's attributions of atheism became far more numerous than his exonerations. For example, there was extensive atheism in France, including that of Rabelais, Berigard, Hénault, and many minor Renaissance figures; large numbers of other thinkers, including Bodin, Richard Simon, La Hontan, and Isaac de la Peyrère, were "probably" atheists, although the cases against them were inconclusive. He engaged in similar calculations for Italy, Spain, Poland, Britain, Holland, Germany, and the Ottoman Empire.[53] Two years later, Friedrich Philipp Schlosser, a student of Stoic philosophy, praised and agreed with Reimmann's refusal to label Strato an atheist, but in his very praise he noted how widespread the charge was, citing Cicero, Seneca, Tertullian, Saint Augustine, Lescalopier, Bayle, Buddeus, Thomassius, Jean Le

[47] Reimmann, *Historia Universalis Atheismi*, 24–133. [This follows a separately paginated "*Idea Compendii Theologicii . . .*," of 60 pp.]

[48] Ibid., 133–54.

[49] Ibid., 154–95.

[50] Ibid., 195–16.

[51] Ibid., 216–40.

[52] Ibid., 240–70.

[53] Ibid., 313–541.

Clerc, Leibniz, Samuel Parker, and, most extensively, Ralph Cudworth as authorities who provided people with plausible (but in the final analysis, for Schlosser, uncompelling) grounds for seeing Strato as merely having assigned the term *divinity* to a material nature devoid of consciousness, sensation, and reason.[54] Some reassurance!

. . .

Two of the texts from the emerging "history of atheism" most widely discussed in France were Ralph Cudworth's *True Intellectual System of the Universe*, whose analyses of ancient atheism were widely disseminated in French by Jean Le Clerc's exceptionally long translations and presentations of them in his *Bibliothèque Choisie* of 1703 (and a second edition of 1712), and Buddeus's *Theses theologicae de atheismo et superstitione variis*, first published in 1717, receiving a third Latin edition by 1737, and popular enough to be translated into French by a doctor of the Sorbonne in 1740. Both works were marked by seemingly profound erudition and philosophical depth. An irony of the success of both works, however, was that disagreeing in so many cases about which were false and which were true accusations, the two works between them assigned almost all schools of ancient philosophy to the atheistic side of the scales. A second irony, I shall demonstrate in my subsequent volume, was that each work, while seeking to identify and analyze ancient atheism for purposes of censure, virtually gave lessons in how to think "atheistically."

The underlying apologetic strategy of Ralph Cudworth, and, indeed, of the Cambridge Platonists in general, was enormously complex, involving, in Cudworth's case, a quite heterodox view of "the true Mosaic philosophy," which, he believed, taught that God had infused passive matter with immanent "plastic natures" through which the divine will was executed at one remove.[55] While many admired their ontological bravado, few followed it, and many, indeed, found it paradoxically supportive of atheism itself, making orderly activity a quality that matter could possess of its nature. To argue for this position, however, Cudworth attempted to rewrite, in effect, our understanding of Greek philosophy, and Le Clerc's lengthy excerpts and explications of Cudworth's work popular-

[54] Fridericus Philippus Schlosserus, *Specilegium Historico-Philosophicum de Stratone Lampsaceno Cognomento Physico et Atheismo Hylozoico Vulgo Ipsi Tributo* (Wittenberg, 1728), 1–42.

[55] Ralph Cudworth, *The True Intellectual System of the Universe* (London, 1678). There is an outstanding early-modern and longer-term intellectual contextualization of the issue of "active principles" (such as "plastic natures") offered by J. E. McGuire, "Neoplatonism and Active Principles: Newton and the *Corpus Hermeticum*," in Robert S. Westman and J. E. McGuire, *Hermeticism and the Scientific Revolution* (Los Angeles), 1977, 93–142.

ized and spread it in France. What were its implications for universal consent and the history of atheism?

For Cudworth, Le Clerc accurately explained, atomism in and of itself was in no manner atheistic and, in fact, had been part of the Mosaic understanding. Theistic atomism, however, recognized that atoms had been created by God and infused with formative, immaterial natures that oversaw their motions with design and intelligence. This atomism had been received by the Greeks but had degenerated in the course of time into purely materialistic and deterministic atheistic philosophies: Greek atomists came to believe that the fortuitous, blind motion of eternal atoms accounted for the phenomenal world. From this perspective, atomists who maintained any exclusive "mechanical necessity" were "true atheists [*des véritables Athées*]." An atomistic physics, nonetheless, explained much and could be consistent with belief in God if it were integrated into a larger philosophy in which there were *both* mechanical bodies and immaterial Intelligences, "of which the Divinity, distinct from the world, is the principle." Democritus and Leucippus, however, made "the doctrine of Atoms the foundation of an entire system of philosophy . . . from which it follows that there is not any God, not even when one would say that He were only a body." Democritus and Leucippus, thus, "were the first who joined atoms with atheism."[56]

Plato and Aristotle, Cudworth believed, saw the atheism of this materialistic atomism but recoiled from atomism itself, alas, rather than from simply the materialism and blind determinism of such a system. Given the *physical* correctness of atomism, then, the development of atheism continued apace. The theory of Democritus, Leucippus, and their eventual disciple Epicurus was based, above all else, on the view that the universe was wholly without a principle of intelligence and free choice. From this perspective, Cudworth dismissed charges of atheism against the pre-Socratic corporealists, since even if they saw only matter in the world, they almost all were "nonetheless persuaded that there is a Divinity, although corporeal, and that an Intelligent Nature, placed in matter, formed the world and governed it still at present." Theirs was a false idea of the Divinity, but it was not atheism. It was absurd, for Cudworth, to label atheistic every ancient philosopher who could not conceive of the immaterial, since such a recognition was implicit in every positing of Intelligence as the architect of the world. To discover atheism, one must discover philosophers who accounted for the world "without any superior Intelligence presiding over the whole," and Cudworth believed that he had identified many of those.[57]

[56] *Bibliothèque Choisie*, ed. Jean Le Clerc, 26 vols. (Amsterdam, 1703–1713), I, 63–138; II, 11–77. Cf. Cudworth, *System*, pt. 1, chaps. 1–3.

[57] See n. 56.

There were, he explained, four distinct schools of Greek atheism: (1) the school of Anaximander, the "Hylopathians," who believed that "everything is derived from matter devoid of sentiment"; (2) the school of Democritus, the so-called Atomists, "who make everything come from the fortuitous concourse of the arrangement of atoms"; (3) a major school of the Stoics, "Stoic Atheism," that posited that "a blind Nature, but [one] which acts according to certain laws, presides over all the universe"; (4) the school of Strato, "Hylozoic Atheism," whose adherents "attribute to matter I know not what [sort of] life, without sentiment and without intelligence."[58] For Cudworth (as for so many commentators, however diversely they categorized specific philosophies), the manifest distinction to be drawn was between theists, even if materialists, who saw a material universe directed by "Intelligence," and atheists who attributed all to chance, blind mechanical law, or the nature of brute matter alone. In his analysis, the latter included some very significant schools of Greek thought.

What added to Cudworth's list of atheists was his view that many major thinkers had recognized "Intelligence" in nature, but describing only physics, had produced disciples who did not, a phenomenon that he believed had begun with Thales himself. Thus, while there was no systematic atheism before Leucippus and Democritus, there were many actual atheists of belief, as both Plato and Aristotle had recognized. With such a criterion, Cudworth sought to unmask the atheism of his own age. In modern times, for Cudworth, Hobbes simply had revived intact the system of the ancient atheists. Descartes, like Thales, himself believed in such "Intelligence," but his mechanistic philosophy ignored so thoroughly the intelligent guidance of bodies that his disciples were increasingly unequivocal atheists (a judgment from which Le Clerc was quick to dissent).[59] Le Clerc's lengthy translations and explications of *The True Intellectual System* were popular enough to enjoy a second edition in 1712 and 1713. Cudworth needs to be restored to his vital place among the influences on early-modern French culture.

· · ·

Buddeus's *Theses theologicae de atheismo*, later published as the *Traité d'Athéisme*, was divided into historical and apologetic parts. Although the latter clearly were Buddeus's most essential concerns, his book nonetheless was in many ways one of the most ambitious and well-received of the early-modern histories and analyses of specifically atheistic thought.

[58] The "four schools," though discussed throughout, are concisely summarized by Le Clerc's presentation of Cudworth in ibid., II, 57–73.

[59] Ibid., II, 73–77 and (a separate article) II, 78–130 (cf. Cudworth, *System*, chap. 3).

Its translator, the Sorbonniste Louis Philon, termed it the deepest and most extensive book on the topic ever written, and praised its manner of remaining above all purely sectarian debates.[60] Buddeus had two specifically historical and interpretive goals: first, to identify and analyze unequivocal atheism, ancient and modern, expanding upon the efforts of his earlier *Spinozismo ante Spinozam*; second (and more important to *him*, to judge quantitatively, at least), to identify philosophical positions that led logically to atheism. While at times he kept these categories quite distinct, at times he seemed to conflate them.

Nonetheless, like most savants who addressed the issue of atheism, he deplored the loose condemnation of thinkers as unbelievers, and he insisted on a distinction between "Atheism itself" and "dogmas that follow from atheism or that lead to it," so that one might "do justice" to the individuals involved.[61] In this spirit, and, again, like almost all of his peers in this genre, he devoted an extensive portion of his work to critical discussion of the bibliography of the history of atheism, referring his readers to a very large number of differing accounts of who was and who was not formally atheistic in the history of thought.[62] From that perspective, he must have appeared quite judicious to many readers, for his practice was to cite many authors on behalf of someone's alleged atheism, weigh the claims, and then grant or, in certain instances, dismiss the charges as inconclusive. Thus (which gives one an indication of what *some* of the less erudite literature was like), he exonerated Plato, Hippocrates, Heraclitus, Plutarch, Cicero, Livy, Pliny the Elder, and Euhemerus from the accusations of some scholars (and, for good measure, Socrates from the charges of the Athenians themselves).[63]

When he addressed doctrines in the abstract, he often maintained his original distinction between intentional and logically entailed atheism. When he thought about specific schools and thinkers, however, he made his division far less categorical. Indeed, his explicit efforts to restate the distinction were often far from unequivocal. Thus, in his preface, he clarified his distinction between the "two classes" of atheists as follows: (1) "those who deny the existence of God shamelessly and without evasion,

[60] Johann Franz von Buddeus, *Theses theologicae de atheismo et superstitione variis . . .* (Jena, 1717) [3d Latin ed. (Jena, 1737)]. Translated as Jean-François Buddeus, *Traité de l'athéisme et de la superstition, par feu Mr. Jean-François Buddeus, Docteur & Professeur en Théologie. Avec des remarques historiques et philosophiques*, trans. Louis Philon, ed. Jean-Chrétien Fischer (Amsterdam, 1740). My citations will be from the French translation. The praise from Philon is found in his "Avertissement du Traducteur," which precedes Buddeus's preface.

[61] Ibid., "Préface" and 1–2. See also 96–97, where he deplored the absurd accusations of atheism occasioned by Catholic-Protestant debate.

[62] Ibid., passim, but see especially the notes to 1–97.

[63] Ibid., 16 and n. 2 (Plato); 39–45 (Heraclitus, Hippocrates, Euhemerus, and Plutarch); 47–50 (Cicero, Livy, and Pliny the Elder). The case of Socrates is discussed on 11–14.

or those who, being in bad faith [in disclaiming their obvious atheism], cannot deny or not know that atheism follows necessarily from their principles"; and (2) "those who establish principles . . . which [are] the same thing as if one denied the existence of God, although the authors . . . disavow these consequences and refuse to grant the relationship that they have with their principles." The Epicureans and Spinoza belonged to the first group; Aristotle and the Stoics belonged to the second.[64] Later in his text, he restated the distinction as follows: (1) "atheists . . . who deny the existence of God openly and without employing any evasions, and [who], without caring about the impulses [*mouvements*] or remorse of their conscience, are very willing to persuade themselves and others of it [that God does not exist]"; and (2) "atheists . . . who in truth do not deny in formal terms the existence of God, but who establish principles and hypotheses [theories] from which the doctrine of atheism follows naturally and necessarily, *and in such a manner that they should have [or 'could have'] been aware of it* [*et d'une telle manière qu'ils en auraient pu s'en aperçevoir*]."[65]

In the sections of the work devoted to actual atheism, before he turned his longer attention to those philosophical doctrines that logically led to disbelief, Buddeus specifically *excluded* from his consideration two types of atheism that were, in fact, less threatening to supporters of universal consent: "practical" atheism without manifestation in formal thought; and any "theoretical" atheism based purely on ignorance of or inattention to the phenomena of nature.[66] Instead, he focused on what he termed the two main categories of actual, "first-class" philosophical atheism, "Dogmatic Atheism" and "Skeptical Atheism," and he subdivided dogmatic atheism into four additional "classes" according to the four principal "sects of the philosophers" from which they derived (Epicurean, Stoic, Aristotelian, and Eleatic).[67] Whenever he identified modern atheists, it was in terms of ancient thought: "Atheism," for example, was "the favored dogma of the sect of Eleatic philosophers, from whom Spinoza borrowed his doctrine."[68]

For Buddeus, the proper history of atheism began with Greek philosophy. Granting that there had been corrupt and ignorant atheists of the heart throughout all history, the "fools" of Scripture, Buddeus insisted that we had no evidence of speculative atheism until the period of Ionic philosophy. He found prevailing debates about the extent of atheism among the Chaldeans or Orphic Greeks inconclusive for lack of evidence (a particularly sage determination if his accounts of those discussions are

[64] Ibid., "Préface."
[65] Ibid., 99–100.
[66] Ibid., 105–7.
[67] Ibid., 107–14
[68] Ibid., 29

correct), and he insisted that there was no need to create atheists unnecessarily.[69] As for the explicit issue of universal consent, however, Buddeus argued that it could be maintained only if one specified that there never had been men *properly instructed* about the Divinity who had reached atheism without having had "*the least sense*" that they *might* be wrong. The sad lesson of ancient and modern history, he averred, was that speculative atheists existed in all centuries, men who "either doubt the existence of God, or even make an overt profession of Atheism, or advance, at the least, dogmas from which it follows as a logical consequence that there is no God."[70] Who, then, in all this, dissented from universal consent?

While *all* of the Ionic philosophers, for Buddeus, wrote in a manner favorable to atheism, only certain of them were atheists of the "first class," genuine deniers of Divinity: Anaximander, Anaximenes, and Diogenes of Apollonia. He did claim that exoneration of most of the other Ionics was not certain, however, and referred readers to authors who even believed Anaxagoras to be a naturalistic materialist and atheist. Most of Socrates' disciples were theists, but among them and among the Cyrenaics, he specified Critias, Diagoras, Theodorus, Bion, and Stilpo as explicit atheists who simply "did not believe ['in the existence of the Gods']." Where most authors writing in favor of universal consent quoted certain patristic texts to the effect that such "atheists" were merely enemies of polytheism, Buddeus assured his readers that the Church Fathers were so eager to combat their primary enemy, pagan religion, that they were even willing to use genuine atheists in such a cause.[71]

Referring readers to literature that did find the first (Platonic) Academy atheistic, Buddeus granted the atheistic potential of certain Platonic notions of Divinity and its relationship to matter, but he defended Plato and his first disciples. He reached a similar conclusion, rather equivocally, however, concerning Aristotle, saying that there was great plausibility in the charge of atheism against the Stagirite, given both "his system of the eternity of the world" and his view of "the necessary relationship of God with matter," but Buddeus found it more convincing to see Aristotle as someone who had erroneous ideas about Divinity and nature *that led many of his disciples to genuine atheism* despite his intent.[72] As for the skeptical Academy, especially as it moved toward Pyrrhonian skepticism, he saw it as unequivocally atheistic: "It is certainly *the same thing* to af-

[69] Ibid., 3–10.

[70] Ibid., 1–2.

[71] Ibid., 9–15, 24–26. Buddeus's footnotes, interesting throughout, are particularly interesting about debates concerning the atheism of the Ionic philosophers.

[72] Ibid., 15–16 (Plato), 20–23 (Aristotle). His n. 2 on 16 presented the case he would reject for Platonic atheism; his n. 2 on 20–21 explicated the debate over Aristotle's atheism.

firm without exception that there is nothing certain and to deny the existence of God."[73] Buddeus also found Strato unequivocally atheistic, since the philosopher believed that "the system of the world can subsist even if one does not presuppose any Divinity" and taught that "the Matter of which the world is composed was God Himself," all of which was denial of actual Divinity, pure atheism, and the source of Spinoza's doctrines.[74]

For Buddeus, the Stoics, the atomists, and, indeed, the entire Eleatic school were all atheists who cleverly equated God and nature so that they could feign piety by speaking of "following God" when all they really meant was "following nature." Xenophanes of Colophon, Parmenides, Melissus, Zeno of Elea, Leucippus, Democritus, Diagoras, Protagoras, Prodicus, Epicurus, and Alexander the Epicurean were all explicit atheists, and, again, those who did not see this had been misled by the occasional patristic desire to portray them as merely fellow disbelievers in the specific pagan gods.[75]

For Buddeus, all medieval and modern atheisms were derived from these ancient roots, from the explicit or logically consequential atheism implicit in either Aristotelian, Stoic, Epicurean, or Stratonian sources. "Several scholastics," he insisted, joined "the party of Atheism," led into such dire error by the consequences of Aristotle's arguments against the possibility of creation.[76]

In Italy, above all, after "the reestablishment of belles lettres," the atheistic potential of Aristotelian thought was realized dramatically in a number of "atheists of the first class," including Bruno, Vanini, Berigard, Machiavelli, and "perhaps," the evidence being inconclusive, Cremonius and Ruggerius, plus, given the dangers of Aristotelian naturalism, a significant number of atheists of the "second class." In what again must have given an appearance of considered discrimination to his work, Buddeus examined a large number of charges against alleged atheists that he dismissed as either false, inconclusive, or based on "practical" rather than "theoretical" atheism, exonerating, for example (though explicating all the scholarship to the contrary), Aretino, Poggio, Pomponazzi, Cardan, Campanella, and, rather grudgingly, Cesalpino. He insisted, in the case of Pomponazzi, that fideism could be sincere.[77]

Concerning the alleged atheism of celebrated French thinkers, he found the charges leveled by Mersenne, Garasse, and the like wildly hyperbolic, and he dismissed all accusations against Rabelais (merely a debauched "practical" atheist), Montaigne ("profane," "lively," and "clever," with much of value), and Descartes (a man of "good faith" with "bad proofs

[73] Ibid., 17–20 (see especially n. 2 on 18 and n. 1 on 19).

[74] Ibid., 23–24.

[75] Ibid., 27–50.

[76] Ibid., 50–52.

[77] Ibid., 52–69.

of God"). He found Bayle's claims of fideism, however, to be very problematic and concluded that Bayle's severest critics were probably correct that it was a deliberate ruse to give all intellectual victories to the atheists.[78]

In Holland, van den Ende and Spinoza "openly professed Atheism," and the latter was "the leader and master of the atheists of our century, having recognized no other God than Nature, which is the same thing as if he had denied the existence of God."[79] In England, Buddeus declared, atheism was making great progress, and he counted among its explicit, "first-class" adherents Hobbes, John Toland, and Anthony Collins; nonetheless, he exonerated (again sharing all the charges) Herbert of Cherbury (a "naturalist" who, however, admitted a God) and Thomas Browne (a man simply "indifferent" to religion).[80]

Buddeus's own Germany fared better, with only two explicit atheists, one Matthias Knutzen of Jena, whose heterodoxy appeared to have offended many German theologians and scholars, and, his most anecdotal entry, the anonymous unbeliever who reportedly left an explicitly atheistic note on the preacher's chair in Magdeburg.[81] From the Ionics to the scribbler of Magdeburg, however, the list was long indeed, and if one counted Buddeus's "second-class atheists," who *should* have been such had they only seen the logical consequences of their own principles, the number of disbelievers in God would have constituted a veritable encyclopedia of Western philosophy. When, later in his work, Buddeus sought to demonstrate the existence of God, he mentioned but indeed neither insisted upon nor lingered on the argument from universal consent.[82] As we now have seen, Morgues and Bordelon were not the whole story, to say the very least.

• • •

It is in the midst of these habits and commonplaces of early-modern efforts at a history of philosophy and atheism that we must place Pierre

[78] Ibid., 69–75. The case of Bayle is discussed in n. 1, 75–78.

[79] Ibid., 78–86.

[80] Ibid., 87–95. Buddeus did cite, however, the many continental defenders of Hobbes who quite liked his conclusion that the idea of God was beyond sense experience and ineffable. Nonetheless, he agreed with Hobbes's many English critics who were convinced of his atheism. I shall argue in my subsequent study that Hobbes barely impinges upon French considerations of atheism until the time of d'Holbach. D'Holbach "discovers" the metaphysical side of Hobbes on a trip to England in the mid-eighteenth century, and translates the *Treatise of Human Nature* into French. Diderot, *Correspondance*, ed. G. Roth, XII (Paris, 1965), 45–47, wrote that he was *first* introduced to the philosophical sides of Hobbes by this and was quite swept away.

[81] Buddeus, *Traité*, 95–96.

[82] Ibid., 171–75.

Bayle, himself ironically the eventual *object* of such considerations. Bayle is *not* distinguishable from contemporaries who addressed similar issues by the originality of his assessments, by his erudition, nor by the fact of his attributions of atheism in the history of thought. Indeed, we shall see, he often was more circumspect than many of them in his accounts of disbelief. His sources, unsurprisingly, were the same sources that his contemporaries utilized, and the celebrated "Remarks" of his *Dictionnaire historique et critique* generally referred to the same texts, issues, and scholarship that they also addressed.

Bayle, however, was more explicit and combative than most savants on the status of the argument from universal consent. Further, he insisted in particularly provocative terms on the categorical distinction between the fruits of natural inquiry and the fruits of sin and grace, often illustrating it by an appeal to evidence of praiseworthy natural moral qualities among speculative "atheistic" thinkers or peoples. These traits all served to make him something of a lightning rod on the critical issues of universal consent and of atheism and virtue. If parts of the reading public had remained unaware of the content and implications of erudite vernacular or Latin works on the history of incredulity, Bayle and, above all, his critics made it difficult for readers to remain in such a state. Scholars noted his work along with that of many others, and he did not change the fundamental nature of their debates or conclusions. Critics, on the other hand, took a quite singular interest in him, and, as they did in the case of others in the Chinese rites controversy, they made a cause célèbre of his discussions of disbelief.

• • •

The *Dictionnaire* and the *Oeuvres Diverses* support the most salient conclusions that Elisabeth Labrousse has drawn from them in her magisterial study of Bayle, in this case, concerning Bayle and atheism. As Labrousse argued, he sought to specify by *atheism* the denial of providence and liberty in the First Cause. The reality and the natural moral qualities of "atheists" could not be determined by theory for Bayle but were questions of fact alone. The testimony of history and travel revealed that there indeed had been and were such disbelievers. The same evidence assured us also that while some atheists began in vice rather than speculation and concluded for atheism as a means of seeking assurance of impunity, others clearly began in speculation and concluded in atheism while living discreet and naturally moral lives. Such a finding, however, although merely "factual," was theologically useful for Bayle, reinforcing his conviction that speculation was not a *source* of sin, and that Christian *thought* was very far from a guarantor of virtue. He knew well Plutarch's favorable comparison of atheism to superstition and utilized it on behalf of these views, dissociating atheism from the worst excesses of behavioral depravity.[83] As Labrousse has argued more recently, the thesis that atheism was compatible with a stable state also was extremely useful to a Bayle who wished desperately for a Protestant return to France. If he could convince his French Catholic readers that atheists posed no threat to the order of society, how could they fail to see that the same was true for the "lesser" case of those whom they saw as heretics?[84]

Labrousse's observation, however, that *in contrast to Bayle*, "those who deny the existence of atheists are not extremist skeptics, but, quite to the contrary, theologians" is potentially misleading.[85] As we have seen, there were *so many* theological voices, including the Holy Office in Rome and the Faculty of Theology of Paris, not to mention missionaries, classical scholars, Jansenists, and others, who positively *insisted upon* the reality of atheism, and, in fact, of speculative atheism per se. It was, to say the least, a common theme. Indeed, it was precisely the widespread orthodox refusal *in practice* to deny the existence of atheists that provided Bayle with much of the "factual" basis of a thesis that in many ways was simply a popularization of such views. He was only one of many such voices, and while he may have had a larger audience than any other *one* of them, he did not have a larger audience than they did collectively, and his views were far more an effect than a cause of the breakdown of belief in universal consent. It is, in fact, quite appropriate that in her lengthy intellectual biography of Bayle, Labrousse, who understands him so well, devotes only a single twenty-two-page chapter to the specific issue of Bayle and atheism, and the greater part of that to its relation to his moral concerns.

. . .

Bayle's article on Anaxagoras in the *Dictionnaire* is representative of his work on the history of philosophy. For Bayle, as for others, the answer to one question constituted a most critical divide in natural philosophy: was or was not the world we observed the product of free, intelligent choice by a Divinity categorically distinct from the creatures? From that perspective, he assigned Anaxagoras the exact same place of honor that most of the commentators we have cited assigned to him. In Bayle's words:

[83] Labrousse, *Pierre Bayle*, II, 103–25.

[84] E. Labrousse, "Reading Pierre Bayle in Paris," in *Anticipations of the Enlightenment in England, France, and Germany*, ed. Alan Charles Kors and Paul J. Korshin (Philadelphia, 1987), 7–16.

[85] Labrousse, *Pierre Bayle*, II, 104.

> What was most lovely in the system of Anaxagoras was that in place of how men had reasoned until then about the construction of the world, granting, on the one hand, a most inchoate matter and, on the other, only chance or only a blind fatality that had arranged it, he was the first who supposed that an Intelligence produced the movement of matter and sorted out the chaos [*il fut le premier qui supposa qu'une Intelligence produisit le mouvement de la matière, et débrouilla le chaos*].[86]

Such a view was in no way original, of course, and Bayle never tried to present it as such. Quite to the contrary, for such was seventeenth-century erudition, he built his factual case on as many authorities as he could cite, and he cited many. What were the sources of his view of the pre-Socratics? He was as explicit as he could be: Diogenes Laertius; [pseudo-]Plutarch's *De Placitis Philosophorum* and Plutarch's *Moralia*; Aristotle's *Metaphysica*; Cicero's *De natura deorum*; Plato; and the patristic literature, especially Clement of Alexandria, Eusebius, Saint Augustine, and Irenaeus. He addressed the arguments of those commentators, in this case Lescalopier and Thomassin, who had argued that thinkers before Anaxagoras had presupposed but not written explicitly about the guidance of Intelligence, but he rejected them on the basis of the accounts in these classical and patristic authorities.[87] As he put it, stating the obvious, "One can produce a host of witnesses on behalf of this fact, that Anaxagoras is the first philosopher who assigned the arrangement of matter to the Intelligence of a prime mover." Finally, he tried to turn this to good advantage in terms of the humbling of human arrogance. Addressing the failure of the likes of Thales, Anaximander, and Anaximenes to discern that Intelligence, he asked, "Who will not wonder [at the fact] that such great men had been in so crass an ignorance?"[88]

Yet Bayle almost always withheld the label "atheist" from the pre-Socratic philosophers in the *Dictionnaire*, wavering between his sense, on the one hand, that any equation of God and nature (or God and matter) was the actual denial of God, and his sense, on the other, that benighted mankind quite naturally confused the Creator and His creatures. As Bayle made unambiguously clear in his article on Spinoza, the Dutch philosopher was his model for the actual atheist, the man who explicitly and unequivocally had *equated* God and the world, thereby eliminating God,

[86] Pierre Bayle, *Dictionnaire historique et critique*, 4th ed., rev., corr., and aug., 4 vols. (Amsterdam, 1730), "Anaxagoras." [The *Dictionnaire* was first published in 2 vols. (Rotterdam, 1697).] Quotations from the main text of briefer articles will be cited simply by the title of the article; citations from longer articles will add volume and page from the 4th ed.; the letter of the "Remarks," the reader should know, varies slightly from edition to edition: those given here are from the 4th edition.

[87] Ibid., "Anaxagoras," rems. D and F.

[88] Ibid., "Anaxagoras," rem. F.

and not merely *confusing* Him with the creatures in some odd manner, as so many of the ancients perhaps had done. That was why he termed Spinoza not merely "a systematizing atheist [*un Athée de Système*]," but, indeed, "the first" such.[89] There appears nothing the least bit feigned in Bayle's recoil from Spinoza. In some sense, it was precisely the spectacle of a sincere, rigorous, geometrical mind concluding on behalf of the "absurdity" that God, the world as a whole, and all of the creatures of the world were one and the same substance that made Spinoza such a frightful yet edifying model for Bayle. Spinoza offered a humbling lesson of how unaided human reason could wander into a system so bizarre that, as Bayle explained it, theft would have to be understood as God committing a crime against Himself.[90]

Spinoza's *Ethica*, thus, became the touchstone that Bayle used to assay diverse accounts of ancient or other philosophies in order to determine less the absolute atheism in them than their degree of atheism. For Bayle, given his criterion, atheism was not really an "either-or." Resemblance to the *Ethica* was his most consistent test. Where he could not decide if there were "confusion" or an actual "equation" of God and the creatures, he hesitated to use the damning term. In his article on Jupiter, for example, Bayle noted that Anaximenes and most of the pre-Socratics made God an "immanent cause," a material principle with perpetual movement. This did not distinguish between God and the creatures and was, thus, "at bottom [*au fonds*] Spinozism." Yet he resisted the specific appellation "atheist."[91]

Indeed, whatever Thales' view of God, Bayle, citing Laertius, insisted that Thales "believed that the World was the work of God."[92] The *Histoire des Ouvrages des Savans*, reviewing the *Dictionnaire*, was impressed by Bayle's willingness to go *against* other commentators by presenting Thales as theistic, noting that "there are very few authorities who establish that he [Thales] held this belief [in God as efficient cause], and there are many who give grounds for concluding that he did not hold it."[93] Citing Plutarch on the Stoics, Bayle described them as denying both the eternity and the incorruptibility of the gods, but instead of terming them atheists, he simply noted that "one cannot read without horror what they

[89] Ibid., "Spinoza," passim [IV, 253–71], and rem. A.

[90] Ibid., "Spinoza" and rem. N.

[91] Ibid., "Jupiter," rem. G.

[92] Ibid., "Thales" and rem. A.

[93] *Histoire des Ouvrages des Savans*, nov. 1702, 466–67. This journal, it should be noted, did not see the philosophical sections of Bayle's work as particularly important to the *Dictionnaire*. It observed that "the articles which concern the philosophers are not very numerous, but the majority are quite ample, and contain not only the history of the person, but also the exposition and sometimes even the criticism of his doctrines" (466).

taught concerning the mortality of the Gods."[94] Diogenes of Apollonia, Bayle explained, saw air as the first principle of both matter and divine force, which, he insisted, barely differed from Spinozism, but the difference was enough to limit Bayle's response to a question rather than to a multiplication of atheists: if God is made from air, and effects are less perfect than their causes, how could he have thought his God to be God?[95]

The early atomists, Leucippus and Democritus, may have been illogical about such things, and Democritus may have assigned the term *God* to a Nature that "had neither unity, nor eternity, nor the other attributes which are essential to the divine nature," but, Bayle insisted, atomism was *not* Spinozism. Indeed, he argued, it was far less absurd than the latter, since it maintained "a real distinction among the things that compose the universe," and properly modified by attribution of the creation of the atoms to God, as oriental atomists, he claimed, had done, it could be wholly compatible with theism.[96] In fact, before Epicurus, for Bayle, atomists, by assigning "soul [*ame*]" to atoms, preserved a notion of Intelligence in the formation of things, and it was only with Epicurus and Lucretius that atomism expressed itself as atheism.[97] Far from hunting "high and low," then, for ancient atheists, Bayle followed traditional sources, applied a relatively explicit criterion, and often exonerated or hesitated to label as atheists thinkers thus identified by others.

In discussing the atheists of tradition, Bayle tried to determine whether or not they explicitly had rejected a free, independent God, and he excluded from his list of atheists those whose political explanation of religion had led others to deem them as such. He did not seem particularly eager to find explicit disbelief among them and often equivocated. Rather than terming Critias an atheist, for example, he simply noted that "he has been placed among the number of those who dogmatize against the existence of God," citing Sextus Empiricus and the *De Placitis* as his sources.[98] Protagoras merely made the existence of "the gods" problematic, as opposed to "Diagoras, named 'the Atheist,' " who "denied pure and simple that there were Gods."[99] Theodorus indeed "was a professed atheist," but Bion attached himself to Theodorus only temporarily, and soon became a peripatetic and later quite superstitious.[100] Bayle did not

[94] Bayle, *Dictionnaire*, "Chrysippe" [II, 171–72] and rem. I.

[95] Ibid., "Diogène d'Apollonie" and rems. B and C.

[96] Ibid., "Démocrite" and rems. P and R; "Leucippe" and rem. E.

[97] Ibid., "Epicure" [I, 364–76], and rems. F, G, and L; "Lucrèce," rem. K.

[98] Ibid., "Critias" and rem. H.

[99] Ibid., "Diagoras" and rem. D.

[100] Ibid., "Bion" and rem E. In rem. E, Bayle, commenting on Bion's embrace of religion when ill, noted that "one should not be surprised by this conduct. Almost all those who live

pronounce Prodicus an atheist but merely noted that Sextus Empiricus and Cicero had so classified him because of his view of the origin of religion.[101] In his article on Machiavelli, he remarked that many found *The Prince* atheistic on the same grounds, but he did not agree, claiming that Machiavelli merely had "no religion."[102] Often then, Bayle was *less likely* than many to increase the number of atheistic dissenters from universal consent.

These general tendencies inform his treatment of later philosophy. When he believed he had discerned a resemblance to Spinoza's supposed equation of God and creatures, he could indict almost anyone. Thus, he denounced Abelard's view of universals and the Scotist view of "*universale formale a parte rei*" precisely for their resemblance to Spinoza's monism, insisting that they led to the absurd conclusion that "there is thus only one substance in the universe and all the diversities that we see in the world are only different modifications of this one and the same substance." Thus, "I say that Spinozism is only an extension of this doctrine."[103] Similarly, Cesalpino's particular development of Aristotle, by unifying genus and species, Bayle claimed, was in conformity with Spinoza's doctrine because it destroyed any real distinction between Creator and creatures, and made all things "portions of the substance of God."[104] Even the learned Japanese came "close" to the opinions of Spinoza, since they believed that "there is only one principle of all things," and that this principle was the ubiquitous being of which all things were composed.[105]

---

in irreligion only doubt; they do not arrive at certainty. Thus, finding themselves in the sickbed, where irreligion is no longer of any use to them, they take the safest side."

[101] Ibid., "Prodicus" and rem. G.

[102] Ibid., "Machiavel." We should recall that it was commonplace, indeed virtually universal, for early-modern (and prior) theologians to discuss the usefulness of religion to the order of the state; indeed, one of the considerations that made "atheism" so dreaded was the assumption that the peace and decency of society depended upon belief in God. That was different, of course, from explaining the origins of belief in God by that need, but countless theologians and commentators cited the "political" explanation of religion as proof from "the atheists" themselves that religion was indispensable to mankind. Gabriel Naudé, in his *Considérations politiques sur les coups d'estats* (Paris, 1657), 91–93, saw recognition of the necessity of belief in God to a stable society as part of "the general science of the establishment and conservation of States and Empires." He cited Plato, Aristotle, Cicero, Xenophon, Isocrates, and others, as uncontroversial authors who had recognized that among the "rules received and approved of universally" that were essential to society, one must count "that things do not happen fortuitously nor necessarily; that there is a God, First Author of all things, who cares for them, and who established the rewards of Paradise for the good and the pains of hell for the wicked," etc. For Bayle, it clearly was absurd to describe as "atheistic" someone who shared these common beliefs and saw them as a source of confidence in religious belief.

[103] Ibid., "Abélard," rem. C.

[104] Ibid., "Césalpin," rems. A and C.

[105] Ibid., "Japon" and rem. D.

It is difficult, however, to see such analyses as attempts to identify what Buddeus would term "first-class atheism," rather than as efforts to isolate which philosophical assumptions led by implication to what he saw as a Spinozistic monistic determinism that eliminated the divine from our sense of the world. Having described Spinoza as the first to make an actual atheistic system out of such views, Bayle, it seems clear, was more eager to discern the sources in prior thought of Spinoza's great error than to attribute any intentionally speculative atheism to such "predecessors." The celebrated "Remark A" of the Spinoza article put it plainly enough: although Spinoza *drew from* many ancient and Eastern systems of thought, he was "the first who reduced atheism into a system and made a body of doctrine of it [*le premier qui ait réduit en système l'Athéisme et qui en ait fait un Corp de Doctrine*]."[106]

Where such resemblance to Spinoza was lacking, however, Bayle was always far more ready to exonerate than to convict individuals of atheism. We have seen his refusal to term Machiavelli an atheist. Similarly, it was Aretino's violent attacks on "the disorder of the clergy," not his philosophy, that earned him the false reputation of an atheist.[107] Cardan might often be described as an atheist, but Bayle assured his readers that "I have found in him more of the character of a superstitious man than that of a freethinker [*esprit fort*]," and he cited Samuel Parker as having already seen that clearly.[108] Garasse numbered Charron among the atheists, but there was no basis whatsoever for such an accusation, and he cited the pious abbé de Saint Cyran as someone who had made that clear.[109]

Several savants had argued for the atheism of Mahomet II, the fifteenth-century sultan of the Turks, but from analysis of their accounts, "he was neither an atheist nor an Epicurean."[110] In Bayle's view, the accusation of atheism against Politien was utterly baseless, and despite the accusations against Pomponazzi, it was clear that the latter believed unshakably in the authority of divine Scripture, and that his theological foundations were sincere.[111] Further, it was absurd to accuse of atheism a Hobbes who "sincerely" believed that "there is a God who is the origin of all things," but that "He cannot be enclosed in the sphere of our tiny reason." Far from adding to the number of atheists with Hobbes, Bayle used that article as a platform for an explicit attack against what he himself saw precisely as the absurdity of such a multiplication of disbelievers,

[106] Ibid., "Spinoza," rem. A.

[107] Ibid., "Arétin."

[108] Ibid., "Cardan," rem. D.

[109] Ibid., "Charron," rems. H and I.

[110] Ibid., "Mahomet II" and rem. F.

[111] Ibid., "Politien," rem. K; and "Pomponace" and rems. E, F, and G.

an absurdity that he explicitly identified as a tendency of contemporaneous philosophical criticism. "It is indubitable," he wrote, "that there is no accusation which has fallen into so great an abuse as the accusation of atheism." It had become, he insisted, a charge made by "an infinity of small minds or wicked people" against "all those who limit their affirmations to the great and sublime truths of a great Metaphysics and to the general doctrines of Scripture."[112] Believing himself to possess a clear and purposeful definition of atheism, Bayle consistently had sought to limit such accusations. As he wrote in his *Continuation des Pensées diverses*, for example, in terms scarcely those of the person *responsible* for such a state:

> It is the custom of those who write on the existence of God, or on the divinity of the Gospel, to maintain that impiety runneth over and that a pressing necessity obliges them to stand in opposition to this flood. Be certain that they inflate the matter, that they take for atheists a large number of men who only have proposed some objection with too much vivacity, or who have given themselves license to utter profane jests.[113]

In comparison to many authors, he in fact found little "atheism" in the sixteenth or seventeenth centuries. The number of atheists, he insisted, was not so small as those who insisted on absolute universal consent would have one believe, but it was very far removed indeed from the "multitudes" of atheists that many theologians described.[114] Whatever

[112] Ibid., "Hobbes," rem. M.

[113] Pierre Bayle, *Continuation des Pensées diverses* . . . [first published, Rotterdam, 1705], new ed., corr. (Rotterdam, 1721), III, 257–58. [The *CPD* in this edition comprised vols. III and IV of Pierre Bayle, *Pensées diverses écrites à un docteur de Sorbonne, à l'occasion de la comète qui parut au mois de décembre 1680*, 4 vols. (Rotterdam, 1721), which also included the *Pensées diverses* (I–II, 304), the *Additions* (I, 305–438) and the *Continuation* (III–IV). References to all three of these works will be to that 4-vol. edition.]

[114] Ibid., III, 256–68. Also, on the relative frequency of atheism, see ibid., III, 100–110; and on the relative rarity of atheism see II, 54–62, 91–102. It was not only the theologians, of course, who found "atheism" in so much of sixteenth- and seventeenth-century thought. Among the great anecdotal sources for widespread and indiscriminate charges of atheism were Naudé's accounts of Italian (and other) thought in his amusing tales of Rome. Naudé labeled almost any impiety, doubt about purely rational proof of the immortality of the soul, irreverence, libertinism, or outright love of debauchery atheism and reflected the same sorts of criteria that Garasse and Mersenne had employed. While these were discredited criteria by the more rigorous days of the late seventeenth century, the *Naudaeana et Patiniana, ou singularitez remarquables prises des conversations de Mess. Naudé et Patin*, published with approbation in Paris, 1701 and reissued in Amsterdam, 1703, discussed countless ancient and modern "atheists," including, passim, Borro, Averroes, Cremonius, Machiavelli, Epicurus, Lucretius, Cardan, Pomponazzi, Bembus, Polybius, Cicero, Caesar, Juvenal, Horace, Socrates, Virgil, Euripides, and Boccaccio. The *Patiniana* added, passim, Vanini, Aretino, and diverse "princes, grandees, politicians, men of state, warriors, partisans, and men of wealth" (for the quotation, see ibid. [Paris, 1701], 95–96, or [Amsterdam,

else he was or was not, Bayle was not, and properly knew himself not to be, the source of the early-modern crisis over the *consensus gentium*.

. . .

What Bayle did accomplish, however, was to shock his contemporaries by insisting, explicitly and without equivocation, on the sincerity and good morals of many of those whom he or they saw as atheistic, by defending such judgments as historical fact consistent with sound theology—even after the "dangers" of disseminating such a view had been reiterated to him—and by engaging in a sustained and ever more provocative defense of his criticism of the argument from universal consent. Between Bayle and his critics, the issue of atheism came to center stage at what we shall discover to have been a critical juncture.

There were sincere atheists; some were virtuous; such atheism, though absurd and pitiable, was preferable to superstitious idolatry. There, in a nutshell, is what offended his contemporaries when brought together as an explicit thesis, however much its parts were everywhere. Unimpressed by his critics, Bayle would not concede much to them here. For Bayle, as he explained himself, "things," not "names," mattered, and as long as some thinkers or peoples saw the world as proceeding "by fatality, necessarily," the product of "a cause that acts without any liberty," there clearly was atheism in the world.[115]

Efforts to equivocate about *that*, for Bayle, seemed an absurd fear of simple historical truth and tempted him into arguments that could make his use of *atheism* more capacious than his formal definition. Thus, against the notion that only someone who engaged in a "final perseverance" in atheism until death could be counted against universal consent, Bayle impatiently noted that with such a criterion, we could not know if

1703], 116–17). Reviewing the work, the *Nouvelles de la République des Lettres*, mai 1702, 569–70, noted of Naudé that "the idea he gives us of Italy is not flattering. We learn from him that in his time it was full of libertines, atheists and men who believed nothing." Durand, *La vie de Vanini*, agreed with Bayle that Cardan was superstitious rather than atheistic (18–34) but insisted on Vanini's absolute atheism as "the true key to his pernicious works." For Durand, Vanini's weakness in replying to atheistic objections was purposeful and was not new: he attributed the technique to Carneades, Cicero, Agrippina, and Pomponazzi, among others (37–38). He declared himself amazed that Vanini's *Amphitheatrum* had succeeded in gaining approbations from four theologians, and, declaring his specific agreement with Mersenne's approach to the matter, he deplored the tendency of much modern scholarship to exonerate Vanini of the charge (73–89). Bayle, along with others, he noted, was far too charitable to him (213–58).

[115] Bayle, *Réponse aux questions d'un provincial*, pt. 2, in *OD*, III, pt. 2, 932–34. Pt. 1 of the *Réponse . . .* was first published in Rotterdam, 1704 [1703]; pt. 2 was first published in Rotterdam, 1706 [1705].

anyone were a *theist* until we knew the circumstances of his death, which would *not* strengthen the case for universal consent.[116] Against the notion that only someone who was utterly "certain" in his atheism could be counted, Bayle argued that if you did not believe in a doctrine, you were without the doctrine, and he concluded that "to be not a theist, or [the same thing] an atheist, it is not necessary to affirm that theism is false; it is enough to regard it as a problem."[117]

These provocative formulations attracted attention, but they were not based on any new assertions about what people did or did not believe. When Bayle referred to the travel literature or ancient sources that led him to conclude against universal consent, he did *not* write as someone introducing such works to his audience. "Remark A" of his article on Léry noted precisely that "much attention has been given to a thing that the author observes," namely, the atheism of the Carib Indians.[118] Bayle was matter-of-fact about such topics because he knew his audience to be aware of them. Similarly, he could not understand how anyone still could deny that the examples of Epicurus and Lucretius showed that "atheism is not necessarily united to bad morals [*l'Athéisme n'est pas nécessairement conjoint avec les mauvaises moeurs*]."[119]

. . .

As Bayle frequently would remind his readers, it was the criterion of universal consent, and certainly not the existence of God, that he had raised as a topic in the *Pensées diverses* and in his further replies to his critics. The manifest sequence of his arguments and debates, leaving Bayle's inner self to the gaze of others, confirms such a view and offers yet another example of how assertions made in one context came to influence issues perceived in another. The *Pensées diverses* was ostensibly an attack on what for Bayle was a foolish legacy of pagan superstition within Christendom, the widespread fear of comets as providential ill omens. The only possible support for this opinion of comets, Bayle believed, was the antiquity of and seemingly universal consent to such a view. The target for a critic of such superstition, then, had to be the criterion believed to establish it, universal consent across time and culture, and he proceeded to attack it. If it were a valid criterion, he urged, then, given the history of benighted mankind, it established absurdities that should be abhorrent to

116 Ibid., 690–728.

117 Ibid., 932–34.

118 Bayle, *Dictionnaire*, "Léri," rem. A.

119 Ibid., "Lucrèce," rem. K.

Christian doctrine and critical thought. It was, thus, false that the antiquity or universality of an opinion was a mark of truth.[120]

Against his own specific argument, he presented as a widespread objection the view that "God formed comets so that the pagans would know His providence and not fall into atheism."[121] To resolve *this* "objection," Bayle argued, among other things, that it was theologically absurd to imagine that God intervened in the world merely to replace one "crime" (atheism) with another "crime" (superstitious idolatry).[122] Against the claim that polytheism was superior to atheism and thus worthy of such providential cause, Bayle Christianized Plutarch's thesis and replied with outrage that from both a Christian and a natural moral perspective, atheism was not only no worse than idolatry, but in many ways less heinous and corrupt. Further, he insisted, one could not infer philosophical belief from behavior, as observation of any army of Christian soldiers made plain. While it was perfectly true that corruption of morals could lead to lack of faith, it in no way followed that lack of faith led to corruption of morals (a thesis that he claimed would be theologically dangerous, in fact, extenuating rather than forcing full recognition of the crimes of mankind). There could be wicked believers and virtuous unbelievers.[123] The contest was on!

To support his thesis, Bayle called on the common knowledge of his own culture. If all wickedness were a mark of atheism, then almost all men were atheists, which was absurd and false.[124] He shared precisely the view of the Jansenist Nicole's *Essais de morale*: the virtue necessary to society was not the virtue of grace; self-interest and concupiscence accounted for the basic moral order of fallen mankind; a society of atheists, thus, was in theory possible.[125] If the well-known historical and travel literature were remotely correct, then there existed virtuous atheists.[126] To underline this, he went beyond the narrower definition of atheism operative in the *Dictionnaire*, arguing, in effect, that *from the most pious and irreproachable sources*, atheists often were recognized as men of natural virtue capable of self-sacrifice. "History" showed that "atheists are not distinguished by impurity of morals," and *citing the standard literature*, he named Diagoras, Theodorus, Euhemerus, Hippon, Pliny the El-

[120] Bayle, *Pensées diverses*, I, 1–286.

[121] Ibid., 287–88.

[122] Ibid., 288–92.

[123] Ibid., I, 312–II, 121.

[124] Ibid., I, 379–96,

[125] Ibid., II, 18–54. See the insightful discussion of this theme in Nicole's *Essais de morale* in Dale Van Kley, "Pierre Nicole, Jansenism, and the Morality of Enlightened Self-Interest," in Kors and Korshin, eds., *Anticipations*, 69–85.

[126] Bayle, *Pensées diverses*, II, 54–62, 72–82.

der, Epicurus, Lucretius, Vanini, and Rycaut's Turks, especially their atheistic martyr Mahomet Effendi, to prove his point. He did not want to claim widespread atheism. Indeed, he even specifically referred to his group as "this small number of atheists," but they were sufficient in number, he believed, to establish his general view.[127] There indeed was a voluntary blindness that culminated in a vile, debauched practical atheism. Bayle never challenged that analysis, for he shared it. There also was "an involuntary obscurity of the soul," however, that came from the weakness of mankind and the difficulty of knowing truth, and this occasionally led to a speculative atheism consistent with natural virtue.[128]

. . .

Stunned to find himself accused of atheism for having expressed such views, Bayle, his dander up (that is to say, Bayle), replied to all of his critics, often sharply, and the issues were joined with the sort of passion that attracted the reading public at large. Bayle's *Additions aux Pensées diverses* accused his critics of implying that atheism could be defeated only by miracle and superstition, and reiterated that his "paradox" of an atheism less wicked than idolatry was not intended to apply to the very real category of practical atheism, but only to a speculative atheism that did not acknowledge the existence of God.[129]

The Huguenot edition of the Catholic Renaudot's denunciation of Bayle, interspersed with commentary by Bayle's Huguenot critics, explicitly accused him of either attempting "to establish atheism" in both the *Dictionnaire* and the *Pensées diverses* or, "at the least, of making it pass as equal with all religions."[130] Such charges, and they were widespread, infuriated Bayle, and typical of him, he replied again with yet more (and

[127] Ibid., 54–62, 83–102.

[128] Ibid., 102–6. In ibid., 7–18, Bayle explained his moral theological position quite clearly. Since no natural human persuasion, let alone philosophical belief, was a source of grace, neither natural belief nor philosophy affected the sinful soul. Grace, rather, was "an inner working of the Holy Spirit, so that [one] loves God [*une opération intérieur du Saint Esprit, afin d'aimer Dieu*]." Without it, for Bayle, no intellectual conviction made one more virtuous than a person of different intellectual beliefs. Persuasion of the existence of God was simply categorically distinct from the *love* of God. Surely, for Bayle, if the secular history of Christendom taught anything, it taught that natural human persuasion, even of the highest philosophical kind, was no barrier against the utmost depravities of mankind.

[129] Ibid., 305–403.

[130] Abbé Eusèbe Renaudot et al., *Jugement du Public et particulièrement de M. l'abbé Renaudot sur le Dictionnaire critique du Sr. Bayle* (Rotterdam, 1697), passim. For the quotations, see 11–14 and 33. His sternest critic in this edition, the author of the quotation about establishing atheism, conceded, on 33, that Bayle had undertaken to refute Spinoza, but the critic now complained that there was nothing specifically "Christian" about Bayle's refutation of atheism.

more scholarly) determination. The *Continuation des Pensées diverses* noted that what truly had offended people was his "parallel of atheism and paganism," as if a Christian should care about which was the worse of two absurdities and two errors.[131] His critics had charged, with countless theologians in support, that there could be no sincere atheism. This issue, however, was not a question of revelation and dogma, but a question of history and fact. The argument from universal consent was invalid and thus obviously was of no use to sound theology or philosophy.

To demonstrate this again, he explicitly shared all of Cotta's arguments from *De natura deorum* and declared these confirmed by the vast array of historical, travel, and missionary literature that described sincere atheistic thinkers and peoples.[132] The comparison of idolatry and speculative atheism also was historical, and Léry, Lescarbot, and the whole Chinese rites testimony, he claimed, abundantly and evidently proved his thesis. Surely everyone knew this, he insisted, from accounts of Greece, Rome, Confucianism in general, China in particular, Africa, and the Americas; it was beyond him, he claimed, why any Christian would want to uphold the empirically false view that the superstitious fear of false gods contributed to anyone's good morals, a view which he described as perilously close to the Pelagian heresy.[133]

His defense of his theses only exacerbated the fury of his critics against him, which seemed to amaze him. In his *Réponses aux questions d'un provincial*, he replied again to these critics, reiterating all his prior arguments against universal consent by rehearsing once more the historical evidence for sincere atheism. It was indeed difficult, he noted, to interpret the strange beliefs of strange peoples. Nonetheless, he reminded his read-

131 Bayle, "Avertissement" to *Continuation*, in *Pensées diverses*, III, [unpaginated, i–xxiii].

132 Ibid., III, 25–50, 100–110.

133 Ibid., IV, passim; see especially IV, 98–123, 153–82, 199–229, 561–67. The argument that his opponents' view favored Pelagianism is found on IV, 508–19 (followed by the argument, IV, 520–26, that, apart from that, it simply was *historically* incorrect that fear of false gods contributed to sound morality). Nonetheless, in the *Nouvelles de la République des Lettres*, mars 1705, 325–29, Bernard thought that the proper reply to Bayle was the argument that "the distinction between moral good and evil can be based only on the immutable nature of an intelligent and eternal Being, from which it follows that if there is no such Being, there is no such distinction." The charge of favoring the Pelagian heresy, however, elicited increasingly Baylian concessions from Bernard, who retorted that Bayle's accusation only "would be true, if one maintained that these [good pagan] works were *essentially* good; but those who have taught that the pagans committed [only] *materially* good works without the aid of an efficacious grace never have been accused of Pelagianism." That, of course, was precisely the distinction that Bayle was making with regard to his "atheists." Thus, only a few paragraphs later, Bernard conceded that "it cannot be denied, nonetheless, that Atheists can practice certain virtues and flee certain vices from purely human consideration." Bayle would not have changed a word of that!

ers, it was not he who had created the factual evidence against universal consent; it was others, and he had merely applied their reports to the issue at hand. The *consensus gentium* had been "denied by sober authors [*des Auteurs graves*], who had given us accounts of the new world and . . . of the atheism of several nations discovered in America, in the Orient, and in Africa," accounts, he reminded them, "received as the truth by great theologians of one and the other communion [Catholic and Protestant]." Look at the literature you all know well, Bayle demanded: Jesuits, Dominicans, and other missionaries and travelers on Asia; histories of ancient philosophy; accounts of new discoveries of "a great number of well-populated islands whose inhabitants have no knowledge of the Divinity"; the theologians who have condemned the Ruggieris and Vaninis of not so distant times as atheists. Above all, he demanded, just examine all the well-known literature on China![134] As he wrote to a correspondent in 1698, his critics had to be willing to ignore "those facts, that I have found in books, and that the laws of history obliged me to report," facts that "indeed do no harm to the true religion."[135] Among those "books," some were virtual manuals and handbooks of the learned world, most were impeccably orthodox, and many had attracted intense commentary and discussion. Bayle was indeed their faithful "reporter."

Nonetheless, he provoked a firestorm of criticism, leading to an ongoing explication, refutation, and, thus, advertisement of his views in the popular journals. Again, the thinkability of atheism was made clear to the reading public at large in the context of debates of wonderful drama. The response of the journals to the culmination of Bayle's exchanges with his critics, the publication of part 2 of the *Réponse aux questions d'un provincial* and of diverse hostile replies, was truly singular. Normally, works received one or at most two *extraits* and *comptes rendus*, and fifteen to twenty pages thus devoted would indicate extremely serious review. The *Nouvelles de la République des Lettres*, however, indeed edited by one of Bayle's critics, Jacques Bernard, devoted the following attention to Bayle's positions on atheism, idolatry, and universal consent: in 1705, articles in two of the monthly issues, totaling 94 pages; in 1706, articles in three issues, totaling 99 pages; and in 1707 (among other articles, not counted here, that dealt with other issues raised by Bayle or his critics), articles in seven issues, totaling 227 pages![136]

[134] Bayle, *OD*, III, pt. 2, 690–728, 918–88. His most vivid use of missionary literature is found in ibid., 925–30 where, from a widely available Jesuit source, he added up "eighty-seven" islands whose inhabitants were described as having no knowledge of God at all.

[135] Bayle, *Lettres*, II, 710.

[136] *Nouvelles de la République des Lettres*, fév. 1705, 123–53; mars 1705, 284–348; jan. 1706, 49–77; fév. 1706, 153–87; oct. 1706, 389–426; jan. 1710, 5–33; fév. 1707, 139–74; mars 1707, 256–90; avril 1707, 406–42; mai 1707, 532–51; juin 1707, 636–67; sept.

In one sense, it is tempting to hypothesize that France was exposed to so much of this debate because it avidly read erudite journals originating in a French community in Holland that took its local enfant terrible so seriously. The behavior of the Jesuit *Journal de Trévoux*, however, belies this. Generally, the Jesuit journal gave much briefer accounts of works than Bernard's journal, but it devoted a great deal of attention to Bayle and his foes. In 1705, it demonstrated the deep interest of Catholic France in all this by devoting articles in its issues of June and of July to Bayle's arguments, totaling 45 pages; in 1706, it devoted articles in three consecutive issues to these, totaling 63 pages; in 1707, it did the same in two consecutive issues, totaling 52 pages.[137] Whatever the criticism leveled against Bayle in all of these articles, both journals, as usual, fulfilled their primary obligation to their readers with distinction, providing clear and quite accurate explications both of Bayle's views and of the grounds on which he reached these.

The reviews were not without their interesting ironies. Examine, for example, the lengthy review in the *Journal de Trévoux* of July 1705. In the part of the *compte rendu* that dealt with alleged "virtuous atheists," the *Journal* nominally denied their existence but did so either with extreme equivocation or, indeed, with manifest self-contradiction. Thus, after claiming that it could "challenge almost all his examples," the review argued that "it is not certain that Diagoras was an atheist," and, concerning Buddha, that "since he hid his atheism until the time of his death, perhaps he hid his true views of morality similarly." It conceded the heart of things, however: "Nonetheless, one must agree that the lettered of China join an excellent morality to atheism and that Pliny and Spinoza have offered some beautiful precepts of virtue, and that the Epicureans . . . spoke of morals with much exactitude."[138] In a part of that same re-

1707, 286–330. (When the *early-modern* learned world took something seriously, it didn't dash off a three-page book review two years after a due date! *O tempora! o mores!*)

[137] *Journal de Trévoux*, juin 1705, 919–38; juillet 1705, 1095–1121; mai 1706, 764–83; juin 1706, 950–71; juillet 1706, 1110–23; sept. 1707, 1489–1526; oct. 1707, 1737–52. In the May 1706 review (781–83), the reviewer, momentarily (but never consistently) adamant about the impossibility of atheism, defended Spinoza and "the Spinozists" from Bayle's charge of atheism, averring that they "were wrong only about the essence of God and are in agreement with the human race about His existence," specifying that any recognition of a first efficient cause of any kind whatsoever kept one from atheism. In general, the reviewers of *both* journals tried to advance two rather paradoxical theses: first, that speculative atheism both did not exist and that it was worse than idolatry; two, that there was a universal consent to the existence of God that was threatened by criticism of the argument from universal consent. Bayle, of course, in everything he wrote, derived satisfaction from that embarrassment of his critics. In this particular instance, he noted (*OD*, III, pt. 2, 937–43), that he found their defense of Spinoza both remarkable and in contradiction of their own uses of the term atheist.

[138] *Journal de Trévoux*, juillet 1705, 1116–18.

view criticizing the Cartesian proofs of God that Bayle had urged as more than sufficient alternatives to proof by universal consent, it asked how these ever would change the mind of "the Chinese atheists" or the "atheism" of a Strato.[139] Significantly, when it turned its attention to the specific question of whether idolatry was worse than atheism, the *Journal de Trévoux*, with great honesty, shared its recognition that Bayle merely had repeated what so many orthodox voices had proclaimed:

> He produces a long series of authors who spoke as he did. This list begins with Arnobius and ends with Saint Augustine: their texts formally contain the propositions for which Bayle has been reproached. This host of witnesses must embarrass his accusers, of whatever sect they are; for among the authors cited, there are ancient Fathers of the Church, Catholic theologians, Protestant ministers, philosophers, historians. M. Bayle uses to great profit places where Saint Jerome spoke of heresy as the greatest of all crimes; he even utilized passages in which learned Catholic and Protestant theologians guaranteed that it was better to be an atheist than a Calvinist.[140]

The *Nouvelles de la République des Lettres*, in a review in 1707, found threatening theological implications indeed in Bayle's thesis and, in explicating them, took its readers far beyond any assessment that Bayle himself ever had urged. Bayle had argued that the reality of speculative atheists was a settled matter of fact. His critic, however, argued (as he also had done in 1705) that if Bayle were correct that a philosopher could conclude for atheism sincerely, then it followed necessarily "*that the question 'is there a God' is among the number of those that surpass by far human capacities; that someone can employ all his forces, examine the arguments of the one side and the other without prejudice, and nevertheless conclude in favor of atheism.* . . . I have absolutely denied this principle."[141]

[139] Ibid., 1104–7.

[140] Ibid., 1097–98. Although Bayle replied to every important criticism offered by the Jesuit journal, he clearly was touched by the critical candor of its reviews and by its concessions. In pt. 2 of the *Réponse*, in *OD*, III, pt. 2, 920–25, he noted that "the Jesuits who write the *Mémoires de Trévoux* spoke of the *Continuations des Pensées diverses* with a critical spirit; nevertheless, they recognized that these authors attested to the same thing as Mr. Bayle." In 1719, the Jesuit Baltus, who wished to maintain the argument from universal consent, specifically addressed the issue of the many patristic attributions of explicit atheism to Greek philosophers or schools; according to Baltus, those who thought as he did wanted to say that such attributions were due to "the heat of dispute," but the problem, he averred inconclusively, was that "the Holy Fathers everywhere evidence their care not to exaggerate anything." See Jean-François Baltus, S.J., *Jugement des SS. Pères sur la morale de la philosophie payenne* (Strasbourg, 1719), 30–32.

[141] *Nouvelles de la République des Lettres*, jan. 1707, 13–15. See also ibid., mars 1705, 291ff.

This was fine if one agreed that the evidence of the question was a "principle," but not so reassuring if one had to deal with the consequences of Bayle's "fact." Two months later, thus, when reviewing a section of Bayle's *Réponses* that confronted him with a great array of citations and accounts about sincere speculative atheists, the same reviewer confessed that "I admit that I am not clever enough to sort out all of this chaos" and declared that "I am not very interested in the question of if there are purely speculative atheists."[142] Given what he had said two months earlier, however, it was a question of extraordinary importance.

. . .

For Bayle, as he said explicitly time and time again, the reality of speculative and even virtuous atheism was *not* a question of great import for the issue of belief in God, since the criticism of the argument from universal consent was merely the useful elimination of one illogical and factually incorrect argument from the large number available to the theologian or philosopher. While he grounded his belief in almost all of religious truth upon faith in God's revelation, however, Bayle never had grounded belief in God Himself in the supernatural. As he had argued in his *Theses*, belief in God was a prerequisite of belief in Scripture, since the latter was believed only because it was the Word of God: "Knowledge of divine existence thus precedes knowledge of this revelation, and is presupposed by it, from which it follows that it comes from natural light."[143] Natural light, however, was compelling here, and he frequently referred his readers to other (often Descartes's) proofs. Eliminate the flawed attempted demonstration from the *consensus gentium*, a demonstration unworthy of Christian philosophy, and there remained, he believed, many proofs from which to choose.[144]

The faith, however, as Bayle himself had noted in the *Pensées diverses* and in his *Dictionnaire* article on Zabarella, neither prescribed nor proscribed any particular philosophical path to natural knowledge of God. This worked in two ways: the Christian was free to accept what proofs of God he found compelling; he also was free to criticize and reject what proofs of God he found flawed. As Bayle observed, great theologians and philosophers often had refuted each other's demonstrations, not to establish atheism, but to establish the best possible proofs of God. Indeed, Bayle noted in defending his attack on the proof from universal consent, contemporary learned journals showed that the most devout theologians

[142] Ibid., mars 1707, 258.

[143] Bayle, *Theses philosophiques*, in *OD*, IV, 143–44.

[144] See, for example, his *Systema Totius Philosophiae*, in ibid., 479–82 and 516–19; and *Pensées diverses*, III, 249–57.

of differing philosophical persuasions could reject each other's proofs of God with great intensity and never have their faith or motives called into question.[145] He was correct. What he did not see, however, was precisely how such debates and mutual refutations, especially when they were so popular as to reach the journals, might well erode the belief of at least some readers in God. What if one found all of the well-intentioned mutual refutations of the dialectically skilled and learned equally compelling?

Which brings us, aware of context now, to one of the central dramas of this work. If, as much of the orthodox culture itself taught, belief in God was not a universal principle of all mankind, but, rather, was a necessary philosophical preamble to the faith, subject to "objections" and doubts, then it was the vital task of philosophy or philosophical theology to establish His existence beyond the possibility of sincere and rational disbelief. It was licit, however, to disagree about how that should be done. From this, before the largest reading public the Western world ever had known, in an age increasingly committed to *évidence*, there emerged the mutual fratricide of a Christian learned world philosophically divided over the proper means of demonstrating the single most essential element of the creed. The refutations employed or indeed generated by that great fratricide became the preamble of early-modern atheism in France. Such atheism could not emerge confident, explicit, expressive of the criteria of its culture, and in search of alternative conceptualizations of the world *without a belief that the demonstrations arrayed against it were not compelling*. It was only after such a mutual destruction by the orthodox themselves that the author of one of the earliest clandestine atheistic manuscripts could write so self-assuredly of "a First Being of whom we have no proof."[146]

[145] Bayle, *Pensées diverses*, III, 249–57; *Dictionnaire*, "Zabarella," rem. G.

[146] Bibliothèque de l'Arsenal, MSS. 2558, #2, 101–2.

PART THREE

The Fratricide

Chapter Eight

THE GREAT CONTEST

We turn now not to Aristotle and Descartes, but to the behavior and beliefs of those who embodied their systems diversely in one particular time and place. It is our concern here to discern early-modern Aristotelian and Cartesian schools of thought as historical entities and actors, not as philosophical "ideal types." By the latter term, I mean the interpretations of Aristotle and Descartes that philosophers today find most consistent with their own analyses of the inherent logic of Aristotle or Descartes. Such analyses may be essential to ongoing *philosophical* debate, but the capacity of systems of thought to undergo diverse mutations and outright metamorphoses is so manifest a reality that logical analysis simply cannot replace empirical inquiry in intellectual history. Thus, we seek to understand the behavior of the learned world of the late seventeenth and early eighteenth centuries rather than to adjudicate in any way among competing interpretations of Aristotle or Descartes. Our concern is with how that learned world read and understood authors, and with how it thought and debated from what it took to be Aristotelian and Cartesian perspectives. Above all, we are concerned here with the nature and consequences, in early-modern perspective, of the great Aristotelian-Cartesian debates of the second half of the seventeenth century, and, the true object of our inquiry, the effects of these upon the emergence of disbelief.

If the debates did not turn on matters of such extraordinary substance as how the human mind ought to understand, structure, and transmit its experience of the world in which it found itself, it might be tempting to see the great Aristotelian-Cartesian contest of early-modern France simply as a struggle for eminence, influence, and institutional power among clerks and philosophers of competing schools. In its deepest terms, however, it was nothing less than a contest for a status in which the highest ideal aspirations and the rawest ambitions touched and reinforced each other: the right to teach others in the name of Christendom. Catholic Aristotelians and Catholic Cartesians shared the same creed—although at times they barely could concede *that*—but they faced each other across a philosophical divide that so many of them believed could not be bridged.

Their Church, their universities, their collèges, their seminaries, their religious orders, their texts, their instruction of the world, so many seemed to believe, had to be on one or the other side of that divide. That was why their debates were not only about metaphysics and physics, but about the Eucharist, about the patristics, and about the institutions, responsible positions, and sinecures of the Church and learned world. Aristotelian-Cartesian contestation, as a historical phenomenon, both arose from and evoked some of the deepest philosophical, theological, religious, and institutional tensions in the Christian, and, more specifically, French Catholic world. Their debates both reflected and drew upon ancient philosophical, theological, and attitudinal divisions: Platonists versus Aristotelians; rationalist versus empiricist impulses; Augustinian versus Thomistic tendencies.[1] The emergence of Malebranchism from Cartesian thought only exacerbated the intensity of the disagreements. As ever, skeptics and fideists observed and commented, often using the arguments of each side against the other, to advance their own claims about the impotence of human reason (and, in the case of the fideists, about the consequent need to rely upon faith for the grounds of belief). Their debates also reflected and drew upon the most divisive contemporary religious differences: Jansenist versus Thomist versus Molinist. They also reflected and became enmeshed in the most intense institutional rivalries: Jesuits versus Oratorians or Benedictines; the University of Paris versus the provincial universities or the groupings of philosophers and savants outside the university structures. Aristotelians and Cartesians, in short, struggled for nothing less than the soul and mind of France, and for the satisfactions and rewards of winning that struggle. We shall narrow our focus to their debates about proving the existence of God, but we should understand that these were the effect, not the cause, of deeper and broader divisions.

Both camps believing, on the whole, that there could be only one victor between them, they each sought in their polemics to deliver the coup de grace to their rivals. How better to deliver that than to demonstrate that one's opponents could not satisfy the most minimal of the essential roles of Christian thinkers, the defeat of "the atheist"? Having created the theoretical model of their antithesis from the history of philosophy and from the "objections" of their own minds, they invited him along on their debates, taunting each other with the charge of incapacity to overcome the imagined archenemy. When the dust from their seventeenth-century and early eighteenth-century debates had settled, they discovered that not only did they face the deistic Voltaires and Montesquieus of the Enlightenment contesting the Church's collective right to teach the world, but that their archenemy himself had come to life, not discovered any longer

[1] There is a particularly interesting view of the affinity of Augustinians for Descartes and the Cartesians (and vice versa) in Henri Gouhier, *Cartésianisme et Augustinisme au XVIIe siècle* (Paris, 1978).

by *their* sense of implication, but declaring himself explicitly, without ambiguity, equivocation, or even linguistic concession. Ironically, but, if one thinks on it, quite naturally, that archenemy borrowed every weapon that Christian Aristotelian and Christian Cartesian ever had turned against each other. Given the dialectical skills of both schools, it was an arsenal! Between them, Aristotelians and Cartesians offered large numbers of demonstrations of the existence of God that for each exponent established the *praeambulae fidei*. Between them, in their mutual assaults, in texts published with imprimatur and royal privilege, they offered, in an age in which formal *évidence* mattered critically, widespread grounds for rejecting every one of these.

. . .

Aristotle's notions of causality are not unhelpful here, at least metaphorically, in understanding the role played by Aristotelian-Cartesian debate about each other's proofs of God in the emergence of disbelief. As Aristotle had taught, to have an entity, a bronze statue, for example, you need four things. There must be a matter capable of being a statue, in this case the bronze, the material cause, the *materia* of which the statue in fact can be made. There must be a specific form in which the bronze can occur, in this case the statue, the formal cause, the *forma* in which the bronze can realize one of its many possibilities. In addition, there must be something to actualize the form from the material, in this case, the sculptor and his tools, the efficient or proximate cause, the *efficacitas* that makes the possibility actual. Finally, there must be a reason, purpose, or motive that leads the sculptor to act as efficient cause, in this case the desire for art, glory, or commission, the *teleos* or final cause (the end, the *finis*) of its being. The creation of "objections," the recovery and consideration of ancient texts and commentary, and the consideration of universal consent all had given early-modern France the *materia* and the *forma* of a negation of belief in God, the material for atheism and the shape that material might assume. What brought the form out of that material? What, as an Aristotelian would ask, was the efficient or proximate cause by which that *potentia* of the Western mind came into actuality? Let me offer one explanation that, at the least, grounds the emergence of atheism in the dynamics of the learned culture in which it actually occurred, including its notions of *évidence* and of the logical sequence of Christian theistic belief: the mutual destruction of Christian philosophical theology. It is also an explanation that may allow us to make new sense of the content and definition of issues in the texts of eighteenth-century French atheism. Without understanding the toll of Christian theological fratricide, we cannot understand in context how it became possible for minds to be "a-theistic," without theism, unpersuaded by any claims that "God exists." The great debate educed, in certain minds, the *évidence* for disbelief. As for *teleos*, we leave that for another day.

• • •

As the seventeenth century itself knew, such contestations over proofs of God were certainly not new in the history of Christian theology. Some of the most celebrated doctors of the Church, including Saint Thomas Aquinas, Duns Scotus, William of Ockham, Nicolas d'Autrecourt, Henry of Ghent, Cardinal Pierre d'Ailly, and other widely respected theologians and commentators had established and perpetuated a long and venerable tradition of dialectical, philosophical, and theological criticisms of particular or general modes of demonstration of God's existence. The most theologically learned in the early-modern world even knew of major theologians who had argued in diverse contexts that such proof could not be accomplished and was utterly unessential to Christian peace of mind or soul, and who indeed had been condemned for such "fideistic" views.[2]

Such debates, however, had been both brief and circumspect asides in the course of such men's diverse theological and philosophical concerns, and, essentially, *intra muros*, among the theologians themselves. They had been of limited concern to the more circumscribed lay cultures of their times, and, on the whole, not subject to widespread dissemination and discussion. They certainly did not occur amid widespread considerations of the "problem" of atheism or in cultures tempted by the priority of natural knowledge—even when they believed that knowledge to lead with certainty to God—over religious experience. To say the very least, none of those circumstances that mitigated the broad influence of such contestations still obtained by the second half of the seventeenth century. It was a different, broader, and inexhaustibly curious reading public before which the new debates occurred. It also was a different kind of a contest, a very public brawl fought *extra muros*, and it drew this public to the great theological fratricide that such mutual contestation now entailed. To understand the contest, we also must understand the context.

Some minds found much to profit from in both the Aristotelian and the Cartesian traditions, and some men tried, in vain, to keep the peace between the two Christian philosophical camps. Not even Bossuet himself, however, could accomplish that. There is much that could be written

[2] I am smitten by the parenthetical observation on this by Anthony Flew, *The Presumption of Atheism and Other Philosophical Essays on God, Freedom and Immortality* (London, 1976), 36: "(No one, it seems, told them that the belief in the possibility of natural theology was going to become an essential part of their religion)."

about those widespread irenic philosophical efforts, for they represent very major strains of early-modern thought. For many theologians—and the account that follows should not make one lose sight of this—the diversity and abundance of proofs of God offered by the various philosophical camps in Christian theology was a great benefit, and something to be celebrated.[3] For most who chose to write on such matters, however, mutually exclusive choices had to be made.

For countless authors and readers, of course, the immediacy of early-modern religious experience made the whole discussion of proper proofs irrelevant to belief, or, indeed, distasteful. We are not examining how a whole culture came to disbelief (it did not), but only how it became possible for some minds that were products of that culture to reach the conclusion that God did not exist, and to do so in a manner that they deemed consistent with that culture's criteria of proper assent or negation. For some, indeed, the whole marriage of theology and philosophy was inconsummate and should be annulled. For so many readers, however, the great debates and the claims of mutual exclusivity were more riveting than either peacemaking or calls to disdain such efforts, and, for our purposes, such debates and claims were a vital agency of change. Minds came to adulthood in an intellectual world sharply polarized between two primary conflicting visions of appropriate philosophical language, conception, and demonstration. They were asked to consider the most fundamental issues in the light of that division, and, by each camp, to reject each other's proofs of God. To understand their dilemmas, we must understand that polarization. It had its deep intellectual sides; it had its personal and institutional sides as well.

Intellectually, it is by no means clear that a polarized rather than eclectically syncretic Christian philosophical voice had to emerge from the Cartesian encounter with Scholastic philosophical theology. As Gilson has shown, Cartesians and Scholastics shared far, far more than they (or their chroniclers) were prepared to concede, even in their proofs of God.[4] It is differences among strong and proud minds, however, not similarities, that have a way of dominating intellectual (and other) encounters. Besides, as Bayle always argued, behavior, to say the least, does not always

[3] See, for example, Diroys, *Preuves et préjugez*, who used them all and clearly felt that there were enough proofs to satisfy members of all philosophical schools. Bossuet, Fénélon, and bishop Jean-Claude Sommier were equally eclectic in their demonstrations of God.

[4] Etienne Gilson, *Index Scolastico-Cartésien* (Paris, 1912); *Etudes sur le rôle de la pensée médiévale dans la formation du système cartésien* (Paris, 1930); *L'Athéisme difficile* (Paris, 1979), 54–58. Gilson, in the last work, argued plausibly, after logical analysis of Thomistic demonstrations, that in Aquinas's a posteriori proofs, "there is thus foreknowledge of God anterior to the proofs." That may be, but that was *not* how it appeared to most of his seventeenth-century disciples.

follow the theoretical logic of speculation. The bitterness of philosophical rivalry crystallized, exaggerated, and hardened differences, and led to widespread mutual recriminations, including, from each school's perspective, the charge that its antagonist could not establish the preamble of the faith. The coexistence of Aristotelian and Cartesian in early-modern France was not peaceful.

. . .

As indicated by the very name for Christian, generally Thomistic Aristotelians, "the Scholastics" or "Schoolmen" had dominated precisely the formal institutions of learning in Catholic Europe, and, certainly, in France. The intensity and the stakes of Aristotelian-Cartesian encounter reveal themselves most clearly in the Scholastic effort to repress any challenges to that status. In the sixteenth and early seventeenth centuries, Aristotelian Scholastics saw themselves as the sole guardians and propagators of philosophical and theological rigor, orthodoxy, tradition, and common sense in a learned world that they believed to be in danger of losing its solid moorings in received science and wisdom. From that sense of things, they believed themselves to have manned the ramparts courageously and triumphantly against wild Platonists, magicians, radical mystics, alchemists, Pyrrhonists, astrologers, neo-Pythagoreans, excessively naturalistic Averroists, and diverse incoherent innovators or renewers of ancient errors. They even had stemmed the Huguenot tide and preserved a Catholic France. The last great challenge before Descartes had been Ramus, and the Scholastics, it appeared, had won. Aristotle seemed, on the surface, more firmly entrenched than ever before in the curriculum and official texts of the learned world.[5]

Through a combination of polemic, institutional advantage, repression, victories at Trent, linkage of "innovation" or ancient revival with "heresy," and even (as with Vanini or Bruno) an occasional exemplary burning at the stake, the Scholastics maintained their official control over intellectual life. The dissatisfactions with and perceived restraints or limits of Scholastic thought never could be eliminated, however, and the sev-

[5] Again, just for the pleasure of citing someone who put it so well, here is C. B. Schmitt's reminder, to students of early-modern skeptical revival, of the perspective they should not forget. C. B. Schmitt, "The Rediscovery of Ancient Skepticism," in *The Skeptical Tradition*, ed. Miles Burnyeat (Berkeley, 1983), 240: "Moreover—and this needs to be emphasized—the continuity of the Aristotelian tradition was of such vigor that it remained the dominant philosophy of Western Europe until at least the second half of the seventeenth century. Skepticism did come increasingly into its own during the period separating Montaigne and Bayle, but it represented a mere trickle alongside the veritable flood of Aristotelian doctrine."

enteenth century would generate a great diversity of further challenges. Above all, there was Descartes, and, what gave him his importance, there were those who claimed to find both *scientia* and *sapientia* in his works. As the Carthusian monk and scholar Alexis Gaudin recounted it, the Ramist challenge to Aristotelianism had created great disturbances in the world of Christian thought and education, but authority overcame innovation, and the Ramist "sect" did not persist. "Thus," Gaudin wrote, "one remained with Aristotle, until Descartes appeared."[6]

In 1705, the Scholastic philosopher Jean Du Hamel published a collection of all prior formal condemnations of Cartesian philosophy, reminding his audience that each still remained in place. The *Quaedam recentiorum philosophorum ac praesertim Cartesii propositiones damnatae ac prohibitae* was both published separately and bound into his anti-Cartesian course on Aristotelian philosophy, the *Philosophia universalis.*[7] It was a compilation of a whole series of anathemas against, prohibitions and censures of, and (coerced) agreements not to teach Cartesian philosophy, and, above all, not to teach it in any area where it disagreed in any way with Scholastic doctrines. Most of these documents had been disseminated in the vernacular as well. These efforts to suppress the Cartesian alternative had linked it with Calvinist views of the Eucharist, with Jansenism, and with errors in metaphysics and physics that endangered the foundations of the faith. The condemnation of Descartes, he argued explicitly, was not simply a question of philosophy, but a question of law.[8]

Although Du Hamel's collection began with a sequence of medieval condemnations that he claimed convicted the Cartesians implicitly, it quickly turned to a recapitulation and full provision of the texts of the seventeenth century's use of *force majeure* in matters philosophical.[9] First, there was control of Paris; then, control of other universities and of religious congregations whose members had been drawn towards Carte-

[6] Alexis Gaudin, Carthusian, *Abrégé de l'histoire des sçavans, anciens et modernes* (Paris, 1708), 260–68.

[7] Jean Du Hamel, *Quaedam recentiorum philosophorum ac praesertim Cartesii propositiones damnatae ac prohibitae* (Paris, 1705). (It also was bound into the fifth volume of his *Philosophia universalis, sive Commentarius in universam Aristotelis philosophiam, ad usum scholarum comparatam*, 5 vols. [Paris, 1705].) Du Hamel had taught philosophy at the collège du Plessis and was now a "professeur émérite" of the University of Paris, and, at the time of this publication, canon of Notre Dame. [He should not be confused with Jean-Baptiste Duhamel, also a philosopher, who wrote a *Philosophia Vetus et Nova.*]

[8] Ibid., 1.

[9] Ibid., 2–7, where he presents the condemnations of 1277 as directed against giving philosophy priority over theology and against neglect of the supernatural, both of which he believed were essential to Cartesianism. He also saw Descartes as implicated in various fourteenth- to sixteenth-century condemnations of Averroism. Since each of the seventeenth-century documents that he presents constitutes a discrete text, I shall footnote them separately for anyone who might wish to cite them.

sian thought. In 1624, the Faculty of Theology of Paris had condemned all criticism of "Aristotle's doctrines [as] commonly received."[10] In 1662, the Faculty of Theology of Louvain had condemned what it took to be gross Cartesian errors that led to "atheism."[11] In 1671, the Faculty of Theology at Paris repeated its condemnation of Descartes and specifically forbade the teaching of Cartesian theories of substance.[12] In 1673, the dean of the Faculty of Medicine at Paris proclaimed the same ban, which was confirmed by the faculty senate.[13] In 1675, the crown, or, more precisely, the *conseil d'état*, itself had responded to Scholastic requests and imposed upon the University of Angers the same prohibition against "the teaching of the opinions and sentiments of Descartes." Following this command that Cartesianism not be taught there "in any way or manner whatsoever," the officers of the entire university had joined in such a condemnation.[14] In that same year, the Benedictines of the influential Maurist congregation at Saint-Germain-des-Près officially were instructed that they "must abstain from teaching the new [Cartesian] opinions" in metaphysics and physics.[15] In 1677, the Faculty of Theology at Caen was placed under the same ban.[16] In 1678, the august Congregation of the Oratory was coerced into an agreement to cease and desist from all teaching of Jansenism and Cartesianism, including Descartes's principles in all philosophy, from physics to metaphysics.[17] In 1678, the same agreement was forced upon the Congregation of Sancta Genovefae in all of France: no Jansen; a return to Saint Thomas; and an order explicitly forbidding Génovéfain philosophers from "teaching the opinions of Descartes."[18] In 1691, the rector and the professors of philosophy at Paris agreed to refrain from Cartesian logic, physics, and metaphysics.[19] In 1693, the eminent société de Sorbonne reiterated its insistence that students never be taught new doctrines that usurped the authority of Aristotle.[20] In 1704 and 1705, the professors of philosophy at the Faculty of Arts at Paris renewed their acceptance of the royal ban against Cartesian philosophy, including explicit agreement never to depart from the doctrine that, *contra* Descartes, spirit had extension.[21] Needless to say, such bans indicate that *both* camps had broad support.

[10] Ibid., 7–11.
[11] Ibid., 11–15.
[12] Ibid., 15–18.
[13] Ibid., 19–21.
[14] Ibid., 22–27.
[15] Ibid., 28–29.
[16] Ibid., 29–30.
[17] Ibid., 30–31.
[18] Ibid., 32.
[19] Ibid., 33–34.
[20] Ibid., 35.
[21] Ibid., 43–45.

The condemnation of 1691 in Paris attributed to the Cartesians "intolerable" opinions that related directly to proof of God. Descartes's argument that doubt should precede conviction by *évidence* was paraphrased as follows by its Scholastic censurers: "One *must* doubt if there is a God until one has clear knowledge of it [*Il faut douter s'il y a un Dieu, jusqu'à ce qu'on en ait une claire connoissance*]." More revealing, perhaps, of the implications of Cartesian-Aristotelian debate was another proposition that the Scholastics claimed to find in Cartesian philosophy: "One should reject all the arguments which theologians and philosophers have utilized until now with St. Thomas to demonstrate that there is a God."[22] As Eustache Le Noble noted, however, in his *Uranie, ou les tableaux des philosophes* (enjoying its widest circulation with the publication of his *Oeuvres* in 1718), the edicts, the power of the University of Paris, and the great credit enjoyed by Aristotelian doctrine were *not* "a sufficient restraint."[23] Most Cartesians or Malebranchists who signed agreements to abide by such bans clearly felt under no rightful obligation to what they saw as intolerable and inappropriate coercion of purely philosophical belief.

In the 1680s, theologians such as Charles-Joseph de Troyes and the Jesuit La Ville revived (or, more accurately, kept boisterously alive) the old accusation that Descartes's metaphysics was incompatible with the mystery of the Eucharist, the former attempting to transform the issue into a question of outright heresy.[24] Observing from Holland, but always

[22] Ibid., 33–34. See also Jourdain, *Histoire de l'Université de Paris*, I, 445–50. The Cartesian and Jansenist priest Adrien Baillet, *Auteurs déguisés* (Paris, 1690), 285–86, understood full well how "individuals" gave their opinions "a so much greater weight" by having them voiced by "entire Faculties of a university."

[23] Eustache Le Noble (baron de Saint-Georges et Tonnelière), *Uranie, ou les tableaux des philosophes*, in *Les Oeuvres de M. Le Noble*, 19 vols. (Paris, 1690–1718), XVI, 294–300. As was the case with virtually all anti-Aristotelians, Le Noble stressed (ibid., 293) that "the first Fathers of the Church, and with them all Christians who had some science, had been Platonists."

[24] Père Charles-Joseph de Troyes [Tricassino], *La philosophie de Monsieur Descartes contraire à la foy catholique, avec la réfutation d'un imprimé fait depuis peu pour sa défense* (Paris, 1682); Louis de La Ville [Le Valois], S.J., *Sentiments de M. Descartes touchant l'essence et les propriétés du corps, opposés à la doctrine de l'Eglise et conformes aux erreurs de Calvin sur le sujet de l'Eucharistie* (Paris, 1680). Despite the titles, it was Charles-Joseph de Troyes, who published extensively on St. Augustine, who suggested intentional heresy and La Ville who stressed simply the consequences of Descartes's ontology. Charles-Joseph de Troyes (*Philosophie de Descartes*, 40) wrote that the only way to be both a Catholic and a Cartesian was to believe that something could be "false according to Faith but true according to philosophy," a position which, he reminded his readers, the Church unambiguously had rejected for centuries. In an unpaginated "Préface historique," he arrayed the sixteenth-century Lateran Council under Pope Leo X, the 1678 ban against Oratorian Cartesianism, and the bans of the Universities of Caen, Angers, and Paris, among other prohibitions, against what he took to be the heart of Cartesian philosophical doctrine. La Ville (*Sentiments de Descartes*, 89) wrote, with some moderation (but giving us some sense of more

well-informed about France, Bayle wrote of a kind of "Inquisition" by the Scholastics against the disciples of Descartes and published a series of essays on and chronicles of the Aristotelian-Cartesian wars. According to Bayle, he had to fill in the French public about these, since anxious *approbateurs* had become loathe to approve of anything on the topic during such a period, were holding manuscripts for three or four years, and were ordering authors "to suppress what [the authors] most esteem in [their] writings."[25]

In addition to many pieces dealing with the Eucharist and Cartesian metaphysics, Bayle offered his avid readers the full text of the "Concordat between the Jesuits and the Fathers of the Oratory," the humiliating cover letter to the king in which the Oratorians promised to accept Aristotle and to refrain from "attaching [ourselves] to the new doctrine of M. Descartes," and a commentary on the whole affair. In the letter from the Oratorian superior Sainte-Marthe to Louis XIV, the congregation agreed to a most specific restraint in matters of metaphysical theology. It would not seek to prove the existence of God from His essential attribute of perfection, the Cartesian mode par excellence (so to speak), but would establish His existence prior to any discussion of His attributes: "In Metaphysics, *after* having proven the existence of God, one can make it obvious by necessary consequences what are His attributes." It further accepted the obligation to do this "without treating of any [attribute] in particular, nor going beyond that in matters of theology."[26] In anonymous commentary on the "Concordat," the reader was assured that if the Oratorians had not agreed to it, "the King . . . was ready to remove their collèges from them."[27]

Textbooks may describe a Scholasticism in retreat and a Cartesianism in the ascendancy by the late seventeenth century, but such a view would have sounded odd to the Oratory in the 1680s. As the commentator noted: "They surrendered, thus, both to please the King and to avoid and protect themselves from the storm that threatens them. . . . It is thus the

common tones) that "it is not my intention to fly into a rage against M. Descartes here, or to accuse him of atheism, impiety, or wild folly, as his adversaries do every day with more passion than reason. . . . [Whatever dangers some of his specific arguments pose to the faith] he elsewhere has evidenced so much submission to the Church that one indeed has the right to say that he went too far, that he gave his mind too much freedom, and that these places [where he errs] deserve to be condemned, but one cannot say that he was an atheist or an unbeliever."

[25] Pierre Bayle, ed., *Recueil de quelques pièces curieuses concernant la philosophie de Monsieur Descartes* (Amsterdam, 1684), "Avis au lecteur."

[26] Ibid., 1–4 (the "Concordat"), and 4–13 (the letter from A. L. de Sainte Marthe, *supérieur général* of the Oratory, to the king).

[27] Ibid., 23–26. (The entire text of the "Remarques sur le Concordat entre les Jésuites et les PP. de l'Oratoire" is ibid., 17–45.)

cowardice of the Fathers of the Oratory which saved them for this time from the complete ruin prepared for them, but they saved themselves by subjecting themselves to the Jesuits."[28]

For the commentator, the pretext was Jansenism, the ostensible target was Descartes, but there were two real issues that were primary in this affair: first, whether Aristotle or Saint Augustine was the *maître* of Catholic theology; and second, the rivalry between clerical corps. Each community of theologians, he insisted, should be free "to choose a guide." The Jesuits, in his view, had proscribed not only Saint Augustine and Descartes, but the very "liberty [of mind] that is acquired by natural right and that the Law of God left to us in its entirety." It was a scandal to link Christian theology by fiat to any particular philosophical system.[29] Their ability to do this, however, was, he averred, political, not theological. "They govern the conscience of the King," he complained, from which flowed their control of benefices, their ability to aid their allies and harm their adversaries, and their intimidation of the archbishop of Paris, the one figure who ought to be able to stand up to them. The Jesuits, he insisted, had "three principal goals that govern all of their proceedings" in affairs such as this: (1) to establish their Aristotelian doctrines against all opponents, "at whatever cost [*à quelque prix que ce soit*]"; (2) "to weaken the authority of the Holy Fathers [the patristics], which is almost always contrary to their opinions," a reference to what he took to be their aversion to Saint Augustine and the Platonic or neo-Platonic fathers; (3) to destroy or to subjugate "all of the [clerical] societies [*Compagnies*] whose merit causes them resentment and who can share with them the ecclesiastical employments over which they claim to be the completely sole masters."[30] In brief, Aristotelian-Cartesian debate was about far more than metaphysical issues.

Decades earlier, Antoine Arnauld, Augustinian and Jansenist in his theology, and profoundly influenced by and sympathetic to Cartesian philosophy, had denounced the condemnation of Descartes's works by the Congregation of the Index in Rome in even stronger terms. What "great service they render to the Church by their prohibitions," he observed sardonically, when they allow students to read critics of "the most solid proofs of the existence of God and the immortality of the soul," while "it is not permitted to them to read the author who would have persuaded them of these truths."[31] In 1671, the Oratorian theologian Nicolas Joseph Poisson, a fervent Cartesian, explained that neither Inquisition nor Council could make an article of faith out of what was indifferent to faith,

[28] Ibid.
[29] Ibid., 26–45.
[30] Ibid., 17–21.
[31] Arnauld, *Oeuvres complètes*, III, 396 (a letter to du Vaucel).

insisting upon the *philosophical* liberty of the believing Christian. No one in the Church should interfere with "the liberty of opinions that should be left to philosophers," he insisted, and he reminded his readers, with no small degree of sarcasm, that despite the fact that medieval Councils and, indeed, the University of Paris itself once had banned the teaching of Aristotle, Scholastics indeed still retained "the liberty to teach and follow the doctrine of Aristotle that they condemned."[32] In 1761, referring to this seventeenth-century "quarrel" of clerical orders, Irailh spoke of "the eternal wall of division between the Oratorians and Jesuits" and recalled that while the Oratory "rarely" gave Jesuit works to its students, the Jesuits "never" presented Oratorian works to theirs: "The Society [of Jesus] sees poison on every page of their writings." It was across such "walls" and in the context of such mutual contempt that the charges of theological incapacity to prove God would be hurled by each camp against the other.[33] As an ex-Jesuit from this period had noted about the persecution of the handful of Cartesians within the Society, "Penalties quickly bring a Controversy to an Issue."[34]

There were clever ways around such penalties, and the willingness to use them in the face of dangers shows how deeply such philosophical commitments could be felt. Edmond [or Edmé] Pourchot was one of the eminent professors of philosophy at the University of Paris. His course, which, in published form, enjoyed a fourth edition by 1717, betrayed many an aversion to Aristotle and many a liking for Descartes, but to reassure his superiors, he published what virtually everyone (including the twentieth-century *Dictionnaire de théologie catholique*) took to be a safe and purely Scholastic presentation of Aristotelian philosophy, the *Exercitationes scholasticae* (1700). In the course of this work, however, he ironically used Aristotle to establish Descartes's proofs of the existence of God, never mentioning Descartes by name, but giving the Cartesian proof of God from His perfection as *an example* of what Aristotle surely meant by certain knowledge "from cause." Indeed, Pourchot, for all of his nominal "Aristotelianism" here, argued that Aristotle's notion of *scientia* entailed a (Cartesian) criterion of "clear and distinct ideas" as the *évidence* of truth, entailed (the Cartesian view) that we had "prior ideas" of divine

[32] Nicolas Joseph Poisson, Oratory, *Commentaire ou remarques sur la méthode de Mr. Descartes. Où l'on établit plusieurs principes généraux nécessaires pour entendre toutes ses ouvrages* (Paris, 1671), 235–37.

[33] Abbé Augustin Simon Irailh, *Querelles littéraires, ou Mémoires pour servir à l'histoire des révolutions de la république des lettres, depuis Homère jusqu'à nos jours*, 4 vols. (Paris, 1761), IV, 1–52.

[34] François de La Pillonnière, *An Answer to the Reverend Dr. Snape's Accusation . . . Containing an Account of His Behaviour and Sufferings amongst the Jesuits. Of His leaving their Society, and afterwards turning Protestant . . .* (London, [1717]), 15.

and spiritual qualities before sense experience, and entailed (Descartes's) concept of the "objective being" of ideas eminently distinct from their "formal being."[35] All of these conclusions were anathema to seventeenth-century Aristotelians but were positions that Pourchot refused to abandon. It was not accidental, thus, that in his preface, Pourchot expressed his adherence to the University of Paris's condemnation of Aristotle's critics not with reference to any seventeenth-century regulation, but in terms of article 41 of the statutes of 1598, which merely called on professors to reject "inane" challenges to Aristotle's *Physics*.[36]

In their own society, the Jesuits rigorously acted against members sympathetic to Descartes or Malebranche, in particular, against François de La Pillonnière, Rodolphe Du Tertre, and Yves-Marie André. They threatened these "dissidents" with isolation and rebuke, removal from teaching, exile from Paris or all cosmopolitan cities, and, to put it simply, unpleasant tasks in unpleasant places.[37] André wrote to Malebranche and others about the endless pressures he was under: his superiors demanded that he sign formulas denouncing Descartes and Malebranche; he was threatened with being found guilty of formal violation of his vows; he was stripped of his beloved duties as a professor; he was assigned to kitchen duties and hard manual labor; he was removed from Paris; he was told to yield or be sent to China or Japan.[38] He wrote to Malebranche about his anguish: discipline impelled him to subscribe to "the [Aristotelian] opinions of the order"; "the sincerity that I owe to God" impelled his recognition of Cartesian and Malebranchist truth; Christian "charity"

[35] Edmond [sometimes, Edmé] Pourchot, *Exercitationes scholasticae in varias partes philosophiae, praesertimque in Aristotelis Metaphysicam, sive Series disputationum ontologicarum naturali ordine dispositarum, quibus praemissum est breve compendium philosophiae* (Paris, 1700), 130–48, 372–400. The *Exercitationes scholasticae* were in a 3d ed. by 1711 and a 4th ed. by 1717. Pourchot, who lived to be eighty-three, was rector of the University of Paris seven times and served for forty years as syndic. He taught philosophy first at the collège de Grassins, and later at the new collège des Quatre-Nations. From 1700 on, he also taught Hebrew. (On the misreading of the *Exercitationes*, see *Dictionnaire de théologie catholique*, art. "Pourchot.")

[36] Ibid., "Praefatio," 1–4.

[37] See, in particular, the papers of the formidable Jean Hardouin, S.J., Bibliothèque Nationale, MSS.: Fonds français, 14705–6; La Pillonnière, *Answer*, and *Mr. Francis De La Pillonière's Further Account of Himself . . . And of His Advances in His Inquiries after Truth* (London, 1729); Malebranche, *Oeuvres complètes*, XIX and XX; and Yves-Marie André, S.J., *Oeuvres philosophiques. Avec une introduction sur sa vie et ses ouvrages tireé de sa correspondance inédite*, ed. Victor Cousin (Paris, 1843); André, S.J., *Documents inédits pour servir à l'histoire philosophique, religieuse et littéraire du XVIIIe siècle, contenant la correspondance de ce père avec Malebranche, Fontenelle, et quelques personnages importants de la Société de Jésus*, ed. A. Charma and G. Mancel, 2 vols. (Caen, 1844–[1857]); and André, S.J., *La Vie du R. P. Malebranche*, ed. Père Ingold (Paris, 1886) [*Bibliothèque Oratorienne*, vol. VIII]. Also, see infra, pt. 3, chap. 10.

[38] André, *Documents inédits*, I, 1–175, passim.

impelled him never to withhold truth from his students.[39] He wrote to those chosen to change his views that in the depth of his conscience he believed in the profound Catholic orthodoxy of Descartes and Malebranche, and he begged his would-be mentors not to force him into a "false and ridiculous" condemnation of these two philosophers that he believed would be "totally contrary to charity."[40] He was advised to be "more humble" and was assailed for having "praised them [Descartes and Malebranche]" and for having "spoken with disdain of Aristotle and of the theologians who follow him with St. Thomas." A former friend enlisted to dissuade him of his "obstinacy" wrote to him in 1707 about the dangers of supporting Descartes or Malebranche: "The affair is serious, for we are resolved not to tolerate in the order not only those who follow these authors, or who praise them, but those who do not condemn them, and who are not zealous against their doctrine. . . . Disabuse yourself!"[41]

Malebranche advised André, Du Tertre, and La Pillonnière to consult with each other, and the three anti-Scholastic Jesuits provided mutual moral support for as long as they could. In the end, however, only André found ways to reconcile his vow of obedience to his superiors with his belief that Descartes and Malebranche were the ideal Christian philosophical theologians.[42] When at last Du Tertre gave in, he wrote to his friend André about his "very great worry with regard to you," given the punishments he had heard bandied about. "In the name of God," he advised him in 1713, bend to the demand to recant your Cartesian and Malebranchist positions, before suffering "consequences yet more painful perhaps than what at present can be foreseen." The issue, one should note, was not even indirectly Jansenism here, but purely one of philosophical theology. Obedience, Du Tertre wrote, makes more of a demand on conscience than philosophical opinions. At the bottom of his letter, a lonely André wrote, for no one in particular, "I have resolved to remain firm in the truth at the expense of my peace and of my happiness."[43]

André also understood full well, however, that issues of institutional control were as important in all of this as any pure appeal to truth. In a letter of 1715 to a Cartesian friend, the abbé Marbeuf, he wrote:

[39] Ibid., 50–53 (8 August 1709).

[40] See, in particular, ibid., 162–75, and, also, 99–104, 108–13, 127–36, 152–56.

[41] Ibid., 156–61. Four years later, the same friend wrote that "in the final analysis, since the Company wants it, I should be a peripatetic, as some [others] are Scotist, or Thomist, and should be convinced that it is not appropriate for an individual to be opposed to the doctrine of his *corps*."

[42] Ibid., 53–57.

[43] Du Tertre, S.J., to André, S.J., 31 January 1713, in André, S.J., *Oeuvres philosophiques*, cxxvii–cxxviii.

> We should not deceive ourselves, Monsieur. We praise our Descartes and our Malebranches, all of our philosophical heroes, in vain. Our philosophy never will be universally regarded as the philosophy of good sense until it is received in the collèges. That is a thought that is always on my mind.[44]

The reason he cared about such institutional issues, however, was that he cared so deeply about "the truth." We teach Christian youth Scholastic pedantry, he went on in that letter, while true Christian philosophy should begin with compelling demonstration of "primary and fundamental truths" such as the existence of God.[45]

To prove his own new loyalty to Aristotelian notions of "the truth," Du Tertre in 1715 wrote a work of pure Scholastic denunciation of Descartes and Malebranche, presenting the choice as being between Aristotle and heresy.[46] André was more than attuned to the question of how the public might respond to this. In a letter to Malebranche in 1715, just before his former friend's work was to appear, he wrote: "I don't know if you have learned of the distressing death of Father Du Tertre's publisher. He threw himself into a well, headfirst. This tragic episode delays a bit the comedy being prepared for the public [*Cet épisode tragique recule un peu la comédie que l'on prépare au public*]."[47] In the journal *L'Europe Savante*, the Cartesian Miron bitterly replied to Du Tertre, "You are correct that it is better to be an Aristotelian than a heretic, but I do not agree with you that the new philosophy leads to heresy, or even to error."[48] It was across these divisions, also, that the issue of demonstration of God would be raised with such venom and urgency.

. . .

Ideas are embodied in the dynamics of particular times and places, and thinkers learn these ideas (and, indeed, these dynamics) not from a "society" in the abstract, but from those mediating institutions, relationships, and conflicts in which real human beings lead actual lives. The use of "atheism" in Aristotelian-Cartesian debate makes no purely logical sense. It makes great human sense, however, when one understands how personal and contestatory the experience of that division could be. Charles Cotolendi wrote, in 1695, of crossing a forest and being disturbed by a loud argument between two Franciscans walking from

[44] André, S.J., *Documents inédits*, I, 365–70.

[45] Ibid.

[46] Rodolphe Du Tertre, S.J., *Réfutation d'un nouveau système de métaphysique* . . . , 3 vols. (Paris, 1715).

[47] André, S.J., *Documents inédits*, I, 94.

[48] *L'Europe Savante*, III, pt. 2, 296–310 (the quotation is on 296–97).

Nemours to Paris: "The one believed in Descartes as if in God; the other defended the ancient philosophy as if it were the Gospel."[49] As so many saw, participants in the Aristotelian-Cartesian debates always argued about each other with the public at large but rarely did more than argue past each other in actual dialogue. In Bayle's observation, "Speak to a Cartesian or a Peripatetic [Aristotelian] about a proposition that does not agree with the principles toward which he is biased; you will find that he thinks far less about fathoming what you are saying to him than about inventing arguments to combat it [*Parlez à un Cartésien, ou à un Péripatéticien, d'une proposition qui ne s'accorde pas avec les principes dont il est préoccupé; vous trouverez qu'il songe bien moins à pénétrer ce que vous lui dites, qu'à imaginer des raisons pour le combattre*]."[50] They ignored their common ground and insisted on the categorical differences between them. Reviewing Malebranche's *Conversations chrétiennes* in 1703, a work about the very grounds for being Christian, the Jesuit *Journal de Trévoux* noted that it would appeal and seem consistent only to most Cartesians:

> He speaks only to Cartesian philosophers; and he undertakes to prove that from the principles of these gentlemen, one cannot refrain from embracing the Christian religion. . . . Those who are still attached to the philosophy of Aristotle, or who believe that Descartes's Metaphysic is not solid, must not expect to find *anything* that persuades them. It is not for them that his book has been done. It presupposes the principles of Cartesian philosophy to be true, and it is only with regard to those who accept this supposition that one claims here to justify the religion and the morality of Jesus Christ.[51]

The eminent Cartesian Clerselier, writing a preface to the posthumously published mathematical essays of the Cartesian Rohault, was struck by the personal and theological animus against his camp. Philosophy and the human sciences, he urged, should be based on "a spirit of peace and charity, without mutual condemnations," but instead, he claimed, Scholastics, uncomfortable with and hyperbolic about new ways of thinking, have described and analyzed Cartesian thought as dangerous to the faith. He was outraged, for example, that because of Rohault's Cartesianism, his priest, before administering last rites to the expiring

[49] Charles Cotolendi, *Livre sans nom. Divisé en cinq dialogues* (Lyon, 1695), 156–57. [Opinion seems divided on whether this work is by Cotolendi or by Laurent Bordelon.]

[50] Bayle, *Pensées diverses*, I, 323.

[51] *Journal de Trévoux*, jan. 1703, 69–70. I use the term *noted*, since Malebranche had written, in the "Avertissement" he first added to the *Conversations Chrétiennes* in the 4th ed. of 1693 (*Oeuvres, complètes*, IV, 4–5): "Experience teaches well enough that it is not possible to convince a Cartesian by the principles of Aristotle, nor a peripatetic by those of Descartes."

natural philosopher, dared to question him at length about his views of the Eucharist.[52]

The furor that Clerselier described at Rohault's death was nothing compared to the effect that Rohault's Cartesianism might cause during his active life. Among his papers, Rohault kept a copy of a remarkable letter that he had felt obliged to write to a syndic of the Sorbonne, justifying himself amid the storm that his very appearance had caused in Aristotelian territory, despite the fact that he was so respected elsewhere for his quantitative natural philosophy that he was made the official instructor of the dauphin in physics. As Rohault attempted to explain to the syndic, he had been passing Saint-Germain-des-Près and had met an erstwhile friend, now a theologian at the Sorbonne, who, "stopping me and taking me by the arm," complained of Rohault's Cartesian physics, whatever his talents as a mathematician. Recalling what a pleasure it used to be to talk with doctors of the Sorbonne, Rohault explained, he decided to visit his old friend there and discover what it truly was that he objected to in "my philosophy." Rohault reported that it was with relief that he heard his host at the Sorbonne explain that his disagreement was in philosophy, not theology. Pressed to explain those differences, Rohault explained, his friend could only specify that twelve years earlier a bachelor of theology whom he knew had been " 'strongly infatuated' " by Cartesian philosophy but found that he had to abandon it to be a theologian. Pressed further, his theological friend simply stressed the need to hold to Aristotle. Rohault replied, he claimed, that Descartes was not that far from Aristotle, since both denied the void, and both used the language of privation, matter, form, substance, quality, essence, and accident. " 'I know nothing about all that,' " the theologian replied; however, he knew that Cartesians not only held " 'extremely shocking opinions' " but even believed that they could make a wooden rabbit afraid of a wooden wolf. Only my respect for my former friend, Rohault added, prevented me from laughing. They concluded their discussion, according to Rohault, with a long debate about the Eucharist, the theologian insisting that everyone knew it was incompatible with Descartes's physics and Rohault insisting that it was an article of faith that did not even relate to physics. "There, Monsieur," Rohault assured the syndic, "is what happened during the visit that I made to the Sorbonne." Why, however, did Rohault have to justify himself at all? The reason, the letter revealed, was that the presence of a leading Cartesian at the center of Aristotelian orthodoxy had caused the Sorbonnistes to notify the syndic of this, even though he had been away from Paris at the time. The syndic obviously had demanded an ex-

[52] C. Clerselier, "Préface," xii–xxvi, in Jacques Rohault, *Oeuvres posthumes*, ed. C. Clerselier (Paris, 1682).

planation from Rohault, and this was his reply. He let the syndic know that he found the circumstances absurd:

> It had been two years since I had set foot in the Sorbonne, when I was there last Friday to visit M[onsieur] N., and although I spoke to no one [except him], neither during nor after, I did notice that the report [*bruit*] of it had spread, and that, as if it were an utterly extraordinary thing, or something that merited that you be alerted to it, care had been taken to make you know of it some thirty leagues from here two days after it had happened.[53]

Cartesians often declared themselves incredulous at the sorts of responses they evoked from Aristotelians. Rohault had copied by hand a "Mémoire" presumably by Arnauld against efforts in the early 1670s to have the parlement of Paris "condemn every Philosophy other than that of Aristotle." The "Mémoire" warned against the "quarrels [*les brouilleries*]" that this would cause, and against its assault on a Christian's *philosophical* "liberty"; it compared it to failed thirteenth-century attempts to repress Aristotelian philosophy itself, and the absurdity of having had Louis XI intervene in nominalist-realist philosophical debates; it denied that there was *one* Aristotelian view, warned against confusing philosophy and theology, and insisted that it was Aristotle, not Christianity, that proponents of such intervention by civil authorities sought to protect. Finally, and "perhaps the most convincing" reason, it warned, it would break a brief peace and give "subject for quarrel" to all those just "looking for the chance."[54] As we have seen, such interventions continued apace well into the eighteenth century.

The priest and controversialist Pierre Valentin Faydit, standing on what he took to be the philosophical theology of Plato, Saint Augustine, and Descartes, explicitly criticized Aristotle, Saint Thomas, Duns Scotus, Ockham, and their disciples (and, one should add, Malebranchists as well). "It is inconceivable," he urged, that "Christian Schools and professors of philosophy can be obliged to support the doctrine of Aristotle," and that "Scholastics, as much Thomists as Scotists, Ockhamites, and Nominalists," while they disagree on all other things, agree to condemn proper Cartesian philosophical theology.[55] "I believe firmly," he defiantly

[53] Bibliothèque Nationale, MSS.: Fonds français, 14837, fols. 211–23.

[54] Ibid., fols. 225–36. The Bibliothèque Nationale attributes this "Mémoire" to Arnauld and dates it at 1673, based on the copy in Arnauld's hand in the Fonds français, 16999. The copy in Rohault's hand is among his papers from 1671. Is it possible that Arnauld copied it from Rohault, and not vice versa?

[55] Abbé Pierre Valentin Faydit, *Nouvelles remarques sur Virgile et sur Homère . . . Dans lequel on réfute les erreurs des Spinosistes, Sociniens & Arminiens, et les opinions particulières et hétérodoxes des plus célèbres auteurs, tant anciens que modernes* (n.p., 1710), passim, but especially 547–52 (where one finds the quotation). Faydit argued (40–45) that St. Thomas's "metaphysical subtleties" in pt. 1 of the *Summa Theologiae* had absolutely noth-

insisted, "that if Saint Peter, Saint Paul, and Saint John returned to the world, they would understand nothing in the scholastics," who, he urged, had "smothered the roses [of Christianity] under a pile of thorns."[56] He also recalled what had happened to him for having expressed similar views before, assuring readers of his preface that he would not commit again "all the faults that aroused the public and armed the first magistrates of the kingdom and the powers of the court not only against my book but against my person." That first attack on Scholastic depredations against true Augustinian theology, he recalled, had led to his "being exiled to 100 leagues from Paris, in a region of mountains, where literature is held in horror and men of study are less common and less cherished than wolves or boars."[57] As we have observed, it could get personal. As we also have seen, as in the Chinese rites controversy, the "victims" of pressures often associated with the Jesuits could give as well as take.

Pierre-Daniel Huet, close friend and associate of the Jesuits (with whom he took all of his spiritual retreats), scholar, critic, eventually a bishop, and, we later shall see, a growing philosophical skeptic, was first drawn to Cartesian thought with great love and intensity, but came to dissent from it and eventually to be one of its most widely read and successful critics. In his autobiography, he recalled that when he abjured his Cartesianism, "swarms of Cartesians rose against my dissertation," since "the sect is so petulant and impatient of contradiction." Former friends, he remembered, ceased talking to him or treated him "with rage and violence." He noted that even before the University of Caen "had been agitated by any gale of Cartesianism," he himself had initiated the university's celebrated philosopher Pierre Cally, his good friend, into Cartesian enthusiasms. Huet's censure of Descartes, however, changed all that: "When he understood that I was an open opponent of this philosophy, he so entirely renounced the friendship between us of many years standing, that not only all our former intercourse was at an end, but, giving way to intemperance of language, he spoke of me in a manner unworthy both of me and himself."[58]

---

ing to do with God or Christ, and that Christians should "hold fast to the theology of St. Augustine." Descartes, on the other hand, he argued (53–54), was the first philosopher in "almost 6,000 years" to understand in natural philosophy the distinction between soul and body that the Fathers of the Church had known theologically.

[56] Ibid., 40–45. ("*Je croi fermement que si Saint Pierre, Saint Paul et Saint Jean revenoient au monde, ils n'entendroient rien dans les scholastiques. . . . Ils [the scholastics] ont tout barboüillé et étouffé les roses sous un tas d'épines.*")

[57] Ibid., "Préface" [unpaginated].

[58] Pierre-Daniel Huet, *Memoirs of the Life of Peter Daniel Huet, Bishop of Avranches, Written by Himself . . . with copious notes, biographical and critical . . .* , ed. and trans. John Aikin, 2 vols. (London, 1810), II, 350–53. This is a translation of *P.-D. Huetii Commentarius de rebus ad eum pertinetibus* (The Hague, 1717).

This was not the *universal* response to his Cartesian apostasy, Huet noted. Rohault and Clerselier "patiently suffered their opinions to be controverted," but Bossuet, who "had attached himself to the Cartesians . . . [although] he cautiously dissembled his opinions in public," expressed impatience and disappointment at what he [Huet] had done. Where Cartesians often talked about Aristotelians as a virtual church, Huet saw it in reverse, describing himself as having attacked "the Cartesian sect . . . and its dictator Descartes."[59]

Huet's own manuscript copies of his censures of Cartesian philosophy reveal interesting hesitations about how far to go and how strong his language should be. Perhaps he had precisely these friends in mind. Every page was reworked extensively, precisely to find the appropriate nuance of condemnation, and usually to soften his initial formulation.[60] On the relationship between Descartes's philosophy and Christian theology, for example, he first had written "ruinous consequences," crossed it out and wrote "pernicious consequences," and crossed that out also to conclude with "dangerous consequences."[61] On the relationship between Descartes's idea of God and God Himself, he first had written that there was "no" relationship ["*qui ne luy resemblera point*"], but crossed that out and changed it to "not much [*qui ne luy resemblera pas beaucoup*]."[62] Given his description of the responses of his Cartesian friends to his work, he need not have sought such distinctions, but clearly, from his successive drafts, he had tried.

The tidal shifts of opinion that alter received loyalties slowly over generations are not always perceptible to those alive in stable but contestatory times, and the immediate struggle is for the young (in early-modern France, for control of education) and for that small group of independent minds who on occasion actually change their commitments on the basis of arguments and objections. In a polarized world, the latter can be hard to find. In 1702, the *Nouvelles de la République des Lettres* reported as a remarkable fact the story of a philosopher in Paris named Langenhert who, after offering public lectures on philosophy and publishing them in Latin and in French, was the object of a set of critical objections against his system. He "did not respond," the journal noted, "and even discontinued his lectures, because . . . he could not resolve several objections made against his singular opinions."[63] Le Gallois reported as equally unusual the mood that prevailed at the salon of Bourdelot, where "Aristotle was

[59] Ibid., 353–55.

[60] Bibliothèque Nationale, MSS.: Fonds français, 14702–3.

[61] Ibid., 14702, 2v (from "*conséquences ruineuses*" to "*pernicieuses*" to "*dangereuses*"). There is no ambiguity about the sequence of changes.

[62] Ibid., 31r.

[63] *Nouvelles de la République des Lettres*, fév. 1702, 230.

not less favorably listened to than Descartes," and where "the world is free to believe what it wants."[64] The philosopher Bouillier wrote of his embrace of the new philosophy, his hesitations in the face of sound criticisms of it by the old, and his return to ancient beliefs after coming to feel that he had lived among paradoxes too long. "I know of nothing more humiliating for the human mind," he concluded, "than this flux and reflux of opinions which is seen among the philosophers of different centuries."[65] In an age in which it was perilous not to be "connected," intellectually as well as socially and institutionally, such independence was rare indeed.

The Oratorian Richard Simon questioned why each Dominican and each Jesuit, for example, should have to embrace and accept a particular philosophical theologian determined by his order. It was not always like that, he claimed, citing prior Dominican criticism of Saint Thomas Aquinas himself. He asked, of Aquinas, "has he become a fifth evangelist because he has been placed among the saints?"[66] Yet he himself merely cited Saint Augustine to settle the issue of whether there could be actual atheism among the Chinese, and he declared that compared to the Faculties of Theology of the Universities of Louvain and Douai, the Sorbonne was of almost no use in the struggle against heresy because it stood on Scholastic theology rather than on the patristic (he meant, above all, Augustinian) tradition.[67]

It also was a theological and philosophical world whose members had been given a remarkable sense of their mission and their powers and did not suffer opposition lightly. In a society where most of their fellow creatures worked the soil or labored manually in the cities and towns, theologians and philosophers, from their childhoods, had been singled out for exemption from such toil. They not only had learned to read complex prose, as had many others who worked on purely worldly affairs, but had conquered Latin, mastered difficult texts, defended themselves and attacked others in countless disputations and exercises, and been told, again and again, that theirs was the highest calling to which the natural faculties of the species could be devoted. Their status was lofty and their pride immense, and intellectual concession came particularly hard to them. This was one of the reasons why so many titles began with "Reply to," "Reply to the Reply to," and, indeed, "Reply to the Reply to the

[64] Pierre Le Gallois, *Conversations tirées de l'Académie de Monsieur l'abbé Bourdelot contenant diverses recherches et observations physiques* (Paris, 1672), 62. [The "Privilège" lists the abbé Pierre Bourdelot himself as the author of the *Conversations*.]

[65] David Renaud Bouillier, *Essai philosophique sur l'âme des bêtes* . . . (Amsterdam, 1728), 1–2.

[66] Simon, *Bibliothèque critique*, II, 371–76.

[67] Ibid., II, 62–63 (re Chinese atheism); II, 1–2 (re Louvain and Douai).

Reply to." Who could give any critic the last word, leave any challenge unanswered, or remain silent with his reputation exposed? They fought with each other tooth and nail. La Bruyère put it well: to read the disputes of "men of party and cabal . . . one must read a great number of strong and injurious terms said of each other by serious men *who from a contested point of doctrine or fact create a personal quarrel*."[68] It was not an uncommon observation. As the *Histoire des Ouvrages des Savans* noted concerning the ongoing debate between Malebranche and Arnauld, "The dispute that began as a question of theology degenerates somewhat here into a private quarrel and into personal reproaches."[69]

The abbé de Lubières remarked, in *L'Esprit du siècle* (1707), that ambition ruled the university. Although he himself had the innovators in mind in his particular account of professorial vanity, he also noted that ambition ruled the whole Church as well, from cloister to faculty of theology to congregation and order. Some at the collèges, he observed, want "to be a savant without having the reputation for it," but the others want "to pass for learned without being a savant." Among the professors, he observed at the dawn of our age,

> the least of geniuses, puffed up with a vain doctrine, is never prouder than when, raised to the Chair of Professor, he proffers his alleged new systems to a young band of students, devotees of commendation. He regards himself as a St. Thomas, imagines himself to be inspired by the same spirit as this Angel of the School, and offers his conclusions as oracles.[70]

The Oratorian polymath Bernard Lamy, a Cartesian and Augustinian, once distinguished his own work from that of others in terms that most major thinkers came to internalize at some level in their sense of self. His *Entretiens sur les sciences*, he wrote, "is not one of those that ambition alone or the desire to make books causes to appear. I believe that I obey God by writing it."[71] Writing for God about God, why not raise the spec-

[68] La Bruyère, *Les Caractères de Théophraste*, I, 101.

[69] *Histoire des Ouvrages des Savans*, sept. 1687, 45.

[70] Abbé de Lubières, *L'Esprit du siècle* (Paris, 1707), 13–14, 27–28 (the longer quotation is from 14). ["Cultural studies" take note!]

[71] Bernard Lamy, *Entretiens sur les sciences, dans lesquels, outre la méthode d'étudier, on apprend comme l'on doit servir des sciences pour se faire l'esprit juste et le coeur droit & pour se rendre utile à l'Eglise. On y donne des avis importans à ceux qui vivent dans les maison écclésiastiques* (Lyon [and Grenoble, 1684]), "Lettre Préliminaire." Readers who persist in misconceiving such works as in any way marginal to early-modern thought should note that the Oratorian's *Entretiens* had an augmented 2d ed. (Lyon, 1694; Lyon, 1700); a revised and augmented 3d ed. (Lyon, 1706; Lyon, 1724; Amsterdam, 1724); and a "new and last ed.," (Lyon, 1751), most with several printings. There is now an outstanding critical edition of the *Entretiens sur les sciences . . .*, ed. Francois Girbal and Pierre Clair (Paris, 1966) [based on the 3d ed. (Lyon, 1706)], in which the quotation is found on 23. Bernard

ter of atheism in one's criticisms of one's rivals' works? The contestation of ideas touched the deepest aspects of self-image and calling in the early-modern learned world.

. . .

We must never underestimate that world's attraction for the things of the mind. Although savants of the seventeenth century could complain endlessly about the decline in intellectual quality occasioned by that spread of education and printing of which they were the beneficiaries, their works fascinated each other as both intellectual feasts and intellectual provocations. Despite their complaints, they loved the dialectic, the logic, the exhaustive and exhausting mastery of the principles of formal thought upon which, they believed, all purely human coherence depended. They loved a good fight, with arguments arrayed against each other like regiments on a tactical battlefield or pieces on a chessboard. Despite their frequently expressed impatience with the terms and disputations of the Schools, their behavior indicated that in many ways, they loved these too. They almost all believed that mind could not be simply accidental, and were certain that it had a substantial and purposeful relationship to the divine design of things. The processes of mind, for almost all of them, represented to us and participated in an intellectual and spiritual order that could be demonstrated to be true from the very qualitative and, for many, quantitative analysis of being in virtually any and every form. Some minds still deemed extraordinary by our own learned world, and the seventeenth century had many, sought above all to bring system out of the deductively mathematical and were certain that the order they disclosed pervaded not merely the sciences of mathematics and logic, but the science of being in general, of the whole of reality. Almost all seventeenth-century thinkers wanted to understand the *qualities* of things, in particular or in general, certain that these too expressed the coherence and order that prevailed under God's ineffable wisdom. Applying mind to the analysis of quality and quantity was never *just* an exercise or route to fame and influence for them: it was participation in the relationship of mind to order, of mind to the divine source of order itself.

The *Journal de Trévoux*'s description of "the theologians" was true of so much of the whole learned culture in essential ways: "men accustomed to quibble about the least things, and contradictors by profession [*gens*

Lamy, who should not be confused with the Malebranchist Benedictine philosopher François Lamy, was one of those Cartesian Oratorians whose philosophical teachings led to the scandal which provoked the ephemeral Concordat of 1678. He had studied theology under the Augustinian André Martin (Ambrosius Victor), who, like Lamy, was more than sympathetic to Plato and to Descartes.

accoutumez à vétiller sur les moindres choses, et contradicteurs de profession], who use a part of their erudition to confront the diverse systems of authors and point out where they agree and where they differ." They sought fame; they indeed "quibbled about the least things"; they obsessed on differences. They also sought, as the *Journal* added, "to draw the truth from the bottom of the well."[72]

. . .

The stakes, then—personal, institutional, intellectual, and spiritual—were high. Many recent (and other) studies have deepened historical knowledge of the world of early-modern higher education and shed light on the context in which these stakes were being contested. It was a France that had undertaken a great extension of education and learning, in which tens of thousands of students from all social classes attended collèges, universities, and seminaries in any given year (only half of whom, although a much larger percentage in the major cities, were drawn from noble, bourgeois, merchant, and, increasingly, office-holding strata combined). It also was a France in which essential issues were being debated before the ever more diverse reading public created, in part, by educational reforms. The Church had favored a great increase in education to secure the faith in a new age begun by the challenge of the Reformation, and, as part of that endeavor, to increase the number and the quality of well-educated clergy and believers. It succeeded in essential ways in that mission, but it could not control the awesome consequences of that undertaking. Those who dissented from received culture and creed had been formed by received culture and creed.[73] Books opened worlds for this newly educated public, and by 1701, there were seventy-five printer-booksellers on the rue St. Jacques and neighboring streets near the University of Paris alone.[74] Almost all scholars agree: the crown and royal

[72] *Journal de Trévoux*, juillet 1718, 113.

[73] See the works cited supra, chap. 3, n. 7. Pierre Chaunu, *La mort à Paris: XVIe, XVIIe et XVIIIe siècles* (Paris, 1978), 216–17, discussing the remarkable growth of Catholic education at all levels in early-modern France, noted: "In fact, we are in the presence of successive and as if superimposed continuities. The first, in depth, unites at the popular level the end of the Middle Ages and modernity, from 1300 to 1750, in sum, a collective piety located on the plane of gesture, of festival, of emotion, and of the sacred. *The other, at the apex, asserts itself between 1600–1610 and 1650 . . . , right up toward 1670–1680, and perpetuates itself gradually in an intellectual, enlightened Catholicism that, without great transition, opens the route to the Enlightenment [L'autre, au sommet, s'affirme entre 1600–1610 et 1650 . . . , jusque vers 1670–1680 and se prolonge insensiblement en un catholicisme intellectuel, éclairé, qui ouvre, sans grande transition, le chemin aux Lumières].*"

[74] Chaunu, *La mort à Paris*, 207–11. See Chaunu's whole discussion (207–17), where, among many other things, he notes the remarkable size (in number of volumes) of the great libraries of Paris, many of them monastic, open to a selected reading public.

officialdom worried greatly about all this, deeply concerned about how to maintain proper social and economic relations with so many people being educated; the Church, and, in particular, the religious orders, had few doubts about the wisdom of educating as deeply as possible as many Christian minds as could be reached.[75] Bossuet might complain, as in the case of Richard Simon, that there were debates that simply had to remain in Latin, for "*savants*" alone, but he himself specified that it was "women" and "the vulgar" whom he wanted protected.[76] Bossuet, of course, did not even keep his own counsel here, writing in French on controversial matters indeed. The blessing, Pandora's box, or Promethean

[75] François Furet and Mona Ozouf, *Reading and Writing: Literacy in France from Calvin to Jules Ferry* (Cambridge, 1982), 63–64, note that Richelieu had warned against the effects of the unchecked spread of education on farming and trade but was vigorously opposed in this by almost all elements of the Church. Commenting on the continuation of this tension into the eighteenth century, they observe "where the paradox lies: On the whole, the 18th-century *intendant* was less concerned with elementary education than were the bishop or the parish priests. . . . Far from being a monolithic, obscurantist force, interested solely in keeping the people ignorant, the Catholic Church was the driving force behind a major effort of elementary education; it invented and dignified the figure of the '*maitre d'école*,' the ancestor of the teacher. Such forces hostile to education for the masses as there were under the *Ancien Régime* were generally recruited from the administrative and political elites of the kingdom, and from the Enlightenment intelligentsia." (*Reading and Writing* is a translation of the first part of Furet and Ozouf, *Lire et écrire* . . . [Paris, 1977], the second part of which extended to a remarkable series of regional studies.) Lebrun, Venard, and Quéniart, *De Gutenberg aux Lumières*, 237, note that what some had taken to be a demographic "decline" at the French universities during the seventeenth century was a profound misreading of the data: many new independent collèges attracted students formerly at collèges officially affiliated with universities; many *foreign* students (above all from Protestant countries) now chose to remain in their home countries and at their own universities; many new "académies" opened. All this *added* to the number receiving higher education. As they remind us (342–61), the number of Jesuit collèges increased in France from twelve in 1572 to seventy by 1640—including a great increase in the number of *collèges en pleine exercise* that took the student from grammar, humanities, and rhetoric to formal study of philosophy—and similar expansion was resulting from the efforts of other religious orders and congregations. From a survey taken in 1627, they assert that there were 60,000 students learning Latin at collèges in France in that year, *before* the period of greatest expansion. Dainville, *L'éducation des jésuits*, 122–48, from the same survey, put the figure at 40,000. Discussing the many complaints of Richelieu, officials, and notables about the "overabundance" of collèges, and the effect of higher education and Latinity in diminishing (they feared) the number of farmers, soldiers, and taxpayers, he observed, however, that such education rapidly was becoming "the indispensable stepping-stone to all social advancement," and that "*the number of collèges, far from being reduced, did nothing but grow from 1625 to 1665*." Dainville also notes a series of anguished inquests, memoirs, and warnings, almost all from royal officials, about the great harm being done to the "rights of birth" by the extraordinary multiplication of students at the collèges and universities. For Dainville, not until the toll of the wars made itself felt, from 1685 to 1715, was there first a "stagnation" and then an eventual diminution in the number of students.

[76] Bossuet, *Oeuvres*, I, 521.

fire of education had been set loose in the world. Large numbers of Latin works went into multiple editions, the journals explicated them for those who limited their reading to French, and, increasingly, there were few issues of controversy that did not make their way into the vernacular. Niceron reminded his readers that a century before, in 1607, publication of a French translation of Saint Thomas's *Summa Theologiae* had been suspended by the Faculty of Theology in Paris, which could not tolerate "that things that it believed should be reserved to the theologians be exposed to the eyes of the public."[77] It was too late for all that now.

For Naudé, the watershed was the fall of Constantinople, which brought a host of curious and erudite Greek Christians to Europe, where their hunger for knowledge and novelty changed the Western world.[78] For the sixteenth-century scholar André Thevet, whose history of the savants of four continents was republished in 1670–1671, and for the late seventeenth-century deist Marana, it was printing that had changed it all. Writing in 1586, Thevet had seen the phenomenon with great optimism. By means of printing, he wrote, "we can insure that the law of God extends to the barbarous and savage nations lost in ignorance." By means of printing, "all the sciences have been made illustrious and greatly ennobled."[79] Printing, the more skeptical Marana stressed a century later, meant that every error as well as every truth could reach a multitude.[80]

Journals were an essential part of what printing and the expansion of education had made possible. The first copy of the *Journal des Sçavans* explained in 1665 that "the purpose of this journal [is] to make known what is happening that is new in the Republic of Letters." Its scope would be everything "worthy of the curiosity of men of letters."[81] Among the things that proved "worthy" of such "curiosity" were the personal intellectual quarrels that so captured the fancy of the age. As the *Journal de Trévoux* noted in 1707, "The quarrels of men of letters are the most avidly read [*curieuses*] subject matter of a journal," and journals fulfilled their responsibility here "when they conserve in faithful and disinterested selections the items of the literary suits; trials which in truth rarely contribute to the clarification of the questions which gave rise to them, but which serve very well to make known the savants engaged in these quarrels [*quand ils conservent dans des extraits fidelles & desinteressez les pièces des procès litéraires; procès qui à la verité contribuent rarement à l'éclaircissement des questions qui leur ont donné lieu, mais qui servent*

[77] Niceron et al., *Mémoires*, III, 11.

[78] Naudé, *Considérations politiques*, 213–24.

[79] André Thevet, *Histoire des plus illustres et sçavans hommes de leurs siècles, tant de l'Europe que de l'Asie, Afrique et Amérique*, 8 vols. (Paris, 1670–1671), VII, 109–14.

[80] Marana, *L'Espion Turc*, II, 378–80.

[81] *Journal des Sçavans*, I (1665), 5 ("L'Imprimeur aux Lecteurs").

beaucoup à faire connoître les Sçavans engagez dans ces querelles]."[82] As the *Journal de Trévoux* itself admitted in 1712, the learned journals edited by Huguenots in Holland enjoyed the greatest popular success in France, which was the reason that the duc du Maine had undertaken to fund the Jesuit journal.[83] Nonetheless, even the Jesuits continued to be impressed by and to recommend to their own readers such journals.[84] The Huguenot and other Dutch journals appreciated their wide audience in France and tried, at least, to honor the commitment made by the *Nouvelles de la République des Lettres* in the preface to its very first volume: "It is not a question [here] of Religion [sect]; it is a question of Science; and we must lay aside all the terms which divide men into different [sectarian] factions and consider only the point in which they are united, which is the [shared] quality of illustrious man in the Republic of Letters. In that sense, all savants must look upon each other as brothers or as equally good, the ones and the others."[85] Indeed, the learned journals would be almost the *last* place to look for the bitterness and rancor surrounding the revocation of the Edict of Nantes. From their issues, one would be largely unaware of the intensity of the drama unfolding in that domain.

The most essential reason for the journals' collective success and growth, however, perhaps was best expressed by the *Histoire des Ouvrages des Savans* itself in 1692: they were the place of contact between the truly erudite and the broader reading public. Thus:

> The journals were invented for the relief [*le soulagement*] of the readers. Our century passionately loves abridgments, and there reigns a *je ne sais quoi* that some would name laziness . . . that causes one to ask only for easy ways of becoming a clever man [*devenir habile homme*] without much effort. The journals . . . can put a reader in a proper condition to talk about an infinity of things without his having made much of an effort.[86]

In such circumstances and by such means, fundamental debate among leading Christian thinkers about the proper philosophical theology for the faith reached a broad educated public and became causes célèbres. Personal quarrels arising from such debates held that public spellbound, and the issues engaged moved not only *extra muros*, but into journals that themselves could define their readers as men who now would "talk about an infinity of things without . . . having made much of an effort." There is another way to think about this, though: as more people were informed

[82] *Journal de Trévoux*, août 1707, 1347–48.
[83] Ibid., fév. 1722, 218–24.
[84] Ibid., avril 1719, 643–44.
[85] *Nouvelles de la République des Lettres*, mars 1684, "Préface."
[86] *Histoire des Ouvrages des Savans*, mars 1692, 327–28.

of such debates, so there would be more (and more diverse) responses to them. That is why even if such mutual contestation had occurred in every century since the thirteenth, it could not possibly be the same this time.

. . .

It was not the subject matter of the debates about proper proof of God's existence that determined their tone. The contestants did not really think of each other as "atheists" or friends of "the atheists" at all. It was, rather, the extraordinary division and the polemical drama of the early-modern learned world. As the *Journal de Trévoux* noted in 1701, the whole world of learning "is now divided between two kinds of philosophers . . . those who call themselves disciples of Aristotle and those who have embraced the new opinions."[87] On the whole, the two camps could not change each other's minds. Reviewing a long sequence of Aristotelian and Cartesian attacks and counterattacks on their mutual proofs of God that had taken place in the most widely read learned journals, the theologian Niceron noted that after two years of constant exchanges, "everyone will remain, following the custom, in his original opinion."[88] A generation before, Bayle had been struck by precisely the same phenomenon.[89] In all early-modern debates, the spectacle of revered thinkers assailing each other attracted a crowd. As the *Histoire des Ouvrages des Savans* noted in 1687, when two great figures attack each other with great reproach and energy, "the reader feels his curiosity redoubled in this case, from the pleasure that he takes in seeing a clever man pressed a bit, and . . . in a peril worthy of him."[90] What, however, was the nature of this spectacle? Reviewing a book that was part of a bitter debate over grace, in 1706, the *Journal de Trévoux* (itself, at times, such admonition notwithstanding, as unforgiving as could be) exclaimed: "These disputes, which undoubtedly have their usefulness for the clarification of certain points of theology, would be a source of much pleasure if the two sides knew how to be moderate and to limit themselves to the search for truth, always preserving decorum. But this moderation between authors is a very rare thing."[91]

The self-image of the learned world most assuredly did not favor "moderation." That self-image, we have seen, involved far more than simply deep schooling in disputation and great pride in dialectical skills;

[87] *Journal de Trévoux*, nov.–déc 1701, 38–41.
[88] Niceron et al., *Mémoires*, vi, 380–81.
[89] Bayle, *Dictionnaire*, "Zabarella."
[90] *Histoire des Ouvrages des Savans*, nov. 1687, 308–9.
[91] *Journal de Trévoux*, nov. 1706, 1843–44.

it was also a sense of a calling and a special relationship to God Himself. In 1666, a reviewer in the *Journal des Sçavans* put it this way:

> As God made use of the simplest and most common persons [*des personnes les plus simples et les plus grossières*] for the establishment of Christianity, so he has used, for its progress, the most learned and the most enlightened. And having made His power shine forth in the former, he has made His wisdom admired in the latter. And certainly, after the Church was founded by the zeal of the apostles, and confirmed by the constancy of the martyrs, it was necessary for God to give doctors to it, to convince men of the truth of what it taught. And something would be lacking from the perfection of the Christian religion if its doctrine, having been established by miracles, was not still maintained by [compelling] arguments.[92]

All the participants in the debates over the correct philosophical voice for fundamental Christian metaphysical theology believed in God. Unlike the participants in debates over grace, it was never the conclusion about which they argued, but simply the modality by which to reach it. As Bayle had noted, however, they excelled at attack, not defense.[93] For Bayle, it was in theory all supposed to proceed according to simple rules of disputational good faith:

> Someone says to you: I believe, sir, as well as you, that there is a God; we will have no dispute on that point. But perhaps you base yourself on reasons that differ strongly from my own. In that case, we well could dispute against each other, for if you propose proofs to me that do not appear solid, I will tell you freely that you are wrong, and thus, although we are in agreement about the fact, I will oppose my reasons against yours, and you will be obliged to submit yourself to all the laws of disputation, and if you have the right to push me all the way to the innermost recesses of dialectic [*me pousser jusques aux derniers recoins de la dialectique*], I also have that right.[94]

Institutional identities, philosophical and theological commitments, efforts to advance, maintain, or defend one's reputation, and the most altruistic aspects of self-image all merged in a commitment pursued "to the innermost recesses of dialectic" to unmask one's adversaries' fallacious proofs of the existence of God. That "altruism" often spoke the language of service to the faith. Unconvincing arguments for God's existence, the Sorbonne's L'Herminier explained, caused the greatest harm and prejudice to theology and gave the greatest comfort to incredulity.[95] "It is of

[92] *Journal des Sçavans*, 15 fév. 1666, 262.

[93] Pierre Bayle, *OD*, IV, 725–26.

[94] Bayle, *Pensées diverses*, III, 86 [in *Continuation* . . .].

[95] Nicolas L'Herminier, *Summa Theologiae ad usum scholae accommodata*, 3 vols. (Paris,

extreme importance," the Benedictine Robert Desgabets warned, "to let nothing enter into proofs of the existence of God but what is utterly solid."[96] As the *Journal de Trévoux* put it in 1708, in matters of theology, "it is more disadvantageous to be badly defended than to be strongly attacked."[97] Canon Simon Foucher, justifying his deep criticisms of Malebranche, including Malebranche's proofs of God, sought to make the higher framework clear: "There is this difference between Truth and the majority of the other possessions that we seek: that provided that we possess these [other] goods, we have grounds for being content with them, even when we are beholden to chance; whereas it is not enough that we have Truth, if we do not know by what right [*à quel Titre*] we possess it; by what means and in what manner we have begun to be in possession of it [*nous avons commancé d'en joüir*]."[98]

In demonstrations of God, then, for a great variety of reasons, eliminating the flawed proofs of rivals and determining the proper grounds for natural conviction were seen as essential roles, and at those deepest corners of logical dispute, one simply revealed that with arguments no better than he had, one's adversary might just as well be a speculative atheist. Although he waited until page 604 of his work to do it, the ex-Oratorian Faydit sought to explain and justify his use of this mode against Malebranche:

> I believe myself obliged to warn the reader that although I confuse Father Malebranche with Spinoza sometimes . . . I am very far from believing that this virtuous and learned priest is caught up in the same errors. . . . *I meant only that one can draw consequences from his principles in favor of [such] doctrine*. I beg of him here and now, and also his disciple l'Elevel [Henri Lelevel], to forgive [me] if they find in this work several expressions a bit too hard and too lively, that the heat of the dispute inadvertently could have made me use [*quelques termes un peu trop durs et trop vifs, que la chaleur de la Dispute aura pû me faire échapper*].[99]

1701–1703), I, 40–44. (L'Herminier taught theology at the University of Paris from 1689 to 1707, when he was called to a high ecclesiastical appointment by a Jansenist bishop.)

[96] Desgabets, O.S.B., *Critique de la Critique*, 86. Desgabets was an anti-Aristotelian philosopher, eventually a disciple of Malebranche, who was sent by his Benedictine order to Paris as its *procureur général*; in Paris, he frequented Cartesian and then Malebranchist philosophical and theological circles.

[97] *Journal de Trévoux*, avril 1708, 721.

[98] Simon Foucher, *Critique de la Recherche de la vérité. Où l'on examine en même-tems une partie des principes de Mr. Descartes* . . . (Paris, 1675), 20. Foucher was a canon of Dijon. This was the work criticized by Desgabets.

[99] Faydit, *Remarques sur Virgile et sur Homère*, 604. This was the work that led to Faydit's exile from Paris. Faydit had been an Oratorian priest who had been dismissed from the Congregation in 1671 for his uncompromising promulgation of the Cartesian view of soul, at a time when the Congregation was under intense pressure to restrain its Cartesian enthu-

After Pierre Bayle had argued that the Cambridge Platonist Ralph Cudworth's philosophical defense of theism led to atheism, the late Cudworth's daughter wrote to Le Clerc in shock and outrage. Bayle wrote to Pierre Coste to please explain to her that *only* the specific Cartesian proofs had been spared his criticism, and that nothing personal had been meant by his argument that Cudworth's demonstrations were more suitable to establish disbelief: "I only alleged that Mr. Cudworth's principles were exposed to the same difficulties as the ordinary principles of peripatetic philosophy, or all non-Cartesian philosophers," and had no force against "the atheists." In brief:

> No one is unaware that in disputes, one objects to one's adversaries as many inopportune consequences as one can from their principles [*on objecte à ses adversaires autant de fâcheuses suites qu'on peut de leurs principes*] be it by alleging that they acknowledge these consequences (and sometimes we are unjust in that), or by making an abstract of them whether they acknowledge them or not, or by declaring that they do not acknowledge them. It is thus [in this last way] that I proceeded, for I said that MM. Cudworth and Grew exposed themselves, without realizing it [*sans y penser*], to the retortion of one of the proofs that we oppose to atheism.[100]

After Pierre-Daniel Huet had undertaken his celebrated censure of Cartesian proofs, Antoine Menjot, whose *philosophical* skepticism made him suspicious of all "schools," wrote to congratulate him. Descartes's proofs of the existence of God, he wrote, were "so forced and so muddled [*si guindées et si embrouillées*] that they would be capable of persuading [people of] the opposite, if the natural lights of the human mind did not oppose that." What further offended Menjot was that Descartes, he believed, had dismissed the arguments of the most learned theologians and enlightened philosophers of all prior centuries and presented his own demonstrations as "the *only* ones capable of establishing the Divinity." What followed from that, Menjot added, clearly had escaped the Cartesians' notice: no one who was not a Cartesian logically should believe that God existed, and "the Atheists have only begun to be in error in the

siasts. He was always a figure of controversy and scandal. His works on "Virgil and Homer," in fact, had virtually nothing to do with either poet but focused on what he saw as the chasm between patristic truth and the errors of *both* Scholastics and Malebranche. *Only* Descartes, he believed, was consistent with the patristic tradition. Since Faydit offended a great variety of powerful people on a great variety of grounds, it is not possible to specify the relative weight of purely philosophical issues in causing his exile.

100 Bayle, *Lettres*, III, 1018–23. In n. 4 on 1020, Des Maizeaux, editor of Bayle's letter, noted that when Bayle expressed himself publicly to this effect, Cudworth's daughter withdrew the complaint that she had sent to Le Clerc for publication.

century in which [these] other new proofs have appeared."[101] Commenting on the debate among French Catholic theologians over Chinese atheism, the *Histoire des Ouvrages des Savans*, as early as 1687, had seen that "it is the celebrated doctors among the Catholics who, to avenge their personal resentments, betray the common cause and furnish arms to the [atheistic] heretics." The irony of this, the journal added, was that "piety is the sole motive of all their insults and of all their quarrels."[102]

Yet, as Bayle noted, the debate about proofs of God was destined to continue. Commenting on the claim that the eminent sixteenth-century Catholic theologian Maldonat rashly had arrayed against each other the strongest possible arguments for and against the existence of God, he reminded his readers that Maldonat had done what Christian theology was obliged to do. It was only by such a means that God's existence could be proven conclusively. The existence of God, he wrote, as so many had written before him, was not a "principle," but a "thesis" in need of demonstration, and the holiest of men had sought to prove it and to secure it "sheltered from objections."[103] Saint-Evremond, we may recall, had found it absurd that his civilization punished overt atheism by death yet asked in the Schools if God existed.[104] An anonymous critic replied that Saint-Evremond had misunderstood the issue completely: "When theologians ask if there is a God, it is not in order to doubt His existence, but to provide indubitable proofs of it, and to confound the atheists."[105] Theologians and philosophers indeed took with utmost gravity their responsibility to provide indubitable proofs and to assail those that they found dubious. They may have inhibited some potential atheists by this endeavor. The evidence suggests very strongly, however, that they brought others into being.

[101] Antoine Menjot, *Opuscules posthumes . . . contenant des discours & des lettres sur divers sujets . . .* (Amsterdam, 1697), 139–46. Menjot had been a medical doctor with the titles of *médecin ordinaire du roy* and *conseiller du roi.*

[102] *Histoire des Ouvrages des Savans*, déc. 1687, 495–96.

[103] Bayle, *Dictionnaire*, "Maldonat," rem. L.

[104] Saint-Evremond, *Oeuvres*, I, 184–85.

[105] *Dissertation sur les Oeuvres mêlées de Monsr. de Saint Evremond* (Paris, 1698), 216. [Bayle himself referred to this work.]

Chapter Nine

THE ASSAULT ON CARTESIAN PROOFS OF GOD

BY THE LATE seventeenth century, there were some nine proofs of the existence of God broadly but diversely favored by the French theological and philosophical communities. First, there was proof from Christian experience itself, which might take the form of the "evidence" of grace and miracle (external in others or internal in one's own life); or of Scripture as necessarily divine; or of the providence believed visible in the history and life of the people and Church of God. It was widely conceded, however, as we have seen, that such proof begged the question for all but Christians; for most theologians, while such phenomena ought to be persuasive, they constituted "moral" rather than "demonstrative" proof. Next, there was the classical argument from "universal consent," a proof that for many obviated the need for other demonstrations, showing either that awareness of God was ineradicably engraved in our souls by God Himself or that it was so obvious an inference from the world that no one sound and sincere had failed to grasp it. We have seen the difficulties posed to some minds concerning the validity of this proof, which also generally was deemed, even by its most fervent advocates, to be "moral" rather than "demonstrative." The goal of philosophical theology with reference to the first article of the creed, however, was taken by most to be precisely the provision of *compelling demonstration* of this truth. There were seven that dominated the literature.

For the Scholastics, Saint Thomas Aquinas had provided five such compelling philosophical demonstrations, linked to or derived from, it was widely believed, the most evident principles and conclusions of the most rigorous elements of Aristotelian philosophy. Among Scholastics, there had been and still was lively debate, from the thirteenth century well into the seventeenth, on particular aspects of these demonstrations: the extent to which some of these proofs depended upon physics or metaphysics (i.e., upon "motion" as conceived by "physics" or upon "act" or "change" as conceived by "metaphysics"); the nature of a "series" or "sequence" to which one legitimately could apply the notion of the impossibility of infinite regress; the need to demonstrate the "possibility" of the object of proof before its "actuality." By the seventeenth century, however, these were secondary issues, and most Scholastic theologians seemed to believe that however one redefined specific trees, the forest of Aristotelian or Thomistic proof of God stood tall and imposing. Further, the question of almost all of these intra-Scholastic disputes was not one of the validity or invalidity of the demonstrations, but of precisely how they should be formulated in order to be made utterly compelling.[1]

In general, however Aquinas might be read today, seventeenth-century authors, theological and lay, proponents and critics, understood Saint Thomas's "Five Ways" as follows. One, from the *motion*, *change*, or *activity* of the beings we observe, we knew that there must be a *First Mover*, for there could be no infinite regression of acquired or dependent motion (or acquired or dependent change). Two, from the *sequence of dependent cause and effect* in the beings we observe, we similarly knew that there must be an independent *First Cause*. Three, from the *contingency* of all

[1] For Scotus, to try to put the matter simply, the First Mover reached by any possible proof from *physics* was not necessarily the infinite God, and *metaphysics* must prove God independently of arguments from physical motion alone. His criticisms of using terms from Aristotle's *Physics* rather than *Metaphysics* in Aquinas's "First Way," and the supporting commentary of his most celebrated commentators, were widely available in the seventeenth century in France, in the remarkable edition of Scotus's works edited by Luke Wadding, O.F.M., and in the independent commentaries of the Cordelier professor at the University of Paris, Claude Frassen, O.F.M. (see supra, chap. 3, n. 10). While disciples of Scotus naturally remained loyal to him in his criticism of St. Thomas, Scotist-Thomist differences in the seventeenth century, let me emphasize again, were *not* over the validity of the "First Way," but over its proper formulation. More importantly, these differences did not become even minor disturbances in the world of learning and did *not* spill over into the concerns of the broader reading public. Thomas de Vio Cajetan—in his commentary on the *Summa Theologiae*, widely available in a great diversity of editions of St. Thomas—when he addressed the "First Way" in his discussion of Ia, q.2, a.3, simply referred to Scotus's rejection of Aristotle's principle of motion from the *Physics* in the proof but asserted that when the "First Way" was read in the context of the broader discussion of the *Summa Contra Gentiles*, and the First Mover shown to be identical with God, it remained valid. One of the strongest statements of a Scotist criticism of St. Thomas's use of the *Physics* in his first proof was by F. Stümellius, O.F.M., *Primum & Perenne mobile*, 2 [fol.] vols. (Cologne, 1680), which, while it was sold in Paris (see *Journal des Sçavans*, 13 jan. 1681, 11–12), did not seem to cause much stir. There is an interesting discussion of Scotus's position and its relationship both to his contemporaries and to late-medieval and Renaissance commentators in Roy R. Effler, O.F.M., *John Duns Scotus and the Principle "Omne quod movetur ab alio movetur"* (Louvain, 1962). (The most interesting Scotist challenges concerning natural knowledge of God were posed by the remarkably problematic *Theoremata*, which received interesting commentary in the Wadding edition. It was *not* a work, however, that seemed to focus any debates or commentaries beyond the responses of the Wadding edition commentators. As the late Ira O. Wade once remarked to me concerning Voltaire, the objects of our study do not always act with our convenience in mind! Neither Scotists nor their students tended to go beyond his more celebrated works for their sense of his theology, and discussion of the *Theoremata* is hard to find. Scotus's deserved reputation as "the Subtle Doctor" appears to have made many seventeenth-century critics and commentators less than enthusiastic about engaging his most difficult works.)

the beings we observe, their capacity to come into being and pass away, we similarly knew that there must be a *Necessary Being*. Four, from the *degrees of perfection* in the finite beings we observe (for example, in goodness, wisdom, or powers), we knew that there must be a *Supreme Perfection* of whose absolute perfection they were partial negations (or in whose absolute perfection they participated). Five, from the *benevolent purposes, harmony, and order* of the world that we observe, we knew that there must be a *Providence*, that is to say, a supremely wise and beneficent governor of the world. Seventeenth-century Scholastics were committed, in epistemological theory at least, to Aristotle's celebrated dictum that nothing entered the mind except by way of the senses, and here, from our experience of the world, were five compelling a posteriori demonstrations whose force had stood the test of time and criticism.[2]

For Cartesians, Descartes's "revolution" in thinking about knowledge, his theory of certainty based on "clear and distinct ideas," and, above all, his denial of the priority of sense experience in the acquisition of true and certain *scientia*, created (and, for the most theologically fervent among them, arose from) the need for demonstrations of the existence of God consistent with this exaltation of "idea" and this denigration of induction from the "uncertain" senses in fundamental philosophy. For Scholastics, Descartes—to whatever extent he was not just another misguided "innovator"—merely had revived, in his demonstrations of God, the initially well-intentioned arguments of theologians who had been properly criticized by Aquinas and by Thomistic (and other) commentators. Many believed, depending on their degree of charity, that only deliberate malice, ambition, superficiality, fatuity, or ignorance could lead someone to restate what already had been disposed of as useless to the faith, or even, since bad arguments for true propositions created unnecessary doubts, as dangerous to it. For Cartesians, however, Descartes's proofs of God were so convincing that they believed that he had made it literally impossible to doubt in any sincere manner the truth of philosophical knowledge of the existence of God.

In the view of so many Cartesians, Descartes had revivified the soul of metaphysical philosophy, ended the "tyranny" of Aristotle, and restored Christian thought to the more "Platonic" affinities of the patristics and, above all, of Saint Augustine. By the late seventeenth century, *a posteriori* and *a priori* referred above all to the *source* of natural demonstration and whether it was "after" or "before" knowledge of *effects* derived from

[2] Although Aquinas addressed the question of proof of God's existence diversely in a variety of places, the "Five Ways" that came to be synonymous with "his" demonstration of God are found in any edition of the *Summa Theologiae* 1a, q.2, art. 3.

sense experience of the world. In theory, the distinction could well refer to what was logically or ontologically prior or posterior, but it was almost invariably understood to distinguish between proof from sensible effects and proof from cause or essence grasped by the mind.

Although we generally associate Augustinian theology with a more pessimistic version of the consequences of the Fall for natural theology, the Scholastics also stressed those consequences but focused on a different set of supposed effects. For the Scholastics, it was the pure intuitive light that we had lost: only Adam as a natural philosopher had known God a priori; the Fall had condemned all the rest of us in matters natural to rely upon the senses and our experience. To the Cartesians, on the other hand, which was not without appeal to Augustinians, it was our corporeal sensory experience of the world that reflected the consequences of the Fall far more starkly. Reason, for the Cartesians, was not of the concupiscent body, and though easily enslaved by perverse volition and easily ignored in the sensual business of life, it had remained, as pure spirit, an unerring guide to truth. For the Cartesians, first truths were to be disclosed a priori, that is, as they understood it, by reason alone, independently of sense experience, as in geometry or logic. Descartes, his disciples believed, had offered two such purely rational proofs, both following solely from logical analysis of the idea of God as a perfect being.

Although twentieth-century philosophers debate both whether Descartes advanced two or three proofs in the *Meditations* and whether or not these proofs were in fact (from modern notions) a priori, almost all seventeenth-century defenders and critics of Descartes (though not necessarily Descartes himself) understood him to have advanced two distinctly a priori demonstrations. Early-modern thinkers tended to reverse the sequence of "first" and "second" proof as currently labeled, and we shall follow them in this. One, there was proof from the idea of God as the most perfect being of whom we can conceive, entailing His actual existence as a necessary property of perfection. What has come to be termed Descartes's "ontological proof" was understood by his contemporaries as follows: what we conceive as necessarily entailed by the essence or nature of an entity truly belongs to it (e.g., of a triangle, three angles whose sum equals that of two right angles); since actual existence is necessarily entailed by the essence of the most perfect being (for its nonexistence would contradict its essence as most perfect being, making a nonexistent God as self-contradictory as a four-sided triangle), the perfect being necessarily and, thus, actually exists. Two, there was Descartes's proof from the "objective being" of the idea of God. This demonstration, for seventeenth-century readers, was based on a distinction between the nature of an idea as a modification of the mind (its "formal being") and as a representation of some particular entity or object (its "objective being"). For Descartes, one could in all instances, save one, analyze what an idea represented to us, without thereby knowing whether such a represented being, the "object" of the idea, had actual existence. The exception was the case of a perfect being, for on the principle that no cause could have less perfection than its effect, the cause of the "objective being" of the idea of infinite perfection must itself be infinitely perfect. Stated less formally, and without the explicit notion of "cause," the source of the idea of a perfect being could not be an imperfect mind or any imperfect being, since they could have no infinite perfection to be represented in such an idea. Rather, only an actual perfect being could be the source of the idea of infinite perfection, such that analysis of the idea of God demonstrated with certainty that an infinitely perfect being exists.[3] The seventeenth century generally did not see such a demonstration as a posteriori from effect to cause, but as an attempted a priori proof from analysis of the idea of God alone.

For the Scholastics, these two Cartesian "proofs" were utterly fallacious, dangerous in their weakness, and revealed Cartesianism clearly for the philosophical confusion they took it to be. Descartes's proofs, for them, were interlopers that threatened to unsettle what should be settled in all minds. Let us turn first, then, to Scholastic perception and refutation of them, bearing in mind the very large number of Cartesians who were the objects of such "refutation" of their grounds for believing in the demonstrability of God. Textbooks and historians of philosophy focus, on the whole, on the sets of objections and replies concerning these proofs

[3] These demonstrations are found in the third and fifth meditations in any edition of Descartes's *Meditations on First Philosophy*, first published as *Meditationes de prima philosophia in qua Dei existentia et animae immortalitas demonstratur* (Paris, 1641); 2d ed. (Paris, 1642); French translations (Paris, 1647; Paris, 1661; Paris, 1673). For a sample of conflicting modern analyses and interpretations of Descartes's proofs, see M. Guéroult, *Descartes selon l'ordre des raisons*, vol. I: *L'âme et Dieu* (Paris, 1953); the response to this by H. Gouhier, "La preuve ontologique de Descartes (A propos d'un livre récent)," *Revue Internationale de Philosophie* VIII, no. 29 (1954), 295–303; and the reconsideration by Guéroult, *Nouvelles réflexions sur la preuve ontologique de Descartes* (Paris, 1955). See also E. M. Curley, *Descartes against the Skeptics* (Cambridge, Mass., 1978), 125–69; A. Kenny, *Descartes* (New York, 1968), passim; L. J. Beck, *The Metaphysics of Descartes: A Study of the Meditations* (Oxford, 1965), 231–37; B. Magnus, "The Modalities of Descartes's Proofs for the Existence of God," in *Cartesian Essays: A Collection of Critical Studies*, ed. B. Magnus and J. B. Wilburd (The Hague, 1969), 77–87; W. Doney, "The Geometrical Presentation of Descartes's A Priori Proof," in *Descartes, Critical and Interpretive Essays*, ed. M. Hooker (Baltimore, 1978), 1–25; H. Gouhier, *La pensée métaphysique de Descartes* (Paris, 1962), 143–61; and J. Rée, *Descartes* (London, 1974), 135–40, 162–64. This is simply a small selection of twentieth-century readings of Descartes, and I beg authors excluded from this list to take no offense.

published in the very first edition of the *Meditations*.[4] In fact, however, it was in the two generations that followed Descartes's death that the *historically* most significant contestations occurred.

. . .

Scholastics assailed these two Cartesian proofs with a self-confident ferocity that derived from the most essential elements of their education, predisposing them both to categorize the proofs as a priori and to reject even the theoretical possibility of their validity. They were Aristotelians, and they were generally disciples of Aquinas in fundamental philosophical theology. What did they learn at those fonts that pertained to the Cartesian demonstrations they would encounter?

First, of course, there was what was taken to be the whole sensationalist orientation of Aristotelian philosophy, the belief that one cannot in matters of natural philosophy attain knowledge of an intelligible reality by intuition or natural illumination, but that one must begin in the sensible and proceed *from* that *to* recognition of a Divinity, a recognition that then allowed for some ultimate (if limited) rational understanding of the universe. This sensationalism was precisely what made the Jesuit *Journal de Trévoux* initially quite sympathetic to John Locke.[5] Aquinas had put the matter directly:

> According to its manner in the present life, the intellect depends on the sense for the origin of knowledge; and so those things that do not fall under the senses cannot be grasped by the human intellect except in so far as the knowledge of them is gathered from sensible things. . . . [B]eginning with sensible things, our intellect is led to the point of knowing about God that He exists.[6]

In natural knowledge, for the Scholastics, only principles and axioms could be known immediately or by intuition. Demonstrations applied these to derive truths from other things that were known. In the *Posterior Analytics*, Aristotle distinguished between demonstration *propter quid* and demonstration *quia*. The first was from the cause to the consequences of the cause, and was the ideal of logical scientific demonstration: knowledge and analysis of the cause entailed certain truths about its consequences or effects. It was this logical mode that Scholastics found so rewarding a tool in the deduction of further truths from divine revelations

[4] Descartes, *Oeuvres philosophiques* (Alquié ed.), II, 507–890.

[5] *Journal de Trévoux*, jan.–fév. 1701, 116–31, where Locke is called "a penetrating mind who meditates much and who is convincing." The reviewer particularly praised Locke's sensationalism with reference to proof of the existence of God and, indeed, of the existence of all things beyond our own selves.

[6] Aquinas, *Summa Contra Gentiles* l.I. c.3. par.4 (Pegis translation).

that could be taken as certain because of their source. Demonstration *propter quid* was what Scholastics and Cartesians saw as a priori demonstration. For the Aristotelians, such demonstration required a proposition known to be true with certainty, and if the *question* was, Does God exist? it obviously (for them) begged that question to answer yes on the basis of what followed as a consequence from a cause as yet unknown.[7]

Aquinas's *Summa Theologiae*, in fact, had addressed (quite briefly) Saint Anselm's and others' belief that God was self-evident from reflection upon or analysis of the terms of His nature as a being than which nothing greater or more perfect could be conceived. In one sense, Aquinas had treated "self-evidence" as an issue that depended to a significant degree on the factual question of whether or not there were those who did not believe it (if there were, it was not "self-evident"). Nonetheless, with Saint Anselm's *Proslogion* as his seeming model, he had stated the case for self-evidence in language that related directly to what his disciples would see as Descartes's own proof. Although he would reject it, he understood it as follows:

> A proposition is self-evident if we perceive its truth immediately upon perceiving the meaning of its terms: a characteristic, according to Aristotle, of first principles of demonstration. . . . Now once we understand the meaning of the word "God" it follows that God exists. For the word means "that than which nothing greater can be meant." Consequently since existence in thought and fact is greater than existence in thought alone, and since, once we understand the word "God," He exists in thought, He must also exist in fact. It is therefore self-evident that there is a God.[8]

Thus, so many students of the *Summa Theologiae* did not believe Descartes to have said anything new in this regard. As Pierre-Daniel Huet put it in 1711, Descartes had tried to claim originality by insisting that he had never read Saint Anselm; this was dishonest for Huet, since the argument could be found in a source he surely had read: Descartes's "demonstration of the existence of God, which has caused such a clamor [*qui a fait tant de bruit*] . . . is from Saint Anselm, . . . found in the *Summa* of Saint Thomas."[9]

Devising an "objection" to such a demonstration, Aquinas noted that

[7] Aristotle, *Posterior Analytics* I and II. Most students in France after the mid-seventeenth century would have used the *Aristotelis Opera Omnia* . . . , ed. Guillaume Du Val, 3d ed., 4 [fol.] vols. (Paris, 1654). (The prior seventeenth-century editions were Paris, 1619 and Paris, 1629.)

[8] Aquinas, *Summa Theologiae* I.1, q.2, art. 1 (Blackfriars translation). [The discussion is virtually identical in Aquinas, *Summa Contra Gentiles* I.I. c.22.]

[9] Pierre-Daniel Huet, bishop of Avranches, *Nouveaux mémoires pour servir à l'histoire du Cartésianisme* (Paris, 1711), 7.

"nobody can think the opposite of a self-evident proposition," and he cited the Psalmist about the "fool" who denied God. In his own conclusion, however, Saint Thomas formally distinguished between a proposition that was "self-evident in itself [*per se nota secundum se est*]" and a proposition that was "self-evident to us [*quoad nos*]." Since, for Aquinas, God's essence and existence were inseparable, "the proposition God exists is self-evident in itself," but the proposition was "*not* self-evident to us" and could only be made evident in natural philosophy by demonstration *from effects*, that is, by demonstration a posteriori. In brief, in terms of how the seventeenth century read Aquinas, *after* God's existence had been demonstrated a posteriori, one *then* understood that as He was a perfect being, His existence and essence were one. The proposition "God exists" indeed was analytically true, but barring the miracle of direct illumination by Truth itself, the human mind could know it to be true only after sensible proof of His existence:

> Someone hearing the word "God" may very well not understand it to mean "that than which nothing greater can be thought," [and] indeed, some people have believed God to be a body. And even if the meaning of the word "God" were generally recognized to be "that than which nothing greater can be thought," *nothing thus defined would thereby be granted existence in the world of fact, but merely as thought about. Unless one is given that something in fact exists than which nothing greater can be thought—and this nobody denying the existence of God would grant—the conclusion that God in fact exists does not follow.*[10]

As Aquinas further explained, "Yet because we are not able to conceive in our minds that which God is, that God exists remains unknown [in terms of "self-evidence"] in relation to us." It is only once we know the nature of a "whole," he explained by analogy, that the proposition "the whole is greater than its part" becomes self-evident to us. It would require prior knowledge of the nature of God to know that "God exists" is a true and certain proposition.[11]

This distinction between two kinds of analytic propositions—those true in themselves and true for us, on the one hand, and, on the other, those true in themselves but not true for us—sounds odd, perhaps, to modern ears. Seventeenth-century Scholastics, however, did not find it curious. As a reflection upon a God already known and demonstrated as a perfect being, it followed from analysis that He existed necessarily. Since such an analysis, however, could only *follow* demonstration of the object of analysis, it was absurd to them *to assume* such a being and *to*

[10] Aquinas, *Summa Contra Gentiles* l.i.c.11. (Pegis translation).
[11] Ibid.

begin with such an analysis. For them, the fallen human condition was not a state of perfect knowledge, to say the least, and it was not at all surprising that what was true for God was not apparent to us.

Besides, and for many this sufficed, it was a distinction that Saint Thomas himself had maintained explicitly. So many students of Saint Thomas in the seventeenth century, which is to say, so many of those who dominated the educational structures of France, took Saint Thomas to be "the Angelic Doctor" par excellence of their faith. It is difficult to exaggerate the degree to which early-modern disciples of Saint Thomas admired him, prompting, you will recall, the Oratorian Richard Simon's barbed comment that they had made a "fifth evangelist" of him. In the late seventeenth century, Bishop Louis Abelly wrote a meditation for 7 March of "the Christian year," the saint's day of Thomas Aquinas. After briefly detailing Thomas's "virtue of chastity," he wrote at length upon "the completely celestial doctrine with which his soul was adorned, and by which he enlightened and still enlightens the entire Church." He added:

> This science merits being approved not only from [the authority of] the entire Church, but even from the very mouth of Jesus Christ. For this holy doctor being one day at prayer before a crucifix, he heard a voice which emerged, which calling him by his name, said to him: "Thomas, you have written and spoken very well of me in your books."[12]

Given such a view, the Dominican professor Antoine Regnault (Antonio Reginaldo) could find it both "ignorant" and "criminal" to criticize the doctrine of Saint Thomas, whose teaching had been confirmed by the Church, and specifically, he believed, by her Councils and popes.[13]

For seventeenth-century Scholastic Scotists, similar arguments against a priori proof of God were available from their mentor's most widely cited works, the Parisian and Oxford teachings. In the former, Duns Scotus had argued that God's being could not be known a priori, since we

[12] Louis Abelly, bishop of Rhodes, *La Couronne de l'année chrétienne, ou Méditations sur les principales et les plus importantes vérités de l'Evangile de Jésus-Christ . . .*, new ed., 2 vols. (Lyon, 1796), I, 473–75. By comparison, the fête of St. Augustine moved him to note (II, 249–51) that he was "one of the brightest lights of the Church" because of his assaults on heresy and infidelity, his dignity as a good pastoral bishop, and his foundation of a religious order. Abelly died in 1691, and this is a reprint of the *12*th ed. of Paris, 1706. The 1st ed. was Paris, 1657, and the 11th ed., Paris 1698. The 12th ed. also had been reprinted in 1720.

[13] Antoine Ravaille Regnault (Antonio Reginaldo), O.P., *Doctrinae Divi Thomae Aquinatis tria principia cum suis consequentiis, ubi totius doctrinae compendium & connexio continetur*, 3 vols. (Toulouse, 1670), I, "Praefatio." The "three principles" were "*Ens est trancendens*"; "*Deus solus est actus purus*"; and "*Absoluta specificentur à se; relativa ab alio.*"

had no prior demonstration of the essence of God to serve as a middle term for any *propter quid* demonstration of His existence.[14] In the latter, he had specified that any a priori knowledge of God's essence, from which His existence could be demonstrated, depended upon a prior concept of God, which begged precisely the question at hand and depended upon a certainty unavailable through natural philosophy about the relationships among our human and therefore composed concepts of divine essence. God's existence, then, for Scotus, could not be derived from the terms of any of our definitions of Him.[15]

Even the leading Capuchin professor and disciple of Saint Bonaventure, who stressed that he and many theologians in his order were not Thomists, nor Scotists, "but Bonaventurists," and who complained about the exclusion of Saint Bonaventure from the curricula of non-Franciscan orders, offered his readers a Saint Bonaventure forced (at some violence, perhaps, to the intent of the *Itinerarium mentis*) into the closest possible agreement with Saint Thomas on this question.[16] In his *Cursus Theologicus, ad mentem Seraphici Doctoris S. Bonaventurae* (1687), Bartholomaeus Barberiis cited Saint Bonaventure's argument that since God's existence was identical with His essence, "we cannot conceive that God does not exist." He employed this argument, however, only to demonstrate that the Seraphic Doctor agreed with Saint Thomas against Duns Scotus about the relationship of existence and essence in God (Duns Scotus having presented that relationship, in Barberiis's analysis, as modal rather than predicative).[17] He cited Saint Bonaventure's arguments that God was "without possibility of not being" and, thus, that "this proposition, God exists, is self-evident," proven by "connection between subject and predicate." He used this argument, however, *not* to prove the existence of God, but only to distinguish between the being of created things and the being of God.[18] In fact, he too insisted on a categorical distinction between what was "self-evident" about God *after* one knew Him and what was demonstrable "according to [the condition of] the creatures," concluding explicitly that "God's existence is demonstrable by natural reason not a priori but a posteriori [*Deum esse est demonstrabile per rationem naturalem, non a priori, sed a posteriori*]." In our fallen state, he insisted, we had such a defective knowledge of *what* God is, of His essence, that it was wholly evident that nothing probative fol-

[14] Duns Scotus, *Rep. Paris.* I. d.2. q.2.

[15] Duns Scotus, *Opus Oxon.* I. d.2. p.1. q.1–2.

[16] Bartholomaeus [de] Barberiis, O.F.M., Capuchin, *Cursus Theologicus, ad mentem Seraphici Doctoris S. Bonaventurae*, 2 tomes in 1 vol. (Lyon, 1687). The reference to the status of (and his loyalty to) St. Bonaventure is found in I, "Ad lectorem benignissimum."

[17] Ibid., I, 12–15 (and see, especially, his nn. 30–32).

[18] Ibid., 13 (and see, especially, his nn. 33–35).

lowed from our notion of Him. *We* could not know God "absolutely, but only in relationship to the creatures and a posteriori." The question "if He is" *must* precede, in human knowledge, the question "what He is," because "existence cannot be proven from essence [*non potest existentia per essentiam probari*]."[19]

Supporting Saint Thomas's refutation of the "self-evidence" of God's existence, which is to say, in seventeenth-century understanding, his refutation of a priori demonstration of God, the Dominican Jean Nicolai, editor of the major seventeenth-century edition of Aquinas's works, merely referred his readers, without commentary, to Aristotle's *Posterior Analytics*.[20] To understand those readers, we must, like them, read Descartes through the filter of Aristotle's *Organon*. Aristotelianism, as they were taught it, was the intellectual air that they breathed, their common language. It was Aristotle's most general analyses of demonstrations that gave them their grounds for refutation and attack.

In the *Topica*, Aristotle had defined *definition* as "a phrase indicating the essence of something."[21] Descartes, Scholastics believed, merely had *defined* God as the most perfect being of which we can conceive and deduced His necessary actual existence from that. Aristotle had taught them, however, most explicitly in the *Posterior Analytics*, that a definition proved nothing and could not conceivably prove anything either by syllogism, by analysis, or by hypothesis. "To define the nature of a unit," Aristotle had insisted, "is not the same as to assert its existence." "Definitions," he taught, "make no assertion of existence or non-existence." Further, the master instructed, questions of existence always must precede questions of essence: "When we know that the subject exists, we ask what is it." It was "evident," Aristotle had written, not only "that not everything that is definable is demonstrable," but (with obvious relevance to his seventeenth-century disciples as they read the Cartesians), "that in no case is it possible to have both definition and demonstration of the same thing. Thus, it is clear also that definition and demonstration cannot be the same, and that neither can be included in the other." In no demonstration, Aristotle insisted, can essence appear in the premise or middle term before a determination about existence. If it did, "we are assuming what we are required to prove," an example of "*petitio principii*," the crude fallacy of begging the questions at hand.[22]

[19] Ibid., 13–14 (n. 35).

[20] Nicolai, O.P., ed. *Summa Theologica S. Thomae Aquinatis* I. q.2, a.1, note K. In Nicolai's notes to the "Five Ways," he refers the first proof exclusively to Aristotle's *Physics*.

[21] Aristotle, *Topica* I.v.101b.40–102a.1 (translation from the Loeb ed. of *Organon*, vol. II, ed. and trans. E. S. Forster [Cambridge, Mass., 1960]).

[22] Aristotle, *Posterior Analytics* I–II.viii (translation from Ibid., ed. and trans. Hugh Tredennick).

A definition of *X* and a demonstration of the existence of *X*, Aristotle taught, were categorically distinct. One may *assume* meaning, but one must *demonstrate* existence. Thus, *knowledge* of the essence of any actual thing assumed that its existence had been demonstrated, and no definition of essence could entail any such demonstration of its own validity or of the actual existence of the essence defined. "It is evident," in Aristotle's words, "that those who define do not prove the existence of the definiendum [that which is defined]." Further, "Definitions do not include evidence that it is possible for what they describe to exist, nor that it is identical with that which they claim to define." The question of the existence [*an est*] of any being must *precede* the question of its essence [*quid est*] in the order of scientific knowledge.[23] To students of Aristotle, Cartesians seemed to have failed to grasp the most elementary principles of logic.

Aristotle, for the Scholastics, had described *petitio principii* definitively, and for the life of them, they never quite could grasp how any serious philosopher could disagree with them that this fallacy was at the heart of Descartes's proofs. In the *De Sophisticis Elenchis*, Aristotle had defined this paralogism in simple terms and provided the means to identify it: "Fallacies due to assuming the original point and stating as a cause what is not a cause are clearly exposed by means of the definition . . . ; again, the conclusion should follow without the original point being included, which is not true of arguments based on the begging of the original point."[24] Such a paralogism, for Aristotle, easily led to "the case where the result follows in word only and not in reality."[25] As we shall see, this was precisely the main line of Scholastic assault upon Cartesian proof. Aristotle, for the Scholastics, had shown in either the *Physics* or the *Metaphysics* or both that there was, indeed, as he phrased it in the latter, "a primary being, eternal and unmovable and separate from sensible things."[26] He had demonstrated this, however, they believed, not from any definition and arbitrary assumption of such a being, but from the applications of the principles of rigorous reasoning to sensibly acquired knowledge of the world.

In Pierre Barbay's *In universam Aristotelis philosophiam introductio* (in a fifth edition by 1707) and in his diverse commentaries on Aristotelian philosophy, the eminent Parisian Scholastic philosopher fully accepted what Aquinas had seen in his own discussion of natural knowledge of existence and essence in God: once one knows by sensible means *that* God exists, one *then* understands that His necessary existence and His

[23] Ibid., II.

[24] Aristotle, *De Sophisticis Elenchis* VI.168b.22–26 (translation from the Loeb ed. of *On Sophistical Refutations*, ed. and trans. E. S. Forster [Cambridge, Mass., 1955]).

[25] Ibid., VIII.170a.5–10.

[26] Aristotle, *Metaphysica* XII.7.1073a (Richard Hope translation).

essence are inseparable. Only principles, however, such as that something cannot both be and not be at the same time, are not in need of proof. In this world, one must prove, and not assume, the existence of an entity with this or that essence, and no demonstration can follow from a mere hypothetical assumption.[27] As he indicated in his *Commentarius in Aristotelis Metaphysicam*, in a second edition of 1676, as much as one would wish to make the proposition "God exists" a principle of natural metaphysics, one may not, but must proceed to demonstrate such a thesis by application of the principle of identity and contradiction to the world as we know it.[28] Further, for Barbay, in a lesson that would come to mind for many Scholastics when they considered both of Descartes's proofs, causality itself has no prior cause (or else there would be infinite regress), and God, as first cause, has "no cause of Himself."[29] Yet from Scholastic perspective, Cartesian proof of God a priori was proof of God *from cause*, which meant conceiving of God as effect, which was self-contradictory.

Barbay also emphasized the Aristotelian distinction between "beings of reason" and "beings of the actual world." Whenever Scholastics considered Descartes's proofs of God from an idea, they thought precisely of a "being of reason," something that might well exist just as a phantasm or modification of the human mind, without any referent in the actual world. The atheist's "no God," the polytheist's "many Gods," and the Christian's "one God," for Barbay, were all thoughts in human minds, from which nothing about their actual existence possibly could follow. The atheist and polytheist, however, could not demonstrate the content of their thought to be actual in the world beyond their thought, and thus they thought only on "beings of reason." The theist, however, could demonstrate his one God from the visible world and knew from this that his thought was of an actual being in the actual world. Since God is the First Cause, He obviously cannot be demonstrated a priori, but He can be demonstrated "from the creatures or effects," that is, Barbay offered, from the order of the cosmos, and from the series of essentially dependent causes we observe.[30] Saint Anselm and Descartes, Barbay noted, as Aquinas had shown, confused something true about the God we came to know by a posteriori demonstration or revelation—that His existence is insep-

[27] Pierre Barbay, *In universam Aristotelis philosophiam introductio*, 5th ed., rev. (Paris, 1707), 173–74; *In Aristotelis Metaphysicam*, 66–74, 89–93, 361–72 (within which, 368–72, his specific rejection of Descartes's proof and his use of Aquinas's reply to Anselm's proof). Barbay's metaphysics is essentially Aristotle and Aquinas as commented upon by Suarez.

[28] Barbay, *In Aristotelis Metaphysicam*, 24–29.

[29] Ibid., 89–92.

[30] Ibid., 310–25.

arable from His essence—with something unknowable to us in the course of seeking natural demonstration of His existence.[31]

In the Jesuit Georges de Rhodes's *Philosophia Peripatetica, ad Veram Aristotelis Mentem* (1671), a priori certainty was defined as "certain and evident knowledge" by means of a "necessary connection" between a "cause" that is known and an entailed effect or consequence. Since no cause of the First Cause is possible, and since knowledge of immaterial entities must be derived from experience of the sensible world, it followed ineluctably for him, as for Barbay, that "we do not know God and the angels *except by means of material things* [*Deinde non cognoscimus Deum et Angelos, nisi per res materiales*]."[32] This posed no difficulty whatsoever for de Rhodes, since we knew God both through His production and conservation of the world, and through His purposes that were so manifest in it.[33] As the Parisian-trained theologian Bésian Arroy wrote, God only could be known either by direct communication of His glory to the just, which had nothing to do with philosophy, or from His works, "outside of Himself [*hors de lui*]," from which we inferred both His existence and His perfections. In our human state, causes are known from their effects.[34] The Aristotelian Jean Vincent, a professor of theology and a priest of the Congregation of Christian Doctrine, did *not* believe that

[31] Ibid., 361–72; his discussion in ibid., 373–450, attempts to demonstrate how one may deduce the divine attributes from the being first established by a posteriori proofs.

[32] Georges de Rhodes, S.J., *Philosophia Peripatetica, ad Veram Aristotelis Mentem. Libris quatuor Digesta & Disputata; Pharus ad Theologiam Scholasticam* (Lyon, 1671), 75, 606–704 (the lengthy quotation is from 620).

[33] Ibid., 154–79, 268–73.

[34] Bésian Arroy, *Le prince instruit en la philosophie en français* . . . (Lyon, 1671), 299–309. Arroy argued (ibid., 326–334) that "the three most learned metaphysicians" in the history of mankind had been King David, Aristotle, and St. Thomas. Despite Aristotle's having been "an infidel," Arroy urged, St. Thomas was "the irreproachable *approbateur* of the metaphysical perfection of Aristotle, since he used him to give clarity to the certainty of the faith which we have in its obscurity; thus . . . Aristotle himself is [also] an irreproachable witness of the metaphysical knowledge of St. Thomas." (It was this sort of thing that drove Platonizers, Augustinians, and Cartesians to despair!) In his candid "Au Lecteur" [unpaginated], Arroy announced that he was eighty years old, and had taught philosophy in Latin and in Greek with great pleasure for years, but now wanted to write in French. Above all, he declared, he hoped to address *not* "the students of Paris," who were comfortable with Latin and with "all savant philosophers," but, rather, the provincial priests who came "for the most part from poor families" and were not going to read Latin tomes. Explaining his book's title, he said that he had taught nobles and members of the royal court in addition to priests, and that they had the same need. He recorded his surprise that in such a contentious philosophical age as this, the first five theologians to whom he submitted his work for approbation had approved of it, but he noted that two were friends of his who happened to be Thomistic doctors of the Sorbonne and had overpraised it; two were Carmelite theologians who at least had found it "solid"; and one was a theologian who at least had claimed to like it.

we could learn of God's perfections from the creatures, but only of His existence. To know the quiddity or essence of God was not within the powers of the natural creature; to know "*that* He exists," however, was precisely what we learned from universal consent, and from motion, causality, contingency, degrees of perfection, the order and disposition of the world, and the desire of intelligent creatures for beatitude.[35]

• • •

When the Doctrinaire Vincent specifically turned his Aristotelianism against the Cartesians, in his *Discussio peripatetica in qua philosophiae Cartesianae principia, per singula fere capita seu Articulos dilucide examinantur* (1677), he expressed his bitter disappointment that Cartesian philosophy had made such progress despite so many official censures and condemnations, including those of the "three great tribunals" of the Sorbonne, the parlement of Paris, and Rome. He found much to condemn in Descartes, including the definition of body as extension, which he deemed incompatible with the Catholic doctrine of the Eucharist. He also declared himself both offended and philosophically appalled by Descartes's proofs of God. First, he was offended by the suggestion that demonstration should proceed from methodological "doubt" to conviction by "clear and distinct ideas" since, he believed, this called upon the Christian to suspend belief in God. What was appalling to him, however, was that having led the believer into such a suspension of belief, awaiting persuasion, Descartes should attempt to prove God from the idea of the infinite, despite, he insisted, both countless demonstrations that this could not be done and the manifest inadequacy of any human conception of the infinite to be a source of any certain consequence. In brief, for Vincent, any consistent Cartesian logically should suspend belief in God's existence and remain permanently in that state.[36]

For more than two generations, in every form of theological and philosophical media—courses, textbooks, formal Latin tomes, serious vernacular treatises, sardonic parodies, book reviews, and exchanges in the popular learned journals—the Aristotelians scornfully analyzed the Cartesian proofs of God, seeking precisely to show that, in effect, no Cartesian had the right to believe in God on the basis of the proofs he had accepted. They did this precisely during the period when large numbers of French thinkers believed themselves to be Cartesians. The tone and

[35] Vincent, Doctrinaire, *Cursus philosophicus*, v, 599–619.

[36] Jean Vincent, Doctrinaire, *Discussio peripatetica in qua philosophiae Cartesianae principia, per singula fere capita seu Articulos dilucide examinantur* (Toulouse, 1677), passim. See the "Praefatio" for his shock at the persistence of Cartesians despite official censures.

content of these attacks were not surpassed by later eighteenth-century atheistic critics of these Cartesian "demonstrations."

. . .

For the Scholastics, Descartes's proof from the necessary existence of a perfect being simply assumed what in fact it was obligated to demonstrate. François-Marie Assermet, a leading Cordelier (and Scotist) professor of theology, tried to sum up for his students those two generations of criticism in his *Theologia scholastico-positiva* (1713). An opponent of Jansenism and of all attempted use of Saint Augustine against the Scholastics, he found it difficult to believe that even such hapless theologians as his targets could take Descartes's proof seriously. All that the Cartesians had done, he wrote, was to pronounce their own definition of God to be an innate idea in all mankind, and since their definition included necessary existence, they declared themselves to have demonstrated the existence of God by means of their philosophy. Not only was this inane, Assermet asserted, since everyone truly learned understood why God's existence could not be proven a priori, but it was contradicted by the very opposition that they encountered. First, there could not possibly be proof a priori of God, since there was no conceivable *cause* of God's existence. Further, if all men possessed the idea of a necessarily existent perfect being, there would not be even a need for demonstration, let alone such widespread opposition to Descartes's supposed proof.[37]

Michael Morus, professor of philosophy at the University of Paris (and later at the collège royal) and principal of the collège de Navarre, sought to explain what he saw as the essential illogical nature of Descartes's proofs to his students and readers, in a work specifically addressed to Aristotelian-Cartesian debates. It was true, he noted, that the proper "idea" of God, derived from proper proof, correctly included necessary existence, but the mere and ambiguous "name" of God did not. It was so very obvious to him that one could not simply declare one's nominal definition a proper idea. First, one must demonstrate a posteriori that a perfect being existed, and only then, as Saint Thomas had seen, could one understand that such a perfect being existed necessarily "*quoad se*," with reference to His own nature. To attempt to demonstrate that with reference to our ambiguous ideas was absurd. Aristotle's five proofs (he attributed them to Aristotle and not to Saint Thomas) demonstrated such a

[37] François-Marie Assermet, O.F.M., *Theologia scholastico-positiva* . . . , vol. I: . . . *De Theologiae Principibus, Prolegomenis, De Deo Uno, Ejusque Attributis* (Paris, 1713), 111–46.

being from the things of this world, and the superiority of Aristotle to Descartes was categorical and manifest.[38]

François Perrin, a Jesuit who taught theology to seminarians at Toulouse and then was professor of theology at the University of Strasbourg, attacked Descartes's proof in his *Manuale Theologicum, sive Theologia Dogmatica et historica ad usum seminariorum*, published in Toulouse, 1710, and in a second edition in Paris, 1714. The Cartesians, he charged, never had bothered to discover if their "idea of God" were absolute or conditional, a mental being or an actual being, real or chimerical. "Why," he asked, "cannot an idea of chimerical existence enter the mind?" It could, of course, he insisted, but the Cartesians had not considered that. Their claim that the idea of God entailed His existence, he argued, begged the whole question of the essential distinction between mental and actual beings. If someone said, "There is no other God," for example, he would have the *idea* of another perfect being (the "other God" whom he denied), and by Cartesian logic, that "other God" also would have actual existence. Indeed, he concluded, the proof was so inane that it was highly dubious that Saint Anselm or any other genuine theologian ever had meant anything similar at all, and its solidity crumbled, as Saint Thomas had seen, the moment one thought seriously on it. For Perrin, the existence of God was indeed evident to all but the "fool" described by Scripture, but it was evident from nature, not from the Cartesian "idea of God." What made the existence of God manifest were a posteriori proofs: the "metaphysical" proof from the contingency of observed beings to a necessary being; the "physical" proofs from the structure of the universe, from movement, and from purpose; the "moral" proof from universal consent. The irony for Perrin was that with their new attempt to demonstrate God from an alleged "innate idea" of Him, it was precisely "these followers of the new philosophy," the Cartesians, who threatened to "cast shadows from another source over this most evident truth," and it was intolerable that "they set their feet in Theology."[39] Inundated by such charges, Cartesians could well relate to the letter from Descartes to Chanut that the Cartesian and Jansenizing priest Adrien Baillet reprinted in 1691: " 'A minister [Voët, in Holland] undertook to convince people that I was an atheist without adducing other reasons except that I tried to prove the existence of God.' "[40]

Even the eminent eclectic and generally anti-Aristotelian Minim profes-

[38] Michael Morus, *De Existentia Dei et Humanae Mentis Immortalitate secundum Cartesii et Aristotelis doctrinam disputatio* (Paris, 1692), 56–79, 196–313.

[39] François Perrin, S.J., *Manuale Theologicum, sive Theologia Dogmatica et historica ad usum seminariorum* (Toulouse, 1710), 5–9.

[40] Adrien Baillet, *La vie de Monsieur Des-Cartes*, 2 vols. (Paris, 1691), II, 282–83.

sor of theology Emmanuel Maignan, often sympathetic to Descartes, assailed his attempt to prove God by analysis of our idea of Him. Perhaps more influenced by Gassendi's early "Objections" than by any remnants of Aristotelianism, his *Philosophia Sacra* (1661) argued that "*if* God exists," He exists necessarily, but an attempted a priori proof of the essential connection between God and His necessary existence ignored the "if," which was precisely the question at hand. One could argue a posteriori from the aggregate of contingent beings to a necessary being, but *not* from the idea of a necessary being to its actual existence.[41] The Jesuit Théophile Raynaud, in his *Theologia Naturalis*, published in his *Opera Omnia* (1665), rejected the proof from contingent beings, arguing that "the atheist" would have no difficulty asserting an infinite cycle of contingencies, and urged that natural proof focus on the series of subordinated efficient causes we observe which entailed the necessity of a First Cause. He agreed emphatically, however, that God could not be demonstrated a priori, since both the evidence of atheism and the human condition made it impossible that God's existence could be "self-evident to us." Descartes's proof was Saint Anselm's, and its subtlety could not hide its sophistical nature.[42]

One of the most popular Latin censures of Cartesian proofs of God (and of Cartesianism in general) was by Pierre-Daniel Huet, a leading man of letters, a critic, an eventual bishop and member of the Académie française, and (we know in retrospect) a man rapidly moving toward extreme skepticism in matters *philosophical*. At the time of the *Censura Philosophiae Cartesianae*, however, the skepticism was not manifest to his contemporaries, and, extremely close to the Jesuits, he was perceived generally as simply a particularly effective Aristotelian voice against Descartes. The *Censura* was published in 1689, reprinted in 1690, and in a *fourth* edition by 1694.[43]

Huet's sense of Descartes's proof was clear enough: one could no more "conceive of an infinite and most perfect thing that does not exist" than

[41] Maignan, Minim, *Philosophia Sacra*, 57–104 (see especially 89–90).

[42] Raynaud, S.J., *Opera Omnia*, v, 205–17. He also thought that proofs from Aristotle's physics, from teleology and from the gradations of perfections among the creatures were satisfactory proofs (ibid., 21–40, 217–90).

[43] Pierre-Daniel Huet, bishop designate, *Censura Philosophiae Cartesianae* (Paris, 1689; Kampen, 1690); many reprintings and editions, culminating in a 4th ed. (Paris, 1694) and many reprintings in the 1720s. At the time he wrote it, Huet was bishop designate of Soissons. He eventually became bishop of Avranches but abandoned this position to devote himself full-time to scholarship and polemics. He wrote the *Censura* in French, from which he then made his Latin translation for publication (see Biblioteque Nationale, MSS.: Fonds français, 14702, an interesting window onto his hesitations and equivocations in choosing the formulas of his criticisms).

one could conceive of a triangle without "three angles equal to right angles" or "mountains without valleys." The essential flaw of that demonstration, he believed, was manifest: Descartes had failed to make the elementary Scholastic distinction between "beings in-the-mind [*a parte intellectus*]" and "beings in-the-actual-world [*a parte rei*]." Since the relationship between the two was the very issue at stake in Descartes's demonstration, the proof was hopelessly confused and question-begging. Clarification of an *idea*, Huet insisted, was *not* deduction of any truth about its supposed object.[44] Regnault's textbook on Thomistic philosophy had explained that the truth of our ideas about actuality did not pertain to "actual being [*esse realem*]" or "being of reason [*esse rationis*]" considered apart from each other, but precisely to a relationship of conformity between the two that further conformed to the understanding held by God.[45] For Huet, thus, Descartes's analysis referred only to an idea itself. Descartes, in his view, furtively had defined the "*est*" that pertained to the properties of an idea (known thus far to exist only in the understanding) as "*est a parte rei*," which, unfortunately for Descartes, was the very issue in dispute for the unbeliever. What had to be added to each proposition of Descartes's proof, Huet insisted, was the phrase "in the manner that it exists," such that "*if* [God] existed *only in the understanding*, He existed necessarily *only in the understanding*."[46] To put the matter more simply, *if* a unicorn actually existed in the manner in which we conceived of it (which would require proof from sensible experience), it must be as a creature with one horn; *if* God actually existed in the manner in which we conceived of Him (which also would require proof a posteriori), it must be as a being with necessary existence. That, for Huet, was *all* that Descartes had shown.

Prevailing Scholastic ontology reinforced this criticism. As Jean Du Hamel explained it, ideas were only "modifications of the mind" and thus were categorically distinct from "external objects"; no formal proof could deduce the latter from the former. An "atheist" would claim, Du Hamel noted, that nothing supremely perfect could exist *a parte rei*; it never would occur to the unbeliever to doubt that the *idea* of such a being could exist.[47] For the eminent Michael Morus, the Cartesians could not establish their doctrine of innate ideas (the very existence of atheists demonstrating that the idea of God, in particular, was not innate), nor account for their formation and being. The arrogant and illogical flaw at

[44] Ibid., 103–36 (c.4).

[45] Regnault, O.P., *Doctrinae Divi Thomae Aquinatis*, 118–20.

[46] Huet, *Censura*, 103–36.

[47] Jean Du Hamel, *Lettre de Monsieur Du Hamel, ancien professeur de philosophie à l'Université de Paris, pour servir de réplique à Monsieur Régis* (Paris, n.d. [ca. 1699]), 7.

the heart of their theology was that they consulted not the world, but merely their own arbitrary definitional terms. Their very use of the term *God*, he argued, was thus not a reference to the known Supreme Being whose existence was demonstrated by the data of the world itself, but, rather, was simply an ambiguous name assigned to an assumed being about whom they knew nothing.[48] As the Jesuit François Perrin put it in his *Manuale Theologicum* (1710), all particular ideas required comparison to experience and authority. Men often conceived of "chimerical existence," he observed, and were certain that they were "aware" of chimerical beings. What the seeker after knowledge of God required, however, was a judgment a posteriori about divine existence, *not* contemplation of his own fancies.[49]

For Jacques-Nicolas Colbert, doctor of theology, member of the Société de Sorbonne and later archbishop of Rouen, in a work published in the very year that he was received as a member of the Académie française (by Racine himself), Descartes simply had failed to grasp the most elementary aspects of serious theology. Colbert's *Philosophia vetus et nova ad usum scholae accommodata* referred his students to Aquinas's reply to Anselm's "proof" from the idea of God. Once we knew Divinity a posteriori, we indeed understood that God existed necessarily of His own essence. No one denied that God's necessary existence was always true *for* God. Descartes, however, had confused divine and human vantages: for human beings condemned to the tutelage of the senses in matters of natural knowledge, such truth could only be gained from the external things of the world. Absent beatitude, our idea of God always would be "obscure" and "confused."[50] Even if it were not obscure, however, as Michael Morus explained, "the idea of a thing is its definition," and nothing more.[51] Even if an idea could be more than a definition, as the Scholastic Robert Basselin, professor of philosophy at the collège des Grassins at the University of Paris explained, ideas originate in the senses, the source of our notions of things.[52]

In an immensely popular work in the vernacular, the powerful Jesuit Gabriel Daniel succeeded in bringing home these criticisms of Descartes's proofs to an exceptionally wide audience. His *Voyage du Monde de Des-*

[48] Morus, *De Existentia Dei*, 47–79, 196–221, 238–47, 292–313.

[49] Perrin, *Manuale*, 5–9.

[50] Jacques-Nicolas Colbert, *Philosophia vetus et nova ad usum scholae accommodata* . . . , 4 vols. (Paris, 1678), II, 488–98. He became archbishop of Rouen in 1691. Despite his fundamental Aristotelianism, this philosophical text was not without its sympathies toward Plato and the philosophical sides of St. Augustine.

[51] Morus, *De Existentia Dei*, 56–67.

[52] Robert Basselin, *Dissertation sur l'origine des idées, où l'on fait voir contre M. Descartes, le R.P. Malebranche and MM. de Port-Royal, qu'elles nous viennent toutes des ses et comment* (Paris, 1709). The entire work is 75 pp.

cartes was published in 1690 and 1691, enjoying multiple printings, a revised edition in 1702, and an augmented edition in 1703, in which an "Avertissement au Lecteur" noted without hyperbole that it had been one of the great successes of the past thirteen years.[53] Daniel argued to his many readers that Descartes's proof was the very model of "a pure paralogism," since it obviously *began* with its putative conclusion, presupposing that the idea whose necessary attributes were under examination was "a real being, that is to say, [one] which represents a real, at least a possible object." From the idea of "a knowing, feeling horse," he explained, Descartes could not deduce its actual sentience, for first, the possible and actual existence of such a horse would have to be assured. For Daniel, Descartes's "proof" precisely did *not* establish the "*évidence*" that the idea of God was a real rather than chimerical idea. Indeed, he insisted, without "ordinary demonstrations" drawn from "reflection on the [sensible] things that prove the existence of God," the idea of a supremely perfect being seemed, in and of itself, far more chimerical than real. It in no way belonged to the essence of "Being" to be "supremely perfect Being."[54]

Further, Daniel charged, as Jean Vincent had done, that Descartes never had satisfied his own injunction "that one must doubt of everything" until convinced by "clear and distinct ideas." The *Meditations* had based its criterion of truth, "clear and distinct ideas," on a consequence drawn from demonstration and analysis of the being of God, namely, that a perfect being could not deceive. In short, for Daniel, Descartes was trapped in a vicious circle: he could not have a criterion of truth without a proof of God, but he could not prove God without a criterion of truth. And this from a man who told us to doubt everything until truth were perfectly clear! "The circle," he wrote, "always will be a circle." Thus:

> To all mankind, it always will be pitiable and ridiculous to want to demonstrate the existence of a good God who does not deceive, in order to be convinced that "what one conceives clearly is true," since it is just as impossible to demonstrate this existence without being convinced beforehand of this principle as it is to arrive at a destination without using the means that alone could get one there. . . . No one could be touched or persuaded [by this

[53] Gabriel Daniel, S.J., *Voiage du Monde de Descartes* [later, *Voyage*, in all subsequent editions] (Paris, 1690; reprint, Amsterdam, 1690 and Paris, 1691); new ed., rev. and aug. (Paris 1702); new ed., rev. and aug. [with a "Cinquième Partie"] (Paris, 1703). The "Avertissement" begins the latter edition. [He also published a *Nouvelles difficultez proposées par un péripatéticien au voyageur du monde de Descartes* (Paris, 1695), which also enjoyed a reedition in 1706 under the title of *Suite du Voyage du monde de Descartes* . . . (Amsterdam, 1706).]

[54] Ibid. (1691 ed.), 163–74. He insisted that Aquinas's proofs of God were "one hundred times more compelling," a curious comparison to "a pure paralogism."

proof] unless he had resolved with determination above all other things to let himself be convinced, and to appease at any price whatsoever the anxiety of his mind.[55]

. . .

For the Scholastics, then, as they insisted far and wide, Cartesian attempts to prove the existence of God were hopelessly confused about both the nature of demonstration and the nature of ideas. This latter confusion, in its critics' view, revealed itself most tellingly in Descartes's alleged proof from the "objective being" of the idea of God. Indeed, Scholastic and other critics were so mordant on the subject of Cartesian use of the term *objective being* that the prominent Cartesian Pierre-Sylvain Régis felt obliged to retort, in 1692, that "philosophers are free to define words as they wish, provided that they are explicit about it."[56] For anti-Cartesians, however, the problem was not only definitional, but explicitly theological.

The most frequent Scholastic objection to the Cartesian proof from the "objective being" of the idea of a perfect being was simply that no entity in the human mind could possess in *any* significant sense the perfection of God. Gabriel Daniel, again summing up more than a generation of Scholastic criticism of this proof, believed in fact that neither Descartes nor any Cartesian even had proven the principle that underlay the demonstration, namely, that "the cause of the idea must contain formally or eminently all [of the idea's] perfections." This obviated the proof for him, but he found that less interesting than the objections that remained against it even if one granted the Cartesian principle. Simply put, the Cartesians, Daniel argued, had failed to see the absolutely essential difference between "representing" and "possessing" perfection or its degrees. If the idea of perfection truly "possessed" actual perfection, he argued, then Descartes's principle, if valid, would pertain to the issue. The idea of God, however, he insisted, merely "represented" perfection to us, and since no human idea could "represent" anything except in a manner consistent with the manifest *imperfections* of the human mind, it "repre-

[55] Ibid. (1702 ed.), 524–25.

[56] Pierre-Sylvain Régis, *Réponse aux Réflexions du M. Du Hamel sur le système cartésien de la Philosophie de M. Régis* (Paris, 1692), 5–8. Régis had attended Rohault's "public" lectures on Cartesianism in Paris and then himself offered scheduled and celebrated public lectures on Descartes's philosophy in Toulouse, Montpellier, and then Paris, where, apparently disturbed by their immense success, the archibishop of Paris at least nominally forbade him to lecture publicly. His published courses on Cartesian philosophy were exceptionally popular, however, and he was extremely active in defending Cartesian philosophy, both physical and metaphysical, from all critics. In 1699, he became a member of the Académie des Sciences.

sented" perfection imperfectly. Representing perfection "imperfectly," then, the idea of God obviously could have an *imperfect* cause of its being, and, thus, did not establish the existence of God. In short, "the perfection of an idea is not measured by the nobility of the object it represents, but by the manner in which it represents it, which being very imperfect in the case in question, cannot be infinite."[57]

Responding to Cartesian explanations that such criticisms would be appropriate *only* if the Cartesians had attempted to prove God from the "formal" rather than the "objective" being of the idea of God, Jean Du Hamel replied sharply that this critical Cartesian distinction was "confused" and "false." Cartesians were trying to distinguish between (1) ideas as modifications of the human mind and (2) ideas as representations of a particular object, but, he argued, the two were inseparable. The "power of representing," he wrote, was merely *an attribute* of the "formal being" of human ideas, of the kinds of things that ideas were. Since human thought was manifestly imperfect, the formal being of human ideas was precisely the power to represent objects and modify the mind *imperfectly*. A proper concept of the "objective being" of ideas, thus, was not the active power to represent, but the passive power to be represented imperfectly, from which one certainly never could infer the existence of any perfect being. To make *that* inference, one would have to prove that God Himself was represented in all of His infinity and infinite perfection in an imperfect human idea. All Cartesians, however, Du Hamel noted, willingly admitted that men did not know God "in an infinite and comprehensive manner," so they logically could *not* conclude the existence of God from the "objective being" of the idea we have of Him. The alternative, Du Hamel insisted, would be the extraordinary fallacy of supposing that "the idea of God" is "the actual perception of God." Surely, he argued (incorrectly, we shall see, with reference to the Malebranchists), all philosophical camps agreed on the preposterousness of *that*. Whether one believed the idea of God to be innate or acquired, representing infinite perfection positively (as the Cartesians believed), analogically (as many Scholastics believed), or by negation of finite imperfections (as many other Scholastics, including Du Hamel, believed), it surely was obvious to all that the manner in which a human idea represented God (or, indeed, anything) was always finite and imperfect.[58] These were standard criticisms.[59]

Régis, the veritable spokesman of the "orthodox" (that is, non-Male-

[57] Daniel, S.J., *Voyage* (1691 ed.), 174–75.

[58] Jean Du Hamel, *Réflexions critiques sur le système cartésien de la philosophie de Mr. Régis* (Paris, 1692), 12–16, 68–78.

[59] See, for example, their matter-of-fact presentation to seminarians in Perrin, S.J., *Manuale*, 5.

branchist) Cartesians, replied for his camp. Obviously, he conceded, we did not know God comprehensively, but Descartes's proof was indeed compelling for "a being in which we know as many perfections as we are capable of knowing."[60] To this, Du Hamel retorted scornfully that such a redefinition of infinity into a finite human idea had nothing to do with God's infinity. The creed, he wrote, did not announce the most perfect being of which imperfect human minds could conceive, but "a being in which there are infinite perfections," the divine perfections that the mind of man in no way could contain, a God, in short, whom the Cartesians were unable to prove.[61] As Colbert sought to explain, the human mind simply could not achieve Descartes's "clear and distinct idea of God's perfection." The flaw, he noted, obviously did not reside in the object of the idea, but in its subject, the human thinker. Given the imperfection of man, this attempted proof always would fail.[62] In Michael Morus's explanation, what *we* possessed could only be an imperfect mental being, a finite human idea modifying a finite human mind. The perfection of God resided in God, not, in any manner, in our idea of Him.[63]

Further, from any remnant of an Aristotelian perspective, this was clearly a proof that could not avoid self-contradiction as an a priori demonstration. The Jesuit Estenne Petiot's *Démonstrations théologiques* (1674), the prestigious Parisian philosopher Guillaume Dagoumer's *Metaphysica* (1703), and the Franciscan Assermet's *Theologia scholastico-positiva* (1713) all made the same point with particular force: real perfection could have no prior "cause" and thus could not be amenable in any way to proof that categorized it as "effect" under the guise of "objective being." If the *idea* of God possessed real infinite perfection, it would *be* God, an obvious absurdity.[64]

Both of these criticisms of what we now term Descartes's first proof were given prominence in Huet's popular *Censura*. Huet described this demonstration as a Cartesian "game," wholly dependent on an arbitrary, unwarranted assumption that in fact begged the entire question, namely,

[60] Régis, *Réponse aux Réflexions*, 40–42.

[61] Du Hamel, *Lettre*, 7.

[62] Colbert, *Philosophia*, II, 488–98.

[63] Morus, *De Existentia Dei*, 71–79, 292–313.

[64] Petiot, S.J., *Démonstrations*, 19; Guillaume Dagoumer, *Philosophia ad usum scholae accommodata*, vol. III: *Metaphysica* (Paris, 1703), 235–39; Assermet, O.F.M., *Theologia*, I, 111–46. Dagoumer was professor of philosophy at the prestigious collège d'Harcourt. He was suspected of Cartesian sympathies but after reassuring the authorities and securing his reputation as someone who would not wander too far or explicitly from Aristotle, he enjoyed brilliant academic success. He served as rector of the University of Paris for the unusually long periods of 1711–1713 and 1723–1725, and as administrative head of the collège d'Harcourt 1713–1730 (see Jourdain, *Histoire de l'Université de Paris*, II, 38, 76–78, 112–13, 127, 172–74).

that the "object" of an idea was identical with the actual being represented. Since human thought was imperfect, no human idea could embrace God's actual infinity and infinite perfection, from which it was patently clear that we indeed *could* have an *idea* of an infinitely perfect God even if that God did not exist. Once one recognized that "the idea of an infinite and infinitely perfect entity that is in us is finite," the absurdity of the putative proof, he argued, was evident. The only Cartesian alternative, he insisted, was indeed to equate two categorically distinct entities, the "idea of God" and "God Himself," which for Huet was a *reductio ad absurdum* of the whole proof. The real fallacy, however, he believed, was crystal clear: since ideas were merely "modifications of our minds," all ideas, including the idea of an infinitely perfect being, could be attributed to finite causes.[65]

In brief, then, to the critics of Descartes, in a culture demanding *évidence* and philosophical demonstration of the preambles of the faith, the Cartesian proofs failed absolutely in their efforts to establish the existence of God. The charges we have encountered were made to a culture much of which indeed was smitten by Descartes, and they were made not by freethinkers, but, in this case, by believers all. Listen carefully to the conclusion that Gabriel Daniel, soon to be *supérieur de la Maison Professe* of the Jesuits in Paris, offered to his wide audience: "*If there were no other demonstrations of God but these, there would be none at all [s'il n'y avait point d'autres démonstrations de l'existence de Dieu, que celles-là, il n'y en aurait point du tout].*" Given this, the theologian warned disciples of Descartes *not* to criticize the common Thomistic proofs: "So the advice that I would give to your philosopher and his disciples would be at the least not to give preference to his demonstrations over those commonly utilized [*De sorte que l'avis que je donnerais à vôtre Philosophe et à ses disciples, serait au moins de ne point préférer ses démonstrations à celles dont on se sert communément*]." The reason for this widely circulated warning was direct indeed:

> For if it were true that the other [Aristotelian proofs] were not more compelling in comparison to these [Cartesian proofs], *one would conclude from this principle exceptionally wicked consequences against the existence of the First Being [Car s'il était vrai que les autres n'eussent pas d'évidence, en comparaison de celles-là, on tirerait de ce principe de fort méchantes conséquences contre l'existence du Premier Etre].*[66]

Historically speaking, that appears to be precisely what occurred! As we shall see in the following chapter, the drama of early-modern French

[65] Huet, *Censura*, 103–36.
[66] Daniel, S.J., *Voyage*, 174–75.

philosophical theology was precisely that Cartesians could no more abide by Daniel's warning than Scholastics could refrain from refuting Descartes. As we have seen, the stakes, diversely conceived, altruistic and base, were simply too high, and the weapon of reduction of one's rivals to impotence against "atheism" was simply too inviting to ignore. The advent of the Malebranchists in force would raise the temperature of these debates yet higher. Further, as we shall see from study of the popular learned journals, the arguments of this mutual fratricide, coinciding in time with the great debates over Chinese atheism and universal consent, were considered neither esoteric nor arcane. Quite to the contrary, they increasingly obsessed the culture, both as issues of substance and as the endlessly fascinating clash of titans. The "one" that Daniel either feared or invoked was indeed a spectator and, indeed, was taking notes. The "one" was not many (though certainly a French "*on*" and not an English "one"), but the "consequences" drawn indeed could constitute philosophical grounds for rejecting belief in the demonstrability of God, in an age when so many orthodox voices proclaimed precisely the necessity of philosophical demonstration.

Chapter Ten

THE ASSAULT ON PROOFS FROM THE SENSIBLE WORLD

THE POWERFUL WAVES of Scholastic criticism of Descartes's proofs of God broke not just against the shores of natural philosophy, but also against those of a passionate theology. However we read Descartes today, there was a seventeenth-century Descartes whose vision of truth, order, and substantive knowledge inspired some of the most influential minds and sensibilities of two generations. How difficult it is to recapture that simply by analysis of arguments! There was a Cartesian moment, when, for large parts of a culture, the light of understanding shone rapturously. It was a theological moment, too, and Cartesian philosophical theology of the late seventeenth and early eighteenth centuries needs to be understood not only in its metaphysical constructs, but also in its larger human terms, including the intense loyalty that it inspired. To understand more fully why pious Cartesians so assailed their adversaries on proofs of the existence of God, we need to apprehend some of *their* sense of a struggle worth contesting. Descartes had touched, among other things, a religious chord.

Listen to the priest Adrien Baillet, in his popular and influential *Vie de Monsieur Des-Cartes* (1691). Baillet was a peasant's son, initially educated at the *petit séminaire* of Beauvais, who, prevented by his bishop from becoming a Trappist monk, became a Jansenist and ascetic priest, a vicar known for his deep Catholic faith, his erudition, his work on the Virgin Mary and on the lives of saints, and his constant worry about the spread of heresy and irreligion.[1] He also was a fervent Cartesian, unmoved by the decades of bans, prohibitions, and censures of Descartes's philosophy. "*Never*," he wrote, "has a philosopher appeared more profoundly respectful toward the Divinity than M. Descartes." His Descartes respected all of the mysteries of the Trinity and Incarnation, he was unable to bear "the temerity of certain theologians" who confounded the provinces of reason and faith, and "he spoke of God . . . always in a noble and exalted manner." Baillet quoted admiringly from the published letters of Descartes:

[1] Gregory Sebba, "Adrien Baillet and the Genesis of His *Vie de M. Des-Cartes*," in *Problems of Cartesianism*, ed. Thomas M. Lennon et al. (Montreal, 1982), 9–60.

"For the existence of God is the first and most eternal of all the truths that ever can be, and the sole from which all the others proceed. But what makes it easy in this case to err is that most men do not consider God as 'an infinite and incomprehensible being' who is the sole Author on whom all things depend. They ordinarily go no further than the syllables of His name; and they believe it sufficient to know that *God* means the same thing as what is called *Deus* in Latin and what is adored by mankind. Those who have no higher thoughts than that easily can become Atheists."[2]

For men such as Baillet, who longed so deeply for the faithful to go "further than the syllables of His name," that was a religious as well as philosophical theme. So many of the themes of Cartesian theological vision were in that letter: God as the source of all truth and knowledge of truth; God considered as a being at once infinite and incomprehensible; God represented not by "name," but by our highest thoughts.

It was unbearably ignorant and unjust, Baillet complained, that a Descartes who understood so properly and circumspectly "the part that human Reason can have in knowledge of the divine" ever should have been accused of atheism or of aiding it. To the contrary, this incomparable philosopher had believed and had shown that "philosophy properly employed is of great aid in supporting and justifying the Faith in an enlightened mind." For Baillet, all ecclesiastical suspicion of Descartes's works arose not from piety, but solely from personal intrigue. Descartes, Baillet assured his readers, never put reason above faith; rather, it was he who placed reason fully and efficaciously in the service of the faith. His efforts surely pleased God, however much they may have displeased certain men who tried so hard to stifle them. In philosophy, it was truth, not antiquity, that mattered: "[Descartes's] philosophy is more favorable to the Christian religion . . . than that of Aristotle adopted in our schools."[3]

It was not the Eucharist or notions of substance and space that Baillet had primarily in mind here, but a choice between parts of the human self in which one might ground one's natural approach to things divine. Baillet quoted from a letter that Descartes had written to his friend, the Minim monk Mersenne, about proof of God. Proper demonstration of the Divinity, it explained, depended essentially on something so difficult for so many in the world: " 'to disengage the mind from the senses.' "[4] That disengagement from the concupiscence of the senses was not, to say

[2] Baillet, *Vie de Des-Cartes*, II, 503–6. (The work was so successful that it was issued in a one-volume abridgement, *Abrégé de la Vie de Descartes* [Paris, 1692], which enjoyed a 2d. and rev. ed. in Paris, 1693.)

[3] Ibid., 503–29.

[4] Ibid., I, 284–85.

the least, without its deep Christian appeal. For Baillet, Descartes, by rendering untenable all opinions *not* based on a true distinction between what pertained to body and what pertained to mind alone, "seems to have destroyed the principal stronghold of libertines and atheists."[5] There even was evidence of this. No one, the Jansenist priest claimed, ever had lost belief from reading Descartes's *Meditations* and *Principles*, "but by a benediction that it pleased God to honor them with, they converted several Atheists by a simple reading of them [*mais par une bénédiction dont il a plu à Dieu de les honorer, ils ont converti quelques Athées par leur simple lecture*]."[6]

. . .

This was a far cry from another kind of favorable response to Descartes with which many students of the seventeenth century are familiar, embodied well in letters from a friend to the count de Bussy, advising him and his family to read the philosopher: "I have given myself over to the Philosophy of Descartes. . . . His Metaphysic pleases me also. Its principles are easy. . . . Why don't you study it? It will entertain you with the Mesdemoiselles de Bussy." Shortly after, the same friend wrote: "The Mesdemoiselles de Bussy will learn it faster than any game. For myself, I find it delicious. . . . Without it, we would have died of boredom in this province."[7] As a clerical correspondent of Bussy-Rabutin had written him, it was a century "which divides its day between *la Messe et la Comédie*."[8] Let us stay awhile with those who focused more upon the Mass. For another generation, at least, they had the larger audience.

. . .

The Oratorian priest Louis Batterel, writing in 1729, recalled that the founders and first superiors of the Oratory had admired Descartes deeply, and he claimed proudly that the admiration was mutual. Descartes's own favorite theologian on the subject of man's relationship to God, he wrote, had been the Oratorian superior Guillaume Gibieuf, whose death, he said, the philosopher had mourned deeply.[9] Despite proscriptions and persecutions, the flame of Cartesianism had been kept alive in the Con-

[5] Ibid., II, 115.

[6] Ibid., 508.

[7] De Rabutin, comte de Bussy, *Lettres*, I, 135–36, 141–42.

[8] Ibid., III, 212.

[9] Louis Batterel, Oratory, *Mémoires domestiques pour servir à l'histoire de l'Oratoire* . . . [written 1729], ed. A.M.P. Ingold (Paris, 1902), 233–60.

gregation. It of course would emerge and be transformed with such particularly startling force in the work of Malebranche, but he was one of so many Oratorians who were drawn to Descartes. One of the Congregation's most influential theologians was the eminent Louis Thomassin, who taught first philosophy and then theology within the Congregation, advancing from Lyon to the collège de Juilly, to Saumur, and finally to the seminary at Saint-Magloire. At the height of the persecutions of Cartesianism, he taught a course explicitly grounded not in Aristotle and Saint Thomas, but in Saint Augustine, and he espoused a philosophical theology manifestly based on Plato, Saint Augustine, Descartes, and Malebranche. Although he never mentioned the latter two by name, his first and foremost proof of God was from the infinite perfection of our idea of Him and the inconceivability of the nonexistence of perfection, discovered in the course of the soul's exploration of its own innate ideas.[10] As we have said, however, he had much company in his love of Descartes, which of course was why the "Concordat" had been imposed on the Oratory in the first place.

In his *Commentaire . . . sur la Méthode de Mr. Descartes* (1671), the Oratorian priest Nicolas Joseph Poisson defended Descartes against the "calumnies" and "insults" of critics, linked him to the authority of Saint Augustine, asserted his great superiority to Aristotle and his wondrous consistency with Christian theology, declared that he occupied the same "rank" among true philosophers of this century that Plato and Aristotle had occupied among the ancients, and proclaimed Cartesian thoughts to be "immortal in the mind of savants."[11] The Scholastics, Poisson wrote, "smother" our understanding with "subtleties." "By contrast," he wrote, "Descartes believed that just as it is only children and the simple who should enter the Kingdom of Heaven, it is similarly necessary to be very simple to enter the Kingdom of Reason, and that the truths which clear

[10] Louis Thomassin, *Dogmatum Theologicorum . . .*, vol. I: *De Deo, Deique proprietatibus* (Paris, 1684), l.I, c.1–20. See also his *La méthode d'étudier et d'enseigner chrétiennement et solidement la philosophie par rapport à la religion chrestienne . . .* (1685).

[11] Poisson, Oratory, *Commentaire*, passim. (For the quotations on his "rank," "immortal" thoughts, and the nature of his critics, see his dedicatory "Epistre." For the most striking comparisons to Aristotle and St. Augustine, see 5–63 and 96–112. On 112, he wrote that in moral theology, to speak "*fort Chrestiennement*" is to speak "*fort Cartésiennement*." On 139–99, he argued that Descartes's physiology and physics were wholly complementary to and consistent with the Catholic faith, including his Copernicanism, where the Church must leave philosophers "liberty" with regard to "a problematic question." On 195–203, he defended Descartes's proof of God from the charge of a "vicious circle" (the claim that the certainty of the demonstration of God's existence depended on God as the guarantor of certainty) by arguing that a true "vicious circle" involved two *identical* propositions, where Descartes's proof involved the "relationship [*liaison*]" of his propositions.

the way there must be treated with simplicity and without ornamentation, for fear that the glitter of the colors do not so take hold of our senses."[12] There it is again: it was the senses, from which, of course, a posteriori proofs began, that denied us the kingdom of truth. It was Descartes who spoke for a "Reason" that offered a different way.

. . .

Poisson, in a remarkable "Avis au Lecteur," also wrote of his defense of Cartesianism in a more personal vein. What long had dissuaded him from writing on Descartes, he explained, was his belief that since his time was God's, not his own, his religious calling and clerical talents "[obliged] me to spend it on things holier in themselves than those that concern Philosophy and Mathematics." Nonetheless, he wrote, after much soul-searching and consultation, it was the same sense of duty to God and to his calling that broke his earlier resolve "to remain a simple spectator and not to take part in the contentions [*les demeslez*] that today divide all the schools and academies of Europe." What led him to this presentation and defense of Cartesian philosophy, he claimed, was coming to understand the full implications of Saint Augustine's teaching that "Truth" is "Goodness" and "Error" is "Evil."

What we lost in Adam's Fall, Poisson explained, was our knowledge of truth, and it was our common task to work with all of our particular talents and energies "to redeem [*réparer*]" that loss. Christian thought must restore the truth. That was "the design [for us] of God Himself." Truth, being God's, linked us to God. We knew the route to truth: prayer, humility, and the illumination of external or internal things according to our capacities. How, he asked, could I refuse to do that, referring to a decision to explicate and defend the thought of René Descartes, especially since Christian "charity" commanded it also? His religious vocation, thus, was to master and explain Cartesianism, despite the difficulty of the "philosophy," "mathematics," and "theology" involved, and despite the need to respond to hundreds of "malicious reproaches" that had been directed against Descartes. The old Aristotelian method, the priest-philosopher wrote, could not attain the end the Church had sought from it: discovery of truth. Its former critics, Valla, Agricola, Vives, and Ramus, had done no better. Francis Bacon had been a ray of light, but, above all, Descartes and the *Logic* of the Jansenists of Port-Royal that he inspired (the *Art de Penser* by Arnauld and Nicole, "that can be called," Poisson observed, "the 'Supplement' to Descartes") showed us the new way.

[12] Ibid., 2–4.

Scholastic sensationalism—that is, its reliance on the senses as the path to truth—was ruinous to Christianity. If Descartes's philosophy were a crime, his accomplices were the greatest doctors in the history of the Church. He concluded by informing his readers of where in Paris they could purchase the relevant Cartesian works.[13]

. . .

Poisson's fellow Oratorian priest and savant, Bernard Lamy, best known for his mathematics, natural philosophy, and Cartesian-Malebranchist sympathies (but who also wrote on Christian morality and on the synoptic Gospels) described the Paris Oratory as a "community of virtuous and savant ecclesiastics" who lived "at great remove [*éloignement*] from the world and with a great disdain for what [the world] calls great and pleasant." Devoted above all, in his description, "to the service of the Church," they also were ever "studious," and "they have worldly commerce only with their books which constitute *their* pleasure." Except when they were involved in devotions or other pious activities, he confessed, they were "restless" to return to their studies.[14] The self-image of the Paris Oratory and its practices were well recorded in his observation that from this "love of truth" there arose a sense of the "sweetness of study" and a "love for letters" that superiors had to control, lest the priests lose sight of their primary duties. "Nonetheless," he noted, "when we find some penetrating and broad mind who has a rare genius for the sciences [of any worthy kind], *he is discharged from all other business* [italics his, perhaps to explain his own mathematical and erudite studies], and we do not believe that he could offer any more useful service to the Church than by studying." Without such savants, he noted, students never would know how to resolve "difficulties" or where to place final confidence in matters of human learning and debate.[15] Reviewing the first edition of Lamy's quite Cartesian *Entretiens sur les sciences* (1684), Bayle, in the *Nouvelles de la République des Lettres*, must have greatly pleased Lamy. "What is very praiseworthy in his ways of proceeding," Bayle wrote, "is that he never loses sight of the principal end of our actions, which is to relate everything to God." "All men," Bayle advised, "and men of letters even more than all others need to be reminded of that."[16] That was precisely the Cartesian and later Malebranchist theological self-image: unlike the sensationalist Aristotelians, who related all

[13] Ibid., "Avis au Lecteur" [11 pp., unpaginated].

[14] Lamy, Oratory, *Entretiens sur les sciences*.

[15] Ibid., 180–81.

[16] *Nouvelles de la République des Lettres*, déc. 1684, 468–78.

things to the particulars of the sensible world, they, by contrast, related all things to God.

. . .

Cartesian piety and Cartesian worldliness often met. The Carthusian Bonaventure [Noel] d'Argonne, who wrote of worldly things under the pseudonym of "Vigneul-Marville," himself attended Rohault's lectures on Cartesian philosophy in Paris. He admired Descartes enormously and, speaking explicitly of the philosopher's need to move to Holland in order to work freely, pronounced it a peculiar trait of French character "to neglect what we possess." While French Cartesians still found themselves under censure, he noted, "they teach, in the North, the Philosophy of Descartes against which we pronounce anathema here."[17] Even Descartes's severest French critics, he urged, were forced to recognize the genius and elevation of his works.[18] He cited with pleasure the assertion made by a Cartesian to several Aristotelian visitors at Rohault's lectures that one was "always free in philosophy."[19] He termed the eminent Cartesian Clerselier "a completely *honnête homme*, a truly Christian philosopher, an eminently likable sage, and a wonderfully elegant mind" who had made whatever had been obscure in Descartes "so very clear."[20] Descartes, he opined, was one of the six best minds of the entire century (Galileo, Bacon, Digby, Grotius, and Gassendi were the others).[21] Descartes's opinions, he was convinced, were derived from patristic sources and consistent with Saint Augustine.[22] Like many savant friars, he pronounced the joys of study superior to all the favors and fortunes of the world.[23]

Knowing intimately the Parisian world of Cartesian ecclesiastics, and

[17] Bonaventure [Noel] d'Argonne, Carthusian [under pseud. of Vigneul-Marville], *Mélanges d'histoire et de littérature*, 4th ed., rev., corr., and aug., 3 vols. (Paris, 1725), I, 177. In ibid., I, 22, he told a wonderful story about Rohault's lectures on Cartesian philosophy: "The first wife of M. Rohault, the disciple of M. Descartes, whose Philosophy he explained in public lectures, placed herself on those days at the door of her home, and refused entry to those who did not have an air of quality, convinced that it required this air to deserve to hear her husband. This good man was wearing himself out telling her that fortune does not always give rich clothes to philosophers; she wanted to see silks and satins and would not yield."

[18] Ibid., 185.

[19] Ibid., 118–24.

[20] Ibid., 379–80.

[21] Ibid., 422.

[22] Ibid., II, 348–49. He had great praise for St. Augustine, (ibid., III, 196–98); in II, 323, he pronounced it good to embrace St. Augustine theologically but agreed with the authorities that some had gone to "excess" in what they took to be Augustinian views.

[23] Ibid., II, 306–10.

given to anecdote, d'Argonne offered lively views of the relationship of Cartesianism and clerical life. He claimed to have heard from the Oratorian priest Salmon and others that Malebranche had stumbled upon Descartes's *Le Monde* by chance, browsing in a bookstore, an encounter, as d'Argonne told it, that led him from simple piety to metaphysical and moral philosophy, and from there to his status as "the Plato of our times."[24] He told a story, perhaps apocryphal, but perhaps with a kernel of truth, of Richard Simon's belated examination in philosophy in the Oratory, before his expulsion in 1678, at a time when the pressure was intense on the Congregation to tolerate no Cartesianism at all. The examiner, in d'Argonne's account, dutifully warned Simon against "a certain . . . Cartesian Philosophy that poisoned many people [*une certaine Philosophie Cartésienne . . . qui empoisona bien des gens*]." D'Argonne's version of what happened next, if even remotely based on fact, showed the depth of cynicism among Oratorians toward the formal prohibition of Descartes:

> "I am a peripatetic for life," M. Simon replied, smiling; "and I for the money," replied the examiner. "Isn't it the case," he continued, "that if Descartes had written in Greek, in a very obscure style, and if he were 2000 years old, his principles, being neither read nor understood by anyone, would have more approvers [*approbateurs*] than at present, when he is read and understood by everyone?"[25]

. . .

For most religious spirits drawn to Descartes, however, it was difficult indeed to be cynical about the issues involved. The Génovéfain canon René Le Bossu, comparing Cartesian and Aristotelian natural philosophy, cautiously but earnestly sought to show the superiority of the former. His *Parallèle des principes . . . d'Aristote, & . . . de René Des Cartes* (1674) stressed the freedom of Christian thought in matters philosophical, arguing that "truth has several perspectives" and that "the temple in which she is adored has more than one avenue [leading to it] and more than one door."[26] Although he spoke of "accommodating" the two natural philosophies, of finding points of "reconciliation" in their first principles, and of their lack of "contradiction,"[27] he found the *spirituality* of Cartesian

[24] Ibid., I, 25.

[25] Ibid., 284–85.

[26] René Le Bossu, Génovéfain, *Parallèle des principes de la physique d'Aristote, & de celle de René Des Cartes* (Paris, 1674), 1–9.

[27] Ibid., passim. Often, however, as on 27–31, he utilized these putative similarities to

physics far worthier of Christian thought about the world. Where Aristotle, in Le Bossu's view, would not make the Divinity the principle of *his* physics, since he wished to begin with the most accessible particulars of sensory experience, Descartes had made God central to his entire natural philosophy:

> [Descartes employs] knowledge of immaterial entities as principles, in order to draw *from them* the clear and certain knowledge of bodies and of material beings. . . . He begins by knowledge of himself and of his soul, and even by knowledge of God, whose nature and infinite perfection serves him as the unique principle for establishing and for demonstrating all nature.[28]

When Le Bossu turned from Descartes's physics to his metaphysics, the Génovéfain's most fundamental thoughts and feelings about the theological implications of Descartes emerged with yet more force. Descartes's *Meditations* was not merely a philosophical text, it was "this Temple consecrated to God and to the immortality of our souls." Since Cartesianism began its inquiries with an examination of one's own soul, he argued, perhaps it was compatible with Aristotle's insistence that knowledge of the creatures preceded knowledge of God. The difference, however, was that for Descartes, God was "the first principle" of all knowledge. It was Cartesian philosophy that understood that there could be no natural certainty without knowledge of God. From this, it followed that where they differed, Descartes was invariably the more spiritual and Christian of the two, and Le Bossu proposed a relationship of the systems that gave the victory and the laurels of a pious Christian philosophy to Descartes. Let us all *begin* our education with Aristotle, he suggested. Then, following Descartes's method, let us agree to doubt everything not wholly certain. To overcome that doubt, let us accept what Descartes had taught us: "the necessity of knowledge of ourselves and of God, in order to be perfect and complete philosophers, and in order to know in a manner much more noble, more excellent, more certain, and more worthy of a man *and of a Christian*, what there is of truth and of vanity in the creatures, and in all that we search for by means of the science of natural things."[29]

For Le Bossu, thus, Christian humility and Cartesian philosophy went hand in hand. The *Parallèle*, one should add, was in no way a work unacceptable to the leaders of the Génovéfain Congregation. It was published with the explicit approbations and permissions of Le Bossu's most eminent superiors, Blanchart, the abbé of Sainte Geneviève de Paris and

---

support Cartesian theses: in this case, they both recognized, he claimed, "this necessity of doubting in order to learn," and they both taught one "to rid oneself of ancient prejudices."

[28] Ibid., 22–27.

[29] Ibid., 304–11.

supérieur général of the regular canons of the Congregation for all of France, and du Molinet, *Père supérieur général* of the Congregation.[30]

. . .

It was precisely this perceived spirituality of Cartesian philosophy, its presumed reliance upon divine illumination of the soul, that made it seem so exquisitely superior to Aristotelian sensationalism in the judgment of many theological and religious minds. It was this that made it seem to them so reflective of what they took to be patristic rejection of pagan bondage to the body and its senses. Commanded again and again to abandon Descartes and Malebranche in favor of Aristotle, the Jesuit André, we have seen, could not. If you accuse me of holding views inimical to the faith, André wrote to a superior in 1709, you also accuse "the most celebrated of the holy Fathers." I prefer Saint Augustine to Aristotle, he insisted with great bitterness, since the latter's maxims, above all, his view " 'that there is nothing in the mind which did not enter by way of the senses,' overturns quite obviously all of the sciences and, above all, overturns morality." The passion of Cartesian and Malebranchist theological opposition to Scholasticism, and to the sensual basis of its proofs of God, ran deep. The particulars of Aristotle's sense experience, André explained, were "ephemeral [and] contingent," while ideas were the divine source of truth. André never would consider renunciation of his Jesuit vows, but not for a moment would he consider acceptance of an Aristotelian voice for Christian faith, a voice, he believed, that would condemn his creed to reliance upon the fallen senses and to rejection of the grace of intellectual light:

> I declare to you, thus, my reverend father, and to all of the Society, that I hold as indubitable that Jesus Christ, as eternal Word and Wisdom . . . is, as St. John says, the true light that illuminates all men, and, as St. Augustine says, the essential truth which encloses in its divine substance all the immutable truths, and, as Father Malebranche says, the universal reason of minds.[31]

His own philosophical works continued to reflect this Cartesian and Malebranchist impulse in early-modern Catholic theology. In his "Discours sur la Nature des Idées," he argued that ideas were to sensory perceptions what light was to shadow.[32] In his "Essai sur le Beau," in which beauty and intellectual order were identical, he begged his reader to leave

[30] Ibid., [prior to text].
[31] André, S.J., *Oeuvres philosophiques*, ciii–cvi.
[32] Ibid., 241–42.

"this material and terrestrial world" to join him in "the country of beauty [*le pays du Beau*]":

> in the region of minds, or, as St. Augustine phrases it, in this intelligible world that is the abode of light and of truth. There, if we make ourselves in the least attentive to our first ideas, we will see all the others that we know: God, created spirit, matter, each placed in the rank that marks its place in the universe, its degree of essence and of perfection.[33]

In his "Discours sur la Nature et les Merveilles du Raisonnement," he wrote that while the senses and everything derived from them lead us astray, we truly cannot err if we admit only what cannot be doubted because of "an irresistible *évidence*."[34] For theologians committed to Cartesian proofs, their opponents were proposing nothing less than to deprive Christian thought of the divine light itself. Philosophy, for them, was in and of itself a primary religious experience.

The Jesuits' generally effective restraint of their own Cartesians, if the latter may be believed, did not always succeed in preventing that sense of Christian thought from being communicated to the Society's own students and charges. André wrote unabashedly to confidants about his ways of letting students know his true beliefs.[35] Du Tertre, before his philosophical apostasy, also wrote to André of his own Malebranchist successes in this domain:

> Last Friday, which was my last class [of the year], the best of our students . . . explained, with regard to demonstration of God, the entire system of ideas during three whole quarters of an hour, and proved that our ideas could only be the intelligible substance of God. You never saw more astonished men than the majority of those who heard him. I can assure you that the majority of our students are quite *au courant* and well grounded on good principles. There are also four or five prefects who are on the right road. . . . but they are fearful of being known . . . for you could not believe how far the terror has spread. There are those who even fear being taken for one of my friends.[36]

As the Jesuits themselves would discover within a half-century, even during periods of persecution there were ways to testify. Using the common false imprint for Jansenist and, when times were perilous, Cartesian works, "Cologne . . . Pierre Marteau," the abbé de Lanion, although a brother of the powerful Breton *noble d'épée*, adopted a pseudonym and published a Cartesian *Méditations sur la Métaphysique* in Paris, in 1678,

[33] Ibid., 22–23.
[34] Ibid., 271–72.
[35] Ibid., ccxiii–ccxvii.
[36] Ibid., cxxiii–cxxvii.

to which Bayle gave much broader circulation a few years later. He wrote of having explored skepticism to the point of doubting if we could know that there was a God, until he grasped the luminous truth of Descartes's proofs from the objective being of the idea of God, whose only conceivable source could be God Himself, and from the entailed actual existence of infinite perfection clearly and distinctly perceived.[37] As another Cartesian cited in Bayle's *Recueil* of 1684 observed, "In addition to reason, Cartesians still have the authority of the Fathers and the tradition of the Church" on their side.[38] How could Christians who experienced or believed such things abandon the field to the Scholastics?

. . .

Among the Benedictines, both within the prestigious Congrégation de Saint-Maur of Saint-Germain-des-Près, and within the Congrégation de Saint-Vanne, many distinguished savants and teachers expressed their sympathies for both Descartes and Malebranche, in an order where devotion to patristic sources, love of Saint Augustine, and attraction to aspects of Jansenism all ran high.[39] Dom Robert Desgabets, one of these teachers at the Congrégation de Saint-Vanne, wrote in 1676 that he felt himself part of a moment in history when an entire philosophical order was giving way to another: "The affairs of the Empire of letters are in a situation in which they never were and never will be again," he wrote; "we are passing now from an old world into the new world, and we are working seriously on the first foundation of the sciences."[40] He also wrote to the Cartesian Clerselier, in 1663: "I will tell you, sir, that I have worked with such success that there is no other order of regulars [monks] in France where the philosophy of M. Descartes is more in vogue than ours. There is not a course given in philosophy in which it is not declaimed [*débitée*] with praise, and we even have gotten it accepted in theology, in which I have not neglected it these past years."[41]

We know something of these courses. Like the Génovéfain Le Bossu, Desgabets found Descartes's natural philosophy ideal for a Christian. In a manuscript of his lecture on "the foundations of Christian philosophy

[37] Guillaume Wander [abbé de Lanion], *Méditations sur la Métaphysique* (Cologne [Paris], 1678); reprinted in Bayle, *Recueil*, 267–333. See also Bayle, *OD*, III, 547.

[38] Bayle, *Recueil*, 122–26.

[39] Paul Le Maire, *Le Cartésianisme chez les Bénédictins. Dom Robert Desgabets: son système, son influence et son école, d'après plusieurs manuscrits et des documents rares ou inédits* (Paris, 1902).

[40] Dom Robert Desgabets, O.S.B., letter of 18 September 1676 to unknown correspondent, in Malebranche, *Oeuvres complètes*, XVIII, 122.

[41] Cited in Le Maire, *Cartésianisme*, 290.

and mathematics," Desgabets said of Descartes that "he not only *discovered* these foundations . . . but sanctified, so to speak, all philosophy and mathematics by the particular attachment that he showed the sciences to have to the sovereign perfection of God."[42]

Such Cartesian enthusiasms were, to say the very least, compatible, we have seen, with the most intense piety. The most celebrated Cartesian of the Maurist Benedictine Congregation in Paris was Dom François (not to be confused with Bernard) Lamy, a well-educated noble who abandoned a military career in his twenties to become a monk, taking final vows in 1658. A century later, in his order, he still was remembered for two things above all: his brilliance as a philosopher, and the extremity of his monastic rigors, his "painful and humbling exercises [*des exercises pénibles et humilians*]." At Saint-Germain-des-Près, he had wanted to work as a baker or tinker, but a reputation from his university days for having been a brilliant student of philosophy preceded him, and his superiors instructed him to prepare to teach philosophy and theology. The chronicler of his order told it this way: "Having found the Philosophy of M. Descartes in the library, he read it, developed a taste for it, and abandoning the prejudices that he had held until then, he was the first who taught it openly in the Congrégation de St. Maur." He became, it was said, "the arbiter of all difficulties" in the Congregation on matters of philosophical theology.[43]

In his celebrated *De la connoissance de soi-même*, first published in 1697 and in a second edition by 1701, he argued that "the mind of man finds itself as if situated between God and its body." The appeal for him of Descartes (and particularly of Malebranche, toward whose occasionalism he was rapidly drawn) was evidenced by the conclusion which he drew from this, namely, that such a location gave men a choice in their understanding of the real source of their knowledge of truth, "body" or "God." Where so many denounced Cartesian and Malebranchist proofs from the idea of God as "speculative" in comparison to Scholastic proofs, Lamy reversed the equation. The pious Christian, he believed, lost nothing by eschewing "a knowledge of God" copied from the physics of "the pagans," dependent upon body and not soul, a knowledge that was

[42] Cited in ibid., 95.

[43] Dom René Prosper Tassin, O.S.B., *Histoire littéraire de la Congrégation de Saint-Maur, Ordre de S. Benoît, où l'on trouve la vie & les travaux des auteurs qu'elle a produits, depuis son origine en 1618, jusqu'à présent* (Brussels [and Paris], 1770), 351–56. According to Philippe Le Cerf de la Viéville, O.S.B., *Bibliothèque historique et critique des auteurs de la Congrégation de St. Maur* (The Hague, 1726), 185–95, Lamy desperately wished to withdraw from active scholarly pursuits, and indeed withdrew for a long stretch to the seclusion of the abbey of St. Dénis, until his superiors convinced him that it was a "criminal obstinacy" to withhold "the products of his mind" from the world.

"*wholly* speculative, abstract, dry, [and] insipid," and which concluded not in a perfect being but merely in some "first being" or "first mover." The most pious Christian, however, he insisted, from cloistered monk to secular clergy to layman, needed to overcome the ignorance of original sin by "entering himself," by reflecting upon the content of his immortal soul. There, he would find the idea of infinite perfection and know God in his own soul, in an affective and, indeed, salvific manner.[44]

Lamy wrote that such a path could be traveled alone, but that he himself owed so much to the philosophers and theologians who had taught him this. Here, again, in a somewhat different mode, was the Cartesian theological impulse that saw itself linked to Christian philosophical liberty and to the inward means of knowing eternal truth:

> They taught me (and this is particularly the obligation that I have toward them) that I could think alone; that it was not necessary that I be led always by the hand; and that on matters that depend only on reason [*sur les sujets qui ne relevent que de la raison*], there was no obligation to think either according to the ancients or according to the moderns . . . [but] that tranquil and intent on consulting this public and inner light [of reason], I even could advance to discern who of the ancients or moderns best had consulted it . . . and I recognized that these great [philosophers] were only, as in my case, students of the eternal Truth . . . and that . . . they were distinguished with regard to it only by their greater or lesser application and docility.[45]

Responding, in this second edition, to charges that *he* worshiped at the throne of abstraction rather than at the throne of God, Lamy distinguished in effect between the insipidly abstract being derived from Aristotelian sense experience and the affectively abstract being identified by consideration of the light within: "Don't be deceived: the true objects of piety are truth, justice, and wisdom. Is there anything more elevated or more abstract?" He replied also to the accusation that he had sought to overstep the bounds of philosophical theology, to know by natural knowledge "the hidden God." His answer revealed how for those who felt inspired by Cartesian or Malebranchist notions of detachment from the senses in knowledge of God's existence, the distinction between philosophy and experiential theology was not a meaningful one:

> Our God, the God that we adore, and who is the object of our cult, is a hidden God; a God who hides Himself *only in order to oblige us to search*

[44] Dom François Lamy, O.S.B., *De la connoissance de soi-même*, 2d ed., rev. and aug., 6 vols. (Paris, 1701), I, passim, and especially 1–23; II, passim, and especially 466ff. Again, he should not be confused with Bernard Lamy of the Oratory. The *De la connoissance de soi-même* was published with the approbation of a great many doctors of theology also sympathetic to Jansenism.

[45] Ibid., III, "Dessein Général," secs. 14 and 16 [unpaginated].

> *for Him with all the attention and application of which we are capable. . . .* True adoration, adoration in mind and in truth [*en esprit et en vérité*], cannot subsist without some metaphysic; and the most perfect Christians are the most metaphysical, often without knowing it. I say without knowing it, for *when God opens the heart to truth and to justice, as He does to a thousand good souls, He soon gives to them a pure idea of the one and the other, and a comprehension [une intelligence] disengaged from all image and all phantasm.*[46]

In his *Lettres philosophiques* (1703), Lamy stated the matter more directly and simply: we must stop philosophizing by means of "taste and opinion" and do so only by means of "light and reason." Philosophy of the latter kind, he wrote, was the search for "propositions of immediate insight" and the "*évidence* . . . [of] what one sees clearly and distinctly."[47]

Antoine Legrand's widely read *Apologia pro Renato Des-Cartes* (1679) argued that Descartes's method of seeking knowledge of God partook of the spirituality of Saint Augustine. For Legrand, Cartesian natural philosophy understood and demonstrated that only a notion of God originating from and demonstrated by our idea of an infinitely perfect being could represent what was divine to us. Compared to it, a notion of God that we might have by the senses failed in the same way that a portrait of a material dove failed to give us an apprehension of the Holy Spirit.[48] There was more than philosophy involved in the choice between a posteriori and a priori proofs!

Malebranche so often complained that theologians spoke of God in terms more appropriate to a corporeal or anthropomorphic being than to that being known in "the idea of the infinitely perfect being" to which detachment from the senses and attention to contemplative reason could lead.[49] For Malebranche, as he wrote in his demonstration of God in the widely beloved *Conversations chrétiennes*, to know of God was precisely to ignore the senses, to tear one's mind and soul away from "this exterior and sensible man who is incapable of comprehension." Rational philosophy and religious experience could be one. Malebranche advised the seeker of knowledge of the existence of God in these terms: "Learn . . . to return inside yourself, to be attentive to interior Truth. . . . The attention of the mind is the natural prayer that we offer to interior truth, so that it will make itself known to us [*L'attention de l'esprit est la prière naturelle*

[46] Ibid., VI, 508–10.

[47] F. Lamy, O.S.B., *Lettres philosophiques sur divers sujets importans* (Trévoux, 1703), 1–32.

[48] Antoine Legrand, *Apologia pro Renato Des-Cartes* . . . (London, 1679), 105–15.

[49] See, for example, Malebranche, *Oeuvres complètes*, V, 26–27, 75, 116, 168–69; XII, 171, 183, 186, 197, 201.

que nous faisons à la vérité intérieure, afin qu'elle se découvre à nous]."[50] For Malebranche, we were *not* condemned to derive our ideas by means of the body. As Fontenelle remarked of him with breathtaking insight, "He wanted to know only what Adam had known."[51]

Clerselier's long preface to the 1677 one-volume edition of Descartes's *L'Homme* and *Le Monde* stated what he saw as the essential Cartesian contribution to knowledge of the existence of any entity, and by implication, to natural knowledge of the existence of God: "Reason teaches us that to judge of the Essence *and Existence* of any substance, we can do so only by means of the attributes, properties, or qualities whose ideas we have in us, and which we conceive to belong to that substance." To believe in God, by reason or by faith, Clerselier insisted, required *first* the "recognition that He is supremely perfect." Knowledge of *what God was* had to precede knowledge *that God was*. Descartes and Saint Augustine had understood that.[52]

If such were the case, however, then the struggle between Cartesianism and Aristotelianism was, from a Cartesian perspective, one on which the very ability to know that God existed depended. Bayle, thinking of the problem of evil, had written that without the Christian revelation, it was so difficult to convince an atheist that God existed. He added, however, that it also had been so difficult to accomplish that before Cartesian philosophy.[53]

From such a perspective, it was fitting that Clerselier included in the edition of 1677 both Louis de La Forge's "Remarks" on Descartes's essay on the formation of the fetus and a French translation of Schuyl's original Latin preface to *L'Homme*. La Forge asserted that "there was something extraordinary in this man [Descartes], whom we call Divine with far more right to the title than Plato, and of whom we can believe, with far more truth than some have claimed for Aristotle, *that he was sent by God to teach us to philosophize well*."[54] Schuyl went even further and said explicitly what so many Cartesians clearly believed. Descartes, Schuyl wrote, represented the triumph of truth over confusion, wisdom over prejudice, and philosophical freedom over philosophical slavery. Descartes had restored philosophy, established method, defeated atheism, proven demonstratively the existence of God, and, indeed, by grounding

[50] Ibid., IV, 10–12.

[51] Fontenelle, *Eloge du P. Malebranche*, in ibid., XIX, 100.

[52] Clerselier's [unpaginated] "Préface" to René Descartes, *L'Homme de René Descartes . . . A quoy l'on a ajouté Le Monde, ou Traité de la lumière . . .*, ed. Clerselier, 2d ed., rev. and corr. (Paris, 1677). (This is such an exquisite edition: the bibliophile, historian of material culture, or aesthetically minded reader should make a point of consulting it!)

[53] Bayle, *Pensées diverses*, IV, 244–84.

[54] "Remarques de Louis de La Forge," in Descartes, *L'Homme/Le Monde*, 367.

all truth in Him, had made the existence of God clearer than even the truths of mathematics. At last, philosophy now could work for the glory of God. Having abolished all of the fatal errors of the Aristotelians, Descartes had "posed and established" his new philosophy as "this solid foundation of piety . . . to destroy and exterminate . . . atheism once and for all." "*By a wholly singular favor of Heaven*," Schuyl wrote, "*René Descartes came to make his appearance* [*Par une faveur toute particulière du Ciel, René Descartes est venu à paroître.*]"[55] At the very least, so many believed what a reviewer in the *Journal des Sçavans* had said of Descartes in 1667: "There is no philosopher who worked more than he to demonstrate the existence of God and the immortality of the reasonable soul."[56] The philosopher Gérard de Cordemoy explicitly described him as occupying the place in philosophy that Moses held in revelation, and stressed their complementary relationship.[57] The Huguenot Isaac Jacquelot wrote that before "the incomparable Descartes," we had no "proper idea of the nature of a spirit," nor, thus, of what we meant by the incorporeality of God.[58]

In 1716, the *Nouvelles littéraires* informed its readers that a superb philosophical poem, published in France, "attracts a great deal of attention." "Savants esteem it," the journal reported, "and [even] the less clever have a taste for it." It was a poem that "develops the entire system of the new philosophy, and uses it to prove the existence of God." The reviewer recommended its translation into Dutch, assuring a potential publisher that it would have a success equal to that it had enjoyed in France.[59] The Cartesian poem was by the abbé Charles Claude Genest, member of the Académie française and *aumônier ordinaire* of the duchesse d'Orléans. Genest may merely have been looking for a rhyme for "*s'explique*," but he made Descartes the voice of God in the seventeenth and eighteenth centuries: in the Cartesian system, everything falls into place and is explained; "The Author of the Universe communicates through him [*Dans son système heureux . . . tout s'y tient, tout se suit, tout s'arrange, s'explique; L'Auteur de l'Univers par lui se communique*]."[60] Men who felt that way were not about to heed the warning

[55] French translation of Schuyl's "Préface" to *L'Homme*, in ibid., 369–403.

[56] *Journal des Sçavans*, 31 jan. 1667, 33–37.

[57] Gérard de Cordemoy, *Copie d'une lettre écrite à un sçavant religieux de la Compagnie de Jésus, pour montrer: 1. que le système de M. Descartes et son opinion touchant les bestes n'ont rien de dangereux; 2. & que tout ce qu'il en a écrit semble estre tiré du premier chapitre de la Genèse* (n.p., 1668). The *Lettre* was translated into English and published as *Discourse Written to a Learned Frier* [sic] . . . (London, 1670) (to which was appended François [*not* Pierre] Bayle's course in Cartesian philosophy).

[58] Isaac Jacquelot, *Avis sur le tableau du Socinianisme* (n.p., 1690), 24–27.

[59] *Nouvelles littéraires* IV (1716), 303–4.

[60] Genest, *Principes*. The poem received the approbation of the royal censor Fraguier,

issued by Gabriel Daniel. How could they? They too, it appeared, had their "fifth apostle." No wonder some sought to extend Cartesian philosophy to explication of the very Eucharist itself.[61]

. . .

In brief, then, on the one side, a lionization of Descartes, including a theological celebration, and a great championing of his proofs of God's existence, for some, indeed, the *only* possible compelling demonstrations. On the other side, a ceaseless flow of criticism, refutation, and dismissal of those same proofs as inane, undemonstrative, and illogical by the leading teaching order in all of France, the Jesuits, and by whole university faculties, by respected academic authorities, by subtle and influential dialecticians, and, these all believed, by the evident authority of Aristotle, the prince of logic, and Saint Thomas, the Angelic Doctor of the Church. Obviously, the more widespread the first phenomenon became, the more damage could be done to the grounds of philosophical (or for some, perhaps, experiential) belief by the second, and the appeal of Descartes's philosophical theology was broad indeed.

. . .

It intrigued almost everyone, this proof of God from the idea we have of Him, and almost anyone could be tempted or charmed by its elegance. Fénélon—who warned in his "Lettre sur l'idée de l'infini" that in philosophy, it was not Descartes or Aristotle who had authority, not "names" or "citations of authors who can err," but "proofs"—wrote that he found wisdom in both philosophical traditions.[62] At the beginning and end of the pages in which he expressed his wonder at the Cartesian proof, he came close to conceding the core of what for Scholastics invalidated its probative claim, namely, in Fénélon's terms, that since the idea of God was, after all, a human idea, the infinitely perfect was "known infinitely imperfectly," and, "once again, that this knowledge and this love do not

---

who noted that it "already had been received by the public with applause" and that it "would bring honor to our century." It was dedicated to the regent, the duc d'Orléans. In his unpaginated "Préface," Genest wrote that he learned "the excellent method" of Descartes from Rohault, from François Lamy, O.S.B., from Malebranche, and from the Cardinal de Polignac (whom he did not mention by name, but whose poem against Lucretius he mentioned). He noted that it was "absurd" that Descartes still should be under assault.

[61] See Richard A. Watson, "Transubstantiation among the Cartesians," and Ronald Laymon, "Transubstantiation: Test Case for Descartes's Theory of Space," in Lennon et al., eds., *Cartesianism*, 127–48, 149–70 respectively.

[62] François de Salignac de la Motte Fénélon, archbishop of Cambray, *Lettres sur divers sujets concernant la religion et la métaphysique* (Paris, 1718), 221–31.

have a perfection equal to their object." Nonetheless, he could not resist it: "Nothing is so astonishing as the idea of God . . . ; it is the infinite contained in the finite. . . . I do not understand how I could have it in my mind, but nonetheless I have it. It is useless to examine how I could have it, since I do have it. The fact is clear and decisive."[63]

Bossuet was equally tempted at times. "How could it be," he wrote, "that the unbeliever does not know God, that so many nations . . . have not known Him, since one bears the idea in oneself with that of perfection?" It could only be from an excessive attachment to the senses instead of to the realm of the rational, he answered: "a lack of attention," because "man, given over to the senses and to the imagination, does not want or cannot commune with himself [*se recueillir en soi-même*] nor attach himself to pure ideas." Man, "whose mind is burdened with gross images," he concluded, "cannot bear the simple truth" that one cannot know what is imperfect *before* one knows the perfect.[64] Believing that men were "given over to the senses," however, Bossuet always offered and never assailed sensible proofs of God also. The true Cartesians, however, for reasons we have seen, would not do that.

Even those who would be among the most influential and the most intense critics of the Cartesian proofs of God could remember or still feel the lure of them. The learned Jesuit Tournemine, a leading editor of the *Journal de Trévoux*, who in ten years would create a scandal by declaring Fénélon's use of Cartesian proofs intentionally and solely ad hominem, reflected in 1703 on the Aristotelian-Cartesian debate about ideas. He admitted, just this once, his awe at "the idea of complete perfection . . . comprising the effect and the cause . . . inseparable from the soul . . . and that the Cartesians are right to call an 'innate' idea, although they demonstrate it as badly as can be done."[65] Huet—whose fall from Cartesian certainty began an odyssey that ended in fideism, the Christian mirror image, perhaps, of philosophical disbelief—recalled that he had begun with a passion for geometry, which made him an early admirer of Descartes. "I cannot easily express the admiration this new mode of philosophizing excited in my young mind," he remembered, "when, from the simplest and plainest principles, I saw so many dazzling wonders brought forth." "In fact," he wrote in his autobiography, "I was for many years closely engaged in the study of Cartesianism . . . attached to it as by a kind of fascination." His description of his break, however, echoed both the formal criticism of his *Censura* and his later sense that reason, deductive or inductive, was only good for criticism and refutation: "I long wan-

[63] Ibid., 62–66.

[64] Bossuet, *Oeuvres*, IV, 624.

[65] *Journal de Trévoux*, juin 1703, 1072–82 [the article is specifically attributed to Tournemine].

dered in the mazes of this reasoning delirium, till mature years, and a full examination of the system and its foundations compelled me to renounce it, as I obtained demonstrative proof that it was a baseless structure and tottered from the very ground [foundation]."[66]

For an Augustinian Jansenist who admired but resisted Descartes, Pierre Nicole, what the Cartesians and their theological admirers thought possible in fact could not be: with the Fall, we lost "this simple contemplation of the truth that Adam enjoyed."[67] As he wrote to a Benedictine correspondent at Saint-Germain-des-Près, the danger in all philosophy was presumption, and while Descartes was perhaps more reasonable than Aristotle, it was unbelievable and sad that the best schools for monks should teach his philosophy, and that the pious should "openly profess" a philosophical sect and "make themselves noticed in this war of the children of the century [*qu'on se fasse remarquer dans cette guerre des enfans du siècle*]." "In truth," he warned, "the Cartesians are not worth more than the others, and are often prouder and more self-satisfied." Don't go too far, he advised![68] Who, however, would not lay siege to an enemy's capital in a "war . . . of the century"? That capital was the essential task of Christian philosophy: the *évidence* of God.

. . .

Finally, before turning to that siege, we should remind ourselves, one last time, without belaboring the obvious, that Cartesian celebration of spirit over bodily senses as a Christian philosophical route to knowledge of God merged powerfully with broad anti-Scholastic currents of thought and sensibility. Institutional rivalries affected these unions, intensified intellectual contestation, and raised all of the stakes. In particular, these anti-Scholastic (and often explicitly anti-Thomistic) tendencies were particularly pronounced among those (often overlapping) Jansenists, Augustinians, Benedictines, and Oratorians who wished the Catholic thirst for understanding to be quenched at what they took to be the different, purer, and sweeter waters of the more Platonic Fathers of the Church, and, of course, in particular, of Saint Augustine. The primary sources are almost limitless here, and their codes are often clear: on the one side, each often forced into serving as proxy for the others, Plato, the Platonizing Fathers, Saint Augustine, Descartes, and Malebranche; on the other, in the same relationship, Aristotle, Saint Thomas and the great Thomistic doctors, and the seventeenth-century Jesuit, Dominican, and other Scholastic professors and teachers who spoke or claimed to speak in their names.

[66] Huet, *Memoirs*, I, 18–30.
[67] Nicole, *Lettres*, I, 292.
[68] Ibid., 437–44.

The configurations, however, we also should know, were *by no means* always clear or consistent. In the diverse contexts of debates engendered by issues of grace, Gallicanism, probabilism, physical premotion, quietism, *Unigenitus*, monastic education, mysticism, occasionalism, Mariology, fideism, hagiography, *péché philosophique*, Chinese rites, and diverse ecclesiastical rivalries, the permutations become a Rubik's chiliahedron for anyone seeking perfect correlations. What alone is obvious is that so many Aristotelian-Cartesian debates were motivated by or played out in the name of other, often deeper, often more ancient contestations.[69] Henri Gouhier's distinction between Augustinized Carte-

[69] In addition to the well-known works of particularly well-known authors that would form pieces of the puzzle (those of Arnauld, Pascal, Malebranche, Fénélon, Bossuet, Nicole, Barbay, Thomassin, Maignan, Pourchot, Alexandre, and the like), the reader beginning an exploration of Cartesian and Scholastic multivalence with other particles of thought and religiosity should look also at Jacques Fournenc, Oratory, *Universae philosophiae synopsis accuratissima, sinceriorem Aristotelis doctrinam cum mente Platonis passim explicata et illustrata, et cum orthodoxis SS. Doctorum sententiis breviter dilucideque concinnans*, 3 vols. (Paris, 1655); André Martin, Oratory [under the pseud. Ambrosius Victor], *Philosophia Christiana Ambrosio Victore theologo collectore, seu Sanctus Augustinus de philosophia universim*, 3 vols. (Paris, 1656); 2d ed., 5 vols. (Paris, 1667); 3d ed. (Paris, 1671); the commentary in and reviews of the remarkable (and remarkably harassed) Maurist editions of St. Augustine and other "controversial" Fathers; Dom Jean Mabillon, O.S.B., *Traité des études monastiques*, 2d ed., rev. and corr., 2 vols. (Paris, 1692) (and his very public disputes with the abbé de La Trappe over this work); Pierre Cally, *Universae philosophiae institutio*, 5 vols. (Caen, 1695); abbé Pierre Valentin Faydit, *Alteration du dogme théologique par la philosophie d'Aristote, ou fausses idées des scholastiques sur toutes les matières de la religion* (n.p., 1696), and *Remarques sur Virgile et sur Homère* (and the controversies and further self-defenses that these stirred: see, in particular, Louis-Charles Hugo, Premonstratensian, *Réfutation du sistême de Monsr. Faidy sur la Trinité* . . . [Luxembourg, 1699]; Faydit, *Apologie du Sisteme des Saints Pères sur la Trinité* . . . [Nancy, 1702]; and Hugo, Premonstratensian, *Réponse à l'Apologie du Systême de . . . Faydit* . . . [Paris, 1702], paying attention to their sets of "Approbations"); Bonaventure [Noel] d'Argonne, Carthusian, *Traité de la lecture des Pères de l'Eglise* . . . (Paris, 1688); Matthieu Souverain, *Le Platonisme dévoilée, ou Essai touchant le Verbe Platonicien* (Cologne, 1700); Jean-François Baltus, S.J., *Défense des SS. Pères accusez de platonisme* (Paris, 1711) and *Jugement des SS. Pères sur la morale de la philosophie payenne* (Strasbourg, 1719); Claude Fleury [priest and abbé du Luc-dieu], *Traité du choix et de la méthode des études* (Paris, 1686); Jean-Baptiste Du Hamel [not to be confused with Jean DuHamel], *De consensu veteris et novae philosophiae libri duo* (Paris, 1663); André Dacier's notes and exposition of Plato in his edition of *Les Oeuvres de Platon*, 2 vols. (Paris, 1699); Louis Ellies Dupin, *Traité de la doctrine chrétienne et orthodoxe* . . . (Paris, 1703). Against arguments that no one named a Saint by the Church could have written the doctrine of the *Summa Theologiae*, Jacob Echard, O.P., felt compelled to write the *Sancti Thomae Summa suo Auctori vindicata* . . . (Paris, 1708). When the extremely eminent Jesuit scholar, editor, librarian, and teacher Jean Hardouin wrote that no one named a saint by the Church could have written most of St. Augustine's works, or those of most of the Platonizing Fathers, and that they were medieval forgeries, his own Society forced him to renounce such views, issued a public declaration that it wished these particular works by Hardouin "never had seen the light of day, or had remained in

sianism and Cartesianized Augustinianism, and his emphases, in many ways, on who was using whom against what, are simultaneously brilliant, overdrawn, heuristically useful, and falsely concrete.[70]

Let us understand it, rather, this way: in philosophical theology, there were affinities, sympathies, and family resemblances that linked individuals diversely to Aristotle or "the new philosophy," and people were deeply moved by them. The heart of it all for so many was not simply an issue of natural epistemology, but an even deeper issue of the Christian route to truth, and, perhaps, of the very relationship between body and soul. For so many, an essential or polemically useful battleground on which the clash between these two august tendencies of early-modern philosophical theology could be settled was the question of proof of God's existence. To defeat their rivals, many Cartesians and Malebranchists sought to show that demonstration of God, which would constitute the preamble of the faith, could not be attained by a posteriori proof, but *only* by the light of the mind undimmed by the shadows of the senses. Having seen the assault upon one set of putative proofs, let us turn, now, to the assault upon the other.

. . .

The essence of the Cartesian and Malebranchist critique of Scholastic philosophical theology is already evident: the errant senses could not initiate a journey to certainty. One did not have to agree with the Malebranchist Henri Lelevel, who had written that "God necessarily loves bodies less than minds," in order to hold such a view.[71] As the Benedictine Desgabets's course expressed it, proofs a posteriori never could convince the rigorous atheist of the existence of God, for such alleged demonstrations *presupposed* the reliability of the senses and of the induction on which they depended. Before one could posit any useful ways of learning from experience, one first had to demonstrate, a priori, a God on whom

oblivion," and was embarrassed by the efforts of its delighted foes to keep them in circulation (see *Journal de Trévoux*, fév. 1709, 367–71; *Nouvelles de la République des Lettres*, jan. 1709, 95–101). The extraordinary Hardouin deserves a biographer of unsurpassed erudition, Latinity, and wit. (I bequeathe the effort!)

[70] Gouhier, *Cartésianisme et Augustinisme*. Gouhier, in this insightful and provocative book, is primarily concerned with issues of how Cartesians used St. Augustine to polemical advantage and how Augustinians used Descartes in similar fashion, focusing above all on issues of strategy during the persecution of the Cartesians, and on the Eucharist, Jansenism, and efforts at philosophical synthesis. I hope the tone of my textual observation does not detract from the profound respect I have for a scholar who has illuminated so much of the seventeenth century for his readers in so many of his works.

[71] Henri Lelevel, *La philosophie moderne . . . contenant la logique, la métaphysique, & la physique. Avec un Traité sur l'art de persuader*, 3 vols. (Toulouse, 1698), 180.

all certainty depended. The skeptical atheist would remain an atheist "for as long as one utilizes the testimony of the senses to prove the existence of God."[72]

For those who employed Thomistic-Aristotelian demonstrations, Aquinas's fifth way, for example, from "governance," humbled any would-be skeptic by its array of the evidence of divine purpose in the world's structure and operations. Cartesians such as Desgabets, however, focused not on what might seem pious and reasonable in such a proof (the claim of a world of visible divine purpose), but on what they saw as the presumption of its confidence that *by use of our senses we could understand in any manner whatsoever the ways of God.* All teleology, he taught, was "of little use, because we do not know the reasons that God proposed to Himself for acting, and that He keeps hidden in the secret of His Providence."[73] That "*we do not know*" was the meeting point of the pious Desgabets and his polemically useful "atheist."

. . .

There are such paradoxes in the history of early-modern (and, undoubtedly, all) thought! The "mechanics," physics, and astronomy of the seventeenth century were generally explicitly anti-Aristotelian, but common perceptions of the disclosures of these sciences did so much to maintain the form of a sensationalist natural *theology* against which Cartesian and Malebranchist anti-Aristotelians struggled. The widespread belief that these sciences had discovered whole new modes of "order," "law," and "purpose" in the universe reinforced the certainty of so many early-modern Christians and deistic freethinkers that the providence of God in the natural order was yet more visible to them than to their ancestors (the Enlightenment, after all, would be preponderantly theistic). It was a powerful current of Christian philosophical theology, however, that, long before Hume, sought to vitiate the use of such "evidence" as a proof of God. What we now term science did far more than theology to keep Saint Thomas's "fifth way" vital for many minds, at least until the Darwinian rev-

[72] Dom Robert Desgabets, O.S.B., "Supplément à la philosophie de M. Descartes," cited in Le Maire, *Cartésianisme*, 224–30.

[73] Ibid., 208. From the "Supplément," we learn that Desgabets was teaching a modified Cartesianism that he deemed to have improved by means of Descartes's own doctrine and method. He denied the need for hyperbolic doubt. He was much more sensationalist in his physics and more explicitly occasionalist in his relation of mental and physical phenomena. He approved of Cartesian criticism of Scholastic proofs but claimed that Descartes's were in need of refinement and clarification. There would seem to be a certain tension in Desgabets between moving in more Malebranchist modes and in more Lockean (or perhaps Gassendist) modes. There is clearly more ambiguity in his teaching than in his published works. He is explicitly Cartesian, but not quite sure where to give unqualified assent.

olution in natural history and diverse reconceptualizations of physical science and physical "law" altered, in various ways, broad currents of Western thought. It was not from early-modern "science," but from the great debates of philosophical theology, that the assault upon empirical natural theology arose. Some debates originated in fideism, and they shall occupy us elsewhere. Some of the most striking of these debates, however, originated precisely in the contestations that concern us here.

. . .

Cartesian and Malebranchist epistemologies, of course, constituted a formidable objection to proof of God's existence from *any* phenomenon of nature, since they insisted that prior knowledge of God was necessary to enable us to know even that an external world existed apart from our dreams or imagination, and to establish the validity of any putative knowledge of that material world. Malebranche, whose stature was so high as the eighteenth century dawned, at times could appear to go the furthest here. In his *Entretiens sur la métaphysique et sur la religion* (1688), he argued that since there could be "no *necessary* relationship" between "the infinitely perfect being" and "any creature, . . . it is not possible to demonstrate precisely that there are bodies." Indeed, he wrote, "There is thus no way other than revelation that can assure us that God indeed willed to create bodies [*Il n'y a donc point d'autre voie que la révélation qui puisse nous assurer que Dieu a bien voulu créer des corps*]."[74]

Further, strict Cartesian mechanism, with its antifinalism, its denial of inductive *knowledge* of ends or purposes, militated against the entire foundation of proof *ex gubernatione rerum*. For almost all Cartesians and Malebranchists, the providence of God, His intelligent ordering and governing of the world, was either *deduced* from the self-evident actual perfection of God, or it was best approached as a matter of faith. Either way appealed both to their denigration of a posteriori philosophical theology and to their piety. *We* could not learn from *our* sensual experience of the world *anything* essential about God. God alone taught us of His providence (or of any other of His essential attributes, including existence), either from the idea of Him already in our minds, or from His mysterious revelation. Saint Thomas's fifth way, to them, was sheerest arrogance.

Thus, congratulating Leibniz on his proof a priori of the world's providential excellence, Malebranche wrote of the awful dangers of attempting to establish providence a posteriori, "because we are only too given to judging God by ourselves [our human standards], and to judging the plan of His work, although we know almost nothing of it." In such a

[74] Malebranche, Oratory, *Oeuvres complètes*, XII, 137–40.

state, we drew analogies more appropriate to the relationships among men than to the relationship between perfect being and creature, thus exposing the faith to all of the traditional "specious arguments" against God and providence from our human experience of this world.[75] Indeed, Malebranche once even argued that Descartes's theory of the insensate automatism of animals followed deductively from God's perfection, since, otherwise, "animals suffer pain, each more miserable than the other," despite the fact that "they never have sinned." Under the Scholastic suppositions of sensate animals and natural inference, Malebranche wrote, "God is unjust."[76]

In theory, of course, there need not have been any conflict between a priori and a posteriori proofs *of* God's providence. One could attempt to *deduce* providence from the being established by any of Saint Thomas's other a posteriori proofs of God, on the one hand, and, on the other, one might be stimulated to look for the actual manifestations of providence in the creation once having established it a priori. In historical fact, however, there indeed was a war between two schools of philosophical theology, and for so many Cartesian and Malebranchist theologians, it was precisely our inability to attain knowledge of God from confused and confusing sensory experience that underlined the value of their theology as the *only* source of certainty beyond faith. What better claim could they make for their philosophical method? To argue *that*, of course, was to argue that sensory knowledge could not establish that very providence of God which the Aristotelians claimed as an a posteriori proof of His existence.

To make this argument most forcefully, Cartesians and Malebranchists often insisted that the *last* thing one would infer from observing this sorry world, until reason overpowered the misleading senses, was its intelligent design or governance. Thus, for example, the Carthusian (and Cartesian) monk Alexis Gaudin, in his *La distinction et la nature du bien et du mal* (1704) stressed the priority of purely rational, a priori certainty of providence over what he saw as the skeptical or disbelieving natural *inference* one would be tempted to draw from sensory experience. The philosophical debates of our age, Gaudin insisted, had raised this issue to urgent prominence, for from sense experience, men believed themselves to know of all the "evils" and "imperfections" of the universe. Fortunately, however, we knew with certainty *from our idea of God* that He existed as a perfect being, and thus that evil and imperfection could not be His work. Such qualities in the effects would indicate imperfections in the cause, but such "defects," we knew *logically*, "could not be found in the . . . Creator,

[75] Ibid., XIX, 813.

[76] Ibid., XVIII, pt. 1, 513–18: *Défense . . . contre l'accusation de Monsr. De la Ville . . .* (Cologne [Paris?], 1682).

who only can be conceived as an infinitely perfect being." If one trusted to the senses, one would admit "imperfections" as real qualities in the world, and *atheism would follow as a consequence*: "Will we remove existence from God," he asked rhetorically, "to give it to evil?" From analysis of our idea of a perfect being, however, we knew that both His existence and His freedom from defect followed necessarily.[77]

Jacques Bernard, in his *De l'excellence de la religion* (1714) put the matter more simply and more dramatically in a discussion of reason's theological role. Our experience, he wrote, is of a universe of endless confusion, suffering, pain, and uncertainty. Just as the machines of men "easily break down," so in the machine of the world open to our gaze, "I see, every day, certain parts . . . that perish . . . [and] others that appear to me to leave their appropriate order and place." He confessed that "the more lights and knowledge I have, the more examples of this disarray I see." Sunspots made him fear that the sun would be extinguished, and all that he observed "terrifies me": "thunder, lightning, storms, winds, tempests, excessive rains, excessive droughts, earthquakes, sterility, plague, war, the malice of the wicked." (And this from someone, let us recall, who was appalled by Bayle's articles on the indispensability of faith for belief in providence!) "Every creature," he concluded, "can do me harm; how can I can be reassured?" Fortunately, he answered, reason and analysis of the *idea* of God suffice to calm the doubts of all men concerning providence (which was why Bayle had been rash!). The truth of God's providence did not depend upon our sad *experience* of the world but followed from a logical consideration of the nature of God. A being of infinite perfection entailed, necessarily, infinite wisdom and infinite goodness. One might not discern the providence of God in nature, but one could know with certainty that it was there.[78]

When the abbé Claude-François Houtteville's *Essai philosophique sur la providence* had cataloged all of the empirically derived objections against providence, he noted that they were irrelevant to the issue, since providence was an attribute deductive with certainty from the infinite perfection of God.[79] The *Journal de Trévoux* invited its readers both to note that "one sees . . . that the author has read Malebranche" and has established the Oratorian and Descartes as "his authorities," and to conclude, with the reviewer, that Houtteville's statement of these objections

[77] Alexis Gaudin, Carthusian, *La distinction et la nature du bien et du mal* . . . (Paris, 1704), "Préface," and passim. Gaudin cites St. Augustine (whose *De Natura Boni contra Manichaeos* he translated from the Maurist Latin edition and published with this work) and not Descartes or Malebranche in support of these views. His approbation was from an Oratorian theologian. The networks are interesting.

[78] Bernard, *De l'excellence de la religion*, I, 94–100.

[79] Abbé Claude-François Houtteville, *Essai philosophique sur la providence* (Paris, 1728), 47–149.

was far stronger than his "Cartesian" response to them.[80] In earlier reply to all such efforts, and explicitly against Malebranche, the Jesuit journal had written that all attempted a priori demonstrations of the providential beauty and harmony of the world were in fact assaults on the *liberty* of God to create and govern as He would, and that ultimately there was only one acceptable demonstration of providence: "that the world with its alleged defects bears in its beauty and its constant arrangement the marks of an infinite power and wisdom, . . . that, finally, God knows how to draw a greater good from what appears to us an evil." It was the task of philosophical theology to demonstrate these claims a posteriori.[81]

For the Malebranchist Henri Lelevel, for whom a posteriori proof of God was impossible, the existence of God was knowable by His self-evidence, but providence was *only* knowable by revelation and Christian faith.[82] As the Benedictine André Roze explained, since God *could have created* a world infinitely more beautiful than this one, how could anyone dare think that he could find God's perfection in a human judgment of its operations?[83] The Cartesian Pierre Villemandy agreed with all of them, arguing that it was perfectly comprehensible that before the clarification of revelation, "almost all the world was in this error, that God had very little part in what occurred in nature." Without knowledge of Scripture, Villemandy insisted, man could not know that "[God's] sovereignty presides over all events."[84] We merely have sampled here, since criticism of a posteriori proof of God, not the issue of providence per se is our present object of concern, but it already should be abundantly apparent that the Cartesian Benedictine Dom Robert Desgabets was not alone.

. . .

As the Oratorian Cartesian Poisson explained it, all knowledge proceeded from what was known to what was unknown by virtue of a proper "*via*," "*medium*," "*moyen*." Without a proper *medium*, no enterprise of knowledge could succeed.[85] The fatal flaw of Scholasticism for him was its assumption that the content of intellect entered reason by the *medium* of

[80] *Journal de Trévoux*, août 1728, 1505–30.

[81] Ibid., juillet 1708, 1134–43.

[82] Henri Lelevel, *Entretiens sur ce qui forme l'honneste homme et le vray sçavant* (Paris, 1690), 61–98, 221.

[83] Dom André Roze [sometimes spelled Rose], O.S.B., *Nouveau sistême par pensées sur l'ordre de la nature* (Paris, 1696), "Avertissement" and 20–21.

[84] Pierre Villemandy, *Traité de l'efficace des causes secondes contre quelques philosophes modernes, dans lequel on prouve cette efficace par des principes également clairs et solides* . . . (Leiden, 1686), 4–5. As his title indeed indicates correctly, Villemandy was an anti-Malebranchist "orthodox" Cartesian. This issue was critical for him, since he explicitly stated here that denial of providence was atheism.

[85] Poisson, Oratory, *Commentaire*, 84–91.

the senses. In addition to charging that this made the corporeal body the master of spiritual reason, resulting in "this completely sensual philosophy [*cette philosophie toute sensuelle*]," he explicitly argued that it made any proof of God utterly impossible, since the senses *only* could give us ideas of "corporeal things." Things above the corporeal "are not subject to their jurisdiction." If Scholastics were correct that all ideas derived from sense experience, there *could not be* any authentic idea of God.[86] Where, for Desgabets, then, the senses could not provide any certainty of God, for Poisson, they could not provide even an incoherent or uncertain idea of any real being beyond the material world. One needed no freethinkers in early-modern France to be able to hear or read arguments such as that. It was the Benedictine François Lamy who taught in his *Premiers élémens des sciences* (1706), whose subtitle announced that it was written to be "accessible to tradesmen [*à la portée des commerçans*]," that *neither faith nor the sensible world could first let us know of the existence of God*, since confidence in either depended upon prior conviction by reason, with absolute certainty, of the existence of God.[87]

In the course he taught at the Protestant academy at Sedan, Bayle had instructed his students that reason did establish the existence of God with complete certainty: the Cartesian criterion of truth was compelling, and the Cartesian proofs of God were absolutely demonstrative. He also taught his students, however, that a posteriori proofs of God were not only undemonstrative but, as the Cartesians taught, were flawed by the very concept that any notion of God could arise from the objects of sense experience.[88] Chevigny's *La science des personnes de la Cour* continued to argue, in its many editions, that while knowledge of bodies could be had by the senses, knowledge of God could not possibly be reached by such a path, since from the corporeal one learned only about the corporeal.[89] Only metaphysics could provide us with knowledge of God, provided that it did so "independently of material things."[90]

. . .

Thus, while one half of the learned world taught that there was no way to distinguish the Cartesian or Malebranchist "idea of God" from a pure

[86] Ibid., 124–38.

[87] F. Lamy, O.S.B., *Les premiers élémens des sciences*, 68–94.

[88] Pierre Bayle, "Synopsis Metaphysicae," in his *Systema Totius Philosophiae* [taught between 1675 and 1677 at Sédan], in *OD*, IV, 475–82, 516–19.

[89] Chevigny, *La science*, 5th ed. (1717), III, 238–39. (The ed. of 1707 was composed of only 2 vols.)

[90] Ibid., new ed. (1707), I, 16.

fancy, since it did not originate in the sensible world or entail actuality, the other half explicitly argued that God could not possibly be known by sensible experience or, indeed, by complex induction from sensible experience. The *Logique* or *Art de penser* of Port-Royal, Nicole's and Arnauld's influential "best-seller" and anti-Scholastic *Organon*, taught that if we were limited to some idea of God derived from the senses, we *could not have* an idea of a being that did not partake of corporeal attributes, such as finitude, materiality, or divisibility, that is, we could not have an idea of a perfect being, of God. That was why so many people thought of God not as a perfect spiritual being, but as "a venerable old man." The *Logique* argued that the belief that we were dependent upon the senses for our ideas was not an *analysis* of the Fall, but a *consequence* of the Fall, and a dangerous one at that. The critical question for philosophy, it claimed, was whether or not it was true that all ideas originated in the senses. Such a position (which it obviously found false) would be "as opposed to religion as to true philosophy."[91] Certainty, the *Logique* insisted, never can be inductive; rather, it must be based upon the Cartesian principle that " 'what is contained in the clear and distinct idea of a thing can be affirmed with truth about this thing.' " If *that* principle were destroyed, all "*évidence*" would be destroyed with it, and only Pyrrhonism would prevail.[92]

Legrand's *Apologia pro Renato Des-Cartes* argued that God had no affinity with material things and thus could not possibly be known by means of them. No knowledge of God whatsoever was possible "from consideration of the things of the world." One could *not* attain a notion of God by "progression" from or by "amplification" of anything accessible to the senses, nor by negation, since any idea of God had to be not only positive, but "overflowing." From the senses, only "the simulacra of material things" could arise, that is, things even more inferior. Those who attempted to use Saint Paul in Romans 1 as scriptural support for a posteriori proof from the sensible world misread him, for in natural knowledge, God was an object of intellect alone. Saint Augus-

[91] Antoine Arnauld and Pierre Nicole, *La logique, ou l'Art de penser, contenant, outre les règles communes, plusieurs observations nouvelles, propre à former le jugement*, crit. ed., ed. Pierre Clair and François Girbal (Paris 1965), 40–49. [based on 5th ed. (Paris, 1683), with references to the 1st through 4th eds.]. I use the term *best-seller* without hesitation: the *Art de penser* was first published in Paris, 1662 [3 printings]; 2d ed. (Paris, 1664); 3d ed. (Paris, 1668); 4th ed. (Lyon, 1671; reprint, Paris, 1674; Lyon, 1674; Lyon, 1675; Amsterdam, 1675); 5th ed. (Paris, 1683; reprint, twice in Lyon, 1684; Amsterdam, 1685). There was a posthumous 6th ed. printed at least eight times between 1697 and 1727; a Latin ed. printed more than a dozen times; and five English eds. printed in London between 1685 and 1717.

[92] Ibid., 315–19.

tine, by his own account, Legrand wrote, first became able " 'to think about my God' " when he stopped allowing his mind to be "darkened by corporeal images" and turned to the idea of the most perfect being that he found there. If one rejected the Cartesian proof of God, there was no proof, since "there was no other way open to the human intellect."[93]

One now can understand with fuller force why the condemnation of the Cartesians by the University of Paris in 1691 attributed to them the view that "one must reject all of the reasons which theologians and philosophers have used with St. Thomas until this day to demonstrate that there is a God."[94]

• • •

Baillet's *Vie de Des-Cartes* quoted its hero explicitly: many " 'pious and serious theologians have refuted . . . St. Thomas's proofs concerning God's existence.' " Baillet agreed that those proofs were invalid. Either we were certain of God's existence a priori or we were not certain of it at all.[95] The leading non-Malebranchist Cartesian philosopher of the late seventeenth century, Régis, went beyond even the concept of "certainty." Since no finite thing conceivably could be the source of any knowledge or notion of the infinite, either the idea of God was innate, essential to the soul, and compelled belief both by its very terms and by the necessity of God alone as source of its objective being, or there could be no real notion of God, let alone of His existence, and we were just playing with words. It was impossible that the idea of God was "formed" by the mind from knowledge of the world: "The soul could not form the idea of God without [first] knowing God," he insisted, "and if it knows Him, it has no need to form the idea of Him."[96]

For Régis, whose audience was vast, Saint Thomas's proofs were "moral," not "metaphysical," that is to say, they had a surface plausibility (given our prior *idea* of God), and they might be affectively influential in practice, but they were in no manner logically compelling. The imperfect world to which Saint Thomas appealed in a posteriori argument could not possibly give us knowledge of God. If Descartes's demonstration were not compelling, "[one] could advance *no* wholly necessary proposition to prove His existence."[97]

In the preface to his *Dissertations sur l'existence de Dieu* (1697), Isaac

[93] Legrand, *Apologia*, 120–36.

[94] Du Hamel, *Quaedam recentiorum philosophorum*, 33–34.

[95] Baillet, *Vie de Des-Cartes*, II, 283–85, 507; see also, I, 181.

[96] Régis, *Réponse aux Réflexions*, 71–79.

[97] Pierre-Sylvain Régis, *Système de philosophie*, 3 vols. (Paris, 1690), I, 59, 79–87.

Jacquelot, a Huguenot theologian and critic with a wide following in France, wrote that it would be wonderful if there were no great debate about the existence of God, but that this obviously could not be the case. That being so, he opined that Cartesianism was the only genuine philosophical barrier to atheism, since a posteriori proofs from sensible experience could not conclude in God. The issue was not one of "words," he claimed, since anyone equivocally could pronounce the name "God." Whatever words one used, however, it was the case that from a posteriori proof one might mean by *God* "no more than the matter of the universe."[98]

In the popular *Histoire des Ouvrages des Savans*, three years later, and as part of a raging debate in the journals about proofs of the existence of God, Jacquelot was even more explicit. Nothing derived from the senses, he insisted, could represent to us a necessarily existent perfect being, that is, God, for the senses "represented merely material beings [to us], which, unable to be perfect, contain no necessary existence. One must listen, thus, to reason alone." Descartes's proofs, he insisted, would be evident if only the senses and imagination "did not distract the understanding, and did not occupy it with corporeal objects." The Thomistic arguments for God's existence, all drawn from such a flawed source, might well be *consistent* with our a priori knowledge of God once the latter was attained (the obverse of Thomistic claims about proof by self-evidence), but they were unconvincing as proofs, for they depended entirely on our prior rational knowledge that "necessary existence" was real, which they could not establish. To those who found Descartes's proofs "too metaphysical and too subtle," he urged the same caution that the Jesuit Daniel had urged upon those who found Saint Thomas uncompelling: they had best be silent, for these were the *only* certain proofs.[99] François Lamy, we have seen, had warned not only that the very use of sense data in demonstrations depended upon a priori knowledge of the existence of God, but that the very use of revelation depended on it also, such that Scholastic criticisms placed the faith in peril indeed.[100] The simple truth, Baillet quoted Descartes as saying, was " 'that it is not possible to know the certainty and evidence of reasons which prove the existence of God . . . except by remembering distinctly those [reasons] that make us see the uncertainty in all knowledge that we have of material beings.' "[101] Again, readers explicitly were invited to draw a startling conclusion: if criticism of Carte-

[98] Jacquelot, *Dissertations*, "Préface."

[99] *Histoire des Ouvrages des Savans*, mai 1700, 199–222 [written as a critical response to Werenfels, *Judicium de argumento Cartesii pro existentiâ Dei petito ab ejus ideâ* (Basel, 1699)]. On the excitement in the journals concerning these debates, see infra.

[100] F. Lamy, O.S.B., *Le nouvel athéisme renversé*, 5–8. See also supra, n. 87.

[101] Baillet, *Vie de Des-Cartes*, II, 284–85; see also I, 181, and II, 507.

sian proofs were valid, there was *no* demonstration of the preamble of the faith.

. . .

Although "orthodox Cartesian" and "Malebranchist Cartesian" differences would occasion a whole new set of debates and problems concerning the existence of God, both schools of philosophical theology, we already have seen, agreed on the deficiencies of a posteriori proofs. For some, it could not conceivably be necessary to infer an infinite and perfect cause from finite and imperfect effects. For others, there simply could not be a finite source of knowledge of the infinite. What did it matter if there were a "necessary being" or a "first being" or a "first mover," or a cause of order, or a source of attributes we deemed finite instances of something positive, if such an entity (or such entities) could be an eternal material world itself, or its atoms, or its forces alone? If one denied the self-evidence of God *for us*, Malebranche warned the Scholastics in the *Recherche de la vérité*, then "*all the ordinary proofs of the existence and perfections of God drawn from the existence and perfections of His creatures . . . are not convincing*." In this work, which enjoyed six editions in his own lifetime, he explained that the issue was not whether there were *anything* superior to men, but whether or not there were a God. A posteriori proofs indeed proved "that there is *some* power superior to us," but, he insisted, "they do not demonstrate fully that there is a God or an infinitely perfect being."[102] As he explained in his *Entretiens sur la métaphysique et sur la religion* (1688), if one accepted the Scholastic notion that one could not know God as infinite perfection, one could not know what one talked about when one said "God":

> For otherwise, when you asked me if there is a God, or an infinite being, you would be putting a ridiculous question to me, by means of a proposition whose terms you would not understand. It would be as if you asked me, is there a "Blictri," that is to say, a something, without knowing what.[103]

. . .

The "orthodox Cartesians" would make a similar argument against Scholastics who criticized Descartes's proof of God from the "objective being" of our idea of Him. Indeed, they were convinced, such criticism placed nothing less than fatal weapons in the hands of the atheist, and they sought to make that plain. When Régis agreed with his critics that

[102] Malebranche, *Oeuvres complètes*, II, 371–72.
[103] Ibid., XII, 56.

"our mind, which is finite, cannot enclose the power of God, which is infinite," he deemed it a triumph, not a concession, for it was precisely the certainty of that principle which demonstrated God from the objective being of our idea of Him: its source could not be the imperfect world appealed to in a posteriori proof.[104] To the countless rejoinders that no idea could represent God in His perfection to us, Régis replied directly that if our idea of the infinitely perfect being were *not* a true idea of such a being, *how could one know if any a posteriori proof established the existence of such a being*? (How could you know if you had found a "unicorn" in the actual world if your mind could not comprehend the notion of "horn" or "one horn"?) "One cannot know that a thing exists," he concluded contemptuously, "without knowing generally what it is."[105] The Cartesians, in short, turned the Scholastic charge that the idea of God could not represent infinite perfection into the dramatic counteraccusation that if this were correct, then *no* knowledge of God was possible. As readers of the *Histoire des Ouvrages des Savans* read of it, "If [Descartes's] argument [from the objective being of the idea of God] is not demonstrative, one must admit that one no longer can know any entity, nor speak of it, because we know them, judge of them, and speak of them only with regard to our lights, and in conformity with the ideas that we have of them."[106]

La Coudraye's Cartesian *Traité de métaphysique* (1693) warned that if our idea of God were not, in fact, a clear and distinct idea of an infinitely perfect being, then we simply had no knowledge of God. La Coudraye agreed fully that God was "above us," but he cautioned Descartes's critics (and all his readers) that "they must take care that from wanting to give an exalted notion of Him, they do not make us lose sight of His true idea, which is nothing other than that of the infinitely perfect being." By insisting that no idea could contain real representation of God's perfection (which, he conceded, was not the same as full "comprehension" of that perfection), and by limiting their "knowledge of God" to what could be represented by the imperfect world, Scholastics threatened to destroy the very idea of God. What we derived from the senses were, at best, "purely human opinions," and, at worst, pure chimeras. None of these, he emphasized, could give knowledge of "the real and positive perfections" that alone constituted God. These actual and positive perfections could be known *only* by their necessary connection to the essence of God as represented objectively in the idea of God. If one denied that, one denied knowledge of the existence of God. To say merely that "God is," as the

[104] Régis, *Système de philosophie*, I, 59, 79–87.
[105] Régis, *Réponse aux Réflexions*, 219–51.
[106] *Histoire des Ouvrages des Savans*, mai 1700, 217–18.

conclusion of any of Saint Thomas's five ways, was to posit merely "*a*" being, without knowledge of its essence. Yet God *is* His essence! God *is* His perfections! If the mind could not know these, the mind could not know that the being posited was in fact God! The Scholastics, far from proving God, "have confused Him with *a certain phantasm that their imagination has formed from the collection of the negations of all that they do know*," the imperfections of the world. One could avoid this awful pitfall only by ignoring the senses and "consulting, uniquely, and with strict attention, the idea of the perfect being." It was that, or nothing![107] As Arnauld and Nicole put it in the *Art de penser*, if we didn't have a real idea of God, we had only "these four letters *D, i, e, u*."[108]

• • •

Who needed freethinkers? Who needed a few articles in Bayle? Who needed Hume? A legion of pious Scholastics insisted that all of the Cartesians' supposed proofs of God were merely definitional, presupposed what they needed to prove, could not establish His reality, and left them worshiping merely the figments of their own minds! A host of pious Cartesians insisted that Scholastics had no valid criterion of truth, could not infer the qualities or existence of God from the data of the world, employed a word, *God*, to which no coherent idea could correspond in their system, had no way of knowing even what kind of being they thought was entailed by the fallacious conclusions of their would-be proofs, and left them worshiping the phantasms of their own imagination! The public, we shall see, was enthralled, and all sides continued to appeal to public opinion. Enter the Malebranchists, and the public witnessed the emergence of dramatic and powerful new participants in these debates, and ever more charges that the atheists were now triumphant. The wonder, perhaps, is not that a current of atheistic disbelief arose in the early eighteenth century, but that the current remained so circumscribed.

[107] Denis de Sallo, sieur de La Coudraye, *Traité de métaphysique démontrée selon la méthode des géomètres* (Paris, 1693), "Préface" [unpaginated: xxii–xxviii]. La Coudraye was a man of letters and the founder and first publisher of the *Journal des Sçavans*. Although he is generally described as a Malebranchist, and did admire him, his posthumously published *Traitez* offered a far more "orthodox" Cartesian perspective, accepting the proof from "objective being" that, we shall see, Malebranche so vehemently rejected.

[108] Arnauld and Nicole, *Art de penser*, 41. The editors of the critical edition (ibid., 374, n. 37) believe that this argument referred to the original objections of Hobbes and Gassendi to the *Meditations*. As should be obvious now, the issue was far more timely than that.

Chapter Eleven

MALEBRANCHE; THE FIRESTORM; THE TOLL

THE EMERGENCE of Malebranchism from Cartesian thought modified these debates in complex ways, having an effect quite distinct from the Oratorian's irenic intentions. It is difficult to convey the combinations of awe and rapture, on the one side, dismay and anger, on the other, with which Christians in the two or three generations before the Enlightenment read and discussed Malebranche. Pascal, Arnauld, Bossuet, and Fénelon all had admirers; Malebranche had disciples. We have seen the sort of intellectual and religious passion he could inspire in priests and thinkers such as the Jesuit Yves-Marie André. The audience of the *Nouvelles de la République des Lettres* read the following description of him in August 1684:

> This author has done so much to make us aware that he goes further than the others in all the parts of philosophy that he has examined so far. . . . [No philosopher] has shown so strongly the union of all minds with the Divinity, and the obligation they are under to love and fear this infinite being. . . . [He is] the foremost philosopher of this century [and he reasons] perpetually on principles that suppose with absolute necessity an omniscient, omnipotent God, the unique source of all good, the immediate cause of all our pleasures and all our ideas. It is a more powerful presumption in favor of the good cause than a hundred thousand devotional volumes written by authors of small mind.[1]

Readers of the *Journal de Trévoux*, on the other hand, read this merciless description of his theology in 1708: "Malebranche . . . annihilates the Divinity."[2]

His influence on French thought, directly and indirectly, was immense, and, in his lifetime, immeasurably more than that of Spinoza and Leibniz combined. His fate, ironically, may have been the one commonly assigned to Spinoza: that however intoxicated he was by his sense of God, his legacy was disbelief. For now, let us examine his effect on the development of grounds for doubt that demonstrations of God's existence were compelling for all sound minds. In the final analysis, Malebranchism would

[1] *Nouvelles de la République des Lettres*, août 1684, 22.

[2] *Journal de Trévoux*, juillet 1708, 1134–43; see also ibid., déc. 1708, 1985–2004.

serve to discredit further the claims of a posteriori knowledge of God and, by reformulating the nature of Descartes's own a priori proof, would expose the latter to the most outraged assault it ever had endured.

. . .

Ironically, Malebranche sought to have a calming effect on the increasingly strident debates over the establishment of the most essential preamble of the faith. He conceded that most minds were indeed "sensual" and ought to be provided with sensible proofs. He claimed that these existed in profusion, since "everything that God has done proves Him . . . everything that we see, everything that we feel proves Him."[3] Indeed, he once wrote, "there is no truth which has more proofs than that of the existence of God."[4]

He meant such things in his own manner, however, within his system of occasional causes, a system that informed all of his work. In Malebranche's occasionalism, God was the only (and only conceivable) efficacious cause. This system, from whose premises "everything . . . proves God," indeed allowed a demonstration of Divinity from each and every "effect," since among its principles was the impotence of both matter and soul to exist, act, or interact of their own substantial natures or attributes, entailing God as the real cause of all phenomena. The apparent secondary or natural causes were merely "occasions" of divine act.

As we already have seen, Malebranche made it abundantly clear that he agreed wholeheartedly with the essential Cartesian critique of a posteriori proof of God, namely, that any discussion, knowledge, or a posteriori demonstration of the Supreme Being *presupposed* the self-evidence of God's existence as infinitely perfect being. Indeed, in the *Recherche de la vérité* he braved the charge of circularity against Descartes's proof by insisting that all certainty, including certainty of God's existence, depended upon the self-evidence of God's existence as infinite perfection and the consequence entailed by that perfection, that God could not deceive us.[5]

In the *Recherche*, he offered Descartes's proof of God from the necessary existence of perfect being as an example of precisely the sort of compelling metaphysical demonstration to which all men would consent were it not for the distractions of the senses. It was axiomatic in metaphysics, he wrote, and "even more evident than the axiom that the whole is greater than its part," that "one is assured of a thing that one conceives

[3] See, for example, Malebranche, Oratory, *Oeuvres complètes*, II, 19, 103–4; IV, 14–30; XV, 11–18.

[4] Ibid., II, 103–4.

[5] Ibid., II, 52, 372; see also IV, 11–14.

clearly to be contained in the idea that represents it." Descartes's proof was absolute and categorically compelling: necessary existence clearly was contained in the idea of infinitely perfect being. Just as the mind must consent to the "greater" quantity of the "whole" compared to the "part," or to the "four angles of a square," or to the "valley" necessarily beneath any "mountain," so must it consent to Descartes's conclusion. To the Scholastic charge that it was a circular argument that followed only if one *assumed* God to exist, Malebranche replied with contempt that no one added to the necessary four angles of a square the phrase "if it is 'supposed' that a square has four angles." There was only one possible deduction from Descartes's demonstration: "Thus, God or the infinitely perfect being exists necessarily."[6]

It was as a Cartesian, thus, that Malebranche received *some* of his criticism. The canon Foucher, for example, argued that while it was true that analysis from terms was compelling, it was because such alleged "proof" was in fact mere repetition of terms. Who thinks "2 plus 2" concedes "4," Foucher noted, because nothing new has been learned: one merely has stated that "2 + 2 = 2 + 2."[7] Malebranche's demonstrations, Foucher charged, lack certainty, are arbitrary in their principles, and presuppose the criterion of necessary truths that they must demonstrate. Further, he noted, the assumption that God could not deceive us moves from philosophy with great rashness into mysteries of faith: of course God could deceive us if He chose. God was perfectly free to reserve truth to Himself alone.[8]

Malebranche, however, had two critical difficulties of his own with Descartes's proofs. The heart of his first problem lay in his understanding of the terms *idea* and, thus, *the idea of God*, which differed essentially from Descartes's. For Malebranche, to try to put the complex simply, "ideas" were *not* modifications of the human mind, but "archetypes" *in God* of that which He created (from which Malebranche's most cele-

[6] Ibid., II, 90–95.

[7] Simon Foucher, *Réponse pour la Critique à la seconde volume de la Recherche de la vérité, Où l'on examine le sentiment de M. Descartes, touchant les idées* (Paris, 1686), 21–213.

[8] Foucher, *Critique de la Recherche de la vérité*, 1–35. In ibid., 4–6, he opined that "Cartesians" and "peripatetics" never would succeed in refuting each other, since they both borrowed from each other when necessary for defense and both argued largely "*ad hominem*," resulting in "confusion" and "trouble" rather than "light." See also his *Dissertation sur la Recherche de la vérité, contenant l'Apologie des académiciens . . . Pour servir de Réponse à la Critique de la Critique, etc. . . .* (Paris, 1687) and his *Dissertations sur la Recherche de la vérité . . . Avec plusieurs réflexions sur les sentimens de M. Descartes* (Paris, 1693). The attention of the reader is called once again to the remarkable work by Watson, *The Downfall of Cartesianism*, which is concerned above all with Foucher's polemic with Malebranche on the status of ideas.

brated and repeated saying, that we see all things in God). Second, whatever the nature of ideas, Malebranche *agreed with* the logic of one essential Scholastic criticism of Descartes, the refutation of his proof from "objective being" by consideration that nothing finite could represent the infinite to us. Cartesians, we have seen, made the very ability to know of God dependent upon the validity of that Cartesian proof. Malebranche added his weight to the attack against it and, in attempting to preserve the proof from the necessary existence of perfect being *without* a representational idea of God, ignited a firestorm.

Since, for Malebranche, ideas were not modes of the human mind, the whole Cartesian understanding of the distinction between the "formal" and "objective" being of any idea was based on a false assumption. Cartesians such as Régis, he believed, compounded this error by asserting that what they took to be a finite modification of a finite mind nonetheless could "represent" to us the infinite perfections of God. On *this aspect* of Cartesian proof, Malebranchist criticism could sound indistinguishable from that of the Scholastics.

In the *Recherche de la vérité*, Malebranche denounced the "gross error" of "those who support this proposition, that the finite can represent the infinite."[9] Almost a decade later, in reply to Arnauld's defense of both the Cartesian concept of ideas as representational mental modes and the proof from the "objective being" of our idea of God, Malebranche charged that Arnauld was attempting to uphold "the most insupportable opinion that can be imagined, namely, that the modality of his soul is actually representative of God Himself and of infinity."[10] In 1693, replying to Régis, he reiterated his conviction that "all the modifications of a finite being are necessarily finite, for the modification of a substance [is] merely its manner of being."[11] In 1704, ending his twenty-year public debate on this topic with the now deceased Arnauld, Malebranche posed the issue with utmost clarity: "Is it indeed evident that an infinite cause is necessary to give to the soul a finite modality?" He answered that what was evident was that "the modalities of the soul cannot be representative of the infinite in all senses, that is to say, of God or the infinitely perfect being."[12]

His sometime disciple Henri Lelevel, who had studied philosophy at an Oratorian collège (in Alençon), devoted the second chapter of his *La vraye et la fausse métaphysique* (1694), a critique of Régis's orthodox Cartesianism, to a defense of the proposition that "*the soul does not have enough reality to contain the idea of God*" and to a sustained criticism of

[9] Malebranche, *Oeuvres complètes*, II, 96–101.
[10] Ibid., VI, 169.
[11] Ibid., XVII, pt. 1, 283.
[12] Ibid., IX, 947–50.

the Cartesian proof from "objective being." The distinction between "formal" and "objective" being, he urged, was incoherent and question-begging. Régis could not proceed from the finite, what is "in him, what is his own," to the infinite, "what is outside of him." He should concede to the Scholastics that his mind does not contain "the idea of God," but merely a finite perception. Thus, there could be no proof from an "idea of God," and the Scholastics were correct that the Cartesians "cannot boast of having devised any demonstration of the existence of God." For Lelevel, Régis's Aristotelian critic Du Hamel, in his exchanges with Descartes's disciple, correctly had understood that any human "idea of God" was merely "one of the creatures." If we accepted Régis's principles, we should conclude that "*the infinite being . . . exists only in the understanding, and, as a consequence, has no objective reality.*"[13]

Arnauld had challenged Malebranche precisely on the issue of how the Oratorian failed to reach Lelevel's conclusion, that Descartes had accomplished nothing. Arnauld charged that despite Malebranche's professed loyalty to Descartes's proof of the necessary existence of the perfect being, and his claim, Arnauld reminded him, that this was "the most beautiful proof" of God, his principle that nothing finite could be the idea of God "had ruined [it]."[14] Malebranche replied that far from ruining it, he had enhanced it and removed the final barrier to people's ability to grasp its self-evidence. By eliminating the notion of a *representational* idea of God, he claimed, he had made Descartes's proof from our idea of a perfect being "more complete and more convincing."[15]

The contestation between two of the most redoubtable figures of the early-modern period was not just an event in the history of theories of ideas and knowledge, or even of philosophical theology broadly conceived. It was a personal drama that held its audience spellbound. As Fontenelle remarked: "Europe scarcely had ever offered two such Athletes. But where to find the Referees? [*A peine l'Europe eût-elle fourni encore*

[13] Henri Lelevel, *La vraye et la fausse métaphysique, où l'on réfute les sentiments de M. Régis, et de ses adversaires, sur cette matière* (Rotterdam, 1694), 22–39. From his published systematic course on philosophy (Lelevel, *Conférences sur l'ordre naturel et sur l'histoire naturelle . . .* [Paris, 1699], xiv–xvi, 1–8, 108–10, 374–82), it is clear that he believed proof of God from occasional causes (from the inefficacy and impotence of both mind and matter and, in particular, from the synchronization of mind-body phenomena) the most satisfying proof of God. He also shared, without criticism (ibid., 401–56), the proof from contingency and (not inconsistent with occasionalism if one thinks on it) from design.

[14] Antoine Arnauld, *Des vraies et des fausses idées, contre ce qu'en enseigne l'auteur de la Recherche sur la vérité* (Cologne [Paris], 1683), 285–88; and *Troisième lettre . . . au R. P. Malebranche* [written 1694; published 1698], published in Malebranche, *Oeuvres complètes*, IX, 1027–41.

[15] Malebranche, *Oeuvres complètes*, IX, 947–48.

deux pareils Athlètes. Mais où prendre des Juges?]."[16] It was indeed Olympic sport! Bayle wrote to Minutoli, after one of Arnauld's replies, "Father Malebranche will have much difficulty replying to this," and, a year later, that "M. Arnauld has replied to the Response of Father Malebranche, and indeed has flown into a rage against him, alleging that he has been offended against all right and reason [*et s'est mis bien en colère contre lui, prétendant qu'il a été offensé contre tout droit et raison*]."[17] The *Nouvelles de la République des Lettres* informed its readers, after more than twelve months had passed between replies: "Everyone was beginning to grow bored from seeing no new work from M. Arnauld since last year. But here is the Reply that we made you hope for in our *Nouvelles* of April."[18] A year later Bayle wrote of the expectation that a second round of exchanges would be followed by a third (it was!) and, the year after that, wondered if Malebranche had delayed replying to yet another exchange because of the strength of Arnauld's reply (he had not!).[19] Even those who could not follow the philosophy could find the stuff of usual brawls in all of this. As the *Nouvelles de la République des Lettres* explained:

> One almost never has seen two authors write against each other without each complaining thousands of times that his opinions have been disguised, falsified, misunderstood, and miserably mutilated by his adversary. One had grounds for hoping that such would not be seen in the contestations occurring between Monsieur Arnauld and Father Malebranche. For, since these are two extraordinary minds, great philosophers and [men] of the strictest morality, one expected that they would understand each other mutually, that they would act in good faith, and, thus, that they would not hurl at each other the reproaches that ignorance or malice cause to prevail elsewhere among those who refute each other. Nevertheless, experience shows us that these two great men are no more pleased with each other than if they were minor authors.[20]

. . .

Addressing Arnauld in 1684, in this closely watched "contestation," Malebranche expressed his amazement that Arnauld should pose objections to his use of Descartes's proof now. He always had maintained, he

[16] Bernard Le Bovier de Fontenelle, *Oeuvres diverses* . . . , new ed., 3 vols. (The Hague, 1728–1729), III, 209–10.

[17] Bayle, *Lettres* (ed. of 1729), I, 199, 221.

[18] *Nouvelles de la République des Lettres*, juillet 1684, 535.

[19] Bayle, *Lettres*, I, 234–35, 270.

[20] *Nouvelles de la République des Lettres*, juillet 1685, 777–87.

claimed, "without difficulty" for Descartes's demonstration, that "with regard to the infinite, one knows it by itself, and not by an 'idea,' because I know that there is no archetype on which God has been formed, and that nothing can represent God."[21]

Malebranche was correct in this description of his views. In the very first volume of the *Recherche*, he had assured readers that "one cannot conceive that the idea of an infinitely perfect being, which is that which we have of God, is something created" and had offered that impossibility as proof that the infinitely perfect being is known directly in itself and, thus, exists. God was known "by an immediate and direct view."[22]

Forced to clarify what he possibly could mean by "the idea of God" in such a case, Malebranche, in volume II of the *Recherche*, had offered a "Clarification of Descartes's Proof." Of every entity known save one, he wrote, "we do not see it in itself or by itself . . . but only by the vision [*vue*] of certain perfections that are in God, that represent it." Thus, the essence of no created thing entails its existence, since no necessary existence is contained in the idea that represents it precisely as a finite thing. In the case of the infinitely perfect being, however, "one cannot see Him except in Himself, for there is nothing finite that can represent the infinite. One cannot see God, thus, except that He exists: one cannot see the essence of an infinitely perfect being without seeing its existence." Thinking of God, then, was direct proof of "the efficacity [and existence] of His substance," for "the infinite has not and cannot have an idea distinct from itself, that represents it."[23]

Later in the *Recherche*, he set forth quite explicitly what he truly meant: "One sees [*On voit*] that there is a God as soon as one sees the infinite, because necessary existence is contained in the idea of the infinite, *or, to speak more clearly, because one can see the infinite only in itself.*"[24]

. . .

What perhaps prevented some readers from seeing the full implications of Malebranche's position was that, as we just have seen, he indeed used the phrase "the idea of God" in his praise of Descartes's proof. As he specified to Arnauld in 1684, however, "Sometimes I use the word 'idea' generally, for what is the immediate object of the mind when one thinks," but with reference to the Divinity, "this 'idea' *will be God Himself.*"[25] In the *Entretiens sur la métaphysique* (1684), he ceased to use the term *idea*

[21] Malebranche, *Oeuvres complètes*, VI, 165.
[22] Ibid., I, 441–42, 449–50.
[23] Ibid., II, 96–101.
[24] Ibid., 371–72.
[25] Ibid., VI, 166–67.

in its "general" sense and stated the drama of human knowledge of God's existence without reservation: "God or the infinite being is not visible by means of an idea that represents Him"; God is known "without idea, . . . in Himself."[26] In 1707, he reiterated the formula of self-evidence: "Since nothing finite can represent the infinite, *the idea of God can be nothing but God.*"[27] What Huet and the Scholastics had offered as a *reductio ad absurdum* of Cartesian proof of God indeed had come to pass as a positive claim.

Such a formulation, as evidenced by the reverence with which so many read Malebranche, was not without its appeal. In effect, it sought to destroy, once and for all, any distinction between philosophical theology and direct religious experience. No wonder philosophers such as André could associate knowledge of God in Malebranche's system with awareness of the grace of Christ within. No wonder the Jesuits believed that far more than issues of philosophical choice were involved.

Indeed, that appeal could extend beyond the immediate and growing circles of Malebranche's disciples. The eclectic theologian Jean-Claude Sommier, for example, doctor of theology from the University of Dôle, apostolic protonotary and, later, archbishop, explicitly argued in his *Histoire dogmatique de la religion* (1708–1711) that the idea of God was indeed God Himself. Without attribution to Malebranche, Sommier merged the "objective" and "formal" being of the "idea of God," stated as axiomatic in philosophy the principle that nothing finite "could represent or copy" the infinite, and concluded that our awareness of God as the most perfect being was a direct, immediate apperception of the substance of God. For Sommier: "*When our soul knows and perceives the infinite being, there is nothing between our soul that knows and God who is known.*"[28] Such views provoked new and additionally acrimonious levels of controversy into theological debate.

• • •

First, for the Cartesians who had maintained the concept of an idea as a representational modification of the mind, Malebranche's "clarification," as Arnauld had written, destroyed rather than strengthened Descartes's proof of God. What allowed Descartes to demonstrate God, Arnauld specified, was precisely that His existence was entailed by something that did *not* presuppose His existence, namely, our idea of God, absolutely distinct from God, from which His existence necessarily followed. Elimi-

[26] Ibid., XII, 53–54.
[27] Ibid., IV, 11–12.
[28] Sommier, *Histoire dogmatique*, I, 23–35.

nate that distinction, and, indeed, the demonstration would be a *pétition de principe*. Malebranche's proof, then, was no proof at all; it precisely "presupposed" what it must prove, namely, a perfect being "intimately united to my soul." If Malebranche were correct about the inability of an "idea" to represent God, there was no proof of God at all.[29] Indeed, Arnauld wrote in his study of "true" and "false" ideas, the very notion of knowledge without representational idea was unintelligible and put all issues of clear and distinct knowledge into question. It was an invitation to utter Pyrrhonism, fatally undermining not only the force and lucidity of Descartes's proof of God, but, indeed, of all proof per se. It separated irrevocably the "object known" and the "perception of the object known," since these could be linked only by "a representational being."[30] For Arnauld, the power of Descartes's proof, then, was precisely that one particular entity, the idea of God, logically entailed the existence of another particular entity, the God represented by the idea. How else could one demonstrate God?

In 1708, Malebranche's *Entretien d'un philosophe chrétien et d'un philosophe chinois* sought at one and the same time to enhance his readers' understanding of God's infinity, to strengthen, thus, the proof of God's existence from awareness of that infinity, and to do so by denying that this proof depended on any intermediary connection between particular beings. He clearly believed that by doing this, he would enable his readers to understand why it was self-evident that only God could be the direct object of a consideration of infinity. "God" was *not* "a particular being," Malebranche explained, "a this or a that." Rather, he asserted, He is "the Being that contains in His essence all that there is of reality or perfection in all things, the infinite Being in all senses, in a word, Being." Although it is "incomprehensible" to the finite mind, Malebranche averred, the nature of God's infinity could be specified: "[He is] Being without any restriction or limitation. He contains in Him . . . all the perfections, all that there is of true reality in all beings created and possible . . . even everything that there is of reality or perfection in matter, [in] the least and most imperfect of beings."[31]

Given that, how could anything "represent" God to us? How could what we took to be "the idea of God" be anything other than awareness of Being itself in all its self-evidence? To contemplate infinity was to know the necessary existence of the divine object of one's contemplation!

Such formulations of God's infinity had been implicit, if not quite so concisely explicit, in Malebranche's metaphysical theology, and Régis,

[29] Arnauld, *Troisième Lettre*, in Malebranche, *Oeuvres complètes*, IX, 1031ff.

[30] Arnauld, *Des vraies et des fausses idées*, 285–88.

[31] Malebranche, *Oeuvres complètes*, XV, 3–7.

for the Cartesians, had charged him in 1694 with reducing our understanding of God to the general idea of universal nature and with making all beings formally parts of His essence.[32] One did not need to read Spinoza's difficult *Ethica* to be aware of such conceptions. Further, recall how many historians of philosophy asked readers to discern atheism in any equation of God and universal nature, the consequence that Régis believed Malebranche to have offered inadvertently.

For the Jesuit *Journal de Trévoux*, Malebranche at last had betrayed himself. Reviewing the *Entretien*, the *Journal* challenged Malebranche furiously before its vast audience: God *is* "a particular being," it insisted, "a this or a that," known from works whose reality was wholly distinguishable from that of the divine essence. Malebranche's manner of writing about God, it charged, "*can well be congruent with the idea of the totality of the universe*." In Malebranche's system and in Malebranche's proof of what he termed "the Infinite Being," God is "all being" and touches our mind directly with His essence; were this the case, however, we would possess knowledge of all beings in all their reality, which surely we do not. Whatever Malebranche's intentions, his "proof from infinity" reduced itself to proof from "merely an infinity that contains in itself the reality of an infinity of things *of which our mind conceives*." That was a conception categorically distinct from God, whose particularity was precisely that He was "infinity in all perfections . . . and by His very infinity distinguished from everything else." Such a proof, the *Journal* concluded, "is not very much to advance for the existence of God." It might establish the reality of some poor human conception, but it advanced "*an idea that annihilates the Divinity by reducing it to the totality of the world*."[33]

The papers of the Jesuit Jean Hardouin reveal quite clearly his influence in moving his Society toward such a view of Malebranchism (a philosophy that he saw as a logical development of Cartesian thought). Further, André, Du Tertre, and La Pillonnière all testified, in letters and other writings, to Hardouin's ceaseless efforts in this regard. In the manuscripts of his courses and expositions to the Jesuits on the dangers of "the new [Cartesian-Malebranchist] philosophy," Hardouin, professor of theology at the collège de Louis-le-Grand from 1684 to 1714, termed it "atheism," pure and simple, and analyzing what "followed" from its premises, gave virtual lessons on how to think atheistically.[34] All they had done, Har-

[32] Pierre-Sylvain Régis, *Seconde réplique de M. Régis à la Réponse du R.P. Malebranche touchant la manière dont nous voyons les objets qui nous environnent* (Paris, 1694), art. 23.

[33] *Journal de Trévoux*, juillet 1708, 1134–43, and déc. 1708, 1985–2004.

[34] Hardouin's notes, a fascinating set of documents, in which he generally copies passages from Malebranche and then offers his own commentary on them as either heretical or explicitly atheistic in almost all aspects of the Oratorian's essential theology, are in Bibliothèque Nationale, MSS.: Fonds français, 14705–6. The editors of Malebranche, *Oeuvres*

douin sought to explain, was to equate the terms *God* and *Truth* such that "every mathematician or geometer is united to God."[35] Worshipers of "reason," not "God," they equated the two so that they could make human reason the standard of all things.[36] All Malebranche meant by *God* was "reality" however it occurred to mankind, and his definition of Him as "Being in general" was nothing but a metaphysical abstraction that had far *less* reality and perfection than any particular being.[37] Cartesians and Malebranchists merely applied the term *Divinity* to a nature that they saw as "blind" matter in necessary mechanical motion.[38] Obviously, one cannot deny existence to "Being" without contradiction, but "God" is *not* "whatever exists," which was the authentically atheistic formula of Malebranche's thought.[39] He taught his students and Society how to decipher the "new atheists' " code: "*When the new philosophy says 'God,' always understand 'the reality of things,' or 'their truth,' or 'Nature,' or 'the Necessity of the laws of motion'; you will enter into their thought.*"[40] For Malebranche, in his view, "there is no other God but Nature."[41]

There were Scholastics who saw the *consequences* of the Cartesian and Malebranchist denial of substantial forms as necessarily concluding in an atheistic natural philosophy, and who asked their adversaries to choose, in effect, between peripatetic philosophy and an ontology that dispensed with God.[42] There were Cartesians and Malebranchists who saw the *con-*

---

complètes conveniently have assembled letters pertaining to his activities in vols. XIX–XX, passim. See also supra, chap. 10, and the works cited by André and La Pillonnière.

35 Bibliothèque Nationale, MSS.: Fonds français, 14705, 4.

36 Ibid., 6–13.

37 Ibid., 77–98.

38 Ibid., 35, 126.

39 Ibid., 134–36.

40 Ibid., 239–40.

41 Ibid., 39. Here, Hardouin first had written that for Malebranche "*le Créateur n'est que la Nature*," then crossed it out and specified that in Malebranchism "*il n'y a point d'autre Dieu que la Nature*," concluding that all that Malebranche ever meant when he spoke of "the will of God" was "Nature." For Hardouin, Malebranchists used theological language "poetically" to refer to nature and disguise their "new school of atheism."

42 See, for a good example, Jean-Baptiste de La Grange, Oratory, *Les principes de la philosophie, contre les nouveaux philosophes Descartes, Rohault, Regius, Gassendi, le P. Maignan, etc.* (Paris, 1675), 7–19, 30–36, 51–176. The *reductio* to atheism of each other's *physics* is a theme to which I shall return in my next volume, for these polemical debates truly constituted courses in why one *should* think atheistically from certain premises. It was not the Cartesians who "atheized" Descartes's mechanism (indeed, they continued to expand the role and the necessity of God within it); it was the Scholastics who for two generations attempted to demonstrate that consistent Cartesians should dispense with God. See also Daniel, S.J., *Voyage*, (2d ed.), 144–53; Du Hamel, *Réflexions critiques sur le système Cartésien de Mr. Régis*, 220–25, 330–44; the priest J. Gallimard, *La philosophie du prince, ou La veritable idée de la nouvelle et de l'ancienne philosophie* (Paris, 1689), 53–216; and

sequences of substantial forms as necessarily doing the same, and who asked Scholastics to choose between occasionalism, for example, and an ontology that dispensed with God.[43] These were standard, if awesome, polemical techniques that urged, as with proofs of God, incapacity against the hypothetical atheist. Hardouin and those who accepted his views were saying something more dramatic: that a whole school of philosophy *had dispensed with God*—intentionally, in Hardouin's view; unintentionally, in the view of the Jesuit Marquer who wrote the review of Malebranche's *Entretien*. If they believed that, then whatever they wrote about "the fool," they believed that atheism was more than possible within the conceptual world of early-modern France. In their polemics, they even taught how it could be achieved.

• • •

For others, the "problem" with Malebranche's proof was equally ominous, but in a different sense, and it reflected upon the entire Cartesian enterprise. In 1687, the Huguenot theologian Pierre Poiret, who recently had been a Cartesian himself, now, on an odyssey toward extreme mysticism, warned that the Cartesians were making "an idol" of "the idea of God so celebrated at the present time." Such an entity was not without "its dignity," Poiret agreed, but "the idea of God . . . is not God Himself." Indeed, he admonished, "posited very inappropriately in the place of the living God, despite its being merely the work of the creature, [the 'idea of God'] leaves the soul truly atheistic and empty of the true God."[44] The Jesuit Perrin, in 1710, compared the Cartesians to "the atheists" they claimed to refute, for the Cartesians also ignored the existence of the actual God known from his works, believing that they knew Him when in fact they knew only an idea whose conditional nature they failed to understand.[45] When the Jesuit Rodolphe Du Tertre consummated his break

---

R. Du Tertre, S.J., *Réfutation*, I and II. Note that these were all written in the vernacular. The process of "transmission" is not always the same, I shall argue, as the imagined "logic of ideas" being played out *in the minds of proponents*.

[43] See, for example, F. Lamy, O.S.B., *L'incrédule*, 78–118; *Lettres philosophiques*, 33–95. Again, it was the Cartesians and the Malebranchists who drew "atheistic" physical theories from Aristotelian premises.

[44] Pierre Poiret, *L'oeconomie divine, ou Système universel et démontré des oeuvres et des desseins de Dieu envers les hommes*, 7 vols. (Amsterdam, 1687), II, 568–73. For Poiret's prior Cartesianism, see the *first* edition *only* of his *Cogitationes rationales de Deo, anima et mâlo* (Amsterdam, 1677), which will give a good indication of how far he moved. The *Nouvelles de la République des Lettres*, avril 1685, 410, described him this way: "He is a man of a recognized probity, and who, from being a great Cartesian, has become so devout, that in order better to muse on the things of Heaven he has broken almost all commerce with the earth."

[45] Perrin, S.J., *Manuale*, 5–9.

with Malebranchist philosophy by publishing his *Réfutation d'un nouveau système de métaphysique* (1715), he denied that the finite mind, before beatitude, could have any "knowledge" of the infinite that was not merely negation of the finite, and, thus, that it was impossible for us to see God "in Himself," as Malebranche had claimed, "by an immediate and direct vision [*vue*]." More dramatically, he charged that Malebranche and his disciples—all of whom were themselves disciples, he insisted, of Descartes—had substituted the idea of God for God Himself, and, in the final analysis, only worshiped and only knew a "God" who was purely "a being of [human] logic," conceived as the Being of the world in general. This was atheism, he concluded, but one should not charge the "new school" with intentionally seeking it.[46]

Such caution, we have seen, was not exhibited by Jean Hardouin. While his views on Cartesian and Malebranchist "atheism" were not *published* in full until his posthumous *Opera varia* (1733), he lectured formally and informally to all and sundry on the topic, and he circulated his manuscripts. Indeed, his analyses were so well known that in 1715, La Pillonnière (who had abandoned the Jesuits in his own odyssey that, by the end, would take him from Scholasticism, to Malebranchist rationalism, to fideism, to Protestantism, to the occultism of the Paracelsians) published an abstract of Hardouin's views. This work, *L'Athéisme découvert par le R.P. Hardouin*, focused on the substitution of the idea of God for God and was reprinted in Thémiseul de Saint-Hyacinthe's *Mémoires littéraires* in 1716 to satisfy the curiosity of the public. Now the view that Cartesians and Malebranchists deliberately denied the real God to worship merely at the feet of reason and nature was explicitly before the world. "The goal of Descartes," Hardouin concluded here, "was thus to establish that there is no other God but the being of the things that we can know," and "there is his atheism." La Pillonnière himself decided that during his Malebranchist years he indeed had come to worship "a chimerical God," and that the debates of the philosophers established nothing. Belief in God, he now concluded, was an utterly supernatural gift, achieved by "faith," not natural lights.[47]

. . .

Such fideism was in theory not an acceptable *philosophical* conclusion for Catholic theology. Sommier warned his readers that "it would be heresy

[46] R. Du Tertre, S.J., *Réfutation*, I, 277–319; II, 11–99, 139–220.

[47] François de La Pillonnière, *L'Athéisme découvert par le R.P. Hardouin* . . . (n.p., n.d. [1715]), which was reprinted in Saint-Hyacinthe, *Méms. litts.*, II, 403–35. See also La Pillonnière, his *An Answer to Reverend Dr. Snape's Accusation . . . Containing an Account of His Behaviour and Sufferings amongst the Jesuits* . . . (London, [1717]) and . . . *Further Account of Himself . . . And of His Advances in His Inquiries after Truth* (London, 1729).

to say that one cannot know the existence of God without faith."[48] Nonetheless, its appeal grew throughout the late seventeenth and early eighteenth centuries, as did the reputation of Pascal, who had written, in the *Pensées*, that it was generally in vain that we looked for proof of God in nature or in our reason, when He was only truly known in the heart and through the grace of Christ.[49] Such a position was far more an assertion of the priority of faith and religious experience over philosophy than a formal embrace of any philosophical position on demonstration of the existence of God, but it was a far cry from the attitude toward *praeambulae fidei* being taught elsewhere. Nonetheless, it is more than interesting to note its appeal in a culture that professed to believe that atheism was an act of will whose madness was made manifest by the luminous evidence of God to the natural mind.

La Pillonnière was not the only direct participant in these contestations to move toward fideistic skepticism. The posthumous publication of Pierre-Daniel Huet's treatise on "the weakness of the human mind" surprised and intrigued those who thought they knew him. In his "Préface," addressed to "my friends the philosophers," Huet explained that he was in the end "profoundly shocked by these continual disputes of the philosophers," and that he had found his peace in philosophical skepticism and, from recognition of the weakness of the human mind, in faith as the source of his beliefs.[50] In the body of his treatise, he applied all of the criticism of Sextus Empiricus against both knowledge by reason alone and knowledge derived from the senses, denying the certainty of both. He addressed Scholastic critiques of Cartesian a priorism against the rationalists, and Cartesian critiques of Scholastic sensationalism and induction against the Aristotelians. We needed "some means more useful" than our natural faculties to achieve certainty of any kind, he concluded: "Now, this means is the Faith by which, during his life, man acquires some knowledge of God and of things divine." That means, he opined, was a gift of God to those who were not presumptuous about the powers of their minds.[51] He noted, as a major objection to his position, that all

[48] Sommier, *Histoire dogmatique*, I, "Discours préliminaire, ou Apologie de la raison et de la foy contre les pyrrhoniens et les incrédules," i–iii.

[49] Blaise Pascal, *Pensées de M. Pascal sur la religion, et sur quelques autres sujets, qui ont esté trouvées après sa mort parmy ses papiers* [the so-called Port-Royal ed., with preface by Etienne Perier] (Paris, 1670), 55–65, 190–93, 153. In ibid., 190–93, Pascal argued that St. Paul did not say that God was obvious to all in nature, but merely that He was indeed there. The *Pensées* was published with an unparalleled eleven pages of approbations and enjoyed edition after edition.

[50] Pierre-Daniel Huet, *Traité philosophique de la foiblesse de l'esprit humain* (London, 1741), 1–10. The *Traité* was first published (posthumously) in Latin (Amsterdam, 1723). It was found among his papers in both Latin and French. As was his wont, Huet had written it first in French and then translated it into Latin.

[51] Ibid., passim. The quotation about "things divine" is found on 211.

schools of philosophy claim the absolute certainty of proof of the existence of God. In the final analysis, however, he argued, all human proofs were at best merely probable, and it was "clear" from the way that "clever philosophers openly have fought these principles" that even here, "in this natural knowledge that we have of God," "one does not achieve a perfect and complete certainty on all points." Each school of philosophy succeeded in putting the "first principles" of each other school into doubt, while "Faith does not depend on first principles, but presupposes them as certain." That was the better route.[52] All human belief required faith.[53]

Huet's friend and fellow academician, the abbé d'Olivet, translator of Cicero's *De natura deorum*, defended his memory against the host of critics who either denied that the pious Huet could have written this or who were appalled by what they saw as his assault upon natural certainty of the existence of God. It is a sad day, d'Olivet noted, when a man is treated like an atheist for having written that the natural human mind has "no means of achieving the knowledge of any truth" without "faith, a pure gift of God," our only "infallible" guide.[54] If one recalls the portrait of "the atheist" with which this book began, however, one can understand, in context, the shock.

. . .

Even theologians untempted by pure fideism, however, clearly were sensitive to the ravages effected by Cartesian-Scholastic-Malebranchist debate. In 1712, the Capuchin Nicolas Anaclet du Havre noted for his students the views of pious theologians who believed that they could "prove that one cannot demonstrate the existence of God." His own explication of their arguments revealed the inroads of Aristotelian-Cartesian polemic, laying out the most essential positions of both camps against even the theoretical possibility of, on the one hand, a priori and, on the other, a posteriori proof. The answer to such problems, the theologian advised the teachers of his order, was to consult the great theologians who had written on the existence of God, and he referred them to the authorities: Saint Thomas *and* Malebranche; Huet *and* François Lamy; the Jesuit Petau *and* the Cartesian Thomassin *and* the fideistic Pascal. In short, he referred them to the very problem itself.[55]

For others sensitive to these dilemmas, the task became to find what

[52] Ibid., 275–90.

[53] Ibid., 284.

[54] Abbé Joseph d'Olivet, *Histoire de l'Académie Française depuis 1652 jusqu'à 1700* (Paris, 1729), "Addition," 362–69.

[55] Anaclet du Havre, O.F.M., Capuchin, *Sujet de conférences*, I, pt. 3, 48–49, 61–62, and II, 1–2.

remained standing and solid after the assaults of the diverse theological and philosophical camps against each other's citadels. The Capuchin Basile de Soissons, in his "Traité de l'Existence de Dieu" (1680), wished that the Church did not see fideism as "a violence against truth" but acknowledged the need to prove God. He apologized for having to refer to Aristotle, who, after all, he reminded his readers, believed in the eternity of the world, and he apologized for using "several [Scholastic] philosophical terms rather barbarous in our ordinary language," but he believed that there was *one* philosophical argument that could overcome the most demanding critic: the proof from contingent beings.[56] The Jesuit Boutauld, in *Le théologien dans les conversations avec les sages et les grands du monde* (1683), declared it "a great abuse to run and ask [the philosophers] if it is true that there is a God" and denied the need for "demonstrations drawn from the books of Aristotle or Saint Thomas." There was only *one* proof of God beyond the certainty of faith, he concluded: the *moral* proof from the order of the world. "If you want to know [it] better by speculations and convictions," he warned, "tomorrow you will know it no longer." In short: "Absolute God though He is, He has not had any other argument or any demonstration than this one to make known His Divinity to men."[57]

Thus, even among those who rejected all a priori proof, there no longer was a consensus that the "five ways" of Saint Thomas were all invulnerable to refutation, and many theologians were conscious of the explicit toll taken by these mutual refutations. In 1680, the abbé Armand de Gérard addressed a Christian laity that he believed to be increasingly confused and appalled by the divisions within the Catholic intellectual community. Although he favored the Thomistic arguments as *illustrations* for those who already believed, he asserted that *both* Aristotelian Scholasticism and Cartesian innovation stood condemned by their manifest inabilities to prove the God known by authority. Against the Cartesians, he argued that if God is infinite and perfect, He cannot be known by our finite and imperfect ideas. Against the Scholastics, he argued that if God is spirit, He cannot be known by the corporeal senses from the beings of the corporeal world. If creation, design, and governance were obvious, he asked, then why did "the two greatest geniuses of antiquity," condemned to think without the grace of faith, not see it? Aristotle himself had believed the world eternal and had denied that divine providence extended to the terrestrial world. Epicurus had believed the world the product of

[56] Basile de Soissons, O.F.M., Capuchin, "Traité de l'Existence de Dieu . . . Contre les Infidelles et les Athées de notre siècle," paginated separately [45 pp.] at the end of *Fondement inébranlable de la doctrine Chrétienne* . . . , 3 vols. (Paris, 1680–1683), I.

[57] Michel Boutauld, S.J., in Coton and Boutauld, *Le théologien*, 16–47. This was in a fourth printing by 1696.

the fortuitous concourse of atoms and had denied all providence entirely. It was not philosophy that taught us the existence of the true God, but Genesis. After a "recourse to faith," we then looked for the evident marks of the Creator in the universe and found them.[58] In brief, he had accepted the Scholastic critique of Cartesianism. He also had accepted the heart of Cartesian critique of scholastic proofs, that a posteriori proof was only useful *after* one already knew God.

The implications of such a position were made patently (and perhaps painfully) clear to learned readers and students of philosophical theology in Nicolas L'Herminier's *Summa Theologiae*, first published in 1701–1703 and having a second edition in 1718–1719. L'Herminier was a professor of theology at the Sorbonne, and a Jansenist sympathizer with little respect for either the Scholastics or the Cartesians in their mutual contestations. In his summa, he rejected Descartes's proofs of God (and all a priori demonstration by cause or "necessary conjunction") as question-begging, agreeing with Scholastic critics that such demonstrations presupposed the very object of their proof. He agreed that the "formal" being of ideas obviated the possibility of proof from their "objective" being, and that the very existence of atheists refuted the premises of Descartes's chain of argument.[59] When he turned to Saint Thomas's "five ways," however, he revealed the profound influence on his theology of the Cartesian argument that unless an a posteriori proof established "a perfect being," it had failed to demonstrate the existence of God against the objections of the would-be atheist.

Saint Thomas's proofs from contingent being, motion, and efficient cause, he reasoned, were clearly *not* demonstrative. No one, he argued, conceivably denied that there was *a* necessary being, given contingency; *a* prime mover, given motion; and *a* first cause, given a sequence of effects. Saint Thomas, however, wholly had begged the question of whether or not such entities had to be "a *perfect* being." Assume, the theologian explained, eternally existing atoms with inherent essential motion, as so many of the ancients did, and one has assigned just as plausibly to such atoms the status that Saint Thomas assigned to God. If the issue were whether or not *any* cause existed of the phenomena we observe, Saint Thomas triumphed. Atheists, alas, demanded further demonstration that such causes could be found only in a perfect being, and Saint Thomas merely presupposed the very issue in dispute. Turning to Saint Thomas's proof from degrees of perfection, L'Herminier concluded that it too begged the central issue in dispute. If there were, in fact, "degrees of per-

[58] De Gérard, *La philosophie*, "Epître," "Préface," and 1–54 (see, especially, 33–35). On his view of appropriate a posteriori argument, see 116–86.

[59] L'Herminier, *Summa Theologiae*, I, 24–40, 49–55.

fection," Saint Thomas had demonstrated that such things could only have a perfect cause. The argument, however, presupposed perfection, and it would be wholly *inefficacious* against the thinker who believed that all we observed was merely the result of the fortuitous arrangements of atoms, and who believed that human judgments about qualities were merely arbitrary pronouncements about how such arrangements affected our physical senses and well-being. Further, he charged, the whole argument about "negations" of perfection obviously told us merely what was *not*. Only the argument from providential governance triumphed, L'Herminier concluded, for only providence demonstrated qualities—intelligence, benevolence, and will, for example—that could *not* be attributed to corporeal entities.[60] As we have seen, however, in our analyses of "objections," doubts, the history of philosophy, and of Cartesian criticisms of Scholastic proofs, the argument from providence was, for many, problematic indeed.

. . .

Debates about proof of God, and, in particular, Cartesian-Scholastic mutual refutation, occupied a salient place in the popular learned journals, reaching a very wide audience among the educated public. Virtually every work I have cited in the last three chapters received extended explication, review, and, often, refutation in these journals. Apart from reviews, other forms of exchanges among participants in these debates—articles, replies, letters, and brief essays—all assaulting one another's efforts to prove the existence of God, were prominent in these popular forums. At almost any moment during two generations, these contestations commanded attention. The remarkable recriminations of Arnauld and Malebranche, which so rent the Cartesian camp, each claiming that the other could not prove God, found their forum in what was in many ways the *least* learned (although chronologically the first) of these journals, the *Journal des Sçavans*, which, in the four consecutive weekly issues of 28 June, 5 July, 12 July, and 19 July of 1694, let the titans go at each other in its pages.[61] Let us stop the clock, so to speak, at the very dawn of the eighteenth century. In May 1700, in the *Histoire des Ouvrages des Savans*, Jacquelot attacked a criticism of Descartes's proofs.[62] In January 1701, the *Journal des Sçavans* let the abbé Brillon reply for the injured critic.[63] In January and Feb-

[60] Ibid., 40–63. Meslier argues very closely to L'Herminier in Meslier, *Oeuvres*, II, 207–8, but more on that in my subsequent volume.

[61] These, of course, were in addition to exchanges in their books. Arnauld and Malebranche both used the journals: in this case, see *Journal des Sçavans*, the issues specified in the text.

[62] *Histoire des Ouvrages des Savans*, mai 1700, 199–222.

[63] *Journal des Sçavans*, 10 jan. 1701.

ruary of 1701, the *Journal de Trévoux* let opposed critics join the issue.[64] For the next two years, in mutually referential and mutually cited debates across the journals, the fratricide continued. Why did the journals so focus on the question? They did so because the subject was profound, the names were grand, the public loved a quarrel—and once the public loved a quarrel, the journals did so too. What symbiosis! In November 1701, the *Nouvelles de la République des Lettres* informed readers of the status of the debate and the interlocutors, cited and summarized what had transpired in other journals (though generally assuming that its readers had read those too), published letters from two participants, and—after presenting Jacquelot against Werenfels against Jacquelot against Brillon against Dom François Lamy against La Montre (who, it claimed, "was content merely to transcribe" the view of Régis)—commented, in a revealing phrase, "Here is a Dispute which is going to be in fashion [*Voilà une Dispute qui va devenir à la mode*]."[65] These and wholly new contestants had a vast field on which to set their arguments. The *Nouvelles de la République des Lettres* gave space to such mutual refutations in September and November of 1701; May, July, and September of 1702; February and August of 1703. The *Histoire des Ouvrages des Savans* did the same in May of 1700, and in February, May, and September of 1701. The *Journal de Trévoux* did so, at exceptional lengths, in January–February 1701, and in July–August and September–October of that same year, and in July and September 1702 (by which time it had moved to monthly issues). These were *not*, to say the very least, private debates.[66]

. . .

Such a climate also meant that everyone had "the atheist" (in the guise of an adversary or reader unpersuaded by one's own arguments) always looking over one's shoulder, and, perhaps, increasingly internalized as a critical presence. It was, for some, one gets the distinct impression, exhausting. No one could avoid or ignore the arguments of potential dialec-

[64] *Journal de Trévoux*, jan.–fév. 1701, 187–217.

[65] *Nouvelles de la République des Lettres*, nov. 1701, 510–15 (the quotation is found on 513).

[66] These debates preceded these exchanges and followed them, without much change in their terms, which replicated the erudite literature we have explored. Note the length of many of them. For these debates at the dawn of the eighteenth century, see *Nouvelles de la République des Lettres*, sept. 1701, 317–58; nov. 1701, 483–509; mai 1702, 272–77; juillet, 1702, 31–41; sept. 1702, 293–96; fév. 1703, 188–200; août, 1703, 163–71; *Journal de Trévoux*, jan–fév. 1701, 187–217; juillet–août, 1701, 3–14, 190–91; sept.–oct. 1701, 203–7; and *Histoire des Ouvrages des Savans*, mai 1700, 199–222; fév. 1701, 43–49; mai 1701, 226–29; and sept. 1701, 420–28. For the scholar interested in a closer look, I have Xeroxes of hundreds of such exchanges, from many years of the journals, that I should be pleased to share.

ticians waiting to find the arbitrary assumptions, logical fallacies, and failure to anticipate objections in one's work. There were too many of them; they were all too clever; they ignored the object of one's efforts and derided one's work before the world. Perhaps some of the appeal of fideism lay there. The editors of the first edition of Pascal's *Pensées* had conceded that those who wanted "proofs and geometric demonstrations of the existence of God" would be disappointed, but they denied the efficacy of empirical, metaphysical, and commonplace proofs. Further, they informed the reader, Pascal had written elsewhere that " 'I do not feel myself strong enough' " to prove to doubters "the existence of God."[67] In 1672, a Jansenist supporter defended Pascal for this, quoting him to the effect that "one would seek in vain the traces of God in the dead works of nature."[68] In 1728, the Oratorian priest (and librarian) Desmolets published the remaining fragments of Pascal's *Pensées*, one of which reminded the reader that neither David nor Solomon, the wisest of our fathers, had sought to "prove" his God, and that this was, indeed, "an admirable thing."[69]

Perhaps, despite the outcry, many of them understood Huet's retreat only too well. At the end of a long defense of Malebranche's proof of God's existence against its critics, in a "criticism of a criticism" of a work that he loved, the Benedictine Dom Robert Desgabets took a long breath. He granted that the proof was beset by theoretical objections and difficulties, but, his rationalism suddenly less confident, he pleaded that "there being no other argument but this one that is proportioned to everyone's capacity, . . . there would be peril to disparage it and combat its solidity." Perhaps, he conceded, it convinced us only because God first had revealed Himself to us in Scripture, and perhaps "men corrupted by sin never would have taken it upon themselves to think of God . . . if God first had not made Himself known to man, and if this knowledge had not been passed down from father to son by means of instruction."[70] Gaspard Langenhert, whom we last met retiring from philosophical dispute in the face of objections to which he felt he could not respond satisfactorily, wrote in his *Philosophus Novus* (1701–1702) that a Christian philosopher can *only* be skeptical and should embrace neither Platonic, Epicurean, Aristotelian, nor Cartesian systems. "All science," Langenhert urged, including knowledge of God's existence, "presupposes faith, which . . . cannot . . . be demonstrated by the sole lights of nature." He

[67] Pascal, *Pensées*, "Préface," [unpaginated, but see especially what would be xlvi–xlviii].

[68] Jean Filleau de La Chaise, *Discours sur les pensées de M. Pascal* . . . (Paris, 1672), 5–59 [some attribute this work to Philippe Du Bois-Goibaud].

[69] Pierre-Nicolas Desmolets, Oratory, *Continuation des Mémoires de littérature et d'histoire*, v, pt. 2 (Paris, 1728), 313–17.

[70] Desgabets, O.S.B., *Critique de la Critique*, 85–89.

who wishes to know anything whatsoever of God, he specified, must first believe "by faith" that there is a God. *All* sciences, he noted, *assumed* their objects of study to exist: the mathematician cannot "prove" points and lines to exist; the physicist cannot "prove" bodies to exist; the theologian cannot "prove" God to exist![71]

. . .

If an eighteenth-century manuscript that correctly described much of the atheist Jean Meslier's life and reading is correct in its other claims, the priest who became an atheist knew and presumably read the work of the Jesuit philosopher Claude Buffier, read the abbé Houtteville's treatise on Christianity, and read the Jesuit Tournemine's unauthorized preface to Fénélon's treatise on the existence of God.[72] Since scholars have been known to express amazement that the "isolated" Meslier ever could have emerged from Catholic culture without the influence of free thought, it is not fruitless to ask what he would have or could have encountered in such orthodox works.[73] Buffier's and Tournemine's furious recapitulations of the Scholastic critiques of Cartesian and Malebranchist proofs of God may well have disabused Meslier of any a priori grounds of belief, or, as the culture liked to phrase it, of replies to objections and doubts. Houtteville's treatise had praised Pascal's emphasis on the need for "faith" to know God, his understanding, in Houtteville's words, "that it is not by metaphysical and abstract proofs" that men should "be led to perfect conviction." Natural demonstrations, on the other hand, Houtteville insisted, that is to say, inferences from nature, "depend too much on the imagination and the senses to extend to first principles, sources of all truth." It was not by means of reason or the senses, but "by the heart," that God's existence could be known.[74] Buffier, however able to direct

[71] Gaspard Langenhert, *Philosophus Novus*, 4 tomes in 1 vol. (Paris, 1701–1702), I, 13–73.

[72] Bibliothèque de l'Arsenal, MSS.: 2558, #1, 1–5. I shall address the issue of this manuscript in the next volume. Voltaire derived his own "life of Meslier" by abridging either this source or, more likely, a source common to both.

[73] There are many examples, but see—since it states so well the "problem" that I do not find to be a problem—Jean Fabre, "Jean Meslier, tel qu'en lui-même . . . ," in *Dix-Huitième Siècle*, no. 3 (1971), 107–15, where he argued that Meslier's reading clearly consisted primarily of Christian books that served as "guarantors of the faith," from which he concluded that "this peasant and self-taught curé, liberated from dogmas but not from scholasticism, cleared for himself the path of a merciless atheism." As I hope is now clear, it was precisely in books designed to be "guarantors of the faith" that the machetes to clear a path were found.

[74] Claude Buffier, S.J., *Traité des premières véritez et de la source de nos jugements, où l'on examine le sentiment des philosophes sur les premières notions des choses* (Paris, 1724), passim, and *Elémens de métaphysique* . . . (Paris, 1725), 39–79; René-Joseph Tournemine,

Scholastic objections against the Cartesians, was also aware of the force of rationalist criticisms of Scholastic proofs. In Buffier's philosophy, one cannot "prove" with "absolute evidence" that nature even exists as we conceive of it, that we know true things from it, or that God exists. All a priori proof is question-begging, and all a posteriori proof lacks even the theoretical possibility of "complete demonstration," since it must (and, he believed, should) *assume* "first truths." These first truths, the Jesuit Buffier specified, are principles that are *not* demonstrable themselves, but without which no other demonstrations are possible. Barbay, you will recall, had limited "first truths" to one, Aristotle's principle of noncontradiction, confident that one could get from there to God and to science. For Buffier, these "first truths" incapable of being demonstrated only could be acquired "by way of sentiment," and they included some interesting propositions to be placed beyond possibility of proof: one's own existence; the existence of bodies; the principle that what all men know by "sentiment" and "experience" is true; and (with a priori proof no longer an option), the principle that order "could not be the effect of chance." It is both impossible and malicious, Buffier insisted, to ask for "certain proof" of these "first truths," for they must be presupposed by human thought, and we know they are *not* amenable to demonstration.[75]

• • •

We are a long way from the image of theistic philosophical and intellectual self-confidence that opened our exploration of early-modern French learned culture, and we have consulted scarcely an (early-modern) unbeliever along the way. We need not detach the first speculative atheists of the French eighteenth century from the learned culture that engendered them: its sense of the world; its sense of the past; its own divisions and contestations. Recall where we began: the portrait of the atheist as someone so blinded by depravity that he tried without success to deny the *évidence* of a truth manifest to and agreed upon by all mankind. Recall, also, Lucien Febvre's argument that a cry of pain against the ways of the

S.J., "Réflexions . . . sur l'athéisme . . . ," in Fénélon, *De l'existence de Dieu* (Paris, 1713), where he assured readers that since a priori proofs did not demonstrate God, Fénélon had merely used them ad hominem to aid such poor reasoners in their beliefs; abbé Claude-François Houtteville, *La religion chrétienne prouvée par les faits* . . . (Paris, 1722), cliii–clviii. Tournemine implied an equation of Malebranchism and Spinozism in his "Réflexions," which caused a scandal that brought the issue to everyone's attention. Malebranche sought redress, and the king's confessor Le Tellier ordered Tournemine to apologize for this injury, which he did, ever so grudgingly, in the *Journal de Trévoux*, nov. 1713, 2029–30. Even here, however, he could not refrain from adding: "God said 'I am that I am.' God did not say, 'I am all that is. I am being in general.' "

[75] Buffier, S.J., *Elémens*, 79–132.

world is not atheism until it has reasons for its disbelief. Whatever the motives of disbelief, it now could have its reasons.

These reasons, of course, left the atheist with no end of explaining to do. If there were no God, how account for the widespread belief in Him, how account for mind, the formation of things, the seeming fixity of species, adaptation to environments, in short, the being and nature of the universe? If there were no God, what followed? The atheist had a lot of speculation before him. In the next volume, I shall try to show how the debates, natural philosophy, and scholarship of the world that produced the first modern atheists shaped and informed their disbeliefs and their beliefs, and we shall examine the etiology and dilemmas of early-modern "naturalism," with both its "recovered" ancient and its early-modern roots. We also shall meet in their manuscripts and texts the minds that many had said never truly could be. We also shall discover that on certain subjects, they were, in some essential ways, sailing on their own in uncharted seas. For now, it is my hope that I have explained, indeed, that I have overexplained, how it was possible for a few minds by the early eighteenth century to reject the claims of their culture that only an *insensé* could doubt or reject seriously what almost all of the rest of them believed. History is context, and in this case, context makes things clear. We have seen a complex culture generate its own antithesis, the possibility of which it always had carried within. To portray that singular learned world, or, at least, to portray aspects of it that may be ignored only to the detriment of our historical understanding, also was one of my deepest aspirations for this work.

INDEX